The MANIFESTO in Literature

VOLUME 1

The MANIFESTO *in Literature*

ORIGINS OF THE FORM: PRE-1900

THOMAS RIGGS, *editor*

ST. JAMES PRESS
A part of Gale, Cengage Learning

GALE
CENGAGE Learning·

Detroit • New York • San Francisco • New Haven, Conn • Waterville, Maine • London

The Manifesto in Literature

Thomas Riggs, Editor

Lisa Kumar, Project Editor

LIBRARY OF CONGRESS CATALOGING-IN-PUBLICATION DATA

The Manifesto in Literature / Edited by Thomas Riggs.
  v. cm. — ()
  Includes bibliographical references and index.
  ISBN - 13: 978-1-55862-866-3 (set) -- ISBN - 13: 978-1-55862-867-0 (vol. 1) --
ISBN - 13: 978-1-55862-868-7 (vol. 2) -- ISBN 13: 978-1-55862-869-4 (vol. 3)
  1. Revolutionary literature—History and criticism. 2. Literary manifestos.
3. Political manifestoes. 4. Politics and literature. 5. Authors—Political and social views.
I. Riggs, Thomas, 1963—editor of compilation.
  PN51.M26785 2013
  809.935—dc23

Gale
27500 Drake Rd.
Farmington Hills, MI, 48331-3535

978-1-55862-866-3 (set)   1-55862-866-5 (set)
978-1-55862-867-0 (vol. 1)   1-55862-867-3 (vol. 1)
978-1-55862-868-7 (vol. 2)   1-55862-868-1 (vol. 2)
978-1-55862-869-4 (vol. 3)   1-55862-869-X (vol. 3)

This title will also be available as an e-book.
ISBN-13: 978-1-55862-880-9 ISBN-10: 1-55862-880-0
Contact your Gale, a part of Cengage Learning, sales representative for ordering information.

Printed in the United States of America
1 2 3 4 5 6 7 17 16 15 14 13

# ADVISORY BOARD

CHAIR

Martin Puchner
Byron and Anita Wien Professor of Drama and of English and Comparative Literature, Harvard University, Cambridge, Massachusetts. Author of *The Drama of Ideas: Platonic Provocations in Theater and Philosophy* (2010); *Poetry of the Revolution: Marx, Manifestos, and the Avant-Gardes* (2006); and *Stage Fright: Modernism, Anti-Theatricality, and Drama* (2002). Editor of *The Norton Anthology of World Literature*, 3rd edition (2012); and *The Communist Manifesto and Other Writings* (2005). Coeditor, with Alan Ackerman, of *Against Theatre: Creative Destructions on the Modernist Stage* (2006). Founding Director, Mellon Summer School of Theater and Performance Research.

ADVISORS

Rita Felski
William R. Kenan, Jr. Professor of English, University of Virginia, Charlottesville. Author of *Uses of Literature* (2008); *Literature after Feminism* (2003); *Doing Time: Feminist Theory and Postmodern Culture* (2000); *The Gender of Modernity* (1995); and *Beyond Feminist Aesthetics: Feminist Literature and Social Change* (1989). Editor of *Rethinking Tragedy* (2008). Coeditor of *Comparison: Theories, Approaches, Methods* (2013). Editor of *New Literary History.*

Janet Lyon
Associate Professor of English; Science, Technology and Society; and Women's Studies, Pennsylvania State University, University Park. Author of *Manifestoes: Provocations of the Modern* (1999). Contributor to *Gender in Modernism: New Geographies, Complex Intersections,* edited by Bonnie Kime Scott (2007); *The Cambridge Companion to American Modernism,* edited by Walter Kalaidjian (2005); and *Geomodernisms: Race, Modernism, Modernity,* edited by Laura Doyle and Laura Winkiel (2005).

Peter Nicholls
Professor of English, New York University, New York City. Author of *George Oppen and the Fate of Modernism* (2009); *Modernisms: A Literary Guide,* 2nd

Editorial and Production Staff

Associate Publisher
Marc Cormier

Product Manager
Philip J. Virta

Project Editor
Lisa Kumar

Editorial Assistance
Andrea Henderson, Michelle Lee, and Rebecca Parks

Art Director
Kristine Julien

Composition and Imaging
Evi Seoud, John Watkins

Manufacturing
Wendy Blurton

Rights Acquisition and Management
Kimberly Potvin, Robyn V. Young

Technical Support
Luann Brennan, Mike Weaver

TABLE OF CONTENTS

WOMEN

INTRODUCTION

Among the hundreds of manifestos that are represented in these three volumes, one stands out: *The Manifesto of the Communist Party* (1848). In a collaborative process that spanned several countries and included much trial and error, the two authors, Karl Marx and Friedrich Engels, did nothing less than invent the manifesto as we know it. To be sure, there were earlier texts that called themselves manifestos, but they existed side by side with declarations, proclamations, open letters, admonitions, refutations, theses, defenses, vindications, catechisms, and much more. "Manifesto" was just one more convenient name to give to a document intent on stating publicly—on making manifest—a set of rules or beliefs.

When they were charged with drawing up the beliefs of the newly established Communist League, Marx and Engels experimented with all of these rival forms. For example, they initially thought that the best way of expressing the principles of the new party would be in the form of a catechism, the question-and-answer testing of knowledge introduced by theologians of the Catholic Church. The finished text of the *Communist Manifesto* still bears traces of this early experiment. Gradually, however, the two authors realized that they were facing an unprecedented challenge—a challenge they needed to meet with an entirely new kind of text.

The problem they set themselves in 1847 was how to write a revolution. All across Europe monarchies and empires were entrenched, fortifying their positions of power. They watched jealously for any sign of new revolutionary groups threatening the status quo. The French revolution had long ago receded into history, but it had not been forgotten. Word was going around of a radical new movement sowing discontent abroad, but no one knew anything specific about it. Apparently, it was called communism.

There was something to the rumor. Carefully, Marx and Engels had begun to establish a network of the revolutionaries scattered across the continent. "There is a specter haunting Europe," the *Communist Manifesto* begins. With discontent in the air, the time had come for the secret society to become visible, public—manifest. To accomplish this purpose, the two authors recreated the manifesto as a new genre.

This manifesto did much more than make manifest the principles of communism. Marx, a trained philosopher, had developed a philosophy of history based on the struggle among different classes. This history culminated in the present moment, in the manifesto itself, which declared a kind of point zero: all subsequent history would be shaped by this crucial document. At the center of this turning point stood the proletariat, a newly defined class of workers utterly dependent on the owners of factories and capital. Everyone knew about disenfranchised workers, of course, but the *Communist Manifesto* took the unusual step of describing them as the future sovereigns of Europe and the world.

In addition to articles of belief, Marx and Engels's treatise includes this history of mankind, told at breathtaking speed, leading up to the present and into the future. In order to bring about this revolutionary future, the document introduced a new historical agent—the proletariat—and now had to call this agent into being. The burden of the *Communist Manifesto* was to forge out of the disenfranchised workers a coherent class. This class must be roused to action. If there was going to be a revolution, the manifesto itself must incite it. Ingeniously, Marx and Engels combined the crucial elements—declaration of principle; long view of history; creation of a turning point; introduction of a new agent—and couched them in a style singularly intent on transforming their ideas into action. Out of disparate ingredients the authors created a formula that was exemplified, for the first time, in the *Communist Manifesto*. Without this document, the three volumes presented here would not exist.

The *Communist Manifesto* is a lens through which we can look backward and forward, backward at the prehistory of the genre and forward to the many successors and imitators. A look back reveals a striking fact: many early manifestos were not revolutionary documents. They tended to be declarations by heads of states, emperors, or the Church, utterances by those with the power and authority to make laws and impose a vision of the world. Marx and Engels would cunningly change the genre, turning the manifesto into a tool not for those in power but for those seeking to usurp it.

Alongside these authoritative declarations, other, more subversive texts existed, although they didn't always designate themselves as manifestos. Martin Luther's *Ninety-Five Theses* (1517), nailed to the church door in Wittenberg, had the long-term, if perhaps unintended, consequence of revolutionizing the Church. Other, more explicitly insurrectional documents—for example those (such as the 1649 "Digger's Song") emanating from the so-called Diggers and Levellers in seventeenth-century England, who hoped to claim common property from landlords—explicitly sought to change the status quo. Like Luther, they made ample use of Christian texts to articulate their demands, quoting liberally from the Bible.

Religion was not the only language available to revolutionaries. In the eighteenth century, philosophers began to formulate, more and more cogently, a worldview premised on the human exercise of reason; their beliefs freed humanity from the humble subservience to God that had characterized many earlier revolutionary texts. The new philosophical attitude created a new age, the Enlightenment, and its principal philosopher, Immanuel Kant, authored the seminal text (which might have been called, retrospectively, the Enlightenment Manifesto) "What Is Enlightenment?" This undertaking was not just a matter of philosophy. It aided those hoping to reorganize the social order without recourse to older authorities—to place society on a new foundation.

The most famous experiment along these lines happened not in Europe but in the English colonies of North America, where revolutionaries declared their independence from England and from the monarchy. The Americans expressed the principles of their freedom in a text that soon became world famous and found many imitators of its own: the *Declaration of Independence* (1776). Like the *Communist Manifesto*, the *Declaration of Independence* did not just state new principles; together with the *Constitution* (1787), it called into being a new entity, the United States of America. More particularly, it created a new agent, the people of the United States of America, who would henceforth govern their own fate.

Although these documents and other, lesser-known manifestos tended to be phrased in the radical idiom of universality—as in the opening of the *Declaration of Independence*, which proclaimed, "All men are created equal"—their practice was often a good deal more restrictive, excluding slaves and women, among others. In response these discounted groups began to articulate their demands with recourse to the *Declaration*, holding the document, and those who endorsed it, to its original, radical vision. In 1848 a women's rights convention in Seneca Falls, New York, modeled its *Declaration of Sentiments* explicitly on the *Declaration of Independence*, demanding freedom and independence for the half of the nation that had been excluded in the original *Declaration*. Eighty years earlier, on the French colonial island of Saint-Dominique, a slave revolt inspired by the *Declaration of the Rights of Man and of the Citizen* (1789) had found expression in Jean-Jacques

Dessalines's "Liberty or Death" (1804), which charged Europeans with not living up to their own revolutionary ideas. Despite these forceful new manifestos, it would take centuries for their mandates to receive wider acceptance.

Protest literature, Enlightenment philosophy, a new type of Republican constitution—these were some of the strands that Marx and Engels knit into a new kind of text, the manifesto proper. Despite the later success of this document, which truly changed the world, its immediate effects were disappointing. The timing was right, or almost right—revolutions were erupting across Europe (although the *Communist Manifesto* was published in London, which was relatively isolated from those revolutions, and it was written in German). When the revolutionary energy of 1848 ebbed, however, enthusiasm for the document and its ilk ebbed as well, and it took decades and a concerted program of translation to catapult the *Communist Manifesto* to the forefront again. At the end of the nineteenth century, the treatise finally began its triumphant rise. Marx and Engels's new formula had taken a long time to become popular.

Two developments resulted from the increasingly visible success of the *Communist Manifesto.* The first was that the genre became the preferred form of political expression for the Left: Marx and Engels had inaugurated a long tradition of manifestos seeking to found communist or socialist parties or to update and revitalize the international communist movement. Several of these are collected in the second volume of this set, "The Modernist Movement." They include Emma Goldman's "Anarchism" (1910), in which the author explains the tenets of that movement; the "Zimmerwald Manifesto" (1915), a World War I socialist document condemning the fierce nationalism that held Europe's Left in its grip; and the *Spartacus Manifesto* (1918), a Marxist revolutionary treatise written by Rosa Luxemburg in postwar Germany. From time to time right-leaning groups tried to answer this leftist tradition with manifestos of their own but never with lasting success.

The second development, also represented in volume two, was more surprising. As the *Communist Manifesto* was gaining prominence, artists started to write texts specifically styled as manifestos. Most did not hope to create social revolutions; instead, they wanted to revolutionize the arts. Their treatises adopted many elements from political manifestos: the telling of a grand history (of art) that culminated in a complete rupture; the creation of a new entity or movement; an aggressive denunciation of predecessors or rivals; and lists of demands or actions to be taken. The trend began in the late nineteenth century, when a new group called the symbolists sought to articulate their break with the dominant artistic mode of the time, realism. The art manifesto movement really took off when the obscure Italian symbolist poet F. T. Marinetti recognized the form's potential in the artistic sphere and authored *Futurist Manifesto* (1909). The document created quite a stir, which encouraged Marinetti to write more manifestos until he was flooding the art market with his missives. No futurist artwork had been created yet; the new movement existed simply by virtue of having been founded, defended, and explained through manifestos. With the proclamation of futurism, the new artistic offshoot of the political manifesto had come into its own.

The artistic manifesto, too, had predecessors. Artists had always wanted to articulate their principles and views, sometimes quite succinctly or polemically; examples of these texts appear in the first volume of this series, "Origins of the Form." Percy Bysshe Shelley's *Defence of Poetry* for instance, written in 1821 and published in 1840, exalts Romantic poetry and poets in the face of detractors. Shelley's contemporary William Wordsworth had contented himself with writing the pointed "Preface" to the 1800 edition of *Lyrical Ballads* (poems by Wordsworth and Samuel Taylor Coleridge), which accomplished a similar purpose. Over the course of the nineteenth century, these declarations of aesthetic principles edged closer to the manifesto; Émile Zola's *Naturalism in the Theater* (1880) is a prominent example of this trend. Only after the turn of the century, with futurism, did the genre fully arrive in the world of art.

Once the manifesto gained entry into the artistic sphere, art was never the same again. Groups, splinter groups, and subformations sprang up everywhere, fiercely fighting over minor points of aesthetic doctrine, and most of the fighting was done through manifestos. The immediate effect was a new artistic landscape dominated by a proliferation of "isms." Many artists were no longer content simply to exercise their craft; they now felt the need to be part of a movement—futurism, Dadaism, surrealism, suprematism, and numerous others—until finally the war of the manifestos became more important than the artwork created under the auspices of any particular movement.

The competition even extended to the form of the manifesto itself. Marinetti had perfected a particularly aggressive style, intent on driving home its often extreme points with utmost force. The Dadaists responded with playful, whimsical manifestos that seemed not only to disagree with the content of futurist treatises but also with their bellicose tone. The surrealists differentiated themselves from both of these movements, not only by emphasizing the importance of dreams and of free association but also by writing meandering, essay-like manifestos that mirrored this new emphasis.

A term began to circulate throughout the new landscape: "avant-garde." Originally a military term designating the advanced guard of an army, it now described the ambition of artists to found the latest and most advanced ism through the latest and most advanced manifesto.

The two strands of the manifesto, the political and the artistic, existed side by side, sometimes merging, sometimes diverging. During World War II and its aftermath, however, the fortunes of the manifesto waned as fascism and fascist-leaning regimes took hold in Europe, quelling both leftist revolutionary energy and artistic revolutions. Even movements that had sided with fascism, such as Italian futurism, quieted, and once the war was over, these groups found themselves discredited. The time of the manifesto seemed to have ended.

Not for long. A second wave of both political and artistic manifestos swelled in the 1950s and gained momentum as the 1960s wore on. This next wave, represented in the third volume of this series, "Activism, Unrest, and the Neo-Avant-Garde," was different. The political manifestos, although still primarily leftist, were no longer used predominantly by communist parties but rather by disenfranchised groups seeking recognition and justice, including African Americans, feminists, immigrants, and gays.

Many of these groups could claim a substantial history of manifesto writing. Harlem Renaissance writers of the 1920s and 1930s, including Alain Locke and Richard Wright, outlined the aesthetic and political principles of their art in manifestos or manifesto-like statements, including Locke's "Legacy of Ancestral Arts" (1925) and Wright's "Blueprint for Negro Writing" (1937) (both represented in the second volume of the series). In 1966 the Black Panthers demanded rights for African Americans in a more political and forceful manifesto, the Black Panther Party Platform. They strategically ended their document with the first paragraph of the *Declaration of Independence,* recalling one of the most important documents in the prehistory of the manifesto. In her 1967 *SCUM* (Society for Cutting Up Men) *Manifesto,* Valerie Solanas notably used the standard "we" even though her movement consisted only of herself. She, too, could look back on a long history of feminist manifestos, including Mary Wollstonecraft's *A Vindication of the Rights of Woman* (1792), one of the most important early examples of the form.

Artistic and political manifestos had emerged outside Europe and the United States during the first part of the twentieth century, driven by the global rise of communism, an increasingly international modernism, and the avant-garde movements in the arts. In 1914 the Chilean poet Vicente Huidobro delivered the lecture "Non Serviam" (Latin for "I will not serve"), a manifesto declaring independence from authority in various forms; and in 1917 the future cofounder of the Chinese Communist Party Chen Duxiu wrote "On Literary Revolution," importing the form and its revolutionary zeal to China. By the 1960s the manifesto's international reach was no longer an exception but a commonplace occurrence. Frantz Fanon's *The Wretched of the Earth* (1961) became a manifesto for the independence movements of former colonies all over the world, and Nelson Mandela's 1961 "Manifesto of Umkhonto we Sizwe" played a role in the struggle against Apartheid in South Africa.

By the middle of the twentieth century, writing political manifestos was no longer an original act. On the contrary, it now meant joining a long tradition; it meant pledging allegiance to the institution of leftist thought even as the origin of the tradition, the *Communist Manifesto,* receded into history.

The artistic manifesto was going through a similar experience. Originally conceived as a means of declaring a new point of departure, a complete rupture with all preceding art, avant-garde manifestos now had to admit that they were part of a tradition—a tradition of manifesto writing. What to do? Some artists tried to surpass their early-twentieth-century predecessors by being even more radical and revolutionary; one group, the Situationists (whose founder Guy Debord produced "Situationist Theses on Traffic" in 1959), even declared that they were against the production of anything resembling art. Others found novelty in new technologies, from which they hoped a complete revolution would arise. Donna Haraway's "Manifesto for Cyborgs" (1985) envisioned a new form of existence in the symbiosis of humans and machines, while McKenzie Wark's *Hacker Manifesto* (2004) elevated hacking to the status of a new creative and radical activity.

The end of the twentieth century saw the demise of communism in politics and the emergence of the postmodernist movement in the arts—both seemed to spell, once again, the end of the manifesto. Without communism as a credible alternative to capitalism, how could political activists write in a genre inaugurated by the *Communist Manifesto?* And with the art world declaring that "anything goes," how could activist artists claim to do away with all preceding and rival art forms? If the late twentieth century did not experience the "end of history," as the political scientist Francis Fukuyama predicted in 1992 that it would, it certainly seemed to experience the end of the manifesto.

The manifesto has not disappeared entirely, however. An increasingly global capitalism still breeds resistance and resentment in those left behind; and 9/11 demonstrated that we still live in a world dominated by rival political systems and their sometimes violent clashes. At the same time, the ever-changing social media allow for new forms of revolutionary organizing, and new technological revolutions are changing the face of art even more rapidly now than during the early twentieth century.

The evidence of several hundred years of manifesto writing assembled in these volumes captures a breathtaking history of innovation, a history of men and women trying to make the world anew. The enduring impulse to declare a point zero and to envision a new departure, the audacity to break with tradition and to found new traditions, is nothing less than a history of modernity itself. Manifestos, the most characteristic form in which these ambitions have been expressed, can thus be regarded as the most representative and important documents of the modern world, a literature unto themselves.

Manifestos have routinely predicted the future even as they have tried to bring that future about. They may well continue to shape our world for the foreseeable future.

Martin Puchner,
Advisory Board Chair

EDITOR'S NOTE

The Manifesto in Literature, a three-volume reference guide, provides critical introductions to 300 manifestos throughout the world. As manifestos, all the works share a common trait. They challenge a traditional order, whether in politics, religion, social issues, art, literature, or technology, and propose a new vision of the future.

Among the earliest manifestos discussed in the guide are the *Ninety-Five Theses* (1517), a critique of the Roman Catholic Church by German priest and professor Martin Luther, and the *Politics of Obedience* (1552-53), in which French writer Étienne de la Boétie argues that people allow themselves to be ruled by tyrants out of habit and hope for personal gain. Of the twentieth-century art manifestos covered in the book, "Art, Revolution, and Decadence" (1926), by Peruvian marxist José Carlos Mariátegui, discusses the relationship between revolutionary art and politics, and "Gutai Manifesto" (1956), by Japanese artist Jiro Yoshihara, contends that representational art perpetuates a "fraud" by creating illusions. More recently, *Why Facebook Exists* (2012), by Mark Zuckerberg, the American founder of the social network, offers an idealistic vision for his company, arguing that its mission is not profit but increased interpersonal connectivity throughout the world and thus more democratic social, political, and economic institutions.

The structure and content of *The Manifesto in Literature* was planned with the help of the project's advisory board, chaired by Martin Puchner, Byron and Anita Wien Professor of Drama and of English and Comparative Literature at Harvard University. In his introduction to this guide, he discusses how *The Manifesto of the Communist Party,* written in 1848 by the German theorists Karl Marx and Frederick Engels, helped define the very idea of the manifesto.

ORGANIZATION

All entries share a common structure, providing consistent coverage of the works and a simple way of comparing basic elements of one text with another. Each entry has six parts: overview, historical and literary context, themes and style, critical discussion, sources, and further reading. Entries also have either an excerpt from the manifesto and/or a sidebar discussing a related topic, such as the life of the author.

The Manifesto in Literature is divided into three volumes, each with 100 entries. Volume 1, "Origins of the Form: Pre-1900," has six sections focusing on early concerns of manifesto writers—church and state, citizens and revolutionaries, proletarians, emancipation and independence, women, and artists and writers. "Church and State," for example, contains nineteen entries, such as the *People's Charter* by English activist William Lovett, who advocated electoral reforms aimed at helping British working classes. Volume 2, "The Modernist Movement: 1900-WWII," includes three sections—social and political upheavals, Harlem Renaissance, and avant gardes—the latter two including entries on art and literature manifestos. Volume 3, "Activism, Unrest, and the Neo-Avant-Garde," has eleven sections: art and architecture; film; feminisms; radical politics; queer politics; America left and right; global militants; philosophies; poetry and performance; students, activists, and situations; and technologies.

Among the criteria for selecting entry topics were the importance of the work in university curricula, the region and country of the author and text, and the time period. Entries can be looked up in the author and title indexes, as well as in the general subject index.

ACKNOWLEDGMENTS

Many people contributed time, effort, and ideas to *The Manifesto in Literature*. At Gale, Philip J. Virta, manager of new products, developed the original plan for the book, and Lisa Kumar, senior content project editor, served as the in-house manager for the project. *The Manifesto in Literature* owes its existence to their ideas and involvement.

We would like to express our appreciation to the advisors, who, in addition to creating the organization of *The Manifesto in Literature* and choosing the entry topics, identified other scholars to work on the project and answered many questions, both big and small. We would also like to thank the contributors for their accessible essays, often on difficult topics, as well as the scholars who reviewed the text for accuracy and coverage.

I am grateful to Erin Brown, senior project editor, especially for her work with the advisors and on the entry list; Greta Gard, project editor, who managed the writers; Mary Beth Curran, associate editor, who oversaw the editing process; David Hayes, associate editor, whose many contributions included organizing the workflow; and Hannah Soukup, assistant editor, who identified and corresponded with the academic reviewers. Other important assistance came from Mariko Fujinaka, managing editor; Anne Healey, senior editor; and Janet Moredock and Lee Esbenshade, associate editors. The line editors were Heather Campbell, Cheryl Collins, Tony Craine, Holli Fort, Laura Gabler, Harrabeth Haidusek, Ellen Henderson, Joan Hibler, Dehlia McCobb, Kathy Peacock, Donna Polydoros, Natalie Ruppert, Mary Russell, Lisa Trow, Will Wagner, and Whitney Ward.

Thomas Riggs

CONTRIBUTORS

DAVID AITCHISON

Aitchison is a PhD candidate in literary studies and a university instructor.

GREG BACH

Bach holds an MA in classics and is a freelance writer.

KIM BANION

Banion is a PhD student in English literature and a high school English instructor.

LISA BARCA

Barca holds a PhD in romance languages and literatures and is a university professor.

KATHERINE BARKER

Barker holds an MA in English literature.

CRAIG BARNES

Barnes holds an MFA in creative writing and has been a university instructor and a freelance writer.

MARIE BECKER

Becker holds an MA in humanities.

KAREN BENDER

Bender holds an MFA in creative writing and an MPhil in Anglo-Irish literature. She has taught high school English.

KATHERINE BISHOP

Bishop is a PhD student in English literature and has been a university instructor.

ALLISON BLECKER

Blecker is a PhD candidate in Near Eastern languages.

ELIZABETH BOEHEIM

Boeheim holds an MA in English literature and has been a university instructor.

MELANIE BREZNIAK

Brezniak is a PhD candidate in English literature and has been a university instructor.

WESLEY BORUCKI

Borucki holds a PhD in American history and is a university professor.

JOSEPH CAMPANA

Campana holds an MA in English literature and has been a university professor.

GERALD CARPENTER

Carpenter holds an MA in U.S. intellectual history and a PhD in early modern French history. He is a freelance writer.

CHRISTINA BROWN CELONA

Celona holds a PhD in English literature and creative writing and has been a university instructor and a freelance writer.

CURT CLONINGER

Cloninger holds an MFA in studio arts and is a university professor.

KEVIN COONEY

Cooney holds a PhD in English literature and is a university professor.

ALEX COVALCIUC

Covalciuc is a PhD candidate in English literature. He has been a university instructor and a freelance writer.

GIANO CROMLEY

Cromley holds an MFA in creative writing and is a university instructor.

MARIE DAVOL

Davol holds an MA in writing.

VICTORIA DECUIR

DeCuir holds an MA in art history and is a university instructor.

ANNA DEEM

Deem holds an MA in education and is a freelance writer.

CAMERON DODWORTH

Dodworth holds a PhD in English literature and is a university instructor.

RICHARD ESBENSHADE

Esbenshade holds a PhD in history and has been a university professor and a freelance writer.

TAYLOR EVANS

Evans is a PhD student in English literature and has been a university instructor.

DENNIS FEHR

Fehr holds a PhD in art education and is a university professor.

ELEANOR FOGOLIN

Fogolin is pursuing an MA in English literature.

CAROL FRANCIS

Francis holds an MA in English literature and has been a university instructor.

DANIEL FRIED

Fried holds a PhD in East Asian studies and is a university professor.

DAISY GARD

Gard is a freelance writer with a background in English literature.

GRETA GARD

Gard is a PhD candidate in English literature and has been a university instructor and a freelance writer.

CLINT GARNER

Garner holds an MFA in creative writing and is a freelance writer.

KRISTEN GLEASON

Gleason holds an MFA in creative writing and has been a university instructor.

RODNEY HARRIS

Harris is pursuing a PhD in history and has been a university instructor.

JOSH HARTEIS

Harteis holds an MA in English literature and is a freelance writer.

MICHAEL HARTWELL

Hartwell holds an MFA in creative writing and has been a university instructor and a freelance writer.

RON HORTON

Horton holds an MFA in creative writing and has been a high school English instructor and a freelance writer.

ANNA IOANES

Ioanes is a PhD student in English language and literature and has been a university instructor.

MIRANDA JOHNSON

Johnson is a freelance writer with a background in art history.

EMILY JONES

Jones holds an MFA in creative writing and has been a university instructor.

REBECCA KASTLEMAN

Kastleman is a PhD candidate in English literature and a freelance writer.

KRISTIN KING-RIES

King-Ries holds an MFA in creative writing and has been a university instructor.

LISA KROGER

Kroger holds a PhD in English literature and has been a university instructor.

DAVID LOVE

Love is pursuing an MFA in creative writing and has been a freelance writer.

JENNY LUDWIG

Ludwig holds an MA in English literature and has been a university instructor and a freelance writer.

GREGORY LUTHER

Luther holds an MFA in creative writing and has been a university instructor and freelance writer.

KATIE MACNAMARA

Macnamara holds a PhD in English literature and has been a university instructor.

MAGGIE MAGNO

Magno has an MA in education. She has been a high school English teacher and a freelance writer.

ABIGAIL MANN

Mann holds a PhD in English literature and is a university professor.

THEODORE MCDERMOTT

McDermott holds an MFA in creative writing and has been a university instructor and a freelance writer.

LISA MERTEL

Mertel holds an MA in library science and an MA in history.

STEPHEN MEYER

Meyer holds an MFA in creative writing and has been a university instructor and a freelance writer.

RACHEL MINDELL

Mindell holds an MFA in creative writing and has been a freelance writer.

JIM MLADENOVIC

Mladenovic holds an MS in clinical psychology and is pursuing an MA in library science.

CAITIE MOORE

Moore holds an MFA in creative writing and has been a university instructor.

ROBIN MORRIS

Morris holds a PhD in English literature and has been a university instructor.

JANET MULLANE

Mullane is a freelance writer and has been a high school English teacher.

ELLIOTT NIBLOCK

Niblock holds an MTS in the philosophy of religion.

ELIZABETH ORVIS

Orvis is a freelance writer with a background in English literature.

JAMES OVERHOLTZER

Overholtzer holds an MA in English literature and has been a university instructor.

JONATHAN REEVE

Reeve holds an MA in humanities and an MA in English literature and has been a university instructor.

EVELYN REYNOLDS

Reynolds is pursuing an MA in English literature and an MFA in creative writing and has been a freelance writer.

RICHARD ROTHROCK

Rothrock hold an MA in mass communication and has been a university instructor and a freelance writer.

REBECCA RUSTIN

Rustin holds an MA in English literature and is a freelance writer.

CARINA SAXON

Saxon is a PhD candidate in English literature and has been a university instructor and a freelance editor.

CATHERINE E. SAUNDERS

Saunders holds a PhD in English literature and is a university professor.

JACOB SCHMITT

Schmitt holds an MA in English literature and has been a freelance writer.

NANCY SIMPSON-YOUNGER

Simpson-Younger is a PhD candidate in literary studies and a university instructor.

NICHOLAS SNEAD

Snead is a PhD candidate in French language and literature and has been a university instructor.

HANNAH SOUKUP

Soukup holds an MFA in creative writing.

STEPHEN SQUIBB

Squibb is a PhD candidate in English literature and a freelance writer.

SARAH STOECKL

Stoeckl holds a PhD in English literature and is a university instructor and a freelance writer.

MARTHA SUTRO

Sutro holds an MFA in creative writing and is a university instructor and a freelance writer.

ELIZABETH VITANZA

Vitanza holds a PhD in French and Francophone studies and has been a university and a high school instructor.

GRACE WAITMAN

Waitman is pursuing a PhD in educational psychology. She holds an MA in English literature and has been a university instructor.

JOHN WALTERS

Walters is pursuing a PhD in English literature and has been a university instructor.

JOSHUA WARE

Ware holds a PhD in creative writing and has been a university instructor.

KATRINA WHITE

White is a PhD candidate in Spanish language and literature and a university instructor.

ACADEMIC REVIEWERS

JOSEPH ACQUISTO

Associate Professor of French, University of Vermont, Burlington.

ANN MARIE ADAMS

Professor of English, Morehead State University, Kentucky.

RAPHAEL ALLISON

Assistant Professor of English, MAT Program, Bard College, Annandale-on-Hudson, New York.

JOHN ALVIS

Professor of English and Director, American Studies Program, University of Dallas, Irving, Texas.

NAOMI ANDREWS

Assistant Professor of History, Santa Clara University, California.

PETER ARNADE

Dean, College of Arts and Humanities, University of Hawaiapos;i at Manoa, Honolulu.

BERNARDO ALEXANDER ATTIAS

Professor and Chair, Department of Communication Studies, California State University, Northridge.

SYLVIA BAKOS

Associate Professor of Fine Arts, SUNY Buffalo State, New York.

J. T. BARBARESE

Associate Professor of English and Creative Writing, Rutgers-Camden, New Jersey.

ROANN BARRIS

Associate Professor of Art History, Radford University, Virginia.

ADAM BARROWS

Associate Professor of English, Carleton University, Ottawa, Ontario, Canada.

WILLIAM BAUER

Associate Professor of History, University of Nevada-Las Vegas.

ROSALYN BAXANDALL

Retired Distinguished Teaching Professor, SUNY Old Westbury, New York, and Professor, Bard Prison Project and CUNY Labor School, New York.

JEREMY BEAUDRY

Assistant Professor and Director, Master of Industrial Design Program, University of the Arts, Philadelphia, Pennsylvania.

THOMAS OLIVER BEEBEE

Edwin Erle Sparks Professor of Comparative Literature and German, Pennsylvania State University, University Park.

STEPHEN BEHRENDT

University Professor and George Holmes Distinguished Professor of English, University of Nebraska, Lincoln.

JUSTYNA BEINEK

Assistant Professor of Slavic Languages and Literatures and Director, Polish Language, Literature, and Culture Program, Indiana University-Bloomington.

WILLIAM BELDING

Professorial Lecturer, School of International Service, American University, Washington, D.C.

EVGENII BERSHTEIN

Associate Professor of Russian, Reed College, Portland, Oregon.

ALEX BLAZER

Assistant Professor of English and Coordinator, Teaching Fellows,

Georgia College & State University, Milledgeville.

DAVID BLITZ

Professor of Philosophy and Director, Honors Program, Central Connecticut State University, New Britain.

JULIA BLOCH

Assistant Professor of Literature, MAT Program, Bard College, Annandale-on-Hudson, New York.

SAM BOOTLE

Teaching Fellow in French, University of St. Andrews, Fife, Scotland, United Kingdom.

MARK CAMERON BOYD

Professor of Fine Arts and Academics, Corcoran College of Art and Design, Washington, D.C.

MICHAEL P. BREEN

Associate Professor of History and Humanities, Reed College, Portland, Oregon.

DANIEL H. BROWN

Assistant Professor of Spanish, Western Illinois University, Macomb.

JAMES BROWN

Assistant Professor of English, University of Wisconsin-Madison.

ERNESTO CAPELLO

Associate Professor of History and Latin American Studies, Macalester College, St. Paul, Minnesota.

MICHAEL CARIGNAN

Associate Professor of History, Elon University, North Carolina.

TERRELL CARVER

Professor of Political Theory, University of Bristol, United Kingdom.

MALCOLM CHASE

Professor of Social History, University of Leeds, United Kingdom.

EWA CHRUSCIEL

Associate Professor of Humanities, Colby-Sawyer College, New London, New Hampshire.

ANN CIASULLO

Assistant Professor of English and Women's and Gender Studies, Gonzaga University, Spokane, Washington.

CURT CLONINGER

Assistant Professor of New Media, University of North Carolina, Asheville.

RUSSELL COOK

Professor of Communications, Loyola University Maryland, Baltimore.

RAYMOND CRAIB

Associate Professor of History, Cornell University, Ithaca, New York.

JANE CRAWFORD

Faculty, History and Political Science Department, Mount St. Mary's College, Los Angeles, California.

LESLEY CURTIS

Visiting Lecturer in French, Humanities, and Women's Studies, University of New Hampshire, Durham.

VICTORIA ESTRADA BERG DECUIR

Assistant Director and Registrar, UNT Art Gallery and Art in Public Places, and Adjunct Faculty, Department of Art History, College of Visual Arts and Design, University of North Texas, Denton.

GABRIELE DILLMANN

Associate Professor of German, Denison University, Granville, Ohio.

EDUARDO DE JESÚS DOUGLAS

Associate Professor of Art History, University of North Carolina at Chapel Hill.

ELLEN DUBOIS

Professor of History, University of California, Los Angeles.

HUGH DUBRULL

Associate Professor of History, St. Anselm College, Manchester, New Hampshire.

ELIZABETH DUQUETTE

Associate Professor of English, Gettysburg College, Pennsylvania.

MICHAEL J. DUVALL

Associate Professor of English, College of Charleston, South Carolina.

TAYLOR EASUM

Assistant Professor of Global Histories; Faculty Fellow of Draper Program, New York University.

LORI EMERSON

Assistant Professor of English, University of Colorado-Boulder.

ALEŠ ERJAVEC

Professor of Philosophy, Aesthetics, and Contemporary Art History, Institute of Philosophy, Slovenian Academy of Sciences and Arts, Ljubljana, Slovenia.

SEBASTIAAN FABER

Professor of Hispanic Studies, Director, Oberlin Center for Languages and Cultures, and Chair, Latin American Studies, Oberlin College, Ohio.

BREANNE FAHS

Associate Professor of Women and Gender Studies, Arizona State University, Glendale.

DANINE FARQUHARSON

Associate Professor of English, Memorial University of Newfoundland, St. John's, Canada.

JIMMY FAZZINO

Lecturer in the Literature Department and Writing Program, University of California, Santa Cruz.

ODILE FERLY

Associate Professor of Francophone Studies, Clark University, Worcester, Massachusetts.

JOSHUA FIRST

Croft Assistant Professor of History and International Studies, University of Mississippi, University.

LEONARDO FLORES

Associate Professor of English and Fulbright Scholar in Digital Culture, Universidad de Puerto Rico, Mayagüez.

LISA FLORMAN

Associate Professor, History of Art, Ohio State University, Columbus.

WILLIAM FRANKE

Professor of Comparative Literature and Religious Studies, Vanderbilt University, Nashville, Tennessee, and Professor of Philosophy and Religions, University of Macao, China.

SUSAN GALLAGHER

Associate Professor of Political Science, University of Massachusetts Lowell.

JAMES GIGANTINO

Assistant Professor of History, University of Arkansas, Fayetteville.

DAWN GILPIN

Assistant Professor of Journalism, Walter Cronkite School of Journalism and Mass Communication, Arizona State University, Phoenix.

DALE GRADEN

Professor of History, University of Idaho, Moscow.

PATRICK RYAN GRZANKA

Honors Faculty Fellow at Barrett, the Honors College, Arizona State University, Tempe.

ANDREW P. HALEY

Associate Professor of American Cultural History, University of Southern Mississippi, Hattiesburg.

M. SÜKRÜ HANIOGLU

Garrett Professor in Foreign Affairs, Chair, Near Eastern Studies Department, and Director, Near Eastern Studies Program, Princeton University, New Jersey.

MARK HARRISON

Professor of Theatre and Performance Studies, Evergreen State College, Olympia, Washington.

CHENE HEADY

Associate Professor of English, Longwood University, Farmville, Virginia.

MICHAEL C. HICKEY

Professor of History, Bloomsburg University, Pennsylvania.

STEPHEN HICKS

Professor of Philosophy, Rockford College, Illinois.

BENEDIKT HJARTARSON

Adjunct Professor of Comparative Literature, University of Iceland, Reykjavik.

TAMARA HO

Assistant Professor of Women's Studies, University of California, Riverside.

WALTER HÖLBLING

Professor of American Studies, Karl-Franzens-Universität, Graz, Austria.

PIPPA HOLLOWAY

Professor of History and Program Director, Graduate Studies, Middle Tennessee State University, Murfreesboro.

MARYANNE HOROWITZ

Professor of History, Occidental College, Los Angeles, California. Editor-in-Chief, New Dictionary of the History of Ideas.

BOZENA KARWOWSKA

Associate Professor of Polish Language and Literature, University of British Columbia, Vancouver, Canada.

ANTHONY KEMP

Associate Professor of English, University of Southern California, Los Angeles.

ALICIA A. KENT

Associate Professor of English, University of Michigan-Flint.

MATTHEW KINEEN

Professor of Comparative Literature, St. Louis University-Madrid, Spain.

JASMINE KITSES

PhD candidate in English, University of California, Davis.

SCOTT KLEINMAN

Professor of English, California State University, Northridge.

CHRISTOPHER KNIGHT

Professor of English, University of Montana, Missoula.

ANDREAS KRATKY

Assistant Professor of Media Arts and Interim Director, Media Arts and Practice

PhD Program, University of Southern California, Los Angeles.

CHARLES KURZMAN

Professor of Sociology, University of North Carolina at Chapel Hill.

JOSÉ LANTERS

Professor of English, University of Wisconsin-Milwaukee.

SHARON LARSON

Visiting Instructor of Modern Languages, University of Central Florida, Orlando.

KEITH LAYBOURN

Diamond Jubilee Professor, University of Huddersfield, West Yorkshire, United Kingdom.

BRENT LAYTHAM

Professor of Theology and Dean, Ecumenical Institute of Theology, St. Mary's Seminary and University, Baltimore, Maryland.

KAREN J. LEADER

Assistant Professor of Art History, Florida Atlantic University, Boca Raton.

ESTHER LESLIE

Professor of Political Aesthetics, University of London-Birkbeck, United Kingdom.

ESTHER LEVINGER

Professor of Art History, University of Haifa, Israel.

MARK LEVY

Professor of Art, California State University-East Bay, Hayward.

MARTIN LOCKSHIN

Professor of Humanities and Chair, Humanities Department, York University, Toronto, Ontario, Canada.

XIAOFEI LU

Gil Watz Early Career Professor in Language and Linguistics, as well as Associate Professor of Applied Linguistics, Pennsylvania State University, University Park.

CARY MAZER

Associate Professor of Theatre Arts and English, University of Pennsylvania, Philadelphia.

WILLIAM MCBRIDE

Associate Professor of English, Illinois State University, Normal.

KEVIN MCCOY

Associate Professor of Art and Art Education, New York University-Steinhardt.

PETER MCPHEE

Professorial Fellow of History, University of Melbourne, Australia.

GREGORY METCALF

Adjunct Professor of Art History and Theory & Criticism, University of Maryland; Maryland Institute College of Art, Baltimore.

DARREN MIDDLETON

Professor of Religion, Texas Christian University, Fort Worth.

GRÜNFELD MIHAI

Associate Professor of Hispanic Studies, Vassar College, Poughkeepsie, New York.

GAVIN MURRAY-MILLER

Adjunct Professor of History, Virginia Commonwealth University, Richmond.

DAVID N. MYERS

Professor of History and Chair, Department of History, University of California, Los Angeles.

WENDY NIELSEN

Assistant Professor of English, Montclair State University, New Jersey.

DRAGANA OBRADOVIC

Assistant Professor of Slavic Languages and Literatures, University of Toronto, Ontario, Canada.

ELAINE O'BRIEN

Professor of Modern and Contemporary Art History and Criticism, California State University, Sacramento.

JENNIFER PAP

Associate Professor of French, University of Denver, Colorado. Sanja Perovic Lecturer in French, King's College, London, United Kingdom.

EMMANUEL PETIT

Associate Professor of Architecture, Yale University, New Haven, Connecticut.

MICHEL PHARAND

Director, Disraeli Project, Queen's University, Kingston, Ontario, Canada.

JANET POWERS

Professor Emerita of Interdisciplinary Studies and Women, Gender, and Sexuality Studies, Gettysburg College, Pennsylvania.

EPHRAIM RADNER

Professor of Historical Theology, Wycliffe College, University of Toronto, Ontario, Canada.

MICHAEL RAPPORT

Professor of History and Politics, University of Stirling, Scotland, United Kingdom.

HOLLY RAYNARD

Lecturer in Czech Studies, University of Florida, Gainesville.

JONATHAN REES

Professor of History, Colorado State University-Pueblo.

JOHN RIEDER

Professor of English, University of Hawaii at Manoa, Honolulu.

PATRICIO RIZZO-VAST

Instructor in Spanish and Portuguese, Northeastern Illinois University, Chicago.

HUGH ROBERTS

Associate Professor of English, University of California, Irvine, California.

MOSS ROBERTS

Professor of Chinese, New York University.

LETHA CLAIR ROBERTSON

Assistant Professor of Art and Art History, University of Texas at Tyler.

AARON ROSEN

Lecturer in Sacred Traditions and the Arts, King's College-London, United Kingdom.

ELI RUBIN

Associate Professor of History, Western Michigan University, Kalamazoo.

GREGORY SHAYA

Associate Professor of History and Chair, History Department, College of Wooster, Ohio.

NOAH SHUSTERMAN

Assistant Professor of Intellectual Heritage, Temple University, Philadelphia, Pennsylvania.

JOEL SIPRESS

Professor of History, University of Wisconsin-Superior.

ADAM SITZE

Assistant Professor of Law, Jurisprudence, and Social Thought, Amherst College, Massachusetts.

CRAIG SMITH

Associate Professor of Art, University of Florida, Gainesville.

ROGER SOUTHALL

Honorary Professor in SWOP (Southwest Organizing Project) and Head, Sociology Department, University of the Witwatersrand, Johannesburg, South Africa.

ROBERT SPAHR

Assistant Professor of Media and Media Production, Southern Illinois University, Carbondale.

ANIA SPYRA

Assistant Professor of English, Butler University, Indianapolis, Indiana.

MARY ZEISS STANGE

Professor of Women's Studies and Religion, Skidmore College, Saratoga Springs, New York.

ELIZABETH STARK

Visiting Fellow, Yale Information Society Project, and Lecturer in Computer Science, Yale University, New Haven, Connecticut.

JANET WRIGHT STARNER

Associate Professor of English, Wilkes University, Wilkes-Barre, Pennsylvania.

R. VLADMIR STEFFEL

Professor Emeritus of History and Director, Honors Programs, Ohio State University-Marion.

SARAH STOECKL

PhD, Department of English, University of Oregon, Eugene.

MASON STOKES

Associate Professor of English and Chair, English Department, Skidmore College, Saratoga Springs, New York.

MATTHEW STRATTON

Assistant Professor of English, University of California, Davis.

WOODMAN TAYLOR

Associate Professor of Art History, American University of Dubai.

CHARISSA TERRANOVA

Assistant Professor of Aesthetic Studies, University of Texas at Dallas, Richardson.

DOUGLASS THOMSON

Professor of English, Georgia Southern University, Statesboro.

LARRY THORNTON

Professor of History, Hanover College, Indiana.

JOHN G. TURNER

Assistant Professor of Religious Studies, George Mason University, Fairfax, Virginia.

THOMAS UNDERWOOD

Senior Lecturer (Master Level), College of Arts and Sciences Writing Program, Boston University, Massachusetts.

ELIZABETH VITANZA

French Instructor, Marlborough School, Los Angeles, California.

ALICIA VOLK

Associate Professor of Art History and Director, Graduate Studies, University of Maryland, College Park.

DONALD WELLMAN

Professor of Literature and Writing, Daniel Webster College, Nashua, New Hampshire.

E. J. WESTLAKE

Associate Professor of Theatre, University of Michigan, Ann Arbor.

RACHEL WILLIAMS

Associate Professor of Studio Art and Gender, Women's, and Sexuality Studies, University of Iowa, Iowa City.

SIMONA WRIGHT

Professor of Italian, College of New Jersey, Ewing Township.

RALPH YOUNG

Professor of History, Temple University, Philadelphia, Pennsylvania.

PIERANTONIO ZANOTTI

Adjunct Professor of Japanese Language, Università Ca' Foscari Venezia, Italy.

⌁ ARTISTS AND WRITERS

AGAINST NATURE

Joris-Karl Huysmans

OVERVIEW

Joris-Karl Huysmans's novel *À Rebours,* first published in 1884, announces the author's rejection of the literary school known as naturalism and establishes, in contrast, the principles of the decadent movement. Translated as *Against Nature* (or *Against the Grain*), *À Rebours* chronicles the eclectic experiments and luxurious life of Jean des Esseintes, a degenerate nobleman who retires to the outskirts of Paris to pursue a life of uninterrupted and sometimes perverse pleasure. Weary of the Parisian working and merchant classes (as was Huysmans himself), Des Esseintes seeks amusement in such activities as gilding and bejeweling a tortoise to serve as drawing-room furniture, poring over recondite books of poetry, and constructing a "mouth organ" from a set of interconnected casks of liquor. Along the way, he declares himself in favor of disorienting, open-ended works of art that give free rein to their interpreters.

Huysmans had predicted that *Against Nature,* with its listless narrative and accumulation of esoteric details, would prove to be a "damn fiasco." Certainly it was controversial, drawing criticism from his alienated peers and readers, who were scandalized by its amorality and anticlericalism. However, these elements only underscored the novel's historical significance. In an ironic nod to its ecclesiastical undercurrents, the work soon garnered the nickname of "breviary [i.e., prayer book] of the Decadence," thanks to an essay on Huysmans by Arthur Symons. This movement sought to supersede naturalism with a focus on artificiality, antiquity, and rarefied physical and intellectual pleasures. As such, *Against Nature* provided a retrospective label for authors such as Arthur Rimbaud and a prospective one for later novelists such as Max Beerbohm. For English readers, it became especially notorious as the "poisonous" French novel that captivated and corrupted Oscar Wilde's Dorian Gray. In the years since its publication, *Against Nature* has largely conserved its reputation as the central work of this major fin-de-siècle literary movement.

HISTORICAL AND LITERARY CONTEXT

Huysmans wrote *Against Nature* partly as a declaration that literary naturalism had reached a dead end and partly to suggest a way beyond that impasse. Naturalism, as expounded by the novelist Émile Zola, was the prevailing French literary school of the time, an outgrowth of the mid-eighteenth-century realism exemplified by Gustave Flaubert and Stendhal. Naturalist works, broadly speaking, tended to depict and sympathize with the struggles of the working class in a manner the authors considered true to life. Huysmans found much to admire in the style of his contemporaries but came to believe that their subject matter unnecessarily handicapped them, limiting the scope of their work to a repetitive pattern of human drama. He intended to demonstrate the novel's potential—not as a record of workaday life but as a means of instigating profound aesthetic experiences for an alert and sensitive reader.

By the time he undertook his literary rebuttal of naturalism, Huysmans had already completed a lengthy apprenticeship under Zola. His earliest novel, *Marthe* (1876), had attracted praise from Zola, and his subsequent work, *Les Soeurs Vatard* (1879), evinces many defining "Zolist" traits: its protagonists are factory workers with bleak prospects both in love and in life. In the late 1870s Huysmans was a frequent figure at the literary gatherings Zola hosted at Médan; his short story "Sac au Dos" ("Backpack") appeared in an 1880 anthology published by this "Médan group," alongside works by major naturalist authors Guy de Maupassant and Paul Alexis.

Indeed, in constructing his polemical novel, Huysmans drew upon many of the traits he considered redeemable in naturalist fiction, especially the detailed scene-setting exemplified by such works as Zola's Rougon-Macquart novel cycle (1871-93). Moreover, Huysmans's novel involved painstaking research (another cornerstone of naturalism) into such subjects as the history of literary Latin and trends in contemporary jewel setting. Thus, while Des Esseintes reserves the highest praise for the symbolist authors Charles Baudelaire, Stéphane Mallarmé, and Paul Verlaine, the novel's style itself reflects a more complicated pedigree.

Against Nature was greatly influential in both French and English literary circles. Like his onetime mentor, Huysmans came to be closely associated with a literary school of his own: the decadents, who appropriated their name from a common critical epithet. Not all writers championed by Huysmans were eager to share this label; the poet Jean Moréas took pains in his *Symbolist Manifesto* of 1886 to defend symbolists from the charges rather than exult in

❖ *Key Facts*

Time Period:
Late 19th Century

Movement/Issue:
Decadent movement; Aesthetics

Place of Publication:
France

Language of Publication:
French

DECADENT TO DEVOUT: CHRISTIANITY IN *AGAINST NATURE*

Among its many intersecting motifs, *Against Nature* shows a recurring tension in the protagonist's relationship with religion. Des Esseintes regards the church as an amoral preserver of art and tradition, but he also feels a deep affinity for the religion of his youth, periodically suppressed but never extinguished. This was, according to later autobiographical novels, a pattern familiar to Huysmans himself, who had been raised Roman Catholic but left the church at an early age. His familiar and appreciative treatment of Christian mystical literature in *Against Nature* impressed many Christian authors of his day, though to some it seemed incongruous with Des Esseintes's life of excess. Barbey d'Aurevilly, a prominent Catholic novelist, is quoted in Ellis Hanson's *Decadence and Catholicism* (1997) as saying that the novel left Huysmans with a choice "between the muzzle of a pistol and the foot of the Cross."

Huysmans chose the latter, converting to Catholicism and chronicling the process in his late fiction. Beginning with *Là-Bas* (1891), his final four novels follow the *raisonneur* Durtal in a spiritual trajectory that leads from a brief dalliance with Satanism to life as a Catholic oblate. Yet much in *Against Nature* prefigures this change. First with aesthetic curiosity, then with increasing emotional force (though never with Durtal's depth of conviction), Des Esseintes recalls "the poetic and poignant atmosphere of Catholicism in which he had been steeped as a boy."

them. Perhaps the greatest example of *Against Nature*'s impact on English literature is Wilde's *The Picture of Dorian Gray* (1890), whose hedonistic and malevolent protagonist makes a "poisonous" French novel his veritable guidebook to vice and indulgence. In the course of a highly publicized 1895 libel trial, Wilde identified the novel in question as *Against Nature*, fueling the work's reputation.

THEMES AND STYLE

True to its title, *Against Nature* directly and deliberately reverses many of the defining traits of naturalism. In a 1986 essay by Gail Finney for *Modern Language Studies,* she observes that the novel presents "the cultivation of art and artifice as against the practice of naturalistic imitation … a portrait of wealth and excess as opposed to a picture of poverty and privation; a character study of an isolated, aristocratic dandy versus a depiction of the proletariat acting as a mass." Moreover, by creating in Des Esseintes a restless and deeply reflective interpreter of art, Huysmans not only fills the novel with instances of the decadent style in action, but he also presents the theoretical and aesthetic framework that renders *Against Nature* a full-fledged manifesto. This is evident, for example, in Des Esseintes's consideration of what he values in contemporary literature, namely "Byzantine flowers of thought and deliquescent

complexities of style." The art Huysmans esteems invites a multiplicity of interpretations rather than a single explanation.

Huysmans expounds these decadent values through reference to a wide range of art forms, especially painting and literature. Indeed, in perusing works from across centuries and styles, Des Esseintes establishes that the fundamental qualities of decadent art may be found in historical periods as apparently disparate as second-century Rome and fin-de-siècle Paris. In painting, Des Esseintes favors Gustave Moreau's two depictions of the biblical dancer Salome, seventeenth-century Dutch engravings of torture scenes, and the eerie portraits of Odilon Redon. In literature, he esteems those Latin works "which minds drilled into conformity … lump[ed] together under the generic name of 'the Decadence'"—that is, those of the Silver Age. In narrating a preference for Petronius and Apuleius over Cicero (whom he calls "old Chick-Pea") and Virgil (an "appalling pedant"), Huysmans suggests that the later writers' supposed ornamentations and excesses are instrumental to the decadent experience.

Many of the novel's most memorable passages also have a surreal texture, as the protagonist's consciousness shifts from past to present, from dream to reality, and occasionally into the realm of a fictional work he happens to recall. Thus, Charles Dickens is evoked at considerable length by Des Esseintes's meal in an English restaurant, only to be replaced by a Poean somberness when he orders a glass of Amontillado. Often the individual details are subsumed in a monomaniacal list of particulars, as with the page-length description of the food and furnishings at Des Esseintes's "black feast": "The dining-room, draped in black, opened out on to a garden metamorphosed for the occasion, the paths being strewn with charcoal, the ornamental pond edged with black basalt and filled with ink." Huysmans's narrator proceeds to rove through dozens of such details, from the color of light radiated by the candelabra to the embroidery of the waitresses' slippers to the numerous dishes (all black).

CRITICAL DISCUSSION

In addition to the novel's unmistakable influence on Wilde, *Against Nature* found a somewhat divided audience on both sides of the English Channel. In England, painter James McNeill Whistler expressed admiration for the work, and the poet and critic Symons declared the novel "the breviary of the Decadence" in an 1892 essay on Huysmans. France's Stéphane Mallarmé appreciated the novel's favorable treatment of his poetry and responded with a brief verse tribute to Des Esseintes. Others, however, were less impressed, including Zola, who found his former disciple's about-face dismaying. As Huysmans recounted in the preface to the novel's 1903 edition, Zola reprimanded the younger author for what he perceived as a "terrible blow" to the naturalist tradition. Huysmans replied that he did not necessarily share the values or aesthetics of his eccentric protagonist. The association stuck, however, and Huysmans came to be identified with the work long after he had moved on to other literary projects.

As the archetypal decadent novel, *Against Nature* has furnished scholars with a convenient means of discussing the essential traits of this type of literature and of charting the movement's relationship to naturalism. Finney offers one example of such historical criticism, enumerating the chief stylistic and thematic distinctions between *Against Nature* and Zola's novel *Germinal* (1885). Finney concludes that despite obvious aesthetic and ethical disagreements, the two works actually correspond quite closely: Huysmans displays "the same meticulous attention to detail," the same "particular care in the rendering of sensations" as his predecessor and rival. Moreover, though it is less obvious in Huysmans's case, Finney makes the case that "both works are inspired by a censorious impulse, by a profound dissatisfaction with the status quo."

Recent criticism of *Against Nature* is robust and varied. One emerging theme is Des Esseintes's relationship to his self-fashioned suburban environment. In a 1997 essay for the *South Atlantic Review,* Jennifer Forrest argues that *Against Nature* reflects a changing understanding of the relationship between city and country and suggests that Des Esseintes's retirement to Fontenay-aux-Roses "institutes a more modern, more complex, and certainly more nuanced connection between the center and the peripheral regions." Mary Elizabeth Curtin's 2011 essay in *Victorian Literature and Culture* examines the role of the suburbs in *Against Nature.* Against the common post-World War II interpretation of suburban space as the site of the bourgeois, Curtin contends that places such as Fontenay-aux-Roses, which free the protagonist from both the commercial bustle of cities and the "disappointments of unadulterated Nature," are, in fact, "the only space in which to enact the death of Decadence and symbolically to begin anew."

BIBLIOGRAPHY

Sources

Curtin, Mary Elizabeth. "'Like Bottled Wasps': Beerbohm, Huysmans, and the Decadents' Suburban Retreat." *Victorian Literature and Culture* 39.1 (2011): 183-200. *Literature Online.* Web. 21 Sept. 2012.

Finney, Gail. "In the Naturalist Grain: Huysmans' *À Rebours* Viewed through the Lens of Zola's *Germinal.*" *Modern Language Studies* 16.2 (1986): 71-77. *JSTOR.* Web. 21 Sept. 2012.

Forrest, Jennifer. "Paris à Rebours: Where Huysmans Put the 'Faux' in 'Faubourg'." *South Atlantic Review* 62.2 (1997): 10-28. *JSTOR.* Web. 21 Sept. 2012.

Hanson, Ellis. *Decadence and Catholicism.* Cambridge: Harvard UP, 1997. Print.

Huysmans, Joris-Karl. *Against Nature.* Trans. Robert Baldick. Baltimore: Penguin, 1966. Print.

Symons, Arthur. "Huysmans." *Figures of Several Centuries.* London: Constable, 1917. Print.

Further Reading

Banks, Brian R. *The Image of Huysmans.* New York: AMS, 1990. Print.

Cevasco, G. A. *The Breviary of the Decadence: J.-K. Huysmans's "A Rebours" and English Literature.* New York: AMS, 2002. Print.

Davis, Whitney. "Decadence and the Organic Metaphor." *Representations* 89.1 (2005): 131-49. *JSTOR.* Web. 21 Sept. 2012.

Emery, Elizabeth. "J.-K. Huysmans, Medievalist." *Modern Language Studies* 30.2 (2000): 119-31. *JSTOR.* Web. 21 Sept. 2012.

Gasché, Rodolphe. "The Falls of History: Huysmans's *À Rebours.*" *Yale French Studies* 74 (1988): 183-204. *JSTOR.* Web. 21 Sept. 2012.

Ziegler, Robert. *The Mirror of Divinity: The World and Creation in J.-K. Huysmans.* Newark: U of Delaware P, 2004. Print.

Michael Hartwell

Oedipus and the Sphinx, an 1864 painting by Gustave Moreau. In the novel *Against Nature,* the main character, Jean Des Esseintes, collects reprints of paintings by Moreau. © PETER HORREE/ALAMY

ARS POETICA

Horace

✧ *Key Facts*

Time Period:
1st Century BCE

Movement/Issue:
Aesthetics; Poetics

Place of Publication:
Greece

**Language of
Publication:**
Greek

OVERVIEW

Composed by Quintus Horatius Flaccus (Horace) in about 10 BCE, *Ars Poetica* is a poem on poetics that discusses the decorum of literature and other art forms. Also known as *Epistle 2.3,* or *Epistle to the Pisones,* the poem is in the form of a letter that purports to give advice on poetic composition to the sons of Piso, who was likely a Roman consul. The correct title, date of composition, and genre of this work have been a source of intense debate among scholars, more so than any of Horace's other poems. His longest work, *Ars Poetica* consists of 476 lines with nearly thirty maxims for poets. Following in the Greek tradition, the poem promotes a human-centered, rather than purely mythic, focus in the arts and sciences but in a uniquely Roman way. *Ars Poetica* is notable for its didacticism, humor, common sense, and irony. When the work was composed, during the reign of Emperor Caesar Augustus (27 BCE-14 CE), Horace was recognized as the most significant living Augustan poet, Virgil having died in 19 BCE and Ovid having just begun his career.

Like Horace's *Satires* (35 BCE) and *Epistles* (20-14 BCE), *Ars Poetica* is a lively and entertaining poem written primarily for friends who share similar aesthetic sensibilities. Although evidence is scant, his audience appears to have received the poem with enthusiasm. The Roman rhetorician Quintilian, in the first century CE, was the first to refer to the work as *Ars Poetica,* and the grammarian Pomponius Porphyrio wrote an early commentary in the second century CE. Later Roman authors, including Servius and Lucian, admired the work for its numerous precepts, including the "purple patch," an assertion that excess description is a form of digression. With the exception of Aristotle's *Poetics,* no ancient work of literary criticism has had a greater impact. Horace's unique poem has inspired readers and influenced writers for centuries with its literary principles, wit, and polished style. Prominent among its many admirers were Queen Elizabeth I, Alexander Pope, W. H. Auden, and Jorge Luis Borges.

HISTORICAL AND LITERARY CONTEXT

The Roman Republic, established in about 500 BCE, gave way to the autocratic Roman Empire in the first century BCE. As its first emperor, Augustus needed to popularize his rule, and he charged his friend and political advisor Gaius Maecenas with generating support among the people by creating a distinctly Roman cultural identity. Pre-Augustan writers had often traveled abroad to study at the prestigious Greek academies and tended to mimic Greek literary models. In order to foster independence from foreign influences, the empire promoted schools of rhetoric in Rome where students studied the works of the philosopher Cicero. Acting as a cultural minister and patron, Maecenas sponsored some of Rome's greatest poets, including Virgil, Horace, Propertius, and Ovid, with the aim of glorifying the empire and inspiring its citizens. These masters became known as the Augustan poets.

Horace was aware of the dangers to the empire of perpetuating the ascendancy of Greek aesthetics. Although his early writings are apolitical, his work took on more nationalistic tones after he met Maecenas in 39 BCE. A famous line from *Epistles 2.1* (12 BCE)—"Captive Greece took its Roman captor captive, / Invading uncouth Latium with its arts"— illustrates the aesthetic concerns and anxiety of the Augustan period. In *Ars Poetica* Horace complains that Greece had the "power to speak with eloquent voices," whereas Rome cares for only empire, money, and "doing sums." Although the poem pays homage to Greek literary and rhetorical theory, Horace uses a style replete with both mischief and mores. Along with Livy, the author of the monumental and extremely popular *History of Rome* (ca. 25 BCE), Horace helped to bring national consciousness to new heights. He not only created a Roman poetics but also promoted Augustus's moral reforms (which included fostering religious devotion, penalizing celibacy and the unmarried, restricting divorce and interactions between classes, and severely punishing adultery and bribery), instructing the average Roman citizen on how to live with moral integrity.

Ars Poetica draws from such works of Greek poetic theory as Plato's *Phaedrus* (360 BCE) and Aristotle's *Poetics* (335 BCE). Horace also relies on Greek-influenced Roman writers, such as Cicero, Lucilius, and Varro. The Horatian commentator Porphyrio (ca. 200 CE) wrote that in *Ars Poetica* Horace gathered his central poetic precepts from third-century-BCE Greek critic Neoptolemus of Parium. For example, according to Porphyrio, Horace applied Neoptolemus's tripartite structure of poem, poetry, and poet to his own theories. Neoptolemus's work is lost, however, so scholars are unable to test Porphyrio's claim. Concerning this complex Greco-Roman tradition, Niall Rudd writes in *Horace*: Epistles II *and* Epistle to the Pisones (1989), "We should not assume that Horace had always a specific source in mind … in the [*Ars Poetica*] he presented literary and rhetorical theories drawn from many quarters." *Ars Poetica* is ultimately Horatian in style and theme, promoting a distinct Roman poetics and an Augustan morality.

For more than two millennia, *Ars Poetica* has remained Horace's most influential poem. His younger contemporaries and admirers Ovid and Propertius never explicitly mention the work, but its impact on Ovid's *Metamorphoses* (ca. 8 BCE) is apparent. Many Renaissance poets, notably Ben Jonson, translated the poem and used it as a treatise on poetics. Eighteenth- and nineteenth-century neoclassical literature and aesthetics modeled themselves on *Ars Poetica,* and some modernists, including those in the Imagist movement of the early twentieth century, were indebted to its precepts. Current scholars and writers often return to Horace's masterwork. Recently, David Ferry published a translation (*The Epistles of Horace,* 2002) and Rudd, an exceptional commentary.

THEMES AND STYLE

The artistic intent of *Ars Poetica* is to give advice on poetic composition. Horace declares: "My aim is to take familiar things and make / Poetry of them, and do it in such a way / That it looks as if it was easy as could be / For anybody to do it." The purpose of poetry, he continues, is "to instruct or else to delight; / Or better still, to delight and instruct at once." He discusses the norms and principles of other art forms, providing common-sensical guidance on writing in general, such as "Aspiring writer, be sure to be careful to pick / Material that you're strong enough to handle" and "Order's important." In reference to drama, he states, "The chorus should praise the life of moderation." This and other aphorisms convey his views on proper attitudes toward life, among them, "Obey the conventions" and "All things that mortals do and build are mortal." In addition, the poem addresses literary terms such as mimesis, or art's imitation of life. Horace ends by describing the "crazy poet" who is "a leach that won't let go till he's full of blood," a parody of the poetaster who recites to the unwilling listener until "he reads him to death."

Horace's use of the verse epistle allows him to change tones and connect ideas rapidly, permitting his didactic style to vary from somber to satirical; thus it is the ideal literary form to convey a variety of opinions, information, and advice. The role of the reader resembles that of an eavesdropper listening in on a conversation between intimate friends and thus gaining access to privileged intelligence and instruction. Horace

PRIMARY SOURCE

ARS POETICA

Pick a subject, writers, equal to your strength and take some time to consider what your shoulders should refuse and what they can bear. Neither eloquence nor clear organization will forsake one who has chosen a subject within his capabilities. Unless I am mistaken this will be the special excellence and delight of good organization, that the author of the promised poem, enamored of one subject and scornful of another, says now what ought to be said now and both postpones and omits a great deal for the present....

Also in linking words you will speak with exceptional subtlety and care if a skillful connection renders a well-known term with a new twist. If, by chance, it is necessary to explain obscure matters by means of new images it will turn out that you must devise words never heard by the kilted Cethegi, and license for this will be given if claimed with modesty.

Words that are new and recently coined will be received in good faith if they are sparingly diverted from a Greek source. Why then will the Roman grant to Caecilius and Plautus what is denied to Virgil and Varius? If I am capable of doing it, why am I grudged the acquisition of some few words when the tongue of Cato and Ennius enriched our ancestral language and revealed new names for things? It has always been permitted, and it always will be permitted to bring to light a name stamped with the mark of the present day....

It is not enough for poems to be "beautiful"; they must also yield delight and guide the listener's spirit wherever they wish. As human faces laugh with those who are laughing, so they weep with those who are weeping. If you wish me to cry, you must first feel grief yourself, then your misfortunes, O Telephus or Peleus, will injure me. If you speak ineptly assigned words, I shall either sleep or laugh. Sad words are fitting for the gloomy face, words full of threats for the angry one, playful words for the amused face, serious words for the stern one. For Nature first forms us within so as to respond to every kind of fortune. She delights us or impels us to anger or knocks us to the ground and torments us with oppressive grief. Afterward she expresses the emotions of the spirit with language as their interpreter. If, however, there is discord between the words spoken and the fortune of the speaker, Romans, whether cavalry or infantry, will raise their voices in a raucous belly laugh....

It will make a great difference whether a god is speaking or a hero, a mature old man or someone passionate and still in the full flower of youth, a powerful matron or a diligent nurse, an itinerant merchant or the cultivator of a prosperous field, a Colchian or an Assyrian, one raised in Thebes or in Argos.

SOURCE: Translated by Leon Golend. *Horace for Students of Literature: The 'Ars Poetica' and Its Tradition.* University Press of Florida, 1995. pp. 8, 9, 10, 11.

Fedor Andreevich Bronnikov's 1863 painting *Horatius Reading His Satires to Maecenas* depicts the Roman poet Horace reciting to his patron, Gaius Maecenas. MUSEUM OF REGIONAL STUDIES, SHADRINSK

maintains the epistolary format by directly addressing the Pisos throughout ("Dear Pisos" and "Father and worthy sons") and indirectly referring to the "[a]spiring writer." Although the wide range of subjects gives the appearance of a lack of uniform intent, a thread of decorum runs through the work that transmits the writer's organization and good sense.

Like the heroic poetry of Horace's predecessors, including Homer and Virgil, *Ars Poetica* is written in hexameter; that is, each line is made up of six metrical units. His verse takes on the easy conversational tone of a letter between friends. The voice is confident, knowledgeable, persuasive, and never pretentious. With vigorous spontaneity and intellectual wit, he gives counsel on how to live with integrity, as in the lines "If you don't know what you're doing you can go wrong / Just out of trying to do your best to do right," which evoke the proverb "The road to hell is paved with good intentions." Using unpoetic vocabulary, Horace eliminates Grecisms (sprinkling Latin poetry with Greek words was popular at the time) and restricts his use of archaisms (out-of-date language), common dialect, and comic coinages (such as Aristophanes' exaggerated number "umpteen million"), believing that buffoonery and coarseness weaken artistic and moral effects. The epistle is written with elegant ease and refinement, which never counteract the poem's didactic force and immediacy. Horace writes, "In short, whatever the work is supposed to be, / Let it be true to itself, essentially simple."

CRITICAL DISCUSSION

The initial reaction to *Ars Poetica* in the ancient world is not known. Ovid, who greatly admired Horace, evokes "the mad poet" from *Ars Poetica* in his *Tristia 2* (ca. 9 CE). In *Institutio Oratoria* (ca. 90 CE) Quintilian—who praises Horace as the only Roman poet worth reading—quotes *Ars Poetica* eight times, more often than he quotes any other of Horace's poems. Two commentaries still extant in late antiquity provide evidence of Horace's importance in academic study. The commentary of Porphyrio discusses the works of Horace in nonchronological order and emphasizes the importance of his *Odes* and *Ars Poetica*. The second is a lost Horatian commentary by Roman grammarian Helenius Acro (200 CE).

The later reception of *Ars Poetica* is of far more consequence than that of the Augustan period. Although the works of Virgil and Ovid overshadowed those of Horace during the Middle Ages, when *Ars Poetica* was considered entirely didactic and was utilized primarily as an introduction to poetry, the numerous ensuing translations, imitations, commentaries, and scholarly works centering on the poem testify to its tremendous aesthetic legacy. During the Renaissance it influenced not only major writers such as Jonson but also artists including the French painter Charles du Fresnoy, well-known for his Latin poem *De arte graphica* (*On Graphic Art*, 1668). *Ars Poetica* has been considered not only one of Horace's finest poems but also—as Andrew Laird writes in *The Cambridge Companion to Horace* (2007)—"as a kind of literary 'Magna Carta' for norms and principles that were earnestly applied to literature, drama, and other art forms well into the eighteenth century." Because of the poem's innovation and timeless appeal, scholarly interest in *Ars Poetica* has increased over the centuries. Pope in the eighteenth century and Auden in the twentieth century are just two of the literary luminaries who have emulated its style.

A major trend in scholarship of *Ars Poetica* focuses on the many unknown facts of its genesis. Of all Horace's poems, for example, it is the most difficult to date. In *Shifting Paradigms* (1991), Bernard Frischer examines biographical information, subject matter, meter, stylometrics, word function, and punctuation to date the poem, placing it between 24 and 20 BCE. Other academics such as Rudd, however, assert that the poem was published around 10 BCE, the most widely accepted date. The work's original title may have been *Epistula ad Pisones*. Quintilian, in addition to being the first to refer to the poem as *Ars Poetica* nearly a century after its initial appearance, gave it the subtitle *Liber de Arte Poetica*. Although it is sometimes known as *Epistle 2.3*, *Ars Poetica* in the manuscript tradition does not follow *Epistles 2.1* (a letter addressed to Augustus) and *2.2* (a letter to his friend Florus). Sixteenth-century editors numbered *Ars Poetica* in sequence with the other epistles, but in earlier manuscripts it is listed as an independent work. Believing it to be a poem of serious intent in the tradition of Aristotle's *Poetics* rather than simply a letter in verse, D. A. Russell writes in a 1973 essay in *Greek and Latin Studies,* "Its differences from the *Epistles* are in fact more significant for its understanding than its resemblances to them. It is very much 'a treatise with *Dear so-and-so* at the beginning.'" In *Greece & Rome* (1972), however, Gordon Williams entirely disagrees and emphasizes the poem's "humor and parody" over its purpose as a didactic treatise.

BIBLIOGRAPHY

Sources

Frischer, Bernard. *Shifting Paradigms: New Approaches to Horace's* Ars Poetica. Atlanta: Scholars, 1991. Print.

Horace. *The Epistles of Horace.* Trans. David Ferry. New York: Farrar, 2001. Print.

Laird, Andrew. "The *Ars Poetica.*" *The Cambridge Companion to Horace.* Ed. Stephen Harrison. Cambridge: Cambridge UP, 2007. Print.

Rudd, Niall. *Horace*: Epistles II *and* Epistle to the Pisones. Cambridge: Cambridge UP, 1989. Print.

Russell, D. A. "*Ars Poetica.*" *Greek and Latin Studies: Horace.* London: Routledge, 1973. Print.

Williams, Gordon. "Horace." *Greece & Rome.* New Surveys in the Classics 6. Oxford: Clarendon, 1972. Print.

Further Reading

Brink, C. O. *Horace on Poetry.* Vol. 2. Cambridge: Cambridge UP, 1972. Print.

Freudenburg, Kirk. *Horace: Satires and Epistles.* Oxford: Oxford UP, 2009. Print.

Houghton, L. B. T., and Maria Wyke. *Perceptions of Horace.* Cambridge: Cambridge UP, 2009. Print.

Kilpatrick, Ross. *The Poetry of Criticism.* Edmonton: U of Alberta P, 1990. Print.

McNeill, Randall. *Horace: Image, Identity, and Audience.* Baltimore: John Hopkins UP, 2001. Print.

Tarrant, Richard. "Ancient Receptions of Horace." *The Cambridge Companion to Horace.* Ed. Stephen Harrison. Cambridge: Cambridge UP, 2007. Print.

Greg Bach

ATHENAEUM FRAGMENT 116

Friedrich Schlegel

✥ *Key Facts*

Time Period:
Late 18th Century

Movement/Issue:
Aesthetics; Romanticism

Place of Publication:
Germany

Language of Publication:
German

OVERVIEW

Composed by Friedrich Schlegel, *Athenaeum Fragment 116* (1798) describes the aesthetic qualities, aims, and possibilities of romantic poetry. Schlegel argues that "all poetry is or should be romantic." *Fragment 116* was one of 451 statements of Schlegel's philosophy of aesthetics that were included in the journal *Athenaeum,* which Schlegel founded with his brother August Wilhelm Schlegel in 1798; the statements were collected as the *Athenaeum Fragments.* The journal *Athenaeum* is widely credited with launching German romanticism, and *Fragment 116* is viewed as Schlegel's most succinct expression of the movement's founding motivations and characteristics. *Fragment 116* also marks an important step in Schlegel's progression from his earlier, classicist valorization of Greek poetry to his embrace of modern poetic forms. Central to *Fragment 116* is Schlegel's claim that romantic poetry is able to reach across genres and forms to depict the full complexity of its age.

Though the true significance of *Fragment 116* was not immediately acknowledged by contemporary German intellectuals, it was later recognized as an important crystallization of the ideals of a vital aesthetic movement. In concert with the hundreds of other fragments and various writings in the *Athenaeum, Fragment 116* provides the framework of German romanticism, which was a prominent aesthetic mode throughout the early nineteenth century. The work of numerous writers and other artists can be traced back to the ideas Schlegel broaches in *Fragment 116.* Today, *Fragment 116* is considered an important founding statement of German romanticism and is recognized for its influence on nineteenth-century art of various genres.

HISTORICAL AND LITERARY CONTEXT

Fragment 116 responds to the political, social, and intellectual climate in Europe at the end of the eighteenth century, when the French Revolution, Enlightenment thought, and increasing industrialization upended the old order. As early as 1791, seven years before composing the *Athenaeum Fragments,* Schlegel became sympathetically interested in the progress of the revolution in France, which ended that nation's monarchy and ushered in a republican form of government. A democratic republic, Schlegel believed,

provided the only conditions in which "humanity could be fully realized," according to scholar Fredrick C. Beiser in *Enlightenment, Revolution, and Romanticism: The Genesis of Modern German Political Thought, 1790-1800* (1992). As a result of his democratic fervor, Schlegel idealized Greek culture and art. Contemporary art, he argued, was constrained by society's relative lack of political freedom. Through the mid-1790s, Schlegel published political essays on literature and politics in journals such as the *Lyceum der schönen Künste.*

By 1798, Schlegel's thought had become radicalized. He was no longer interested in conventional political critique and literary criticism; he had become convinced that rational criticism itself should be scrutinized. That year, he and his brother August Wilhelm Schlegel launched *Athenaeum* to provide a forum for this form of radical criticism and, according to Beiser, to "create a revolution in the sphere of culture." Romantic poetry was proffered as the vehicle for this revolution. Romantic poetry, Schlegel argues in *Athenaeum,* is a means of expressing the modern aspiration for a more perfect republican society.

The *Athenaeum Fragments* is a collection of aphorisms that advocate for radical individualism, artistically and ethically. Tradition, law, and convention, Schlegel argues in *Fragment 116,* should all be interrogated and subjugated to the will of the individual; the artist should follow his own genius and inspiration rather than precedent. German writer Friedrich Schiller served as an important influence on the ideas expressed in Schlegel's *Fragments*; Schiller had argued for the liberating potential of contemporary poetry and illustrated for Schlegel the limitations of classical poetry. The fragmentary form that Schlegel adopted was, in part, the result of his reading French writer Nicolas Chamfort's *Pensées, maximes et anecdotes,* a collection of aphorisms.

Fragment 116 helped to inspire a large number of works of German romanticism. Ludwig Tieck, Wilhelm Heinrich Wackenroder, and Novalis, a contributor to *Athenaeum,* were among of the most significant initial adopters of Schlegel's romantic vision. These Early Romantics, as they are known by scholars, produced works of literature that are fundamentally religious and antirational. The Early Romantics were succeeded by the Late Romantics, who became increasingly conservative politically and artistically and who valorized the idea of a collective national past with origins in the common people, or *Volk*. Poet Clemens Brentano collected and published the poetry and fairy tales of the German oral tradition, while writer Joseph von Eichendorff explored the corrupting influence of civilization on nature and religious conviction. Today, German romanticism commands significant scholarly interest.

THEMES AND STYLE

Fragment 116 explores the central theme that romantic poetry offers the ideal aesthetic means of depicting and encapsulating the contemporary world. The fragment opens with a blunt declaration: "Romantic poetry is a progressive, universal poetry." The universality of romantic poetry resides in its ability to encompass and unify a variety of diverse forms: "It tries to and should mix and fuse poetry and prose, inspiration and criticism, the poetry of art and the poetry of nature…." Its universality is not, however, merely formal. Romantic poetry, Schlegel writes, "embraces everything that is purely poetic, from the greatest systems of art … to the sigh, the kiss that the poetizing child breathes forth in artless song." The progressiveness of romantic poetry is demonstrated in its continual reinvention and its infinite ability to adapt. It exists "in the state of

becoming," and this perpetual development is "its real essence." As a result of its inexhaustible ability to incorporate other forms, romantic poetry offers "a mirror of the whole circumambient world, an image of the age."

Schlegel's rhetorical strategy is to use sweeping declarative statements *in Fragment 116* to illustrate rather than discursively argue for his grand claims about romantic poetry. Appearing as it does within the context of hundreds of other aphoristic fragments, *Fragment 116* is not a self-contained document but one part of a much larger rhetorical structure. As a result, *Fragment 116* does not bear the burden of containing a comprehensive argument and is able instead to make claims without necessarily defending or explaining them. Schlegel makes broad declarations—for example, that romantic poetry "alone is infinite, just as it alone is free"—that are unburdened by the weight of argumentation. This makes for a brief text that forcefully outlines the tenets of an entire artistic movement in a single paragraph.

Stylistically, *Fragment 116* employs a combination of aphoristic concision and effusive enthusiasm. As he develops his case for the vitality and value of romantic poetry, Schlegel's syntax starts out plain and grows increasingly ornate. A typical sentence begins as a direct statement—"It is capable of the highest and most variegated refinement"—before branching

Man and Woman Contemplating the Moon by German romantic painter Caspar David Friedrich (circa 1824). Other members of the romantic movement included German writer Ludwig Tieck and his fellow contributors to the periodical the *Athenaeum*. © WORLD HISTORY ARCHIVE/ALAMY

PRIMARY SOURCE

ATHENAEUM FRAGMENT 116

Romantic poetry is a progressive, universal poetry. Its aim isn't merely to reunite all the separate species of poetry and put poetry in touch with philosophy and rhetoric. It tries to and should mix and fuse poetry and prose, inspiration and criticism, the poetry of art and the poetry of nature; and make poetry lively and sociable, and life and society poetical; poeticize wit and fill and saturate the forms of art with every kind of good, solid matter for instruction, and animate them with the pulsations of humor. It embraces everything that is purely poetic, from the greatest systems of art, containing within themselves still further systems, to the sigh, the kiss that the poetizing child breathes forth in artless song. It can so lose itself in what it describes that one might believe it exists only to characterize poetical individuals of all sorts; and yet there still is no form so fit for expressing the entire spirit of an author: so that many artists who started out to write only a novel ended up by providing us with a portrait of themselves. It alone can become, like the epic, a mirror of the whole circumambient world, an image of the age. And it can also – more than any other form – hover at the midpoint between the portrayed and the portrayer, free of all real and ideal self-interest, on tbe wings of poetic reflection, and can raise that reflection again and again to a higher power, can multiply it in an endless succession of mirrors. It is capable of the highest and most variegated refinement, not only from within outwards, but also from without inwards; capable in that it organizes – for everything that seeks a wholeness in its effects – the parts along similar lines, so that it opens up a perspective upon an infinitely increasing classicism. Romantic poetry is in the arts what wit is in philosophy, and what society and sociability, friendship and love are in life. Other kinds of poetry are finished and are now capable of being fully analyzed. The romantic kind of poetry is still in the state of becoming; that, in fact, is its real essence: that it should forever be becoming and never be perfected. It can be exhausted by no theory and only a divinatory criticism would dare try to characterize its ideal. It alone is infinite, just as it alone is free; and it recognizes as its first commandment that the will of the poet can tolerate no law above itself. The romantic kind of poetry is the only one that is more than a kind, that it is, as it were, poetry itself: for in a certain sense all poetry is or should be romantic.

SOURCE: Ludwig Tieck, "Athenaeum Fragments," *Friedrich Schlegel's Lucinde and the Fragments,* edited by Peter Firchow. University of Minnesota Press, 1971. Copyright © 1971 by the University of Minnesota Press. All rights reserved. Reproduced by permission.

CRITICAL DISCUSSION

The 1798 publication of *Fragment 116* alongside Schlegel's other fragments in the first volume of the *Athenaeum* inspired those within Schlegel's close intellectual circle but was mostly overlooked by the public at large, which focused its attention instead on the *Fragments'* radical social stands. According to Beiser, "The *Athenäum* was to launch a revolution not only in aesthetics but in ethics as well." In the fragments, Beiser writes, "Schlegel brought all of modern culture under criticism, its laws, traditions, conventions, and taboos." Schlegel's approval of plural marriages, for example, "shocked his contemporaries," as did his defense of suicide as an individual right. Though *Fragment 116* was less incendiary than those positions, it did serve as an influence on the literary course of writers such as Ludwig Tieck and Novalis.

Fragment 116 inspired the initially idealistic and liberal but eventually cynical and conservative school of German romanticism. This change in the nature of German romanticism was the outcome of growing disillusionment with the notion of radically liberated individualism. Eventually, increasingly political conservative groups within Germany co-opted the movement Schlegel had catalyzed. According to Margarete Kohlenbach in *The Cambridge Companion to German Romanticism* (2009), "The emergence of a conservative and nationalist right and a radical-democratic or socialist left during the nineteenth century was accompanied by interpretations of Romanticism that ignored, misunderstood or reinterpreted the apolitical, philosophical, non-traditionalist and aesthetically innovative concerns of early Romanticism." *Fragment 116* continues to be the subject of a body of criticism that has considered its origins and its influence in literary, social, and philosophical terms.

Many scholars view *Fragment 116* as the key to Schlegel's larger argument in the *Athenaeum Fragments.* As Mirko M. Hall writes in "Friedrich Schlegel's Romanticization of Music" (2009), "Schlegel's project of romanticization is succinctly encapsulated in *Athenaeum Fragment 116.*" Through that project, according to a 2005 piece by Alison Stone in *Inquiry,* Schlegel attempts to re-evaluate "modern poetry, suggesting that it can re-enchant nature in a distinctively modern way, corresponding to its distinctively fragmentary and reflective character, which he rethinks as its *romanticism.*" Rodolphe Gasché, in his 1991 foreword to Schlegel's *Philosophical Fragments,* argues that "Schlegel introduced the form of the fragment into German literature." According to Gasché, Schlegel drew from a tradition of French writers such as Montaigne, Pascal, and Chamfort. However, Gasché argues, Schlegel's fragments and the romantic fragment in general form their own genre. French philosopher and writer Maurice Blanchot, in "The Athenaeum" (1983) is less admiring of Schlegel's use of the fragment, which he deems "a means of

out into a series of grandiloquent clauses—"not only from within outwards, but also from without inwards; capable in that it organizes—for everything that seeks a wholeness in its effects—the parts along similar lines, so that it opens up a perspective upon an infinitely increasing classicism." In this way, Schlegel is able to make a pithy case for romantic poetry while demonstrating the extravagant range and openness of the romanticism he advocates.

complacent self-indulgence, rather than the attempt to elaborate a more rigorous mode of writing."

BIBLIOGRAPHY

Sources

Beiser, Fredrick C. "The Early Politics and Aesthetics of Friedrich Schlegel." *Enlightenment, Revolution and Romanticism: The Genesis of Modern German Political Thought 1790–1800.* Cambridge: Harvard UP, 1992.

Blanchot, Maurice. "The Athenaeum." Trans. Deborah Esch and Ian Balfour. *Studies in Romanticism* 22.2 (1983): 163-72. Web. 12 Aug. 2012.

Hall, Mirko M. "Friedrich Schlegel's Romanticization of Music." *Eighteenth-Century Studies* 42.3 (2009): 413-29. Print.

Kohlenbach, Margarete. "Transformations of German Romanticism, 1830-2000." *The Cambridge Companion to German Romanticism.* Ed. Nicholas Saul. New York: Cambridge UP, 2009. Web. 13 Aug. 2012.

Schlegel, Friedrich. *Philosophical Fragments.* Trans. Peter Firchow. Minneapolis: U of Minnesota P, 1991. Web. 12 Aug. 2012.

Stone, Alison. "Friedrich Schlegel, Romanticism, and the Re-enchantment of Nature." *Inquiry* 48.1 (2005). Web. 12 Aug. 2012.

Further Reading

Behler, Ernst. *German Romantic Literary Theory,* Cambridge: Cambridge UP, 1993.

Benjamin, Walter. "The Concept of Criticism in German Romanticism." *Walter Benjamin: Selected Writings.* Ed. M. Bullock and M. Jennings. Vol. 1. Cambridge: Harvard UP, 1996.

Bernstein, J. M. *Classic and Romantic German Aesthetics.* Cambridge: Cambridge UP, 2003. Print.

Eichner, Hans. "Friedrich Schlegel's Theory of Romantic Poetry." *Proceedings of the Modern Language Association* 71.5 (1956): 1018-41. Web. 12 Aug. 2012.

Forster, Michael N. *German Philosophy of Language from Schlegel to Hegel and Beyond.* Oxford: Oxford UP, 2011. Print.

Gurewitch, Morton. *The Comedy of Romantic Irony.* Lanham: UP of America, 2002. Print.

Speight, Allen. "Friedrich Schlegel." *The Stanford Encyclopedia of Philosophy.* Ed. Edward N. Zalta. Center for the Study of Lang. and Information, Stanford U, 2 Nov. 2011. Web. 12 Aug. 2012.

Theodore McDermott

BALLADS AND ROMANCES

Adam Mickiewicz

❖ Key Facts

Time Period:
Early 19th Century

Movement/Issue:
Aesthetics; Romanticism;
Polish nationalism

Place of Publication:
Poland

**Language of
Publication:**
Polish

OVERVIEW

As a result of his collection *Ballade i Romanse (Ballads and Romances)*, published in 1822, poet Adam Mickiewicz is credited with single-handedly initiating the Romantic Movement in Poland. *Ballads and Romances,* as it has been translated, was published just two years before the poet was arrested and exiled to Russia for his involvement with a student group accused of spreading Polish nationalism. Though he would never return to his native country (he resided mainly in Paris after 1829 and died in Constantinople in 1855), Mickiewicz continued to inspire Polish readers and audiences abroad through extensive publications of poetry, essay, translation, and political writing. Despite his importance, however, Mickiewicz has received relatively little exposure in the West, a fact most likely due to the challenges inherent in translating Polish to English. In addition, readers unfamiliar with the cultural milieu find it difficult to grasp his work's significance. Still, fellow countrymen regard Mickiewicz as a hero of both literary arts and politics, the very embodiment of his renowned idealism.

Ballads and Romances was immediately heralded as a radically innovative poetic success. Mickiewicz gained wide admiration from fellow writers, including Alexander Pushkin, Johann Wolfgang von Goethe, James Fenimore Cooper, Nikolai Gogol, and Margaret Fuller. This early work posed a direct challenge to the currents of rational classicism and Enlightenment philosophy that were dominant at the time, as Mickiewicz decisively introduced Romantic tenets (such as an emphasis on the individual as well as on emotion, mysticism, and folklore) to Polish literature. His poems were received not only as aesthetic triumphs written in a language simple enough to inspire wide readership, but also as political and ethical dictates. Mickiewicz inaugurated a period of nationalistic concern in the arts—one in which the previously unacknowledged difficulties of common people might be addressed with hope and inspiration.

HISTORICAL AND LITERARY CONTEXT

In *Ballads and Romances,* and especially the poems "Ode to Youth" and "Romanticism," Mickiewicz contests an allegiance to classical tendencies that, in his view, are overly rational and uninspiring for younger generations, consequently deadening the spirit. On a

scholarship to the University of Wilno (now Vilna) in 1817, young Mickiewicz became deeply involved with a group of students who called themselves the Philomaths. Their organization originally sought to expand on a university education system they deemed overly conservative; eventually these concerns took on a more philosophical and political tone with the intent to "embrace the moral and patriotic education of youth." Mickiewicz was the chairman of the society's literary division, and it was in this capacity that he first began to share poetry, as well as literary treatises and reviews.

When Mickiewicz's first collection was published in 1822, many Poles could still clearly recall their country's brief restoration under French leader Napoleon Bonaparte at the turn of the century and their subsequent disappointment when Napoleon was defeated by the Russians on his way to Nowogródek in 1812. *Ballads and Romances* emerged in a cultural climate hungry for optimism and ripe to appreciate notions of both independence and national unity. As Stanisław Helsztyński observes in his 1955 introduction to a collection of Mickiewicz's poetry and prose in English, "The traditions of 18th Century liberalism no longer sufficed as an ideological and artistic programme for national literature, which should be a guide for the people in the struggle for independence."

Mickiewicz greatly revered Napoleon, whom he linked inextricably to another dominant personal inspiration: British poet Lord Byron. As Mickiewicz proposes, "I regard it as certain that the flash which kindled the fire of the English poet came from the soul of Napoleon." Mickiewicz held Byron in such high esteem that he later endeavored to translate several of his works into Polish. In the years that directly preceded his first publication, Mickiewicz pored over the work of Romantics such as Byron and, later, the Germans Goethe and Friedrich Schiller. His attention to these works certainly influenced *Ballads and Romances,* as did his intimate familiarity with the native folktales that would inform them. Although he was not the first to write ballads in Poland, none before could match Mickiewicz's virtuosity.

Ballads and Romances quickly propelled Mickiewicz to literary fame and provided the impetus for subsequent work he produced to similarly estimable regard. In 1824, after serving six months in prison for his political activities, Mickiewicz was deported to Russia, where he was received as a revolutionary poet of great import. There he was welcomed into the literary salon culture of the time and was able to create friendships with important Romantic greats, including Pushkin. After a brief trip to Germany (where he met Goethe and the German philosopher Georg Wilhelm Friedrich Hegel) and an unsuccessful attempt to participate in the Polish uprising of 1830, Mickiewicz headed to France. He published his epic poem *Pan Tadeusz* in 1834 and then renounced poetry almost completely in favor of activism.

THEMES AND STYLE

The central theme of *Ballads and Romances* is the vitality of emotional liberation, both in letters and in life. Although several of the included works foster this, none does so as clearly as "Romanticism," a poem focused on the ravings of a strange young woman who attempts to communicate with the dead lover she can supposedly see. A distinction is drawn between the "simple folk," who react to her with kindness and faith, and the old man "whose spectacles are clear," representing cold rationalism. This character harshly associates her vision with the "vulgar throng," calls it "idle, wrong," and accuses everyone of blasphemy. The poet, however, sides with the "common" people: "You delve among dead truths, to men unknown," he tells the old man. Instead, he asserts that "Truth" can only be found in the heart. Thus, "Romanticism" avows that the emotional and mystical bent of everyday people holds more accuracy than a strict reliance on classical study.

"Ode to Youth," included in Mickiewicz's first publication, takes even greater rhetorical strides. The poem is an impassioned entreaty to the Poles of Mickiewicz's generation, bidding them to unite in courage toward a common cause despite sacrifice and in opposition to fear or hopelessness. "Young friends," he writes, "together heed my call! / The aims of all are in the joy of all." Again, an opposition is noted between the old and new, as in the poem's opening: "Here, heartless, spiritless, throng skeleton's in sorry plight … this dead world, curst and bare." Mickiewicz urges the youth to rise above their country's current state of decay, come together and thus "disperse the night." Through an appeal to the distraught and emotional reader, and a clear distinction between the death of the past and life in the future, Mickiewicz creates a lasting and powerful poem, one still recited today by Polish school children.

Stylistically *Ballads and Romances* is intended to appeal to a wide readership. Mickiewicz artfully focuses several poems on folklore, including "The Lilies," the story of a woman who kills her husband and plants flowers atop him; and "Twardorwski's Wife," a popular story, dating back to the sixteenth century, of a woman so evil that even her wicked husband, having sold his soul to the devil, cannot manage her. Mickiewicz selected subject matter that was accessible

CZESŁAW MIŁOSZ AND ADAM MICKIEWICZ

Interesting and valuable connections can be made between the Polish poet Czesław Miłosz, the recipient of the 1980 Nobel Prize in Literature, and Adam Mickiewicz. Miłosz, born in 1911, was affected by the political turmoil of World War One from a young age. He was educated primarily in Wilno and worked for the underground press during World War Two. After the war, Miłosz relocated to the United States, where he served as a diplomat and educator before receiving the Nobel Prize in 1980. Like Mickiewicz, Miłosz wrote all of his poetry in Polish, although Poland banned his work after Miłosz defected to the West in 1951. Not only did Miłosz write extensively about Mickiewicz, calling him "Poland's greatest Poet" in 1955 and referring to him in 1969 as "for Poles what Goethe is for Germans and Pushkin for Russians," but the lives of these two men also resemble each other in significant ways. Both were born in Lithuania and went on to teach Slavic literature in foreign countries. Both studied in Wilno and participated in secretive student organizations. Most notably, both men would spend the majority of their lives as expatriates, building careers abroad while writing in their native tongue. Although Miłosz criticized Mickiewicz for his heavy-handed mysticism and moralizing, he acknowledged that his own work was fully and uncompromisingly indebted to Mickiewicz.

to all and versified it in Polish rather than Latin, which was preferred by many authors in Poland at the time. In simple language that more closely resembles spoken dialect than anything that precedes it, Mickiewicz creates a poetry capable of popular appreciation. By engaging a wide audience, his style supports his argument for unity, emotion, and liberty in art and society.

Portrait of Polish poet and political activist Adam Mickiewicz, by Walenty Wankowicz. MUSÉE ADAM MICKIEWICZ, PARIS, FRANCE/ ARCHIVES CHARMET/THE BRIDGEMAN ART LIBRARY

CRITICAL DISCUSSION

The 1822 publication of *Ballads and Romances* received considerable acclaim and brought the poet social standing. In the *Encyclopaedia Britannica* from 1830, a Dr. Browne wrote, "Of all patriotic bards, Adam Mickiewicz is the head and prince … the muse of freedom is indeed the idol of his poetic worship." He was known across Europe and in the United States as a leading poetic proponent of nationalism, and correspondence attests to his considerable popularity. In a letter to her fellow American Transcendentalist author Ralph Waldo Emerson, Margaret Fuller wrote about visiting with Mickiewicz in 1847, and in 1861 Susan De Lancey Cooper noted the considerable time her husband James had spent with the poet. In 1885, British scholar William R. Morfill declared, "the writings of Mickiewicz are well worth our attention. He is preeminently the national poet of Poland." Although Mickiewicz was highly regarded, he was not without critics, especially after the unauthorized publication of his *Crimean Sonnets* in Warsaw. He was not deterred, however, issuing a preface titled "Reply to the Warsaw Critics" (1829), a group that included adamant followers of pseudo-Classicism.

Ballads and Romances firmly placed Mickiewicz at the forefront of the Romantic Movement in Poland. His work certainly influenced literary endeavors at the time, including the writing of his contemporaries Juliusz Słowacki and Zygmunt Krasinski; together these men are regarded as Poland's "Three Bards." His close relationship with other multinational writers throughout his life had reciprocal effects for all parties. The impact of his work also extended beyond the world of letters to include political inspiration and influence upon other arts. It has been argued that Polish composer Frédéric Chopin's Ballades were very much inspired by Mickiewicz's *Ballads and Romances.*

Beginning in 1945, after Poland was freed from Nazi occupation, publication of Mickiewicz's writing began on a large scale, allowing critical examination of his work to flourish. Several concerns emerged, including the assertion that *Ballads and Romances,* and particularly "Ode to Youth," were still deeply entrenched in classical form, never fully abandoning it in favor of the more radical Romanticism with which Mickiewicz is credited. Further, the poet's strong allegiance to Catholic religion and the extreme nationalism that marked his work have come under recent scrutiny. Critics such as Wiktor Weintraub have linked the latter to a foreign readership's near-total inability to comprehend Mickiewicz's patriotic intent without adept attention to Polish history. Criticism has also been lobbed not at the poet but rather at the linguistic and cultural barriers that prohibit a fully accurate rendering of his work's lyrical and evocative expertise.

BIBLIOGRAPHY

Sources

Brandes, George. "The Romantic Literature of Poland in the Nineteenth Century (1886): Points of Contact in Polish and Danish Literature." *Poland: A Study of the Land, People, and Literature.* London: William Heinemann, 1903. 192-310. Rpt. in *Nineteenth-Century Literature Criticism.* Ed. Jay Parini and Janet Mullane. Vol. 15. Detroit: Gale Research, 1987. *Literature Resource Center.* Web. 7 Sep. 2012.

Fabre, Jean. "Adam Mickiewicz and European Romanticism." *Adam Mickiewicz, 1798-1855: In Commemoration of the Centenary of His Death.* Zurich: UNESCO, 1955. 37-59. Rpt. in *Poetry Criticism.* Ed. Elisabeth Gellert. Vol. 38. Detroit: Gale Group, 2002. *Literature Resource Center.* Web. 3 Sep. 2012.

Kridl, Manfred. "Polish Romanticism before 1830." Trans. Olga Scherer-Virski. *A Survey of Polish Literature and Culture.* Paris: Mouton & Co., 1956. 213-240. Rpt. in *Nineteenth-Century Literature Criticism.* Ed. Denise Kasinec and Mary L. Onorato. Vol. 52. Detroit: Gale Research, 1996. *Literature Resource Center.* Web. 10 Sep. 2012.

Mickiewicz, Adam. *Selected Poetry & Prose.* Ed. Stanislaw Helsztynski. Warsaw: Polonia House, 1955. Print.

Further Reading

Koropeckyi, Roman. *Adam Mickiewicz: The Life of a Romantic.* Ithaca: Cornell UP, 2008.

Mickiewicz, Adam. *Pan Tadeusz.* Trans. Kenneth R. MacKenzie. New York: Hippocrene, 1992. Print.

Miłosz, Czesław. "Adam Mickiewicz." *Russian Review* 14.4 (1955). *JSTOR.* Web. 12 Sep. 2012.

Treugutt, Stefan. "Byron and Napoleon in Polish Romantic Myth." *Lord Byron and His Contemporaries: Essays from the Sixth International Byron Seminar.* Ed. Charles E. Robinson. Newark: U of Delaware P, 1982. 130-143. Rpt. in *Nineteenth-Century Literature Criticism.* Ed. Thomas J. Schoenberg. Vol. 101. Detroit: Gale Group, 2002. *Literature Resource Center.* Web. 13 Sep. 2012.

Zakrzewski, Christopher Adam. "Misers of Sound and Syllable: Reflections on the Poetic Style of Adam Mickiewicz." *Canadian Slavonic Papers* 40.3-4 (1998). Rpt. in *Poetry Criticism.* Ed. Elisabeth Gellert. Vol. 38. Detroit: Gale Group, 2002. *Literature Resource Center.* Web. 13 Sep. 2012.

Rachel Mindell

THE BIRTH OF TRAGEDY

Friedrich Nietzsche

OVERVIEW

Composed by philosopher Friedrich Nietzsche, *The Birth of Tragedy* (1872) attempts a new metaphysics by asserting the importance of music and exploring the relationship between art and science through a discussion of Greek tragedy. The German-born Nietzsche, then twenty-seven years old and a full professor of classical philology, wrote the book at the University of Basel in Switzerland during the Franco-Prussian War. An enthusiastic scholar, he was familiar with the dominant trends in German culture, including Romanticism, transcendental idealism, and Weimar classicism. Directed to a philological and philosophical community that he felt was culturally conservative, *The Birth of Tragedy* uses metaphor and florid language to describe the root of artistic expression: the tension between the Apollonian and Dionysian impulse.

Immediately following its publication, the book came under attack by philologist Ulrich von Wilamowitz-Moellendorf, who published a pamphlet stating that Nietzsche's work was severely lacking in scholarship and disrespectful of academic convention. Nevertheless, the book had supporters, including composer Richard Wagner (to whom the preface of the book is addressed) and scholar Erwin Rohde, both of whom published rebuttals to von Wilamowitz-Moellendorf's critique in the form of open letters. In a preface to the 1886 edition, titled "Attempt at Self-Criticism," Nietzsche stated that the book had its shortcomings. Although *The Birth of Tragedy* has often been the victim of irresponsible scholarship and has been taken out of context to support a number of ideologies, it is today considered perhaps the most important examination of Greek tragedy ever written and an important text in Nietzsche's famous and influential body of work.

HISTORICAL AND LITERARY CONTEXT

The Birth of Tragedy responds to the prevailing academic interpretation of ancient Greece as a noble culture free of darkness and to a modern culture that Nietzsche felt suffered from overly logical restraint. The popular view of Greek culture, held by historians such as Johann Joachim Winckelmann, was that its achievements were the result of Greeks' purity and pursuit of lightness. Nietzsche felt that this view was limited in scope and did not accept the darker forces at play in the Greek world, as represented by Dionysus. While he was writing the book, German culture was dominated by historicism, Romanticism, and Christianity—trends that he felt failed to acknowledge the dark, passionate, and sensual and therefore failed to create conditions favorable to art and life.

Just before the publication of *The Birth of Tragedy,* the Franco-Prussian War had ended, resulting in the unification of Germany in 1871. Nietzsche briefly joined the war effort between 1867 and 1868 and then relocated to Switzerland, relinquishing his German citizenship. There he continued to engage with modern German thought and was influenced by German thinkers such as writer Johann Wolfgang von Goethe and philosopher Arthur Schopenhauer. He had the support of many of his intellectual contemporaries, including professor Friedrich Wilhelm Ritschl, who had recommended the young philosopher for the professorship at Basel, and Wagner—although the latter relationship dissolved following Nietzsche's denunciation of the composer.

Nietzsche's first book as a professor of philology, *The Birth of Tragedy* explores a number of fields, including metaphysics, philosophy, art history, and aesthetics. The text is directly influenced by, and makes explicit mention of, the works and philosophies of Friedrich Schiller, Schopenahauer, Wagner, and Goethe. In its philosophical criticism of earlier metaphysical frameworks—though not in its conclusions—it resembles Immanuel Kant's *Critique of Pure Reason* (1781). It also can be compared to French symbolist texts including Charles Baudelaire's *The Painter of Modern Life* (1863) and Jean Moréas's *Symbolist Manifesto* (1886) for its exploration of aesthetics. "Athenaeum Fragments, no. 116" (1798), an essay on Romantic poetry by Friedrich Schlegel, a key figure in German Romanticism, also may have been an influence on Nietzsche's work.

Since its publication, *The Birth of Tragedy* has inspired a great volume of criticism and has exerted enormous influence on the fields of psychology, metaphysics, philosophy, literature, and music, to name a few. It has had a lasting impact on several aesthetic movements, including early twentieth-century modernism. In fact, German writer Thomas Mann took the title of his famous novel *The Magic Mountain* (1924) from the text of *The Birth of Tragedy.*

❖ *Key Facts*

Time Period:
Late 19th Century

Movement/Issue:
Philology; Aesthetics; Tragedy

Place of Publication:
Germany

Language of Publication:
German

FRIEDRICH NIETZSCHE: FATHER OF EXISTENTIALIST PHILOSOPHY

Friedrich Nietzsche, a German philologist and philosopher, is often named as a father of existentialist philosophy. One of the youngest men ever promoted to a full professorship of philology, he began his teaching career at the University of Basel in Switzerland after an illness ended his service in the Franco-Prussian War. After *The Birth of Tragedy* became the target of a heated attack from philologist Ulrich von Wilamowitz-Moellendorf, the young teacher's classes slowly dwindled in size. He eventually ended his university career in 1879 due to debilitating health problems. However, he continued to write extensively, moving between cities in Switzerland, France, Germany, and Italy.

During this time of dislocation, he wrote many of his most famous works, including *Thus Spoke Zarathustra* (1883-85), *Beyond Good and Evil* (1886), and *On the Genealogy of Morals* (1887). In 1889 he suffered a nervous breakdown in Turin, Italy. Researchers have speculated about the causes of his breakdown, though none of their theories have been proven. After a brief period in a sanatorium, he went to live with his mother. However, following his mother's death, he came under the care of his sister Elizabeth, who took control of his archives, later manipulating his philosophies to promote her anti-Semitic projects. Following the philosopher's death in 1900, his texts were often misread and misrepresented, although as time passed these manipulations have been corrected. Today a more honest representation of his thought has earned him a place as one of the world's most respected philosophers.

Nietzsche's discussion of instinct and impulse has contributed to psychological theory, closely mirroring psychologist Sigmund Freud's concepts of the subconscious. In addition, the book's influence on music is apparent in the works of Gustav Mahler and Richard Strauss. Today the text is read as a prominent influence on philosophers such as Martin Heidegger, Edmund Husserl, and Martin Buber.

THEMES AND STYLE

The Birth of Tragedy explores several central themes, namely that the Greeks achieved greatness by acknowledging and harnessing Dionysian impulse, that Euripidian reason and logic are destructive to art and life, and that a rebirth of tragedy is necessary to reclaim greatness. In the modern age of reason, dominated by moral forces such as Christianity, Nietzsche perceives an environment antagonistic to art and life. He writes of Christianity, "Behind this mode of thought and valuation, which must be hostile to art if it is at all genuine, I never failed to sense a *hostility to life....* Christianity was from the beginning, essentially and fundamentally, life's nausea and disgust with life,

merely concealed behind, masked by, dressed up as, faith in 'another' or 'better' life." He thus contrasts the modern orientation toward morality with the Greeks' acknowledgement of and interaction with the Dionysian impulse, demonstrating how the latter allows for achievement in both art and life.

To achieve its effect, *The Birth of Tragedy* makes use of irony, rhetorical tricks, and a denial of academic convention to represent a new philological and metaphysical view. Nietzsche abandons dry and reasoned discourse in favor of imagistic language: "Greek tragedy met an end different from that of her older sister-arts: she died by suicide, in consequence of an irreconcilable conflict.... When Greek tragedy died, there rose everywhere the deep sense of an immense void." Through this conscious departure from formal, scholarly language, he mirrors his prescribed shift away from destructive reason toward Dionysian lyricism.

Stylistically, *The Birth of Tragedy* is notable for its use of metaphor, repetition, allusion, and dialogue. The language is often complex and wordy. Nietzsche even refers to it in the text as "badly written, ponderous, embarrassing, image-mad and image-confused." He denigrates his language perhaps to draw attention to the central philosophical concerns of the book, which are articulated in a direct address to Euripides: "What did you want, sacrilegious Euripides, when you sought to compel this dying myth to serve you once more? It died under your violent hands ... and just as the myth died on you, the genius of music died on you, too.... Because you had abandoned Dionysus, Apollo abandoned you." Thus, by addressing key Greek figures and their respective symbolic powers, Nietzsche allows his unconventional stylistic choice to achieve a rupturing rhetorical effect.

CRITICAL DISCUSSION

Although well received by some colleagues and friends, *The Birth of Tragedy* was also harshly criticized. As Nietzsche defied philological convention, neglecting to include quotations from source texts or footnotes, von Wilamowitz-Moellendorf attacked the work's lack of scholarship in a pamphlet titled *Future Philology! A Reply to Friedrich Nietzsche's* Birth of Tragedy (1872). In a 2011 essay for the *Journal of Nietzsche Studies,* James Porter quotes the philologist as stating, "Mr. Nietzsche by no means presents himself as ['or acts like'] a scholarly researcher." In response to von Wilamowitz-Moellendorf, Wagner penned an open letter to Nietzsche in support of the text, and Emil Rohde published an open letter to Wagner, titled *Afterphilologie* (1872), which, according to Suzanne Marchand in *Down from Olympus* (2003), calls Wilamowitz-Moellendorf's philology "a horrible distortion of sensible criticism, a truly anal philology" and praises Nietzsche's text for being representative of the "noblest strivings of the present."

Although Nietzsche went on to revise many of the ideas he presents in *The Birth of Tragedy,* the book remains a significant contribution to the study of Greek tragedy. It continues to influence artists and scholars working in a multitude of fields and has remained the subject of scholarly criticism in psychology, literature, music, and philosophy. In an introduction to *The Birth of Tragedy* (2000), translator Walter Kaufmann describes Nietzsche's text as "one of the most suggestive and influential studies of tragedy every written."

Recent scholarship has focused on the philosophical import of *The Birth of Tragedy.* Discussing the influence of Schopenhauer's pessimism, Ivan Soll notes in an essay in *Reading Nietzsche* (1990), "What raises the question mark about the value of human existence ... is the apparent universality and ineluctability of frustration, dissatisfaction, and suffering in life.... Pessimism, as an expression of the despair commonly resulting from the recognition of the inevitability of suffering, becomes one of the central topics of the discussion." Critics have also commented on Nietzsche's interpretation of morality's role in art and life. For example, Alexander Nehamas in a 1996 essay in *Salmagundi* discusses the book's treatment of art, life, and morality, noting, "Nietzsche's attack on the relevance of morality to the good human life depends on at least two controversial assumptions. The first is that literary characters and literary works are appropriate models for understanding human beings and their lives. The second is that, supposing the first assumption is accepted, the moral dimensions of literature are in fact irrelevant to its evaluation."

BIBLIOGRAPHY

Sources

Kaufmann, Walter. Introduction. *Basic Writings of Nietzsche.* Ed. and trans. Walter Kaufmann. New York: Modern Library, 2000. 3-13. Print.

Marchand, Suzanne L. *Down from Olympus: Archaeology and Philhellenism in Germany, 1750-1970.* Princeton: Princeton UP, 2003. Print.

Nehamas, Alexander. "What Should We Expect from Reading? (There Are Only Aesthetic Values)." *Salmagundi* 111 (1996): 27-58. *JSTOR.* Web. 4 Oct. 2012.

Nietzsche, Friedrich. "The Birth of Tragedy, or: Hellenism and Pessimism." *Basic Writings of Nietzsche.* Ed. and trans. Walter Kaufmann. New York: Modern Library, 2000. 14-144. Print.

Porter, James I. "'Don't Quote Me on That!': Wilamowitz Contra Nietzsche in 1872 and 1873." *Journal of Nietzsche Studies* 42 (2011): 73-99. *Project MUSE.* Web. 4 Oct. 2012.

Soll, Ivan. "Pessimism and the Tragic View of Life: Reconsiderations of Nietzsche's *Birth of Tragedy.*" *Reading Nietzsche.* Ed. Kathleen M. Higgins and Robert C. Solomon. New York: Oxford UP, 1990. 104-31. Print.

Further Reading

Acampora, Christa Davis. "Nietzsche Contra Homer, Socrates and Paul." *Journal of Nietzsche Studies* 24 (2002): 25-53. *Project MUSE.* Web. 4 Oct. 2012.

Allison, David B. *Reading the New Nietzsche*: The Birth of Tragedy, The Gay Science, Thus Spoke Zarathustra, *and* On the Genealogy of Morals. Lanham: Rowman & Littlefield, 2001. Print.

Aschheim, Steven E. *The Nietzsche Legacy in Germany, 1890-1990.* Berkeley: U of California P, 1993. Print.

May, Keith M. *Nietzsche and the Spirit of Tragedy.* New York: St. Martin's, 1990. Print.

Porter, James I. *Nietzsche and the Philology of the Future.* Stanford: Stanford UP, 2000. Print.

Silk, M. S. "Nietzsche, Decadence, and the Greeks." *New Literary History* 35.4 (2004): 587-605. Print.

Kristen Gleason

Portrait of Friedrich Nietzsche. © LEBRECHT MUSIC AND ARTS PHOTO LIBRARY/ALAMY

COMPLAINT OF THE SAGE OF PARIS

Jules Laforgue

❖ *Key Facts*

Time Period:
Late 19th Century

Movement/Issue:
Aesthetics

Place of Publication:
France

**Language of
Publication:**
French

OVERVIEW

Jules Laforgue's poem "Complainte du sage de Paris" ("Complaint of the Sage of Paris," 1885)—part of his debut collection, *Les complaintes*—contains the first of his poems to break with the style of Charles Baudelaire, upon which Laforgue had previously relied. In the Paris of Laforgue's time, a *complainte* was a style of popular song. Laforgue chose it for the structure of his collection out of a desire to find a type of verse that was absolutely new. Written in alexandrines, or twelve-syllable rhyming couplets, the poem is most notable for its use of irony. Today Laforgue continues to be known for this irony, found in his use of puns and clownish figures.

Neither Laforgue nor his work was well received by the literary establishment in Paris at the time. The irony and lyrical play in *Les complaintes* would eventually lead the poet to write in *vers libre* (free verse), which he is sometimes credited with inventing. Laforgue's disillusionment with religion and his application of Eduard von Hartmann's theories of the unconscious influenced poets as varied as Wallace Stevens, T. S. Eliot, and Hart Crane. In 1885, however, Laforgue was seen as an immature poet, perhaps owing more to his outsider status than to an actual lack of aesthetic vision. His poetry has come to be seen as important in itself and not merely laying the groundwork for later modernists.

HISTORICAL AND LITERARY CONTEXT

At least since the publication of Baudelaire's prose poem collection *Paris Spleen* in 1869, the atmosphere in Paris had been marked with literature conveying ennui, or dissatisfaction. For Baudelaire, depicting daily experience in all its discomfort and vibrancy was the most important role art could play. He demonstrated this tenet by writing about modern life in his characteristic prose poems, which eschewed the strictures of formal verse. Stéphane Mallarmé fractured language further in his "Un coup de dés" ("A Throw of the Dice"). In the visual arts, impressionism was in vogue, and Laforgue argues in his piece of art criticism "L'Impressionisme" (1903) that the style would stretch the capacity of the eye to perceive and therefore expand the mind's ability to understand the exterior world. For Laforgue, the value he placed on

difficulty could also be extended to complex poetic language.

Between 1880 and 1881, Laforgue worked as a research assistant for the art historian Charles Ephrussi. In 1881 Ephrussi secured Laforgue a position as the French reader for the empress Augusta of Germany, for whom he was scheduled to read twice a day. Both positions afforded Laforgue the time and environment conducive to scholarly study. Today he is frequently cited by historians as one of the most knowledgeable poets of that era. In his studies, he encountered the works of Eduard von Hartmann, particularly his *Philosophy of the Unconscious* (1869). Laforgue then expanded this idea of the unconscious—which differs from the current understanding of consciousness—to include aesthetics.

Laforgue's poetry is not as informal as Baudelaire's and not as chance-driven as Mallarmé's. His experimentation in *Les complaintes* consists of wordplay and innuendos, resulting in a complex and humorous poetry. The poetry that Laforgue wrote before *Les complaintes,* later collected in a volume of thirty-one poems under the title *Le sanglot de la terre* (*Sob of the Earth,* 1897), was considerably less radical. By the time he was composing *Les complaintes,* he had renounced the poems in *Le sanglot* as overly emotional. Shortly after *Les complaintes* was published at the author's expense, he paid to have his second book, *L'imitation de Notre-Dame la lune* (*The Imitation of Our Lady the Moon,* 1886), published. The publication is less experimental but is consistent with his tone, which is at once playful and sincere.

Although Laforgue died in poverty two years after the publication of "Complaint of the Sage of Paris," he received posthumous accolades for his final book, *Derniers vers* (*Towards the Last,* 1890). This led to subsequent publications of collected works, allowing Eliot to easily access his poetry in 1910 while at Harvard. Eliot would later say, "Laforgue was the first to teach me how to speak. I owe more to him than to any one poet in any language." Eliot's early modernist poem "The Love Song of J. Alfred Prufrock," more than "The Waste Land," best resembles *Les complaintes*. The despair that Eliot's speaker feels, his pathetic humor, and the poem's multivocality, all have their direct precedent in Laforgue.

THEMES AND STYLE

In "Complaint of the Sage of Paris," Laforgue experiments with language, weaving religion with the voices of various speakers. The theme from Hartmann's *Philosophy of the Unconscious,* which posits that the world is progressing toward an ultimate consciousness, runs throughout the work. The implicit argument is that experimentation and improvisation lead to a deeper understanding of the world. Religion and morality are called into question and ultimately replaced by an idea of "the whole." Laforgue's opening couplet questions whether "ephemeral skirts," or women, are the only objects to love, or if there might not be something more lasting. Wordplay, rather than being sacrificed for this theoretical position, serves to underline it: "It's the Whole Truth, the Omniversal Umbelliform, / The manchineel under which, my babes, sleep warm."

Irony, too, is used to emphasize Laforgue's notion of the whole. With this technique he juxtaposes high and low culture, usually in an effort to criticize what the majority holds sacred. In one couplet, "the cloth is laid, / the youthful Organ, blindly improvising, played," while the couplet immediately following is even less reserved, evoking a bohemian existence of "ducking marriage, travel, nosey-parkers, treats / Can-cans, and sickly ward-like smell of the same sheets." Laforgue asserts that even following romantic impulses evident in "virtual paradise, / Nights of heredity, limbos of latent dawns" will quickly lead to "infinity without a roof." Laforgue's made-up words in *Les complaintes,* his irony, and his emphasis on originality challenged the reader to engage with the text and come away with fresh insights.

"Complaint of the Sage of Paris," addressed to a familiar "you" (the informal French *tu*), seeks to convince the audience to relinquish passé value systems and follow a more intuitive path. This becomes clear by the sixth couplet: "Don't think the host where sleep your paradisal hours / Is baked with unprecedented or unleavened flours." The informal, chiding, and confident tone comes from an intellectual speaker who is a bit of a fool when it comes to love. Romance may be ephemeral, but its conquest takes precedence: "Oh perfumes, glances, chances. So be it. I'll try too." Laforgue's insistence that the reader embrace the present is reinforced by his reminder of sure death—a "blind lightning" that is "on its way." With this in mind, the poet exhorts his audience to concentrate on "living with no aim, mad with mansuetude."

CRITICAL DISCUSSION

Not only was Laforgue largely ignored in his lifetime, he was later regarded in France as an underdeveloped minor poet. In an essay on Laforgue in *Poem and Symbol: A Brief History of French Symbolism* (1990), Wallace Fowlie tells of "Picasso, Max Jacob, and [Guillaume] Apollinaire once shouting in the streets of

JULES LAFORGUE IN ISOLATION

The term *morbid* is often used to describe Jules Laforgue's poetry, and his life was indeed one of mostly hardship. The poet was born in Montevideo, Uruguay, in 1860. At a young age, his French-born father moved his family back to France, where Laforgue and his ten siblings lived in relative poverty. Laforgue's mother died while giving birth to her twelfth child, and for a time the young Jules was left at a boarding school to study, where he received poor marks.

Cut off socially, he was on the verge of a nervous breakdown when art historian and collector Charles Ephrussi hired him in 1880. Ephrussi would remain strongly supportive of Laforgue until Laforgue's death. In Ephrussi's office, the young poet was exposed to the impressionist paintings that affected his thought and work. To assist Laforgue's poetry career, Ephrussi found him employment with the German empress Augusta. The day he was hired, the twenty-year-old poet discovered his father had passed away. He wrote to his closest sister, Marie, of his heartbreak at being left an orphan, passionately claiming that if she died, he would also. Six years later, he died of tuberculosis at the age of twenty-seven.

Montmartre: '*Vive Rimbaud! A bas Laforgue!*'" ("Long live Rimbaud! Down with Laforgue!"). Nevertheless, Apollinaire and Jacob are considered to have aesthetic affinities with Laforgue's style and techniques. Laforgue's opening "Complaint," which Fowlie refers to as a prayer "to be released from thought," is not so oppositional to the later poets' intuitive poetics: "No, nothing: deliver us from thinking, / Original leprosy, intoxication."

Fowlie likewise discusses modernist writers who have been influenced by *Les complaintes,* including, but not limited to Eliot, Stevens, and Crane. Stevens and Crane took up the more positive aspects of Laforgue's work, seeking to reconcile the relationship between man and the absolute, while Eliot inherited his pessimism. All three utilize Laforgue's sonorous qualities and the theme of personal quest. The dissatisfaction and bitterness that characterize this collection—and that give it humorous overtones—were utilized with frequency during the modernism period that spanned between the two world wars. According to Fowlie, it was "the view of man as being first ridiculous, and then, ultimately, tragic" that Jean-Paul Sartre and Samuel Beckett found most productive in their later period.

Later scholarship has stressed the importance of Laforgue's use of irony as well as his polyvocality. Scholar Warren Ramsey, in *Modern Poets: Surrealists, Baudelaire, Perse, Laforgue, and Others* (1948), insists that irony is an essential tool for conveying modern experience. He equates "ironic poetry" with

Pen and ink illustration drawn by Jules Laforgue and included in *Complainte de l'Oubli et des Morts.* PRIVATE COLLECTION/GIRAUDON/ THE BRIDGEMAN ART LIBRARY

calls—"alexandrine-based narrative poetry" to "an ironic, multi-voiced, dislocated, and dislocating free verse."

BIBLIOGRAPHY

Sources

Fowlie, Wallace. *Poem and Symbol: A Brief History of French Symbolism.* University Park: Pennsylvania State UP, 1990. Print.

Hannoosh, Michele. "Laforgue, Jules. Papiers retrouvés." *Nineteenth-Century French Studies* 36.1 (2007): 175. *Literature Resources from Gale.* Web. 9 Oct. 2012.

Hartmann, Eduard von. *Philosophy of the Unconscious: Speculative Results According to the Inductive Method of Physical Science.* Westport: Greenwood, 1972. Print.

Holmes, Anne. Rev. of *Les complaintes de Jules Laforgue: Ironie et désenchantement,* by Jean-Pierre Bertrand. *Modern Language Review* 93.4 (1998): 1117. *Literature Resources from Gale.* Web. 9 Oct. 2012.

Ramsey, Warren. "Laforgue and the Ironic Equilibrium." *Modern Poets: Surrealists, Baudelaire, Perse, Laforgue, and Others.* Ed. Kenneth Cornell. New Haven: Yale UP, 1948. Yale French Studies 2. 125-139. *JSTOR.* Web. 9 Oct. 2012.

Further Reading

Arkell, David. *Looking for Laforgue: An Informal Biography.* New York: Persea, 1979. Print.

Hannoosh, Michele. "The Poet as Art Critic: Laforgue's Aesthetic Theory." *Modern Language Review* 79.3 (1984): 553-69. *JSTOR* Web. 9 Oct. 2012.

Laforgue, Jules. "Another Complaint of Lord Pierrot." *Modern Poets of France: A Bilingual Anthology.* Ed. Louis Simpson. Brownsville: Story Line, 1997. Print.

———. "Complainte des pianos qu'on entend dans les quartiers aisés." *The Penguin Book of French Poetry: 1820-1950.* Ed. William Rees. London: Penguin, 1990. 329-332. Print.

Morgan, Edwin. "Notes on the Metaphysics of Jules Laforgue" *Poetry* Feb. 1947: 266-72. *JSTOR.* Web. 9 Oct. 2012.

Wettlaufer, Alexandra K. "Jules Laforgue." *Nineteenth-Century French Poets.* Ed. Robert Lawrence Beum. Detroit: Gale, 2000. Dictionary of Literary Biography 217. *Literature Resource Center.* Web. 9 Oct. 2012.

"complex poetry." Taking a different angle, theorist Anne Holmes in a review praises Laforgue's verse but contends that his abject male figure, in addition to influencing modernist writers, had the effect of producing "a denial, an annihilation, even a reification of the female 'other.'" However, both Holmes and Michele Hannoosh emphasize the importance of Laforgue's progression from—what Hannoosh in a 2007 article for *Nineteenth-Century French Studies*

Caitie Moore

CRISIS OF VERSE

Stéphane Mallarmé

OVERVIEW

French poet and critic Stéphane Mallarmé's "Crise de Vers" (1896; "Crisis of Verse," or "Crisis in Poetry") is considered one of the fundamental statements of symbolist ideas. The treatise is an amalgamation of pieces from five different essays by Mallarmé: the introduction to René Ghil's *Traite du verbe* (1886); "Verse et Musique en France," which was originally published in the March 26, 1892, edition of the *National Observer*; *Vers et prose* (1893); and "Lecture at Oxford and Cambridge" (1894) and "Averses ou Critique" (1895), both of which first appeared in *La Revue Blanche*. Mallarmé is known as the father of symbolist poetry, which challenged the conventions of literature in Europe toward the end of the nineteenth century. Realism, naturalism, and even the decadent movement, though it moved toward symbolism, had all attempted to reflect the sensate world in as precise and exhaustive a detail as possible. "Crisis of Verse" objects to this stance by embracing the powers of the subconscious, vision, sound, and syntax to create a reality that readers must then work to grasp. Mallarmé, in his witty yet difficult prose, argues that his contemporaries who managed to break away from formalism and decadence were better able to contribute to an inclusive literature that could encompass music and visual art as well.

Too idiosyncratic and densely written for the majority of readers, Mallarmé's treatise gained little following other than among the radical artists and writers of his day; these, however, included the subsequently illustrious Auguste Rodin, James McNeill Whistler, André Gide, Paul Verlaine, Marcel Proust, Arthur Rimbaud, and Paul Valéry. All attended Mallarmé's weekly salons, which were a vital intellectual element of Paris life. The value of "Crisis of Verse," as with Jean Moréas's earlier *Symbolist Manifesto* (1886; Moréas was the first to use the word "symbolism"), lay in how it positioned contemporary French poetry in a long history of movements that rejected outmoded styles. Mallarmé went further, claiming that modern poetry should be associative and musical, two qualities that continue to mark today's verse.

HISTORICAL AND LITERARY CONTEXT

"Crisis of Verse" reacts against the tendency to make and value poetry with the objective of commanding a wide readership. It envisions a poetics capable of integrating sonority, spatial relationships, and the imagination, propelling thought beyond the trappings of romanticism's emotionalism and realism's faithful descriptions to greater truths. Mallarmé proposes employing the written word as a device to join individual experience with a knowledge that is not accessible through traditional syntax. Because it raised these aesthetic issues, "Crisis of Verse" was fitting for the increasingly industrialized time period that the French poet Theophile Gautier (1811-72) described as having "brought forth in men obscure desires."

The artistic climate in Europe did much to pave the way for Mallarmé's aesthetic claims. In music Richard Wagner was incorporating elements of painting and poetry into his compositions. The impressionist painters had begun to gain acceptance and admiration in Paris. Literature, however, despite the efforts of Verlaine, Rimbaud, Mallarmé, and Valéry to revitalize it, seemed intransigent and stagnant; Mallarmé felt that the stale devotion to a concept of objective reality was impeding poetic pursuits. In 1884 Verlaine edited the essay collection *Les Poètes maudits* ("The Accursed Poets"), which comprised some of his own, Rimbaud's, and others' symbolist poetry as well as reviews by Verlaine of the work of his contemporaries, including Mallarmé. The title alludes to the economic destitution of many poets represented in the volume (like the others, Mallarmé struggled in poverty, though for a time he was able to make a living by teaching English) and to their status as outside the Parisian literary scene. Verlaine's landmark volume helped Mallarmé's work gain the attention it deserved, though the prose in "Crisis of Verse" remained both too obscure and too forward-thinking for many readers.

The visionary nature of the text is indebted to work already undertaken by Charles Baudelaire, whose *Fleurs du mal* (1857; *The Flowers of Evil*) and *Le Spleen de Paris* (1869; *Paris Spleen*) detail life in Paris in the idiom of its inhabitants. Baudelaire's poems were written in free verse, a radical form at the time that liberated poetry from the confines of formal prosody. He defends his choice in a letter included at the beginning of *Paris Spleen,* in which he asks, "Which one of us … has not dreamed of the miracle of a poetic prose, musical, without rhythm and without rhyme, supple enough and rugged enough to

✜ *Key Facts*

Time Period:
Late 19th Century

Movement/Issue:
Aesthetics; Poetics;
Symbolism

Place of Publication:
France

**Language of
Publication:**
French

THE SCOPE OF SYMBOLISM

On September 18, 1886, the French-language Greek poet Jean Moréas published *Le Symbolisme* (*Symbolist Manifesto*) as a supplement in the popular daily newspaper *Le Figaro,* giving the movement its formal starting point. He named Charles Baudelaire (who had died in 1867), Stéphane Mallarmé, and Arthur Rimbaud as the main symbolist luminaries. Mallarmé and Rimbaud, though their styles differed greatly, agreed that poetry had "been visited by some nameless and absolute flash of lightning," as Mallarmé writes in "Crisis of Verse" (1896). These poets and others identified in subsequent attempts to create a cohesive picture of the period that did not necessarily agree with their designation as symbolists, and the term remains relatively open and abstract. Contrary to general assumptions, symbolist works do not have as much to do with symbols as with a rejection of the literary status quo of the time. Indeed, Baudelaire's *Paris Spleen* (1869) and Rimbaud's *Illuminations* (1886) are only grouped together by virtue of their not fitting into previously established categories. Paul Valéry reasons that "aesthetics divided them; ethics united them."

The symbolists' resistance to all that had come before them and to any type of social conformity lent a "quasi-mystical" atmosphere to their poetry; they were nearly religious in their attribution of sacred qualities to words and their assertion that literature could lead to the divine. Mallarmé remarks in "Crisis of Verse" that in poetry, "Mystery bursts forth ineffably throughout the heavens."

adapt itself to the ruggedness of the soul." This legacy freed Mallarmé to suggest something even more provocative, paying homage to and expanding on Baudelaire's vision. "Crisis of Verse" also owes much to the novelist Joris-Karl Huysmans, who published his magnum opus, *À rebours* (*Against Nature*) in 1884, two years before Mallarmé wrote the first draft of "Crisis of Verse." Hoping to widen the scope of fiction, Huysmans wrote that he hoped "to introduce into it art, science, history," a parallel to the Mallarméan ideal of infusing poetry with "orchestral veils" and "works of art."

Mallarmé realized the aesthetic project of "Crisis of Verse" in his most famous poem, "Un Coup de dés jamais n'abolira le hassard" ("Dice Thrown Never Will Annul Chance"), published in the multilingual literary journal *Cosmopolis* in 1897. His impact on the Western canon was profound. Early-twentieth-century poets continued his exploration of song and myth, alluded to other arts, and censured conformist society. Gertrude Stein's poem "Tender Buttons" (1914) and T. S. Eliot's "The Love Song of J. Alfred Prufrock" (1915) both demonstrate Mallarméan values. The radical idea of divorcing words from their referents led to Ezra Pound's insistence that communication is relative, that it needs not be predicated

on acts of direct speech, and that it can indeed be visionary and esoteric. When Mallarmé's work was introduced to the United States, his influence became noteworthy in the poems of Wallace Stevens and Kenneth Rexroth and in the paintings of Robert Motherwell; the inspiration has extended to contemporary poets John Ashbery, Barbara Guest, Nathaniel Mackey, and Rosmarie Waldrop.

THEMES AND STYLE

"Crisis of Verse" insists on interlocking many aesthetic positions at once: "the disappearance of the poet as speaker," a symphonic musicality, suggestion as opposed to literal interpretation, and visual associations. The essay posits that all of these elements must be in place in order for a poem to elicit "the pure notion." While much has been made of the impenetrability of "Crisis of Verse," this assessment refers to the literal meaning of the words themselves, which Mallarmé often deliberately obscures or uses in an ambiguous way. He writes that "languages are imperfect in that although there are many, the supreme one is lacking"; he contends that poetry is the only vehicle that can overcome this obstacle because "verse makes up for what languages lack, completely superior as it is." What he finds superior in poetry is that its musicality and form can combine to create layers of meaning that encompass the complexities of the human condition. He argues that music allows us to overcome difficulties of literal sense. Mallarmé asserts that the poetic "hallucination" should "be counted," because it has the ability to "illumine."

Seeking in "Crisis of Verse" to expose the traditional structure of language, Mallarmé uses words in a way that may appear random, but he never advocates carelessness. His linguistic "difficulty" serves to support his argument that an obscure language will enliven audience engagement. In employing his famously complicated syntax, Mallarmé intended to divest each word of its corresponding familiar association. His attempt "to separate" language into what he saw as its two functions, which he articulates as "the immediate or unrefined word on the one hand, the essential one on the other," creates a tension that his committed readers turn to precisely for the reward they receive when grappling with a complex text. In his few published works, Mallarmé refuses to merely lyricize what readers and poets already know, turning instead to the elusive. He writes, "I say: a flower!" and he hopes that what we will imagine is "the one absent from every bouquet."

The text is uncompromising in its vision of moving modern literature toward symbolism, which he characterizes as a "song, when it becomes impalpable joy," and away from what Mallarmé deems "official" verse—"the silent exchange of money." Unlike other artistic manifestos of the late eighteenth and early nineteenth centuries, notably those of the Italian futurists (in particular Filippo Tommaso Marinetti's

Stéphane Mallarmé
(1876) by Édouard
Manet. Mallarmé was
a strong influence on
several modernist artistic
and literary movements.
© AISA/EVERETT
COLLECTION

1909 "Futurist Manifesto"), the text is neither damning nor aggressive. Mallarmé compels his readers toward engagement with the creative act in a nearly utopian, lyrical tone that declares, "Each soul is a melody which must be picked up again, and the flute or the viola of everyone exists for that."

CRITICAL DISCUSSION

The general public scorned Mallarmé's work, and contemporary critics frequently called it "obscure" and "sterile." Journal editors rejected it, choosing instead to publish the more palatable work of the naturalist school. Mallarmé was lauded by his protégé Paul Valéry, however, who wrote in his tribute "I Sometimes Said to Stéphane Mallarmé" that because readers at the time were marked with "indolence and every form of mental inadequacy," they were not capable of engaging with the puzzles posed by many of the symbolists' texts. According to Valéry, Mallarmé's poems and prose opposed such passivity by "implying and demanding a perpetual exchange between form and substance, sound and sense, action and subject matter." Their grand scope prompted composer Claude Debussy, choreographer/dancer Vaslav Nijinsky, and painter Édouard Manet to honor the poet with homages in their various mediums. When British poet Arthur Symons introduced their work admiringly to the English-speaking world in 1899 in *The Symbolist Movement in Literature,* he characterized it as "a literature in which the visible world is no longer a reality, and the unseen world no longer a dream."

Mallarmé is credited with having changed the face of poetry. In "Mallarmé's Wake" (1995), Robert Greer Cohn writes that the poet "stretched the power of verbal expression beyond normal usage so far that he instituted a quantum leap." His aesthetic arguments were convincing enough that his successors incorporated and added to his work, accepting symbolist rigor as right and effective and viewing themselves as apprentices of history. Imagism, Dada, and surrealism all flowed from his source, as did the modernist interrogation of both linear time and stable subjects that led to the self-conscious and subjective texts of postmodernism.

In the twentieth century, English-language translators struggled to find the most effective ways to render Mallarmé's baffling prose. In the introduction to the standard translation of "Crisis of Verse" (in *Mallarmé: Selected Prose Poems, Essays & Letters*; 1956), Bradford Cook notes that he favored changing Mallarmé's "complex, abstract, condensed, quiet, outwardly cold" prose in a way that would "clarify and concretize" it for the English reader. Scholar Joseph Acquisto's reading of "Crisis of Verse" supports this translation style. According to Acquisto in *French Forum*, "Mallarmé knows that creating a reality where language physically reflects truth would be the death of poetry." Acquisto states that Mallarmé's "cut and paste" composition method signals the poet's faith in "ordinary language." In *Selected Poetry and Prose* (1982), scholar Mary Ann Caws compiles the work of fifteen translators' and her own rendering of "Crisis of Verse." She supplies an alternative approach that is more faithful to the original French. In her preface Caws argues against familiar language, submitting that "Mallarmé would have condemned that roundly." English readers can compare the two versions to get a potentially more comprehensive sense of Mallarmé's meaning and form.

BIBLIOGRAPHY

Sources

Acquisto, Joseph. "Between Stéphane Mallarmé and René Ghil: The Impossible Desire for Poetry." *French Forum* 29.3 (2004): 27-41. *JSTOR.* Web. 6 Nov. 2012.

Baudelaire, Charles. *Paris Spleen.* New York: New Directions, 1970. Print.

Caws, Mary Ann. Preface. *Selected Poetry and Prose,* by Stéphane Mallarmé. Ed. Mary Ann Caws. New York: New Directions, 1982. Print.

Cohn, Robert Greer. "Mallarmé's Wake." *Philosophical Resonances.* Spec. issue of *New Literary History* 26.4 (1995): 885-901. *JSTOR.* Web. 20 Sept. 2012.

Cook, Bradford. Introduction. *Mallarmé: Selected Prose Poems, Essays, & Letters,* by Stéphane Mallarmé. Trans. and ed. Bradford Cook. Baltimore: Johns Hopkins, 1956. Print.

Symons, Arthur. *The Symbolist Movement in Literature.* London: Heinemann, 1899. Print.

Valéry, Paul. "I Sometimes Said to Stéphane Mallarmé." Trans. Malcolm Cowley. *Kenyon Review* 27.1 (1965): 94-112. *JSTOR.* Web. 20 Sept. 2012.

Further Reading

Ashbery, John. *Selected Poems.* New York: Penguin, 1986. Print.

Bersani, Leo. *The Death of Stéphane Mallarmé.* Cambridge: Cambridge UP, 1982. Print.

Cohn, Robert Greer. *Mallarmé's "Divagations": A Guide and Commentary.* New York: Lang, 1990. Print.

Johnson, Barbara. "Poetry and Performative Language." *Mallarmé.* Spec. issue of *Yale French Studies* 54 (1977): 140-58. *JSTOR.* Web. 20 Sept. 2012.

Mackey, Nathaniel. *Splay Anthem.* New York: New Directions, 2002. Print.

Valéry, Paul. "Literature." Trans. William Geoffrey. *Hudson Review* 2.4 (1950): 538-58. *JSTOR.* Web. 20 Sept. 2012.

———. "Poetry and Abstract Thought." Trans. Charles Guenther. *Kenyon Review* 16.2 (1954): 208-33. *JSTOR.* Web. 20 Sept. 2012.

Caitie Moore

A DEFENCE OF POETRY

Percy Bysshe Shelley

OVERVIEW

Percy Bysshe Shelley, a major English lyrical poet and a key figure in the early-nineteenth-century Romantic movement, wrote the essay *A Defence of Poetry* (1840) in 1821 as a refutation of his friend Thomas Love Peacock's satiric "Four Ages of Poetry" (1820), which denigrates the poetic Romanticism popular at the time. Countering with his own philosophy of the history and purpose of poetry, Shelley created a treatise that positions poetry as "the expression of the Imagination," poets as those who contain a "universal sense of the world," and a poem as the "very image of life expressed in its eternal truth." Although it was published posthumously, it was intended to address the educated readership of Peacock's essay, which was originally published in the *Literary Miscellany,* and all those interested in the philosophy of poetry.

While it had a limited readership, Shelley's original draft of *A Defence of Poetry* was embraced by his publisher, his wife Mary Shelley, and his close friends Leigh Hunt and Thomas Medwin. When Mary published it in *Essays, Letters from Abroad, Translations and Fragments* in 1840, it gained widespread recognition. The work was foundational for the poets of the late 1830s and early 1840s—including Alfred, Lord Tennyson and Robert Browning—and for such Pre-Raphaelite poets of the 1860s as Dante Gabriel Rossetti. Even the poet and critic Matthew Arnold, who was notoriously critical of Shelley's poetry, grudgingly praised his *Defence.* Today, the essay is considered a seminal text in studies of poetry and the Romantic movement.

HISTORICAL AND LITERARY CONTEXT

At the turn of the nineteenth century, a group of writers living in England's Lake District gained prominence as the "Lake Poets." Although the influential *Edinburgh Review* consistently reviled their work, they became part of the larger Romantic movement in the arts, education, and politics flourishing on the Continent. Reacting against the rational and scientific emphases of the Age of Enlightenment and the Industrial Revolution, Romanticism exalted emotion, nature, and imagination. Imagination, particularly, was considered central, wielding a creative power comparable to that of nature and even of divinity and at long last asserting its proper place alongside (or above) reason. In the late eighteenth century, *Lyrical Ballads* (1798), a collaborative volume of poetry by William Wordsworth and Samuel Taylor Coleridge, and its influential Preface began to win over detractors; critics hailed it as a triumph of personal expression.

Shelley and his close companions and fellow second-generation Romantics John Keats and Lord Byron were the writers "The Four Ages of Poetry" ridiculed. A contemporary of the three, Peacock had a background in business and a penchant for satire and intellectual criticism. In his tongue-in-cheek analysis of the state of poetry, he argued that English verse of the early nineteenth century no longer possessed intellectual merit. The poetic excellence of the "golden age" of Homer had steadily deteriorated, finally reaching an "age of brass" in which the Romantics were "wallowing in the rubbish of departed ignorance," cultivating a contrived and immature "sort of fairy-land." *A Defence of Poetry* rebuts Peacock's utilitarian views, depicting the history of poetry as the development of one "great poem, which all poets, like the co-operating thoughts of one great mind, have built up since the beginning of the world," a mystical accumulation that immortalizes "all that is best and most beautiful in the world."

Although it was written in response to a contemporaneous essay, *A Defence of Poetry* is heavily indebted to Sir Philip Sidney's Renaissance-period *Defence of Poesie* (1579), which has been called an aesthetic manifesto of humanism. Sidney argued that poetry is superior to philosophy as a form of thought and writing; more enthusiastic and possibly more ethical, it is meant to "teach and delight." Shelley's essay approximated Sydney's framework: he first defines poetry then lauds its ethical value, defends it against detractors, and surveys its history. Both *Defences* admire Plato, working through the Classical Greek philosopher's ideas, despite Plato's famous denigration of poets. *A Defence of Poetry* praises Plato as an "inspired rhapsodist" and "essentially a poet" who anticipated the Romantic fusion of poetry and philosophy. Aristotle's *Poetics* modeled a rebuttal of Plato's contentions, contradicting the view that poetry is merely imitation by claiming, like Shelley, that imagination endows poetic imitation with higher truths. Shelley also drew insight from Wordsworth's famous Preface to *Lyrical Ballads,* which advocates—in place of the wit and urbanity of the Augustan poetry of Alexander

❖ *Key Facts*

Time Period:
Mid-19th Century

Movement/Issue:
Romanticism

Place of Publication:
England

Language of Publication:
English

MARY SHELLEY

Mary Wollstonecraft Godwin (1797-1851) married Percy Bysshe Shelley in 1816. The two had been lovers since they met in 1814. Best known for her anonymously published Gothic novel *Frankenstein; or, The Modern Prometheus* (1818), Mary Shelley also wrote such short stories as "The Sisters of Albano" and "Ferdinando Eboli," both of which appeared in the popular annual magazine the *Keepsake* in 1828; biographies, most notably her three-volume collection *Lives of the Most Eminent Literary and Scientific Men of Italy, Spain, and Portugal* (1837); travelogues, including *Rambles in Germany and Italy in 1840, 1842, and 1843* (1844); children's literature, such as the mythological drama *Midas* (1920), cowritten with Percy in blank verse in 1820; and the occasional poem.

It was Mary Shelley who transcribed and edited early versions of her husband's *Defence of Poetry*. In July 1822, Percy drowned off the coast of Italy. Mary eventually published his poetic treatise in *Essays, Letters from Abroad, Translations and Fragments* (1840), nineteen years after it was composed. She died of a brain tumor in February 1851.

Pope, John Dryden, and others—the use of common speech and its rhythms, the evocation of memory to arrive at emotion, and the poetic inducement of pleasure. The two differ somewhat significantly in their perception of their central poetic subject, all-powerful nature: to Wordsworth it is nurturing, whereas Shelley experiences it as transcendent, dangerous, and indifferent to human needs. Other writers Shelley mentions explicitly as precursors to his contribution to the "great poem" are Homer, Dante, Bacon, Shakespeare, and Milton.

In addition to inspiring poets of his own era and beyond, *A Defence of Poetry* moved subsequent philosopher-poets to meld the two discourses. In the generation immediately following Shelley's, this kind of fusion appears in the writings of Matthew Arnold and, in the United States, Ralph Waldo Emerson. The modernist period retains echoes of Shelley in the writings of the American poet Wallace Stevens. His essay "A Collect of Philosophy" (1951) explains, "It is often the case that concepts of philosophy are poetic" and advises readers to consider the "poetic nature of at least a few philosophical ideas." More recently, the American poet Gabriel Gudding published a collection of poems titled *A Defense of Poetry* (2002) that invokes Shelley's treatise.

THEMES AND STYLE

A Defence of Poetry addresses themes of the poet's role in society and poetry's relationship with "the cause of truth." Taking Peacock's claim that poetic talent

and integrity were in decay as a platform from which to exalt the Romantic endeavor, Shelley refutes Peacock's four ages, arguing that great poets have existed throughout human history, each contributing to an all-embracing poem for the benefit and pleasure of all humanity. This "great Poem is a fountain forever overflowing with the waters of wisdom and delight." Rather than being "empty aimless mockeries of intellectual exertion," poems are intellectual, imaginative, and true; they are the mind acting upon thoughts "so as to colour them with its own light, and composing from them as from elements, other thoughts, each containing within itself the principle of its own integrity." Shelley particularly seizes upon Peacock's accusation that poets have become "a herd of desperate imitators": "Every great poet," Shelley writes, "must inevitably innovate upon the example of his predecessors." He uses Peacock's disparagement as an opportunity to expand our sense of the societal function and responsibility of poets: they "are not only the authors of language and of music [...] they are the institutors of laws, and the founders of civil society, and the inventors of the arts of life, and the teachers." In creating a unique poetic universe, "Poets are the unacknowledged legislators of the world."

Shelley employs all three rhetorical modes of persuasion to great effect in his *Defence*. He begins by defining his terms, a basic appeal to the logos, or reason, of his readers. In "determining what is poetry, and who are poets," he proceeds "to estimate [poetry's] effects upon society" through the use of metaphor, which excites emotion, or pathos; for example, he writes, "A poet is a nightingale, who sits in darkness and sings to cheer its own solitude with sweet sounds" and "poetry is a sword of lightening, ever unsheathed, which consumes the scabbard that would contain it." In this sense, Shelley uses poetry to explain poetry. He also appeals to ethos—virtue and wisdom—by aligning the great poem not only with the great poets but also with noble poetic writers and thinkers such as Pythagoras, Plato, Moses, and Jesus.

In its use of calmly reasoned, nonpolemical language, as well as in treating the past rather than the future, Shelley's *Defence* differs from Wordsworth's Preface, which more nearly resembles a manifesto. The language of *A Defence* combines the emotive expressions of poetry with the analytic language of reason and philosophy. Shelley also addresses the varying styles of poetic language in his essay and in general, explaining that "the parts of a composition may be poetical, without the composition as a whole being a poem." The poetic element of a text may be a sentence or even a single word. In inserting poetic language rooted in metaphor and rhythm into an otherwise dense and thought-driven text, Shelley attempts to emulate Plato. He maintains that the "truth and splendor of [Plato's] imagery, and the melody of his language, are the most intense that it is possible to conceive."

CRITICAL DISCUSSION

During Shelley's lifetime critics ignored the poet and his writing more often than not. In the second half of the nineteenth century, however, his work was taken more seriously. Although Arnold famously called Shelley a "beautiful and ineffectual angel, beating in the void his luminous wings in vain" in his *Essays in Criticism: Second Series* (1888), he conceded that *A Defence of Poetry* would likely withstand the "wear and tear of time" and hold a primary position in the annals of poetry.

By the early twentieth century, Shelley's legacy had been recognized and his reputation as a poet and theorist had solidified. Lilian Winstanley, in her monograph *Shelley's "Defence of Poetry," Browning's "Essay on Shelley"* (1911), writes that "his pamphlet is one of the treasures of English prose—a glowing panegyric of poetry uttered by one who understands the subtlest philosophy of his own art and can express its effect in unrivaled language." In 1927 Roger Ingpen agreed in *The Letters and Poetry of Percy Bysshe Shelley* that the *Defence* is the poet's "most finely wrought piece of prose, but it is also invaluable as the expression of a great poet on his art." More recently, in *The Critical Tradition: Classic Texts and Contemporary Trends* (1998), David H. Richter called Shelley the "most radical English poet since Milton," and he described his essay as "austerely" written, containing an "inspiring vision" of poetry. Today, scholars still consider Shelley's *A Defence of Poetry* a landmark of Romantic, poetic, and literary studies.

Twentieth-century scholarship of *A Defence of Poetry* focused in part on what critics judged to be Shelley's varying degrees of commitment to Platonism. Important studies by Earl R. Wasserman (*Shelley*, 1977) and C.E. Pulos (*The Deep Truth: A Study of Shelley's Skepticism*, 1954) position him as an adherent of skeptical empiricism rather than a philosopher in the Platonic tradition. Tracy Ware's article "Shelley's Platonism in *A Defence of Poetry*" (1983) outlines Shelley's "ambivalent view of the poet" as a Platonic figure, arguing that he promoted a mix of skepticism and Platonism. Ware, Troy Urquhart ("Metaphor, Transfer, and Translation in Plato's *Ion*," 2003), and others examine Shelley's translations of Plato's *Ion* and *Symposium* for clues about the nature and extent of the poet's assimilation of Platonic philosophy. Other critics have compared *A Defence of Poetry* to its precursor Sir Philip Sidney's *Defence of Poesie*. Another strand of scholarship has focused on Shelley's prose style. In *Shelley's Myth of Metaphor* (1970), John Wright sparked a renewal of interest in the essay's use of metaphorical language. More recently, Jerrold E. Hogle's *Shelley's Process* (1989) and Urquhart's article have deconstructed Shelley's

Shelley in the Baths of Caracalla, by Joseph Severn (1845). KEATS-SHELLEY MEMORIAL HOUSE, ROME, ITALY/THE BRIDGEMAN ART LIBRARY

metaphors, arguing that *A Defence of Poetry* is not a work in the Platonic tradition but is, rather, postmodern and anti-logocentric.

BIBLIOGRAPHY

Sources

Arnold, Matthew. "Shelley." *Essays in Criticism: By Matthew Arnold… First and Second Series Complete (CA. 1900)*. Ithaca: Cornell U Lib., 2009. 385-408. Print.

Peacock, Thomas. "The Four Ages of Poetry." *Classic Writings on Poetry*. Ed. William Harmon. New York: Columbia UP, 2003. 317-30. Print.

Richter, David H., ed. "Percy Bysshe Shelley: *A Defence of Poetry*." *The Critical Tradition: Classic Texts and Contemporary Trends*. 2nd ed. Boston: Bedford, 1998. 337-39. Print.

Shelley, Percy Bysshe. *The Letters of Percy Bysshe Shelley: Volume 2*. Ed. Roger Ingpen and W. E. Peek. London: Julian, 1927. Print.

———. *Shelley's Poetry and Prose: Authoritative Texts and Criticism*. Ed. Donald H. Reiman and Neil Fraistat. New York: Norton, 2002. Print.

Stevens, Wallace. "A Collect of Philosophy." *Opus Posthumous: Poems, Plays, Prose*. New York: Vintage, 1990. 267-80. Print.

Ware, Tracy. "Shelley's Platonism in *A Defence of Poetry*." *Studies in English Literature 1500-1900* 23.4 (1983): 549-66. Print.

Winstanley, Lilian. *Shelley's "Defence of Poetry": Browning's "Essay on Shelley."* Boston: Heath, 1911. Print.

Further Reading

Bieri, James. *Percy Bysshe Shelley: A Biography*. Baltimore: Johns Hopkins UP, 2008. Print.

Cox, Jeffrey N. *Poetry and Politics in the Cockney School: Keats, Shelley, Hunt, and Their Circle*. New York: Cambridge UP, 1998. Print.

Fry, Paul H. *A Defense of Poetry: Reflections on the Occasion of Writing.* Stanford: Stanford UP, 1995. Print.

Hogle, Jerrold E. *Shelley's Process: Radical Transference and the Development of His Major Works.* New York: Oxford UP, 1989. Print.

Morton, Timothy. *The Cambridge Companion to Shelley.* New York: Cambridge UP, 2006. Print.

Pulos, C.E. *The Deep Truth: A Study of Shelley's Skepticism.* Lincoln: U of Nebraska P, 1954. Print.

Smith-Hubbard, Julie L. "Cosmopoetics and Politics: Were Those 'Unacknowledged Legislators of the World' Actually Women?" *Forum on Public Policy* (2008): n.pag. *Academic OneFile.* Web. 23 July 2012.

Urquhart, Troy. "Metaphor, Transfer, and Translation in Plato's *Ion*: The Postmodern Platonism of Percy Bysshe Shelley's *A Defence of Poetry.*" *Romanticism on the Net* 31 (2003): n. pag. Web. 7 July 2012.

Verkoren, Lucas. *A Study of Shelley's "Defence of Poetry": Its Origin, Textual History, Sources, and Significance.* New York: Haskell, 1937. Print.

Wasserman, Earl R. *Shelley: A Critical Reading.* Baltimore: John Hopkins UP, 1977. Print.

Wright, John. *Shelley's Myth of Metaphor.* Athens: U of Georgia P, 1970. Print.

Joshua Ware

DEFINITION OF NEO-TRADITIONALISM

Maurice Denis

OVERVIEW

French painter Maurice Denis's "Définition du néo-traditionnisme" ("Definition of Neo-traditionalism"), an artistic manifesto published in the periodical *Art et Critique* in 1890, argues against the idea that a painting's worth should be measured by how closely the artist is able to replicate the natural world. Instead, the essay advocates a formalist aesthetic approach, whereby a painting is valued as an image in and of itself. Denis asserts that confining art to attempts at photorealistic reproduction profoundly limits the artistic imagination, which should be judged by the power of the images it produces rather than the "realism" of those images. "Definition of Neo-traditionalism" served as the mission statement of the Nabis, a symbolist artistic group founded by Paul Sérusier in the late nineteenth century. Along with other manifestos of symbolism, the essay marked a shift away from the mimetic representation that characterized naturalistic and impressionist art. While the term "neo-traditionalism" refers to an appreciation of pre-realist artistic approaches, the text also gestures toward the more abstract focus of later modern art movements, such as fauvism and cubism.

In addition to providing a theoretical foundation for the work of the Nabis, "Neo-traditionalism" was warmly received by the symbolist movement as a whole. The work of symbolists such as Pierre Puvis de Chavannes and Gustave Moreau cohered firmly with the essay's emphasis on iconic images and disavowal of strict realism. In subsequent years Denis's work continued to influence the increasingly abstract avant-garde schools of art that came to prevalence. Today "Neo-traditionalism" is recognized as one of the most important aesthetic manifestos of the late nineteenth century, and its opening sentence—which declares that a painting is "essentially a flat surface covered with colors"—has been widely quoted in aesthetic theory.

HISTORICAL AND LITERARY CONTEXT

Denis's essay responds to the established French artistic scene, which—as part of the Western tradition of painting that emerged in the Renaissance and eventually spread through much of the world—continued to emphasize the objective re-creation of ordinary reality. Yet, by the second half of the nineteenth century, Western art had moved away from the intense emotionality and dramatic subject matter of romanticism. Influenced by society's growing faith in science and human knowledge, artists of the period favored accurate representations of observable, often quotidian phenomena. Impressionism, which came to the fore in the 1870s and 1880s, maintained this naturalistic focus. Impressionists attempted to reproduce the visual impression made by a subject on the eyes of an observer. Although impressionists may not have recorded the "objective" qualities of their subjects, they were nevertheless dedicated to the faithful depiction of a sensory experience.

By the time "Neo-traditionalism" appeared in 1890, the naturalistic ethos of much French art was being challenged by the work of a large number of disparate artists, often grouped under the label of postimpressionism. These artists retained the relatively open artistic purview of impressionism but often pushed beyond that movement's emphasis on remaining faithful to reality. The Nabis belonged to the loose postimpressionist school of symbolism, which sought to convey the emotional state of the artist through metaphor and imaginative symbols. The work of the symbolist painter Paul Gauguin, in particular, was a formative influence on the Nabis—a group that included, in addition to Denis and Sérusier, such renowned artists as Pierre Bonnard and Édouard Vuillard.

"Neo-traditionalism" emerged from a fertile milieu of French aesthetic theory being written in the late nineteenth century. Its most direct theoretical antecedent was perhaps the work of Gauguin, whose aesthetic pronouncements were elaborated by Denis's writings. Gauguin decried impressionism's preoccupation with producing pictorial imitations of human eyesight. He equated this tendency with an excessive interest in scientific rationality, which blinded artists to such fruitful notions as mystery and emotion. Denis shares this conviction, along with Gauguin's belief that art should be an aesthetic manifestation of the artist's imagination. This emphasis on imagination over objective representation may be found in many other symbolist writings of the period, including Jean Moréas's poetry-focused *Symbolist Manifesto* (1886) and other works on visual and nonvisual arts.

⊹ Key Facts

Time Period:
Late 19th Century

Movement/Issue:
Aesthetics; Formalism; Neotraditionalism

Place of Publication:
France

Language of Publication:
French

MAURICE DENIS: ARTIST AND THEORIST

Born on November 25, 1870, Maurice Denis became, at not quite the age of twenty, the primary aesthetic theorist of the Nabis. He is now recognized as one of the major intellectual voices of symbolism and of French artistic theory as a whole. Although Denis may be more noted for his writings than for his artwork, he did achieve considerable renown for the latter. Much of his art depicted religious iconography, as Denis was a devout Roman Catholic. His painting style led his colleagues to call him "the Nabi of the beautiful icons."

As with many of his fellow Nabis, Denis did not limit his work to easel-based painting. His art encompassed a number of murals and other large-scale works commissioned to decorate the interiors of various clients. Believing that art was decorative by its very nature, Denis and the Nabis sought to break down the distinction between decorative and fine art. Meanwhile, as his career progressed, his beliefs about art became progressively more conservative in relation to both the changing avant-garde and to his own prior views. Eventually, his burgeoning classicism largely overtook his previous rebellious pose. Denis died in an automobile accident in 1943.

Denis's essay was massively influential on subsequent aesthetic theory, and its first sentence became one of the most frequently repeated passages within French writing on art. Yet Denis came to deplore the great interest in "Neo-traditionalism," as it tended to overshadow both his art and his copious later writings, many of which were significantly less radical. For example, he vehemently disagreed with the artistic theories of fauvist Henri Matisse, even though the fauvists' free-form, vigorously colored paintings were inspired in part by Denis's own writings. "Neo-traditionalism" remains widely quoted in modern books of art history and aesthetic theory.

THEMES AND STYLE

Central to "Neo-traditionalism" is the conviction that the subject matter of a given artwork is secondary in importance to the artwork's merit as an independent object. The text begins with what at the time was a revolutionary way of defining a painting, focusing on its style or composition rather than its representational qualities: "Remember that a picture, before it is a war horse, a naked woman, or some anecdote, is essentially a flat surface covered with colors arranged in a certain order." Denis goes on to criticize the prevailing artistic definition of "nature" as "the sum of optical sensation." He points out that the relationship between art and human perception is not a one-way transfer of information: "There is an undeniable tendency of painters to assimilate aspects [of objects] perceived in reality with the aspects already observed in painting." In

other words, the subconscious conflation of previously viewed art with one's immediate perception inevitably dooms attempts to replicate objective reality. In light of this, Denis asseverates that the beauty of nature is more truly expressed not through scrupulous realism— "the pettiness of *trompe-l'oeil*"—but through intuitive, symbolic expressions of artistic imagination.

The text's rhetorical approach relies heavily on discussions of past and present artistic theory, as well as on an explicitly religious appeal to the transcendental powers of art. Many of Denis's principles are elaborated not as straightforward declarations but obliquely, through his thoughts on various aspects of the contemporary art world. For instance, he asserts that the impressionists amount to a "presentiment of a return to beautiful things," but, unfortunately, "they spoil the savor of their preliminary sensation … by their disdain for composition and their concern to make it natural!" The religious underpinnings of his convictions are revealed through both his explicit statements about the purpose of art—"art is the sanctification of nature"—and his tendency to use spiritual iconography to illustrate his points: "A Byzantine Christ is symbolic. The Jesus of modern painters … is only literary. In one, the form is expressive; in the other, it is imitated nature which tries to be [expressive]."

Stylistically, "Neo-traditionalism" tends toward rather florid, overwrought language, which befits Denis's approval of artistic emotion and his disdain for dry realism. Rhetorical questions are common, as when, arguing for the supremacy of symbolic over naturalistic representation, he implores the reader to compare the "lion of nature" with the magnificent lions carved by the ancient Assyrians; he then asks, "To which do we kneel?" Meanwhile, wrong-headed approaches to art are passionately denounced in intemperate language: "The wretches who kill themselves to find something original in their servile skulls … [refuse] their worthwhile sensations because they have been taught to deny beauty, because they interpose their concern for *trompe-l'oeil* between the emotion and the work!" Denis's approbation of the work he appreciates is similarly forceful, as is his avowed enthusiasm for the "universal triumph of the esthete's imagination over the efforts of stupid imitation, triumph of the emotion of Beauty over the naturalist lie."

CRITICAL DISCUSSION

Upon its publication in 1890, "Neo-traditionalism" predictably met with warm approval by Denis's fellow Nabis, and it was later appreciated (and appropriated) by fauvists, cubists, and the other more abstract modern artists who eclipsed the Nabis. Charles Edward Gauss, in his 1949 survey of French aesthetic theories, points out that the fauvists' theoretical "point of departure" was the opening sentence of Denis's essay. Denis, however, was not pleased by this popularity; despite the essay's revolutionary stance, his views were never as

Avril, by Maurice Denis, from the Seasons Series. Painted in 1892, two years after Denis wrote his "Definition of Neo-Traditionalism." ERICH LESSING/ART RESOURCE, NY

iconoclastic as they had often been perceived. As Claire Frèches-Thory and Antoine Terrasse observe in their 1991 study of the Nabis, Denis was in fact "struck with horror by the arrival of fauvism and cubism."

Although "Neo-traditionalism" is widely regarded as one of the seminal texts of the symbolist movement, much of its legacy lies in its status as a precursor to modernist art. The increasingly abstract and nonrepresentational qualities of twentieth-century avant-garde art are often traced back to the essay's opening definition of a painting. Indeed, the effect of the rest of the text is arguably weak in comparison to the impact of its initial sentence, which is frequently the only portion of Denis's work quoted in aesthetic writings. Johanna Drucker's assertion, in her 1994 analysis of modernist visual art, that Denis's initial sentence is "the cliché cornerstone of modernity" testifies to its significance in the history of aesthetic theory. That significance is often the subject of contemporary scholarship, as is the article's position within Denis's overall theoretical outlook.

Scholarship on "Neo-traditionalism" often contextualizes the article within both Denis's numerous aesthetic pronouncements and the history of art in general. Michael Andrew Marlais's *Conservative Echoes in Fin-de-Siècle Parisian Art Criticism* (1992), for example, analyzes the relationship between modernism and Denis's theories while emphasizing his inherent conservatism. Likewise, Jean-Paul Bouillon's overview of Denis as a theoretician downplays the supposed radicalism of the essay and contradicts a number of commonly held interpretations of its

aesthetic project. In light of Denis's voluminous critical writings, Bouillon observes that "Neo-traditionalism" is perhaps too well known, as it has "masked the career and work of an artist of much greater scope."

BIBLIOGRAPHY

Sources

Bouillon, Jean-Paul. "The Theoretician." *Maurice Denis: Earthly Paradise (1870-1943).* Ed. Jean-Paul Bouillon. Trans. Josephine Bacon, Caroline Newman, and Shena Wilson. Paris: Éditions de la Réunion des Musées Nationaux, 2006. 33-7. Print.

Denis, Maurice. "Definition of Neo-Traditionalism." Trans. Elizabeth Holt Muench. *From the Classicists to the Impressionists: A Documentary History of Art and Architecture in the 19th Century.* Ed. Elizabeth Gilmore Holt. New York: New York UP, 1966. 509-17. Print.

Drucker, Johanna. *Theorizing Modernism: Visual Art and the Critical Tradition.* New York: Columbia UP, 1994. Print.

Frèches-Thory, Claire, and Antoine Terrasse. *The Nabis: Bonnard, Vuillard, and Their Circle.* Trans. Mary Pardoe. New York: Abrams, 1991. Print.

Gauss, Charles Edward. *The Aesthetic Theories of French Artists: From Realism to Surrealism.* Baltimore: Johns Hopkins P, 1949. Print.

Marlais, Michael Andrew. *Conservative Echoes in Fin-de-Siècle Parisian Art Criticism.* University Park: Pennsylvania State UP, 1992. Print.

Further Reading

Ellridge, Arthur. *Gauguin and the Nabis: Prophets of Modernism.* Trans. Jean-Marie Clarke. Paris: Terrail, 1995. Print.

Harrison, Charles, and Paul Wood with Jason Gaiger, eds. *Art in Theory, 1815-1900: An Anthology of Changing Ideas.* Oxford: Blackwell, 1998. Print.

Kuenzli, Katherine Marie. *The Nabis and Intimate Modernism: Painting and the Decorative at the Fin-de-Siècle.* Farnham: Ashgate, 2010. Print.

Mathieu, Pierre-Louis. *The Symbolist Generation, 1870-1910.* Trans. Michael Taylor. New York: Rizzoli, 1990. Print.

Shiff, Richard. *Cézanne and the End of Impressionism: A Study of the Theory, Technique, and Critical Evaluation of Modern Art.* Chicago: U of Chicago P, 1984. Print.

Thomson, Richard, and Belinda Thomson. "Maurice Denis's 'Définition du Néo-Traditionnisme' and Anti-Naturalism (1890)." *Burlington Magazine* 154.1309 (2012): 260-67. Print.

James Overholtzer

AN ESSAY ON CRITICISM

Alexander Pope

OVERVIEW

In 1711 Alexander Pope published "An Essay on Criticism," advising would-be literary critics to behave with decorum and to ground their work in classical learning. Appearing when Pope was only twenty-three years old, the poem was a consolidation of his early views on literary criticism, the act of writing, and the ideal conduct of authors, as well as the behavior of critics. Written in conversational rhyming couplets, the piece is divided into three parts. First, Pope introduces his topic and outlines the critical precepts of the Greco-Roman period. Then he covers traits that prevent solid judgment, including pride and partiality. Finally, he explains how an ideal critic should behave, using examples from both the ancient and modern world. By approaching the topic of aesthetic theory and criticism in this way, Pope promotes a classically infused approach to reading (and writing) literature, which urges its adherents to conduct themselves in a genteel but rigorous fashion.

As Pope's first major publication on literary theory, "An Essay on Criticism" drew favorable reviews immediately after its publication—though its ideas about aesthetics, and particularly sound's role in poetry, have subsequently been challenged. Still, in 1711 the work introduced Pope as a new young voice in literary criticism, promoting the concepts of decorum (or fittingness) of expression, moderation, and goodwill in overlooking insignificant flaws. By advocating these concepts, first described by writers such as Aristotle and Horace, Pope joins modern critics like Nicolas Boileau in affirming the pertinence of Greco-Roman aesthetic theory to eighteenth-century writing and criticism. He also carves an amiable and witty middle path between fawning approbation and vituperative condemnation. In doing so, Pope's work became a critical benchmark, providing a model of modest but intellectually grounded practice that would influence generations of writers and theorists.

HISTORICAL AND LITERARY CONTEXT

At the beginning of the eighteenth century, Britain was transitioning between ruling houses and reexamining its ideas of culture. In 1688, the year of Pope's birth, the Glorious Revolution ousted the Roman Catholic monarch James II, replacing him on the throne with his Protestant daughter Mary (who reigned jointly with her husband, William of Orange). After fourteen years, Mary's sister Anne assumed the throne; she was succeeded in 1714 by the Hanoverian George I, who brought German customs and ideas to his new position. All these transitions affected the public presentation of religion, international trade, and the balance of power between Parliament and the monarch. In particular, the changes underscored the "outsider" status of Catholics in Britain, while new administrations consolidated the earning power (and increased the spread) of the British bureaucracy.

To discuss and analyze these changes, subjects could visit coffeehouses: open environments where intellectuals—particularly literary figures such as authors and critics—expressed their opinions freely. This coffeehouse culture gave rise to influential publications. At Button's Coffee House, for example, Joseph Addison penned copy for the *Spectator* (a paper to which both Pope and Jonathan Swift would later contribute material). Although coffeehouse culture could be vibrant and engaging, it also encouraged the development of overblown "wits"— literary or cultural critics who engaged in exaggerated, imprecise, or even foolish analysis. "An Essay on Criticism" is a measured response to this trend, attempting to rein in the excesses of the wits while encouraging engaged intellectual activity, with good humor.

A frequent topic of discussion in the early eighteenth century was the relative strength of "ancient" (chiefly Greek and Roman) and "modern" writing. In his 1697 *Battle of the Books,* Swift tackles this issue satirically, describing a literal war between two factions of library volumes. As an editor and a translator, Pope would confront this debate frequently in his work—though never as literally as Swift. Instead, Pope's translations of Homer's *Iliad* (1715-20) and *Odyssey* (1725-26), as well as his imitations of Horace, coexist with his more "modern"-leaning projects; for example, editing the works of the Duke of Buckingham (1723) and publishing his own correspondence with literary figures (1737). As his first foray into the ancients versus moderns debate, "An Essay on Criticism" lays out his perspective: that a grounding in ancient ideas is necessary for full, competent participation in the modern literary world.

In part because it strikes a reasonable balance in this debate, showing the influence of both the

❖ *Key Facts*

Time Period:
Early 18th Century

Movement/Issue:
Criticism; Classicism; Aesthetics; Literary theory

Place of Publication:
England

Language of Publication:
English

THE CATHOLIC POPE

As a Roman Catholic living in predominantly Protestant Britain, Alexander Pope experienced discrimination on a personal level. Forbidden from attending universities and also unable to hold governmental posts, Pope instead pursued a career as a poet, and he positioned himself carefully in his works with respect to religion. In "An Essay on Criticism," for example, he describes the Catholic scholar Erasmus in an ambivalent way, as "the glory of the priesthood, and the shame." Pope also writes that medieval monks "finished what the Goths begun" in ransacking and ruining the legacy of Rome. At the same time, Pope speaks approvingly of the French practice of criticism (particularly Nicolas Boileau's work)—showing his affiliation with Catholic writers on the continent. By highlighting both positives and negatives about Catholic critics and historical figures, Pope advertises himself as a thinker willing to see both sides of an issue. He also hints that Catholics ought to be judged on the merits or fallacies of their actions instead of on their religion alone—an idea that was not yet reflected by British universities or governmental policies.

"modern" French critic Boileau and the "ancient" poet Horace (among others), Pope's poem became the definitive statement of aesthetic theory for the early eighteenth century in England. At the same time, he was not without his detractors. For example, the critic John Dennis became incensed upon reading lines 585-87, accusing Pope of modeling the foolish and judgmental critic "Appius" upon himself. More seriously, Samuel Johnson detected an inconsistency between the text's statement that "sound" and "sense" must work together and the actual function of language within the poem. Although subsequent generations have agreed or disagreed with Johnson to varying degrees, "An Essay on Criticism" remains a sound and amiable portrait of aesthetic theory at the end of the Stuart era.

THEMES AND STYLE

Thematically, "An Essay on Criticism" stresses that the cultivation of an apt critical judgment is vital on both an individual and a cultural level. For the individual, an apt judgment is linked to a sound moral character—creating a critic (and a human being) who is "modestly bold, and humanly severe." On the larger cultural level, the presence of these ideal judges can partially counteract the work of derivative, fawning, or flip-flopping critics who together constitute a "servile herd" of mediocrity. From this perspective, moreover, morality and critical taste become intertwined. At stake for Pope is not simply a method of judging a text but of existing in relationship with both words and

human beings. Ideally, this moral and critical method involves overlooking tiny mistakes, acting humbly but rationally, and following the guidance of nature (which creates standards and assigns "limits fit" to "all things").

To convey and embody these ideas, Pope uses conversational rhyming couplets—creating a chatty, informal atmosphere that urges a moral perspective through wryness and pleasantries. For example, he opens his second verse paragraph with these lines: "'Tis with our judgments as our watches, none / Go just alike, yet each believes his own." With this wry observation, Pope's narrator groups himself together with the audience in a communal "we," signaling that all aspiring critics are subject to individual flaws and idiosyncrasies. The challenge, Pope maintains, is to cultivate a judicious and regulated method of judgment while acknowledging these personal quirks, and this can be done with a thorough knowledge of Greek and Roman writings: "Learn hence for ancient rules a just esteem; / To copy Nature is to copy them." With this argument, Pope asks his readers to embrace a moderate side in the debate between ancients and moderns, grounding their perspectives in ancient ideas, while learning the clarity of vision needed to judge rationally.

Stylistically, Pope's work is characterized by a merger of "sound" and "sense": each line attempts to express an idea not only through logic and rational explanation but through the musical qualities of the language as well. For example, in describing and writing apt poetry simultaneously, Pope offers the famous lines "When Ajax strives, some rock's vast weight to throw, / The line too labours, and the words move slow; / Not so when swift Camilla scours the plain, / Flies o'er th' unbending corn, and skims along the main." With these lines, he presents an optimistic theory of aesthetics that posits an equivalence between ideas and the way those ideas are expressed in words. From the standpoint of aesthetic propaganda, this theory urges writers to reflect actions and notions with vowel and consonant sounds; from the standpoint of moral propaganda, it implies that the most persuasive writing will reach "hearts" through "the power of music."

CRITICAL DISCUSSION

As Richard Terry points out in his 1999 essay in *Modern Language Review*, Pope's treatise was originally praised by Addison but eventually became the subject of a controversy over aesthetic principles. In 1738 Aaron Hill wrote to Pope, quibbling with the "sound" qualities of the "swift Camilla" passage; in 1751 and 1759 Johnson published articles in the *Rambler* that question whether the equivalence of sound and sense has any literary merit at all. (Johnson cites two major reasons: the practice can impede metrical regularity, and "sound" and "sense" can never fully line up.) On a larger level, Terry concludes, this debate became intertwined with the debate over the relationship between poetry and music, which engaged writers such as James Harris, Daniel Webb, and James Beattie.

At the same time, "An Essay on Criticism" remains a clear and coherent statement of Pope's long-term literary precepts—precepts, for the most part, that were admired by Johnson himself. Although Johnson critiqued the piece on aesthetic grounds, he also followed the work's larger injunctions by memorializing Pope in a generally positive way, touting his "genius" and desire to perpetually improve himself. Though the Romantics admired Pope's work for the most part (in particular, *The Rape of the Lock*), the Victorians would largely spurn his style as artificial and contrived. It was in the twentieth century that scholars began to reinvestigate Pope's oeuvre from a historical and aesthetic perspective, reexamining the theories and moral engagements that lie under the sparkling veneer of eighteenth-century satire.

Most recently, scholars have concentrated on the aesthetic theories put forth in "An Essay on Criticism" and on Pope's engagements with classical and continental writings. In his book on Menippean satire, Howard Weinbrot argues that the poem mocks Boileau and his *l'Art Poétique*; reviewer Timothy Erwin, meanwhile, writing for *Modern Philology* in 2008, mentions Pope's established admiration of the French critic. On a larger level, "An Essay on Criticism" is mentioned by scholars investigating the idea of wit itself. In his 2009 essay in *Journal for Early Modern Cultural Studies,* Darryl Domingo posits that the dancing body—invoked by Pope as a metaphor—acts as a cultural host for the argument over apt and foolish wit; more generally, Philip Smallwood has used the poem as a focal point for his argument about modern criticism, calling for a reframing and reexamination of the genre at large. Although its moral injunctions feature less prominently in contemporary scholarship, "An Essay on Criticism" remains a touchstone for arguments about aesthetic theory and literary criticism as a whole.

BIBLIOGRAPHY

Sources

Domingo, Darryl P. "'The Natural Propensity of Imitation': or, Pantomimic Poetics and the Rhetoric of Augustan Wit." *Journal for Early Modern Cultural Studies* 9:2 (2009): 51-95. Print.

Erskine-Hill, Howard. "Pope, Alexander (1688-1744)." *Oxford Dictionary of National Biography.* Oxford UP, 2004. Web. 10 Oct. 2012.

Erwin, Timothy. Rev. of *Menippean Satire Reconsidered: From Antiquity to the Eighteenth Century,* by Howard D. Weinbrot. *Modern Philology* 106:2 (2008): 280-86. Print.

Pope, Alexander. "An Essay on Criticism." *Alexander Pope: The Major Works.* Ed. Pat Rogers. Oxford: Oxford UP, 2006. 17-39. Print.

Porter, Roy. *English Society in the 18th Century.* London: Penguin, 1990. Print.

Rogers, Pat. Introduction. *Alexander Pope: The Major Works,* ed. Pat Rogers. Oxford: Oxford UP, 2006. ix-xxii. Print.

Smallwood, Philip. *Reconstructing Criticism: Pope's* Essay on Criticism *and the Logic of Definition.* London: Associated U Presses, 2003. Print.

Smallwood, Philip. "'To Value Still the True: Pope's *Essay on Criticism* and the Problem of the Historical Mode." *Critical Pasts: Writing Criticism, Writing History,* ed. Philip Smallwood. Lewisburg: Bucknell UP, 2004. 75-94. Print.

Terry, Richard. "'The Sound Must Seem an Echo to the Sense': An Eighteenth-Century Controversy Revisited." *Modern Language Review* 94:4 (1999): 940-54. Print.

Weinbrot, Howard D. *Menippean Satire Reconsidered: From Antiquity to the Eighteenth Century.* Baltimore: Johns Hopkins UP, 2005. Print.

A 1531 depiction of the Greek philosopher Aristotle by Girolamo Mocetto. In *An Essay on Criticism,* Alexander Pope discuses the work of ancient writers like Aristotle. SCALA/WHITE IMAGES/ART RESOURCE, NY

Further Reading

Alderson, Simon. "Alexander Pope and the Nature of Language." *Review of English Studies* 47.185 (1996): 23-34. Print.

Jenkins, Eugenia Zuroski. "'Nature to Advantage Drest': Chinoiserie, Aesthetic Form, and the Poetry of Subjectivity in Pope and Swift." *Eighteenth-Century Studies* 43:1 (2009): 75-94. Print.

Walls, Kathryn. "Pope's *Essay on Criticism,* ll. 205-6: A Source in the *Moriae Encomium* of Erasmus." *Notes and Queries* 55:3 (2008): 315-16. Print.

Nancy Simpson-Younger

LETTERS FROM A SEER

Arthur Rimbaud

OVERVIEW

Composed by the French poet Arthur Rimbaud in 1871, *Letters from a Seer* decries the history of French poetry as paltry and declares the process by which the true poet must make himself a "seer." The first of the two missives, sent to Rimbaud's former school-teacher Georges Izambard, is a harbinger of the second, more complex letter, sent to Rimbaud's friend Paul Demeny, which describes the introspection and ultimate disfigurement of the self that leads to vision-ary poetry. Along with its emphasis on the method of the poet, the letters criticize the dominant poetic group of the day, the Parnassians, whose works were characterized by the skillful but conservative employ-ment of formal constraints. The first letter included Rimbaud's poem "The Stolen Heart," which describes the poet's rape by a gang of soldiers. Of note in the second letter is Rimbaud's six-hundred-word criti-cism of the history of poetry, which he character-izes as the "corpulence and glory of countless idiotic generations."

Letters from a Seer was not explicitly composed as a manifesto, and the recipients' reactions to the cor-respondence reflects its nature as a pair of personal missives. Izambard more or less dismissed Rimbaud's letter, perhaps owing to its insults and obscenities. While Demeny received his letter more warmly, it did not at the time generate any interest outside of their friendship. These letters, did, however, help Rimbaud articulate his artistic philosophy for a career, which despite spanning only five years, established him as one of the major European poets of the nineteenth century. Today, *Letters from a Seer* is considered among the most important correspondences in the history of modern poetry.

HISTORICAL AND LITERARY CONTEXT

Letters from a Seer responds to the state of French poetry during the nineteenth century, which was dominated by the Parnassians. In 1866, five years before Rimbaud's correspondence with Demeny, the first installment of *Le Parnasse contemporain* appeared, an anthology that collected the writings of the Parnas-sian poets, which, according to Graham Robb in his biography *Rimbaud,* "can be seen as a reaction to the failure of Romantic socialism in 1848 and the sub-sequent triumph of the bourgeois Second Empire."

Although Rimbaud was initially enthusiastic about the Parnassians' poems, as evinced by his 1870 letter to poet Theodore Banville, he soon found their strict adherence to formal technique stifling.

Only a few months after Rimbaud wrote his let-ters to Izambard and Demeny, the poetry community in Paris heard rumors of Rimbaud, the young poet prodigy from provincial Charlesville, but it was not the letters themselves that formed his reputation. One of the figures of the Charlesville café scene, Charles Bretagne, offered to give Rimbaud a personal recom-mendation to a Parisian poet named Paul Verlaine. By September of 1871, after receiving two of Rimbaud's letters and several of his poems, Verlaine, who would soon become Rimbaud's lover, spread word of the young poet's gifts throughout the cafés and salons of Paris and helped secure funding to bring Rimbaud to the capital immediately.

Because it was not written as a manifesto, *Letters from a Seer* does not draw on the history of manifesto as much as it does on the history of French verse, specifically the works of Charles Baudelaire. Baude-laire's most famous work, *The Flowers of Evil,* influ-enced much of Rimbaud's poetry, including his early sonnets. Rimbaud gives the highest praise to Baude-laire in his letter to Demeny, and in using the word "seer," he places himself as Baudelaire's poetic heir: "Baudelaire is the first seer," he writes, "king of poets, a real god."

The decades following publication of *Letters from a Seer* provide insight into Rimbaud's creative process. In the summer of 1871, after drafting the let-ters to Izambard and Demeny, Rimbaud composed the first of his poems since his conception of the "seer": "Seven-Year-Old Poets" and "First Commu-nion." During the scant five years in which he wrote poetry, Rimbaud would become, according to Neal Oxenhandler, author of *Rimbaud: The Cost of Genius,* "the creator of French literary modernism." Today, Rimbaud's body of work, including his poetry, prose, and even his letters composed after renouncing poetry for a mercantile career in Africa, command significant scholarly interest. His reputation as a debauched poet, delineated in *Letters,* has influenced generations of writers, poets, artists, and musicians, including Henry Miller, Pablo Picasso, Dylan Thomas, Allen Ginsberg, Bob Dylan, and Jim Morrison.

+ **Key Facts**

Time Period:
Late 19th Century

Movement/Issue:
Aesthetics;
Avant-gardism

Place of Publication:
France

Language of Publication:
French

RIMBAUD: POET GUNRUNNER

To say that Arthur Rimbaud, born in Charlesville, Ardennes, France in 1854, showed early promise is to define understatement. By 1870 he had won a dozen firsts in regional examinations, and that same year, at the age of fifteen, he published his first poem, "The Orphans," in the French literary magazine *La Revue Pour Tous.* A year later he wrote "The Drunken Boat," in which a boat narrates its adventures following the massacre of its crew. He read the poem at a dinner with the Parnassians, the dominant school of poetry at the time. Over the next four years he wrote several other works that revolutionized French poetry, including *A Season in Hell* and *Illuminations,* but by the age of twenty he vowed never to write poetry again.

Instead, Rimbaud, the man who, according to his biographer, Graham Robb, "was one of the most destructive and liberating influences on twentieth century culture," embarked on a career as a merchant. He traveled to dozens of countries, including Egypt, Yemen, and Java, and he worked dozens of jobs—in factories and on docks—and as a sailor, a mercenary in the Dutch Colonial Army, a trader, an explorer, and even a gunrunner. In 1891 cancer in his knee forced him to return to France. Despite the amputation of his leg, he died that same year at thirty-seven.

THEMES AND STYLE

The central theme of *Letters of a Seer* is that the would-be poet must undergo a cultivation and disfigurement of the self in order to arrive at the unknown and write visionary verse. The letters outline this method, saying that "the first study for the man who'd be a poet is knowledge of himself, entire; he seeks out his soul, he inspects it, tests it, learns it. As soon as he knows it, he must cultivate it." This process of introspection and cultivation, however, is only the beginning, according to Rimbaud. In order to make himself a seer, the would-be poet must endure "a long, immense and reasoned *disordering of all the senses.*" The word "reasoned" was lacking from the first letter to Izambard, a fact that John Sturrock, in his introduction to Rimbaud's letters, attributes to a slight shift in the author's conception of his method; instead of a "willed state of mental chaos," which would "hardly be shareable with others," the "true poet must invite temporary dementia" in order to approach the unknown.

The two letters exhibit different rhetorical goals and thus achieve their effects through different means. The letter to Izambard asserts Rimbaud's independence from and intellectual superiority to his former teacher through vicious insults. He accuses Izambard of being a "self-satisfied man who's done nothing, not having wanted to do anything." Of his newly founded concept of the poet as seer, he writes that Izambard

"won't begin to understand, and I almost can't explain to you." The letter to Demeny also includes insults about the state of modern poetry, but the rhetoric is often couched in good-humored irony that allows Rimbaud to take a critical stance while simultaneously disarming his audience. At one point, for example, Rimbaud mocks the French dramatist Jean Racine, calling him "the pure, the strong, the great—If they'd breathed on his rhymes, and jumbled his hemstiches, the Divine Fool would have been unknown today as any old author."

Stylistically, *Letters from a Seer* is distinguished by its bombast and intellectual pretense. Robb writes, "On a first reading, it hardly seems to deserve such a grand title. 'Letter of the Excited Schoolboy' would give a more accurate impression of the torrential arguments and half digested readings." But Rimbaud's confidence and condescension are apparent from the beginning: "I've resolved to give you an hour of new literature," he writes. He refers to former poets as "old imbeciles." In one particularly dismissive sentence he conceives of poetry from the Greeks to the Romantic period as "flabbiness." This incendiary tone, however, belies the insightful nature of much of his criticism, and despite the seemingly bombastic and adolescent view of poet as seer, the efficacy of his method is perhaps best found in his poetry, which was indeed visionary.

CRITICAL DISCUSSION

Initial reaction to *Letters from a Seer* was limited, owing to its nature as personal correspondence to Izambard and Demeny. Indeed, despite being a poet himself, Demeny did nothing to help Rimbaud publish or find an audience. That same year, however, Rimbaud also wrote his most famous poem, "The Drunken Boat"—what Jeremy Harding, in his introduction to *Arthur Rimbaud: Selected Poems and Letters,* calls the "'seer' poem *par excellence.*" Upon hearing it for the first time, Rimbaud's friend Ernest Delahaye claimed that Rimbaud would "enter the world of letters like a bullet." Also during that same year, prior to his arrival in Paris, Rimbaud's "The First Communion," which was circulated through the cafés and studios of Paris by Verlaine, garnered significant interest from the Parisian poets.

After Rimbaud ceased writing poetry in 1875 at the age of twenty, *Letters from a Seer* remained an important document in the history of the poet's brief but brilliant, career. In his critical essay "The Savage Experiment: Arthur Rimbaud and Paul Verlaine," Jeffrey Meyers conceives of the letters as statement of aesthetic freedom by comparing them to the dictum written by Rimbaud's "prophetic soul mate" William Blake: "I must Create a System, or be enslav'd by another Man's." In the 140 years since the letters were written, they have fostered extensive scholarly inquiry that has considered their importance in the history of French poetry.

Much scholarship has been focused on the significance of the literary criticism found in the *Letters*. Robb describes the letter to Demeny as "a gripping piece of literary criticism, a curiously plausible attempt to reconcile the two antagonistic trends of nineteenth-century poetry: the 'bourgeois' belief in endless technological progress and the spiritual aspirations of the Romantics." Significant criticism has also focused on the philosophical significance of the letters' most famous pronouncement, "I is somebody else," which, according to Sturrock, is a claim that the "Cartesian Ego, the self supposedly fully open to introspection, is by no means the whole of a human being, psychically speaking: disorder all of the senses and we may encounter a dimension of the self we hadn't known existed." Sturrock conceives of this other self as a pre-Freudian evocation of the unconscious. The critical and scholarly interest in Rimbaud shows no signs of abating; according to Robb, there are an "average of ten books and eighty-seven articles" a year published on the poet and his works.

A portrait of the French poet Arthur Rimbaud by Fernand Léger. © PHOTOS 12/ALAMY

BIBLIOGRAPHY

Sources

Harding, Jeremy. "Introduction." *Arthur Rimbaud: Selected Poems and Letters*. Trans. Jeremy Harding and John Sturrock. London: Penguin, 2004. Print.

Meyers, Jeffrey. "The Savage Experiment: Arthur Rimbaud and Paul Verlaine." *Kenyon Review* 33.3 (2011): 167. *Gale Academic One File*. Web. 8 Oct. 2012.

Rimbaud, Arthur. *Arthur Rimbaud: Selected Poems and Letters*. Trans. Jeremy Harding and John Sturrock. London: Penguin, 2004. Print.

Oxenhandler, Neal. *Rimbaud: The Cost of Genius*. Columbus: Ohio State UP, 2009. Print.

Robb, Graham. *Rimbaud: A Biography*. New York: W.W. Norton, 2000. Print.

Sturrock, John. Introduction. *Arthur Rimbaud: Selected Poems and Letters,* trans. Jeremy Harding and John Sturrock. London: Penguin, 2004. Print.

Further Reading

Ahearn, Edward. *Rimbaud: Visions and Habitations*. Berkeley: U of California P, 1983. Print.

Rimbaud, Arthur. *Illuminations*. Trans. John Ashbery. New York: W.W. Norton, 2011. Print.

———. *I Promise to Be Good: The Letters of Arthur Rimbaud, Rimbaud Complete Vol II*. Ed. Wyatt Mason. New York: Modern Library, 2004. Print.

Russell, Charles. "The Poet As Seer: Rimbaud." *Poets, Prophets, and Revolutionaries. The Literary Avant-garde from Rimbaud through Postmodernism*. New York: Oxford UP, 1985. 39-61. Print.

Starkie, Enid. *Arthur Rimbaud*. New York: W.W. Norton, 1947. Print.

White, Edmund. *Rimbaud: The Double Life of a Rebel*. New York: Atlas, 2008. Print.

Gregory Luther

Manifesto for an Irish Literary Theatre

Lady Augusta Gregory, Edward Martyn, William Butler Yeats

✢ *Key Facts*

Time Period:
Late 19th Century

Movement/Issue:
Irish Nationalism; Post-colonialism; Aesthetics

Place of Publication:
Ireland

Language of Publication:
English

OVERVIEW

Written by Edward Martyn, Lady Augusta Gregory, and William Butler Yeats, the *Manifesto for an Irish Literary Theatre* (1897) announces a plan to establish an Irish national theater in order to build up an Irish school of dramatic literature. Although the manifesto outlines a goal for a new theater with room for freedom to experiment, the proclamation can be viewed as part of an established tradition in which the revival of the Irish language and culture is employed to conceptualize a distinct national identity. Intended in part as a fund-raising tool, the manifesto claims to have the support of all Irish people "weary of misrepresentation" in the hope that the urge to counteract popular clichés about Ireland will unite an audience that might be otherwise divided by political differences. Central to the manifesto are both nationalistic and aesthetic aims: the writers wish to create a theater that expresses the "deeper thoughts and emotions of Ireland" and attracts innovative plays written with a high ambition.

Initially, the manifesto's assertions sparked controversy among activists working on behalf of an Irish cultural revival. In a letter to the editor of *An Claidheamh Soluis,* nationalist Patrick Pearse asserts that Yeats's literary theater should be "strangled at birth" because of the poet's (and his colleagues') desire to create a tradition of Irish literature written in English. Despite these criticisms, the manifesto led to the creation of the Irish Literary Theatre, which produced original Irish plays from 1899 to 1901. The manifesto inspired the Irish Literary Revival, one of the most significant theatrical developments and literary movements of the twentieth century. It is considered a central text in reestablishing the cultural autonomy of the postcolonial Irish people.

HISTORICAL AND LITERARY CONTEXT

The *Manifesto for an Irish Literary Theatre* responds to the political and cultural crises facing Ireland in the late 1890s, after the defeat and death of Irish parliamentary leader Charles Stewart Parnell had dashed hopes for Irish autonomy through Home Rule. In 1892, Douglas Hyde gave a stirring speech titled "The Necessity for De-Anglicising Ireland." Hyde viewed the revival of the Irish language, which had been slowly eliminated during British rule, as an essential component of Ireland's future. When a second home rule bill was defeated in 1893, some Irish leaders looked beyond parliamentary politics to cultural forums that could influence national taste and opinion.

By the time of the writing of the *Manifesto for an Irish Literary Theatre* in 1897, a number of institutions had been formed to support the revival of the Irish language and culture. Yeats himself started the Irish Literary Society of London (1891) and the National Literary Society in Dublin (1892) as forums for literary criticism. In 1893, Hyde and others formed the Gaelic League. When the *Manifesto for an Irish Literary Theatre* appeared, it created a platform for the discussion of the ambitions of activists and dramatists for an emerging Irish literature. The Irish Literary Revival, the movement engendered by the manifesto, became a dominant cultural force that helped define the independent Irish nation well into the twentieth century, when literature emerged as one of its most significant cultural exports.

The *Manifesto for an Irish Literary Theatre* can be viewed as a continuation of the Irish tradition of literary nationalism. In "On the Study of Celtic Literature" (1867), the English critic Matthew Arnold suggests that traits seen in early Celtic literature could serve as the qualities that would allow Celtic peoples to "conquer their Conquerors." Though Arnold's description romanticizes the Celts, his work influenced others to look to Irish literary texts as a source of political agency. In 1892, Hyde's "De-Anglicising Ireland" urged the Irish people to reestablish their language as a form of resistance to the homogenizing influence of British rule. Similarly, the proposal for the Irish Literary Theatre supported the notion that the Irish people's knowledge of and interest in oratory and storytelling made them well prepared for a national theater.

In the years after it was issued, the *Manifesto for an Irish Literary Theatre* generated public debate about its methods of creating a national literature as well as protest concerning the works that it produced. The perceived religious unorthodoxy of the Irish Literary Theatre's first drama, Yeats's *The Countess Cathleen,* raised the hackles of Catholic nationalists, and subsequent protests in the theater meant that the play had to be performed under police protection. The theater's subsequent works included Yeats's *Cathleen ni Houlihan,* which can be read as a call to arms for an Irish war for independence. The Irish National Theatre became the Abbey Theatre in 1904 and staged controversial works by writers such as J. M. Synge and Sean O'Casey, whose plays provoked riots even as they engaged the manifesto's challenge of representing Irish emotions and concerns.

THEMES AND STYLE

The central theme of the *Manifesto for an Irish Literary Theatre* is that popular dramatizations of the Irish people have failed to represent the Irish nation with dignity. With echoes of Hyde's plea for de-Anglicization, the manifesto opens with a proposal to stage a number of plays in Dublin with the goal of showing that Ireland is not a place "of buffoonery and of easy sentiment, as it has been represented, but the home of an ancient idealism." Implicit in this assertion is the notion that the Irish people have been kept subordinate as a result of mischaracterization and will benefit from being reminded of, in Hyde's words, their "Gaelic heart." To this end, the manifesto proposes that the theater create plays with a "freedom to experiment that is not found in theatres [in] England" as well as works of high artistic merit that are accurate representations of Irish concerns.

The manifesto achieves its rhetorical effect through appeals to an Irish unity that transcends political divisions. This sense of unity comes from the writers' contrasting of the conventions of English theater with their own goal for a theater of Celtic and Irish plays striving for literary excellence and written "with a high ambition." The document declares that cultural sensitivity and awareness will lead to works that accurately reflect the concerns of the national theater's subjects and its audience. Notably, the authors—two of whom (Gregory and Yeats) were Anglo-Irish protestants and one (Martyn) a wealthy Catholic landowner— seem aware of the potentially divisive and inflammatory nature of *any* Irish cultural movement; they stress that their work is "outside all the political questions that divide us." Although Yeats was himself a nationalist, the fledgling theatrical movement avoids inflammatory statements that may have alienated audiences and financial backers.

Stylistically, the *Manifesto for a Literary Theatre* is marked by its ennobling tone. Written to inspire Ireland's dramatists and cultural leaders, the manifesto demands credibility as a thoughtful response to injustices in earlier dramatic representations. The manifesto generates sympathy for its aims by calling upon the readers' general knowledge of the broad caricatures of the Irish in British popular theater. In order to ensure a tolerant reception, the authors soften any resistance to their claims by mentioning their high artistic and apolitical aspirations and by reminding readers of Ireland's "ancient idealism." Although it is a relatively brief statement of purpose, the *Manifesto*

PLAYWRIGHTS OF THE IRISH LITERARY REVIVAL

The *Manifesto for an Irish Literary Theatre* heralded the start of one of the major dramatic movements of the twentieth century. From 1899 to 1901, the Irish Literary Theatre staged dramas penned largely by its creators: Edward Martyn, Lady Augusta Gregory, and William Butler Yeats.

Though the playwrights agreed on the need for a national theater, they had markedly different concerns. Martyn, a wealthy Catholic landowner, favored an Ibsen-esque realism that incorporated the Irish language into drama. Yeats, a fervent nationalist who spoke no Irish, believed in a theater of poetic idealism. Gregory's worldview was shaped by the time she had spent in politically turbulent Egypt. Gregory's pragmatic activism favored cultural preservation, and she became an active documenter of Irish folklore. Her plays often dramatized Irish myths. George Moore, Martyn's cousin, was a fourth author in the movement. Educated in London and Paris, Moore wrote novels in a continental tradition and brought a new realism to Irish theater.

Though the Irish Literary Theatre was short-lived, its legacy endured. The questions it posed—about the nature, subject, language, and responsibility of Irish literature—inspired the Abbey Theatre, the first state-funded dramatic company in Europe, which went on to produce seminal Irish plays by J. M. Synge, Sean O'Casey, and George Bernard Shaw.

William Butler Yeats, Irish poet and dramatist. PRIVATE COLLECTION/THE BRIDGEMAN ART LIBRARY

for an Irish Literary Theatre achieves force by appealing to a general desire among the Irish to be treated as dramatic subjects worthy of thoughtful and nuanced consideration.

CRITICAL DISCUSSION

When the *Manifesto for an Irish Literary Theatre* was issued in 1897, reception within literary and activist circles was mixed. Members of the Gaelic League objected to the idea of English-speaking writers creating an Irish national literature. Even sympathetic dramatists such as George Moore insisted on the centrality of the Irish language to Ireland's revival. Moore wrote to Yeats, "That one child should learn Irish interests me far more than the production of a masterpiece." However, members in the Irish press were supportive. The *Irish Daily Express* wrote: "We do not suppose that there was ever any period when the theatre was a greater national influence than it is today in Great Britain and Ireland, or when that influence was more widely perverted and abused." Despite the manifesto's shortcomings, many rallied around Yeats's goal of creating a national effort to "save the Irish soul."

Though the Irish Literary Theatre endured for only three years before it became what is still the Abbey Theatre, its manifesto remained a touchstone for an Irish national literature and theater. In *The Irish Writer and the World*, Declan Kiberd says of the manifesto: "From this small beginning stemmed one of the major dramatic movements of twentieth-century literature." In the decades since its composition, the manifesto has been considered in historical, political, literary and postcolonial terms.

Much scholarship has focused on the political significance of the *Manifesto for an Irish Literary Theatre* and of the literary works created in its name. Yeats would inextricably link the genesis of an Irish literature to political agency. In *Samhain* (1901), he writes, "All Irish writers will have to decide whether they will write as the upper classes have done, not to express but to exploit this country, or join the intellectual movement which has raised the cry that was heard in Russia in the seventies, the cry 'to the people.'" Modern scholars often cite the fall of Parnell as the moment when, as P.J. Mathews states in "Revival Connections: The Irish Literary Theatre, the Gaelic League, and the Co-Operative Movement," political energy "was diverted to cultural channels." Others dispute the idea that cultural "self-help" movements took the place of political work. Discussing the impact of the manifesto, R.F. Foster notes in his book *Modern Ireland 1600-1972* that, although the turn of the twentieth century was marked by cultural revivalism, "the political relevance of this, in contemporary terms, is less easy to establish." However, Mathews argues that self-help cultural doctrines such as the *Manifesto for an Irish Literary Theatre* worked synergistically to inspire "administrators" and "propagandists" for the new Ireland as the nation became a "Post-British" state.

BIBLIOGRAPHY

Sources

Foster, R.F. *Modern Ireland 1600-1972.* London: Penguin, 1988. Print.

Gregory, Lady Augusta. *Our Irish Theatre: A Chapter of Autobiography.* New York: Oxford UP, 1972. Print.

Hogan, Robert, and James Kilroy. *The Irish Literary Theatre 1899-1901.* Dublin: Dolmen, 1975. Print.

Mathews, P.J. "Revival Connections: The Irish Literary Theatre, the Gaelic League, and the Co-Operative Movement." *Revival: The Abbey Theatre, Sinn Féin, the Gaelic League and the Co-Operative Movement.* Cork: Cork UP, 2003. 5-34. Rpt. in *Twentieth-Century Literary Criticism.* Vol. 222. Ed. Thomas J. Schoenberg and Lawrence J. Trudeau. Detroit: Gale, 2010. *Literature Resource Center.* Web. 23 July 2012.

Kiberd, Declan. *Inventing Ireland.* London: Cape, 1995. Print.

———. *The Irish Writer and the World.* Cambridge: Cambridge UP, 2005. Print.

Yeats, W.B. *Autobiographies.* New York: Scribner, 1999. Print.

Further Reading

"Abbey Theatre in the Irish Literary Renaissance." *Twentieth-Century Literary Criticism.* Vol. 154. Ed. Linda Pavlovski. Detroit: Gale, 2004. *Literature Resource Center.* Web. 23 July 2012.

Brown, Terence. *The Life of W.B. Yeats: A Critical Biography.* Oxford: Blackwell, 1999. Print.

Duggan, G.C. *The Stage Irishman: A History of the Irish Play and Stage Characters from the Earliest Times.* London: Longmans, 1937. Print.

Flannery, James W. *W.B. Yeats and the Idea of a Theatre: The Early Abbey Theatre in Theory and Practice.* New Haven: Yale UP, 1976. Print.

Grene, Nicholas. *The Politics of Irish Drama: Plays in Context from Boucicault to Friel.* Cambridge: Cambridge UP, 1999. Print.

McClintock, Cara B. "'It Will Be Very Difficult to Find a Definition': Yeats, Language, and the Early Abbey Theatre." *W.B. Yeats and Postcolonialism.* Ed. Deborah Fleming. West Cornwall: Locust Hill, 2001. 205-19. Rpt. in *Twentieth-Century Literary Criticism.* Vol. 154. Ed. Linda Pavlovski. Detroit: Gale, 2004. *Literature Resource Center.* Web. 23 July 2012.

Trotter, Mary. *Ireland's National Theaters: Political Performance and the Origins of the Irish Dramatic Movement.* Syracuse: Syracuse UP, 2001. Print.

Karen Bender

Naturalism in the Theater

Émile Zola

OVERVIEW

Émile Zola's *Naturalism in the Theater* (1881), or *Naturalisme au Théâtre*, is a foundational document in the history of the theater and the literary movement known as Naturalism. In this manifesto, Zola argues that French drama must move beyond the conventions of classical tragedy and romantic drama by creating naturalistic drama with realistic characters, lifelike dialogue, and contemporary settings. Bringing together Zola's essays on dramatic criticism that were published in the Parisian newspapers *Le Bien Public* and *Le Voltaire* between 1876 and 1880, *Naturalism in the Theater* articulates a cohesive theory of the evolution of French drama from the Middle Ages to the nineteenth century. The work contends that the major dramatic modes of tragedy and romantic drama, as well as prevailing stage conventions and acting styles, are the expression of an earlier social and political order, and it envisions a new mode that will reflect the social and political realities of the late nineteenth century.

Although *Naturalism in the Theater* calls for an "as-yet-unknown author" whose works will revolutionize the stage, it is clear that Zola is expressing his own theatrical ambitions. Zola hoped to see his theories of Naturalism embodied not only in the novel but also in the theater. Perhaps for this reason, even the contemporary playwrights whom he praises, such as Alexandre Dumas, *fils* and Émile Augier, are described as minor writers because they lack the formula for translating naturalism into art. Despite Zola's ambitions, however, his dramatic criticism in *Naturalism in the Theater* was overshadowed by the public controversy and acclaim that greeted his novels. Throughout his lifetime, Zola's plays achieved little success with critics or the public, but his theories of theatrical Naturalism influenced playwrights such as Eugene O'Neill and Bertolt Brecht, as well as French dramatists from André Antoine to Jean-Paul Sartre.

HISTORICAL AND LITERARY CONTEXT

Along with his preface to *Thérèse Raquin* (1868), a chapter on theater in *The Experimental Novel* (1880), and other dramatic criticism in *Our Dramatic Authors* (1881), *Naturalism in the Theater* is one of Zola's most substantial expositions of Naturalism, especially in terms of its relevance to his historical era and to the genres of the novel and the play. Like other practitioners of Naturalism, Zola derived his theoretical and thematic concerns from a variety of sources: scientific advances in the nineteenth century, especially Charles Darwin's theory of evolution and its implications for heredity; the literary realism of Honoré de Balzac; philosophies of positivism and determinism; the political and economic corruption of French society during the Second Empire (1852-70) and Third Republic (1870-1940); and Zola's own working-class background.

When Zola's manifesto was first printed in 1876 as a series of essays in *Le Bien Public,* Naturalism was regarded as a dirty word in most Parisian literary circles because of the tendency of the movement's authors to focus on such themes as sexual vice, squalor, disease, and the language of the lower classes. In fact, when Zola's novel *L'Assommoir* (*The Dram Shop*) was serialized in the *Le Bien Public,* beginning in April 1876, both it and Naturalism were denounced as immoral in every major periodical in Paris and in public lectures, religious pamphlets, and numerous parodies. Nevertheless, Zola's efforts to champion the movement placed him at the forefront of French Naturalist writers, alongside such authors as Guy de Maupassant, Paul Alexis, and Joris-Karl Huysmans.

When he penned the articles that would later be published as *Naturalism in the Theater,* Zola was an established writer on the verge of his breakthrough into literary celebrity. In 1876, he had already published the first six novels of his defining work, *Les Rougon-Macquart* (1871-93), a series focusing on the descendants of two intertwined families. (*L'Assommoir* would become the seventh installment.) He had worked as a journalist for a decade and had published two collections of his essays. Perhaps most significantly for his essays on theater, Zola had tried his hand at drama by producing five plays: *Enfoncé le Pion* (1856), *La Laide* (1865), *Madeleine* (1865), *Thérèse Raquin* (1873), and *Les Heritiers Rabourdin* (1873-74). Interestingly, two of these plays illustrate the facility with which Zola transformed plays into novels and vice versa; he later rewrote the play *Madeleine* as the novel *Madeleine Férat* (1868), and his play *Thérèse Raquin* was an adaptation of his novel of the same name (1867).

Although less famous than Zola's other manifestos, *Naturalism in the Theater* helped to shape the

⁂ *Key Facts*

Time Period:
Late 19th Century

Movement/Issue:
Aesthetics; Naturalism

Place of Publication:
France

Language of Publication:
French

ÉMILE ZOLA: ICONOCLAST OF THE SECOND EMPIRE

Best known as the preeminent theorist of Naturalism, Émile Zola was a journalist, an art critic, a dramatist, and one of the most important French novelists of the nineteenth century. *Les Rougon-Macquart* (1871-1893), his major work, is a series of twenty novels tracing the fortunes of two intertwined families. Novels such as *L'Assommoir* (1877), *Nana* (1880), *Germinal* (1885), and *La Terre* (1887) are among his acknowledged masterpieces.

Born in 1840, Zola grew up in working-class neighborhoods. In his early twenties, he abandoned a writing style based on romantic idealism for one marked by realism. Throughout his career, he championed Naturalism as the merger of art and science. Stressing the value of experimentation in his influential article "The Experimental Novel," Zola linked Naturalism with the scientific method proposed by Claude Bernard. In 1898, Zola entered the controversy surrounding the Dreyfus Affair, defending Alfred Dreyfus, a Jewish officer, and accusing the French military of a cover-up. The resulting scandal might have led to Zola's death in 1902, when a workman confessed to deliberately blocking up Zola's chimney the day before he died of smoke inhalation.

concept of theatrical realism from the late nineteenth century well into the mid-twentieth and has influenced playwrights internationally. Zola's theories of theater have much in common with those of his contemporaries, Henrik Ibsen and August Strindberg. In addition to influencing French dramatists from Antoine through Sartre, Zola's manifesto had an indirect impact on playwrights as diverse as George Bernard Shaw, O'Neill, and Brecht. Today, Zola's manifesto continues to command significant scholarly interest.

THEMES AND STYLE

The main theme of *Naturalism in the Theater* is that French theater fails aesthetically because it tries to imitate artistic conventions rather than real life. According to Zola, French playwrights' efforts to resurrect the two major modes of French theater, classical tragedy and romantic drama, were fundamentally mistaken because art "is continuously in motion," changing as times, fashions, and modes of living change. Classical tragedy, which dominated the stage from the early 1600s to the French Revolution (1789-99), was marked by its hierarchical structure, rigid formulas, and "majestic tranquility of psychological analysis." However, once France's absolute monarchy was overthrown, classical tragedy ceased to have any relation to French social life, and playwrights' efforts to revive it merely brought out the worst features of its formulas: "outlandish situations, improbabilities, dishonest uniformity, and uninterrupted, unbearable declaiming." Romantic drama, in turn, brought energy and lyricism to French

theater by violating the Aristotelian unities, staging violence onstage, and calling attention to scenery; yet, Zola argues that Romantic drama, like classical tragedy before it, stagnated and no longer spoke to the realities of French society in the latter half of the nineteenth century. Instead, it had become "pastiches of Shakespeare and [Victor] Hugo." Distorting the past, converting characters into abstract ideals, and giving characters dialogue that no one spoke in everyday life, both Romantic drama and classical tragedy ignored the psychological reality that Naturalism would portray.

Zola's manifesto relies on multiple rhetorical strategies: the introduction's portrayal of the author as a theatergoer, the call for a genius who will revitalize the stage, and the metaphor of revolution applied to the stage. By beginning the manifesto with a description of his continual hope and disappointment "[e]ach winter at the beginning of the theatre season," Zola presents himself as a reviewer motivated by an objective love of the theater rather than the promotion of his own career as a dramatist. Similarly, Zola's plea for a writer to create a new expression of reality on the stage is phrased as eager, unselfish expectation: "When will our Corneilles, Molières and Racines appear to establish our new theatre? We must hope and wait." Throughout the manifesto, Zola links the political and theatrical through the metaphor of revolution. If during the classical period "tragedy ruled as an absolute monarch," the appearance of romantic drama was an "insurrection." As with most revolutions, however, the new order led to "excesses of all kinds that go beyond the original aims and degenerate into the despotism of the old, hated system, those very abuses the revolution had just fought against."

The tone of Zola's manifesto is primarily analytical and evenhanded despite his tendency to caricature the excesses of French theater. Thus, although he memorably generalizes that "Romantic heroes are only tragic heroes bitten by the mardi gras bug, hiding behind false noses, and dancing the dramatic can-can after drinking," he balances this caricature with a detailed assessment of both classical tragedy's and Romantic drama's contributions to French theater.

CRITICAL DISCUSSION

When *Naturalism in the Theater* was first published in *Le Bien Public,* it was virtually ignored because of the firestorm over Zola's novels and the failure of his early plays to appeal to the public. Responding to the theories of Naturalism that formed the basis for his novels, reviewers overwhelmingly objected to their moral implications. For instance, many critics in the Catholic and Royalist press, such as Armand de Portmartin, called into question Zola's claim that literature should represent reality unembellished by ideals or moral purpose, declaring that Naturalistic literature would demoralize society and corrupt its readers. Like his novels, Zola's plays often offended many reviewers' moral sensibilities, but perhaps more damning was the fact that some of his fellow Naturalists, such as Edmond de Goncourt, judged his plays as failures for their reliance on melodrama and sentiment.

It was not until late in the twentieth century that *Naturalism in the Theater* was recognized as foundational document in the history of Naturalism and the theater. Early in the twentieth century, Zola's reputation as a theorist of Naturalism rested primarily on *The Experimental Novel* (1880). At that time, according to Philip Walker in *Nineteenth-Century French Fiction Writers: Naturalism and Beyond, 1860-190,* critics made the mistake of "judging his works primarily in the context of his naturalist theories or, worse, of confounding his theory and practice." Because *Naturalism in the Theater* focuses more on the theater itself, scholars did not show much interest in it until a critical reevaluation of Zola began in the 1950s. In 1968, Albert Bermel became the first to publish an (abridged) English translation. Since the 1970s, critics have looked more closely at how his theatrical theories and practices reveal Zola to have been a very different man than simply the theorist of Naturalism.

Recent studies of Zola have looked more closely at the audience dynamics, scientific theories, and theories of representation that underlie Zola's thoughts about the theater. For instance, Bernard Dort argues that Zola's notion of realism was not static but adaptable to the ever-changing audience's sense of what seems realistic. Similarly, William Berg contends that a comprehensive theory of vision underlies Zola's ideas about painting, fiction, and theater. In *Zola and Film* (2005), numerous contemporary critics ponder what cinematic adaptations of Zola's works mean for his legacy in terms of gender, class, nationality, and theories of representation.

French writer Émile Zola in an 1868 painting by Edouard Manet.
© ALFREDO DAGLI ORTI/ THE ART ARCHIVE/CORBIS

BIBLIOGRAPHY

Sources

Berg, William J. *The Visual Novel: Émile Zola and the Art of His Times.* University Park: Pennsylvania State UP, 1992. Print.

Borowski, Mateusz, and Małgorzata Sugiera. "From the Realism of Representation to the Realism of Experience." Preface. *Fictional Realities/ Real Fictions.* Ed. Mateusz Borowski and Małgorzata Sugiera. Newcastle: Cambridge Scholars, 2007. vii-xxviii. Print.

Dort, Bernard, and Maurice Nadeau. Introduction. *Œuvres Complètes d'Émile Zola: Œuvres Critiques II.* Ed. Henri Mitterand. Paris: Cercle du Livre Précieux, 1966. 265-73. Print.

Gural-Migdal, Anna, and Robert Singer, eds. *Zola and Film: Essays in the Art of Adaptation.* Jefferson: McFarland, 2005. Print.

Schom, Alan. *Émile Zola: A Bourgeois Rebel.* London: Macdonald, 1987. Print.

Walker, Philip. *Nineteenth-Century French Fiction Writers: Naturalism and Beyond, 1860-1900.* Ed. Catharine Savage Brosman. *Dictionary of Literary Biography.* Vol. 123. Detroit: Gale Research, 1992. Web. 10 July 2012.

White, Lucien W. "Moral Aspects of Zola's Naturalism Judged by His Contemporaries and by Himself." *Modern Language Quarterly* 23.4 (1962): 360-72. Web. 10 July 2012.

Zola, Émile. "Naturalism in the Theatre." Trans. Albert Bermel. *The Theory of the Modern Stage: An Introduction to Modern Theatre and Drama.* Ed. Eric Bentley. Baltimore: Penguin, 1968. 349-72. Print.

Further Reading

Beitchman, Philip. *The Theatre of Naturalism: Disappearing Act.* New York: Lang, 2011. Print.

Berg, William J., and Laurey K. Martin. *Émile Zola Revisited.* New York: Twayne, 1992. Print.

Carter, Lawson A. *Zola and the Theater.* New Haven: Yale UP, 1963. Print.

Harrow, Susan. *Zola, the Body Modern: Pressures and Prospects of Representation.* London: Legenda, 2010. Print.

Innes, C.D. *A Sourcebook on Naturalist Theatre.* New York: Routledge, 2000. Print.

Nelson, Brian, ed. *The Cambridge Companion to Zola.* New York: Cambridge UP, 2007. Print.

Kevin Cooney

ON REALISM

Fernand Desnoyers

❖ *Key Facts*

Time Period:
Mid-19th Century

Movement/Issue:
Realism; Aesthetics

Place of Publication:
France

**Language of
Publication:**
French

OVERVIEW

Writer and art critic Fernand Desnoyers's "On Realism," the culmination of a prolonged dispute over the introduction of realism in art "as the true depiction of objects," appeared on December 9, 1855, in *L'Artiste,* Paris's premier art journal. Partly a condemnation of the Romantic movement's focus on idealized beauty, "On Realism" declares itself a "manifesto, a profession of faith" and asserts Desnoyers's aesthetic beliefs to the circle of artists and art lovers who comprised the journal's readership. Written just a few years after the French Revolution of 1848 (the third French Revolution, which deposed the Orleans monarchy and set up the Second Republic), the treatise bears several markings of its historical period, including a propulsion toward individual validity rather than state-sanctioned or externally attributed authority.

"On Realism" is now widely recognized as a prophetic turning point in art history, but at the time it simply gained the final word in *L'Artiste* on the legitimacy and superiority of realism. Desnoyers's proclamation that "at last Realism *is coming!*" was proven correct, and his position as a spokesperson for the movement grew as his hopes came to fruition. The works of French artists, most notably Gustave Courbet, later influenced literature, eventually among American authors such as William Dean Howells (*The Rise of Silas Lapham,* 1885) and Theodore Dreiser (*Sister Carrie,* 1890). Scholar George Becker writes in *Documents of Modern Literary Realism* (1963) that Howells fought for realism in the United States "almost singlehandedly," mobilizing his theses in the essay "On Truth in Fiction" in 1891. Dreiser, often called the "American Zola," followed in 1903 with "True Art Speaks Plainly." Such other realists as Russian novelist Leo Tolstoy and American poet Walt Whitman were already publishing, if not theorizing, in accordance with the guidelines for art and writing in "On Realism."

HISTORICAL AND LITERARY CONTEXT

"On Realism" rebels against both political and artistic conservatism. The radical popular impulses of the 1848 revolution had ended in the bloody rout of the June Days Uprising against the increasingly conservative Second Republic. Napoléon III's subsequent 1851 coup d'état and his repressive Second Empire heralded

an end to revolutionary values in government. Desnoyers's insistence on the right to defy illegitimate authority and "to be ourselves, even if we are ugly" reflects a more general opposition to the oppressive politics of the day. Like the revolution's impetus, Romanticism was considered liberal and even radical in its time. Defying industrialization and Enlightenment ideals, it affirmed emotion as a valid basis of aesthetic expression. The movement peaked between 1800 and 1840, and by the mid-nineteenth century it had become the status quo, dominating exhibitions at the Académie des Beaux-Arts, the leading arbiter of artistic taste in Europe. In around 1853 the Romantic poet Charles Baudelaire exclaimed in a letter to Desnoyers, republished in *Selected Letters of Charles Baudelaire: The Conquest of Solitude* (1986), that "there was something irritating and impudent about *Nature* in its fresh and rampant state" and that he was incapable of becoming "sentimental about vegetables." He preferred the symbolic to Desnoyers's more mundane subjects. Pressing for changes in attitude and perspective in both art and society, Desnoyers's treatise reacts against this popular "dream-world of romance" that disparaged the imperfect. In this and his subsequent perpetuation of his vision as a poet, dramaturge, writer, and supporter of the avant-garde disrupted the established art world, he subverted what many felt were elitist, rigid, and exclusionary values.

The public argument in *L'Artiste,* which Desnoyers's article concluded, was sparked when Courbet, the leader of the realist movement, created a one-man show in the summer of 1855 outside the official auspices of the first Exhibition Universelle (a world's fair) art exhibit at the Académie because jurors had rejected some of his major paintings. Courbet hung forty-four works in a nearby temporary structure under a placard reading simply and boldly "Du Réalisme." The title and the show itself challenged the academy's narrow standards and represented—in Courbet's words, as quoted by Becker—a fight for "liberty and independence." However, the public and critics firmly disparaged the effort. French art critic Champfleury (Jules François Felix Fleury-Husson) defended Courbet's actions and his art in a September article in *L'Artiste,* which outraged art critic Charles Perrier. In a scathing reply in the October issue of the journal, Perrier insisted that Courbet's notion of truth was too material and too fixated on the ugly. The discussion revealed that the stakes were higher than aesthetics alone, indicating that the assumptions upon which class and culture were founded were also being redefined.

As a writer with an eye for art, rather than as an artist, Desnoyers followed in the footsteps of early realist French authors Stendhal (Marie-Henri Beyle; *Le rouge et le noir,* 1830) and Honoré de Balzac (*La comédie humaine,* 1842) and of Tolstoy, who had begun a successful career as a realist novelist with his 1852 novel *Childhood.* At the time Desnoyers was formulating his theories, Whitman was writing the poetry collection *Leaves of Grass* (1855), which treated the urbanization of America, and Gustave Flaubert was composing the groundbreaking novel *Madame Bovary* (1856). Realism would also soon spawn the more scientific naturalist movement in literature, the province of Emile Zola, who wrote about social degradation during the Second Empire.

In the decades following the publication of "On Realism," bohemian artists and writers moved toward experimentation and individual expression, promoting artistic visions analogous to Desnoyers's—including Impressionism, naturalism, and eventually modernism—in France and across the world. Realism was first considered an official school after the 1863 alternative exhibition the Salon des Refusés (Desnoyers published the catalogue *Salon des Refusés: Le*

THE RISE OF THE REJECTED: THE SALON DES REFUSÉS OF 1863

In the nineteenth century, the Académie des Beaux-Arts' Salon (or the Paris Salon) was an annual official juried exhibition that could make or break an artist's fortune. In the middle of the century, the artistic community began to protest the jurors' taste more frequently, claiming it was inflexible and elitist. Finally, in 1863, the Salon des Refusés (or the Salon of the Refused) was sanctioned by Emperor Napoléon III to "let the public judge the legitimacy of (the) complaints" against the jurors.

Although it experienced a mixed public and critical reception, the 1863 Salon des Refusés succeeded in that it forced a sea change in judging. A few of the works, such as James McNeill Whistler's *Symphony in White, No. 1: The White Girl* and Édouard Manet's notorious *Déjeuner sur l'herbe* stood out as exceptional. The alternative exhibition revealed the conservative standards of the government-backed Salon. Official support for the Salon des Refusés legitimized new schools of art including Impressionism, naturalism, and other avant-garde offshoots. Desnoyers's catalogue *Salon des refusés: La peinture en 1863* also helped to promote the show. Many of the artists are now firmly established in art history as innovators of the period. Most importantly, the Salon des Refusés supported younger artists in following their own instincts, leading to a blossoming of the type of art prophesied in Desnoyers's "On Realism." The Salon des Refusés returned in 1874, 1875, and 1886.

Young Women of the Village Giving Alms to a Cowherd (1852), by the preeminent painter of the realism movement, Gustave Courbet. METROPOLITAN MUSEUM OF ART, NEW YORK, USA/ THE BRIDGEMAN ART LIBRARY

Peinture en 1863) and entered the public sphere more vigorously as artists became increasingly independent from the government's academic code. The Impressionists held their own exhibitions from 1874 on, and the Salon des Indépendants was inaugurated in 1884.

THEMES AND STYLE

Revolving around the central proposition that real art must represent the mundane and the grotesque as well as the beautiful, "On Realism" repeatedly derides what Desnoyers calls the vapid optimism of the Romantics. He directs his vitriol against convention, tradition, and "rose-colored glasses," asserting, "The landscape artist who does not know how to fill his picture with air and who is only able to render color exactly is not only not a realistic painter, but is not a painter at all." The same, he claims, applies to writers who "can depict men and things only by the aid of known and conventional means." Desnoyers insists that only accurate reflections, rather than a "Romantic dream of the Middle Ages," represent truth and thus constitute true art. He asserts, "I demand for painting and for literature to have the same rights as mirrors have."

Using insults, Desnoyers sets up his foes as not only wrong but also as idiotic. He positions Courbet's detractors as the aggressors in the hotly contentious debate over artistic styles. In an aside, Desnoyers petitions the audience to unite with his cause, explaining that "perhaps some intelligent readers" will not see the purpose of protecting truth in art, but "it is necessary to *defend* since there is an *attack*." The treatise concludes with an invocation suggesting that realism is the artistic equivalent of the 1848 revolution: "Let us have no masters or disciples … the only principles are independence, sincerity, and individuality!" These tripartite values are reminiscent of the revolution's bywords—liberty, equality, and brotherhood—suggesting that a strike against romance is a strike against yet another oppressive regime. Desnoyers's confident rhetoric and intermixture of definitions, arguments, and anti-Romantic derogations push his readers to identify with him and his "faith."

"On Realism" is marked by Desnoyers's use of fervent language to exalt his conception of what art should be: "There is no *true* depiction without color, vital spirit, life and animation, without features and feeling." Art filled with fantasy and ideals is "false, ridiculous, or faded," much like the academic dandies-turned-academics who support it. His tone emphasizes informality while burlesquing Romanticism's decorum; Desnoyers abuts short, simple passages dismissing the Romantics and promoting the value of realism against long, highly descriptive flights of fancy that satirize Romanticism's rococo excesses, as Desnoyers sees them. He hopes to drive readers away from Romanticism through lengthy sentences: "It is through this underbrush, this battle of the Cimbri, this Pandemonium of Greek temples, lyres, and jews' harps, of alhambras and sickly oaks, of boleros, of silly sonnets, of golden odes, of rusty daggers, rapiers, and weekly columns … that Realism has made a breach."

CRITICAL DISCUSSION

Although Desnoyers's contemporaries rarely referred to his treatise, its sentiments were widely restated. The author's positioning of "On Realism" as a manifesto rather than a defense or a plea is mirrored in Edmond Duranty's 1856 *Réalisme,* a periodical dedicated to promoting realism as an aggressive concept mounting a battle against convention. Although it only ran for seven months, the journal's timing was crucial to the spread of the ideals championed by Desnoyers. Champfleury's volumes of critical discussions, *Le Réalisme* (1857), soon perpetuated similar doctrines. These publications, along with the Salon des Refusés and other artistic efforts, contributed to the growth of the movement. The lack of specific critical response to "On Realism," coupled with independent instances of artistic expression around the globe representing similar ideals, indicates that the treatise itself was more prophetic and explanatory than world changing.

"On Realism" captured the artistic climate of a period when such artists as Édouard Manet, Camille Pissarro, and Paul Cézanne, now familiar names, flourished. Nineteenth- and twentieth-century art critics and literary theorists have revived interest in the treatise and the debates in which it took part, particularly in light of their historical legacy. Becker includes the statement in *Documents of Modern Literary Realism* in 1963 inspired further criticism. In *Realism* (1985) Damien Grant translates from Jacques-Henry Bornecque and Pierre Cogny's *Réalisme et naturalism* (1958) to describe Desnoyers's cohesive but relatively simple expression of the tenets of realism as "a sudden start in the need for truth." Martin Puchner's study of manifestos, *Poetry of the Revolution* (2006), cites "On Realism" as an example of a statement whose vision and "literary, poetic, and rhetorical strategies," and the "history of the futures [it] sought to predict, prefigure, and realize," matter more than the change it actually effected. Most often mentioned as a culmination of thought and as a catalyst for the future of the avant-garde, the treatise takes a backseat to the legacy of the movement's most prominent artist, Courbet.

References to "On Realism" primarily appear in texts discussing the artistic and literary developments of realism, Impressionism, and the avant-garde. In *Mimesis* (2006) Matthew Potolsky connects Desnoyers's declaration with works by Zola and others of a scientific bent to describe the trend toward personal observation and experimentation over "imitation and tradition" in the arts in the second half of the nineteenth century. Mary Gluck explains in *Popular*

Bohemia (2008) that this approach varied from that of the "passionate, ethical, and epic values" that belonged to the Romanticism it displaced. She suggests that the realism of the 1850s was associated with a modern "decontextualized and abstract" brand of science. Further, she remarks that an artist born of realism is a "radically individuated self," uniquely free from the tension between present and past. Albert Boime in *Art in an Age of Civil Struggle, 1848-1871* (2008) points to the impulse to fight against convention, arguing that "On Realism" and Courbet's art participated in the same cultural climate of "democracy in art" as Whitman's poetry. Boime writes that all three defy the thematic elevation of the upper classes and recognize democratic social valuations, earthiness, and the value of life's rough edges.

BIBLIOGRAPHY

Sources

Baudelaire, Charles. *Selected Letters of Charles Baudelaire: The Conquest of Solitude.* Ed. and Trans. Rosemary Lloyd. Chicago: U of Chicago P, 1986. Print.

Becker, George J. *Documents of Modern Literary Realism.* Princeton: Princeton UP, 1963. Print.

Boime, Albert. *Art in an Age of Civil Struggle, 1848-1871.* Vol. 4. Chicago: U of Chicago P, 2008. *Ebrary.* Web. 11 Sept. 2012.

Gluck, Mary. *Popular Bohemia: Modernism and Urban Culture in Nineteenth-Century Paris.* Cambridge: Harvard UP, 2008. *Ebrary.* Web. 13 Sept. 2012.

Potolsky, Matthew. *Mimesis.* New York: Routledge, 2006. *Ebrary.* Web. 11 Sept. 2012.

Puchner, Martin. *Poetry of the Revolution: Marx, Manifestos, and the Avant-Gardes.* Princeton: Princeton UP, 2006. Print.

Further Reading

Boime, Albert. "The Salon des Refusés and the Evolution of Modern Art." *Art Quarterly* 32 (1970): 411-27. Print.

Claybaugh, Amanda. *The Novel of Purpose: Literature and Social Reform in the Anglo-American World.* Ithaca: Cornell UP, 2007. Print.

Desnoyers, Fernand. *Salon des Refusés: La Peinture en 1863.* Paris: Azul Dutil, 1863. *Gallica.* Web. 11 Sept. 2012.

Fried, Michael. *Manet's Modernism: or, The Face of Painting in the 1860s.* Chicago: U of Chicago P, 1998. *Google Books.* Web. 11 Sept. 2012.

Grant, Damian. *Realism.* London: Methuen, 1985. Print.

Howells, William Dean. "On Truth in Fiction." *Documents of Modern Literary Realism.* Ed. George J. Becker. Princeton: Princeton UP, 1963. 129-36. Print.

Katherine Bishop

THE PAINTER OF MODERN LIFE

Charles Baudelaire

✜ *Key Facts*

Time Period:
Mid-19th Century

Movement/Issue:
Aesthetics; Early
modernism

Place of Publication:
France

**Language of
Publication:**
French

OVERVIEW

Composed by French poet and literary critic Charles Baudelaire, the essay "Le peintre de la vie modern" ("The Painter of Modern Life"; 1863) describes the ephemeral and eternal nature of beauty and advocates a contemporary art that embraces the "transitory, fugitive" reality of modern life. In the essay, Baudelaire uses professional illustrator Constantin Guys as the archetypal modern artist but keeps Guys's identity concealed. Baudelaire, best known as a poet and for his collection of poems *Les fleurs du mal* (*The Flowers of Evil*; 1857), wrote "The Painter of Modern Life" as part of a lifelong interest in aesthetic theory and art criticism. He first displayed this interest in the essay "Salon de 1845." Known for the passion and urgency of his style, Baudelaire vociferously rejected many of the dominant artistic modes of the era, including neoclassicism and realism. In "The Painter of Modern Life," he praises the work of Guys for "rendering and explaining [life] in pictures more living than life itself."

Serially published in the French newspaper *Le Figaro* in 1863, "The Painter of Modern Life" was praised for its originality and profundity. Much speculation, however, surrounded the identity of the prototypical modern painter, whom Baudelaire only identified as "Monsieur C.G." (or "Monsieur G."). Six years later, when Baudelaire revealed that Guys was the essay's subject, many critics were baffled. Guys was not a fine artist or even a painter. Rather, he was a relatively obscure illustrator for newspapers. Despite critics' and scholars' confusion about Baudelaire's choice, Baudelaire's aesthetic argument endured both as a work of art criticism and as a key to understanding his poetry. In the twenty-first century, "The Painter of Modern Life" is widely considered one of Baudelaire's most brilliant prose works and is viewed as an important anticipation of modernism.

HISTORICAL AND LITERARY CONTEXT

"The Painter of Modern Life" responds to the state of French politics and culture in the mid-nineteenth century, when the nation was undergoing widespread change. The French Revolution at the end of the eighteenth century transformed the nation from an absolute monarchy to a nascent liberal democracy. During the nineteenth century, the transition toward capitalism, industrialization, and democracy was accompanied by conflict. The July Revolution of 1830, which took place during Baudelaire's childhood, and the failed Revolution of 1848, in which the poet participated, were indicative of the turmoil that occurred as the country modernized. During this time of political and cultural change, the nation's art remained rooted in classical forms and style. In essays and articles, Baudelaire advocated a modern brand of art that offered a new way of seeing and depicting the world. Beginning with the essay "Salon de 1845," Baudelaire championed romanticism as a form of modern art and the French painter Eugène Delacroix as the foremost romantic.

By the time "The Painter of Modern Life" was written in 1859 and 1860, some three years before its publication, Baudelaire had begun to look beyond Delacroix and romanticism for a new form of artistic representation that embraced the beauty of the modern world—which he found in the illustrations of Guys. Unlike the works of the romantics, Guys's sketches and watercolors depict the urbanity of contemporary city life, warfare, and fashion, among other subjects. As the scholar Lois Boe Hyslop writes in *Baudelaire: Man of His Time* (1980), "Baudelaire was delighted to find in Guys the modernity which he had found lacking in the visual art of his contemporaries." This modernity was a matter not only of subject but also of technique: Baudelaire praised Guys's ability to distill the fleeting, "contingent" nature of the contemporary world in spontaneous, evocative images.

"The Painter of Modern Life" draws on a varied philosophical tradition that includes the ideas of German thinker Immanuel Kant as expressed in *The Critique of Judgment* (1790). Scholar Timothy Raser writes in *A Poetics of Art Criticism: The Case of Baudelaire* (1989), "Baudelaire recognized the paradoxes of aesthetic propositions and adopted Kantian solutions in order to safeguard his freedom and judgment." Raser argues that Baudelaire's theory of beauty's "double composition" can be read as "an allegory" of Kant's idea of the "*free conformity to law* of the imagination." Another important influence on Baudelaire's art criticism was the work of Denis Diderot, a French encyclopedist, philosopher, and critic. In *Baudelaire the Critic* (1943), scholar Margaret Gilman notes, "Baudelaire, having evidently read and pondered

Diderot, frequently echoes his method and tone, and is close to many of his ideas."

In the years between the composition of "The Painter of Modern Life" and Baudelaire's death in 1867, the poet produced critical essays that further developed his aesthetic arguments. His essay "The Life and Work of Eugène Delacroix," which appeared upon the occasion of Delacroix's death in late 1863, further explores beauty's "double composition" and the modern artist's imperative to capture the "heady bouquet of the wine of life." Baudelaire even borrows some of his own phrasing from "The Painter of Modern Life": the description of "Monseiur G." as being "passionately in love with passion" is echoed when he describes Delacroix as being "passionately in love with passion, and coldly determined to seek the means of expressing it in the most visible way." Baudelaire's art criticism, while not as well known as his poetry, continues to command significant scholarly attention among twenty-first-century academics.

THEMES AND STYLE

The central theme of "The Painter of Modern Life" is that the modern artist must embrace the reality of his age and "extract the eternal from the transitory" in order to make works of enduring truth and beauty.

CHARLES BAUDELAIRE: CONTROVERSIAL ROMANTIC

Romantic poet Charles Baudelaire was born in Paris on April 9, 1821, and died at the age of forty-six on August 31, 1867. He lived a tumultuous, bohemian life. When he was only six, his father died; his mother remarried eighteen months later. He clashed with his stepfather and was expelled from school. Although he enrolled in law school in 1839, he soon contracted a venereal disease from a prostitute, became addicted to opium, and dropped out of school. He ran up an enormous debt, was sent to India by his stepfather, and soon started to write poetry, also participating in the failed French Revolution of 1848.

The poet's outsider image was confirmed in 1857 when he published *Les fleurs du mal* (*The Flowers of Evil*), a volume of poetry that met with outrage. According to scholar Rosemary Lloyd, *Le Figaro,* the primary French newspaper, published a terrible review of the book, declaring, "The odious rubs shoulders with the ignoble, the repulsive blends with the nauseating." In addition to generating a critical backlash and a public outcry, the book attracted the attention of the authorities. Copies were seized by the police, Baudelaire was summoned to court and fined, and the book was bowdlerized. However, the persecution only fueled Baudelaire's creative fire, and over the next decade, he entered the most productive period of his career.

Portrait of Charles Baudelaire by Gustave Courbet. GIANNI DAGLI ORTI/THE ART ARCHIVE AT ART RESOURCE, NY

In making this argument, Baudelaire advocates "a rational and historical theory of beauty." "Beauty," he writes, "is made up of an eternal, invariable element, whose quantity is excessively difficult to determine, and of a relative, circumstantial element, which will be … the age, its fashion, its morals, its emotions." He introduces an anonymous exemplar of modern art (Guys) and examines the ways in which Guys's art satisfies his own definition of beauty. In so doing, Baudelaire provides an in-depth study of the characteristics of modern art: its subject "is the *outward show of life*," including war and fashion. Its ideal attitude is "dandyism," which he defines as "an air of coldness which comes from a determination not to be moved." And its style is at once "transitory, fugitive," and "immutable."

"The Painter of Modern Life" achieves its rhetorical effect through its reliance on concrete details, images, and examples to make its argument. The manifesto opens with a general statement that turns into a vivid scene: "The world—even the world of artists—is full of people who can go to the Louvre, walk rapidly, without so much as a glance, past rows of very interesting, though secondary pictures, to come to a rapturous halt in front of a Titian or a Raphael." Through tangible details, Baudelaire invites readers to enter into the essay and avoids alienating them with abstractions. A high level of specificity continues throughout the essay, especially in the case of the anonymous artist. By invoking "Monsieur C.G.," Baudelaire refers to particular characteristics of the exemplary artist without limiting the argument about modern aesthetics to the case of a single painter.

Stylistically, "The Painter of Modern Life" is distinguished by its urgent lyricism. Baudelaire describes Guys as an artist who appreciates all forms of beauty: "Monsieur G. will be the last to linger wherever there can be a glow of light, an echo of poetry, a quiver of life or a chord of music; wherever a passion can *pose* before him, wherever natural man and conventional man display themselves in a strange beauty, wherever the sun lights up the swift joys of the *depraved animal*!" This piling on of imagery overwhelms the reader with the force of Baudelaire's argument and demonstrates the type of artistic techniques that the essay advocates. Essentially, just as Guys's drawings are "weird, violent and excessive," so is Baudelaire's prose.

CRITICAL DISCUSSION

When "The Painter of Modern Life" was first published in 1863, it was immediately viewed as an important work of criticism. According to scholar Rosemary Lloyd in *Baudelaire's World* (2002), "it was justly heralded as a work of profound criticism, well researched, and highly original." The essay was also the object of much speculation, as many readers wondered about the identity of Baudelaire's exemplary modern painter. Their curiosity was finally satisfied when the essay was republished in the posthumous collection *L'art romantique* (1879) and Guys was named. Many critics were puzzled by Guys as an example of modernity, not only because of his obscurity but also because of Baudelaire's well-known affiliation with more-renowned painters such as Delacroix and Édouard Manet.

After its publication, "The Painter of Modern Life" had a formative influence on the invention of modernist art. Critics have identified Manet, rather than Guys, as the painter who best reflected the ideal artist described in Baudelaire's work. Through paintings such as *Déjeuner sur l'herbe* (1863) and *Olympia* (1863), Manet influenced a revolutionary new style of painting that became known as impressionism, which itself is viewed as initiating a crucial turn from the classical tradition to modernist techniques. As scholar David Carrier notes in *High Art: Charles Baudelaire and the Origins of Modernist Painting* (1996), the argument made in "The Painter of Modern Life" not only "anticipates Impressionism" but also "presents modernism."

In the century and a half since it was written, Baudelaire's essay has been the subject of an extensive body of criticism that has considered the work in aesthetic, political, and historical terms. Much scholarship has focused on Baudelaire's choice of Guys as an ideal modern painter. Raser suggests, "Baudelaire made this choice as a provocation, an effort to unsettle received notions of beauty, and first among them, the notion that beauty is recognized." Commentators have also discussed Baudelaire's definition of beauty. In the introduction to *The Painter of Modern Life and Other Essays* (1964), Jonathan Mayne writes, "Good—whether in art or morality—can only be achieved by conscious (and, one might add, imaginative) effort; by striving after an ideal virtue or beauty, and constantly battling against the powerful, but senseless and undirected impulses of Nature."

BIBLIOGRAPHY

Sources

Baudelaire, Charles. *The Painter of Modern Life and Other Essays*. Trans. and ed. Jonathan Mayne. London: Phaidon, 1964. Print.

Carrier, David. *High Art: Charles Baudelaire and the Origins of Modernist Painting*. University Park: Pennsylvania State UP, 1996. Print.

Gilman, Margaret. *Baudelaire the Critic*. New York: Columbia UP, 1943. Print.

Hyslop, Lois Boe. *Baudelaire: Man of His Time*. New Haven: Yale UP, 1980. Print.

Lloyd, Rosemary. *Baudelaire's World*. Ithaca: Cornell UP, 2002. Print.

———. *Charles Baudelaire*. London: Reaktion, 2008. Print.

Raser, Timothy. *A Poetics of Art Criticism: The Case of Baudelaire.* Chapel Hill: North Carolina Studies in the Romance Languages and Literatures, 1989. Print.

Further Reading

Benjamin, Walter. *The Writer of Modern Life: Essays on Charles Baudelaire.* Cambridge: Belknap, 2006. Print.

Chase, Cynthia. "The Memory of Modern Life (Baudelaire)." *Angelaki: Journal of the Theoretical Humanities* 5.1 (2010): 193-204. *Taylor & Francis Online.* Web. 30 Aug. 2012.

Hiddleston, J.A. "Art and Its Representation." *The Cambridge Companion to Baudelaire.* Ed. Rosemary Lloyd. New York: Cambridge UP, 2005. 130-44. *ProQuest.* Web. 30 Aug. 2012.

———. "Baudelaire, Manet, and Modernity." *Modern Language Review* 87.3 (1992): 567-75. *JSTOR.* Web. 30 Aug. 2012.

Hyslop, Lois Boe. *Charles Baudelaire Revisited.* New York: Twayne, 1992. Print.

McCall, Corey. "The Art of Life: Foucault's Reading of Baudelaire's 'The Painter of Modern Life.'" *Journal of Speculative Philosophy* 24.2 (2010). *JSTOR.* Web. 30 Aug. 2012.

Meltzer, Francoise. *Seeing Double: Baudelaire's Modernity.* Chicago: U of Chicago P, 2011. Print.

Theodore McDermott

THE PHILOSOPHY OF FURNITURE

Edgar Allan Poe

✣ **Key Facts**

Time Period:
Mid-19th Century

Movement/Issue:
Interior decorating

Place of Publication:
United States

**Language of
Publication:**
English

OVERVIEW

"The Philosophy of Furniture" by Edgar Allan Poe is a short, spirited essay on the principles of home decorating. First published in *Burton's Gentleman's Magazine* in May 1840, the essay marks a significant departure for an author best known, then as now, for his horror stories and brooding Gothic poems. Poe argues that Americans, living in a society that privileges wealth above nobility, are imitating European trends without regard for the overall harmony of the rooms they furnish. Declaiming against brightly colored carpets ("the wicked invention of a race of time servers and money lovers"), glass chandeliers (pleasing "to children and idiots"), and above all gas lighting, the author concludes with a detailed description of his own ideally decorated chamber.

Since the essay's initial appearance, readers have exhibited a variety of reactions to Poe's polemical "Philosophy." Some critics, primarily Poe's nineteenth-century contemporaries, have taken issue with his generalizations regarding American tastes and his suggestions for improvement. Those claiming authority as decorators have accused Poe, here as elsewhere, of dilettantism. By the twentieth century, the initial impetus for Poe's outcry was all but forgotten; literary scholars attempted instead to relate this unusual piece to the author's other works, or, in the case of Walter Benjamin, to larger aesthetic shifts taking place in the nineteenth century, which included but exceeded the matter of home furnishing. Critics have observed the essay's underlying principles at work in Poe's tales and poems, in which the evocation of mood through description is a hallmark of his style. Scholars have variously seen in the essay the methodical prose that characterizes Poe's detective stories; the dreamy languor of poems such as "Ligeia" (1838) and "The Raven" (1845); and a disavowal of the garish opulence on display in "The Masque of the Red Death" (1842).

HISTORICAL AND LITERARY CONTEXT

For American and European home decorators, the early nineteenth century represented a watershed in the sheer variety of available furniture styles. In Poe's lifetime, the Gothic, Neoclassical, and Rococo styles entered major revivals, leading to the very real (and, for Poe, quite ghastly) possibility that a room in an affluent home might present a congeries of clashing pieces. More worrisome still for Poe was the idea that the rising middle class in the United States had neither a longstanding furniture tradition to rely upon nor an "aristocracy of blood" to regard as tastemakers and trendsetters.

While Poe takes up the subject of American eclecticism with enthusiasm, the most pressing issue of his essay is lighting, which from 1800 to 1840 had likewise undergone a revolution. In the three decades preceding "The Philosophy of Furniture," gas lamps had risen from an experimental novelty to a mainstay of public lighting in England and America; they were gradually becoming accepted as an economical means of lighting homes as well. Poe, in contrast, strongly favored the smaller-scale Argand oil lamp, invented in 1780: "never was a more lovely thought than that of the [Argand] lamp … [with] its tempered and uniform moonlight rays." The displacement of the Argand lamp appeared to produce something of a crisis for Poe, who found the "harsh and unsteady light" provided by gas "positively offensive" and regarded the cut-glass shades that often accompanied such lamps as "a weak invention of the enemy."

Poe had already established himself as an author of horror stories and poetry, but his readers also knew him as a literary critic and essayist. He had consolidated his reputation for criticism during his years at the *Southern Literary Messenger* in Richmond, Virginia, on whose editorial staff he intermittently served from 1835 to 1837. As a critic, he often satirized emerging literary trends, including those in his own beloved genre of horror, which the 1838 essay "How to Write a Blackwood Article" lampoons for its tendency toward sensational tales with formulaic plots. Poe joined *Burton's Gentleman's Magazine* in 1839; while there, he continued to publish book reviews along with fiction.

History witnesses that Poe's essay had little effect on furniture trends either in the United States or in England. Undaunted, the author himself would continue to evolve his own sumptuous notions of appropriate décor in the many parlors, chambers, and castles of his later fiction. His prescriptions for the proper use of drapery are observed in the breach, for instance, in "The Masque of the Red Death," and even the narrator of "The Pit and the Pendulum" (1843), though trapped in a dungeon, is more sensitive than average to the appearance of his environment.

THEMES AND STYLE

Poe's avowed purpose in "The Philosophy of Furniture" is to expose the numerous misguided practices of home decorating in North America; the "philosophy" of his title is "more imperfectly understood by Americans than by any civilized nation upon the face of the earth." Poe occasionally lights on the political issues he believes underlie this travesty of good taste, namely, the "aristocracy of dollars," which leads "as an inevitable thing" to the confusion of "the two entirely separate ideas of magnificence and beauty." Pursuing this point, the author repeatedly remarks upon the association between the popularity of various furniture items (all of which he happens to despise) and their perceived costliness. In the main, however, "The Philosophy of Furniture" is a collection of specific quibbles with American furniture fashions rather than a sustained examination of the reasons for those trends.

This does not stop Poe from countenancing his efforts with a somewhat incongruous reference to actual philosophy. In a gesture of ironic grandiosity, Poe begins his text with a quotation from the revolutionary German philosopher Georg W. F. Hegel but then shoos the reader along the page by insisting that to explain the quotation would be "wasting time." Maintaining that "there is reason ... even in the roasting of eggs," Poe comically elides the difference between Hegelian philosophy and the personal tastes and anecdotal observations he will offer as its counterpart. Moreover, his assertions leave little room for reply, as he utterly refuses to admit a contrary argument. Nowhere is this more evident than when he speaks of the "*glitter*" of cut glass and mirrors: "in that one word how much of all that is detestable do we express."

Sensing, perhaps, the subjectivity of his argument, the author repeatedly resorts to ad hominem attacks on those who would furnish differently: he calls those whose tastes vary from his own "children of Baal" and "worshipers of Mammon" and declares them unfit "[to] be entrusted with the management of their own mustachios." The author is quite peremptory about the furniture habits not only of Americans but also of many Europeans, including the Dutch, who "have merely a vague idea that a curtain is not a cabbage," and the Italians, who "have but little sentiment beyond marbles and colors." Poe's self-assurance, combined with his offhanded remarks about the decorating defects of his contemporaries, would provoke the ire of a few critics, while others were gleeful or baffled.

CRITICAL DISCUSSION

Early readers of "The Philosophy of Furniture" frequently took the essay at face value: as an exposition of a series of contentious principles for interior decorating. Some nineteenth-century critics made a point of chiding Poe for his presumption, as did the anonymous author of one 1865 article who called Poe an "able man" but no expert in home furnishing and claimed that his "reputation suffers to this day from his own ... hasty discussion of matters not wholly within his ken."

As the gas lamps of which Poe had complained faded into history, critics came to see "The Philosophy of Furniture" as more important to Poe's literary biography than to debates about decorating technique. In his 1968 piece for *American Quarterly*, Charles L. Sanford notes that Poe "deplored the new moneyed aristocracy's degraded rage for 'glitter and glare'" in the essay, while his stories "projected his self-contempt and envy upon the familiar European devil in the form of allegory." The literary critic Walter Benjamin also drew upon Poe's essay to considerable extent in his unfinished *Arcades Project* (1927-40), which posited a convergence of Parisian architectural and decorative fashions with the flâneur—a leisurely urban wanderer—at its center. Pressing the implications of the text much further, Jacques Lacan, in *Écrits I* (1966), used "The Philosophy of Furniture" to present an elaborate argument that domestic spaces in Poe's work were to be read as feminine. However, Servanne Woodward's 1989 essay in *Comparative*

A nineteenth-century portrait of Edgar Allan Poe. © STEFANO BIANCHETTI/ CORBIS

PRIMARY SOURCE

"THE PHILOSOPHY OF FURNITURE"

In the internal decoration, if not in the external architecture of their residences, the English are supreme. The Italians have but little sentiment beyond marbles and colours. In France, "meliora probant, deteriora sequuntur"—the people are too much a race of gadabouts to maintain those household proprieties of which, indeed, they have a delicate appreciation, or at least the elements of a proper sense. The Chinese and most of the eastern races have a warm but inappropriate fancy. The Scotch are "poor "decorists. The Dutch have, perhaps, an indeterminate idea that a curtain is not a cabbage. In Spain they are "all" curtains—a nation of hangmen. The Russians do not furnish. The Hottentots and Kickapoos are very well in their way. The Yankees alone are preposterous.

How this happens, it is not difficult to see. We have no aristocracy of blood, and having therefore as a natural, and indeed as an inevitable thing, fashioned for ourselves an aristocracy of dollars, the "display of wealth" has here to take the place and perform the office of the heraldic display in monarchical countries. By a transition readily understood, and which might have been as readily foreseen, we have been brought to merge in simple "show "our notions of taste itself....

A want of keeping is observable sometimes in the character of the several pieces of furniture, but generally in their colours or modes of adaptation to use. "Very" often the eye is offended by their inartistic arrangement. Straight lines are too prevalent—too uninterruptedly continued—or clumsily interrupted at right angles. If curved lines occur, they are repeated into unpleasant uniformity. By undue precision, the appearance of many a fine apartment is utterly spoiled.

Curtains are rarely well disposed, or well chosen in respect to other decorations. With formal furniture, curtains are out of place; and an extensive volume of drapery of any kind is, under any circumstance, irreconcilable with good taste—the proper quantum, as well as the proper adjustment, depending upon the character of the general effect.

Carpets are better understood of late than of ancient days, but we still very frequently err in their patterns and colours. The soul of the apartment is the carpet. From it are deduced not only the hues but the forms of all objects incumbent....

It is an evil growing out of our republican institutions, that here a man of large purse has usually a very little soul which he keeps in it. The corruption of taste is a portion or a pendant of the dollar-manufacture. As we grow rich, our ideas grow rusty. It is, therefore, not among "our" aristocracy that we must look (if at all, in Appalachia), for the spirituality of a British "boudoir." But we have seen apartments in the tenure of Americans of moderns [possibly "modest" or "moderate"] means, which, in negative merit at least, might vie with any of the "ormolu'd" cabinets of our friends across the water. Even "now", there is present to our mind's eye a small and not, ostentatious chamber with whose decorations no fault can be found. The proprietor lies asleep on a sofa— the weather is cool—the time is near midnight: arc will make a sketch of the room during his slumber.

Literature Studies considered this a misinterpretation: for her, the essay was truly "nothing but a criticism of bad taste in American homes."

Scholarship of "The Philosophy of Furniture" has continued largely in these two veins, treating the work as a touchstone of Poe's other writings as well as of mid-nineteenth-century city life. In a 1996 piece in *Texas Studies in Literature and Language*, Dennis Pahl, en route to an interpretation of Poe's other "Philosophy," notes that the author's ideal room is "as phantasmagorical as any chamber in one of his Gothic stories," possessed of a "dreamlike" and "gloom-inspiring" ambiance and serving as a scene of corpse-like repose. In a rare extended treatment of the essay, Kevin J. Hayes calls for renewed attention to the flâneur figure in Poe and suggests that the essay's publication, coinciding with the customary Moving Day—when all leases in contemporary New York City expired—celebrated a time that "served to break down the barriers between exterior and interior, public and private." Hayes observes that similar motifs—identities encoded in physical objects—pervade Poe's later detective fiction, where the "traces" left by "modern urban dwellers" become a matter not merely of taste but of life and death.

BIBLIOGRAPHY

Sources

Benjamin, Walter. *The Arcades Project*. Trans. Howard Eiland and Kevin McLaughlin. Ed. Rolf Tiedemann. Cambridge: Belknap Press of Harvard UP, 1999. Print.

Hayes, Kevin J. "The Flâneur in the Parlor: Poe's 'Philosophy of Furniture.'" *Prospects* 27 (2002): 103-19. Print.

Lacan, Jacques. *Écrits I*. Paris: Seuil, 1966. Print.

"Our Furniture; What It Is, and What It Should Be." *New Path* 2.4 (1865): 55-62. *JSTOR*. Web. 10 Aug. 2012.

Pahl, Dennis. "De-composing Poe's 'Philosophy.'" *Texas Studies in Literature and Language* 38.1 (1996): 1-25. *JSTOR*. Web. 10 Aug. 2012.

Sanford, Charles L. "Edgar Allan Poe: A Blight upon the Landscape." *American Quarterly* 20.1 (1968): 54-66. Web. 10 Aug. 2012.

Woodward, Servanne. "Lacan and Derrida on 'The Purloined Letter.'" *Comparative Literature Studies* 26.1 (1989): 39-49. *JSTOR*. Web. 10 Aug. 2012.

Further Reading

Apter, Emily. "Cabinet Secrets: Fetishism, Prostitution, and the Fin de Siècle Interior." *Assemblage* 9 (1989): 6-19. *JSTOR*. Web. 10 Aug. 2012.

Banta, Martha. "The Ghostly Gothic of Wharton's Everyday World." *American Literary Realism, 1870-1910* 27.1 (1994): 1-10. *JSTOR*. Web. 10 Aug. 2012.

Hurh, Paul. "'The Creative and the Resolvent': The Origins of Poe's Analytical Method." *Nineteenth-Century Literature* 66.4 (2012): 466-93. *JSTOR*. Web. 10 Aug. 2012.

Ketterer, David. *The Rationale of Deception in Poe.* Baton Rouge: Louisiana State UP, 1979. Print.

Moldenhauer, Joseph J. "Murder as a Fine Art: Basic Connections between Poe's Aesthetics, Psychology, and Moral Vision." *PMLA* 83.2 (1968): 284-97. *JSTOR*. Web. 10 Aug. 2012.

Pollin, Burton R. "Edgar Allan Poe and John G. Chapman: Their Treatment of the Dismal Swamp and the Wissahickon." *Studies in the American Renaissance* (1983): 245-74. *JSTOR*. Web. 10 Aug. 2012.

Teyssot, Georges. "The Disease of the Domicile." *Assemblage* 6 (1988): 72-97. *JSTOR*. Web. 10 Aug. 2012.

Michael Hartwell

A PLEA FOR CERTAIN EXOTIC FORMS OF VERSE

Sir Edmund Gosse

✢ *Key Facts*

Time Period:
Late 19th century

Movement/Issue:
Aesthetics; Formalism

Place of Publication:
England

Language of Publication:
English

OVERVIEW

Written by Sir Edmund Gosse in 1877 and published in the *Cornhill Magazine,* an influential literary journal, "A Plea for Certain Exotic Forms of Verse" was instrumental in introducing English writers and readers to French fixed-forms of poetry. The text disparages the state of English poetry, which had turned away from formal verse toward blank verse. This distinction, perhaps less apparent to modern readers, is between verse that has prescribed numbers of lines along with specific and scant rhyme schemes and verse that is simply written in iambic pentameter. Blank verse is still considered the easiest and most natural form for English speakers, and Gosse argued against it for this very reason. In his view, the poet "properly takes his place beside the sculptor and the painter" when engaging in the act of "conscious artifice." That the poet Austin Dobson wrote "A Note on Some Foreign Forms of Verse" a year later, closely following Gosse's logic by outlining the same fixed forms, verifies the text's influence.

Due to the visibility of his article in the *Cornhill Magazine,* as well as his standing and friendship with some of the major writers of his era (including Dobson, Algernon Charles Swinburne, and Robert Louis Stevenson), the forms Gosse championed became suddenly popular and remained so through the 1890s. However, as early as 1878, Gosse's concrete explanation of the forms' rules was panned as "bungled ... like they almost always are" by French critic Joseph Boulmier. Due to the work's many factual errors, it is not widely studied by scholars today.

HISTORICAL AND LITERARY CONTEXT

"A Plea for Certain Exotic Forms of Verse" responds specifically to a perceived lack of intellectualism characterizing the verse of those poets coming after Alfred, Lord Tennyson, Robert Browning, and Elizabeth Barrett Browning. Its opening argument likening the poet to the visual artist makes an implicit case of "art for art's sake," suggesting that Gosse was aware of the French Parnassian poets and the poet Théophile Gautier's adage *l'art pour l'art.* The French school hoped to reemphasize the craft of poetry as opposed to its content, as poets in both countries were trading musings for what Gosse and Gautier felt was vital: structure.

The French movement would soon give way to symbolism and, with it, a level of experimentation many readers and critics found excessive. In England, however, the literary climate remained considerably more moderate until the end of the Victorian era. Gosse's insistence on the technically adroit and the morally conservative was in keeping with the literary atmosphere of England in 1877, in which many poets, including Gosse, socialized in the bourgeois settings of country clubs. These poets were content to react against the trend of blank verse by retreating to the forms and aesthetics of the past.

Something of a literary opportunist, Gosse was attempting to carve out a place for himself in the academy by introducing subject matter that had little precedent in England. He had been successful with this strategy five years earlier, when he published a review of Henrik Ibsen's poems in *Spectator,* effectively introducing English readership to the Nordic poet. The esoteric nature of both Nordic poetry and Old French fixed forms resulted in few appraisals of his criticism, which contained some factual errors, until years later when Gosse was famously taken to task in the *Quarterly Review* by the scholar John Churton Collins. To his credit, Gosse was able to write poems in each of the forms presented in "A Plea for Certain Exotic Forms of Verse," which can be found in his collections *On Viol and Flute* (1873) and *New Poems* (1879). Gosse was regarded by his peers as a fine, if minor, poet.

Following Gosse's article, books concerning poetic forms in English have rarely neglected to include the six fixed forms that he popularized. Modern prosody handbooks, such as Lewis Turco's *Book of Forms* (1968) and Mary Oliver's *Rules for the Dance* (1998), are structurally modeled on Gosse's text in that they first make a case for formal poetry in modern times before turning to an analysis of the rules of the forms, providing examples for each.

THEMES AND STYLE

The central argument of "A Plea for Certain Exotic Forms of Verse" is that structure elevates poetry from the banal to the essential. Frustrated by the relatively formless work written by second-rate poets, Gosse insists that the fixed form, "instead of appalling us by its difficulty[,] encourages us to brilliant effort." While poets writing in English had long been composing in their own traditional forms, most famously in the sonnet, Gosse bases his argument on the "exotic forms" imported from France. He focuses on six: rondel, rondeaus, triolets, villanelles, ballades, and chants royeaux. For him, there was an inherent logic in French that was lacking in English. Throughout the text, he maintains that the turn toward fixed forms in England predates his article and that the movement "has begun on all sides."

Gosse sets out to convince his readers of the trend by citing the work of prominent poets, offering rondeaus by Dobson and Theodore de Banville, as well as a triolet by Robert Bridges and a ballade by Swinburne. The literary reputation of these poets was substantial enough to cover for the actual scarcity of French fixed-form poems in English; twice Gosse is forced to present his own unpublished poems as models. It is a testament to both his persuasive power and his much-noted charm that this does not seem to undermine his argument that "the actual movement of the time … appears certainly to be in the direction of increased variety and richness of rhyme, elasticity of verse, and strength of form."

Gosse's text follows the congenial tone of much Victorian criticism. Contemporary critic Richard D. Fulton says the Victorian "reader was assumed to have the same tastes as the reviewer, and hence was never preached to, never talked down to." This assertion is supported by "A Plea for Certain Exotic Forms of Verse," in which Gosse openly tells his audience: "I will take the liberty of supposing that those who do me the honour of following my argument unite in this opinion." While for the majority of his treatise Gosse takes pains to not mention mediocre poets by name, his witticisms eventually culminate in his final proclamation: "I hope we may be dead before the English poets take Walt Whitman for their model in style." This was only half a joke to Gosse, as the free verse of the American poet (and its immediate success in the United States) would have been a severe threat to fixed forms.

CRITICAL DISCUSSION

While Gosse is rightly credited with bringing the French forms to the attention of English poets, Dobson's essay the next year, which parrots Gosse's argument, commanded a wider readership as it was included in the anthology *Latter Day Lyrics* (1878). "A Plea for Certain Exotic Forms of Verse" was mentioned only in passing in discussions of the critic's works. Gosse gained more recognition for his work in the biographical genre for an acuity and radicalism he was reluctant to undertake in either his criticism or poetry. Virginia Woolf notes in her essay "Edmund Gosse" (collected in *The Moment: and Other Essays*, 1948) that while his aim in criticism was "to illumine, to make visible and desirable" the literature that was overlooked, "he directs our attention only to its more superficial aspects."

EDMUND GOSSE AND JOHN CHURTON COLLINS AT ODDS

In 1884 Edmund Gosse was awarded a lecturer position at Cambridge. That same year he traveled to the United States, presenting his lecture "From Shakespeare to Pope: An Inquiry into the Causes and Phenomena of the Rise of Classical Poetry in England." Written in his traditional witty and colloquial style, it garnered accolades from the American literary community. However, it was also marred by his usual disregard for correct names and dates, and John Churton Collins, who had recently been turned down for a position at Oxford, found this to be unconscionable. When the lecture was released in book form in 1885, Churton Collins wrote a review that is still known as one of the worst in history, going on for forty-one pages.

Collins's main complaint concerned Gosse's ineptitude as a serious scholar. Lamenting that Gosse had included in his lecture books that he clearly had not read, Collins accused him of having an "utter incapacity for the task," as well as a "habitual inaccuracy with respect to dates." Gosse received letters of sympathy from his many prominent literary friends, but the general consensus was that Collins's assessment was accurate. Ann Thwaite, Gosse's biographer, notes that he retained his position at Cambridge due mostly to his amiable personality.

A few years after Woolf's essay, Ruth Zabriskie Temple's book *The Critic's Alchemy: A Short History of the Introduction of French Symbolism in to England* was published. Temple expresses mixed feelings akin to Woolf's, stating that while Gosse was "among the first of the critics writing for a large audience to

Edmund Gosse, English poet, author, and critic. Drawing by Frank Dicksee. © LEBRECHT MUSIC AND ARTS PHOTO LIBRARY/ ALAMY

study French and English literature from a comparative point of view," he still neglected to "explain the technical experiments of the Symbolists," which for the time was a large omission. Amanda French similarly acknowledges Gosse's shortcomings in the journal *Victorian Poetry* (2010) while still attributing to him the twentieth-century trends toward formalism in the United States, led by poets Dylan Thomas, Theodore Roethke, Sylvia Plath, and later Elizabeth Bishop. It is the breadth of Gosse's influence, rather than the depth of his analysis, that is noted by contemporary scholars.

Gosse's propensity for factual error has meant that his criticism has garnered less respect from current scholars, who demand more precision than those of the Victorian era. In her article, French traces in detail his false history of the villanelle and explains how his narrative came to be accepted as fact after Gosse penned the entry to the 1911 *Encyclopedia Britannica.* However, scholars of biographical research continue to laud what is considered his masterwork, *Father and Son* (1907). The book moves fluidly between the lives of Phillip Gosse (his father) and the author and was seen as genre-breaking for this reason. Writing in *One Mighty Torrent: The Drama of Biography* (1937), Edgar Johnson considers it to be "not the story of the father's life, still less of his son's, but the story of a relationship and struggle."

BIBLIOGRAPHY

Sources

Collins, John Churton. "English Literature at the Universities." *Quarterly Review* 163 (1886): 289-329. *Literature Resource Center.* Web. 9 Nov. 2012.

Gosse, Edmund W. "A Plea for Certain Exotic Forms of Verse." *Cornhill Magazine* 36.211 (1877): 53. *British Periodicals.* Web. 6 Nov. 2012.

French, Amanda L. "Edmund Gosse and the Stubborn Villanelle Blunder." *Victorian Poetry* 48.2 (2010): 243. *Literature Resource Center.* Web. 9 Nov. 2012.

Fulton, Richard D. Rev. of *Victorian Literary Critics,* by Harold Orel. *Victorian Studies* 29.2 (1986): 336-38. *JSTOR* Web. 9 Nov. 2012.

Temple, Ruth Z. "Sir Edmund Gosse." *The Critic's Alchemy: A Short History of the Introduction of French Symbolism in to England.* New York: Twayne, 1953. Print.

Woolf, Virginia. *The Moment and Other Essays.* New York: Harcourt, Brace, 1948. Print.

Further Reading

Cohen, Rachel. "The Very Bad Review." *New Yorker* 6 Oct. 2003: 52. *Literature Resource Center.* Web. 9 Nov. 2012.

Gide, André. *The Correspondence of André Gide and Edmund Gosse, 1904-1928.* Ed. Linette F. Brugmans. New York: New York UP, 1959. Print.

Gosse, Edmund. *Father and Son: A Study of Two Temperaments.* London: Folio Society, 1972. Print.

Thwaite, Ann. *Edmund Gosse: A Literary Landscape, 1849-1928.* London: Secker & Warburg, 1984. Print.

Wyke, Clement H. "Edmund Gosse as Biographer and Critic of Donne: His Fallible Role in the Poet's Rediscovery," *Texas Studies in Literature and Language* 17 (1976): 805-19. *JSTOR.* Web. 9 Nov. 2012.

Amanda French

THE POETS AND THE PEOPLE

By One of the Latter

Oscar Wilde

OVERVIEW

The Poets and the People: By One of the Latter (1887) by Irish writer Oscar Wilde discusses the failure of English poets to address the social unrest spurred by economic depression in England in the late 1880s. The document was directed primarily at the poets of the time and their academic followers in order to draw attention to the faults of their publications; it was also addressed to the people of England who, Wilde believed, were in need of a poet to increase their morale during the financially turbulent atmosphere of the Industrial Revolution. Wilde demands that poets step up to meet the needs of the people and produce poetry that appeals to English people from all classes, lifting spirits and generating a sense of unity instead of focusing on pessimistic writing accessible only to intellectuals.

The lack of response to the work and the tendency of academics to overlook it in their scholarship about Wilde suggest that *The Poets and the People* was largely ignored by scholars and poets alike. While the document supported Wilde's writing style—which garnered success during his time, particularly in the theater—it was the life and trials of the man himself that occupied the interest of his followers. *The Poets and the People* did nothing to damage or maintain that reputation because it provided little new information beyond a short critique of the work of Robert Browning. Even this did not have a great impact, however, and Wilde later published a literary essay outlining his views on the great English poet.

HISTORICAL AND LITERARY CONTEXT

The Poets and the People is primarily concerned with the writing style of critically acclaimed poets and the inaccessibility of that style to the working and middle classes of English society during a time of social turmoil. In a nod to romantic poets' concern for the democratization of poetry, Wilde expresses his view that the language used by the great English poets is too convoluted and too academic to be understood by the common people of England. Furthermore, the subject matter of their poetry is pessimistic and unintelligible, qualities that Wilde writes are detrimental to the moral well-being of the reading audience. He suggests that by producing works in this manner, the poets of his time are ignoring their calling: instead of promoting optimism and morality among their fellow countrymen—as Wilde states is the duty of a poet—the most influential writers, such as Browning, instead prefer to write in a style that does not appeal to the society at large and does not improve morale when it is most needed.

The Poets and the People was published in early 1887, when England was in a depression that resulted in large numbers of unemployed, a mass migration into urban centers, and a significant drop in wages. In London demonstrations had been staged to protest the social stratification occurring in that city, where the vastly wealthy lived alongside the desperately poor. In the midst of these troubles, Wilde, a known proponent of the "art for art's sake" movement with a reputation for promoting eccentricity and irony within his literary works, released *The Poets and the People* as a call for poets to fulfill their duty and uplift the morale of their fellow Englishmen. Although it received little attention, the work fit with Wilde's general literary agenda, which, because of the man's eccentricities, had accumulated a fair amount of fame.

The Poets and the People was written in response to *Parleyings with Certain People of Importance in Their Day* (1887) by Browning and the acclaim it received among literary critics. Wilde was also influenced by criticism about his own poetry collection, specifically from critics who played on his last name, calling Wilde's poetry "tame" because it did not deal with pessimistic ideals or use convoluted language. By writing *The Poets and the People* from the perspective of "one of the latter," Wilde reacts to his critics by drawing attention to the broader impact of poetry that can reach a more inclusive audience.

Despite Wilde's impact on English literature and the massive body of criticism that accompanies his many works, *The Poets and the People* received little notice in comparison to his plays and fiction. The work is a statement of Wilde's opinions about literature and its social importance, but it presents nothing that has not been discussed in his more popular works. Even his opinions of Browning were later published in a critical essay titled "The True Function and Value of Criticism," in which the writer uses the academic medium of literary criticism to address the problems of Browning's work to the audience for which it was written.

❖ *Key Facts*

Time Period:
Late 19th Century

Movement/Issue:
Aesthetics; Poetics

Place of Publication:
England

Language of Publication:
English

OSCAR WILDE AND HIS ECCENTRIC REPUTATION

Born in 1854 in Dublin to a surgeon father and a poet mother, Oscar Wilde was introduced to classic literature through a formal education at Trinity College, Dublin, and Magdalen College, Oxford. He quickly developed a reputation for being eccentric and acquired a cultlike following for his promotion of artifice and the glorification of youth. The years between 1881 and 1887 are generally considered to be his most active in terms of his literary career. He edited *Women's World,* a fashionable women's magazine, and lectured in England and in the United States in addition to publishing his own work, including numerous articles and a poetry collection, *Poems* (1881). He made significant contributions to the British theater in the 1890s.

In 1886 Wilde, in part because of his desire to subvert the moral code of the Victorian era in which he lived, began following his homosexual inclinations with actions that landed him in prison in 1895. His trial and conviction changed the way his works were read, a phenomenon that queer theorists would discuss a century or so after his death. Publications that are often read through the lens of queer theory include *Lord Arthur Saville's Crime and Other Stories* (1891), in which Wilde develops his own feelings as a criminal of society, and *The Picture of Dorian Gray* (1891), in which Wilde discusses the supremacy of youth and beauty.

Portrait of Oscar Wilde by Napoleon Sarony, circa 1882. © ARCHIVE PICS/ ALAMY

THEMES AND STYLE

The main theme of *The Poets and the People* is that the people of England are in need of a poet to create "a spirit of enthusiasm among all classes of society" at a time when the lower classes were facing desperate poverty and the capitalists needed to be saved from their own greed. Wilde asserts that poets are the best people for this task because "the hour has come when the poets should exercise their influence for good, and set fairer ideals before all than the mere love of wealth." The current poets of the time, including the illustrious Englishman Browning, were not rising to the occasion, preferring to write in a pessimistic style or to use such elaborate language that the majority of Englishmen could not understand it. Wilde declares that "England was never in greater need of such a man, and it is Mr. Browning's duty, if he has the ability, to write plain English and act the poet's true part." By reaching only the elite members of society with the diction of his poetry, Browning, according to Wilde, is shirking his proper calling as a poet and doing a disservice to his country.

Wilde develops his argument by contrasting the style of poetry he felt was necessary to lift the spirits of English people with the style of poetry being produced and acclaimed in England at the time. He argues that "tirades of pessimism require but little intellectual effort, and the world is not much the better for them." The ability "to inspire a people with hope and courage," however, and "to fill them with a desire after righteousness and duty" is "work that requires the combination of intelligence and feeling of the highest order." By opposing pessimistic and inspiring styles of poetry in this manner, Wilde establishes a good-bad binary in which he can discuss the works of prominent English poets—such as Browning—as "bad" while the nation needs someone to produce "good" poetry.

Wilde's text plays on the academic organization expected of a work of criticism but uses "plain English." By presenting his arguments in this manner, he is stylistically promoting the type of writing he feels poets should produce in order to reach the people of England. Wilde draws attention to the language in question by calling on "any sensible man" to "dip into the mysterious volume of literary hocus-pocus that has recently been so solemnly reviewed, and see whether he can find a single passage likely to stir the pulses of any man or woman, create a desire to lead a higher, a holier, and a more useful life in the breast of the indifferent average citizen." He demonstrates with his own selection of language that the diction of Browning's work lacks the inspiration needed to reach a population struggling with social and financial issues in late nineteenth-century England.

CRITICAL DISCUSSION

The initial reaction to *The Poets and the People* was lukewarm at best, with many critics overlooking it because of their fascination with the events in Wilde's life over the ideas expressed in his writing. In the essay

"Oscar Wilde: Orality, Literary Property, and Crimes of Writing" (2000), Paul K. Saint-Amour cites a 1900 letter from Robert Ross to Adela Schuster in which Ross expresses the trends of the time, noting that Wilde's "personality and conversation were far more wonderful than anything he wrote, so that his written works give only a pale reflection of his power." This attitude about Wilde reflects the lack of initial reaction to *The Poets and the People* despite the popularity of his ideas and the following he had acquired by this point in his career.

Like Wilde's contemporary critics, modern scholars typically do not mention *The Poets and the People,* although they examine the details of Wilde's life and analyze his writing in terms of the ideas forwarded in the document. Anne Margaret Daniel, in "Wilde the Writer" (2004), notes that Wilde "was born a teller of tales" and that the "power of his art as a writer can have no greater testament than the simple fact that Wilde made people feel." This ability reflects the central theme of *The Poets and the People*—that poets need to fulfill their duty of making readers feel in order to lift their spirits during times of difficulty. Recent scholarship tends to be more interested in the effects of Wilde's writing rather than on this particular work.

Today's scholars often examine Wilde's articles, manifestos, and literary criticism as a group, preferring to focus instead on his poetry, fiction, and plays. In *Oscar Wilde* (1986), Edouard Roditi points out that the "critical views that are scattered throughout" Wilde's works "have been restated in a more organized form in his critical dialogues," which are of more interest to scholars. Joseph Bristow also follows this trend in "Biographies: Oscar Wilde" (2004), admitting that "a number of [Wilde's] editorials on modern poetry count among the finest of the decade" but that they, like the rest of Wilde's "literary ambitions," have been largely overlooked because his readership wanted "to know more about him, since his image—rather than his writings—enjoyed increasing familiarity throughout the culture." Modern scholars examine

Wilde's writings in terms of theoretical structures relating to nationality, asceticism, and sexuality in his more popular works, while lesser-known works, such as *The Poets and the People,* tend to be overlooked.

BIBLIOGRAPHY

Sources

Bristow, Joseph. "Biographies: Oscar Wilde—The Man, the Life, the Legend." *Palgrave Advances in Oscar Wilde Studies.* Ed. Frederick S. Roden. Hampshire: Palgrave Macmillan, 2004. 6-35. Print.

Daniel, Anne Margaret. "Wilde the Writer." *Palgrave Advances in Oscar Wilde Studies.* Ed. Frederick S. Roden. Hampshire: Palgrave Macmillan, 2004. 36-71. Print.

Roditi, Edouard. *Oscar Wilde.* New York: New Directions, 1986. Print.

Saint-Amour, Paul K. "Oscar Wilde: Orality, Literary Property, and Crimes of Writing." *Nineteenth-Century Literature* 55.1 (2000): 59-91. *JSTOR.* Web. 31 Oct. 2012.

Wilde, Oscar. *The Poets and the People: By One of the Latter.* 1887. *Manifesto: A Century of Isms.* Ed. Mary Ann Caws. Lincoln: U of Nebraska P, 2001. 15-16. Print.

Further Reading

Browning, Robert. *Parleying with Certain People of Importance in Their Day: To Wit, Bernard de Mandeville, Daniel Bartoli, Christopher Smart, George Bubb Dodington, Francis Furini, Gerard de Lairesse, and Charles Avison.* Boston: Houghton Mifflin, 1887. *Google Books.* Web. 31 Oct. 2012.

Evangelista, Stefano, ed. *The Reception of Oscar Wilde in Europe.* London: Continuum, 2010. Print.

Salamensky, S. I. *The Modern Art of Influence and the Spectacle of Oscar Wilde.* Hampshire: Palgrave Macmillan, 2012. Print.

Wilde, Oscar. "The True Function and Value of Criticism." *Nineteenth Century* 28.161 (1890): 123-47. Rpt. in *Nineteenth-Century Literature Criticism.* Ed. Janet Mullane and Robert Thomas Wilson. Vol. 19. Detroit: Gale Research, 1988. *Literature Resource Center.* Web. 31 Oct. 2012.

Katherine Barker

PREFACE TO *CROMWELL*

Victor Hugo

✤ *Key Facts*

Time Period:
Early 19th Century

Movement/Issue:
Romanticism; Aesthetics

Place of Publication:
France

**Language of
Publication:**
French

OVERVIEW

The preface to the verse play *Cromwell* (1827) by Victor Hugo is a major statement of the ideals of romanticism, a European cultural movement that sought to supplant the neoclassical values of eighteenth- and early-nineteenth-century art. In a substantial essay introducing his play, Hugo insists upon the total creative freedom of the artist, unhampered by such rules as the Aristotelian unities of drama or the metrical demands of traditional verse. Hugo further maintains that art ought to mingle such elements as tragedy and comedy, sublime and grotesque, following the model furnished by nature. Hugo supports his assertion by sketching a cultural history in which Christianity has made artists aware of the striking dualities of life; this knowledge, in turn, demands a new literary form to replace the odes and epics of previous ages. For Hugo, this successor is the drama, and he considers William Shakespeare, with his genre-defying scenes and characters, its greatest exponent. Hugo surveys later (primarily French) authors in light of this Shakespearean standard, praising or condemning them in proportion to their willingness to flout convention.

Hugo's remarks resonated with many young artists of his generation, among them the novelist Théophile Gautier, who would establish romanticism in more militant terms before partly superseding it with "art for art's sake." By the 1830s the values that Hugo expounds were ascendant in French theater and literature; the romantics had, in essence, won. Today Hugo's preface is widely understood as a greatly influential statement of ideals that would pervade French art and literature during the nineteenth century. Scholars seeking to provide a definition of *romanticism,* a term with notoriously elusive boundaries in literary history, often take the preface to *Cromwell* as their point of departure.

HISTORICAL AND LITERARY CONTEXT

Hugo's preface addressed a French literary public divided in increasingly violent fashion between the neoclassicists (who insisted that drama preserve the Aristotelian unities of time, place, and action) and the romantics (who wished to jettison these conventions in favor of a more natural and lifelike approach). In the wake of Napoleon Bonaparte's defeat at Waterloo in 1815, these positions acquired a heightened political dimension, with the neoclassicists expressing an aversion to foreign literature in general and British literature in particular. In "Shakespeare, Women, and French Romanticism" (2004), Aimée Boutin explains that the performance of Shakespeare's works, increasingly popular in France during the early nineteenth century, represented both "a corrupting foreign influence" and "all that remained inassimilable to French neoclassicism."

Several years after Waterloo, when, according to Boutin, this "moment of French Anglophobia" had largely faded, Shakespeare retained his polarizing status among French theatergoers—especially those who sought to be influential as critics. In fact, a series of 1822 performances of Shakespeare's works in Paris resulted in rioting, with neoclassicist and romantic partisans coming to blows in the theater. Shakespeare would also become a touchstone for the romantic composer Hector Berlioz, the novelist George Sand, and many of Hugo's own *cénacle* (an informal circle of artists taking the place of the earlier salon). Hugo composed his historical play *Cromwell,* along with its polemical preface, in the years following these riots. It is no coincidence, therefore, that his portrayal of the history of art culminates in Shakespeare, who seemed both to his admirers and detractors a romantic avant la lettre.

Rather than a call for a sudden break with tradition, the preface to *Cromwell* is the crystallization of a romantic movement already well under way. As such, it cites a wide range of authors whom Hugo considers to anticipate his vision of artistic liberty; he focuses particularly on playwrights, such as Pierre Corneille and Jean Racine, whose genius Hugo cites as precedent for his own rebellion against the edicts of "good taste." Hugo's frequent references to the cultural commentators of the *feuilletonistes*—that is, the contemporary press—suggest that he considered his own preface to be at odds, stylistically and ideologically, with these conservative critics. Hugo likewise contests the theatrical judgments of Voltaire, who one-half century earlier had fought against the early encroachments of romanticism upon the French theater.

As a cultural call to arms, the preface long outlived the play that accompanied it and reinforced Hugo's status as the cynosure of a group of young French romantic authors. Indeed, the ideas expressed in Hugo's manifesto were widely influential not only among French writers but also in related romantic movements in Germany, Spain, Britain, and elsewhere. Further, as romanticism reached maturity, the leaders of its successor movements often drew upon Hugo's preface as a foundation for their own work. Hugo's essay was revered in particular by a young Gautier, who would expound his credo of "art for art's sake" in the preface to his novel *Mademoiselle de Maupin* (1835).

THEMES AND STYLE

Hugo opens his preface by establishing the basic ideals of romanticism as the inevitable and correct artistic response to human history, especially the cultural history underwritten by religion. He argues that the moral vision of Christianity shows that "the ugly exists beside the beautiful, the unshapely beside the graceful" and, most famously, "the grotesque on the reverse of the sublime." Hugo asserts that poetry at its best mixes these contrary aspects rather than attempting to eliminate or suppress the evil, the grotesque, and the ungainly. This naturalistic mingling of subjects and styles is, for Hugo, the major distinguishing feature of romantic (as opposed to classical) writing.

Shakespeare is the centerpiece of Hugo's argument, much of which rests on a willingness to take the English playwright's genius as peculiarly romantic in character. Citing Shakespeare as the weaver par excellence of the disparate elements he prizes, Hugo accords his predecessor a mythic place in literary history: Shakespeare is not only the "central pillar" of an edifice in which Dante Alighieri and John Milton are "supporting abutments" but also "the god of the stage, in whom, as in a trinity, the three characteristic geniuses of our stage, Corneille, Molière, [Pierre] Beaumarchais, seem united." Rhetorically this approach serves to establish a deep sense of continuity for romanticism, projecting its ambitions across centuries, nations, and (because Hugo construes Dante and Milton as dramatists who happened to write epics) literary genres.

In contrast to this grand historical project, Hugo works—somewhat disingenuously—to maintain a tone of modesty, expressing his reluctance to engage in aesthetic debate at all. He presents himself as "a solitary *apprentice* of nature and truth … who offers good faith in default of good taste, sincere conviction in default of talent, study in default of learning." The author was only twenty-five years old when the preface was published, decades away from the renown he would achieve in his mature career. Nonetheless, Hugo's excuses and apologies serve as an ironic foil to his ability to produce (citing "only what [he] can recall") six or seven examples from international literature to support any point he wishes to make. In further contrast to this sense of effortlessness, Hugo ventriloquizes his classicist opponents as "customs-officers of thought" whose objections are

A portrait of author Victor Hugo, painted by Leon Bonnat. Hugo defined the principles of the romantic movement in his preface to *Cromwell*. GIANNI DAGLI ORTI/THE ART ARCHIVE AT ART RESOURCE, NY

narrow-minded and hyperbolic. A favored tactic is to have them declare as obvious truths some clearly debatable point: "Don't you know that art should correct nature? that we must *ennoble* art?" By portraying his adversaries in this rather ridiculous light, Hugo underscores the vigor of his own arguments.

CRITICAL DISCUSSION

Hugo asserted that he had burdened *Cromwell* with a preface only at the insistence of his friends; the play itself went unperformed, but the preface helped to rally fellow romantics under Hugo's flag. Its effectiveness could be seen in 1830, when Hugo's next play, *Hernani,* was staged to the applause of a raucous and extravagantly dressed "Romantic army," who proceeded to shout down the classicist critics in attendance. In later years the preface to *Cromwell* became all but definitional of French romanticism. Beatrice Young, in a 1932 essay in *Modern Language Journal,* explains that in the century after its publication, the preface was almost "never … questioned as the utterance *par excellence* of romanticism unalloyed, or as nearly unalloyed as romanticism has ever been."

With the preface's reputation in France established beyond doubt, several critics have turned to the task of tracing its impact on other literary cultures. In "The Influence of Victor Hugo on Spanish Drama" (1933), Adelaide Parker and E. Allison Peers argue that Hugo's "precepts" were widely influential in nineteenth-century Spanish drama, though partly because they made "an appeal of familiarity and not of novelty" to a literary culture that held similar values during its seventeenth-century golden age. In her study "Victor Hugo in Russia" (1977), Carole Karp suggests that the preface played a major role in Hugo's mixed reception among Russian literary critics of his

PRIMARY SOURCE

PREFACE TO *CROMWELL*

Behold, then, a new religion, a new society; upon this twofold foundation there must inevitably spring up a new poetry. Previously—we beg pardon for setting forth a result which the reader has probably already foreseen from what has been said above— previously, following therein the course pursued by the ancient polytheism and philosophy, the purely epic muse of the ancients had studied nature in only a single aspect, casting aside without pity almost everything in art which, in the world subjected to its imitation, had not relation to a certain type of beauty. A type which was magnificent at first, but, as always happens with everything systematic, became in later times false, trivial and conventional. Christianity leads poetry to the truth. Like it, the modern muse will see things in a higher and broader light. It will realize that everything in creation is not humanly *beautiful,* that the ugly exists beside the beautiful, the unshapely beside the graceful, the grotesque on the reverse of the sublime, evil with good, darkness with light. It will ask itself if the narrow and relative sense of the artist should prevail over the infinite, absolute sense of the Creator; if it is for man to correct God; if a mutilated nature will be the more beautiful for the mutilation; if art has the right to duplicate, so to speak, man, life, creation; if things will progress better when their muscles and their vigour have been taken from them; if, in short, to be incomplete is the best way to be harmonious. Then it is that, with its eyes fixed upon events that are both laughable and redoubtable, and under the influence of that spirit of Christian melancholy and philosophical criticism which we described a moment ago, poetry will take a great step, a decisive step, a step which, like the upheaval of an earthquake, will change the whole face of the intellectual world. It will set about doing as nature does, mingling in its creations—but without confounding them—darkness and light, the grotesque and the sublime; in other words, the body and the soul, the beast and the intellect; for the starting-point of

day, who, toward the end of the 1800s, were sometimes greater admirers of the author than the French themselves. In her 1977 essay "The Influence of Victor Hugo on Esteban Echeverría's Ideology," Marguerite C. Suarez-Murias shows that Esteban Echeverría, "the ideological leader of the romantic movement in Argentina," likewise incorporated the ideals of the preface into his own, more overtly political variety of romanticism.

Later scholarship has continued to expand its claims for the preface to *Cromwell,* applying its rubric of the grotesque and the sublime not only to later literary movements, such as twentieth-century modernism, but also to the visual arts. For example, Patricia Mainardi, in "The Political Origins of Modernism" (1985), sees in Hugo's celebration of "ugliness" not only a championing of the contemporary artist Eugène Delacroix but also a foreshadowing of works by Gustave Courbet and Édouard Manet. Moreover, these critics have also worked to situate Hugo's statements in the greater context of European political and aesthetic thought, seeking out precedents for the playwright's major ideas. Thus Gene H. Bell-Villada, in his article "The Idea of Art for Art's Sake" (1986-87), considers the preface a "key document for the romantics in their struggle against Classicists" and, in its views on artistic autonomy, the successor to a tradition that includes not only Corneille and Molière but also Immanuel Kant and Anthony Ashley-Cooper.

BIBLIOGRAPHY

Sources

Bell-Villada, Gene H. "The Idea of Art for Art's Sake: Intellectual Origins, Social Conditions, and Poetic Doctrine." *Science and Society* 50.4 (1986-87): 415-39. *JSTOR.* Web. 14 Sept. 2012.

Boutin, Aimée. "Shakespeare, Women, and French Romanticism." *Modern Language Quarterly* 65.4 (2004): 505-29. *Project MUSE.* Web. 14 Sept. 2012.

Hugo, Victor. "Preface to *Cromwell.*" *Prefaces and Prologues to Famous Books.* Ed. Charles W. Eliot. New York: Cosimo, 2010. 354-408. *Google Book Search.* Web. 15 Oct. 2012.

Karp, Carole. "Victor Hugo in Russia." *Comparative Literature Studies* 14.4 (1977): 321-27. *JSTOR.* Web. 14 Sept. 2012.

Mainardi, Patricia. "The Political Origins of Modernism." *Art Journal* 45.1 (1985): 11-17. *JSTOR.* Web. 14 Sept. 2012.

Parker, Adelaide, and E. Allison Peers. "The Influence of Victor Hugo on Spanish Drama." *Modern Language Review* 28.2 (1933): 205-16. *JSTOR.* 14 Sept. 2012.

Suarez-Murias, Marguerite C. "The Influence of Victor Hugo on Esteban Echeverría's Ideology." *Latin Ameri-*

religion is always the starting-point of poetry. All things are connected.

Thus, then, we see a principle unknown to the ancients, a new type, introduced in poetry; and as an additional element in anything modifies the whole of the thing, a new form of the art is developed. This type is the grotesque; its new form is comedy.

And we beg leave to dwell upon this point; for we have now indicated the significant feature, the fundamental difference which, in our opinion, separates modern from ancient art, the present form from the defunct form; or, to use less definite but more popular terms, *romantic* literature from *classical* literature.

"At last!" exclaim the people who for some time past *have seen what we were coming at,* "at last we have you—you are caught in the act. So then you put forward the ugly as a type for imitation, you make the *grotesque* an element of art. But the graces; but good taste! Don't you know that art should correct nature? that we must *ennoble* art? that we must *se-lect*? Did the ancients ever exhibit the ugly or the grotesque? Did they ever mingle comedy and tragedy? The example of the ancients, gentlemen! and Aristotle, too; and Boileau; and La Harpe. Upon my word!"

These arguments are sound, doubtless, and, above all, of extraordinary novelty. But it is not our place to reply to them. We are constructing no system here—God protect us from systems! We are stating a fact. We are a historian, not a critic. Whether the fact is agreeable or not matters little; it is a fact. Let us resume, therefore, and try to prove that it is of the fruitful union of the grotesque and the sublime types that modern genius is born—so complex, so diverse in its forms, so inexhaustible in its creations; and therein directly opposed to the uniform simplicity of the genius of the ancients; let us show that that is the point from which we must set out to establish the real and radical difference between the two forms of literature.

SOURCE: *Prefaces and Prologues to Famous Books,* Vol. 39, edited by Charles W. Eliot. P.F. Collier & Sons, 1827.

can Literary Review 6.11 (1977): 13-21. *JSTOR.* Web. 14 Sept. 2012.

Young, Beatrice. "What Is Meant by Romanticism in France with Special Reference to the Drama." *Modern Language Journal* 16.5 (1932): 429-37. *JSTOR.* Web. 14 Sept. 2012.

Further Reading

Allen, James Smith. "Toward a Social History of French Romanticism: Authors, Readers, and the Book Trade in Paris, 1820-1840." *Journal of Social History* 13.2 (1979): 253-76. *JSTOR.* Web. 14 Sept. 2012.

Athanassoglou-Kallmyer, Nina. "Romanticism: Breaking the Canon." *Art Journal* 52.2 (1993): 18-21. *JSTOR.* Web. 14 Sept. 2012.

Guerlac, Suzanne. *The Impersonal Sublime: Hugo, Baudelaire, Lautréamont.* Stanford: Stanford UP, 1990. Print.

Wilcox, John. "The Beginnings of l'Art pour l'Art." *Journal of Aesthetics and Art Criticism* 11.4 (1953): 360-77. *JSTOR.* Web. 14 Sept. 2012.

Michael Hartwell

PREFACE TO *GERMINIE LACERTEUX*

Edmond de Goncourt, Jules de Goncourt

✥ *Key Facts*

Time Period:
Mid-19th Century

Movement/Issue:
Aesthetics; Naturalism;
Social realism

Place of Publication:
France

**Language of
Publication:**
French

OVERVIEW

Written by Jules de Goncourt and his older brother, Edmond, the preface to *Germinie Lacerteux,* a novel about the life of a servant in Paris that was also written by the Goncourts and published in 1864, presents an approach to novel writing that, in the nineteenth century, was innovative and contrary to both the moralistic social conventions of French society and the overall tastes of the reading public. The preface addresses readers in an apologetic fashion, advising caution to those about to enter the world of the book's protagonist, Germinie Lacerteux. Considered to be a seminal novel of the naturalist, or social realist, movement in literature, *Germinie Lacerteux* seeks to be true to life, wherein the Goncourts aim to portray a hitherto neglected segment of society and to reveal unwelcome verities about the society in which they lived. By carefully observing their society as scientists might study nature in an attempt to seek universal "truths" about their world, the Goncourts aim to enlighten readers with an honest representation of a humble but depraved woman.

At the time it was published, *Germinie Lacerteux* failed to inspire the public's charitable sensibilities for its main character, which was one of the authors' chief ambitions in writing the work. French society was ill prepared to embrace this new brand of starkly honest literature, finding the subject matter to be offensive and infuriating. The tale of Germinie Lacerteux recounts a life of depravity and offers an intimate view of an unpleasant reality, one about which the majority of readers preferred to remain naive. Neither the reading public nor the Goncourts' writing contemporaries could reconcile their incongruous reactions of disgust and sympathy for the novel's protagonist. Only French novelist Émile Zola, who would later be regarded as the father of the naturalist style of writing, praised the novel.

HISTORICAL AND LITERARY CONTEXT

Written during France's Second Empire, the preface to *Germinie Lacerteux* asserts that all classes of society are worthy subjects of great literature. Although members of upper-class French society themselves and nostalgic for the bygone days of the eighteenth century, the Goncourts rejected the style of the romantic era in their writings in favor of a more impressionistic style,

focusing on the "real" rather than the ideal. The "real" character of Germinie Lacerteux was, in fact, based on the Goncourts' own maid, Rose. The Goncourts wanted to convey in words, to the greatest extent possible, their emotional reactions to the world around them. Although far removed in social class from the subjects of their literature, the authors deemed themselves capable of portraying these characters realistically, based upon their nearly scientific observations of their milieu.

The Goncourts presented *Germinie Lacerteux* to the French public during an era of newfound liberties. The concept of a democratic society had been recently reintroduced in France. During an 1859 meeting of the general assembly, moves were made to transition Napoleon III's hitherto absolute empire into a more liberal, egalitarian form of government. This transition was largely due to public outcry over a new free-trade policy with Great Britain that increased competition against French industry and alienated the French business class. With the evolution toward a more democratic society, liberties, such as universal suffrage, freedom of the press, and freedom of speech, began to be restored. In the preface to *Germinie Lacerteux,* the Goncourt brothers insist that, during an era of democracy, the "lower orders" deserve a place in French literature. The preface implies that French society was hypocritical in its outward display of democracy, while it ignored the realities of entire segments of the population. The Goncourts hoped to remedy this disjuxtaposition of sentiment with their novel by using a scientific character study to realistically and truthfully portray a life of misery among the lower classes.

Echoing the sentiments first expressed by Honoré de Balzac in his 1835 preface to *Le Père Goriot,* in which he claims, "All is true," the preface to *Germinie Lacerteux* expands upon the notion of realism in literature, acting as a segue into the naturalistic style, which the Goncourts call *l'écriture artiste* (artistic writing). Before devoting their lives to literature, the brothers had pursued painting, and, as writers, they utilized their artistic background to paint pictures with words. Much like the impressionist painters of the same era, the Goncourts' writing style was not well received by French institutions of the day, such as the Académie des Beaux-Arts, the host of the official Paris

Salon art exhibition since 1725. In 1863 the academy rejected three thousand works of art, including those of Édouard Manet and James Whistler, deeming them unacceptable. With the approval of Napoleon III, these rejected artists exhibited their works exterior to the official salon, but the public and critics alike still reacted with criticism and ridicule. Criticism of innovative forms of artistic expression was not limited to artists. In 1857 Gustave Flaubert was tried and acquitted on charges of obscenity in a court of law for the content of his novel, *Madame Bovary.* Although the Second Empire witnessed a renaissance of the arts, it did so reluctantly.

While much less known than many works of naturalist literature, *Germinie Lacerteux* was a groundbreaking novel. In the decades following its publication, various writers, including Theodore Dreiser, James T. Farrell, and Stephen Crane, devoted their novels to the lives of the lower classes, often portraying sordid lifestyles that society would have preferred to keep hidden. Zola was perhaps the most influenced by the Goncourts' style. His working-class novel, *L'Assommoir* (1877), can be traced back to *Germinie Lacerteux.* Like the Goncourts in their preface to *Germinie Lacerteux,* Zola, in his preface to *L'Assommoir,* declares himself an arbiter of truth and a representative of the lower classes. Throughout the twentieth century, writers such as John Steinbeck, Ernest Hemingway, and John Dos Passos introduced readers to modern versions of realism and naturalism, becoming some of the most notable authors of all time. Perhaps the most enduring legacy of the Goncourts, however, are their journals, begun in 1851, in which they recorded the social, political, and literary life of their era. A selection titled *Pages from the Goncourt Journals* was first published in 1962.

THEMES AND STYLE

The principal theme of the preface to *Germinie Lacerteux* is that truth must be told in literature to give voice to the miseries often suffered among society's neglected classes, even if it disturbs the public's sensibilities. The Goncourts begin the preface with an apology and a caution: "We must ask the public to forgive us for presenting it with this book, and to warn it about what it will find therein." They then abruptly attack the public's tastes in literature, stating, "The public loves untrue novels…. It loves those books that pretend to move in polite society…. The public also likes insipid and consoling reading, adventures with a happy ending." The Goncourts explain that *Germinie Lacerteux* delivers the opposite: gritty truths "from the streets" meant to "challenge its habits and upset its health." The authors' reason for writing was not to shock their readers but to educate them. They felt that it is the democratic right of all members of society "without castes and a legal aristocracy" to be subjects within the nation's canon of literature and that they could "evoke pity as much as … the better parts of society."

LES FRÈRES GONCOURT

Born into nobility, Edmond and Jules de Goncourt were always conscious of their roots. They had an appreciation of the arts and a particular passion for eighteenth-century antiques. By 1848 the brothers were orphans, and they spent time traveling throughout France and Algeria. At first interested in the visual arts, the Goncourts became dedicated to writing literature by the 1850s.

The brothers were inseparable, living together and writing together, until Jules died in 1870. The Goncourts' works include histories such as *Histoire de la société Française pendant la Révolution* ("History of French Society during the Revolution") and biographies including as *Marie Antoinette.* After the death of Jules, Edmond continued his career as a writer, and in 1900 he established the Académie Goncourt, a literary society, in his brother's memory.

The Goncourts use the point of view of the aristocracy, a group to which they belonged, to address their fellow noblemen regarding the literature of the common members of society. They wanted to "show the happy citizens of Paris misery that should not be forgotten." Because of their own place in society, the Goncourt brothers felt the need to defend their choice of subject matter, not only by appealing to the conventions of modern nineteenth-century society, "of universal suffrage, of democracy, of liberalism," but also by harkening back to cherished artistic ideals from the past. They evoke tragedy, "that conventional form of a forgotten literature and a vanished society," which was familiar and acceptable to French nobility of the time. Finally, the Goncourts reference

Portrait of Edmond and Jules de Goncourt by Paul Gavarni. © LEBRECHT MUSIC AND ARTS PHOTO LIBRARY/ALAMY

the aristocracy of yore as a device for arousing understanding and charity among their reading public. They recall "what the queens of olden days let their children see in the hospitals: human suffering, immediate and alive, something which teaches charity."

Stylistically, the preface to *Germinie Lacerteux* uses a combination of humility and persuasiveness, appealing to the country's republican ideals to address the reader, often hypothesizing about their subject in the manner of a scientist, using phrases such as "We became curious to know" or "We asked ourselves whether." They call upon the French republican tradition of egalitarianism, writing, "In this age of equality in which we live, there could be, for writer and reader alike, social classes too unworthy" of inclusion in the nation's body of literature. By maintaining a tone of humility, referring to their "humble novel," and claiming that "it is of little importance if this book is vilified," the Goncourts divert any suggestion that they wrote *Germinie Lacerteux* simply to shock and offend the public.

CRITICAL DISCUSSION

When *Germinie Lacerteux* appeared in 1864, reactions were primarily negative. The largely moralistic public found the subject matter of the novel too disturbing for their tastes, and members of the aristocracy did not embrace the novel. Reviewers also did not appreciate it. In 1866 the *Saturday Review* wrote that it was "ghastly and immoral." Some reviewers were a bit more charitable, such as Yetta Blaze de Bury, who wrote in an 1896 article in the *Fortnightly Review* that "*Germinie Lacerteux* is not a bad book, since it is a 'humane novel,'" but "as for 'glory,' the centuries to come shall decide." Zola was nearly alone in his praise for the work, calling it "a superb study of living, throbbing humanity" in the prologue to Edmond's book, *Les frères Zemganno* (1894)—a work for which Edmond also wrote a preface in which he expands upon some of the issues addressed in the preface to *Germinie Lacerteux*.

The Goncourts' works, including the preface to *Germinie Lacerteux,* were important only in their own era, but their legacy is indisputable. The influence the Goncourts had upon Zola is evident in his preface to *L'Assommoir*. Zola writes, "I do not defend myself. My work will defend me. It is a work of truth, the first novel of the people, who do not lie, and has the smell of the people. And we must not conclude that the whole of the people are bad, because my characters are not bad." Beyond Zola, the realist and naturalist schools of writing remained popular throughout the nineteenth and twentieth centuries. The Goncourts, however, are rarely mentioned in modern scholarship, particularly in the English language, other than a mention of the importance of *Germinie Lacerteux* in setting the stage for other naturalist writers.

Recent scholarship on the preface to *Germinie Lacerteux* is scarce. B.F. Bart, in his essay in the book *Nineteenth-Century French Fiction Writers* (1992)

reaffirms that the Goncourts "played a role of considerable importance in the development of French culture, and especially the novel." With a modern-day perspective on women, Bart also writes, "The Goncourts had further problems in addition to that of public disapproval of their topic ... they had ... great difficulty understanding and depicting women convincingly in any context." Bart concludes, however, that "despite these handicaps, they produced a novel that is certainly their best-known work and perhaps their most significant one."

BIBLIOGRAPHY

Sources

Bart, B.F. "Edmond Louis Antoine Huot de Goncourt." *Nineteenth-Century French Fiction Writers: Naturalism and Beyond, 1860-1900.* Ed. Catharine Savage Brosman. Gale Research, 1992. Web. 9 Oct. 2012.

Bury, Yetta Blaze de. "Edmond de Goncourt." *Fortnightly Review* Sept. 1896: 333-49. *Literature Resource Center.* Web. 9 Oct. 2012.

Goncourt, Edmond and Jules de. "Preface to *Germinie Lacerteux* (1864)." *European Literature from Romanticism to Postmodernism.* Ed. Martin Travers. New York: Continuum, 2001. Print.

Hollier, Denis, ed. *A New History of French Literature.* Cambridge: Harvard UP, 1989. Print.

"Review of *L'Affaire LeRouge*." *Saturday Review* 15 Dec. 1866: 737-38. Gale Research, 1987. Web. 12 Oct. 2012.

Zola, Émile. "Les Frères Zemganno: The Preface." *Bookman* Sept. 1896: 52-53. *Literature Resource Center.* Web. 12 Oct. 2012.

———. "Preface de L'Assommoir." 1877. *In Libro Veritas,* 2006. Web. 12 Oct. 2012.

Further Reading

Auerbach, Erich. *Mimesis: The Representation of Reality in Western Literature.* Trans. Willard R. Trask. Princeton: Princeton UP, 1953. Print.

Coates, Carroll F., ed. *Repression and Expression: Literary and Social Coding in Nineteenth-Century France.* New York: Peter Lang, 1996. Print.

Gershman, Herbert S., and Kernan B. Whitworth. *Anthology of Critical Prefaces to the Nineteenth-Century French Novel.* Columbia: U of Missouri P, 1962. Print.

Goncourt, Edmond and Jules de. *Pages from the Goncourt Journals.* New York : Oxford UP, 1962. Print.

Gouze, Roger. *Les bêtes à Goncourt: Un demi-siècle de batailles littéraires.* Paris: Hachette, 1973. Print.

Heil, Elissa. *The Conflicting Discourses of the Drawing-Room: Anthony Trollope and Edmond and Jules de Goncourt.* New York: Peter Lang, 1997. Print.

Weber, Eugen. *Movements, Currents, Trends: Aspects of European Thought in the Nineteenth and Twentieth Centuries.* Lexington: D.C. Heath, 1992. Print.

Weir, David. *Decadence and the Making of Modernism.* Amherst: U of Massachusetts P, 1995. Print.

Lisa Mertel

PREFACE TO *LEAVES OF GRASS*

Walt Whitman

OVERVIEW

American poet and essayist Walt Whitman wrote the preface to the first edition of *Leaves of Grass* (1855) in order to contextualize his then-groundbreaking free verse as well as his vision of the new American poet. The preface celebrates both the diversity and forward-thinking spirit of America, calling the country "essentially the greatest poem," and the American poet as a paradoxical figure who is "commensurate with the people" and "transcendent and new." Addressed to the general reading public, the preface frames *Leaves of Grass* as a book intended for all Americans: for "the savage or felon" just as much for "the President or chief justice." Whitman encapsulates the preface's egalitarian thrust at the close of the document when he writes: "The proof of a poet is that his country absorbs him as affectionately as he has absorbed it."

Whitman's preface and poems in *Leaves of Grass* met with mixed reactions upon the book's release. In 1856, a year after its publication, Whitman reprinted the collection without the preface. In an 1870 letter written to friend Horace Traubel, the poet wrote that he did "not consider [the preface] of permanent value." Despite Whitman's self-assessment, he reformatted most of the essay as poetry and incorporated it into subsequent versions of his book (for example, "By Blue Ontario's Shore," "Song of Prudence," and "Song of the Answerer"). In his final years he recanted his disparaging opinion of the preface and claimed that he "underrated" the introduction, ultimately considering it "vital and necessary." The poet eventually republished the preface in *Complete Poems and Prose: 1855-1888* (1888). Today, most consider the initial permutation of *Leaves of Grass* to be a foundational document of American literature.

HISTORICAL AND LITERARY CONTEXT

The preface to *Leaves of Grass* responds to the contentious relationship between the North and the South in the United States, which stood on the precipice of civil war, as much as it does to English-influenced American poets such as Henry Wadsworth Longfellow. In 1854, a year before Whitman wrote his preface, Democrats passed the Kansas-Nebraska Act, allowing the newly formed territories to decide whether slavery within their boundaries would be legal. Escalating political tension resulted from the legislation, and southern politicians

began ratcheting up the rhetoric of secession. The preface's belief in the "largeness and generosity" of the American spirit and its claim that the "genius of the United States" does not reside in its "executives or legislatures" speaks to Whitman's hope that the states could remain united in their differences and to his fears that politicians would not resolve the dispute properly.

Around the time Whitman self-published the first edition of *Leaves of Grass,* violence broke out in the territory of Kansas. Abolitionists, known as Free-Soilers, and those in favor of slavery, known as Border Ruffians, met in a series of armed and political confrontations called "Bleeding Kansas." In October of that year, John Brown, a Connecticut-born abolitionist and revolutionary, traveled to Kansas, where he participated in several sieges, raids, and killings of Border Ruffians. He left the state in late 1856 to carry out his antislavery crusade elsewhere. With the publication of *Leaves of Grass,* Whitman intended to mollify the tension between the warring factions within the United States through a pro-American language of unity and a judicious sense of being that accepts lessons "with calmness" and to be "not so impatient" as to take to arms unnecessarily.

The preface to the 1855 edition of *Leaves of Grass* engages a tradition of poetic manifestos inherited from the Romantic poets, including William Wordsworth, Percy Bysshe Shelley, and Ralph Waldo Emerson. While Whitman professed a "radical difference" between himself and his British forebears, he also drew upon them heavily. His belief that the poet "is judgment" echoes Shelley's thought that "poets are the unacknowledged legislators of the world." Likewise, the American bard's praise of the common man and his "manners" and "speech" mirrors Wordsworth's preference for a poetry that reproduced "the real language of men in a state of vivid sensation." Whitman, of course, did not accept these poets and their ideas wholesale. In championing the use of free verse, the preface to *Leaves of Grass* derides poetry "marshalled [sic] in rhyme or uniformity" and instead lauds organic rhythms that "bud" from the landscape "as lilacs or roses." To this extent Whitman not only disavows the British Romantics but also American poets writing under their influence such as Henry Wadsworth Longfellow, who wrote *The Song of Hiawatha* (1855) in strict trochaic tetrameter.

❖ *Key Facts*

Time Period:
Mid-19th Century

Movement/Issue:
American Civil War;
Nationalism

Place of Publication:
United States

Language of Publication:
English

Portrait of Walt Whitman that accompanied the first edition of *Leaves of Grass.*
© LEBRECHT MUSIC AND ARTS PHOTO LIBRARY/ ALAMY

Since the publication of *Leaves of Grass,* Whitman's influence on American literature and culture has been monumental. William Carlos Williams, like Whitman in the preface of *Leaves of Grass,* promoted a poetry written in "plain American"; Allen Ginsberg's poem "Howl" employs a Whitmanesque vision of America updated for the mid-twentieth century; and the critic Harold Bloom has taken great pains to forge a direct connection between Whitman and the contemporary, Pulitzer Prize-winning poet John Ashbery. Even American poets critical of Whitman and his ideas could not escape him. In his essay "What I Feel about Walt Whitman" (1909), the American modernist poet and critic Ezra Pound writes that Whitman "*is* America," which is "disgusting" and "nauseating." Several years later Pound recanted these sentiments in his poem "A Pact" (1913), writing, "Walt Whitman— / I have detested you long enough" and "I am old enough now to make friends." Langston Hughes,

an African American poet associated with the Harlem Renaissance, voiced displeasure with Whitman's handling of race relations in his poem "I, Too" (1925) when he penned, "I, too, sing America. / I am the dark brother."

THEMES AND STYLE

The main theme of the preface to the 1855 edition of *Leaves of Grass* is America's need for great poets, what characteristics a poet needs to be called great, and Whitman's readiness to become one of them. To this extent Whitman believes that "American poets are to enclose old and new" in addition to incarnating the country's "geography and natural life." Moreover, the American poet must employ a "fluency of ... speech" in his poems that exemplifies his particular moment as well as exhibiting a "delight in music." A great poet, ultimately, is one who "knows the soul" and contains the ability to "channel thoughts and thing without increase or diminution," writing in a manner that presents the world as it appears to him through his art. Whitman qualifies these statements, though, by claiming that "America is the greatest poem" and that its citizens assist in composing that poem by acting as "the voice ... of liberty."

The preface employs an inclusive language, often in the form of catalogs. When Whitman mentions the need of an American poet to address geography, he produces an expansive but specific list of places and natural elements that one should write about, such as "Mississippi with annual freshets and changing chutes" or "cedar and hemlock and liveoak and locust and chestnut and cypress and hickory and limetree." Further promoting an inclusive spirit, he claims that there are many "great poets," and "one does not countervail another." It matters little if another poet harbors contradictory thoughts or opinions, for "American bards shall be marked for generosity and affection and for encouraging competitors." In the end it is the absorption of a poet into the country, and the country into the poet, that marks the great poets. Whitman frequently uses ellipses so that one syntactical unit and its corresponding idea can flow into another syntactical unit and its corresponding idea. In doing so he joins discrete ideas through punctuation, thus embracing the inclusive spirit at the level of composition.

The tone of Whitman's preface is exuberant and optimistic. In the opening paragraph, for example, the poet calls Americans "stalwart and wellshaped" and, echoing Darwin's rhetoric, the "fittest for his days." Whitman highlights the text's positive emotional tenor with superlatives, saying that of "all nations the United States ... most need poets" and "have the greatest use" of the "greatest poets." Affirmative absolutes are another technique found in the preface. Whitman believes a poet's duty is to "make every word he speaks draw blood"; when writing of the country's "enormous diversity," he exclaims that the "union always" relates to "all free American" people.

CRITICAL DISCUSSION

The 1855 edition of *Leaves of Grass* and its preface received mixed reviews upon release. Shortly after the book's publication, Whitman sent a copy to essayist, poet, and philosopher Ralph Waldo Emerson, who called it a "wonderful gift" and an "extraordinary piece of wit and wisdom" and longed to "greet him at the beginning of a long career." For the occasion of the 1856 reprinting of *Leaves of Grass,* Whitman excerpted portions of the letter for marketing purposes without permission, and Emerson forced him to retract the material. Rufus Griswold, a critic who, according to Heather Morton, also "ruined Poe's reputation shortly after his death," panned Whitman's work as unpoetic, accusing him of homosexuality and sodomy, which at the time was illegal. Complicating the book's initial reception was the fact that Whitman wrote many anonymous reviews, often championing himself as an independent, "pure American breed" who makes "no allusions to [previous] books or writers."

As the years progressed and Whitman continued to revise, augment, and reprint *Leaves of Grass,* the collection, if not the preface, increasingly received more acclaim from contemporary writers and critics. In his essay "Whitman's Poetic Translations of His 1855 Preface," Willie T. Weathers argues that the disregard Whitman later showed for his preface stemmed from the fact that the poet used it as a "quarry" to be mined for poetry. Once he took all he needed from it, Whitman could "disparage it with a careless word" because it no longer was of use to him. When the preface reappeared in *Complete Poems and Prose: 1855-1888,* Sylvester Baxter wrote in the *Boston Herald* that the introduction to the 1855 version of *Leaves of Grass* was "invaluable" and it should be considered "a masterpiece of composition in the grand style. Its thoughts borne free on the wings of a spontaneous rhythm."

Today scholarship addresses several different aspects of the preface. Morton's "Democracy, Self-Reviews, and the 1855 *Leaves of Grass*" examines the preface as a framing document used by Whitman to "prepare readers to understand [the book] on its own terms" and not according to normative conceptions of poetry. Weathers's essay approaches the preface more analytically, tracing which words, phrases, passages, and sentences found their way into particular poems. In "Walt Whitman and the Poetics of Reprinting" Meredith L. McGill positions the preface

as a document that enabled the poet to experiment with "techniques for extending his poetic voice, using poetic and publishing strategies that draw our attention elsewhere for an account of origins, cultivate a ranges [*sic*] of possible response."

BIBLIOGRAPHY

Sources

Baxter, Sylvester. "Whitman's Complete Works." *Boston Herald* 3 Jan. 1889: 4. *Whitman Archive.* Web. 25 July 2012.

Hughes, Langston. "I, Too." *Poets.org.* American Academy of Poets. Web. 24 July 2012.

McGill, Meredith L. "Walt Whitman and the Poetics of Reprinting." *Walt Whitman, Where the Future Becomes Present.* Iowa City: U of Iowa P, 2008. Print.

Morton, Heather. "Democracy, Self-Reviews, and the 1855 Leaves of Grass." *Virginia Quarterly Review* 81 (2005): 229-43. Print.

Pound, Ezra. "A Pact." *Poetry: A Magazine of Verse* Apr. 1913: 11-12. *The Poetry Foundation.* Web. 24 July 2012.

———. "What I Feel about Walt Whitman." *Poets.org.* American Academy of Poets. Web. 24 July 2012.

Weathers, Willie T. "Whitman's Poetic Translations of His 1855 Preface." *American Literature* 19 (1947): 21-40. Print.

Further Reading

Dana, Charles A. Rev. of *Leaves of Grass,* by Walt Whitman. *New York Daily Tribune* 23 July 1855: 3. *Walt Whitman Archive.* Web. 25 July 2012.

Kaplan, Justin. *Walt Whitman, A Life.* New York: Perennial, 2003.

Marki, Ivan. "*Leaves of Grass,* 1855 edition." *Walt Whitman: An Encyclopedia.* 1998. *Walt Whitman Archive.* Web. 24 July 2012.

Norton, Charles Eliot. Rev. of *Leaves of Grass,* by Walt Whitman. *Putnam's Monthly: A Magazine of Literature, Science, and Arts* 6 Sept. 1855: 321-23. *Walt Whitman Archive.* Web. 25 July 2012.

Schulenberg, Ulf. "'Strangle the Singers Who Will Not Sing You Loud and Strong': Emerson, Whitman, and the Idea of a Literary Culture." *AAA [Arbeiten aus anglistik und amerikanistik]* 31.1 (2006): 39-63. Print.

Tayson, Richard. "Back down to Earth: On Walt Whitman's Preface to the 1855 *Leaves of Grass.*" *Poets.org.* American Academy of Poets. 2005. Web. 24 July 2012.

Whitman, Walt. "Walt Whitman and His Poems." *United States Review* 5 Sept. 1855: 205-12. *Walt Whitman Archive.* Web. 25 July 2012.

Joshua Ware

PREFACE TO *LYRICAL BALLADS*

William Wordsworth

✧ *Key Facts*

Time Period:
Early 19th Century

Movement/Issue:
Aesthetics; Literary
Romanticism

Place of Publication:
England

**Language of
Publication:**
English

OVERVIEW

Preface to *Lyrical Ballads* (1800), written by William Wordsworth, defends the poetics of *Lyrical Ballads,* specifically the collection's use of common speech and rustic subject matter. The original 1798 version, which contains poems by both Wordsworth and Samuel Taylor Coleridge, does not include the Preface; instead, it contains an "Advertisement" that briefly, and much less systematically, describes the reasoning behind the collection's aesthetic. Upon the first reprinting of *Lyrical Ballads* in 1800, Wordsworth details their then-innovative poetry with an extended explanation. The next reprinting, in 1802, opens with a further updated and revised Preface. By defining poetry as "the spontaneous overflow of powerful feelings," the Preface to *Lyrical Ballads* signals a shift from mimetic representation to an expressive theory of art that places the poet/artist at the center of the artistic product. Addressed to a literate English audience, Wordsworth's introduction champions poetry composed in the "real language of men" over "frantic novels, sickly and stupid German Tragedies, and deluges of idle and extravagant stories in verse."

The first edition of *Lyrical Ballads* sold well but met with harsh criticism from reviewers. Shortly after its publication, Robert Southey wrote in an article in the *Critical Review* that Coleridge and Wordsworth's collection had "failed" because it focused on "uninteresting subjects." Likewise, upon its first reprinting, Francis Jeffrey wrote in the *Edinburgh Review* that, although the collection achieved popularity, it was characterized by "perverseness and bad taste." As years passed, though, reaction to Wordsworth's document changed considerably. Today, most consider the Preface to *Lyrical Ballads* to be the first and most important articulation of the Romantic movement in English literature, describing the world, poet, and imagination and the "infinite complexity" that exists between them.

HISTORICAL AND LITERARY CONTEXT

The Preface to *Lyrical Ballads* responds to social, economic, and literary conditions during the close of the eighteenth century in England. With the Industrial Revolution well underway, citizens of the United Kingdom moved in droves from rural environments to urban centers to find work in the increasingly manufacturing-based economy. Wordsworth believed that harsh working conditions, monotonous tasks, and excessively long hours blunted "the discriminating powers of the mind," leading to "a state of savage torpor." The poet thought that common men, to escape from "the uniformity of their occupations," sought "extraordinary incident[s]," and his poems were designed to counteract "this degrading thirst after outrageous stimulation." The imagination, he believed, is most powerfully stimulated by the natural world and man's communion with it.

Another historical factor that influenced the framework of the Preface was the French Revolution, which Wordsworth alludes to when he references "the great national events which are daily taking place." From 1789 through 1799, the people of France, burdened by poverty and hunger, revolted against the monarchy of King Louis XVI. Those leading the revolution promoted political, economic, and social equality among all citizens. Wordsworth writes in praise of poetry that will "give full account of the present state of the public taste," not just verse expressing the language and ideals of the aristocracy, but poetry that will retrace "the revolutions, not of literature alone, but likewise of society itself." Indeed, the poet considered his Preface and subsequent poems to contain a revolutionary impulse.

The Preface announces the collection of poems as a remedy to two prevailing trends in English literature. First, Wordsworth wanted to write and promote poetry that worked in contrast to verse infused with "gaudiness and inane phraseology." Such a claim, no doubt, acted as a recrimination of poetry written during the preceding Augustan Age. Augustan poetry, ornamental and highly stylized, more often than not employed allusions to classical mythology and culture that likely were not common knowledge to rural and working-class people. Second, the Preface openly derides Gothic novels as "frantic." Wordsworth despised this genre, calling it a "general evil," stating he was "almost ashamed to have spoken of the feeble effort with which [he] endeavoured to counteract it."

The ideas found within the Preface spawned several reactions. On the one hand, the document inspired the imaginative poetry of late-Romantic writers such John Keats and Percy Bysshe Shelley; on the other hand, the Preface created a fissure between

Wordsworth and Coleridge, the latter distancing himself from its populist ideas in *Biographia Literaria* (1817). Wordsworth's ideas, as well as his poetry, would eventually give way to Victorian poetry, which neglected the common man in favor of stories that focused on the retelling of classic literature or tales of nobility, such as Alfred, Lord Tennyson's "Ulysses" and "The Lady of Shalott." Today, the Preface functions as a touchstone for poets who champion plainspoken verse, nature poetry, poetry of the imagination, or emotive poetry.

THEMES AND STYLE

Wordsworth's primary argument in the Preface to *Lyrical Ballads* is that the purpose of poetry is to induce pleasure within a reader. He defines poetry as "the spontaneous overflow of powerful feelings." These feelings are reproductions of emotional states the poet previously experienced, which he recalls during a poetic process of meditation. He believes a poem must address "situations from common life" and use "the real language of men in a state of vivid sensation," fitting both into a "metrical arrangement." Wordsworth posits meter as an important aspect of a poem, even though it does not mimic regular speech patterns, because "the pleasure received from metrical language depends" upon "the perception of similitude in dissimilitude." By this he means that emotion in poems can be so strong and often times erratic that it needs the regularity of meter as a counterbalance.

Knowing that his collection of poems employs a different aesthetic from mainstream poetry, Wordsworth labels his project an experiment, providing himself with the conceptual leeway afforded by a test or trial. To his mind, if the poems failed, the audience should at least concede that he was brave to attempt something new. Additionally, because the full Preface was not published until the second printing, he employs an appeal of ethos when he says the first printing "pleased a greater number" than he expected. When addressing specific elements of his poetry, particularly a language stripped of artifice, Wordsworth uses appeals of logos, such as example, cause and effect, and syllogisms, to support his claims. He concludes the Preface with an acknowledgment of the poor reviews the first edition received: "I have one request to make to my reader, which is, that in judging these poems he would decide by his own feelings genuinely, and not by reflections upon what will probably be the judgment of others."

The Preface does not employ the terse imperatives often found within manifestos. In fact, Wordsworth uses phrases that convey humility, for example, saying he was "flattered" when the collection's first printing "pleased a greater number" of people than he thought possible. Likewise, Wordsworth admits he requested that Coleridge contribute to the collection because, as a writer, he understands his "own weakness." As the Preface moves forward, Wordsworth's

A nineteenth-century portrait of poet William Wordsworth. NATIONAL TRUST PHOTO LIBRARY/ART RESOURCE, NY

tone becomes more confident when describing his project and poetry in general. He boldly asserts, "Poetry is the first and last of all knowledge—it is … immortal." When addressing competing aesthetics and genres, he strikes a decidedly antagonistic tone, for example, calling ornamental verse gaudy and "inane." Toward the end, Wordsworth reverts to the humble tone he opened with, using phrases such as "Long as I have detained my reader, I hope he will permit me." He closes the document by shifting agency to the audience, even to the extent that they "will determine how far" he has "attained" his "object."

CRITICAL DISCUSSION

The first printing of *Lyrical Ballads* received mixed reactions. While it sold well, critics did not respond to it well. Robert Southey wrote in the October 1798 *Critical Review* that the narratives of poems like "Idiot Boy" do not deserve "the labour that appears to have been bestowed upon" them. Likewise, he finds Coleridge's contribution "absurd or unintelligible." Southey acknowledges that the Advertisement, which amounts to a proto-Preface, calls the poems "experiments" and functions as a de facto apology, but he is "altogether displeased" with *Lyrical Ballads.* Subsequent printings received similarly scathing criticism. Francis Jeffrey wrote an article about the collection in the October 1807 *Edinburgh Review.* While he acknowledges that Wordsworth's book has been "unquestionably popular," Jeffrey believes "a great source of pleasure" has been "cut off" by the poet's implementation of a "ridiculous" diction. He calls the "lofty, tender, or impassioned conceptions, with objects and incidents" that Wordsworth proposes in the Preface "low, silly, or uninteresting."

Over time, perception of the Preface and its corresponding poems altered dramatically. In 1833 John Stuart Mill invokes Wordsworth's definition of poetry when writing his essays "What Is Poetry?" and "The Two Kinds of Poetry," forwarding the poet's ideas about spontaneity, using external stimuli to create "scenery" that corresponds to "human feeling," and producing pleasure within an audience. In his seminal study on Romantic poetry, M.H. Abrams conceptualizes the Preface as the first public announcement by a poet who conceives of his role in the poem as a "major element generating both the artistic product and the criteria by which it is to be judged." By the mid-twentieth century, scholars of English literature hailed Wordsworth's treatise as a monument to expressive theories of art and poetry.

The Preface's most enduring legacy, arguably, has been its influence on poetry of the English language. American poets of the early twentieth century echoed Wordsworth's sentiments, expressed when he spearheaded the Romantic movement that included Coleridge, Keats, and Shelley. In his 1923 epic meditation on poetry and the imagination, *Spring and All,* William Carlos Williams advocated for poetry written in "plain American" and spoken "from the soul," not in overly florid language, "Sanscrit [*sic*] or... Latin." Wordsworth's obsession with imagination, specifically as an image "recollected" from the external world, resurfaces in the poetry of Wallace Stevens; in "Adagia" (*Opus Posthumous,* 1959) Stevens writes, "In poetry at least the imagination must not detach itself from reality." More recently, in his debut book *Some Trees* (1978), poet John Ashbery published "The Instructional Manual," an imaginative poem in the tradition of Wordsworth's "Tintern Abbey." The insistence on using common language in poetry continued into the twenty-first century—for example, with 2004 poet laureate of the United States Ted Kooser and his belief in "diction drawn from common speech" and subjects "chosen from the everyday world."

BIBLIOGRAPHY

Sources

Abrams, M.H. *The Mirror and the Lamp: Romantic Theory and the Critical Tradition.* New York: Oxford University Press, 1953. Print.

Jeffrey, Francis. "Review of *Poems, in Two Volumes.*" *Edinburgh Review* 11 (1807): 214-31. *English Poetry 1579-1830: Spenser and the Tradition.* Web. 25 June 2012.

Mill, John Stuart. "What Is Poetry?" *Critical Theory Since Plato.* Ed. Hazard Adams. New York: Harcourt Brace Jovanovich, Publishers, 1971: 536-43. Print.

Owen, W.J.B. Introduction. *Wordsworth & Coleridge Lyrical Ballads 1798.* 2nd edition. New York: Oxford University Press, 1971. Print.

Southey, Robert. "Review of *Lyrical Ballads.*" *Critical Review* 24 (1798). *William Wordsworth: News, Commentary, Poetry.* Web. 25 June 2012.

Williams, William Carlos. *Spring and All.* Paris: Contact Publishing, 1923. Print.

Further Reading

Bialostosky, Don H. "Coleridge's Interpretation of Wordsworth's Preface to *Lyrical Ballads.*" *PMLA* 93.5 (1978): 912-24. Print.

Boehnen, Scott. "The Preface to *Lyrical Ballads*: Poetics, Poor Laws, and the Bold Experiments of 1797–1802." *Nineteenth-Century Contexts: An Interdisciplinary Journal* 20.3 (1997): 287-311. *Taylor & Francis Online.* Web. 27 June 2012.

Chandler, James. *England In 1819: The Politics of Literary Culture and the Case of Romantic Historicism.* Chicago: The University of Chicago Press, 1998. Print.

Franta, Andrew. "Wordsworth, Commodification and Social Concern: The Poetics of Modernity." *Eighteenth-Century Studies* 45.1 (2011): 161-63. Print.

Hess, Scott. "Wordsworth's Epitaphic Poetics and the Print Market." *Studies in Romanticism* 50.1 (2011): 55-78. Print.

Perry, Seamus. "Wordsworth, Mill, and the Force of Habit." *Wordsworth Circle* 42:2 (2011): 116-22. *Literature Online.* Web. 27 June 2012.

Williams, Raymond. *The Country and the City.* New York: Oxford University Press, 1973. Print.

Joshua Ware

PREFACE TO *MADEMOISELLE DE MAUPIN*

Théophile Gautier

OVERVIEW

The preface to Théophile Gautier's 1835 novel *Mademoiselle de Maupin* puts forth a new interpretation of Victor Cousin's term *l'art pour l'art* (art for art's sake), which became the governing philosophy of bohemian aestheticism in the mid-nineteenth century. The preface is an essay written in the voice of one of the novel's main characters, Chevalier D'Albert, through whose letters a large portion of the novel is dispatched. Aimed at critics who hold that art and literature should serve some purpose, such as furthering public understanding of morality, Gautier's preface asserts instead that "everything useful is ugly," and that true art exists solely for the sake of being beautiful. The preface acts as a founding charter establishing the standards for modern aestheticism, whereas the novel puts those standards into practice.

The book did not quite sell "at the rate of five hundred copies a minute," as Gautier (presumably jokingly) boasted in the preface that it would. This was due in part to opposition to its sexual content from the moralist and utilitarian critics he was addressing in the preface and from the French government. Because of growing support for the dictums set forth by Gautier in the preface, however, the book later gained the favor of such notable literary figures as Honoré de Balzac and Charles Baudelaire. Although aestheticism as a literary movement enjoyed limited success in the latter half of the nineteenth century, today the shift in artistic ideals proposed by Gautier and enacted by the aesthetes is seen as signaling the beginning of the end of romanticism and as greatly influencing the subsequent emergence of modernism.

HISTORICAL AND LITERARY CONTEXT

The ideas set forth in the preface to *Mademoiselle de Maupin* respond to increased social, economic, and cultural emphasis on utility during the European industrial revolution of the late eighteenth and early nineteenth centuries. This shift began to materialize in the production and discussion of art via the Saint-Simonians, an early French socialist movement. Although their primary focus was on issues of political economy and labor, the Saint-Simonians espoused the ideas of Claude Henri de Rouvroy, comte de Saint-Simon, which included the perception of art as a revered by-product of gainful employment. The group gained favor with prominent European artists, including composer Franz Liszt, and their ideals were later echoed outside continental Europe in the sensibility- and work-oriented social dynamics of Victorian-era Britain.

Gautier released his novel at the height of Saint-Simonian influence in France, addressing the group directly in several passages of the preface. He argues against the spilling over of social sensibility into artistic creation, envisioning the two as distinct from one another. He was criticized for advocating decadence, both in art and in personal conduct. The argument was further leveled when symbolists and decadents—the latter a movement that centered largely on the indulgence of all sensory desires—began citing Gautier as having influenced their philosophies. Ultimately, the symbolists gained more traction than the decadents, and Gautier's ideals were transmitted to future generations most saliently via their publications.

In the preface to *Mademoiselle de Maupin,* Gautier draws from a rich tradition of employing introductory text as a vehicle for an ideological platform. As an admirer of the romantics, Gautier likely draws most heavily from poet William Wordsworth's preface to *Lyrical Ballads* (1798), which acts as a founding charter for the critical theory of romantic literature. In the preface, Wordsworth puts forward the framework for a new species of poetry, one founded in accessible language rather than in the elevated diction typical of eighteenth-century poetry. He provides the now-ubiquitous definition of poetry as "the spontaneous overflow of powerful emotions recollected in tranquility," suggesting the separation of conscious intention from the composing process, and valuing spontaneity and emotional honesty over strained and unnatural figurations for the sake of formal precision.

By 1834 Gautier had grown weary of the melodrama and evangelism of utilitarian and moralist artists and critics. Through his preface, he lays the framework for a radical overhaul of artistic ideals as a whole. Gautier's was not the last such proclamation, as his interpretation of *l'art pour l'art* was modified again—and perhaps taken a step further—in the manifestoes of the movements his work informed, particularly the symbolists'. In 1886 Greek poet Jean

⁌ *Key Facts*

Time Period:
Mid-19th Century

Movement/Issue:
Bohemian aestheticism;
Simonianism

Place of Publication:
France

**Language of
Publication:**
French

GAUTIER AND BAUDELAIRE: FRIENDLY RIVALS

The sincerity of Charles Baudelaire's glowing treatment of Gautier in the pages of *L'Artiste* in 1859 has long been debated, due in no small part to the fact that Gautier had assumed editorship of the review in 1856, implying a certain sense of obligation on the part of Baudelaire to avoid offending a patron of his work. But the two men clearly shared a kinship of spirit, if not an overt affinity. Both were prolific consumers and reviewers of visual art, which has been perceived by those who question Baudelaire's rapport with Gautier as a source of tension.

Of the two, Baudelaire is today considered the more substantive and representative art critic of his time. In their historical moment, however, Gautier was more revered by the artists he reviewed. In fact, in 1862, he was asked to sit as a member of the Société Nationale des Beaux-Arts (National Society of Fine Arts) alongside such major figures as Édouard Manet and Gustave Doré. Some scholars have even suggested that Baudelaire might have harbored a secret resentment of and jealousy for Gautier's success.

Moréas published the *Symbolist Manifesto,* naming Baudelaire and Stéphane Mallarmé among his cohorts in believing artistic expression is a goal in itself.

THEMES AND STYLE

Gautier's preface to *Mademoiselle de Maupin* centers largely on the argument against the idea that a work of art has to have a discernible function—be it practical, political, or moral. He decries the Saint-Simonian watchword *utility* and the group's insistence that every useful thing is the expression of some need. Needs and desires, Gautier argues, "are ignoble and disgusting, like [a man's] own poor and infirm nature." To these critics and to the "moral journalists," he contends, "Neither grand features like Michael Angelo's, nor curiosities worthy of Callot, nor effects of light and shade after the manner of Goya—nothing could find favor in their eyes." In a summative assessment, Gautier says of both types of critic, "They are simply men who have been at college with us, and who have evidently profited less by their studies than we."

In building his case, Gautier employs feigned melodrama in the name of satire, as outdated moralistic melodramas are one of the few types of art he claims critics still seem willing to tolerate. "Virtue is assuredly very respectable," he states in the opening passages, "and we have no wish to fail in any respect to her. God forbid!" Extending the metaphor further, Gautier describes virtue's appearance and disposition, coming to the conclusion that "[s]he is a very agreeable grandmother—but she is a grandmother," and therefore has no place either in works of art or

criticism thereof. Against the utilitarian approach to criticism, particularly that of the Saint-Simonians, Gautier adopts a similarly mocking melodrama. "No, fools, no … a book does not make gelatine soup; a novel is not a pair of seamless boots," he exclaims. "By the guts of all the popes past, present, and future, no, and two hundred thousand times no!"

The tone driving the preface is defiant, at times even militant. In Gautier's estimation, the utilitarians and moralists are not simply offering subjective feedback, they are violently attacking the legitimacy of art itself, which Gautier seems to feel is the only pure thing left in an increasingly tarnished and sordid industrialized world. To the utilitarian argument, he responds, "A hollow cube measuring seven or eight feet every way, with a hole to breathe through, a single cell in the hive, nothing more is wanted to lodge him and keep the rain off his back." He then begins building a case for the hypocrisy of utilitarian critics, arguing that they do not live as minimally as their critical assessments seem to indicate they profess others should. Nor should they, Gautier argues, condensing the basis of his resistance to the utilitarian position to a simple dictum. He writes, "[T]o prevent one's self from dying is not living."

CRITICAL DISCUSSION

Although little criticism of *Mademoiselle de Maupin* or its preface was immediately offered, a sense of the common public response to Gautier's work can be gathered from the historical anecdotes of contemporary scholars. In a 2008 article in *Studies in Romanticism,* Margueritte Murphy reports that Gautier was viciously attacked in the pages of *Le Constitutionnel* for an article he wrote on François Villon, a fifteenth-century poet notorious for being a violent outlaw. The publication labeled his article a work of depravity, and when "a defamation suit launched on behalf of Gautier was dismissed," he set about composing the preface in defense of his position to publicly declare his intention to affect a shift in artistic ideals. Some twenty years after the novel's release, Baudelaire finally began defending Gautier and his position. In an 1859 article for *L'Artiste,* Baudelaire submitted that the preface to *Mademoiselle de Maupin* "had above all the important result of establishing once and for all the exclusive love of the Beautiful, the *Fixed Idea,* as the generating condition of works of art." The article concludes with Baudelaire's overall assessment of Gautier as "the equal of the greatest in the past, a model for those who are to come … A PERFECT MAN OF LETTERS."

Gautier's legacy lies not necessarily in the impact of his creative works but rather in the literary movements that took his dictums as their founding principles. Gautier, as Murphy notes, "articulated an aesthetic posture for the generation of artists and poets who defined modernity," his ideas informing the frameworks of both the French symbolists and the British aesthetes. These two groups, particularly the symbolists, influenced much of the modernist philosophy, or at least the philosophies of some of its star constituents. Most notable among them were Ezra Pound and T. S. Eliot, the latter explicitly noting in an interview for the *Paris Review* the influence of Gautier on Eliot's understanding of the relationship between form and content.

Today scholars uphold both Gautier's preface and the movements that he inspired. Mary Gluck, for example, in a 2000 article for *Modernism/Modernity,* maintains that "The ultimate achievement of Gautier's creative vision was to give voice to a new definition of the modern artist." Gluck sees this definition as distinctly post-Bohemian, one in which the artist is "a speaker of parables and allegories whose task was to translate the esoteric truths of aesthetic experience" rather than to evangelize any one social or moral truth. She suggests that this ethos foretells the modernist vision of the artist as a vessel for truth, rather than the architect thereof.

BIBLIOGRAPHY

Sources

Baudelaire, Charles, and Francis E. Hyslop. *Baudelaire as a Literary Critic.* University Park: Pennsylvania State UP, 1964. Print.

Gautier, Théophile. *Mademoiselle de Maupin.* New York: Modern Library, 1900. Print.

Gluck, Mary. "Theorizing the Cultural Roots of the Bohemian Artist." *Modernism/Modernity* 7.3 (2000): 351-378. *Academic OneFile.* Web. 10 Sep. 2012.

Murphy, Margueritte. "Pure Art, Pure Desire: Changing Definitions of *l'art pour l'art* from Kant to Gautier." *Studies in Romanticism* 47.2 (2008): 147-161. *Academic OneFile.* Web. 10 Sep. 2012.

Svarny, Erik. *"The Men of 1914": T. S. Eliot and Early Modernism.* Philadelphia: Open UP, 1988. Print.

Further Reading

Dorra, Henri. *Symbolist Art Theories: A Critical Anthology.* Berkeley: U of California P, 1994. Print.

Leitch, Vincent B. *The Norton Anthology of Theory and Criticism.* New York: Norton, 2001. Print.

"Presumptions of Progress: Two Prefaces." *New England Review* 23.4 (2002): 199. *Academic Search Complete.* Web. 10 Sep. 2012.

Sova, Dawn B. *Literature Suppressed on Sexual Grounds.* New York: Facts On File, 2006. Print.

Symons, Arthur. *The Symbolist Movement in Literature.* New York: Dutton, 1958. Print.

Ward, Patricia A., and James S. Patty. *Baudelaire and the Poetics of Modernity.* Nashville: Vanderbilt UP, 2001. Print.

Weber, Eugen. *Movements, Currents, Trends: Aspects of European Thought in the Nineteenth and Twentieth Centuries.* Lexington: Heath, 1992. Print.

Clint Garner

Portrait of Théophile Gautier by Jean-Baptiste Clesinger, 1851. GIANNI DAGLI ORTI/THE ART ARCHIVE AT ART RESOURCE, NY

PREFACE TO *THE PICTURE OF DORIAN GRAY*

Oscar Wilde

✤ *Key Facts*

Time Period:
Late 19th Century

Movement/Issue:
British aesthetic
movement;
Anti-Victorianism

Place of Publication:
England

**Language of
Publication:**
English

OVERVIEW

Written as a defense against charges of immorality levied upon the serialized version of *The Picture of Dorian Gray* (1890), Oscar Wilde's preface to *Dorian Gray* (1891) argues that art is amoral and champions the creation of "beautiful things" as the artist's only imperative. Though inspired by earlier artistic theories, the preface is widely viewed as a primary document of the British aesthetic movement, which utilized art to subvert traditional Victorian values and expose the hypocrisy of a society that emphasized above all the appearance of gentility.

The serial publication in *Lippincott's Magazine* of *The Picture of Dorian Gray*—the story of an attractive young man who is granted eternal youth and pursues a life of debauchery, only to find that a portrait of him painted by an enamored artist grows increasingly grotesque with each of his indecent acts—was met with a chorus of outrage and indignation (a review in the *Daily Chronicle* called it a "poisonous book" rife with "moral and spiritual putrefaction"). Wilde refuted the reviews in lengthy letters to the editors of literary publications. Finding those met with similar disdain, he published his preface to the book form of the novel in *Fortnightly Review* in March 1891, arguing, "There is no such thing as a moral or an immoral book. Books are well written, or badly written. That is all." Though the preface did not entirely rehabilitate Wilde's public reputation—he was imprisoned from 1895 to 1897 on charges of indecency—it galvanized the aesthetic movement and established Wilde as its hero. As Bruce Michelson notes in *Literary Wit,* "Wilde's preface ... changed not only the literary and cultural persona of Oscar Wilde but also the literary culture itself," calling it "the most eloquent and durable literary manifesto of the modern era."

HISTORICAL AND LITERARY CONTEXT

The preface to *Dorian Gray* is a product of the social and artistic upheaval of late-nineteenth-century England. The Industrial Revolution produced an upwardly mobile middle class, severely disrupting the traditional social order. Queen Victoria (r. 1837-1901) ushered in a code of strict morality and social conduct predicated on personal responsibility and intended to counteract the perceived depravity of the Georgian era. The elites embraced these conservative values as a way of clinging to their sense of superiority, while the middle class adhered to Victorian morality to signal their newfound refinement and dignity.

By the time Wilde published the preface to *Dorian Gray* in 1891, the polite and virtuous facade of British society had worn thin; Victorian morality did not radically transform citizens' behavior but merely forced them to camouflage their baser instincts. Furthermore, while industrialization brought more people into the workforce, it replaced well-trained craftspeople and artisans with factory workers whose jobs reduced them to little more than living machines producing cheap consumer goods. For Wilde, this emphasis on usefulness and morality transformed social life into a grotesque masquerade. As Derek Hand notes in *A History of the Irish Novel,* "Victorian life by necessity opens up a world of disguise, masking and, ultimately, hypocrisy."

Wilde rejected the repressive effects of industrialism and Victorianism on public life and art. In the early nineteenth century, writers were expected to reinforce the prevalent social values and minimize or ignore class and gender conflicts. In the latter half of the century, however, Charles Dickens, Thomas Hardy, the Brontë sisters, and American expatriate Henry James began to explore the darker side of Victorian society. In his essay "The Art of Fiction" (1884), James attacks "the moral timidity of the usual English novelist," typified by a "cautious silence on certain subjects." Theorist Walter Pater translated French novelist Théophile Gautier's preface to *Mademoiselle de Maupin* (1835), in which the author argues that "nothing is truly beautiful except that which is useless" and espouses "l'art pour l'art," or "art for art's sake." Wilde's preface is frequently compared to Gautier's, as Wilde himself proclaims that "all art is quite useless" in the final line.

Wilde's preface challenges readers to reevaluate their relationship to art by arguing that "it is the spectator, and not life, that art really mirrors." This argument is a subtle break from the realism of Dickens and other late Victorian novelists, implying that the artist is free to set aside the constraints of reality and morality to bring something "new, complex, and vital" into the world, to counteract the regimented ugliness and hypocrisy of Victorian existence with unencumbered beauty. Wilde's preface helped to popularize the aesthetic principles of formal experimentation and artistic freedom that became central to modernism, as exemplified by James Joyce's *Ulysses* (1922). Wilde's preface has become the predominant English text advocating "art for art's sake," leading critic Gene H. Bell-Villada to suggest in 1996 that "when Anglophone readers know anything about Art for Art's Sake, it is usually via this two page text."

THEMES AND STYLE

Wilde's preface is thematically simple: the artist has no responsibility but to create beautiful art, and beautiful art has no intrinsic value but in the feelings that it inspires in the spectator. "Those who find ugly meanings in beautiful things are corrupt without being charming," he argues, suggesting that the pervasive undercurrent of ruthlessness and vice in Victorian society (and in the critics themselves) are what cause critics to decry the supposed immorality of a work of art. In opposition to such "corrupt" spectators, Wilde posits an "elect" and "cultivated" group of individuals "who find beautiful meaning in beautiful things" and to whom "beautiful things mean only Beauty."

Stylistically, the preface is often obtuse and contradictory. As Norbert Kohl notes in *Oscar Wilde: The Works of a Conformist Rebel,* "If one … compares Wilde's theoretical precepts with the novel itself, one cannot help but be struck by certain inconsistencies. How, for instance, is one to reconcile the thesis that 'There is no such thing as a moral or immoral book,' as claimed in the preface, with the description of the yellow book in chapter X as a 'poisonous book'?" Most critics view such inconsistencies as evidence of Wilde's mischievous literary persona, with Michelson likening them to "a sidelong smile" and "a playful wave of the cigarette." Wilde casually grounds his argument in the literary tradition, making several allusions to well-known works that support or amplify his thesis. His support for "the elect to whom beautiful things mean only Beauty" echoes John Keats's 1820 poem "Ode on a Grecian Urn," which concludes with the lines "'Beauty is truth, truth beauty,'—that is all / Ye know on earth, and all ye need to know." He also makes repeated reference to Caliban, the half-man, half-beast of William Shakespeare's *The Tempest* (1623), to describe Victorians' own secret, beastly nature. "The nineteenth century dislike of realism is the rage of Caliban seeing his own face in a glass," he writes, suggesting that critics who attack realism in fact only dislike what it reveals about themselves and their society. Conversely, he argues, "The nineteenth century dislike of Romanticism is the rage of Caliban not seeing his own face in a glass."

PRIMARY SOURCE

PREFACE TO *THE PICTURE OF DORIAN GRAY*

The artist is the creator of beautiful things. To reveal art and conceal the artist is art's aim. The critic is he who can translate into another manner or a new material his impression of beautiful things.

The highest as the lowest form of criticism is a mode of autobiography. Those who find ugly meanings in beautiful things are corrupt without being charming. This is a fault.

Those who find beautiful meanings in beautiful things are the cultivated. For these there is hope. They are the elect to whom beautiful things mean only beauty.

There is no such thing as a moral or an immoral book. Books are well written, or badly written. That is all.

The nineteenth century dislike of realism is the rage of Caliban seeing his own face in a glass.

The nineteenth century dislike of romanticism is the rage of Caliban not seeing his own face in a glass. The moral life of man forms part of the subject-matter of the artist, but the morality of art consists in the perfect use of an imperfect medium. No artist desires to prove anything. Even things that are true can be proved. No artist has ethical sympathies. An ethical sympathy in an artist is an unpardonable mannerism of style. No artist is ever morbid. The artist can express everything. Thought and language are to the artist instruments of an art. Vice and virtue are to the artist materials for an art. From the point of view of form, the type of all the arts is the art of the musician. From the point of view of feeling, the actor's craft is the type. All art is at once surface and symbol. Those who go beneath the surface do so at their peril. Those who read the symbol do so at their peril. It is the spectator, and not life, that art really mirrors. Diversity of opinion about a work of art shows that the work is new, complex, and vital. When critics disagree, the artist is in accord with himself. We can forgive a man for making a useful thing as long as he does not admire it. The only excuse for making a useless thing is that one admires it intensely.

All art is quite useless.

SOURCE: London: Ward, Lock and Company, 1891.

The language of the preface is authoritative and lively but somewhat disinterested, as if the whole fiasco surrounding the novel is nothing but an inconvenience for Wilde. Bell-Villada calls the preface "high-wire intellectual juggling at its most self-assured and masterful." Wilde's preface—and ultimately his entire literary output—comes across as a playful antagonism of readers who would denigrate transcendent works of art by forcing them to conform to arbitrary notions of morality. "When critics disagree the artist is in accord with himself," Wilde writes. Of course, he was also concerned with maintaining his livelihood, so the preface takes on a quasi-apologetic tone, embodying what Michael Patrick Gillespie

Watercolor portrait of Oscar Wilde (1895) by Henri de Toulouse-Lautrec. ERICH LESSING/ART RESOURCE, NY

The preface represents a watershed moment in the transition between romanticism and modernism and a death knell for Victorianism. Michelson writes, "It proved to be a breakthrough, or a breakout, in the practice of literary manifestoes, popping the gas-filled balloon of pietistic and reasonable genteel Victorian disputation." Though aestheticism was relatively short-lived, the movement introduced several literary and artistic principles that remain in practice and under debate, and the preface to *Dorian Gray* stands as its central document. And yet, as Michelson rightly points out, "in the midst of a storm of fine publication about Wilde's aesthetics, his martyrdom, and his impact on modern and postmodern culture, there is very little in the way of sustained commentary on the preface as a discrete text."

Indeed, most studies of the preface treat it as an extension of the thoughts developed in *The Picture of Dorian Gray,* perhaps rightfully so given that it was written as a sort of primer for critics that would, as Kohl suggests, "inculcat[e] them with the 'right' set of artistic values in the hope of influencing their reviews." While many of the ideas in the preface are now commonplace in philosophical debates over the nature of art and beauty, literary critics of Wilde tend to study his works in relation to his literary persona, particularly in psychoanalytic, gender studies, and Queer Theory circles, and thus view the preface as further evidence of his iconoclastic and progressive disposition in the face of a stultifying social milieu on the brink of collapse.

describes in his essay in *Oscar Wilde and the Poetics of Ambiguity* (1996) as "the equilibrium that he sought to establish between an inclination toward accommodation and a disposition toward outrageousness."

CRITICAL DISCUSSION

Wilde's insistence that a beautiful work of art has no meaning beyond what the spectator subconsciously brings to it was predictably attacked by his unrelenting critics. Some accused him of "decadence" in an attempt to associate him with Charles Baudelaire, Paul Verlaine, and Arthur Rimbaud, but like these authors, Wilde wore the term as a badge of honor that distinguished him from his Victorian contemporaries. Others published parodies of the preface in prominent weeklies. As Joseph Bristow points out in his introduction to *The Complete Works of Oscar Wilde Vol. 3,* the satirical magazine *Punch* "trivialized Wilde's aphorisms by stating that the numerous bold asterisks that separated each epigram in the *Fortnightly Review* made it plain that this document was nothing more than a 'literary flower-bed,' one in which the reader could sniff the derivative nature of his maxims." Nevertheless, the preface was widely read along with the novel and contributed to Wilde's status as one of the wittiest and most vexing authors of his day.

BIBLIOGRAPHY

Sources

Bell-Villada, Gene H. "The Diffusion of the Doctrine I: England." *Art for Art's Sake and Literary Life: How Politics and Markets Helped Shape the Ideology and Culture of Aestheticism, 1790-1990.* Lincoln: U of Nebraska P, 1996. 57-96. Print.

Bristow, Joseph. Introduction. *The Complete Works of Oscar Wilde,* vol. 3. New York: Oxford UP, 2005. xi-lx. Print.

Gillespie, Michael Patrick. "Cultural and Aesthetic Responses in Wilde's Essays: Approaching *The Picture of Dorian Gray.*" *Oscar Wilde and the Poetics of Ambiguity.* Gainesville: UP of Florida, 1996. 36-56. Print.

Hand, Derek. "Living in a Time of Epic: The Irish Novel and Literary Revival and Revolution, 1891-1922." *A History of the Irish Novel.* Cambridge: Cambridge UP, 2011. 114-43. Print.

Kohl, Norbert. "Culture and Corruption: *The Picture of Dorian Gray.*" *Oscar Wilde: The Works of a Conformist Rebel.* Cambridge: Cambridge UP, 1989. 138-75. Print.

Michelson, Bruce. "A Calendar and a Preface: Mark Twain's *Pudd'nhead Wilson's Calendar* and Oscar Wilde's Preface to *Dorian Gray.*" *Literary Wit.* Amherst: U of Massachusetts P, 2000. 37-72. Print.

Wilde, Oscar. *The Picture of Dorian Gray.* London: Ward, Locke, 1891. Print.

Further Reading

Brown, Julia P. *Cosmopolitan Criticism: Oscar Wilde's Philosophy of Art.* Charlottesville: UP of Virginia, 1997. Print.

Constable, Liz, Dennis Denisoff, and Matthew Potolsky. *Perennial Decay: On the Aesthetics and Politics of Decadence.* Philadelphia: U of Pennsylvania P, 1999. Print.

Danson, Lawrence. *Wilde's Intentions: The Artist in His Criticism.* Oxford: Clarendon, 1997. Print.

Dowling, Linda C. *The Vulgarization of Art: The Victorians and Aesthetic Democracy.* Charlottesville: UP of Virginia, 1996. Print.

Foldy, Michael S. *The Trials of Oscar Wilde: Deviance, Morality, and Late-Victorian Society.* New Haven: Yale UP, 1997. Print.

Mendelssohn, Michèle. *Henry James, Oscar Wilde and Aesthetic Culture.* Edinburgh: Edinburgh UP, 2007. Print.

Jacob Schmitt

REALIST MANIFESTO

Gustave Courbet

✣ *Key Facts*

Time Period:
Mid-19th Century

Movement/Issue:
Aesthetics; French
Revolution of 1848

Place of Publication:
France

**Language of
Publication:**
French

OVERVIEW

Gustave Courbet's "Realist Manifesto," written in 1855, describes the artist's belief that art should depict the realities of contemporary life rather than be restricted to grand or historical themes. It also conveys the political implications of Courbet's artistic choices within the tumultuous climate of mid-nineteenth-century France after the Revolution of 1848 and during the Second French Empire of Napoleon III, which began in 1852. Courbet penned the four-paragraph statement after three of his works, including *The Painter's Studio* (1854-55) and *The Burial at Ornans* (1849-50), were rejected by the jury of the Universal Exposition in Paris. In response, Courbet organized a private show, called the Pavilion of Realism, to display his work. Although he demurred that the title "Realist" was artificially imposed, his document provided a coherent statement of the aesthetic and political aims

that he and other Realist painters shared. The manifesto is a statement against romanticism, idealism, and neoclassicism, styles typified by the "official" artists of the Exposition, including Eugène Delacroix and Jean-Auguste-Dominique Ingres. "To be able to translate the customs, the ideas, the appearances of my epoch … in a word to create living art, that is my goal," Courbet writes.

Courbet further expanded on this brief manifesto in an open letter he published in 1861, in which he emphasizes his disagreement with the academic teaching of art, both in its preferred subject matter and its hierarchical organization. For Courbet, realism was not about the perfect repetition of line or form—instead, it was a rough and spontaneous application of paint that evoked the irregularity and immediacy of nature. Both his subject matter and his techniques led some critics to accuse him of deliberately "courting uglincss." Courbet's political convictions eventually led to a six-month jail term and self-imposed exile in Switzerland after the failure of the Paris Commune, but his art had a significant influence on the developing impressionist movement and later artists.

THE ARTIST'S STUDIO: A VISUAL MANIFESTO

One of the most famous of Courbet's paintings displayed at the Pavilion of Realism in 1855 was the vast *The Painter's Studio, a real allegory summing up seven years of my artistic life* (141.33 by 235.43 inches). This painting is often considered a manifesto in itself, a visual summation of Courbet's view of the artist and his role in society. "It's the whole world coming to me to be painted," he writes, "on the right, all the shareholders, by that I mean friends, fellow workers, art lovers. On the left is the other world of everyday life, the masses, wretchedness, poverty, wealth, the exploited and the exploiters, people who make a living from death."

The figures on the right side of the painting include the poet Charles Baudelaire, art critic Champfleury, philosopher and anarchist Pierre-Joseph Proudhon, and art collector Alfred Bruyas. Figures on the left include a priest, a merchant, a worker's wife, an Irishwoman nursing a child, and a hunter resembling Napoleon III. The guitar and dagger on the floor to the left are often seen as symbolic rejections of traditional academic painting. The painting treats artists and Courbet's own work on the epic scale of history paintings: Courbet sits painting a realist landscape in the center of the work, beside an innocent child and a model whose contemporary clothing is at her feet.

HISTORICAL AND LITERARY CONTEXT

French Realist art emerged prominently after the Revolution of 1848 and the publication of Karl Marx and Friedrich Engels's *Communist Manifesto* that same year. Ross Finnochio writes in "Nineteenth-Century French Realism," "As French society fought for democratic reform, the Realists democratized art by depicting modern subjects drawn from the everyday lives of the working class." Courbet and the other realists were not interested in history painting, the genre favored by the Paris Salon at the time and the predominant style in many national artistic academies. History painting was primarily associated with a grand style and scale, depicting famed historical figures or subjects from Scripture and classical literature. These works often had a moral theme, in contrast to the less highly esteemed "genre paintings" depicting everyday life.

Realism also coincided with the development of photography, which challenged aesthetic definitions of realism while also documenting some of the motifs realist painters depicted, particularly scenes of peasant and working-class life. Realist painting was further influenced by the emerging style of realist literature,

typified by French authors such as Honoré de Balzac and Gustave Flaubert. Courbet's work grew out of the earlier romantic movement, which was characterized by an interest in the simplicity of rural life and folk traditions, as is seen in the work of painter Jean-François Millet. He was further influenced by the rapidly growing popular press, which featured such artists as Honoré Daumier, who produced lithographs dealing with everyday life and social themes. In an 1851 letter, Courbet declared, "I am not only a socialist, but also a democrat and a republican, in a word, a partisan of revolution and, above all, a realist, that is, the sincere friend of the real truth." He styled his manifesto after other political manifestos and essays circulating at the time.

In addition to scenes of rural life, Courbet was particularly influenced by the Dutch masters, including Rembrandt and Frans Hals. Works by these artists strengthened Courbet's conviction that painters should focus on depicting the world around them. His early works, especially self-portraits such as *The Desperate Man* (1844-45), also show the influence of the romantic movement. Courbet's circle included the poet Charles Baudelaire, the art critic Champfleury, and the anarchist Pierre-Joseph Proudhon. Courbet repeatedly emphasized his independence, both political and artistic, at one point saying, "I am fifty years old and I have always lived in freedom; let me end my life free; when I am dead let this be said of me: 'He belonged to no school, to no church, to no institution, to no academy, least of all to any régime except the régime of liberty.'"

In addition to scenes of rural life, Courbet applied his concept of realism—"the negation of the ideal," as he put it—to other subjects, including erotic nudes (deemed pornographic by some at the time) and seascapes. Courbet is considered a significant influence on many painters, including the impressionists (particularly Édouard Manet, Claude Monet, and Paul Cézanne), the German Leibl circle, and Americans James McNeill Whistler and Edward Hopper. More generally, the realist movement profoundly inspired artists of all types to choose subjects based on the lives and struggles of ordinary people rather than focus solely on the famous and powerful.

THEMES AND STYLE

By penning his manifesto and staging his own show, Courbet self-identified as a "Realist" and laid out the basic aesthetic principles of the movement: the dedication to painting scenes of everyday life and the rejection of the official academic tradition. This artistic decision was deeply political at the time, representing a rejection of the old monarchical and imperial traditions. Although the subjects Courbet addressed had been depicted previously, his works were considered radical because of the political implications of elevating peasant life to the same epic scale as grand subjects of history paintings. Whereas rural scenes often had been treated sentimentally, as nostalgic or idyllically pastoral, Courbet created vast scenes that are geographically and temporally specific. While his 1849 painting *After Dinner at Ornans* begins to lay out the themes and styles of his later, more politically controversial works, the content is comparatively neutral and, in fact, won him a medal at the Salon, which technically allowed him future entry into the Salon without jury approval and enabled him to display pieces that viewers found more politically challenging. In "Gustave Courbet," Jeanne Willette says that the paintings he submitted for the next Salon, including *The Burial at Ornans* and *The Stonebreakers* (1849-50), "asserted the social importance and historical

Gustave Courbet's painting *Burial at Ornans* (1849-50). After the 1855 Paris Universal Exposition rejected this painting and other works, Courbet wrote the "Realist Manifesto." © THE ART GALLERY COLLECTION/ALAMY significance of the petit bourgeois class and the *sans coulottes.* Unlike the middle class elites, these classes had lost all the revolutions of the past four decades, especially the one of 1848."

Courbet's manifesto, brief and to the point, relies on the impact of the accompanying, outsized paintings to help convey his message. For example, describing *The Burial at Ornans* in his book *Realism and Social Vision in Courbet and Proudhon,* James Rubin writes that "the huge canvas with life-sized figures flaunted Courbet's challenge to assumptions about what was worthy of large-scale artistic representation, and his ostensibly coarse technique evoked a worker's handicraft." Likewise, Arnold Hauser, in *The Social History of Art,* writes, "The passion which fills Courbet and his supporters is, however, fundamentally political; their self-assurance comes from their conviction that they are the pioneers of truth and the forerunners of the future." Courbet himself described *The Burial at Ornans* as "in reality the burial of Romanticism." The painting pointedly lacks sentimental emotions or a clear dramatic narrative, demanding attention for its *petit bourgeois* subjects on their own unidealized merits.

Courbet's emphasis on art as a concrete subject that should consist of the representation of "real and existing things" leads him to be highly critical of the academic emphasis on history paintings. "I hold the artists of one century basically incapable of reproducing the aspect of a past or future century—in other words, of painting the past or the future," he says. Further, he charges that the preference for historical subjects over contemporary subjects is an indication of misplaced social and aesthetic priorities: "An age which is not capable of expressing itself through its own artists has no right to be represented by subsequent artists." Realism requires artists to be attuned to the issues of the day and all classes, not merely to glorified history or the elite.

CRITICAL DISCUSSION

Many critics of the day disliked Courbet's work, finding it ugly, offensive, or simply bewildering. Regarding the reception of *The Burial at Ornans,* art historian Sarah Faunce writes in *Courbet Reconsidered,* "In Paris the *Burial* was judged as a work that had thrust itself into the grand tradition of history painting, like an upstart in dirty boots crashing a genteel party." His decision to stage his own show was also seen as both a political challenge to Napoleon III's Exposition and an affirmation of Courbet's arrogance, an epithet the artist gleefully accepted. Courbet's friend, the art critic Champfleury, said of the Pavilion of Realism: "It is an incredibly audacious act, it is the subversion of all institutions associated with the jury, it is a direct appeal to the public, some are saying it is freedom. It is a scandal, it is anarchy, it is art dragged through the mud."

From his death in 1877 until the mid-twentieth century, critics tended to downplay Courbet's major political works and emphasize the strictly formal aspects of his painting, particularly the landscapes and portraits from his later career. He was also considered to be an inspiration to the impressionists; critic Clement Greenberg even suggests that Courbet's solo show was the inspiration for the famous exhibition organized by Monet, Pierre-Auguste Renoir, and Camille Pissarro in 1874 that gave the impressionists their name. In addition, Meyer Schapiro's 1941 essay "Courbet and Popular Imagery" brought new attention to Courbet as a political artist. *New York Times* critic Michael Kimmelman observes, "To trace the course of scholarship on Courbet is in a sense to sketch the history of art-history and its relation to politics during roughly the last century." Recently, historians have provided more nuanced readings of Courbet's political leanings and how they interacted with his artistic sensibilities.

Today, Courbet is seen as significant not only for his political themes and his painting techniques but also for his self-promotion, his embrace of controversy, and his forging of a path for artists outside of the traditions of the academy. Courbet's Pavilion of Realism is considered by some critics to be a turning point in artistic marketing; single-artist retrospectives were rare at the time and represented a new avenue for artists seeking to gain attention and earn money without official honors or endorsements. In *The Most Arrogant Man in France: Gustave Courbet and the Nineteenth-Century Media Culture,* Petra ten-Doesschate Chu states that Courbet "paved the way for modernism in art"—not only by introducing new themes and techniques but also by challenging the way artists were expected to interact with critics, politics, and the marketplace.

BIBLIOGRAPHY

Sources

"Courbet at the Met." *New Criterion* 26.9 (2008): 52+. *Fine Arts and Music Collection.* Web. 30 June 2012.

Danto, Arthur Coleman. "Courbet." *Nation* 23 Jan. 1989: 97+. *Academic OneFile.* Web. 25 June 2012.

Finocchio, Ross. "Nineteenth-Century French Realism." *Heilbrunn Timeline of Art History.* Metropolitan Museum of Art, 2000. Web. 8 Aug. 2012.

"Gustave Courbet." Musée d'Orsay, 2006. Web. 24 June 2012.

Kimmelman, Michael. "Critic's Notebook: Ever-Provocative Courbet Examined Anew." *New York Times,* 29 Dec. 1988. Web. 22 June 2012.

Parks, John A. "The First Realist: The Paintings of Gustave Courbet." *American Artist* June 2008: 28+. *Fine Arts and Music Collection.* Web. 29 June 2012.

Willette, Jeanne S. M. "Gustave Courbet." *Art History Unstuffed,* 3 Sept. 2010. Web. 24 June 2012.

Further Reading

Amic, Sylvain. *Gustave Courbet.* Ostfildern: Hatje Canz, 2008. Print.

Chu, Petra ten-Doesschate. *The Most Arrogant Man in France: Gustave Courbet and the Nineteenth-Century Media Culture.* Princeton: Princeton UP, 2007. Print.

Clark, T.J. *Image of the People: Gustave Courbet and the 1848 Revolution.* London: Thames, 1999. Print.

Faunce, Sarah, and Linda Nochlin. *Courbet Reconsidered.* New Haven: Yale UP, 1988. Print.

Hurley, Clare. "The Art of Gustave Courbet in His Epoch and in Ours." *World Socialist Web Site.* Intl. Committee of the Fourth International, 10 Oct. 2008. Web. 23 June 2012.

Nochlin, Linda. *Courbet.* London: Thames, 2007. Print.

Rubin, James Henry. *Realism and Social Vision in Courbet and Proudhon.* Princeton: Princeton UP, 1981. Print.

White, Harrison C., and Cynthia White. *Canvases and Careers: Institutional Change in the French Painting World.* Chicago: U of Chicago P, 1993. Print.

Marie Becker

THE RENAISSANCE
Studies in Art and History
Walter Pater

✥ **Key Facts**

Time Period:
Late 19th Century

Movement/Issue:
Aesthetics; Revived
interest in the
Renaissance

Place of Publication:
England

**Language of
Publication:**
English

OVERVIEW

The Renaissance: Studies in Art and History, originally published in 1873 as *Studies in the History of the Renaissance,* is a collection of essays in which Walter Pater discusses various artists and works of the Renaissance as a means of exploring his own aesthetic theories, which center on the intensity of experience and personal reactions to isolated moments of beauty. In the essays, many of which had previously appeared in other magazines, Pater turns his attention to the Renaissance and uses his discussion to make broader points about an "ideal" form of art and life that he believes transcends historical periods. He suggests that the Renaissance stands out in history because of its "excitement and enlightening of the human mind" and "unity of spirit," which led to a "visionariness" of many of its artists. Pater emphasizes the manner in which Renaissance artists struggled with conflicting humanistic and religious views, as well as with questions of art and form. Focusing on philosophical and aesthetic questions, Pater's work is aimed at an upper-class audience, such as the students and tutors at Oxford, where he spent all of his student and working life.

The Renaissance was a foundational text for the so-called aesthetes and decadents of the fin-de-siècle, such as Oscar Wilde (who termed *The Renaissance* "the holy writ of beauty") and Vernon Lee. More-conservative readers were uncomfortable with, and critical of, what they perceived as *The Renaissance*'s endorsement of hedonism and amorality. Although critics pointed out that Pater did not achieve a true historical study (which is why he changed the original title of the collection), his work provoked a new interest in the period. His essay on Sandro Botticelli was the first published in the English language and led to a revival of both popular and scholarly interest in Botticelli's works and in those of other lesser-known Renaissance artists.

HISTORICAL AND LITERARY CONTEXT

The Renaissance focuses on art as a highly individualized experience that inheres within specific, intense moments. Pater argues that art may be found in single lines of poetry or in specific areas of a painting, if not in the work as a whole, and that the critic plays a crucial role in recognizing and highlighting such moments. Pater also espouses what might be termed a Neoplatonic conception of art, or one that is interested in a spiritual ideal rather than in concrete details. For Pater, art "is always pressing forward from the outward beauty ... to apprehend the unseen ... abstract form of beauty." His emphasis on art as an abstract, ephemeral form reflects his concern with art's role in a modern world, which he sees as marked by "conflicting claims," "entangled interest," and "distracted ... sorrows."

Pater wrote during a period of growing interest in earlier historical ages and in new aesthetic approaches and techniques. Before Pater's work was published, one of the most important aesthetic works of the age was John Ruskin's *Stones of Venice* (1851), which praised the art of the Gothic period as superior to the "pestilent" art of the Renaissance. In contrast, Pater's work read the Renaissance's emphasis on movement and change as far superior to the wholehearted realism that Ruskin praised.

The Renaissance can be placed within a diverse set of Victorian writings about culture and modernity. With its deep interest in Greek culture, Pater's work responds to Matthew Arnold's ideas about Hellenistic and Hebraic frames of mind. Whereas Arnold sees a need for balance between the "sweetness and reason" of Hellenistic culture and the religiosity and justice of the Hebraic, Pater argues for the "freedom" of Hellenism. Although *The Renaissance* focuses on times long past, Pater developed many of his ideas in works on contemporary artists such as Samuel Taylor Coleridge and William Morris. In fact, Pater's essay on Morris contains paragraphs that were later included in *The Renaissance*'s highly controversial conclusion.

Pater most significantly influenced the closely related symbolist, aesthetic, and decadent movements of the 1890s and the modernists who followed in the early part of the twentieth century. Writer Oscar Wilde considered Pater a crucial influence, as did many early modernist authors such as James Joyce, W.B. Yeats, and Ezra Pound. Pater's ideas about portraying the passage of time shaped the subjective stream-of-consciousness style of modernist novels. As a critic, Pater influenced the focus and techniques of art and literary criticism. His emphasis on subjectivity and the importance of the viewer helped to justify many of the modern approaches to understanding the meaning and effects of literary texts. Today Pater's emphasis on the importance of even fleeting beauty continues to inspire those interested in aesthetics.

THEMES AND STYLE

The central theme of *The Renaissance* is Pater's attempt to define art as something both privately evocative and responsive to its environment. He refuses to define any absolute rules of beauty, instead arguing that the critic must note fleeting moments of beauty. The emphasis on interpretation not only elevates the importance of the critic but also the individual, subjective experience. In his famously controversial conclusion, Pater argues, "not the fruit of experience, but experience itself, is the end. A counted number of pulses only is given to us of a variegated, dramatic life. How may we see in them all that is to be seen in them by the finest senses?" His much-quoted answer—which is often taken out of context—is "[t]o burn always with this hard, gemlike flame, to maintain this ecstasy, is success in life."

Pater's work stands out because of the literary and poetic manner in which he expresses his philosophical points about art. His style is almost epigrammatic: he incorporates wisdom in brief, beautifully phrased sentences. At other points, he engages in much longer poetic descriptions that evoke mood more often than tangible details. For instance, he famously describes Leonardo da Vinci's *Mona Lisa* as "older than the rocks among which she sits; like the vampire, she has been dead many times … and all this has been to her but as the sound of lyres and flutes, and lives only in the delicacy with which it has moulded the changing lineaments, and tinged the eyelids and the hands." This passage enacts his theory that minute details (Mona Lisa's eyelids and hands) can be "the beautiful" in a work because of the way they echo the fleetingness of time and deeper meanings rather than merely reflect reality.

Although Pater writes in a richly poetic descriptive mood, his style is deliberately inclusive so that the reader feels guided and encouraged, not lectured. "Our education," he writes, including the reader as a critic, "becomes complete in proportion as our susceptibility to these impressions increases in depth and variety." He goes on to directly address the reader about this susceptibility: "perhaps you have sometimes wondered why those peevish-looking Madonnas, conformed to no acknowledged or obvious type of beauty, attract you more and more, and often come back to you when the Sistine Madonna and the Virgins of Fra Angelico are forgotten?" For Pater, this inclusion of the reader allows him to instruct the reader as to how to act: "we have an interval," he points out, "and then our place knows us no more. Some spend this interval in listlessness, some in high passions, the wisest, at least among 'the children of this world,' in art and song."

WALTER PATER: TEACHER

In *The Renaissance: Studies in Art and History,* Walter Pater emphasizes the importance of teaching art and spreading influence, ideals he espoused in his own life. Little is known about Pater's personal life despite the fact that Victorians tended to chronicle their lives in voluminous detail through diaries and letters. One area of his life that is well documented, however, is his role as teacher and mentor. He spent his career at Oxford University as a tutor with expertise in German philosophy. In this role, he mentored a number of writers, either as students or as friends, including Arthur Symons, Edmund Gosse, Vernon Lee, Michael Fields, Gerard Manley Hopkins, and most famously Oscar Wilde.

Pater's mentoring relationships seem to have been a motivating factor in his writing. For instance, when he removed the conclusion from the second edition of *The Renaissance* he explained that he had done so because "it might possibly mislead some of those young men into whose hands it might fall." The seriousness with which he took his role as a teacher tends to support this explanation and weaken the view that Pater was merely justifying his capitulation to public opinion.

CRITICAL DISCUSSION

Many of Pater's contemporaries responded to *The Renaissance* with discomfort and anger due to what they perceived as its hedonistic approach to life. In 1876 W.H. Mallock parodied Pater in the *New Republic,* depicting the critic as an effete aesthete. Such parodies cost the critic several promotions. The famous Catholic poet Gerard Manley Hopkins, who was Pater's pupil and close friend at Oxford, eventually cut all ties with him. As a result, Pater tried to tone down the effect of his atheism in *The Renaissance* by removing the conclusion from the second edition. He also attempted to return to more-conventionally Christian views in 1885's *Marius the Epicurean.*

Although much of conventional Victorian society rejected Pater's views and style, his ideas were, for others, a refreshing new take on morality and culture. In an essay printed in *Walter Pater: The Critical Heritage* (1980), John Morley, for instance, praises Pater for raising "to the throne lately filled by religion" a new creed of "inspiring earnestness and gravity." Carolyn Williams in *Transfigured World: Walter Pater's Aesthetic Historicism* (1989) argues that Pater is a crucial transitional figure, as he deals with "intensified awareness that the problem of 'objective' knowledge and the problem of 'subjectivity' are intractably one and the same." Consequently, for the decadents, whose movement focused on an artistic, stylized response to the transience and potential meaninglessness of life, Pater was seminal. Wilde called *The Renaissance* "my golden book; I never travel anywhere without it" and W.B. Yeats adapted a

Detail of Sandro Botticelli's painting *La Primavera* (1477). ERICH LESSING/ART RESOURCE, NY

examine Pater's art in terms of music and music theory. Finally, recent queer studies have suggested that the coded homoerotic elements in Pater's writings, as well as in his lifestyle, may have been the source of the public's discomfort with some of his work.

BIBLIOGRAPHY

Sources

Bucknell, Brad. "Re-Reading Pater: The Musical Aesthetics of Temporality." *Modern Fiction Studies* 38.3 (1992): 597-614. *Project Muse.* Web. 29 Aug. 2012.

Gallagher, Catherine. "Formalism and Time." *Modern Language Quarterly* 61.1 (2000): 229. *Academic Search Complete.* Web. 30 Aug. 2012.

Morley, John. "Mr. Pater's Essays." *Walter Pater: The Critical Heritage.* Ed. R.M. Seiler. Boston: Routledge and Kegan Paul, 1980. 57-61. Print.

Pater, Walter. *The Renaissance: Studies in Art and History.* New York: Cosimo Classics, 2005. Print.

Williams, Carolyn. *Transfigured World: Walter Pater's Aesthetic Historicism.* Ithaca: Cornell UP, 1989. Print.

Further Reading

Donoghue, Denis. *Walter Pater: Lover of Strange Souls.* New York: Knopf, 1995. Print.

Franke, Damon. "The 'Curious' Pagan Spirit of Pater's *The Renaissance.*" *Nineteenth-Century Prose* 31.1 (2004): 170-90. *Academic OneFile.* Web. 30 Aug. 2012.

Inman, Billie Andrew. "The Intellectual Context of Walter Pater's 'Conclusion.'" *Walter Pater: An Imaginative Sense of Fact.* Ed. Philip Dodd. Totowa: Cass, 1981. 11-28. Print.

Leighton, Angela. *On Form: Poetry, Aestheticism, and the Legacy of a Word.* Oxford: Oxford UP, 2007. Print.

Levine, Caroline. *The Serious Pleasures of Suspense: Victorian Realism & Narrative Doubt.* Charlottesville: U of Virginia P, 2003. Print.

Newman, Beth. "Alice Meynell, Walter Pater, and Aestheticist Temporality." *Victorian Studies* 53.3 (2011): 495-505. *Project MUSE.* Web. 30 Aug. 2012.

Potolsky, Matthew. "Decadence, Nationalism, and the Logic of Canon Formation." *Modern Language Quarterly* 67.2 (2006): 213-44. *Academic Search Complete.* Web. 30 Aug. 2012.

Roberts, Gabriel. "'Analysis Leaves Off': The Use and Abuse of Philosophy in Walter Pater's *Renaissance.*" *Cambridge Quarterly* 37.4 (2008): 407-25. Web. 29 Aug. 2012.

Siegel, Jonah. "Leonardo, Pater, and the Challenge of Attribution." *Raritan* 21.3 (2002): 159-87. *ProQuest.* Web. 29. Aug. 2012

Abigail Mann

section from it into his own poetry. Beyond offering an aesthetic approach, Pater's greatest influence on the decadents might have been his richly dense, rhythmic language, which sought to create beauty even—or perhaps especially—at the sentence level.

Contemporary criticism continues to probe Pater's effects on decadence and on modernism while examining Pater's greater literary and cultural contributions. Catherine Gallagher, in a 2000 article for *Modern Language Quarterly,* argues that Pater did not just inspire a handful of writers but had a huge effect on twentieth-century formalism, with its emphasis on ephemerality and the impossibility of capturing a perfect moment. This interest in ephemerality is reflected in Pater's famous insistence that great art should approximate music, inspiring several studies that

St. Cloud Manifesto

Edvard Munch

OVERVIEW

Written by artist Edvard Munch on New Year's Eve, the "St. Cloud Manifesto" (1889) is a diary entry describing his reaction to an experience of quintessential nineteenth-century Parisian nightlife. The piece signifies a severe stylistic change in Munch's paintings, which helped birth visual art's movement into expressionism. While living a drunken and isolated life in Saint-Cloud, a cheap suburb of Paris, the Norwegian artist used private journal entries to document a series of insights he had in response to mundane life events, marking a shift in his consciousness and his relationship to the world around him. This, along with other journal entries from the 1890s, became a personal call to action to paint in a way that gives faithful form to the artist's emotional self through the most expressive of the formal elements: color. Throughout the short manifesto, Munch processes his reaction to the modern life of Paris, seeing the emptiness in its excess while focusing on the harmony of music, color, and emotions to give clear expressive form to the pure sensations of life.

Because it was a private journal entry, the "St. Cloud Manifesto" did not have an immediate influence on the artistic climate of the time. Instead, Munch's subsequent body of work can be seen as the presentation of his manifesto. Although the general public was continually disturbed by the raw intensity of Munch's work, his paintings had a significant impact on the way artists were thinking about the relationship between color, vision, and emotions. Despite a disastrous solo exhibition of his work in Berlin in 1892, Munch became popular in the artistic and intellectual German underground for finding the visual language to express sensations and emotions simultaneously. The abrupt stylistic change brought about by the "St. Cloud Manifesto" places Munch in a prominent position on the timeline of visual art's movement from spontaneous impressionistic vision to pure nonrepresentational expression.

HISTORICAL AND LITERARY CONTEXT

The "St. Cloud Manifesto" is a passionate response to the emotional vapidity of contemporary Parisian nightlife, illustrating Munch's opposition to the impressionist painting style and subject matter popular in the 1880s. Avant-garde artists who were showing in impressionist exhibitions between 1874 and 1886 responded to Charles Baudelaire's legacy by painting what they saw around them. After Baron Haussmann's redevelopment of the city, a see-and-be-seen café culture emerged along with the detached gaze of the flâneur artist who painted prostitutes, performers, barmaids, and drunkards in a manner that expressed them physically and spontaneously. This allowed the viewer to remain detached without, for instance, making the hallucinatory journey of Edouard Manet's *Absinthe Drinker* or participating in the small talk of Edgar Degas's *Women on a Café Terrace*. Painted in the impressionistic style, these pieces became mere interior scenes, the type Munch vowed to no longer paint.

By the time Munch arrived in Paris in 1889, the public had recognized the impact of artists such as Manet and Paul Cézanne, and artists such as Paul Gauguin were already exhibiting works exploring symbolism, which Munch viewed at the 1889 Volpini Exhibition. This period of transition from naturalism to symbolism mirrored artists' waning interest in the blind decadence of urban Paris for the emotional and spiritual insights of simplistic rural culture. Although Munch worked independently of other artists of the time, witnessing this transition allowed him space to explore how different artists were expressing their subjects. This new generation of postimpressionist artists, which included Gauguin and Émile Bernard, used color to express emotions and symbolize spiritual truths, creating a total effect that aimed to bring new insight to and evoke sentiments within the viewer. Similarly, Munch realized during his New Year's Eve escapade that the way to arouse in the viewer a connection to all that had ever existed would be to create on canvas a symbiotic dance between music and color.

Thanks to the stylistic equanimity of avant-garde painters before him, Munch was afforded the opportunity to explore his own style and create one so unique that it marked a clear division within his own body of work. Mid-century naturalist artists such as Gustave Courbet and Manet welcomed modern life onto the canvas and into the Salon de Paris. Impressionist artists broke from this mold completely, focusing on their unique modes of vision while bringing their works directly to the public. As Michel Melot explains in his essay "Camille Pissarro in 1880," Pissarro, like most of the impressionist painters, was

Key Facts

Time Period:
Late 19th Century

Movement/Issue:
Aesthetics;
Expressionism

Place of Publication:
France

**Language of
Publication:**
Norwegian

Night in St. Cloud, painted by Edvard Munch during the winter of 1890 in St. Cloud, France. SCALA/ ART RESOURCE, NY

interested in depicting precisely what the eye saw without identifying exactly what those objects were. This method exercised a direct and spontaneous connection between an artist's eye and hand. Munch, who was known to have seen an exhibit of Pissarro's work while in Paris, rejected this method in the "St. Cloud Manifesto" for his own interest in a more complete experience that could be found by traversing the inward path from eye to psyche to hand. Munch would communicate the effects of that inward path through expressive color.

After his written revelation in the "St. Cloud Manifesto," Munch began expressing the intangible parts of life on the canvas through vibrant swaths of colors, arousing the same emotional reaction in the viewer that he was personally experiencing and conveying. Soon after, he began working on new paintings in this style and entering them in juried competitions. Always bouncing between being well received and horrifically rejected, Munch continued to win scholarships supporting his new work while simultaneously being criticized for being bizarre. His new style had very little influence on his Parisian peers, as artists he was showing with, such as Monet and Degas, had very well-patented styles. It was not until his showing in Berlin in 1892 that he found his audience in the German underground. Today the impact of Munch's exhibition in Berlin is clearly seen, as he is now known as one of the grandfathers of Europe's fin-de-siecle expressionist movements.

THEMES AND STYLE

Throughout the "St. Cloud Manifesto," Munch relates his emotional experience in the ballroom to what he believes the purpose of all visual art should be, in light of its contemporary state. The people he describes are fashionable—the line "top hat by top hat" suggests chicly detached flâneurs with similarly well-hatted ladies—but Munch experiences them as empty. While looking for a beautiful woman, he finds one who, upon her discovery of being noticed, stiffens and her face and becomes "mask-like." This attention to surface within the nightlife of Paris stands juxtaposed to the emotional rapture Munch witnesses onstage. While reflecting upon this moment of connectivity between two performers, Munch sees the thread that links humanity throughout the history of the world: "these two in the moment when they are not themselves but only a part of a chain of the thousand generations that connect generations to generations." Like the contrast between audience and performers in the ballroom, Munch calls himself to paint pictures that bring viewers to "understand the sacredness and power of this moment" and to no longer paint "people who read and women who knit." This places Edvard Munch, spiritual artist, in direct opposition to the most popular Norwegian artist of his time, Gustav Wentzel, who painted predominantly interior domestic scenes.

Munch's private writings in his diary create an emotional appeal to himself, ultimately impelling an inner transformation. The initial picture he paints of the ballroom creates the awareness that this is his personal vision, charged by his emotional self as he sits isolated within a crowd. He then describes the performance using such painterly and emotional language that it is difficult to decipher the onstage activity. "It was love and hate, yearning and reconciliation—and beautiful dreams—and the gentle music melted into the colours." The internal experience of the performers elicited such a passionate emotional response within him that he demands change in the way he approaches painting—and consequently in the way viewers experience paintings.

Although the beginning of the "St. Cloud Manifesto" creates a swirling, lyrical picture of a specific episode, it abruptly transitions to Munch holding himself accountable for the transformation

PRIMARY SOURCE

"ST. CLOUD MANIFESTO"

I must give form to this as I saw it just now, but in the blue haze....

People must understand the sacredness and power of this moment and remove their hats as if they were in church.

I must produce a number of such pictures. Interiors should no longer be painted, people who read and women who knit.

There must be living people who breathe and feel, suffer and love.

I felt I must do this—it should be so easy. The flesh would take on form and the colours come to life.

of painting, thereby giving form to the things that connect humanity. The colors and movement of the dreamy New Year's Eve initially give way to a suggestive plea: "I should do something." This is followed by repetitive demands for action: "I must give form to this" and "I must produce a number of such pictures." From his action, audiences will inevitably be moved to the same realizations: "people must understand the sacredness and power of this moment." This internal dialogue worked out on paper becomes an example of Munch's focus on the importance of the emotional subjectivity of artists. He has the power to enact change in individuals by himself being emotionally connected to his experiences and then representing that emotion in a personal way.

CRITICAL DISCUSSION

The works Munch created directly after the "St. Cloud Manifesto" brought him widespread criticism and a small but important number of counterculture supporters. His showing in Berlin in 1892 elicited extreme public outcry. Kaiser Wilhelm and other officials made speeches calling for the exhibition to be closed, and after six days it was shut down "out of reverence to art and artistic effort." Affronted by this control of creativity, young Berliner artists spoke out against the establishment, created their own artists' association, and brought about the Berlin Secession, a movement that would encourage other secessionist movements in Europe.

Munch's "St. Cloud Manifesto" revelation about how successfully to weave the thread of humankind throughout his paintings also found written form in later diary entries over the next three years. In his diary, he expounds on the importance of not just painting an object but painting the artist's reaction to the object. In an entry from 1889 he writes, "It is not the chair which is to be painted but what the human being has felt in relation to it." This type of limitless representation provided a precedent for expressionist artists after the turn of the century to represent their feelings of isolation and discontent using colors, even if the colors were not representational. As Stanisław Przybyszewski, one of the organizers of the 1892 Berlin exhibit, explains in an essay republished in *Art in Theory: 1815-1900* (1998), "lines which a child might have scratched out on a slate now acquire a mighty pulsing life of their own, enter into relation with the most intimate stirrings of our psychic life, and fuse themselves with the moving forms of the soul itself." The formal elements of the painting—line and color—become the most important method by which to express emotion. If the objects are removed from Munch's paintings, the overall emotions remain expressed.

Although the "St. Cloud Manifesto" marks a significant change in Munch's work, it has received very little critical attention. Scholars point out the shift in Munch's work and consciousness around 1890 without looking in detail at the musings that precipitated the change. In *Edvard Munch: Behind* The Scream (2007), Sue Prideaux devotes an entire chapter to Munch's life in Saint-Cloud, with a close look at both the manifesto and the mood leading up to its writing. The chapter offers only a faint impression of how the "St. Cloud Manifesto" affected his future work. Carla Lathe's 1983 article in *Journal of the Warburg and Courtald Institutes* makes a typically brief mention of the work as being what inspired "a series of pictures showing 'living people, who breathe and feel, suffer and love.'" The "St. Cloud Manifesto" remains a watershed moment without receiving the detailed attention it deserves as an extension of Munch's craft.

BIBLIOGRAPHY

Sources

Gluck, Mary. *Popular Bohemia: Modernism and Urban Culture in Nineteenth-Century Paris.* Cambridge: Harvard UP, 2005. Print.

Lathe, Carla. "Edvard Munch's Dramatic Images 1892-1909." *Journal of the Warburg and Courtald Institutes* 46 (1983): 191-206. Web. 27 Sept. 2012.

Melot, Michel. "Camille Pissarro in 1880: An Anarchist Artist in Bourgeois Society." *Critical Readings in Impressionism and Post-Impressionism.* Ed. Mary Tompkins Lewis. Berkeley: U of California P, 2007. 205-225. Print.

Munch, Edvard. "Impressions from a Ballroom, New Year's Eve in St. Cloud, 1889." *Art in Theory: 1815-1900.* Ed. Charles Harrison. Oxford: Blackwell, 1998. 1040-41. Print.

Prideaux, Sue. *Edvard Munch: Behind* The Scream. New Haven: Yale UP, 2007. Print.

Przybyszewski, Stanisław. "Psychic Naturalism (The Work of Edvard Munch)." *Art in Theory: 1815-1900.* Ed. Charles Harrison. Oxford: Blackwell, 1998. 1044-50. Print.

Further Reading

Aurier, G. Albert. "From 'Symbolism in Painting: Paul Gauguin.'" *Art in Theory: 1815-1900.* Ed. Charles Harrison. Oxford: Blackwell, 1998. 1025-29. Print.

Clarke, Jay A. *Becoming Edvard Munch: Influence, Anxiety, and Myth.* New Haven: Yale UP, 2009. Print.

Gauguin, Paul. "Fable from 'Notes Esparses.'" *Art in Theory: 1815-1900.* Ed. Charles Harrison. Oxford: Blackwell, 1998. 1037-39. Print.

Heller, Reinhold. "Concerning Symbolism and the Structure of Surface." *Art Journal* 45.2 (1985): 146-53. *JSTOR.* Web. 15 Oct. 2012.

Munch, Edvard. "From the Violet Diary, Nice 2 January 1891." *Art in Theory: 1815-1900.* Ed. Charles Harrison. Oxford: Blackwell Publishing, 1998. 1042-43. Print.

———. "Notebook Entry on Subjective Vision, 1889." *Art in Theory: 1815-1900.* Ed. Charles Harrison. Oxford: Blackwell, 1998. 1041-42. Print.

Schröder, Klaus Albrecht, ed. *Edvard Munch: Theme and Variation.* Vienna: Albertina, 2003. Print.

Sprinchorn, Evert. "The Transition from Naturalism to Symbolism in the Theater from 1880 to 1900." *Art Journal* 45.2 (1985): 113-19. *JSTOR.* Web. 15 Oct. 2012.

Steinberg, Norma S. "Munch in Color." *Harvard University Art Museums Bulletin* 3.3 (1995): 1-3, 7-54. *JSTOR.* Web. 15 Oct. 2012.

Wood, Mara-Helen, ed. *Edvard Munch: The Frieze of Life.* London: National Gallery, 1992. Print.

Miranda Johnson

LE SYMBOLISME

Jean Moréas

OVERVIEW

First appearing in a supplement to the September 18, 1886, issue of *Le Figaro,* Jean Moréas's *Le Symbolisme,* also known as the *Symbolist Manifesto,* outlines the conceptual framework and aesthetic tendencies of the newly formed symbolist movement. Even before the movement had a name, several French writers and artists in the mid- to late-nineteenth century, such as poets Charles Baudelaire, Stéphane Mallarmé, and Paul Verlaine and painters Gustave Moreau and Dante Gabriel Rosetti, were using symbolist techniques of experimentation and abstraction. Moréas's manifesto positions symbolism as an antidote to the staleness of naturalism, a prominent aesthetic movement emphasizing realism and verisimilitude, which Moréas found banal and commonplace. Addressed primarily to members of French literary and artistic circles who remained faithful to the naturalist and impressionist movements, *Le Symbolisme* announces the arrival of a decadent, complex style of literature that communicates ideas through "the sumptuous trappings of external analogies" and "pure sounds, densely convoluted sentences, [and] mysterious ellipses."

Le Symbolisme initially met with harsh criticism, including a backlash from those associated with the naturalist and impressionist movements. In addition, Remy de Gourmont, a writer loosely affiliated with the symbolists, found fault with the document and formed his own faction of symbolism. Internal divisions among the symbolists led Moréas to break with the movement in the spring of 1891 in order to pursue poetry steeped in classical traditions and to begin the *école romane,* or the Roman school, which championed ancient Greek and Roman literature. Today, *Le Symbolisme* is significant for articulating the poetic concerns of a canonical group of French writers and for being widely considered the first literary or artistic manifesto on the strength of its declarations of collectivity and explanations of various movements and their labels.

HISTORICAL AND LITERARY CONTEXT

Le Symbolisme responds to naturalism, the predominant trend in European continental literature during the mid- to late-nineteenth century, and to impressionism, albeit to a lesser extent. Naturalism employs highly descriptive, realist writing, often as a means to convey social and environmental conditions. As early as 1876 the naturalist writer Émile Zola pejoratively used the term *symbolism* to describe the paintings of Gustave Moreau. Ten years later, "Les Poetes decadents" (1885), an article written by Paul Bourde in *Le Tempes,* mocked writing that employed symbolist methods. Bourde's essay prompted Moréas to compose his manifesto in an effort to demonstrate the central differences between naturalism and symbolism.

By the time *Le Symbolisme* appeared, naturalism and impressionism were losing their artistic dominion over European culture. In 1886 the impressionists held their final collective exhibit, and Zola, considered the figurehead of naturalism, was in the twilight of his publishing career. Although Moréas acknowledges indebtedness to his predecessors in the manifesto, he announces the arrival of a new movement featuring poets such as Mallarmé, the deceased Baudelaire, and Arthur Rimbaud, and visual artists such as Paul Gauguin, Paul Cézanne, and, to a lesser extent, Georges Seurat. These artists and writers focused on communicating a personal, often spiritual vision through associations between words or images.

Baudelaire's writings, which predate Moréas's manifesto, are considered the basis of symbolist literature. Postulating a universal harmony between the tangible and intangible, Baudelaire believed that poets could perceive traces of the extrasensory within real-world objects. He referred to this capacity within the poet as *dedoublement* and described it as producing a trance in which everyday objects are experienced as conduits of the spiritual realm. According to Baudelaire, these trances, born of the unconscious mind, appear as conflicting or contradictory elements in a poem. Echoes of Baudelaire's beliefs and aesthetic traits can be heard in Moréas's call for poetry containing "mysterious ellipses" and "multiform tropes." Moréas's neoclassical tendencies mirror Baudelaire's claim that abridgments and distortions of artworks from archaic cultures are necessary for poets to successfully express abstract thought. Moréas also references the obscure writings of such authors as Voltaire, Pindar, and Dante, and he argues that symbolists should employ "the rich and joyous French language of before," as used by Rabelais and Philippe de Commynes, though in a "modernized" form.

✦ *Key Facts*

Time Period:
Late 19th Century

Movement/Issue:
Aesthetics; Symbolism

Place of Publication:
France

Language of Publication:
French

ARTHUR RIMBAUD: SYMBOLIST POET

Arthur Rimbaud (1854-1891), a French symbolist poet, published several collections of verse during his teenage years but ceased writing by age twenty in favor of traveling the world. He first came to prominence after symbolist poet Paul Verlaine read Rimbaud's "The Drunken Boat." Realizing the young man's poetic ability, Verlaine immediately took him into his home, where Rimbaud and Verlaine worked closely and became lovers. Soon thereafter, Rimbaud published his two most famous works: *A Season in Hell* (1873) and *Illuminations* (1874). He died on November 10, 1891, after a short and painful battle with cancer.

The most well-known symbolist poet to contemporary audiences, Rimbaud has remained prominent thanks to translations by Donald Revell (*A Season in Hell* [2007]) and John Ashbery (*Illuminations* [2011]). The French poet's legacy is also alive in popular culture. For example, the motion picture *Total Eclipse* (1995), starring Leonardo DiCaprio, is an adaptation of Rimbaud's life. Rock icon Bob Dylan in his memoir *Chronicles, Volume 1* (2005) writes, "I came across one of [Rimbaud's] letters called 'Je est un autre,' which translates into 'I is someone else.' When I read those words the bells went off. It made perfect sense. I wished someone would have mentioned that to me earlier."

The influence of *Le Symbolisme* can be seen in the creation and development of other literary and art manifestos, especially in Europe during the early twentieth century. A former member of the symbolist movement, Filippo Tommaso Marinetti, spearheaded the futurist revolution by writing and publishing *Le Futurisme* (1909), later retitled *Manifesto of Futurism,* in *Le Figaro.* The text's original title and focus on explicitly stating the concerns of an art collective—along with the futurists' discontent with mainstream aesthetic trends and the manner in which the manifesto labels the collective as an ism—demonstrate a linguistic and rhetorical indebtedness to Moréas's manifesto. Although Moréas defected from the symbolists in order to pursue his interest in classical literature, the symbolists' focus on associations, particularly those that are playful or absurd, continued to influence artists such as Henri Matisse and Pablo Picasso at the turn of the century. Conceptually, Moréas most directly influenced the surrealists, who announced themselves in the "Manifesto of Surrealism" (1924) and embraced the unconscious, automatic writing, and dream logic.

THEMES AND STYLE

The main argument of *Le Symbolisme* is that mainstream trends in literature and art during the late-nineteenth century had grown stale and that symbolism was needed to infuse the arts with a new

energy and vigor. The manifesto opens with the statements, "Like all arts, literature evolves" and "each new phase in artistic evolution corresponds precisely with the senile decrepitude, the ineluctable end of the school just before it." Moréas claims that the ill will publicly expressed by advocates of naturalism and impressionism was an affirmation that the "inevitable manifestation of a new art" was well underway: "We have already proposed the name *Symbolism* as the only reasonable designation of the present tendency of the creative spirit in art." *Le Symbolisme* outlines the conceptual and aesthetic principles of the movement, including the idea that poetry "tries to house the Idea in a meaningful form" that "will never appear without the sumptuous clothing of analogy." According to Moréas, analogical poetry "needs an archetypal complex style" expressed through "pleonasms," or the use of more words than necessary; "mysterious ellipses"; "the hanging anacoluthon," or an abrupt shift in syntax; and "every daring and multiform trope imaginable."

The manifesto achieves its rhetorical effect by employing a problem-solution model and appealing to the authority of classicism. Moréas asserts that realistic depiction of the material world in writing has become worn, its effect weakened through overuse; therefore, associative writing marked by experimental uses of language is an appropriate remedy. To strengthen his argument, Moréas compares symbolism and classical literature: "Readers will accuse this aesthetics of obscurity … Weren't Pindar's *Odes,* Shakespeare's *Hamlet,* Dante's *Vita Nuova,* Goethe's *Faust Part II,* Flaubert's *Temptation of Saint Anthony* said to be ambiguous?" By aligning symbolists with canonical authors and their most prominent texts, *Le Symbolisme* attempts to quell "the silly jokes" and "all the ill temper" directed at the stylistic innovations of symbolism. The manifesto calls for a rhythm in poetry that is "a rejuvenation of the old metrics; a cleverly ordered disorder," with rhymes that are "fluid and abstruse," alluding to the cyclical nature of the arts and the role of symbolism in the return to classical aesthetics.

In order to communicate with readers accustomed to the naturalist and impressionist modes of writing, *Le Symbolisme* fails to follow its own prescription of using obscure language rooted in overly complex or ambiguous linguistic formations. Instead Moréas uses clear, declarative language to illuminate surrealists' deliberate artistic choices and intellectual opposition to dominant literary and artistic trends. By adopting the language of his opponents, he demonstrates his understanding of naturalism and impressionism while depicting the rise of symbolism as part of a logical, natural movement from one school of art into another. Ironically, the contradiction between the aesthetic aims of symbolism and the style of the manifesto led many symbolists to ignore its significance as a symbolist work.

CRITICAL DISCUSSION

Upon publication, *Le Symbolism* drew criticism from naturalists and impressionists, as well as from symbolists who disagreed with Moréas's method and characterization of symbolism. Remy de Gourmont criticizes the manifesto's claim that symbolism is a form of poetic innovation, pointing out that the poetic devices Moréas describes so closely resemble the common technique of metaphor that there is nothing new or progressive about them. Furthermore, Gourmont faults the document, in which Moréas states symbolism is rooted in mystery and ambiguity, for making symbolist theory too clear. In an 1892 article for *Mercure de France,* Gourmont writes that by explaining symbolists' work in a way that removes its complexity and ambiguity, Moréas moves symbolism away from pure art and creates the need for another new form of expression.

While symbolism eventually gave way to a series of other isms that swept through continental Europe during the first decades of the twentieth century, the movement's influence on subsequent trends in art and literature was powerful. Martin Puchner, in his comprehensive history of the manifesto, *Poetry of the Revolution: Marx, Manifestos, and the Avant-Garde* (2006), situates *Le Symbolisme* as the "text that is often considered one of the first genuine art manifestos" because it "belongs to a world in which art is produced collectively and where collective declarations invest much energy in labels such as naturalism, symbolism, decadence, naturism, and many lesser-known coinages." These traits were later incorporated into the manifestos of the futurist, dadaist, surrealist, and situationist movements, which also sought to place themselves in their art historical context and to define their collective methods and purpose.

Today, scholars view *Le Symbolisme* as marking what Pierre-Louis Mathieu in *The Symbolist Generation: 1870-1910* (1990) calls the de facto "birth of literary Symbolism." In *Symbolist Art Theories: A Critical Anthology* (1994), Henri Dorra notes that most postimpressionist artists, regardless of medium, "were broadly and profoundly affected by the principles of symbolism … subordinating the naturalist ideals of proportion and lighting to expressive effects of line and color, as well to a concern for harmony, and sometimes discord." Anna Balakian, in *The Symbolist Movement: A Critical Appraisal* (1977), more clearly addresses this profound affect, acknowledging that in the wake of symbolism, poets became obligated "to find new ways to cope with reality, to make [their] peace with nature, [and to] find new sources of beauty in harmony with a new apprehension of the forces of the natural world."

BIBLIOGRAPHY

Sources

Balakian, Anna. *The Symbolist Movement: A Critical Appraisal.* New York: New York UP, 1977. Print.

Caws, Mary Ann. *Manifesto: A Century of Isms.* Lincoln: U of Nebraska P, 2000. Print.

Dorra, Henri. *Symbolist Art Theories: A Critical Anthology.* Berkeley: U of California P, 1994. Print.

Dylan, Bob. *Chronicles, Volume 1.* Bath: Chivers, 2005. Print.

Mathieu, Pierre-Louis. *The Symbolist Generation: 1870-1910.* New York: Rizzoli International Publications, 1990. Print.

Puchner, Martin. *Poetry of the Revolution: Marx, Manifestis, and the Avant-Gardes.* Princeton: Princeton UP, 2006. Print.

Further Reading

Butler, John D. *Jean Moréas: A Critique of His Poetry and Philosophy.* The Hague: Mouton, 1967. Print.

Poster advertising the 7th Exhibition of the Salon des 100, depicting Paul Verlaine and Jean Moréas. Moréas was strongly influenced in his writings by the poet Verlaine. BIBLIOTHÈQUE DES ARTS DECORATIFS, PARIS, FRANCE/ ARCHIVES CHARMET/THE BRIDGEMAN ART LIBRARY

Doody, Noreen. *An Influential Involvement: Wilde, Yeats and the French Symbolists.* Dublin: Four Courts, 2001. Print.

Gerould, Daniel Charles. "The Symbolist Legacy." *PAJ* 31.1 (2009): 80-90. Print.

Grigorian, Natasha. *European Symbolism: In Search of Myth (1860-1910).* Oxford: Lang, 2009. Print.

McGuinness, Patrick. *The Language of Politics in Symbolist and Decadent Polemic: From Le Décadent to the Ecole romane.* Oxford: Lang, 2011. Print.

Olderr, Steven. *Symbolism: A Comprehensive Dictionary.* New York: McFarland, 2012. Print.

Joshua Ware

TEN O'CLOCK

James Abbott McNeill Whistler

OVERVIEW

"Ten O'Clock," originally delivered as a lecture by American expatriate painter James Whistler on February 20, 1885, at Prince's Hall in London, champions a belief in art for art's sake and disparages perceptions of art as primarily a moral, emotional, or intellectual matter. Later printed in essay form in Whistler's collection *The Gentle Art of Making Enemies* (1890), the lecture condemns several competing trends in art criticism in late nineteenth-century England, including veneration for the Pre-Raphaelites, who sought to emulate early Renaissance artistic techniques and principles. Whistler also responds to art critic John Ruskin's insistence on "truth to nature" as a criterion of achievement, arguing that nature, as commonly conceived, often presents crude materials capable of substantial improvement in the hands of a gifted painter. Addressed primarily to British artists and critics, the lecture suggests that the projection of any symbolic, nonaesthetic value onto artworks impoverishes the critical discussion of past masterpieces and contemporary works.

Presented on a lecture circuit that included London, Oxford, and Cambridge, "Ten O'Clock," named for the time at which it was held, received mixed reactions from audiences, who were attracted by the painter's status as an inflammatory figure in the British art world. The lecture was celebrated by Whistler's friend and fellow aesthete Oscar Wilde, whose newspaper review of the event suggested that listeners were by turns relieved, dumbfounded, and irritated at the painter's irreverent take on art history. After his death in 1903, the painter quickly became known as "the newest of the Old Masters." Ensuing biographical interest gave "Ten O'Clock" and Whistler's other writings renewed prominence for art historians. Today, Whistler's lecture is considered one of the major products of his involvement with the late nineteenth-century aesthetic movement, informing studies of his paintings created before and after 1885.

HISTORICAL AND LITERARY CONTEXT

An essential problem for Whistler in the "Ten O' Clock" lecture is the privileging of nonaesthetic values in art criticism. He takes particular aim at the short-lived but highly influential Pre-Raphaelite Brotherhood (1848-1850), which had become known as one of the most significant British art movements of the nineteenth century. The Pre-Raphaelites brought with them several artistic desiderata, such as allegorical subject matter; preoccupation with historical and literary themes, especially Biblical and medieval ones; and attentiveness to nature as a model of artistic perfection.

By 1885 Whistler had scuffled with the Pre-Raphaelites' critical proponents in the press but none more notoriously than Ruskin, with whom the painter was involved in a costly and highly publicized lawsuit. Ruskin, responding to Whistler's impressionistic *Nocturne in Black and Gold: The Falling Rocket* (1877), carped that he "never expected to hear a coxcomb ask two hundred guineas for flinging a pot of paint in the public's face." Whistler characteristically objected in the strongest terms and filed suit for libel. The case yielded him only a farthing in damages and cemented his reputation as a polarizing figure in the late Victorian art world. Moreover, it more clearly delineated the terms of the division between aesthetes like Whistler (and, for a time, Wilde) and those like Ruskin and the late J.M.W. Turner who believed that art could capture intellectual and moral truths.

Lectures in the form of "Ten O'Clock" were common in Victorian England, both at universities and in public settings. In fact, Ruskin gave enough art lectures to fill multiple volumes of printed works. Speaking in a forum accustomed to expositions of the meaning and value of art, Whistler questioned the arguments and even the utility of lectures, such as Ruskin's, that expounded on the "truth" contained in art. As Wilde notes in his review of the lecture, the painter, in his "first public appearance as a lecturer on art … spoke for more than an hour with really marvelous eloquence on the absolute uselessness of all lectures of the kind."

Whistler further developed his stance on art criticism, including his judgments of Ruskin and even Wilde, in a series of lectures and essays collected in the 1890 volume *The Gentle Art of Making Enemies*. Although there is little evidence that Whistler's literary or rhetorical style was especially influential, "Ten O'Clock" is said to have inspired the postimpressionist painter Georges Seurat. In addition, as J.P.H. House in a 1980 essay for *Journal of the Royal Society of Arts* suggests, postimpressionist artist Paul Gauguin was influenced by Whistler's severe rejection of naturalistic ideals.

⁘ Key Facts

Time Period:
Late 19th Century

Movement/Issue:
Aesthetics

Place of Publication:
England

Language of Publication:
English

THEMES AND STYLE

The primary theme of "Ten O'Clock" is that art is a purely artistic endeavor and that critics have misled the public by attempting to find new meanings in works of art. Whistler begins by attacking the notion that art should improve society and by personifying art as "selfishly occupied with her own perfection only—having no desire to teach—seeking and finding the beautiful in all conditions and all times." He addresses a set of historical influences that he sees as responsible for the confusion of beauty with "virtue," laying blame on the industrial manufacture of consumer goods and on the ascendance of art critics. The former, for Whistler, supplants handcrafted objects of artistic value, whereas the latter distracts the public from the visual perfection that some works of art achieve. Finally, he posits another obstacle to

appreciation of the beauty of art: the prevailing belief that "Nature is always right." He contends, "Nature is usually wrong … seldom does [it] succeed in producing a picture."

The lecture achieves its rhetorical effect through metaphor, in particular through a fable about the origins of art, which serves to illustrate his arguments regarding mass-production, nature, and art criticism. He sketches a prehistoric society in which, for perhaps hundreds of generations, artists produce crafts required by their tribe. These primeval artists are set apart by their aesthetic sense, and since the objects they produce are useful, they are permitted to fashion ever more-elaborate vases, furniture, and so forth. The ancients quickly exceed the "slovenly suggestion of nature," producing forms from their own imaginations without brooking the opinions of dilettantes and outsiders. Thus, Whistler concludes, painters have an implicit rightness in the aesthetic hierarchy of the tribe: "And the people questioned not, and *had nothing to say in the matter.*"

Despite his modest suggestion that he will "preach" only "with great hesitation and much misgiving," Whistler proceeds to expound his opinions with an air of unapproachable authority. (The irony of this promise would have been all the more acute for members of London society familiar with Whistler's flamboyant, domineering personality.) The speaker couches his initial argument in the style of a wartime polemic, rallying his listeners to their own defense against the invasion of art into every aspect of their formerly quiet, decent lives. Throughout, he employs a flippancy that Wilde, at least, found charming, and he often offers comic images as a means of forestalling further argument on an issue. For instance, on the subject of naturalism, he maintains, "to say to the painter, that Nature is to be taken as she is, is to say to the player, that he may sit on the piano."

CRITICAL DISCUSSION

Contemporary reactions to "Ten O'Clock" were in part a referendum on Whistler's controversial character. His critics dismissed this latest incarnation of his argument for art for art's sake, even as his friends praised the lecture. Wilde, who attended the February 20 performance of the lecture, wrote in the next day's *Pall Mall Gazette* that he was delighted with Whistler's rendition of "a miniature Mephistopheles, mocking the majority!" Although Wilde's enthusiasm reflects his friendship with Whistler, the relationship between the two soon soured, as Anne Bruder notes in her study of Whistler and Wilde, published in *English Literature in Transition, 1880-1920* (2004). Whistler felt Wilde was encroaching on his intellectual territory and Wilde began to align himself with Ruskin. Robert Slifkin in a 2006 essay for *Oxford Art Journal* suggests that Whistler had another, more cryptic critic in

H.G. Wells, whose novella *The Invisible Man* (1897) may be interpreted as a literary caricature of Whistler's aesthetics.

In spite of his reputation for bitter arguments with critics, Whistler created a body of work that constitutes a significant part of the Western artistic canon. Although his lecture did not launch a countermovement in support of the notion of art for art's sake, "Ten O'Clock" is notable as a point of reference for Whistler's artistic practice. In addition, Rebecca Beasley in a 2002 essay for *American Literature* notes that the lecture appealed to American poet Ezra Pound, whose career rivaled Whistler's in notoriety and who was greatly influenced by the painter. Beasley writes that Pound, in a typescript asserting Whistler's superiority to Ruskin, claims his own opinions about the nature and virtues of art are merely restatements of "things that Whistler has said with final beauty in his ten O clock" [sic].

Today, many art historians read "Ten O'Clock" in terms of Whistler's career prior to 1885, discerning the biographical basis for the lecture's values and even some of its apparent quirks. According to Linda Merrill in a 1994 essay in *Burlington Magazine*, the central parable of the lecture "recalls a critical period in Whistler's own career, when a community of aesthetes assisted his escape from realism." Merrill locates this period in the years circa 1865 when Whistler took a keen interest in the patterns of Chinese porcelain. Somewhat further afield, scholars have found use for Whistler's aesthetic observations in discussion of similar problems in literature. For example, Charles Martindale in a 2001 essay for *Arion* applies the ideas of Whistler, Immanuel Kant, and Friedrich Schiller to his construction of a "plea" for renewed interest in aesthetics among classicists.

BIBLIOGRAPHY

Sources

Beasley, Rebecca. "Ezra Pound's Whistler." *American Literature* 74.3 (2002): 485-516. Web. 26 Aug. 2012.

Bruder, Anne. "Constructing Artist and Critic between J. M. Whistler and Oscar Wilde: 'In the Best Days of Art There Were No Art-Critics'." *English Literature in Transition, 1880-1920* 47.2 (2004): 161-80. Web. 26 Aug. 2012.

House, J.P.H. "Post-Impressionist Visions of Nature." *Journal of the Royal Society of Arts* 128 (1980): 568-88. Web. 26 Aug. 2012.

Martindale, Charles. "The Aesthetic Turn: Latin Poetry and the Judgement of Taste." *Arion* 9.2 (2001): 63-89. Web. 26 Aug. 2012.

Merrill, Linda. "Whistler and the 'Lange Lijzen.'" *Burlington* Oct. 1994: 683-90. Web. 16 Aug. 2012.

Slifkin, Robert. "James Whistler as the Invisible Man: Anti-Aestheticism and Artistic Vision." *Oxford Art Journal* 29.1 (2006): 53-75. Web. 21 Aug. 2012.

Wilde, Oscar. "Mr Whistler's 'Ten O'Clock'." *Pall Mall Gazette* 21 Feb. 1885. Web. 21 Aug. 2012.

PRIMARY SOURCE

"TEN O'CLOCK"

Art is upon the Town!—to be chucked under the chill by the passing gallant—to be enticed within the gates of the householder—to be coaxed into company, as a proof of culture and refinement.

If familiarity can breed contempt, certainly Art—or what is currently taken for it—has been brought to its lowest stage of intimacy.

The people have been harassed with Art in every guise, and vexed with many methods as to its endurance. They have been told how they shall love Art, and live with it. Their homes have been invaded, their walls covered with paper, their very dress taken to task—until, roused at last, bewildered and filled with the doubts and discomforts of senseless suggestion, they resent such intrusion, and cast forth the false prophets, who have brought the very name of the beautiful into disrepute, and derision upon themselves.

Alas! ladies and gentlemen, Art has been maligned. She has naught in common with such practices. She is a goddess of dainty thought—reticent of habit, abjuring all obtrusiveness, purposing in no way to better others....

Humanity takes the place of Art, and God's creations are excused by their usefulness. Beauty is confounded with virtue, and, before a work of Art, it is asked: "What good shall it do?"

Hence it is that nobility of action, in this life, is hopelessly linked with the merit of the work that portrays it; and thus the people have acquired the habit of looking, as who should say, not at a picture, but *through* it, at some human fact, that shall, or shall not, from a social point of view, better their mental or moral state. So we have come to hear of the painting that elevates, and of the duty of the painter—of the picture that is full of thought, and of the panel that merely decorates....

A favourite faith, dear to those who teach, is that certain periods were especially artistic, and that nations, readily named, were notably lovers of Art.

So we are told that the Greeks were, as a people, worshippers of the beautiful, and that in the fifteenth century Art was engrained in the multitude.

That the great masters lived in common understanding with their patrons—that the early Italians were artists—all—and that the demand for the lovely thing produced it.

That we, of to-day, in gross contrast to this Arcadian purity, call for the ungainly, and obtain the ugly.

That, could we but change our habits and climate—were we willing to wander in groves—could we be roasted out of broadcloth—were we to do without haste, and journey without speed, we should again *require* the spoon of Queen Anne, and pick at our peas with the fork of two prongs And so, for the flock, little hamlets grow near Hammersmith, and the steam horse is scorned.

Useless! quite hopeless and false is the effort!—built upon fable, and all because "a wise man has uttered a vain thing and filled his belly with the East wind."

Listen! There never was an artistic period.

There never was an Art–loving nation....

Further Reading

Anderson, Ronald, and Anne Koval. *James McNeill Whistler: Beyond the Myth.* New York: Carroll & Graf, 1995. Print.

Farr, Dennis. "James McNeill Whistler—His Links with Poetry, Music, and Symbolism." *Journal of the Royal Society of the Arts* 122 (1974): 267-84. Web. 26 Aug. 2012.

Spencer, Robin. "Whistler's Early Relations with Britain and the Significance of Industry and Commerce for His Art. Part II." *Burlington Magazine* 136 (1994): 664-74. Web. 16 Aug. 2012.

Thorp, Nigel, ed. *Whistler on Art: Selected Letters and Writings of James McNeill Whistler.* Washington, DC: Smithsonian Institution, 1994. Print.

Whistler, James. *The Gentle Art of Making Enemies.* London: Heinemann, 1994. Print.

Michael Hartwell

CHURCH AND STATE

1890 MANIFESTO

Wilford Woodruff

OVERVIEW

Issued by Wilford Woodruff, president of the Church of Jesus Christ of Latter-day Saints, the *1890 Manifesto* officially disavowed polygamy. The manifesto was a response to mounting pressure by the U.S. government, which had passed three antipolygamy statutes and disincorporated the Mormon church. The federal government was also on the verge of seizing the church's assets and disenfranchising all Mormons if they continued in their refusal to cease plural marriage. Woodruff had long been a vociferous defender of polygamy, which the church considered a divine mandate, yet he concluded that continuing the practice would undermine the viability of the church. The 360-word proclamation, initially published in the church-owned newspaper the *Deseret Weekly,* was addressed primarily to a non-Mormon audience and was couched as a direct response to news stories alleging that the church had "encouraged and urged the continuance of the practice of polygamy."

Although the church's leadership immediately and unanimously approved the manifesto, the document drove a wedge into the church's membership. On one hand, the change in church doctrine eventually led to the creation of a fundamentalist Mormon sect that refused to obey Woodruff's proclamation and thus became increasingly marginalized. On the other hand, it moved the official Mormon church closer to mainstream America. In 1896 the Utah Territory, where the church was based, was granted statehood, which had long been denied because of the practice of polygamy. Today the *1890 Manifesto* is credited with spurring Mormonism's greater accommodation of, and acceptance by, American law and culture.

HISTORICAL AND LITERARY CONTEXT

The *1890 Manifesto* was issued in response to U.S. government efforts to end polygamy, a practice the church had accepted since the 1830s, although members had not openly observed it until the early 1850s. The Morrill Act of 1862 expressed official disapproval of polygamy by prohibiting plural marriage, making bigamy punishable by fine and imprisonment, and restricting the church's ability to own property. However, the church ignored the law, and the government did not enforce it. In 1882 the Edmunds Act

made plural marriage a felony, mandating jail time, fines, and disenfranchisement for those convicted. Five years later, the Edmunds-Tucker Bill directed the government to confiscate all major church assets and instituted new mechanisms for prosecuting polygamists.

When Wilford Woodruff became church president in 1889, he sought to mitigate the conflict with the government and to smooth the path to Utah's statehood. He quickly changed church policy to refuse permission for further plural marriages. However, U.S. Supreme Court decisions that upheld the legality of the government's seizure of church property and the disenfranchisement of Mormons in Idaho convinced Woodruff that a more emphatic end to polygamy was necessary. On September 24, he presented a draft of the *Manifesto* to a group of the general authorities of the church, who modified and approved it, publishing it the next day. That October the church's General Conference accepted the proclamation as "authoritative and binding."

Woodruff's intent was twofold: to convince believers of the edict's religious truth and to demonstrate to outsiders its legal validity. The manifesto is a direct response to Section 132 of the *Doctrine and Covenants of the Church of Jesus Christ of Latter-day Saints,* which records a revelation of church founder Joseph Smith on July 12, 1843, establishing the tenet of the "plurality of wives." In contrast to the revelation, which is written in the high style of the King James Bible and attributes its authority to the direct word of the Lord, Woodruff's manifesto uses plain language befitting publication in a newspaper. The approach is legalistic rather than revelatory because Woodruff's aim is to convince outsiders (particularly government authorities) of his resolve without contradicting the received word of God and thereby offending his flock.

In the years following the manifesto's publication, Woodruff elaborated on the meaning and source of his proclamation. In a series of addresses, he claimed that the language was "manifested" to him and that the Lord revealed to him what would happen if the church continued to allow polygamy. He also emphasized the divine origin of his decision in order to quell doubts and divisions among church members. In 1908 the manifesto was printed in the

Key Facts

Time Period:
Late 19th Century

Movement/Issue:
Polygamy in the Mormon Church

Place of Publication:
United States

Language of Publication:
English

WILFORD WOODRUFF AND PLURAL MARRIAGE

Although Wilford Woodruff is remembered as the man who ended plural marriage in the Mormon church, he was a committed polygamist reported to have been married to between five and nine women. He was a vociferous defender of the practice for many years, and in 1879 he wrote his rationale for observing polygamist doctrine rather than federal law: "Now who shall we obey? God or man? My voice is that we will obey God."

When the Edmunds Act took effect in the mid-1880s and U.S. federal officials entered Utah to prosecute polygamists, many male polygamists went into hiding to evade capture. The network of safe houses, farms, fields, and compartments (called "polygamy pits") that harbored these men became known as the Mormon underground. In February 1886 Woodruff, too, went into hiding, and when church president John Taylor died in exile the following year, Woodruff led the church from an underground location near St. George. Woodruff's change of mind came with his realization that in order to survive in the United States, the church would have to accommodate the U.S. government. Federal officials had been unrelenting in their pursuit of polygamists and church leaders, driving Mormons into Mexico and Canada to establish settlements. Thus, when Woodruff emerged from hiding in 1889, he assumed the church presidency and announced his intention to bring Mormon marriage into conformity with American law.

church's *Doctrine & Covenants,* a collection of revelations (mostly from Joseph Smith) that Latter-day Saints regard as scripture. It is known today as "Official Declaration-1." Only one other Mormon document, which also expresses a reversal of church doctrine, has been made an Official Declaration—a 1978 letter from church president Spencer W. Kimball declaring that all men could serve in the priesthood "without regard for race or color."

THEMES AND STYLE

The principal theme of the *1890 Manifesto* is that—with regard to polygamy—the Mormon church would acquiesce to the federal rule of law rather than follow received church doctrine. In a sober tone, with reference to the mechanisms of American government, Woodruff makes a secular, rather than divine, pledge: "In as much as laws have been enacted by Congress forbidding plural marriages, which laws have been pronounced constitutional by the court of last resort, I hereby declare my intention to submit to those laws, and to use my influence with the members of the Church over which I preside to have them do likewise." To reinforce the church's commitment to cooperation, Woodruff not only pledges to abide by the law but also forcefully confronts and

denies specific charges that the church has been surreptitiously breaking the law by sanctioning plural marriages.

Woodruff's manifesto achieves its aim by accommodating the law without contradicting religious authority. Rather than directly address his flock, Woodruff begins by responding to "press dispatches," which he claims have been sent for "political purposes." In the third paragraph, he cites a report of a church-sanctioned polygamous marriage ceremony "in which the parties allege that the marriage was performed in the Endowment House, in Salt Lake City, in the Spring of 1889." Instead of responding to the attack with a moral or theological argument, Woodruff adopts the form and mode of his detractors, as if issuing a press release or debuting a legal argument: "In consequence of this alleged occurrence the Endowment House was, by my instructions, taken down without delay." Thus, Woodruff eschews any appeal to religious authority by plainly denying the charge of criminal wrongdoing and reasserting his obedience to the law of the land.

Stylistically, the manifesto is distinguished from other religious pronouncements by its legalistic diction and tone. The document opens not as the church's revelatory pronouncements typically do, with "Thus Saith the Lord," but with the prosaic salutation "To Whom It May Concern," immediately signaling the proclamation's grounding in secular logic. He reinforces the bureaucratic nature of his proclamation through objective, specific language, referring to the Utah Commission, the Supreme Court, and Congress rather than to God or heaven. Instead of claiming a divine mandate, he makes a detached, legal argument, closing with a word of "advice" to followers—"refrain from contracting any marriage forbidden by the law of the land"—thereby punctuating his aim of appeasing outsiders without upsetting believers.

CRITICAL DISCUSSION

When the *1890 Manifesto* was issued, readers within and outside the Mormon church received it with skepticism. The *Salt Lake Tribune,* a secular newspaper, declared that the "manifesto was not intended to be accepted as a command by the President of the Church, but as a little bit of harmless dodging to deceive the people of the East." Mormon believers were divided in their response: To many, including plural wife Lorena Eugenia Washburn Larson as she stated in her autobiography, "it seemed impossible that the Lord would go back on a principle which had caused so much sacrifice, heartache, and trial." To others, it represented a new beginning for the church. Although the church officially accepted the manifesto at its General Conference, "many church leaders viewed the Manifesto as purely a political proclamation," according to Richard S. Van Wagoner in *Mormon Polygamy: A History* (1989).

Despite the manifesto's solemn oath that the church would no longer sanction any more plural marriages, and mainstream Mormons' acceptance of its edict, the process of eradicating the practice was long and uneven. As Van Wagoner writes, "the manifesto did not produce the abrupt about-face in the Church's position that Mormons today tend to imagine." The practice persisted even as the church's public opposition to it, heralded by the *1890 Manifesto,* hastened statehood for Utah (in 1896) and initiated Mormonism's eventual acceptance of traditional marriage.

Many scholars have examined the ways in which the *1890 Manifesto* negotiated theological and practical concerns to bring about slow but lasting change in the Mormon church. In *Mormonism in Transition: A History of the Latter-day Saints, 1890-1930* (1986), Thomas G. Alexander writes that Woodruff's proclamation "marked the end of one phase of Mormon history and ushered in the transition to the second." According to Alexander, the second phase was marked not only by an end to polygamy but also by a "shift away from a closed community" and by a turn toward greater involvement with national politics and affairs. Woodruff's *Manifesto* was the start of a slow and sometimes painful accommodation to American values and political realities.

The St. George Utah Temple in St. George, Utah, was built in 1871-77. Wilford Woodruff, author of the *1890 Manifesto,* was the temple's first president.
© JIM WEST/ALAMY

BIBLIOGRAPHY

Sources

Alexander, Thomas G. *Mormonism in Transition: A History of the Latter-day Saints, 1890-1930.* Urbana: U of Illinois P, 1986. Print.

Church of Jesus Christ of Latter-day Saints. *The Doctrine and Covenants of the Church of Jesus Christ of Latter-day Saints.* Salt Lake City, UT: Church of Jesus Christ of Latter-day Saints, 1989. Web. 31 May 2012.

Embry, Jessie L. "The History of Polygamy." *Utah History Encyclopedia.* Salt Lake City: U of Utah P, 1994. Web. 28 May 2012.

"History of the Church." *Frequently Asked Questions about the Church of Latter-day Saints.* BYU Studies. Web. 1 June 2012.

Larsen, Lorena Eugenia Washburn. Autobiography. Provo, UT: Brigham Young UP, 1962. Print.

Van Wagoner, Richard S. *Mormon Polygamy: A History.* 2nd ed. Salt Lake City: Signature, 1989. Print.

"Woodruff, Wilford (1807–98)." *The New Encyclopedia of the American West.* 1998. Web. 31 May 2012.

Further Reading

Alexander, Thomas G. *Things in Heaven and Earth: The Life and Times of Wilford Woodruff, a Mormon Prophet.* Salt Lake City: Signature, 1991. Print.

Bennion, Lowell C. Rev. of *Solemn Covenant: The Mormon Polygamous Passage,* by B. Carmon Hardy. *BYU Studies* 33.2 (1993): 350-55. Web. 31 May 2012.

Cannon, Kenneth L. "Beyond the Manifesto: Polygamous Cohabitation among LDS General Authorities after 1890." *Utah Historical Quarterly* 46.1 (1978): 24-36. Print.

Ellsworth, Maria S., ed. *Mormon Odyssey: The Story of Ida Hunt Udall, Plural Wife.* Urbana: U of Illinois P, 1992.

Embry, Jessie L. *Mormon Polygamous Families: Life in the Principle.* Salt Lake City: U of Utah P, 1987. Print.

Hardy, B. Carmon. *Solemn Covenant: The Mormon Polygamous Passage.* Urbana: U of Illinois P, 1992. Print.

Hunter, J. Michael. Rev. of *Modern Polygamy: The Generations after the Manifesto,* by Brian C. Hales. *BYU Studies* 47.4 (2008): 178-84.

Kerstetter, Todd M. Rev. of *The Politics of American Religious Identity: The Seating of Senator Reed Smoot, Mormon Apostle,* by Kathleen Flake. *BYU Studies* 46.3 (2007): 169-72. Print.

Theodore McDermott

THE ADI BRAHMO SAMAJ TRUST DEED PRINCIPLES

Rammohun Roy

✧ *Key Facts*

Time Period:
Mid-19th Century

Movement/Issue:
Religious pluralism;
Social reform

Place of Publication:
India

**Language of
Publication:**
English

OVERVIEW

Composed by the Indian social and religious reformer Rammohun Roy, *The Adi Brahmo Samaj Trust Deed Principles* (1830) prescribe guidelines for the use of a Brahmoist house of worship by the religious society known as the Brahmo Sabha ("One God Society") he founded in 1828. Each principle advances a pluralistic religious theme by encouraging practitioners to worship only a generalized and inclusive "eternal unsearchable and immutable being" who is the "author and preserver of the universe." The principles also forbid the use of specific religious names and any uniquely sectarian religious practice. Although Roy (sometimes styled as Ram Mohun Roy) was born a member of the wealthy Hindu Brahman elite, he rejected the social and religious constraints of the Indian caste system. He advocated for social reform and a more monotheistic religious practice based on an egalitarian interpretation of Hindu scripture and the Vedic tradition. Roy originally put forward *The Adi Brahmo Samaj Trust Deed Principles* for use by the congregation worshiping at the first Brahmo Samaj consecrated house of prayer in Calcutta, a group originally known as the Brahmo Sabha. The service was open to all creeds and represented one of the first attempts at pluralistic religious practice in nineteenth-century India.

The Adi Brahmo Samaj Trust Deed Principles were strongly criticized by conservative Brahman Hindus as a concession to English influence, especially the efforts of Christian missionaries. Conversely, Christian missionaries, especially Unitarians, welcomed the development of the Brahmoist movement, believing it represented a transitional step in the progress of the Indian people away from traditional Hindu beliefs and toward monotheistic Christianity. The vague and inclusive nature of the language of *The Adi Brahmo Samaj Trust Deed Principles* allowed for significant variation in Brahmo Samaj practice, and the community experienced multiple divisions in the decades following Roy's death in 1833. The introduction of *The Adi Brahmo Samaj Trust Deed Principles* remains a landmark event in the history of pluralistic religious practice and social reform in India.

HISTORICAL AND LITERARY CONTEXT

The Adi Brahmo Samaj Trust Deed Principles address several developments in Hindu and colonial Indian history. Roy believed that many historical Hindu practices, such as polytheism, idolatry, barring women from education, and suttee (the practice of a widow self-immolating upon her husband's death), were based on incorrect interpretations of Hindu religious texts by Brahman priests. By reinterpreting these texts—and by making them available to all Hindus regardless of caste—Roy argued that these errant practices could be eliminated and a more historically pure Hinduism returned. Born a member of the religious and economic Brahman elite in 1772, Roy was educated in Persian, Arabic, Sanskrit, and Bengali. He was also exposed to the social and religious culture of India's British colonial rulers, most notably European political, social, and religious history; Enlightenment thought; and Unitarian Christian practice. Roy also subscribed to the eighteenth-century European deist principle that God's existence was proved by the complexity of reality.

After leaving Bengal as a youth to study Buddhism in Tibet, Roy later worked for the British East India Company. Upon returning to Calcutta, he attempted to put his religious ideas into practice by founding in 1815 the Atmiya Sabha ("Friendly Association"), which met at his home to recite Hindu scriptures, sing hymns, and discuss religious and social issues. The Atmiya Sabha disbanded in 1819. Roy later organized the Brahmo Sabha in 1828, for which in 1830 he provided the trust deed (a legal agreement between the joint owners of property) for use in a place of worship by the Brahmo Sabha. This document is now popularly known as the *Adi* ("Original") *Brahmo Samaj Trust Deed Principles* after a Brahmoist schism in the 1860s. On the strength of this organization, Roy traveled to England in 1829, where he was met enthusiastically by the Unitarian Church establishment and received an audience with King William IV. After Roy's death in 1833, Brahmo Sabha practice—whose adherents had only numbered in the hundreds—faded in India but was revived a decade later by the son of one of Roy's close friends,

Debendranath Tagore. Under Tagore, the Brahmo Sabha community became known as the Brahmo Samaj in 1846.

Roy's composition of *The Adi Brahmo Samaj Trust Deed Principles* was influenced not only by Christian Unitarian writings that emphasized the monotheistic oneness of God and the importance of interfaith dialogue but also by his extensive knowledge of the Hindu Vedas, Upanishads, and Vedanta-Sutra. He translated both the Upanishads and Vedas from Sanskrit into Bengali, Hindi, and English, in violation of Brahman tradition and despite criticism from the orthodox Hindu community. He also published several works urging social and religious reform, including *A Gift to Deists* (1804), *A Conference between an Advocate for and an Opponent of the Practice of Burning Widows Alive* (1818), and *Precepts of Jesus, the Guide to Peace and Happiness* (1820), an excerpt of the ethical teachings of Christ drawn from the four gospels. Roy also founded one of the first bilingual journals in India, *Brahmmunical Magazine,* in 1821.

The Adi Brahmo Samaj Trust Deed Principles have been reinterpreted and modified numerous times since their original presentation, often by the various, sometimes schismatic groups that grew out of the original Brahmo Sabha into the modern Brahmo Samaj. Most notably, a subsequent *Deed of Trust* issued by Sib Chunder Deb for use by the Sadharan ("General") Brahmo Samaj reiterated Roy's original principles in 1880. Tagore first codified the Brahmo religion based on *The Adi Brahmo Samaj Trust Deed Principles* in the *Brahmo Dharma* (1850), a work that rejected the authority of the Vedas and deemphasized the role of Roy's conception of a Vedantic unitary God. Tagore's *Brahmo Dharma* evolved into the modern *Prime Adi Principles* associated with the Adi Dharm religion, the modern term for the Adi Brahmo Samaj religion dating from 1861.

THEMES AND STYLE

The central theme of *The Adi Brahmo Samaj Trust Deed Principles* is that Brahmoism and Brahmoist places of worship are open to anyone regardless of specific faith, providing they acknowledge the existence of one nonsectarian unifying spirit overseeing all existence. Roy writes in the first and second principle that a Brahmoist place of worship will be open to "all sorts and descriptions of people without distinction … for the worship and adoration of the One Eternal Unsearchable and Immutable Being … but not under or by any other name, designation or title peculiarly used for … any being or beings by any man or set of men whatsoever." The remaining principles consist of a series of generalized prohibitions forbidding Brahmoists from engaging in sectarian religious practices such as idolatry, sacrifice, feasting, and divisive speech, with the last prohibition receiving special emphasis. Roy writes that

J.T. SUNDERLAND MEETS THE BRAHMOISTS

In 1895 fifty-three-year-old American Unitarian missionary J.T. Sunderland traveled from the United States to India to meet with members of the Brahmo Samaj. Like many other missionaries to the Samaj, he was familiar with Rammohun Roy's work *Precepts of Jesus, the Guide to Peace and Happiness,* as well as P.C. Mazumdar's *Oriental Christ* (1869), a Brahmoist work popular among missionary Christians owing to Mazumdar's emphasis on Jesus's elevated status in the theology and liturgy of the Brahmo Samaj. Sunderland had also met Mazumdar at the 1893 World Parliament of Religions in Chicago and wrote before his arrival in India that, while the Brahmo Samaj "does not explicitly call itself Christian … it is essentially a Unitarian Church that has sprung up on the soil of India."

Upon his arrival, Sunderland was invited to attend a Brahmo service and was stunned to find "clapping of hands and swaying of the body and violent dancing." He noted that "the men sweat and it seemed to me they would drop down in exhaustion." He admitted to being surprised to find that Brahmo services were not identical to Unitarian services. His Brahmoist hosts did not apologize for their religious practices but later reassured him by emphasizing their commitment to social reform and the building of educational institutions. Sunderland returned from his mission in 1896 convinced that India's spiritual interests were best served by Indians themselves rather than by Western missionaries.

"no sermon, preaching, discourse, prayer or hymn" shall be used in the service except those that "have a tendency to the promotion of charity, morality, piety, benevolence, virtue and the strengthening of bonds … between men of all religious persuasions and creeds."

Roy's rhetorical strategy in *The Adi Brahmo Samaj Trust Deed Principles* is based on striking an effective balance between prohibition and inclusivity. Because the principles are worded in the negative ("that none of the following shall be allowed…") and presented as codified legal precepts similar to the Christian Ten Commandments, Roy's explanation of Brahmoist religious practice is deceptively forceful and clear. However, each principle is left open to broad interpretation based on categorical definition and allows for religious groups with widely disparate views to engage in Brahmoist religious practice. In this sense, *The Adi Brahmo Samaj Trust Deed Principles* echo the works of Christian Unitarians and religious humanists who also employ seemingly definitive yet realistically pliable guidelines to define their beliefs, a strategy intended to make the group attractive to a wider variety of potential followers.

The language of *The Adi Brahmo Samaj Trust Deed Principles* is intensely legalistic, with Roy making

extensive use of categorical specificity to define each principle. One example is his prohibition of any "graven image, statue, or sculpture, carving, painting, picture, portrait, or the likeness of anything" inside a Brahmoist place of worship, which is, in turn, described alternatively as a "messuage, building, land, tenements and heraditaments and premises." This kind of exhaustive concrete specificity also invites wider religious participation by eliminating exceptions that might attract one faith while driving away another. In this way, Roy again opens Brahmoist practice to a wider potential audience.

CRITICAL DISCUSSION

Roy's death in 1833 and the subsequent fading of the Brahmo Sabha movement in Calcutta limited initial critical reaction to *The Adi Brahmo Samaj Trust Deed Principles*. The principles were criticized in Roy's lifetime by a conservative Hindu group, the Hindu Dharma Sabha, which claimed Roy's beliefs represented too much of a concession to colonizing English missionaries at the expense of traditional Hindu belief. Tagore's revitalization of the Brahmo Sabha into the Brahmo Samaj in 1846 received criticism from English Christian missionaries in India, notably Alexander Duff, for his renunciation of Roy's more pluralistic views and emphasis on the superiority of Hindu religious practice. The Brahmo Samaj movement experienced large growth throughout India in the 1860s, with Keshab Chandra Sen leading a large faction of Samaj members in demanding social reform and performing a controversial intercaste marriage in 1862. The modern Sadharan Brahmo Samaj split off from Sen's group in 1878 over Sen's refusal to introduce a democratic constitution into the Brahmoist church. Western newspapers and journals took greater notice of the Brahmoist religion in the 1880s, with the *Methodist Quarterly, Independent,* and *Reformed Quarterly Review* publishing exploratory articles on Brahmoist beliefs and reviews of Brahmoist publications.

Western scholarship on *The Adi Brahmo Samaj Trust Deed Principles* in the twentieth century focused on some of the misconceptions of nineteenth-century Western observers of the Brahmoist movement, with Kenneth W. Jones calling the work a "sketchy statement of principles for Sabha" in his essay in *Socioreligious Reform Movements in British India* (1989) and noting how the lack of a more concrete codification of beliefs by Roy led to the rapid decline of the Brahmo Sabha upon his death. Prominent Brahmoist scholar David Kopf has argued that Roy did not embrace Christianity as much as many contemporary Christian missionary groups believed and, instead, used Christian analysis and value systems to philosophically validate India's own religious texts. Historical studies of the Brahmoist movement also focused on the role of intercaste marriage controversies under India's Adi Dharma Law.

The Adi Brahmo Samaj Trust Deed Principles have continued to guide the Brahmo Samaj community into the twenty-first century, with Brahmoists winning recognition for Brahmo marriages to Hindus, Jains, Sikhs, and Buddhists in Bangladesh in 2002. In 2004 the Supreme Court of India dismissed the government of West Bengal's thirty-year legal effort to classify Brahmoists as Hindus. Western scholars have noted that Roy was the first Indian to apply the ideas of the French and American revolutions to Indian society, and Paul E. Teed has continued to explore the complicated relationship between Christian missionaries and the Brahmo Samaj community in India at the close of the nineteenth century.

BIBLIOGRAPHY

Sources

Adi Dharm. Brahmo Samaj Community. Web. 24 Oct. 2012.

"History of the Brahmo Samaj." *www.thebrahmosamaj.net.* Brahmo Samaj Community, n.d. Web. 24. Oct. 2012.

Jones, Kenneth W. "Bengal and Northeastern India." *Socio-religious Reform Movements in British India.* Cambridge: Cambridge UP, 1989. *Cambridge Histories Online.* Web. 24 Oct. 2012.

"Rom Mohun Roy." *Encyclopedia Britannica Online.* Encyclopedia Britannica, 2012. Web. 25 Oct. 2012.

Sadharan Brahmo Samaj. Sadharan Brahmo Samaj Community. Web. 24 Oct. 2012.

Teed, Paul E. "Interfaith Encounter and Religious Pluralism: J.T. Sunderland's Mission to the Brahmo Samajes of India, 1895-96." *American Studies* Spring/Summer 2009: 51-69. *Project MUSE.* Web. 24 Oct. 2012.

Further Reading

Ahmed, Salahuddin A.F. *Social Ideas and Social Change in Bengal, 1818-1835.* Leiden: E.J. Brill, 1965. Print.

Killingley, Dermot. *Makers of Modern Indian Religion in the Late Nineteenth Century.* Oxford: Oxford UP, 2002. Print.

Kopf, David. *Orientalism and the Bengal Renaissance: The Dynamics of Indian Modernization, 1773-1835.* Berkeley: U of California P, 1969. Print.

———. *The Brahmo Samaj and the Shaping of the Modern Indian Mind.* Princeton: Princeton UP, 1979. Print.

Morearty, John. "The Two-Edged Word: The Treacherousness of Symbolic Transformation: Rammohun Roy, Debendranath, Vivekananda and 'The Indian Golden Age.'" Ed. Warren Gunderson. *Studies of Bengal.* East Lansing: Michigan State UP, 1976. Print.

Craig Barnes

AN ADMONITION TO THE PARLIAMENT

John Field, Thomas Wilcox

⁘ Key Facts

Time Period:
Mid-16th Century

Movement/Issue:
Reformation; Puritan conflict with the Church of England

Place of Publication:
England

Language of Publication:
English

OVERVIEW

Published illegally in 1572, *An Admonition to the Parliament* by John Field and Thomas Wilcox announces the demands of radical Protestants, often called Puritans, for far-reaching changes in an English church they felt had been insufficiently reformed. Appearing at a moment when debate was raging over the doctrines and government of the Church of England, Field and Wilcox's *Admonition* gave voice to the beliefs of the most radical reformers. The book calls for Parliament to adopt a fully Presbyterian form of church government in which all clergy would be equals and for the English monarchy to give up its claim to supreme governorship over the church. While they addressed their demands to Parliament, Field and Wilcox also hoped to mobilize public opinion in favor of their position.

The appearance of *An Admonition* set off one of the most heated controversies of the Elizabethan period. Official reaction was swift and harsh. The authors were arrested and incarcerated in London's Newgate prison for more than a year, and the government tried to suppress the book by forcing booksellers to hand over all copies in their possession. Despite such censorship efforts, *An Admonition* remained present in the public consciousness, largely because of the subsequent pamphlet war, known as the Admonition Controversy, which continued the debate over the issues Field and Wilcox had raised. Supporters of the official church could not let *An Admonition* go unanswered and produced a proliferation of texts to rebut it. These rebuttals were countered, in turn, by supporters of Field and Wilcox. Nevertheless, the Puritans inspired by Field and Wilcox did not succeed at changing the fundamental doctrines or organizational structures of the Church of England.

HISTORICAL AND LITERARY CONTEXT

An Admonition voices the concerns of Puritans, who felt that the Reformation in England had not yet produced a church sufficiently purged of the errors they associated with Catholicism. Puritans especially objected to the Church of England's requirements that clergy wear Catholic-like robes during services and that ministers read stock homilies from a state-produced book instead preaching to their congregations as they wished. Puritans compared the English church unfavorably to the more thoroughly reformed Presbyterian churches found in parts of Germany, Switzerland, and the Netherlands and in neighboring Scotland. London-based Puritans such as Field and Wilcox needed to look no further for models of their ideal church than the so-called "strangers' churches," Presbyterian congregations that Protestant refugees from Europe had been allowed to set up in the English capital.

When *An Admonition* appeared, tensions between Puritans and conservatives who favored the status quo in the English church had been increasing for several years. Immediately before the book's publication, Parliament had deliberated a bill that would have allowed Puritan ministers to depart from the order of worship established in the Book of Common Prayer (which clergymen were legally required to use), enabling Puritan clergy to devote more of their services to the preaching and Bible-reading practices they viewed as especially important. Although the bill was relatively moderate, Queen Elizabeth strongly opposed it and intervened in Parliament to defeat it. Frustrated by such actions against further reformation by the Queen and the bishops, Puritans such as Field and Wilcox sought to use the press to win public support for their views.

An Admonition draws upon the theories of proper church government and the importance of preaching set forth by European religious reformers such as John Calvin. As an admonition, the book also implicitly functions as a kind of printed sermon. As Kenneth J. E. Graham writes in *The Performance of Conviction: Plainness and Rhetoric in the Early English Renaissance* (1994), the act of admonishing is "a branch of ecclesiastical discipline, the mildest form of church censure and the first step toward excommunication." Thus, Field and Wilcox used the work's genre as an implied warning that unless the English government reformed the church properly, godly ministers would have to pronounce more severe censures in the future.

By inspiring the subsequent proliferation of pro- and anti-*Admonition* pamphlets, the piece had significant literary influence in its own time. In addition, the issues it raised and the controversy it generated influenced the works of Elizabethan poets and dramatists, including William Shakespeare. Perhaps most importantly, by providing what some radical Puritans saw as a denunciation of the English church's sinfulness, *An Admonition* inspired some readers to entertain the extreme possibility of leaving it and forming their own churches. Among those so-called separatists who took such action were the predecessors of the Puritans, who in 1620 left England on the *Mayflower* to seek religious freedom in America.

THEMES AND STYLE

An Admonition argues that the English church needs further reform, particularly in three areas: "preaching of the worde purely, ministring of the sacraments sincerely, and ecclesiastical discipline." On the topic of preaching, the authors complain that English clergymen are forced to perform services by rote from the legally mandated prayer book instead of preaching the Gospel as God moves them. Field and Wilcox claim this practice leaves worshippers poorly instructed in the Christian faith. They further allege that the sacraments are administered in ceremonies too closely resembling Catholic worship, listing several practices in both the Communion and baptism rituals first introduced by papal decrees that the English prayer book retains. The last and most controversial point concerns church government. The authors demand that "instead of an Archbishop or Lord bishop, you must make equalitie of ministers." The community of clergy would then elect "Seniors or Elders" to help them govern while ministers focused on teaching and disciplining their congregations. This demand is especially sensitive because it takes the power of appointing church leaders away from the monarch and gives it to ordinary clergymen.

An Admonition directly addresses its audience to solicit support, as evidenced by its concluding reminder: "God hath set these examples before your eyes to encourage you to go foreward to a thorow and a speedy reformation." The treatise also makes heavy use of the rhetorical technique of antithesis to make unfavorable comparisons between the contemporary situation and the idealized primitive church of the Apostles. For example, the authors claim: "Then the ministers wer preachers: now bare readers.... In those dayes knowne by voice, learning, and doctrine: now they must be discerned from other by popish and Antichristian apparel." These antitheses serve to illustrate the faults of the present-day English church in brief but memorable style.

An Admonition is divided into two parts that are quite different stylistically. The first part (written by Wilcox), also called "An Admonition to the Parliament," employs clear but dispassionate language. Rather than wading through abstruse theological arguments, Wilcox uses antitheses to offer brief examples of the abuses the authors hope to see corrected. The second part, written by Field and titled "View of popish abuses," raises almost exactly the same arguments as the first but in a scathing, passionate style. Field's denunciation of the Book of Common Prayer as "culled & picked out of that popishe dunghill, the Masse booke" is representative of

THE BOOK OF COMMON PRAYER

First introduced in 1549 during the reign of the Protestant King Edward VI and revised in 1552, the Book of Common Prayer was outlawed during the time Catholic Queen Mary sat on the throne. When the Protestant Queen Elizabeth became sovereign after Mary's death in 1558, she favored reintroducing the prayer book. Although many pro-Catholic bishops initially resisted, Elizabeth achieved Parliamentary approval for restoring the Book of Common Prayer in 1559. The Elizabethan version was mostly based on the 1552 edition but jettisoned some of its more radically Protestant features.

The Book of Common Prayer was the blueprint for religious practice in early modern England. It contains instructions for how ministers were to perform services, including the prayers to be said; the Psalms and scriptural texts to be read at given times; and the ceremonies to be followed during the rites of baptism, communion, marriage, and burial. As the text that prescribed how these important events should be observed, the Book of Common Prayer permeated the lives of early modern English people. Its language influenced notable English authors such as William Shakespeare and John Donne, and many phrases from it—such as "ashes to ashes, dust to dust"—are now part of the common lexicon.

his authorial voice. The two authors also supplement their texts with a large number of marginal references to biblical verses, lending scriptural authority to the argument. Both parts of *An Admonition* thus come to resemble sermons like those Field or Wilcox might have preached.

CRITICAL DISCUSSION

An Admonition provoked passionate responses, favorable and unfavorable alike, when it appeared. In addition to imprisoning the authors, the English government waged a printed counterattack on their ideas. Bishop John Whitgift assailed *An Admonition* soon after its publication in his *An answere to a certen Libel*, while other bishops assaulted it in sermons. The bishops' anti-*Admonition* proclamations prompted other Puritans to respond with defenses of Field and Wilcox's book. The most notable pro-*Admonition* pamphlet is Thomas Cartwright's answer to Whitgift, *A Replye to an answere*, which became a Puritan classic in its own right. Whitgift responded to Cartwright's *Replye*, and these two rivals engaged in several more rounds of pamphlet warfare. The controversy did not end with these writers, though. Two decades later, Richard Hooker's defense of religious conformity in his *Laws of Ecclesiastical Polity* was still responding to challenges first raised in *An Admonition*.

The first of its kind instating an overtly Puritan position on issues such as church government and preaching, *An Admonition* "served to keep these issues before the public mind for twenty years," if not longer,

John Field and Thomas Wilcox's *Admonition to Parliament* calls for Queen Elizabeth I, depicted here, to banish remaining aspects of Roman Catholicism from the Church of England. BPK, BERLIN/NATIONAL PORTRAIT GALLERY, LONDON, GREAT BRITAIN/ JOCHEN REMMER/ART RESOURCE, NY

publication roughly coincides with an important change in the character of the English reformation. Since the 1530s religious reform in England had been driven by the monarchs and by Parliament, but in the 1560s and 1570s the reformation took on a more popular character as ordinary folk such as Field and Wilcox argued that the changes imposed from above were inadequate and the church needed reform beyond what the authorities were willing to countenance. In addition, *An Admonition*'s publication is often cited as marking a moment when English Protestants began to contend with each other over religious issues as violently as they had with Catholics in the previous decades.

BIBLIOGRAPHY

Sources

Collinson, Patrick. *English Puritanism*. General Series 106. London: The Historical Association, 1983. Print.

Duffy, Eamon. *The Stripping of the Altars: Traditional Religion in England, c. 1400-c. 1580*. New Haven: Yale UP, 1992. Print.

Field, John, and Thomas Wilcox. "An Admonition to the Parliament." *Puritan Manifestoes: A Study of the Origin of the Puritan Revolt*. Ed. W. H. Frere and C. E. Douglas. London: S. P. C. K., 1954. 1-39. Print.

Graham, Kenneth J. E. *The Performance of Conviction: Plainness and Rhetoric in the Early English Renaissance*. Ithaca: Cornell UP, 1994. Print.

Howard, Leon. *Essays on Puritans and Puritanism*. Ed. James Barbour and Thomas Quirk. Albuquerque: U of New Mexico P, 1986. Print.

Kirk, James. "'The Polities of the Best Reformed Kirks': Scottish Achievements and English Aspirations in Church Government after the Reformation." *Scottish Historical Review* 59 (1980): 22-53. *JSTOR*. Web. 29 Aug. 2012.

Further Reading

Booty, John E. "History of the 1559 Book of Common Prayer." *The Book of Common Prayer 1559: The Elizabethan Prayer Book*. Ed. John E. Booty. Charlottesville: The UP of Virginia, 1976. 327-84. Print.

Collinson, Patrick. *The Elizabethan Puritan Movement*. Berkeley: U of California P, 1967. Print.

Eppley, Daniel. *Defending Royal Supremacy and Discerning God's Will in Tudor England*. Aldershot: Ashgate, 2007. Print.

Kneidel, Gregory. "'Mightie Simplenesse': Protestant Pastoral Rhetoric and Spenser's 'Shepheardes Calendar.'" *Studies in Philology* 96.3 (1999): 275-312. *JSTOR*. Web. 4 Sept. 2012.

MacCulloch, Diarmaid. *The Later Reformation in England 1547-1603*. New York: St. Martin's Press, 1990. Print.

McGinn, Donald Joseph. *The Admonition Controversy*. New Brunswick: Rutgers UP, 1949. Print.

Simmons, J. L. "A Source for Shakespeare's Malvolio: The Elizabethan Controversy with the Puritans." *Huntington Library Quarterly* 36 (1973): 181-201. Print.

Solt, Leo F. *Church and State in Early Modern England, 1509-1640*. Oxford: Oxford UP, 1990. Print.

writes Patrick Collinson in *English Puritanism*. Many of the same issues remained contentious long into the seventeenth century, and disagreement over them played no small part in the outbreak of the English Civil War in the 1640s. *An Admonition* remains of interest to scholars of early modern England because it is often taken to represent the beginning of Puritanism as a distinct position within the Church of England.

Modern scholarship on *An Admonition* tends to focus on its role in initiating the fierce debate over church government, practices of administering the sacraments, and preaching that divided the Church of England for almost a century. As the statement of "a new and radical development in the English reformation," writes Leon Howard in *Essays on Puritans and Puritanism* (1986), *An Admonition* represents an important new stage in the complex history of religious conflict in sixteenth-century England. According to historian Eamon Duffy in *The Stripping of the Altars* (1992), its

John Walters

BRUNSWICK MANIFESTO

Geoffroy de Limon

OVERVIEW

Written by minor French politician Geoffroy de Limon, the *Brunswick Manifesto* (1792) not only enumerates the uncompromising terms of the Prussian and Austrian coalition forces' war against the French revolutionary government that had replaced King Louis XVI but also threatens the total destruction of Paris if the royal family or its residence in the Tuileries were attacked or harmed. Fearing the spread of revolution throughout Europe and the destabilization of other monarchies, commander of the Prussian and Austrian armies Charles William Ferdinand, Duke of Brunswick, signed the manifesto on July 25 at Koblenz, Prussia (now in Germany), where many émigré French noblemen, fearing the peasant uprising against the wealthy, had fled after the Revolution began. The aristocrats had rejected an earlier, more moderate draft, preferring the menacing version written by Limon, who believed in fully restoring the privileges of the French monarchy. Addressed to French citizens, the manifesto threatens death to those who oppose the advancing coalition forces and calls for the immediate restoration of the king to his pre-Revolution level of power.

The *Brunswick Manifesto* was derided in the French press as illegal and the product of royal collusion with Austria. Its threatening tone only heightened the fear and tension in revolutionary France, confirming for many that the king, who was already unpopular for his choices in wielding what limited power he had, was a traitor and unfit to lead. Brunswick, whose troops were expelled from France just two months after the signing of the document, is rumored to have stated that he would give his life to take back his signature. Historians later described the document as the catalyst of the August 10 storming of the Tuileries Palace, the royal residence in Paris where the king and his family were being held. In twenty-first-century scholarship, the manifesto is thought to be just one of several social and political forces that provoked the attack, which proved a turning point in the Revolution.

HISTORICAL AND LITERARY CONTEXT

The threatened aggression in the *Brunswick Manifesto* only served to strengthen revolutionary France's will to defeat the ineffectual French monarchy. The War of the First Coalition—an attempt by other European powers to once again place the French monarchy in power—began with revolutionary France's declaration of war against Austria on April 20, 1792, which it followed nine days later with a failed invasion of the Austrian Netherlands. Among other territorial points of friction was the Comtat-Venaissin, which for centuries had been part of the Holy Roman Empire, then also part of the Austrian Empire. In 1791 the Comtat-Venaissin was declared a part of France. French kings had been trying for centuries to wrest it from successive popes, but it took a people's plebiscite to make it happen. Still other contentious domains were the French Alsace and Lorraine, in which German princes had long held extensive properties. The Revolution suppressed the princes' rights and those of French noblemen in the region, overturning a centuries-old system of fiefdoms.

In spite of the initial failure of the French invasion of the Austrian Netherlands, the French Revolution enjoyed popular support there, and within France nationalist sentiment continued to rise, especially with the deliverance of the *Brunswick Manifesto*. On July 11, 1792, the National Assembly had issued a brief statement, *La patrie en danger* (The Homeland in Danger), a rallying cry for citizenship and freedom, as the Austro-Prussians gathered their forces along the border. When the high-handed force of the manifesto was made known to the people of France at the end of the month, it served as the final push to unite the country against the invaders.

It was common practice in European warfare for participants to issue various declarations and proclamations. This tactic often served as a means of garnering support from other powers by attributing blame to the other side; such issuances also could be used to take advantage of internal strife in the opposing side's realm. For instance, in 1742 the empress of Russia forced Sweden to accept her preferred candidate as heir to the Swedish throne as a condition for peace during one of the three wars between the two powerful entities in the eighteenth century. Russia issued many declarations to maintain its preferred conditions and had forces assembled on Swedish soil to back them up.

The *Brunswick Manifesto* was shouted down in the National Assembly before it could be heard; all

Key Facts

Time Period:
Late 18th Century

Movement/Issue:
Monarchism; French Revolution

Place of Publication:
France

Language of Publication:
French

PROCLAMATIONS, DECLARATIONS, PRONOUNCEMENTS, AND THREATS

Forceful diplomacy has been used throughout history with varying consequences. During the Prussian campaign against Amsterdam in 1787, Charles William Ferdinand, Duke of Brunswick, signed a threatening manifesto and led his forces to an easy victory against the Dutch Patriot revolution. After the French royal family's failed attempt to flee the country in June 1791, Leopold II, Holy Roman emperor and brother to Marie Antoinette, issued the Pilnitz Declaration in August. It exhorted the principal monarchs of Europe to join forces to defeat the French Revolution and restore the French monarchy.

One of the most powerful documents to emerge from the French Revolution was *Déclaration des droits de l'homme et du citoyen* (1789; *Declaration of the Rights of Man and of the Citizen*), which drew on the ideals of the Enlightenment to posit a new sovereignty of the people. One of the few women writers of the time, French social reformer Olympe de Gouges, wrote a feminist version, *Déclaration des droits de la femme et de la citoyenne* (1791; *Declaration of the Rights of Women and of Female Citizens*), but the leaders of the Revolution were unprepared to allow for new consideration of the role of women in society. After several more pamphlets critical of the Revolution, Gouges was executed in 1793.

of the elements were already in place for the succession of events that would lead to the abolishment of the monarchy and the establishment of the republic in September 1792. On August 10, the Tuileries were stormed. In early September, rumors of a counterrevolution being planned by prisoners compelled murderous attacks on jails in Paris and other French cities. French forces rallied to defeat the Austrian coalition's armies on September 20 at the Battle of Valmy. Barely six months after the manifesto was issued, on January 21, 1793, Louis XVI was guillotined after being found guilty of counterrevolutionary actions. Limon went on to write *La vie et le martyre de Louis XVI ... avec un examen du décret régicide* (1793; The Life and Martyrdom of Louis XVI, with an Examination of the Regicidal Decree). Although scholarly interest in the *Brunswick Manifesto* exists in the twenty-first century, it is the history of the events surrounding the work that receives the most attention.

THEMES AND STYLE

The *Brunswick Manifesto*'s guiding principle is that the French Revolution is an illegal farce, perpetrated by a radical minority on a cowed population that wanted to see the king restored to full power. It posits the Austro-Prussian alliance as the savior of the French people:

> Convinced that the sound part of the French nation abhors the excesses of a faction which dominates it, and that the greatest number

of inhabitants look forward with impatience to the moment of relief to declare themselves openly against the odious enterprises of their oppressors, his Majesty the Emperor and his Majesty the King of Prussia, call upon them and invite them to return without delay to the ways of reason, justice, order and peace.

The manifesto lists eight points: the two monarchs have no territorial aspirations; the royal family must immediately be set free and the king allowed to reconfigure the government as he sees fit; cooperative towns and villages will be protected; the National Guard must obey the invading armies or be treated as rebels; the entire French army must rededicate itself to the king; all regional administrators responsible for any type of resistance to the invading army will pay with their lives; civilians who resist the invading armies will pay with their lives; and, lastly, if any harm befalls the royal family, the entire city of Paris will be laid to waste. A final paragraph envisions the royal family being escorted to "the city in his kingdom nearest the frontiers" in order to set up a provisional government for the imagined transitional period to follow.

Two of the most frequently used words in the *Brunswick Manifesto* are "submit" and "violence." Inherent to the traditional belief that the monarchy held their power by divine right is the idea that to deprive them of that right would arouse the wrath of God. The manifesto's wording was thus subliminally appealing to what remained of religious sentiment among the populace, as well as to common superstition. The other two most frequently used words are "liberty" and "security," both key principles of the Revolution as they pertained to the common man; however, in the *Brunswick Manifesto,* the words are used on behalf of the king. Borrowing from the language of the Enlightenment and the Revolution, the manifesto aims "to restore to the King the security and liberty of which he is deprived." The imagery appeals directly to the emotions, as though the king were synonymous with the "boroughs and villages," the "towns and country districts."

CRITICAL DISCUSSION

When the *Brunswick Manifesto* reached Paris at the end of July 1792, it met with reactions ranging from disbelief to ridicule. Some people questioned its legality in terms of the law of nations, and the king, in a disingenuous attempt to save face, claimed it was forged. As noted by historian Elizabeth Cross, the July 28-August 4 edition of *Les révolutions de Paris* reported that "most people thought this *régiocomique* piece was written at the Tuileries." The moment when the people could be intimidated by haughty noblemen had passed. Noted history professor H.A. Barton, in his article "The Origins of the *Brunswick Manifesto*," observes, "by August 7 the *Moniteur* was complaining about 'all the Austrian, Prussian, and Brunswickian manifestoes, declarations, and counterdeclarations.'"

The *Brunswick Manifesto* failed to undermine—and may even have bolstered—the Revolution, and its stated goals proved impossible, but the rhetorical devices it deployed have remained notable features of manifestos of all types. Manifestos are typically marked by moral outrage, a call to immediate action, repeated actions, and unequivocal demarcations of opposing sides of a conflict. In her introduction to *Manifestoes: Provocations of the Modern* (1999), Janet Lyon describes the conditions that give rise to such writing: "manifestoes proliferate at the cloverleafs of class war, gender politics, ethnic identification, and national struggle." Critical attention toward the *Brunswick Manifesto* has focused on its significance with regard to historicizing the French Revolution, its position within the ideological framework of the Enlightenment, and its role in the changing nature of European warfare and international law.

Many scholars have assessed the *Brunswick Manifesto* as a galvanizing factor in the Revolution: "The effect of the manifesto was precisely the opposite of its purpose," says Robert Roswell Palmer in his book *The Age of the Democratic Revolution* (1970). Barton, examining the *Brunswick Manifesto*'s origins, reveals "how little the Revolution in France was understood by those who sought to combat it." Tracking the interventions of a surprising number of aristocrats involved in its composition and invested in the outcome of the manifesto, Barton notes Marie Antoinette's opinion that it "should dissociate itself publicly from the pretentions of the émigrés, should identify itself with no particular faction in France, should not appear to interfere in French internal affairs, and should avoid too much mention of the king." The manifesto, however, failed to conform to her suggestions.

BIBLIOGRAPHY

Sources

Barton, H.A. "The Origins of the *Brunswick Manifesto*." *French Historical Studies* 5.2 (1967): 146-69. Print.

Cross, Elizabeth. "The Myth of the Foreign Enemy? The *Brunswick Manifesto* and the Radicalization of the French Revolution." *French History* 25.2 (2011): 88-213. Print.

Lyon, Janet. *Manifestoes: Provocations of the Modern.* Ithaca, NY: Cornell UP, 1999. Print.

Palmer, Robert Roswell. *The Age of the Democratic Revolution: A Political History of Europe and America, 1760-1800.* Vol. 2. Princeton: Princeton UP, 1970. Print.

Robinson, J.H., ed. "The Proclamation of the Duke of Brunswick, 1792." Hanover Historical Texts Project. Hanover College. Web. 13 Aug. 2012.

Traugott, Mark. "The Duke of Brunswick's Manifesto." *History 171 Syllabus Reading.* Santa Cruz: U of California. Web. 26 June 2012.

Further Reading

Bell, D.A. *The First Total War: Napoleon's Europe and the Birth of Warfare as We Know It.* Boston: Houghton Mifflin, 2007. Print.

Bouloiseau, Marc. "A propos du 'Manifeste de Brunswick.'" *Annales historiques de la Révolution française* 265.265. *Persée: Portail de revues en sciences humaines et sociales.* Web. 26 June 2012.

Edelstein, Dan. "War and Terror: The Law of Nations from Grotius to the French Revolution." *French Historical Studies* Spring 2008. *Bibliothèque et archives nationales du Québec.* Web. 26 June 2012.

Mayer, A.J. *The Furies: Violence and Terror in the French and Russian Revolutions.* Princeton: Princeton UP, 2000. Print.

Schama, Simon. *Citizens: A Chronicle of the French Revolution.* New York: Random House, 1989. Print.

Rebecca Rustin

The Farewell of Louis XVI to His Family, painted by Jean-Jacques Hauer in 1795, depicts the king departing for his execution in 1793. ALFREDO DAGLI ORTI/THE ART ARCHIVE AT ART RESOURCE, NY

CHRISTIAN NON-RESISTANCE

Adin Ballou

✧ *Key Facts*

Time Period:
Mid-19th Century

Movement/Issue:
Nonresistance
(nonviolent protest);
Abolitionism; Christianity

Place of Publication:
United States

**Language of
Publication:**
English

OVERVIEW

Christian Non-Resistance (1846), written by Universalist minister, socialist, and antislavery activist Adin Ballou, represents both a comprehensive description and vigorous defense of the pre-Civil War nonresistance movement. His book describes the ethic of Christian nonresistance—better known today as nonviolence— as it applied to a young United States divided over issues of slavery, war, and justice. *Christian Non-Resistance* is "soberly and frankly addressed to the reason, conscience, and higher sentiments of mankind," and implicitly functions as a call for all "true Christians" to engage in passive resistance against what Ballou saw as the un-Christian practices of slavery, war, and capital punishment. Although pitched as a moral call based on the life and teachings of Jesus, Ballou aims for nothing less than a new sort of government that gains its legitimacy not from military might but from "superior justice, forbearance, meekness, forgiveness, and charity." To this end, his manifesto is notable for its insistence on nonparticipation in government, rallying Christians to forgo voting and instead to simply live by the Christian ethic of nonresistance.

Initially embraced for its lucid and comprehensive defense of early-nineteenth-century nonresistance, *Christian Non-Resistance*'s call for governmental nonparticipation became contentious as the United States descended into the Civil War. Ballou was one of few pacifists who continued to live by his nonresistance ideology during the Civil War, despite pressure from abolitionists to join the Union's cause. In many ways, Ballou's book was a short-term failure: it engendered no great nonresistance movement, nor did it lead to the abolishment of slavery or prevent the massive and bloody Civil War. However, it did lay the groundwork for future nonviolent movements, and Ballou's ideas were reflected in some of the twentieth century's most successful nonviolent figures, such as Mohandas Gandhi and Martin Luther King, Jr.

HISTORICAL AND LITERARY CONTEXT

Christian Non-Resistance is a comprehensive argument for nonresistance in an era when the United States was growing into a colonial power. For many American Christians, the question of military activity became ambiguous after the War of 1812, sometimes called the Second War of Independence. The young United States

had decisively defended its borders, gaining Britain's begrudging acceptance of its sovereignty. Thus, further military activity was less about self-defense and more about colonial ambition. The bellicose tone struck by the United States in this period was considered by many in power to be justified, but it was also at odds with America's historical origins as a "A City upon a Hill," a phrase signifying that the country should be an example of Christian virtue for the rest of the world.

Ballou's text was published in the shadow of the annexation of Texas by the United States (1845), an event that precipitated the Mexican-American War (1846-1848). The United States' eventual victory, and the territorial expansions that came with it, became a flashpoint in the national debate over slavery. Ballou's book functions as an alternative vision of a future that eschews violence in favor of "pure Christian government." This vision was shared by many people, including noted abolitionist William Lloyd Garrison (1805-1879). The ideology of nonresistance became an important part of opposition movements in the United States' early period of expansion and persisted well into the twentieth century, when it became a key component of the civil rights era.

Ballou's book participates in a longer tradition of nonresistance movements; in particular, it is grounded in readings of the New Testament. Parts of his text reflect his position as a prominent abolitionist, echoing his 1843 address "The Voice of Duty." In composing *Christian Non-Resistance*, Ballou also drew from the experience he gained as the founder of the socialist Hopedale community. This town was a utopian experiment grounded in the religious idealism that drives his book. Founded in 1842, the commune was designed around Ballou's belief in a "Practical Christianity," which asserted that true Christians should live by biblical ideals in their everyday lives.

Initially embraced by like-minded pacifists, *Christian Non-Resistance* fell out of favor in the decades following the Civil War, in part because the slavery issue had been resolved through acts of considerable violence. In the years of the Civil War, many pacifists on both sides of the Mason-Dixon Line backed away from a strict ideology of nonresistance in order to contribute to the war effort. Many abolitionists, more concerned with the institution of slavery than ideological nonresistance, also shifted their support toward the Union's efforts. Throughout the war, Ballou stayed true to his belief in nonresistance, but in the years following it, he lost much of his original audience. Nevertheless, history treated him kindly: his ideas eventually had a profound influence on Russian novelist and nonresistance advocate Leo Tolstoy, who, in turn, influenced the work of Gandhi and King.

THEMES AND STYLE

Christian Non-Resistance argues that Christianity is a fundamentally nonviolent religion and that the "true Christian" should therefore strive to lead a life of complete nonresistance. It opens by defining the key terms in the movement, starting with "Christian Non-Resistance" itself: "It is that original, peculiar kind of non-resistance, which was enjoined and exemplified by Jesus Christ, according to the scriptures of the New Testament." Once his definitions are clearly established, Ballou works through chapters of scriptural proof, answers spiritual and general objections, and ends with a long description of nonresistance in relation to government. Throughout the book, Ballou maintains an emphasis on the importance of nonresistance as a day-to-day ideology: "Righteousness is an aggregate of the little things of life. He that is faithless habitually in small matters is not to be depended on in great matters."

Ballou achieves his rhetorical effect through appeals to both biblical authority and common sense. The entire text is structured as a straw man argument, posing both potential and actual objections as questions that he then answers at length. Ballou grounds his argument first in lengthy biblical proofs and then moves through as many biblical objections, explaining why the apparent contradiction in each case is actually in agreement with his beliefs. Ballou also makes significant use of rhetorical questions. For example, he asks, "Can there be any doubt that Jesus Christ, his apostles, and the primitive Christians, held, taught, and exemplified the doctrine for which I am contending?" Although Ballou writes from a first-person perspective, his many rhetorical questions and appeals to biblical authority serve to elevate his argument beyond the realm of one man's opinion.

Christian Non-Resistance is stylistically reminiscent of an extended sermon. Despite being a static text, it actively involves its readers by borrowing from the oral conventions of the pulpit sermon that Ballou had honed through his years as a preacher. He often adopts a preacher's cadence of call and response: "Have I not triumphantly demonstrated that the Holy scriptures teach the doctrine of non-resistance as defined in the first chapter of this work? ... It seems to me that candid minds, after seriously investigating the subject, can come to no other conclusion." By drafting *Christian Non-Resistance* as an extended sermon, Ballou demonstrates his theological bona fides and, in turn, the theological soundness of his appeal to nonresistance. Taken as a whole, his style is tailored

THE INTERNATIONAL INFLUENCE OF A FORGOTTEN WORK

Leo Tolstoy, perhaps best known for his novels *War and Peace* (1869) and *Anna Karenina* (1877), may seem like an unlikely advocate for the American preacher Adin Ballou. However, closer examination reveals that the two were a good fit: besides being one of the world's most famous novelists, Tolstoy was devoutly Christian and committed to nonviolence. In the late 1880s, Tolstoy became aware of Ballou's works and liked them enough to write him a letter from Russia detailing his thoughts and some objections. Still sharp in his old age, Ballou responded to Tolstoy's critique, beginning a correspondence that lasted until Ballou died on August 5, 1890.

Tolstoy later incorporated Ballou's ideas into his influential nonfiction book *The Kingdom of God Is Within You* (1894). An eloquent argument in favor of nonviolent resistance, the book had a profound impact on a young Mohandas Gandhi, who later wrote of its influence on his philosophy. Gandhi, in turn, became central to twentieth-century nonviolence movements and was important in framing the ideas of a young Martin Luther King, Jr., who emerged as a towering figure in the civil rights movement of the 1960s.

to appeal to those Christians who broadly accept his religious premises but have yet to embrace his nonresistance conclusion.

CRITICAL DISCUSSION

When *Christian Non-Resistance* was first published in 1846, it was warmly embraced by the abolitionist movement. Excerpts of his argument were

Adin Ballou penned *Christian Non-Resistance*. In addition to being a nonviolent theorist, he also was an abolitionist and a socialist. © UNIVERSAL IMAGES GROUP LIMITED/ ALAMY

PRIMARY SOURCE

CHRISTIAN NON-RESISTANCE: IN ALL ITS IMPORTANT BEARINGS

Now let us examine Matt. 5:39. "I say unto you, resist not evil..." This single text, from which, as has been stated, the term non-resistance took its rise, if justly construed, furnishes a complete key to the true bearings, limitations and applications of the doctrine under discussion. This is precisely one of those precepts that may be easily made to mean much more, or much less, than its author intended. It is in the intensive, condensed form of expression, and can be understood only by a due regard to its context. What did the divine Teacher mean by the word "evil," and what by the word "resist?" There are several kinds of evil: 1. pain, loss, damage, suffered from causes involving no moral agency, or natural evil; 2. sin in general, or moral evil; 3. temptations to sin, or spiritual evil; and 4. personal wrong, insult, outrage, injury – or personal evil. Which of these kinds of evil does the context show to have been in our Savior's mind when he said, "Resist not evil?" Was he speaking of fires, floods, famine, disease, serpents, wild beasts, or any other mere natural evil agent? No. Then of course he does not prohibit our resisting such evil. Was he speaking of sin in general? No. Then of course he does not prohibit our resisting such evil by suitable means. Was he speaking of temptations addressed to our propensities and passions, enticing us to commit sin? No. Then of course he does not prohibit our resisting the devil, withstanding the evil suggestions of our own carnal mind, and suppressing our evil lusts. Was he speaking of personal evil, injury personally inflicted by man on man? Yes. "Ye have heard that it hath been said, 'An eye for an eye and a tooth for a tooth'; but I say unto you that ye resist not evil," *i.e.* personal outrage, insult, affront – injury. The word "evil" necessarily means, in this connection, personal injury or evil inflicted by human beings on human beings.

published, for instance, in the New Lisbon, Ohio, *Anti-Slavery Bugle,* and advertisements for copies of his book appeared for years after its initial publication. As scholar Lewis Perry relates in *Radical Abolitionism: Anarchy and the Government of God in Antislavery Thought,* Ballou's book was valuable to the nonresistance movement because there was a need for someone "to give their doctrine a theological defense." *Christian Non-Resistance* eventually made its way to Russia, where it caught the eye of Tolstoy. In his 1894 book *The Kingdom of God Is within You,* Tolstoy expresses shock to find that Ballou has been nearly forgotten in the United States: "one would have thought Ballou's work would have been well known, and the ideas expressed by him would have been either accepted or refuted; but such has not been the case."

During and after the American Civil War, *Christian Non-Resistance* was largely forgotten, both by his allies and his opponents. The nonresistance advocated in the text seemed a quaint relic of an idealistic past. It was in his correspondence with Tolstoy that Ballou's work lived on. As related in Ballou's autobiography, he received a letter in July 1889 from Tolstoy that read: "I have seldom experienced so much gratification as I had in reading Mr. Ballou's treatise and tracts. I cannot agree with those who say that Mr. Ballou 'will not go down to posterity among the immortals.'" To that end, Tolstoy translated Ballou's work into Russian and included it in his wide-reaching discussions on Christian nonviolence. However, beyond Tolstoy's intervention, Ballou has largely been lost to posterity, generating interest mostly as a footnote to other, more famous twentieth-century nonresistance practitioners.

Today, Ballou's legacy resides in a small group of dedicated scholars who maintain a website dedicated to his life and works, and in the lives of his better-known intellectual descendants: Tolstoy, Gandhi, and King. Most scholarship on Ballou comes in discussions of nonviolent movements in general. For instance, in her book *Civil Disobedience,* Maria Jose Falcon y Tella describes the genealogy of "passive resistance's characteristic means": "Passivity of means, however, does not coincide with a passivity of either will or emotion." It is here that Ballou's

The necessary applications of the doctrine are to all cases in human intercourse where man receives aggressive injury from man, or is presumed to be in imminent danger of receiving it – *i.e.,* to all cases wherein the injury of man upon man is either to be repelled, punished or prevented. There are four general positions in which human beings may stand to resist injury with injury: 1. as individuals; 2. as a lawless combination of individuals; 3. as members of allowable voluntary associations; and 4. as constituent supporters of human government in its state or national sovereignty. Standing in any of these positions, they can resist injury with injury, either in immediate self-defense, in retaliation, or by vindictive punishments. As individuals, they may act immediately by their own personal energies, or they may act through their agents – persons employed to execute their will. Connected with a lawless combination, they may act directly in open co-operative violence, or clandestinely, or through select agents, or in a more general manner through their acknowledged leaders. As members of allowable voluntary associations, they may exert a powerful influence, without any deeds of violence, by means of speech, the press, education, religion, etc., to delude, corrupt, prejudice, and instigate to evil the minds of mankind one toward another. Thus designedly to stimulate, predispose and lead men to commit personal injury, under pretence of serving God and humanity, is essentially the same thing as directly resisting injury with injury by physical means. The mischief may be much greater, the moral responsibility certainly no less. As constituent supporters of human government (whether civil, military, or a compound of both), in its state or national sovereignty, men are morally responsible for all constitutions, institutions, laws, processes, and usages which they have pledged themselves to support, or which they avowedly approve, or which they depend upon as instrumentalities for securing and promoting their personal welfare, or in which they acquiesce without positive remonstrance and disfellowship.

place in this history of civil disobedience becomes clear: "Ballou, who influenced Tolstoy and, through him, Gandhi, tried to fuse non-resistance and passive resistance together, into the notion of 'moral resistance.'"

BIBLIOGRAPHY

Sources

Ballou, Adin. *Christian Non-Resistance.* Philadelphia: J. Miller McKim, 1846. Print.

Ballou, Adin. "Non-Resistance." *Anti-Slavery Bugle,* 28 Aug. 1846. *Chronicling America.* Web. 1 Oct. 2012.

Ballou, Adin. *Autobiography.* Lowell: The Vox Populi Press, 1896. Print.

Jose Falcon y Tella, Maria. *Civil Disobedience.* Herndon: Brill Academic Press, 2004. Print.

Perry, Lewis. *Radical Abolitionism: Anarchy and the Government of God in Antislavery Thought.* Knoxville: U of Tennessee P, 1995. Print.

Tolstoy, Leo. *The Kingdom of God Is within You.* Trans. Constance Garnett. Lincoln: U of Nebraska P, 1984. Print.

Further Reading

Brock, Peter. *Freedom From War: Nonsectarian Pacifism 1814-1914.* Toronto: U of Toronto P, 1991. Print.

Dower, Nigel. *The Ethics of War and Peace.* Malden: Polity Press, 2009. Print.

Hughes, Peter. "The Origins and First Stage of the Restorationist Controversy." *Journal of Unitarian Universalist History* (2000): 1-57. Print.

Hunt, James. "Adin Ballou, Tolstoy, and Gandhi." *Friends of Adin Ballou.* 2002. Web. 1 Oct. 2012.

———. *An American Looks at Gandhi: Essays in Satyagraha, Civil Rights, and Peace.* New Delhi: Promilla & Co. Publishers, 2005. Print.

Peter Brock, *Freedom From War: Nonsectarian Pacifism 1814-1914.* Toronto: U of Toronto P, 1991. Print.

Tolstoy, Leo, and Adin Ballou. "The Christian Doctrine of Non-Resistance ... Unpublished Correspondence Compiled by Rev. Lewis G. Wilson." *The Arena* 13 (1890): 1-12. Print.

Wolfe, George. *The Spiritual Power of Nonviolence.* Austin: JOMAR Press, 2011. Print.

Taylor Evans

Fifty Nine Particulars Laid Down for the Regulating Things, and the Taking Away of Oppressing Laws, and Oppressors, and to Ease the Oppressed

George Fox

✛ *Key Facts*

Time Period:
Mid-17th Century

Movement/Issue:
Quakerism; Religious
freedom and tolerance

Place of Publication:
England

**Language of
Publication:**
English

OVERVIEW

Written by George Fox and published in 1659, *To the Parliament of the Common-wealth of England: Fifty Nine Particulars Laid Down for the Regulating Things, and the Taking Away of Oppressing Laws, and Oppressors, and to Ease the Oppressed* is a list of fifty-nine political, social, and religious demands for reform that concludes with a substantial addendum arguing for the importance of religious tolerance. Published in the form of a pamphlet, the manifesto is addressed to the English Parliament on behalf of the Children of Light, or Friends of the Truth, a religious sect of which Fox was a principal founder and whose members later became popularly known as Quakers. It was also intended for other English religious sects of the day and reflects an attempt by Fox's followers to solidify various gains made by the early Quakers during the English Civil Wars (1642-1651) and the commonwealth period. Published prior to the restoration of the English monarchy in 1660, *Fifty Nine Particulars* also represents the desire of multiple English religious radical groups to realize some of the reforms of the civil wars and the commonwealth period.

Parliament ignored *Fifty Nine Particulars,* and religious sects failed to address the pamphlet. Fox and the majority of other Quaker leaders disavowed the demands of *Fifty Nine Particulars* early in the following decade, and thereafter, Quaker scholars either ignored the work or suppressed its inclusion in Quaker texts out of concern for its radicalism. The manifesto represents a crucial turning point in early English Quaker history from socially active agitation toward a more inward conservatism and a general policy of tolerance and nonconfrontation with the state.

HISTORICAL AND LITERARY CONTEXT

Fifty Nine Particulars expresses Fox's fears that the political and social gains of the Children of Light and other English religious revolutionaries would be wiped away by the restoration of the English monarchy. The early Quaker movement had experienced significant growth in the previous decade, while Lord Protector Oliver Cromwell ruled England. By the late 1650s, Fox and other Quaker leaders hoped for broader popular conversion to the Quaker movement and saw the restoration of the Church of England and the English monarchy as impediments to this goal. Chief among Fox's concerns was the ongoing Quaker persecution by church and state officials.

When *Fifty Nine Particulars* appeared in 1659, England's government was experiencing a period of instability. Oliver Cromwell had died in September 1658, and his son, Richard, became the new lord protector. Richard's rule was short; after struggling with the country's financial troubles, a poor relationship with the army, and repeated calls for a return to a monarchy, he resigned in May 1659. In May 1660 Charles II, who had been living in exile, returned to England and assumed the throne. Distributing his pamphlet prior to Charles's return, Fox used *Fifty Nine Particulars* to advocate for the implementation of Quaker political and social agendas into law.

Fifty Nine Particulars does not appear in any of Fox's collected works published in his lifetime or in the decades following his death. Notably, Fox's *The Lamb's Officer Is Gone Forth with the Lamb's Message* (1659), a radical work condemning the corruption of English priests that was published in the same year as *Fifty Nine Particulars,* does appear in his *Gospel Truth Demonstrated* (1706), suggesting that not all of Fox's radical writing was ignored or suppressed by early Quaker scholars.

While historians occasionally note the existence of *Fifty Nine Particulars,* the manifesto has largely escaped scholarship, and author Hugh Barbour does not mention it in his book, *Quakerism in Puritan England* (1962), widely considered to be a definitive twentieth-century work of early English Quaker history. As a result, *Fifty Nine Particulars* has had a relatively small influence on Fox's reputation as an early Quaker theologian, although it remains an important example of the revisionist literary impulse of Fox's religious contemporaries.

THEMES AND STYLE

The central theme of *Fifty Nine Particulars* is the right of Quakers and other dissident religious groups to practice their religion unmolested and to reform society. Additional themes include the importance of religious pluralism in general and the need for social reform, including moral reform. The fifty-nine demands that constitute the work outline concerns resulting from Quaker experience and from a desire to improve morality and address societal inequality. For example, demand twenty-four, a concern drawn from Quaker experience, states, "Let none that meet together in the fear of God, in several houses, waiting upon the Lord, praying, or exhorting, & edifying one another in the most holy faith, let them not have their houses broken, their windows broken … as many have been." Demand fifty-three is a general societal concern. It states, "Let all the Gaols be in wholesom places, that the Prisoners may not lye on their own dung, and Piss, and straw like Chaffe … and let these things be mended." The long addendum to *Fifty Nine Particulars* focuses primarily on the urgent need for religious tolerance.

The demands in *Fifty Nine Particulars* range from concise and concrete directives to longer and more abstract pleas to limit the power of English priests and to transform society. The first demand, for example, is just one sentence that states, "Let no man be prisoned for Tithes, which have been set up by the Apostates (the Papists) since the days of the Apostles," while demand thirty-three is a paragraph that begins, "Let all the poor people, blinde and lame, and creeples be provided for in the Nation." Some demands are short-term and specific, such as demand fifty-four: "And let all these jangling of Bells cease, which do feed people's pleasures and vain minds." Others suggest broader long-term reform, such as demand thirty-nine: "Let no Judge, nor Justice, nor Sherif that is ambitious, Highminded, bear rule … for such are out of the fear of God … the Creator." The addendum is not stylistically similar to the initial list and takes the form of a rhetorically expansive sermon.

The language in *Fifty Nine Particulars* is forceful and declarative. Almost all of the demands begin with "Let not the following," which is an exhortation form reminiscent of religious commandments. The language in the addendum is more nuanced, and scholars suggest that Fox might have intended to publish it as a separate work. Scholars also argue that the more-nuanced, less-strident addendum may reflect

A Quakers Meeting, painted by Egbert van Heemskerk the Elder in the seventeenth century. Quakerism had been founded by George Fox earlier in the century. PRIVATE COLLECTION/ JOHNNY VAN HAEFTEN LTD., LONDON/THE BRIDGEMAN ART LIBRARY

PRIMARY SOURCE

FIFTY NINE PARTICULARS LAID DOWN FOR THE REGULATING THINGS, AND THE TAKING AWAY OF OPPRESSING LAWS, AND OPPRESSORS, AND TO EASE THE OPPRESSED

FRIENDS,

Who are the Parliament of the Common–Wealth, who are to regulate things for the taking away of oppressing Lawes, and oppressors, and to stop the oppressors....

9. Let no man be fined, and his goods be spoiled, because for con-science sake towards Christ and his commands he cannot swear. Let no man be put out of place or office or service because he cannot swear, because he doth what he doth faithful to God, at yea and nay to serve in his place where he is....

24. Let none that meet together in the fear of God, in several houses, waiting upon the Lord, praying, or exhorting, & edifying one another in the most holy faith, let them not have their houses bro-ken, their windows broken, and they pulled out of their houses, and knockt down and beat, and houses unthatched, and many pulled down, and men plucked out, and knocked down, as many have been....

37. Let all this observing of holidayes, and Saint's days, (which hath been set up by them who were out of the power of God), as Michalmas, and Candlemas, and Christmas, Whitsontide, Easter, and many of the Saint's days which they were killed on, those that sottish people feast on, let this abomination be taken away....

52. Let neither Beggars nor Blind people, nor Fatherless, nor Widows, nor Cripples go a Begging up and down the streets, but that a house may be provided for them all, and meat, that there be never a Beggar among you; and let those great Fees of Gaolers and Garnish money be taken away. Through those Fees many have layn long in Prison.

53. Let all the Gaols be in wholesom places, that the Prisoners may not lye on their own dung, and Piss, and straw like Chaffe, having never a House–of–office in the Prison; Therefore let there be a House–of–office in all Gaols, and let these things be mended.

54. And let all these jangling of Bells cease, which do feed people's pleasures and vain minds.

55. Let all those Ballad–singers, and Ballad–makers, and Jest–bookmakers which stir up people's vain and light minds, be taken away.

56. And let all this wearing of gold Lace, and costly attire, more like Anticks than sober men, let this be ended, and cloath the naked, and feed the hungry with the superfluity. And turn not your ear from the cry of the poor, for if you do, you turn away from the Law that pro-vides for them.

Justice and Righteousness exalteth a Nation; But sin is a shame to both Rulers and people.

SOURCE: Thomas Simmons, 1659.

Fox's suspicion that his initial list of demands would be ignored by Parliament and his desire to conclude on a more conciliatory note, thus placing the Quaker movement in a more cooperative position with the English government.

CRITICAL DISCUSSION

Fox found Parliament's failure to respond to *Fifty Nine Particulars* and the general lack of critical consider-ation of the pamphlet to be personally devastating. As a result, he is said to have taken to bed at a friend's home for ten weeks at the end of 1659. Scholars point to his endorsement of the Quaker 1661 *Peace Testi-mony*, which announces the state has nothing to fear from Quakers, as evidence of Fox's later conversion to a more-conservative, less-radical view of the Quaker role in England. In the following years, Fox discouraged the radical Quaker sentiment he espouses in *Fifty Nine Particulars*, ostensibly in the hopes of preserving the Quaker movement under the threat of state suppres-sion. Contemporary religious history scholar H. Larry Ingle notes that some of Fox's radical language in *Fifty Nine Particulars* is echoed in muted form in Fox's later, more-conservative writings.

In the centuries following the publication of *Fifty Nine Particulars*, the pamphlet was consistently neglected, aside from occasional scholarly notes that in passing dealt with its existence. In the case of Quaker history scholars, it is possible that the lack of recognition of the work may have resulted from a concern for maintaining Fox's reputation and for sup-pressing the radical origins of English Quakers. After its initial publication, *Fifty Nine Particulars* was not republished for 340 years.

In 2002 the Quaker Universalist Fellowship republished *Fifty Nine Particulars* as a pamphlet and an e-book with the intention of increasing aware-ness of the obscure work. In her preface, editor Rhoda R. Gilman notes, "Fox makes a passionate plea for religious liberty" in the addendum to the pamphlet and that "history illustrates repeatedly the close relationship between such liberty and univer-salism." Ingle provides the introduction, in which he argues that, after *Fifty Nine Particulars* failed to influence the English government or find a recep-tive audience, "Fox led Quakerism into laying aside an exuberant radical past whose members spoke of capturing the nation and the world for their version of Christianity."

BIBLIOGRAPHY

Sources

Barbour, Hugh. *The Quakers in Puritan England.* New Haven: Yale UP, 1964. Print.

Fox, George. *A Journal of Historical Account of the Life, Travels, Sufferings, Christian Experiences, and Labour of Love, in the Work of the Ministry, of the Ancient,*

Eminent, and Faithful Servant of Jesus Christ, George Fox. 4th ed. Vol. 1. New York: Collins, 1800. Print.

———. *To the Parliament of the Common-wealth of England: Fifty Nine Particulars Laid Down for the Regulating Things, and the Taking Away of Oppressing Laws, and Oppressors, and to Ease the Oppressed.* Ed. Rhoda R. Gilman. *Quaker Universalist Fellowship.* Quaker Universalist Fellowship, 2002. Web. 28 Aug. 2012.

Ingle, H. Larry. "George Fox, Millenarian." *Albion: A Quarterly Journal Concerned with British Studies* 24.2 (1992): 261-78. Print.

Further Reading

Braithwaite, William C. *The Beginnings of Quakerism,* 2nd ed. Ed. Henry J. Cadbury. Cambridge: Cambridge UP, 1961. Print.

Davies, Adrian. *The Quakers in English Society.* Oxford: Clarendon, 2000. Print.

Frost, William J. "The Dry Bones of Quaker Theology." *Church History* 39.4 (1970): 505-25. Print.

Ingle, H. Larry. *First among Friends: George Fox and the Creation of Quakerism.* New York: Oxford UP, 1994. Print.

Middleton, Warren C. "The Denunciations of George Fox Viewed Psychologically." *Journal of Religion* 11.4 (1931): 589-609. Print.

Vann, Richard T. *The Social Development of English Quakerism 1655-1755.* Cambridge: Harvard UP, 1969. Print.

Craig Barnes

MAGNA CARTA

Feudal barons of King John of England

✥ Key Facts

Time Period:
Early 13th Century

Movement/Issue:
Constitutionalism; Civil rights

Place of Publication:
England

Language of Publication:
Latin

OVERVIEW

Magna Carta, widely considered to be one of the most important legal documents in the history of democracy, is a charter written by a group of English barons and granted by King John of England on June 15, 1215. Containing sixty-three clauses, the charter addresses the complaints of the feudal barons and defines the regulation of feudal customs and taxations; its purpose was to limit the powers of the king and to protect the privileges of the barons. Magna Carta became the basis of English constitutional law and served as a model and guide for other countries around the world.

Forced to agree to Magna Carta to avoid civil war, King John soon sought to have Pope Innocent III nullify it. Two years earlier the king had sworn allegiance to the Pope, thereby making England part of the pontiff's papal holdings. Therefore, any affront to King John was also an affront to Pope Innocent. Just ten weeks after the king granted the charter, the Pope nullified it and threatened to excommunicate anyone who continued to revolt. The result was a civil war, known as the First Barons' War (1215-1217). Magna Carta, however, did not remain nullified forever. It was revised and reissued several times, eventually becoming one of the most famous and influential documents in the English-speaking world and serving as a template for some of democracy's greatest documents, including the Declaration of Independence and the U.S. Constitution.

HISTORICAL AND LITERARY CONTEXT

Angry feudal barons created Magna Carta because they were upset about King John's exploitation of his rights over them and his ruthless administration of justice. According to author James Lacey in a 2010 article for the journal *Military History*, many historians agree with the assessment of medievalist William Stubbs, who in 1875 referred to King John as "the very worst of all our kings." The majority of the sixty-three clauses contained in Magna Carta deal with specific grievances. Some of the clauses specify the treatment of widows and children of barons who died. For example, the king had the right to demand a tax be paid by the deceased baron's heirs, and he had the right to sell guardianship of children to the highest bidder. Widows and daughters could also be sold into marriages of the king's choosing. There are clauses on the use of the royal forest, the payment of debts, and even special treatments for specific types of merchants.

While the original Magna Carta was only in effect for ten days, it was revised and reissued several times after King John's death in October 1216. The following month William Marshal, the Earl of Pembroke and the guardian and regent to King Henry III, the nine-year-old son of King John who had assumed the throne upon his father's death, issued a new charter, based on forty-two of the original sixty-three clauses, in order to acquire support of the barons for the boy king. Marshal issued another version in 1217 at the end of the First Barons' War, increasing the number of clauses from forty-two to forty-seven. In 1225 Henry III himself reissued Magna Carta with thirty-seven clauses, and it was the first version to enter English law. In 1297 King Edward I reissued the charter only to have it annulled by Pope Clement V in 1305. Finally, during the reign of Edward III, Parliament passed six statutes between 1331 and 1369 that reinforced the protections of Magna Carta. They also redefined the term "free man" and introduced the phrase "due process of law."

The feudal barons modeled the 1215 version of Magna Carta on another charter created more than a century earlier known as the Charter of Liberties. In the year 1100, Henry I, fourth son of William the Conqueror, had himself quickly crowned king after his older brother William was killed in a hunting accident and the next older brother, Robert, was away crusading. The action angered many barons who were loyal to Robert. In order to quiet the revolt, Henry had the Charter of Liberties created, and it offered many concessions to both the barons and the church. The charter contains fourteen clauses that read almost exactly like the clauses in Magna Carta.

Magna Carta has been a tremendous influence not only upon British constitutional history but also upon the history of many other English-speaking nations. It was the template for numerous early American documents, including the Massachusetts Bay Company Charter, the Virginia Charter of 1606, the U.S. Constitution, and the Bill of Rights. Other countries that based their constitutional laws upon Magna Carta include Australia, New Zealand, and Canada.

THEMES AND STYLE

The main theme of Magna Carta is freedom from oppression and fair and equal justice for all "free men." In 1215, however, "free men" referred to barons, earls, and other wealthy men who owned land, servants, and even military forces—and not to peasants or slaves. Throughout the document there is an obvious and conscious attempt to be fair to all "free men." For example, clause four states, "The guardian of an heir who is thus under age, shall take from the land of the heir nothing but reasonable produce, reasonable customs, and reasonable services." There are several clauses that forbid certain actions without a baron's permission. Clause thirty warns, "No sheriff or bailiff of ours, or other person, shall take the horses or carts of any freeman for transport duty, against the will of the said freeman." There are several clauses that specify that property may not be taken from a debtor if he is able to pay in "moveable goods." Clause thirty-nine, which prohibits the punishment of a free man without first establishing his guilt in a fair trial, eventually evolved into the modern legal concepts of due process, trial by jury, and habeas corpus.

The original charter of 1215 and its subsequent revisions were designed to benefit the barons and not the king. Clause sixty-one of the 1215 version even provided for twenty-five of the barons to monitor

KING JOHN OF ENGLAND

King John of England ruled from April 6, 1199, until his death in October 1216. John was the youngest of five sons of King Henry II and Eleanor of Aquitaine. His oldest three brothers, William, Henry, and Geoffrey, all died young, leaving brother Richard I, better known as Richard the Lion-Hearted, to ascend the throne in 1189. John made an unsuccessful attempt to take the throne while Richard was away fighting in the Third Crusade. Richard died in 1199, finally allowing John to become king of England. Although John was a fairly successful military tactician, his financial and interpersonal skills were lacking. His treatment of Breton, Norman, and Anjou nobles created many enemies for him and resulted in the collapse of his holdings in northern France in 1204. An argument with Pope Innocent III over who should be the next archbishop of Canterbury led to his excommunication in 1209, and a military campaign against Philip II of France not only failed but was also costly in terms of money and lost allies. Upon his return to England from the French campaign, John was set upon by angry barons who were unhappy with his reckless and abusive use of power. Magna Carta resulted from their negotiations, but John, unwilling to live up to the stipulations of the agreement, convinced the Pope to nullify the document. He died in October 1216 of dysentery while on another military campaign in the eastern part of England.

One of four surviving exemplifications of the Magna Carta issued in 1215. The Magna Carta was an important precursor to the rise of constitutional law, which diminished the power of monarchs. HIP/ART RESOURCE, NY

the behavior of King John and gave them the power to seize his castles and possessions as punishment or compensation if he defied any part of the charter. There are even clauses protecting the property of feudal barons from the greedy reach of their king after the death of a baron. Clause eight of the 1215 charter, for example, states, "No widow shall be compelled to marry, so long as she prefers to live without a husband." At that time women were considered property, and prior to the 1215 charter the king could lay claim to all of a dead baron's possessions, including his widow. The king would then sell the widow into marriage. Clause eight kept the widow in the baron's family.

The English barons who created Magna Carta in 1215 did so because they had been financially or even physically harmed in some manner by King John, and while the overall purpose of the document was to protect them from the king, approximately two-thirds of the sixty-three clauses address specific complaints. The first clause, affirming the freedom of the church, is in reaction to King John's dispute with Pope Innocent over the election of Stephen Langton as archbishop of Canterbury. Clauses that specify use of the royal forest reflect another source of animosity between King John and the barons. The king's regular annexation of private lands, claiming them as part of his own forest, did much to create a hostile disposition toward the king.

CRITICAL DISCUSSION

Although the first version of Magna Carta in 1215 was a quick and decisive failure, the spirit of the charter did not die so easily. When it was revised and reissued in 1217, it created a precedent, making it easier for further revisions to be made in the future. After its 1225 reissue, Magna Carta became the blueprint for the Provisions of Oxford of 1258, England's first written constitution. The Ordinances of 1311, a collection of regulations restricting the powers of King Edward II, mentions Magna Carta specifically in clause six, which states, as quoted by Peter Linebaugh in his book *The Magna Carta Manifesto,* "The Great Charter shall be observed in all its particulars." Its flexibility and timelessness made it a source of great discussion and debate among law scholars for centuries.

The fundamental importance of Magna Carta was not seriously recognized until the early 1600s, when Sir Edward Coke, a former chief justice of both the Common Pleas and the King's Bench, wrote that Magna Carta was "the fountain of all the fundamental Laws of the Realm," according to author Geoffrey Hindley in his book *A Brief History of the Magna Carta.* It was Coke's inspiration in framing the Petition of Right of 1628, a statement of civil liberties that Parliament sent to King Charles I that became an important supplement to Magna Carta. The humanist philosopher John Selden, a contemporary

of Coke's, was instrumental in interpreting habeas corpus as part of clause twenty-nine in Magna Carta. According to Linda E. Mitchell in her essay in the book *Events That Changed Great Britain,* medievalist William Stubbs described the Magna Carta as "the first great public act of the nation, after it has realised its own identity … the whole of the constitutional history of England is little more than a commentary on Magna Carta."

Scholars worldwide acknowledge both the importance and the profound influence that Magna Carta has had in forming societies around the world. According to Linebaugh, "the [U.S. Constitution's] Fourteenth Amendment's due process clause constitutes the most decisive legal translation from Magna Carta to America." Ralph Turner, in an article in a 2003 issue of *History Today,* writes,

> Today, Magna Carta seems to enjoy greater prestige in the United States than in the United Kingdom. Indicative of this is the monument at Runnymede [the field in England where King John signed the Magna Carta] erected in 1957 by the American Bar Association to commemorate the Charter … Americans' dedication to fundamental law increased in the years after 1688, an age when British political thinkers were discarding it in favor of parliamentary sovereignty. Their commitment to such higher law as Magna Carta fortified their inclination toward written constitutions.

BIBLIOGRAPHY

Sources

Hindley, Geoffrey. *A Brief History of the Magna Carta: The Story of the Origins of Liberty.* Philadelphia: Running Press, 2008. Print.

Lacey, James. "1215 and All That." *Military History* 27.1 (2010): 50-57. Web. 4 Sept. 2012.

Linebaugh, Peter. *The Magna Carta Manifesto: Liberties and Commons for All.* Berkeley: U of California P, 2008. Print.

"The Magna Carta." 1915. *Constitution Society.* Web. 4 Oct. 2012.

Mitchell, Linda E. "The Magna Carta 1215: Interpretive Essay." *Events That Changed Great Britain: From 1066 to 1714.* Ed. Frank W. Thackery and John E. Findling. Westport: Greenwood, 2004. Print.

Turner, Ralph V. "The Meaning of Magna Carta since 1215." *History Today* 53.9 (2003). Web. 4 Sept. 2012.

Further Reading

Breay, Claire. *Magna Carta: Manuscripts and Myths.* London: British Library, 2002. Print.

Daniell, Christopher. *From Norman Conquest to Magna Carta: England, 1066-1215.* London: Routledge, 2003. Print.

Fryde, Natalie. *Why Magna Carta? Angevin England Revisited.* London: Transaction, 2001. Print.

Howard, A.E. Dick. *The Road from Runnymede: Magna Carta and Constitutionalism in America.* Charlottesville: UP of Virginia, 1968. Print.

Loengard, Janet S., ed. *Magna Carta and the England of King John.* Rochester: Boydell, 2010. Print.

Prescott, Andrew. *English Historical Documents.* London: British Library, 1988. Print.

Sandoz, Ellis, ed. *The Roots of Liberty: Magna Carta, Ancient Constitution, and the Anglo-American Tradition of Rule of Law.* Indianapolis: Liberty Fund, 1993. Print.

Stenton, Doris M. *After Runnymede: Magna Carta in the Middle Ages.* Charlottesville: UP of Virginia, 1965. Print.

Swindler, William F. *Magna Carta.* New York: Grosset & Dunlap, 1968. Print.

Thompson, Faith. *The First Century of Magna Carta: Why It Persisted as a Document.* Minneapolis: University of Minnesota, 1923. Print.

Jim Mladenovic

A MANIFESTO OF THE LORD PROTECTOR OF THE COMMONWEALTH OF ENGLAND, SCOTLAND, IRELAND, &C. WHEREIN IS SHEWN THE REASONABLENESS OF THE CAUSE OF THIS REPUBLIC AGAINST THE DEPREDATIONS OF THE SPANIARDS

John Milton

✧ **Key Facts**

Time Period:
Mid-17th Century

Movement/Issue:
Anglo-Irish War;
Colonialism

Place of Publication:
England

**Language of
Publication:**
Latin

OVERVIEW

Written by English poet John Milton during his term as secretary of foreign correspondence, *A Manifesto of the Lord Protector of the Commonwealth of England, Scotland, Ireland, &c. wherein Is Shewn the Reasonableness of the Cause of This Republic against the Depredations of the Spaniards* (1655) seeks to justify the Anglo-Spanish War of 1655-60 to the English government and its people. Oliver Cromwell, protector of the short-lived British republic of 1653-59, controlled the Independent party, which had triumphed in the English Civil War and had executed King Charles I. He commissioned the manifesto as part of his plan of Western Design, which called for conquest of Spanish holdings in the West Indies and military action against Catholic Spain in order to promote English Protestant colonies across the world. Addressed to the people of the British Isles, the manifesto lists Spain's transgressions against England, alleging abuse of English colonists abroad, in order to recast England's recent military actions as self-defense.

The manifesto drew mixed reaction. Many Royalists and other enemies of Cromwell recognized the document as a thinly veiled justification for pursuing an unauthorized and expensive war. Moreover, they accused Cromwell of attempting to establish a new monarchy and of lying about events in the New World. English merchants argued that trade with Spain was more important than any political wrongdoings, and several English fleet captains refused to act against Spain. Ultimately, the manifesto did little to change public opinion about the invasion of the West Indies or to garner support for further colonization. The manifesto was revived in 1739, a year after it was translated from Latin into English, when Parliamentary leader Robert Walpole used it to declare war on Spain. Today the manifesto is notable for its political influence and its famous author.

HISTORICAL AND LITERARY CONTEXT

Manifesto of the Lord Protector responds to Spain's commission of atrocities against indigenous peoples and English settlers in the New World. Milton lists the acts of violence as "murdering, and sometimes even in cold blood butchering, any of our countrymen in America," as well as undertaking to "seize upon their goods and fortunes, demolish their houses and plantations, [and] take any of their ships." He chronicles the history of the struggle for empire between England and Spain, compiling grievances that extend as far back as the 1588 sailing of the Spanish Armada into the English Channel.

When the manifesto was written in 1655, Cromwell's tacit goal was to cut off Spanish trade routes and to end Spain's monopoly on New World trade and religion. He also was determined to spread his Puritan brand of Protestantism wherever Catholicism took hold. Tensions in England between Protestants and Catholics, which had intensified under Charles I, nurtured English fears about the influence of Catholic Spain. In 1654 Cromwell began promoting a plan called the Western Design, under which he made two secret but failed attempts to invade Hispaniola. English military leaders also decided to capture Jamaica, infuriating King Philip II of Spain, whose plans for an alliance with England had been thwarted by Cromwell's actions.

Manifesto of the Lord Protector follows in a tradition of English tracts examining empire building in Central and South America. Such works as explorer George Peckham's *True Report of the Late Discoveries and Possession Taken in the Right of the Crown of England, of the New-Found Lands, by that Valiant and Worthy Gentleman, Sir Humphrey Gilbert, Knight* (1584) and poet and explorer Sir Walter Raleigh's *The Discovery of the Large, Rich, and Beautiful Empire of Guiana* (1595) justify English colonization and make reference to successful English and Spanish exploits and colonies. Milton's manifesto is most heavily influenced by Spanish historian and missionary Bartolomé de las Casas's *A Short Account of the Destruction of the Indies* (1552) and by proimperialist writer Richard Hakluyt's *Discourse Concerning Western Planting* (1584). One of many religious and political treatises written by Milton, *A Manifesto of the Lord Protector* uses the same persuasive style that marks his other works, including *Areopagitica* (1644), his fervent and historically momentous defense of freedom of speech and of the press.

Milton's authorship did not have a significant effect on the manifesto's initial reception, though his name was later used by Walpole for political gain. Walpole penned *The Grand Question, Whether War or no War with Spain, Impartially Consider'd: In Defence of the Present Measures against Those That Delight in War* (1739) to examine the reasons for his somewhat reluctant war against Spain, using Milton's manifesto—and Milton's reputation—to support the argument for war. Today *Manifesto of the Lord Protector* is of interest to scholars not only for its historical value but also for its illustrious author.

THEMES AND STYLE

The manifesto's main themes are that English attacks against Spain's West Indian colonies are justified and that the Spanish government's cruelty must be stopped. In order to persuade the audience of the noble intentions behind Cromwell's war, the manifesto focuses on the violent behavior of the Spanish as they colonized the New World: "That the Spaniards themselves are the occasion of this war, will evidently appear to every one who considers how … they find opportunity, without any just cause, and without being provoked to it by any injury received." Other themes include England's innocence, the desire for peace, and "promoting the Glory of God, and enlarging the bounds of Christ's kingdom." At the heart of the document is Cromwell's goal of converting the world to the Christian faith, implicitly by spreading Protestantism. (The manifesto does not explicitly mention Catholics or Protestants.)

Rhetorically, the manifesto appeals on emotional grounds to members of the Commonwealth of England, Scotland, and Ireland in an attempt to unite them against a common enemy, despite diverse political affiliations and religious views. Milton refers to the "ancient glory of the English nation" and calls on the people of Britain to "[avenge] the blood of the English." He uses the first person plural throughout as an appeal to unity, creating an us-versus-them dynamic in order to incite collective anger and "vengeance on the Spaniards." After calling the Spanish "absurd" and "ridiculous," he provides a list of the grievances Spain has committed against the English and aligns the English with the Native Americans as innocent victims.

The style of the manifesto is reminiscent of Milton's other works, which share the document's

JOHN MILTON: POET AND POLITICAL THINKER

Perhaps best known for his epic poem *Paradise Lost* (1667), John Milton was in his time a well-known author and civil servant. Years before writing the *Manifesto of the Lord Protector,* he had been active in English politics. His *Eikonoklastes* of 1649 defended the recent execution of King Charles I, and his *Defensio pro Pupulo Angelico* (1651) and *Defensio secunda* (1654), more popularly known as the First and Second Defenses, were written in response to Royalist tracts that opposed Cromwell's republican rule. Just before the restoration of the English monarchy, he published *The Ready and Easy Way to Establish a Free Commonwealth* (1660), advocating for the necessity of popular government.

By the time he began work in 1658 on *Paradise Lost,* his magnum opus, he was blind. Through dictation, he finished the book-length poem, now considered one of the greatest epic poems in the English literary canon. The text recounts the biblical story of Adam and Eve and the fall of man in order to illustrate themes central to Milton's anti-imperialist and Protestant beliefs. Scholars have read *Paradise Lost,* like *Manifesto of the Lord Protector,* in terms of Milton's views on colonization, liberty, and equality.

formal, Christian tone. Appealing to the Protestant audience that Cromwell wished to target, Milton writes in a lofty, sophisticated style that mirrors the attitude of a people who have "patiently borne" Spanish aggression. The manifesto's restrained eloquence portrays the English as a moral and civilized Christian nation in contrast to the wild and barbarous Spanish. The victims of Spanish cruelty are "poor Orthodox Christians" and the New World colonists are "Christian brethren in America." The manifesto closes by suggesting that the purpose of defeating Spain is to spread God's word "to all who are free of those prejudices which hinder people from clearly discerning the truth." Thus, he masterfully disguises the argument for war as a plea for peace.

CRITICAL DISCUSSION

Dismissed by many as propaganda, the *Manifesto of the Lord Protector* had limited success in rallying support for Cromwell's cause. Some, including members of Cromwell's Council of State, agreed that a war against Spain could be useful in promoting Protestant mission work abroad. In 1656 Milton's nephew John Phillips translated Las Casas's *Short Account,* and in his introduction to the text, Phillips calls on Cromwell to avenge the wrongs perpetrated against the Indians, alleging that Spain is guilty of brutal acts in the New World and that Cromwell is the Protestant warrior who will bring peace to the conflict. Despite support from writers such as Phillips, however, Milton's

manifesto did little to change perceptions of English imperialist designs.

For almost a century, *Manifesto of the Lord Protector* went unnoticed. When Walpole adapted the 1738 English translation as part of what David Armitage in an essay for *Historical Journal* (1992) calls "a flood of propaganda [that] harped on the shame and injustice" of the Spanish wrongdoings against the English, the manifesto experienced renewed significance. During Walpole's time, the subject of Spanish injustices was popular, and the public eagerly purchased copies of Milton's manifesto. Centuries later the manifesto garnered critical attention for its imperialist language and its insight into Milton's personal beliefs about colonization.

Modern academic criticism has focused on Milton's language in order to determine his view on colonization in the New World. Antonia Fraser, in her 1973 book *Cromwell: The Lord Protector,* suggests that one of the manifesto's goals was to extend missionary work to the New World, a goal which was "borne up… by Protestant enthusiasm." Other critics complicate this idea, arguing that Milton's language suggests that he saw the natives in the New World as anything but equal. In an essay written in 2006 for *Philological Quarterly,* Elizabeth Sauer contends that, although

Milton may have despised the Spaniards' poor treatment of the indigenous population, he considered the conquered peoples inferior to the English: "Milton associates the Amerindians with ruined innocence at best and barbarism most often." Other critics, such as John T. Shawcross, attempt to place Milton outside of the English canon and situate his political works within a more global pattern, particularly by examining them through a Spanish lens and by placing Milton in the context of Spanish writers rather than English ones.

BIBLIOGRAPHY

Sources

Armitage, David. "The Cromwellian Protectorate and the Languages of Empire." *Historical Journal* 35.3 (1992): 531-55. *JSTOR.* Web. 6 June 2012.

Fraser, Antonia. *Cromwell: The Lord Protector.* New York: Knopf, 1973. Print.

Milton, John. "Manifesto of the Lord Protector of the Commonwealth of England, Scotland, Ireland, &c. wherein Is Shewn the Reasonableness of the Cause of This Republic against the Depredations of the Spaniards." *The Prose Works of John Milton.* Vol. 2. Ed. Rufus Wilmot Griswold. Philadelphia: Moore, 1847. *Online Library of Liberty.* Web. 5 June 2012.

Sauer, Elizabeth. "Toleration and Translation: The Case of Las Casas, Phillips, and Milton." *Philological Quarterly*

85.3/4 (2006): 271-91. *Academic Search Premier.* Web. 9 June 2012.

Shawcross, John T. "John Milton and His Spanish and Portuguese Presence." *Milton Quarterly* 32.2 (1998): 41-52. *Project Muse.* Web. 9 June 2012.

Further Reading

Evans, Martin. *Milton's Imperial Epic:* Paradise Lost *and the Discourse of Colonialism.* Ithaca: Cornell UP, 1996. Print.

Greenspan, Nicole. "News and the Politics of Information in the Mid Seventeenth Century: The Western Design and the Conquest of Jamaica." *History Workshop Journal* 69 (2010): 1-26. *Project Muse.* Web. 9 June 2012.

Lewalski, Barbara K. *The Life of John Milton: A Critical Biography.* Oxford: Blackwell, 2000. Print.

Lim, Walter H.S. *John Milton, Radical Politics, and Biblical Republicanism.* Newark: U of Delaware P, 2006. Print.

Lisa Kroger

NATURE

Ralph Waldo Emerson

✣ *Key Facts*

Time Period:
Early to Mid-19th
Century

Movement/Issue:
Transcendentalism;
American romanticism

Place of Publication:
United States

**Language of
Publication:**
English

OVERVIEW

Ralph Waldo Emerson's *Nature* (1836) is a landmark publication in American literature, a classic statement of transcendentalism that perhaps more than any other document influenced the literary imagination of the Romantic period in the United States (approximately 1830-60). In his essay, originally published anonymously as a ninety-five-page book, Emerson provocatively advocates religious living based on experience rather than tradition, asking his readers to find spiritual sustenance not in organized religions such as Christianity but in communion with nature. Nature, Emerson writes, is to be understood in two ways: commonly as all that pertains to the natural world, and more philosophically as everything that is distinct from the soul. The essay is heavily indebted to German idealist philosophy, which came to Emerson as interpreted through the work of English Romantic poet and critic Samuel Taylor Coleridge.

Many early reviewers of *Nature* found much to praise and just as much to criticize in Emerson's writing and thinking. In particular, they appreciated his religious devotion but not his idealism: They characterized him as a "dreamy," "idiosyncratic," and "eccentric" author of a work that was sometimes difficult to the point of being impenetrable in its ideas and expression. More affirmatively, the essay marked the emergence of American transcendentalism as a major philosophical and cultural movement whose fundamental belief is that God is immanent within all nature and humanity. The text proved especially influential in the realm of literature, with Emerson's ideas directly inspiring and shaping the work of some of the most celebrated writers of the mid- to late nineteenth century, including Henry David Thoreau, Margaret Fuller, Herman Melville, Walt Whitman, and Emily Dickinson.

HISTORICAL AND LITERARY CONTEXT

In his attempt to define a new theology, Emerson criticizes his age, which he describes as being so preoccupied with achievements of the past that it has given up on certain fundamental experiences. Individuals are compelled to engage in secondhand reflections on, rather than original relations to, life in the universe. The problem is especially acute in the realm of organized religion, where the tendency to focus on history distracts the faithful from discovering their own immediate relationships to God and nature. Emerson seeks to remedy this in *Nature* by asking his contemporaries to rethink who and what they are—as creatures dependent not on doctrines or histories but on self-knowledge, self-reliance, and a divine correspondence with the world around them.

By the time *Nature* was published, Emerson had spent time as a junior pastor at Boston's Unitarian Second Church; he was ordained in 1829, but his growing interest in science and the death of his wife led him to resign in 1832. After leaving the ministry, he went a tour of Europe and had a life-altering moment in the Jardins des Plantes in Paris—an overwhelming and invigorating sense of the interconnectedness of all the life around him. He describes the "animated forms—the hazy butterflies, carved shells, birds, beasts, fishes, insects, snakes, and the upheaving principle of life everywhere incipient." After his tour, Emerson became a public lecturer on the lyceum circuit. His Paris experience became the subject of his first lecture, "The Uses of Natural History," in which he lays out key ideas that he develops in *Nature*.

Emerson's departure from the Unitarian church was not a rejection of religion; rather, the point was to cast off institutional trappings in the hope of defining a *truer* religious experience—one returning revelation and inspiration to everyday life. The works of Plato, Emanuel Swedenborg, and Immanuel Kant (as interpreted by Coleridge) helped Emerson refine these ideas, and the influence of each is evident in *Nature*. The essay draws not only on European philosophies but also on the Old and New Testaments (Luke, Corinthians, Ezekiel, Matthew); the Western literary canon (Homer, William Shakespeare, George Herbert, John Milton); and contemporary thinkers such as Coleridge and Thomas Carlyle, both of whom Emerson had met in Europe.

Some of the most enduring works in nineteenth-century American literature owe their vision and style to Emerson's theory of the correspondence between humankind and nature, including Thoreau's *Walden* and Whitman's *Leaves of Grass*. The opening poem in *Leaves of Grass,* "Song of Myself," is in many ways a direct response to *Nature* and another Emerson essay, "The Poet," which together ask for new political and poetical understandings of human's relationship to the universe. Thoreau's experiment in living in the woods recorded in *Walden* similarly takes up Emerson's grand themes of self-reliance and seeking the divine in nature. The influence, in turn, of these texts on subsequent generations of artists and thinkers is still felt today, especially in the fields of American studies, environmentalism, and ecocriticism.

THEMES AND STYLE

Emerson is particularly interested in vision and perspective and how individuals are situated within particular "horizons" of perception and activity. These thematic concerns inform one of the essay's most enduring—and also one of its strangest—literary images: "In the woods," says Emerson, "we return to reason and faith…. Standing on the bare ground;— my head bathed by the blithe air, and uplifted into infinite space;—all mean egotism vanishes. I become a transparent eyeball; I am nothing; I see all; the currents of the Universal Being circulate through me; I am part and particle of God." The point is to imagine a pure perception, immersed in the natural environment but attuned to the divine spirit infusing it, so that the individual realizes that he or she shares that divinity. Described here, if not explicitly spelled out, are some of Emerson's grandest themes: that people can know the mind of God without recourse to either doctrine or tradition and that in solitude they can meet their deepest needs.

Emerson sets out in his introduction a series of questions to which the ensuing chapters offer responses: Comparing "our age" to that of "foregoing generations," he asks, "Why should not we also enjoy an original relation to the universe? Why should not we have a poetry and philosophy of insight and not of tradition, and a religion by revelation to us, and not the history of theirs?" His answer, of course, is that we should. To make it so, however, he insists that people must reconsider the fundamental role nature plays in their lives—as select chapter headings indicate, not only as commodity (yielding materials and life processes) but also as a blueprint for the love of beauty, as the source of language ("words are signs of natural facts"), as a "discipline" of sorts (nature has lessons for all), and—above all—as bearer of spirit ("Nature is the organ through which the universal spirit speaks to the individual").

Emerson's language is dense and allusive yet economical, delighting often in packed but succinct statements. He opens the essay with short but forceful sentences: "Our age is retrospective. It builds the sepulchers of the fathers. It writes biographies, histories, and criticism. The foregoing generations beheld God and nature face to face; we through their eyes." Relying on vocabulary and phrasing drawn from the New Testament (paraphrasing here from Luke 11:47 and Corinthians 13:12), Emerson

PUBLIC LECTURES AND THE LYCEUM CIRCUIT

The Lyceum Circuit, in which Emerson began his career as a public lecturer, was made up of a number of voluntary associations across the country that sponsored lectures, concerts, dramatic works, and debates. Situated mostly in the northeastern and midwestern states, the lyceums played a crucial role in the moral and social education of adults in the United States. The Lyceum—founded in 1826 by Massachusetts teacher and lecturer Josiah Holbrook and named after the public space in which Aristotle had lectured to Greek youths—began as an informal venue for local speakers. In time, however, it paid lecturers and entertainers to come from other towns and states.

Touring the "circuit" of these venues, Emerson delivered a staggering 1,500 lectures in his lifetime; more than a hundred of these talks are still in print. Other notables who lectured on the circuit include Susan B. Anthony, Frederick Douglass, Nathanial Hawthorne, Mark Twain, and Daniel Webster. In seeking to educate and inform the public, the lyceum movement initially had much in common with early attempts to form public libraries and museums. After the U.S. Civil War (1861-65), however, organizers were more likely to book dancers, singers, and magicians for popular entertainment in the vaudeville style.

strikes a high—even prophetic—tone and establishes a fitting voice for one who is used to preaching. Provided the reader recognize his allusions, he makes his point subtly—that people all too readily orient themselves by the thoughts and expressions of long-dead generations.

CRITICAL DISCUSSION

Leading Emerson scholar Lawrence Buell notes that following its publication, "*Nature* was reviewed attentively, receiving the extremes of praise and blame according to the reviewer's orthodoxy and commitment to systematic reasoning." Educator and reformer Amos Bronson Alcott describes *Nature* as a "beautiful work," while an anonymous critic goes further, writing, "We would call all those together who have feared that the spirit of poetry was dead, to rejoice that such a poem as *Nature* is written." Frances Bowen, too, found "beautiful writing and sound philosophy in the little work" but arrived at the verdict that "the effect is injured by occasional vagueness of expression, and by a vein of mysticism that pervades the writer's whole course of thought."

The ideas developed in *Nature* continued to receive critical acclaim throughout the nineteenth century and into the early twentieth century and are credited with influencing some of the most notable workers in American philosophy and social reform— including William James and John Dewey—as well

A photograph of Old Manse, a Concord, Massachusetts, house that at different times was the home for American writers Ralph Waldo Emerson and Nathaniel Hawthorne. © LEE SNIDER/PHOTO IMAGES/CORBIS

philosophical frame of reference." Interest in Emerson as a philosopher continues in the twenty-first century, with his engagements with transcendentalism singled out for serious study by Cavell and David Hodge, Joel Myerson, and Lance Newman. More recently, Randall Fuller, John C. Rowe, and Mark Vásquez have turned their attention to the political implications of Emerson's writings. Meanwhile, the environmentalist dimensions of *Nature* have come to the fore in studies by Douglas Anderson, Andrew McMurry, and Christopher Windolph. Emerson's focus on pragmatism has also influenced African American modernist texts; Ralph Ellison's *Invisible Man,* for example, is heavily indebted to Emerson. Modern criticism on one the most influential figures—and one of the most influential essays—in American literary history is substantial and shows no signs of exhaustion.

BIBLIOGRAPHY

Sources

Anderson, Douglas R. "Emerson's Natures: Origins of and Possibilities for American Environmental Thought." *New Morning: Emerson in the Twenty-First Century.* Ed. Arthur S. Lothstein. Albany: State U of New York P. 2008. Print.

Cavell, Stanley, and David J. Hodge. *Emerson's Transcendental Etudes.* Stanford: Stanford UP, 2003. Print.

Jacobson, David. *Emerson's Pragmatic Vision: The Dance of the Eye.* University Park: Penn State UP, 1993. Print.

McMurry, Andrew. *Environmental Renaissance: Emerson, Thoreau, and the Systems of Nature.* Athens: U of Georgia P, 2003. Print.

Windolph, Christopher J. *Emerson's Nonlinear Nature.* Columbia: U of Missouri P, 2007. Print.

Further Reading

Bell, Ian F. A. "The Hard Currency of Words: Emerson's Fiscal Metaphor in Nature." *ELH* 52:3 (1985): 733-53. Print.

Ihrig, Mary Alice. *Emerson's Transcendental Vocabulary: A Concordance.* New York: Garland, 1982. Print.

Lundin, Roger. *From Nature to Experience: The American Search for Authority.* Lanham, MD: Rowman & Littlefield, 2005. Print.

Marr, David. "Face to Face with Emerson." *New Morning: Emerson in the Twenty-First Century.* Ed. Arthur S. Lothstein. Albany: State U of New York P, 2008. Print.

Myerson, Joel, ed. *A Historical Guide to Ralph Waldo Emerson.* New York: Oxford UP, 1999. Print.

Robinson, David M., ed. *The Spiritual Emerson: Essential Writings.* Boston: Beacon, 2003.

Wilson, R. Jackson. "Emerson's *Nature*: A Materialistic Reading." *Subject to History: Ideology, Class, Gender.* Ithaca: Cornell UP, 1991. Print.

David Aitchison

as underwriting the emergence of a secularized faith rooted in self-reliance and individualism. In the 1920s and 1930s, however, Emerson fell out of favor in the academy and was thought to be muddle-headed in his thinking; it was not until the 1940s that scholars began to reconsider his legacy more favorably. Since then, interest in *Nature* has continued apace, with scholars giving increasing attention to his understanding of theology, politics, and aesthetics.

In the 1990s, as the work of Stanley Cavell and David Jacobson shows, critics reawakened their interest in Emerson's thinking and what it means in particular for the philosophy of pragmatism. As Jacobson notes in *Emerson's Pragmatic Vision: The Dance of the Eye* (1993), critics up to then had mostly been "reluctant to read [Emerson's] essays and lectures within a

NINETY-FIVE THESES

Martin Luther

OVERVIEW

Allegedly nailed to the door of Castle Church in Wittenberg, Germany, on October 31, 1517, Martin Luther's *Ninety-Five Theses,* or *Disputation on the Power and Efficacy of Indulgences,* ultimately proved to be the definitive catalyst for the Protestant Reformation. Composed following the form of sixteenth-century academic debates about theology, Luther's manifesto centers on a critique of the Roman Catholic Church's sale of indulgences, guarantees of divine remission of punishment for sin, which were authorized by the pope and sold aggressively to help fund the construction of the new St. Peter's Basilica in Rome. Although there is some debate among scholars as to how far-reaching Luther had intended the manifesto's audience and ramifications to be, there is little doubt of the conviction present in its pages or the influence it had on longstanding Christian debates over paths to salvation (focusing, example, on the nature and role of sacraments, the role of the clergy in administering sacraments, and the power of the gospels in the vernacular). Luther's condemnation of indulgences and the damage they did to the church and its Christians was so powerful that it pulled a broad constellation of theological questions into its orbit, beginning the Reformation.

After Luther sent a copy of his *Disputation on the Power and Efficacy of Indulgences* to Archbishop Albert of Mainz on October 31, 1517, the archbishop was outraged. In Barbara A. Somervill's biography, *Martin Luther: Father of the Reformation,* she reports that the scandalized Albert exclaimed "God on High!" and questioned, "Is this how souls entrusted in your care are taught?" The concerned archbishop sent a copy of Luther's letter directly to Pope Leo X; although the pope would later come to excommunicate Luther, he initially dismissed the theses as stemming from a purely academic debate among monks. As Luther's theses circled through the streets and university halls of Wittenberg, the questions asked by this upstart Augustinian began to find echoes, launching a tumultuous, unprecedented reformation of the church.

HISTORICAL AND LITERARY CONTEXT

While Luther's *Ninety-Five Theses* came to be the representative text for myriad grievances within a broad challenge to the papacy, the crux of the manifesto itself is Luther's strong disapproval of how indulgences were

being sold throughout Christendom in 1517. About four decades prior, in 1476, Pope Sixtus's papal bull *Mare magnum* exponentially extended the purview of the previously exceptional sale of plenary indulgences (full remission of punishment for sin). This proclamation not only allowed indulgences to be sold incessantly (as opposed to only on particular holidays) or to fund a crusade or special church building project but also extended their redemptive efficacy to include souls already in purgatory; for the first time in Christian history, one could buy an indulgence to save the deceased.

When Luther penned his theses in 1517, there was a quiet but swift undercurrent of concern about un-Christlike corruption within the papacy flowing beneath much of Christendom. Rival popes, one in Avignon, France, and one in Rome, spent decades arguing and excommunicating one another (Papal Schism, 1378-1417), and because of political infighting (with an additional dose of hubris), the papacy was unable to protect Constantinople, now Istanbul, from being taken by the Ottoman Turks in 1453. The papacy's popular credibility as the unimpeachable heir to Christ seemed shaky throughout much of the fifteenth century. Still, when Pope Leo X, a member of the powerful Medici family, was elected in 1513, the papacy's religious and political powers were formidable.

The growth of urban universities during the late Middle Ages, along with the beginnings of humanism therein, provided the fertile soil in which Luther's *Ninety-Five Theses* would flourish. The growth of cities in the High Middle Ages helped foster the growth of universities, and from the thirteenth century the number and importance of universities was on the rise throughout Europe. In his article "The Universities of the Renaissance and Reformation," Paul F. Grendler highlights the crucial role of universities in providing the infrastructure for what would become Luther's reformation; not only, according to Grendler, was the strong structure of German universities ideally suited "to introduce change into religion and society" but also, especially in early sixteenth-century Germany, it was increasingly common to see scholars using disputations, such as Luther's theses, to reach out to a broader audience beyond the university itself. In addition, as Byzantine Christians filtered into Europe following the fall of Constantinople in 1453,

✤ *Key Facts*

Time Period:
Early 16th Century

Movement/Issue:
Theology; Protestant Reformation

Place of Publication:
Germany

Language of Publication:
Latin

An illustration by Angus McBride depicting Martin Luther posting his *Ninety-Five Theses* on the door of Wittenberg Church. PRIVATE COLLECTION/© LOOK AND LEARN/THE BRIDGEMAN ART LIBRARY

the resultant influx of Greek texts helped to spark the growth of humanism in the Latin West. Luther's intellectual formation was strongly influenced by this new trend in European thought; as renowned Reformation historian Bernd Moeller notes in his essay "The German Humanists and the Beginnings of the Reformation," "without Humanism, no Reformation."

Luther's manifesto produced a profound societal change in his day and beyond. Though his translation of the Bible would be one of the (if not the most) formative texts for the linguistic evolution of modern German, Luther's *Ninety-Five Theses* themselves were not aesthetically groundbreaking. As Grendler puts it, "The ideas in the *Ninety-Five Theses* (or *On the Power of Indulgences*) were revolutionary. But the theses were written in academic disputation prose, which was just as dreary as it sounds." Nevertheless, though the style may have been drab, the impact of the ideas rose far above the drudgery of the prose. Few tracts in the history of literature have had as profound, or as lasting, an influence on society as Luther's theses.

THEMES AND STYLE

In the *Ninety-Five Theses,* Luther principally objects to the sale and portrayal of papal indulgences, suggesting that almsgiving and sincere penitence are vastly preferable routes to the remission of sin. It should be noted, however, that even as he warns Christians who spurn charity in order to purchase pardons that they only earn "the anger of God" and even as he says that anyone who believes the pardon from indulgences alone is sufficient for salvation "will be eternally damned along with their teachers," Luther nevertheless also affirms the true power of indulgences. Though he rails against its abuse, he also assures his reader that an indulgence

"imparted by the Pope is by no means to be despised, since it is, as I have said, a declaration of the Divine remission," going so far as to explicitly curse anyone "who speaks against the truth of apostolical pardons." And yet, even as Luther accedes to the efficacy of indulgences bestowed by the apostolic succession, he also equates that efficacy to only one percent of the grace to be gleaned from the Gospel itself, saying that were papal pardons celebrated with a single bell, then, by contrast, the Gospel "should be preached with a hundred bells."

As Grendler has pointed out, Luther's manifesto is composed according to the form of academic debates common in sixteenth-century universities. Graham White, in his book *Luther as Nominalist,* traces the medieval lineage of Luther's logic, suggesting that the structure of his thought in the theses "can be regarded, to a very great extent, as a continuation of medieval critiques." Although this text would become the paradigmatic example of protest against corruption in the church, Luther takes care to frame his theses as decidedly orthodox, in the most literal sense of the word: correct teaching. By repeatedly beginning some of the theses with the phrase "Christians should be taught…," Luther casts his manifesto as a defense of—rather than a diatribe against—Christian orthodoxy, which, according to Luther, is being routinely misunderstood, abused by the wanton sale of indulgences.

This air of orthodoxy is key to Luther's rhetorical strategy in the theses, as the language he uses sets him up as an ally of the church, while concurrently critiquing it. Luther not only emphasizes what "Christians should be taught" in concord with orthodox doctrine but also presumes to speak on behalf of the pope, suggesting that if "pardons were preached according to the spirit and mind of the Pope, all questions would be resolved with ease." In so doing, Luther is able to both align himself with orthodoxy, with the papacy, while nevertheless issuing a challenge to the pope to make things right. Although there is some debate about the extent to which Luther intended his theses to inaugurate a reformation within—or even a break from—the Roman Catholic Church, theses such as number thirty-seven, in which Luther unequivocally proclaims that God's grace is offered regardless of papal pardons, pepper the text with hints that Luther may have had a grander design in mind. In *The Reformation: Roots and Ramifications,* the great twentieth-century Luther scholar Heiko A. Oberman calls the theses "an out-and-out manifesto … pitched for a new and much larger stage than that of the Wittenberg lecture hall."

CRITICAL DISCUSSION

Popular interest in Luther's *Ninety-Five Theses* spread quickly in the lands surrounding Wittenberg. In his biography *Luther: Man Between God and the Devil,* Oberman reports that only "two weeks after being posted, the theses had circulated all over Germany," with Luther himself responding that it ought to be expected, "for all the world is complaining about indulgences." Rome soon found out, and by the end of January 1518, the Dominican Johann Tetzel and many of his fellow mendicants were preaching in Germany against Luther's theses. Although David Bagchi, in *Luther's Earliest Opponents,* highlights how frequently Luther's detractors stuck to the style of academic disputation—not least because it was unwelcoming of lay participation—there were also a number of Dominicans who preached that Luther was an outright heretic.

If Luther envisioned his *Ninety-Five Theses* as "an out-and-out manifesto" challenging the papacy, he could have hardly foreseen the seismic shifts that manifesto would spark. The religio-political rifts that opened along the fault line of Luther's manifesto embroiled Europe in a series of religious wars for more than a century, inaugurating the worst internecine conflict within Christendom since—and far surpassing—the siege of Constantinople during the Fourth Crusade in 1203. Though the theses can be seen as the catalyst for the Eighty Years' War (1568-1648), the French Wars of Religion (1562-1598), the Thirty Years' War (1618-1648), and a number of other conflicts, Luther's manifesto also carries a more noble legacy; in the twenty-first century, many Christians the world over view the *Ninety-Five Theses* as an emblematic profession of faith in the face of corruption.

The body of scholarship on Luther and his manifesto is enormous. One notable trend revolves around the question of whether Luther in fact affixed his theses to the door of Castle Church on October 31, 1517. Both Martin Brecht in *Martin Luther: His Road to Reformation 1483-1521* and Richard Marius in *Martin Luther: The Christian between God and Death* doubt that Luther immediately nailed his theses to the door, suggesting instead that their public posting

was subsequent to Luther's letter to the archbishop of Mainz.

BIBLIOGRAPHY

Sources

Bagchi, David. *Luther's Earliest Opponents: Catholic Controversialists, 1518-1525.* Minneapolis: Fortress, 1991. Print.

Grendler, Paul F. "The Universities of the Renaissance and Reformation." *Renaissance Quarterly* 57.1 (Spring 2004): 1-42. Print.

Moeller, Bernd. "The German Humanists and the Beginnings of the Reformation." *Imperial Cities and the Reformation: Three Essays.* Ed. and Trans. H. C. Erik Midelfort and Mark U. Edwards Jr. Durham, NC: Labyrinth, 1972. 19-38. Print.

Oberman, Heiko A. *Luther: Man between God and the Devil.* Trans. Eileen Walliser-Schwarzbart. New Haven: Yale UP, 1989. Print.

Oberman, Heiko A. *The Reformation: Roots and Ramifications.* Trans. Andrew Colin Gow. Grand Rapids, MI: Eerdmans, 1994. Print.

Somervill, Barbara A. *Martin Luther: Father of the Reformation.* Minneapolis: Compass Point, 2006. Print.

White, Graham. *Luther as Nominalist: A Study of Logical Methods Used in Martin Luther's Disputations in the Light of Their Medieval Background.* Helsinki: Luther-Agricola-Society, 1994. Print.

Further Reading

Brecht, Martin. *Martin Luther: His Road to Reformation 1483-1521.* Trans. James L. Schaaf. Philadelphia: Fortress, 1985. Print.

Leroux, Neil R. "Luther's Use of Doublets." *Rhetoric Society Quarterly* 30.3 (Summer 2000): 35-54. Print.

Marius, Richard. *Martin Luther: The Christian between God and Death.* Cambridge, MA: Belknap, 1999. Print.

Waibel, Paul R. *Martin Luther: A Brief Introduction to His Life and Works.* Wheeling, IL: Harlan Davidson, 2005. Print.

Elliott Niblock

OSTEND MANIFESTO

James Buchanan, John Y. Mason, Pierre Soulé

✦ *Key Facts*

Time Period:
Mid-19th Century

Movement/Issue:
Imperialism; United
States Foreign Policy

Place of Publication:
United States

**Language of
Publication:**
English

OVERVIEW

Authored by three U.S. diplomats—James Buchanan, John Y. Mason, and Pierre Soulé—the *Ostend Manifesto* (1854) describes various strategies for the United States to acquire Cuba from Spain. The manifesto was addressed to Secretary of State William Marcy and directed to President Franklin Pierce, who wished to add the prosperous island territory to the young American nation for various economic, political, and military reasons. At the time, Cuba was a leading sugar producer and a strategically valuable shipping hub. In February 1854 authorities at a Havana, Cuba, port seized a U.S. ship carrying cotton. This act incensed many Americans and elicited popular cries for President Pierce to take a more confrontational attitude toward Spain over Cuba. Buchanan, Mason, and Soulé—U.S. ministers to England, France, and Spain, respectively—were called to Ostend, Belgium, to discuss America's options regarding Cuba. The result was the *Ostend Manifesto,* a communiqué that was meant to be private but that was leaked to the public. Although much of the document is mild and objective in tone, its most notable element is a suggestion that the United States could be compelled by circumstance to take Cuba from Spain.

Although an array of Americans supported Pierce's efforts to extend American control into the Caribbean, the stance of the *Ostend Manifesto* undermined his ability to do so. In the 1854 congressional elections, Democrats had lost in a landslide to Republicans and the Know-Nothing Party, largely because of their support for the controversial Kansas-Nebraska Act, and many northerners viewed the manifesto's recommendations as part of a larger plot by the South to extend the institution of slavery. Although Pierce immediately rejected the report's recommendations, the manifesto was the source of much controversy and suspicion when it became public in 1855. As a result of the leaked *Ostend Manifesto,* Pierce abandoned all efforts to acquire Cuba. Modern scholars view the manifesto as a key document in the history of imperialist U.S. foreign policy.

HISTORICAL AND LITERARY CONTEXT

The *Ostend Manifesto* reflects America's growing imperialist aspirations and mounting conflict over slavery in the nineteenth century, when the young nation was seeking to extend its influence in the Western Hemisphere. In the early 1840s President James K. Polk, with his territorial ambitions, embraced the doctrine of Manifest Destiny, the concept that the United States was destined to expand. Southerners were particularly interested in adding territory in the Caribbean, a region they believed would help bolster support for slavery. In 1848 Polk offered Spain $100 million to purchase Cuba but was rebuffed. Between 1848 and 1854 numerous American adventurers known as "filibusters" planned and launched unsuccessful schemes to foment revolution in Cuba. In 1853 Spain threatened to abolish slavery on the island to deter perceived threats from the United States. In light of the fears of rebellion and black control over the government, white southerners saw emancipation as a grave threat and agitated for a preventative takeover.

When the *Ostend Manifesto* was composed in 1854, the nation was divided over the issue of annexing Cuba. The North and the South had long been at odds over the question of slavery. The Kansas-Nebraska Act of 1854 opened the territories of Kansas and Nebraska to the option of slavery, thereby intensifying the regional conflict and igniting southerners' interest in making Cuba a new slave territory. Pierce, a Democrat, was sympathetic to the South. In 1853 he had appointed Soulé, a Louisiana senator who favored expansion, to the crucial post of minister to Spain. Then, in February 1854 Spanish authorities unjustifiably seized an American ship. Many southerners urged Pierce to use this incident as a pretext for war. Meanwhile, the former brigadier general and military governor John Quitman organized a group to liberate and annex Cuba. Quitman depended on Pierce's tacit support for success. It was in this milieu that Pierce suggested a conference of his ministers in Spain, England, and France to recommend a course of action. They debated the relative merits of attempting to purchase Cuba, of invading the island, and of supporting filibusters, such as Quitman. The document that resulted from those discussions, the *Ostend Manifesto,* supported purchase above the other options but would ultimately undermine all three of these options for gaining Cuba.

The *Ostend Manifesto* draws on a tradition of expansionist American political writing that can be traced to the Monroe Doctrine of 1823. Issued by President James Monroe as part of a speech to

Congress, the Monroe Doctrine responded to the collapse of the Spanish Empire and the general weakening of European influence in the Americas. The document established the U.S. policy of forbidding European involvement in the affairs of the Western Hemisphere and justified U.S. intervention in the affairs of Latin America and the Caribbean. The propositions laid out by Monroe would help guide the authors of the *Ostend Manifesto* more than thirty years later.

In the decades following its publication, the *Ostend Manifesto*'s argument for U.S. intervention in Cuba resonated in the escalating tension between the United States and Spain over the island. In 1859 Buchanan, who had since been elected president, renewed the effort to acquire Cuba and requested support from Congress. Although this attempt also failed, the United States did intervene in Cuba in 1898 during the Spanish-American War. Cuban rebels had been fighting for independence from Spain for decades, and the argument in the United States in favor of intervention paralleled the rationale of the *Ostend Manifesto*. A dispatch to President William McKinley from Steward Woodford, the American ambassador to Spain, echoed the *Ostend Manifesto*, recommending an invasion of Cuba on the basis of U.S. self-interest. Unlike the 1854 manifesto, Woodford's dispatch resulted in war. Today the *Ostend Manifesto* is viewed as a key document in the history of the country's fraught relationship with Cuba and in the development of U.S. foreign policy.

THEMES AND STYLE

The central theme of the *Ostend Manifesto* is that the U.S. government should consider taking Cuba from Spain due to the likelihood of a slave rebellion that could adversely affect American interests and particularly the interests of the pro-slavery American South. With the rationale of the Monroe Doctrine underlying their position, the dispatch's authors assert that "the Union can never enjoy repose, nor possess reliable security, as long as Cuba is not embraced within its boundaries." They argue that the sale of Cuba is in Spain's best interest as well. If, however, Spain refuses to sell the island, the authors ask the president to consider whether continued foreign possession of Cuba would "seriously endanger" the United States. If so, the authors declare in their strongest and most controversial passage, "then by every law, human and divine, we shall be justified in wresting it from Spain." Though the bellicose suggestion is followed immediately by a sentence that places this justification in the context of American interests, it was viewed by many as a recommendation for war.

The manifesto achieves its rhetorical effect through an appeal to the inevitability of the document's conclusions. Rather than simply call for an invasion, the authors outline numerous reasons why

JAMES BUCHANAN: STATESMAN

When James Buchanan met with his colleagues in Ostend and then in Aix-la-Chapelle in Prussia to draft the *Ostend Manifesto,* he was in the midst of a long political career that would take him to the very pinnacle of U.S. government and a four-year term in the White House. Originally from Pennsylvania, Buchanan began his political life at age twenty-three as the youngest member of his home state's legislature. In 1820, after serving six years, he was elected to the U.S. House of Representatives. He remained there until 1832, when he was named ambassador to Russia by President Andrew Jackson. Buchanan was then elected to the U.S. Senate in 1834. He served as secretary of state from 1845 to 1849 under James K. Polk, who expanded the country's territory more than any other president. During his career as a legislator, Buchanan earned a reputation as a supporter of states' rights, as a southern sympathizer, and as an advocate of minimal central government.

In 1844 Buchanan made his first of four presidential bids, but the Democratic nomination went to Polk. Buchanan lost the nomination again in 1848 and in 1852; President Franklin Pierce made him minister to Great Britain after his third defeat. In the 1856 election, Buchanan used his role in the *Ostend Manifesto* controversy to curry favor with southern voters and was at last elected president. He served one term as the leader of a deeply divided—and further fracturing—nation that was on the brink of civil war. Afterward he retired to his native state, relieved to leave politics after more than fifty years of service.

the transfer of Cuba makes practical sense and insist that it is indeed a historical certainty: "We firmly believe that, in the progress of human events, the time has arrived when the vital interests of Spain are as seriously involved in the sale, as those of the United States in the purchase, of the island, and that the transaction would prove equally honorable to both nations." The U.S. acquisition of Cuba, the authors argue, can be justified not only by self-interest but also by "the great law of self-preservation." To make this case, they invoke the metaphor of a person "tearing down the burning house of his neighbor, if there is no other means of preventing the flames from destroying his own house." In this way the manifesto portrays the taking of Cuba as necessary and inevitable, as well as based on strategic concerns outlined in the Monroe Doctrine.

Stylistically the *Ostend Manifesto* is distinguished by its formal and logical tone. Written as a diplomatic dispatch to the secretary of state, the manifesto assumes the objective perspective of an official document. It refers to such details as Cuba's "numerous navigable streams, measuring an aggregate course of some 30,000 miles" and "the system of immigration and labor lately organized within

[Cuba's] limits." In making their case, the authors allude repeatedly to the security, prosperity, and interests of the United States as the aim of their recommendations. They also consistently situate their arguments within the context of international law. Although the manifesto proposes a highly contentious territorial takeover, it achieves its argumentative weight through the manipulation of diplomatic and bureaucratic rhetoric.

CRITICAL DISCUSSION

When the *Ostend Manifesto* was received by Pierce and Marcy, they were concerned about potential political ramifications and rejected its recommendations out of hand. In a response to Soulé, who had sent the dispatch, they told him that seizure of Cuba was not an option. Within two weeks of the president's receipt of the document, it had been leaked and published in newspapers. Public opinion, particularly in the North, was deeply negative and suspicious of both the manifesto and the conference that had produced it. According to historian Lester D. Langley in *The Cuban Policy of the United States* (1968), "Antiadministration newspapers in the United States painted the conference as a Southern conspiracy. The three ministers and the entire Pierce administration underwent abusive criticism." As a result, Soulé resigned his position in Spain, and Buchanan and Mason attempted

to distance themselves from the controversy and the document.

The publication of and public response to the *Ostend Manifesto* led to the eventual end of America's longstanding colonial ambitions in Cuba. According to historian Michael J. Connolly in his 2009 article in *American Nineteenth Century History*, "The firestorm of criticism was so intense that Pierce was forced to shelve any desire for Cuban annexation." Although acquiring Cuba remained an official goal of the federal government until the Civil War, the United States never again came as close to doing so as it had in the moment before the *Ostend Manifesto* was issued. Despite the effective end to America's Cuban ambitions, the *Ostend Manifesto* remained prominent in American politics during the lead-up to the Civil War. Republicans used it as evidence of the South's nefarious ambition to extend slavery. Democrats, meanwhile, elected Buchanan president in 1856, in part because of his role in writing the manifesto.

Much scholarship has focused on the manifesto's place in the history of America's imperialist foreign policy. According to scholar Robert E. May, the rationale for the country's colonial ambitions in Cuba was largely related to expanding the American racial state. "Many white Americans felt superior to the generally darker people inhabiting lands to the south," May explains in his book *The Southern Dream of a Caribbean Empire, 1854-1861* (1973), "and expansionists catered to these prejudices, claiming that it was the United States' duty to uplift those people through annexation." Other scholars have viewed the manifesto in the context of pre-Civil War politics. "The absorption of Cuba, a policy that Pierce believed would mitigate the slavery debate," notes Langley, "was in fact a proposal that resurrected the dispute in its most virulent form."

BIBLIOGRAPHY

Sources

Connolly, Michael J. "Tearing Down the Burning House: James Buchanan's Use of Edmund Burke." *American Nineteenth Century History* 10.2 (2009): 211-21. Web. 26 June 2012.

Dent, David W. *The Legacy of the Monroe Doctrine: A Reference Guide to U.S. Involvement in Latin America and the Caribbean.* Westport: Greenwood, 1999. Print.

Langley, Lester D. *The Cuban Policy of the United States: A Brief History.* New York: John Wiley and Sons, 1968. Print.

May, Robert E. *The Southern Dream of a Caribbean Empire, 1854-1861.* Baton Rouge: Louisiana UP, 1973. Print.

———. "A 'Southern Strategy' for the 1850s: Northern Democrats, the Tropics, and the Expansion of the National Domain." *Louisiana Studies* 14 (1975): 333-59. Print.

Potter, David Morris. *The Impending Crisis, 1848-1861.* New York: Harper and Row, 1976. Print.

Further Reading

Baker, Anne. *Heartless Immensity: Literature, Culture, and Geography in Antebellum America.* Ann Arbor: U of Michigan P, 2006. Web. 25 June 2012.

Brown, Charles Henry. *Agents of Manifest Destiny: The Lives and Times of the Filibusters.* Chapel Hill: U of North Carolina P, 1980. Print.

Ettinger, Amos A. *The Mission to Spain of Pierre Soulé, 1853-1855: A Study in the Cuban Diplomacy of the United States.* New Haven: Yale UP, 1932. Print.

Holden, Robert H., and Eric Zolov, eds. *Latin America and the United States: A Documentary History.* New York: Oxford UP, 2000. Print.

Katz, Irving. "August Belmont's Cuban Acquisition Scheme." *Mid-America: An Historical Review* 50 (1968): 52-63. Print.

Meinig, D.W. *Continental America, 1800-1867.* New Haven: Yale UP, 1993. Print.

Moore, J. Preston. "Pierre Soulé: Southern Expansionist and Promoter." *Journal of Southern History* 21 (1955): 203-23. Print.

Schoultz, Lars. *Beneath the United States: A History of U.S. Policy toward Latin America.* Cambridge: Harvard UP, 1998. Print.

Smith, Peter H. *Talons of the Eagle: Latin America, the United States, and the World.* New York: Oxford UP, 2008. Print.

Webster, Sidney. "Mr. Marcy, the Cuban Question, and the Ostend Manifesto." *Political Science Quarterly* 8.1 (1893): 1-32. Print.

Theodore McDermott

A REFUTATION OF DEISM

Percy Bysshe Shelley

❖ *Key Facts*

Time Period:
Early 19th Century

Movement/Issue:
Religious skepticism;
Atheism; Romanticism

Place of Publication:
England

**Language of
Publication:**
English

OVERVIEW

Composed by Percy Bysshe Shelley, *A Refutation of Deism* (1814) asserts that both Deism, a popular philosophical religion of the seventeenth and eighteenth centuries, and traditional Christian belief are logically untenable and that classical skepticism, if not outright atheism, is the only logical course. The book questions the biblical account of Creation, attacks the Deist argument for God's design of nature, holds up scriptural passages for parody, and catalogs the ills of organized religion. Written during a period of strong reactionary conservatism among European religious authorities, the work ostensibly leaves room for the possibility of Christian belief and the existence of God based upon the power of revelation, but Shelley's exact intent with this inclusion is the subject of much scholarly debate. *A Refutation of Deism* has been categorized alternately as an example of early romanticism, philosophical anarchism, and classical skepticism and is considered one of Shelley's most ambiguous and inconclusive works.

Originally self-published by Shelley, *A Refutation of Deism* was not widely read upon publication and reached a marginally larger audience only upon a subsequent publication in 1815. Although the book did not garner significant critical review, its incendiary nature can be traced to one of Shelley's earliest works, *The Necessity of Atheism* (1811), which he composed with his Oxford classmate Thomas Jefferson Hogg and for which Shelley was ultimately expelled. *A Refutation of Deism* can be read as a significantly more nuanced expansion of *The Necessity of Atheism* and as an attempt by Shelley to express his controversial religious convictions in a way that would hold broader appeal. In this sense *A Refutation of Deism* represents an important turning point in Shelley's evolution as a writer concerned with religious themes and in the broader transition from European eighteenth-century Enlightenment rationalism to nineteenth-century romanticism.

HISTORICAL AND LITERARY CONTEXT

A Refutation of Deism speaks to nascent early nineteenth-century intellectual dissatisfaction with both eighteenth-century Deist philosophical religious beliefs and traditional Christian theology. The dissatisfaction with Deism stemmed from a logical continuation of eighteenth-century Enlightenment intellectuals' dedication to rationalism: when carried to their logical extent, the same principles of rational analysis that had encouraged the growth of Deism now made that philosophy untenable. This extent also marked the limits of rational analysis and called for the renunciation of all religions that were not based upon personal revelation. Regarding traditional Christian theology, the dissatisfaction grew out of perceived ongoing abuses by religious authorities, especially in the wake of the French Revolution. In this sense *A Refutation of Deism* represents a historical departure from previous attempts to reconcile rationalism with religion.

By the time *A Refutation of Deism* was published, religious and political authorities across Europe had retreated to a position of staunch conservatism regarding political, social, and intellectual reform. This retreat can also be attributed to the French Revolution and European authorities' ongoing fears that the same radical political and religious sentiments that had toppled the French government and church might take hold in other European nations. As a result of popular sentiment, the writings of many seemingly radical intellectuals were actively suppressed or were not widely disseminated. Shelley's *A Refutation of Deism,* with its catalog of ills purportedly caused by organized religion, can be read as an attack on the historical prejudice of the moment.

For literary influence, *A Refutation of Deism* draws on a long list of seventeenth- and eighteenth-century Enlightenment rationalist writings, such as *An Essay Concerning Human Understanding* (1690) by John Locke, *Dialogues Concerning Natural Religion* (1779) by David Hume, and *The Age of Reason* (1794) by Thomas Paine. Other influences include *De natura deorum* (45 BCE) by Cicero, *Tractatus Theologico-Politicus* (1670) by Benedict de Spinoza, and the writings of Paul-Henri Thiry, Baron d'Holbach (1723-89). *A Refutation of Deism* can also be read as a companion piece to Shelley's philosophical poem *Queen Mab* (1813), which explores the variant evils of religious authorities and governments and the slow progress of humanity toward civilization.

In the years following the publication of *A Refutation of Deism,* the book was eclipsed by Shelley's romantic poetry and ranks as one of the author's lesser-known prose works. Shelley did expand upon some of the ideas he originally expressed in *A Refutation of Deism* in a subsequent work, *Essay on Christianity* (1816). The book remains an important work in the study of Shelley's evolution as a Romantic writer and as a political, social, and religious radical.

THEMES AND STYLE

The central theme of *A Refutation of Deism* is the failure of both Deist and traditional Christian belief to withstand the test of rational foundation. In the book both belief systems are subjected to a trial of logic and are found wanting. The result is a de facto rejection of both belief systems, suggesting the necessity of finding an alternative or rejecting religion altogether. Shelley outlines this purpose in his preface to the work: "The object of the following dialogue is to prove that the system of Deism is untenable. It is attempted to show that there is no alternative between atheism and Christianity; that the evidences of the Being of a God are to be deduced from no other principles than those of divine revelation."

The book takes the form of satirical argument between a Christian believer, Eusebes, and a Deist believer, Theosophus. In the successful attempts of each to undermine the belief system of the other, the two ironically show both belief systems to be in logical error. Both speakers make their attacks by noting the inconsistencies of the other's position and holding up that position for ridicule. In one example of the Christian attack upon Deism, Eusebes concludes, "Surely the Deity has not created man immortal and left him forever in ignorance of his glorious destination. If the Christian religion is false, I see not upon what foundation our belief in a moral governor of the Universe, or our hopes of immortality, can rest." In his response, the Deist representative, Theosophus, asks why God—as represented in the Bible as having created "man with certain passions and powers" and "surrounding him with certain circumstances"—would then "condemn him to everlasting torments because he acted as omniscience had foreseen, and was such as omnipotence had made him."

The rhetorical strategy of *A Refutation of Deism* is notable for its clever use of straw-man arguments on behalf of both speakers and the balance of satirical and philosophical irony in the dialogue—the latter in the sense of classical skepticism's willingness to engage in rational argument but refusal to accept the conclusion of the argument as fully valid. Scholars have also noted the subtlety of the language of the preface, arguing that Shelley intended for contemporary readers, many of whom would have been ostensible Christian believers, to read the preface as a promise that *A Refutation of Deism* would favor traditional Christian belief rather than attack both belief systems. In this way he theoretically increased his receptive readership and mitigated the anger of conservative religious authorities.

TUMULT BETWEEN PUBLICATIONS

Percy Bysshe Shelley experienced a great deal of upheaval in his personal life between his initial publication of *A Refutation of Deism* in 1814 and its subsequent publication in the *Theological Inquirer* in 1815. In that time period his marriage to Harriet Westbrook collapsed, and he eloped to Switzerland with Mary Godwin, future author of the novel *Frankenstein; or, The Modern Prometheus* (1818) and the daughter of Shelley's former mentor William Godwin. Mary Godwin's stepsister, Claire Clairmont, traveled to Switzerland with the couple. The elopement angered William Godwin to the point that he vowed never to speak to Shelley, although he continued to demand money from him in writing. Godwin's anger reportedly shocked Shelley. Homesick and destitute, Shelley, his wife, and her stepsister returned to England in 1815 in time for the second publication of *A Refutation of Deism*.

CRITICAL DISCUSSION

A Refutation of Deism was largely ignored upon its initial publication. In the preface to the work, Shelley claims that the expense of the printing was "inimical" to "the general diffusion of knowledge" and "was adopted in this instance with a view of excluding the multitude from the abuse of a mode of reasoning liable to misconstruction on account of its novelty." *A Refutation of Deism* reached a marginally larger audience upon its subsequent republication in the magazine the *Theological Inquirer* in 1815. The magazine's editor, George Cannon (who edited under the pseudonym Erasmus Perkins), was an acquaintance and occasional collaborator of Shelley. Along with *A Refutation of Deism*, Cannon published a long review of Shelley's previously unpublished poem *Queen Mab* in the same issue. One-third of the review was a long quote from the poem. The *Theological Inquirer* did not enjoy a large readership, and Shelley's contribution was soon eclipsed in his intellectual circles by speculation over his tumultuous personal life.

As Shelley's reputation as a Romantic writer grew, so did interest in his early prose works. Scholars would later mark *A Refutation of Deism* as a key point in his artistic evolution, specifically in his treatment of the subject of God and religiosity. Twentieth-century scholars alternately championed the manifesto as an example of political radicalism, empiricism, Platonism, Christian devotion, and classical skepticism, with the last enjoying a mid-twentieth-century critical resurgence. Other scholars have examined the use of irony in *A Refutation of Deism*, debating Shelley's intent in setting the opposing Deist and Christian schools against each other in a dialogue of mutual destruction. In his book *The Deep Truth: A Study of Shelley's Scepticism* (1962), C.E. Pulos argues, "If our classification

Portrait of Percy Bysshe
Shelley, author of
A Refutation of Deism.
© LEBRECHT MUSIC AND
ARTS PHOTO LIBRARY/
ALAMY

Shelley's status as a nineteenth-century social, political, and religious radical. Of particular interest is the transmutation of Shelley's early seemingly atheistic views into an embrace of divine revelation in his verse. Michael Henry Scrivener argues this point in his book *Radical Shelley: The Philosophical Anarchism and Utopian Thought of Percy Bysshe Shelley* (1982). Scrivener suggests that "there is not much difference between the 'nature' of the *Refutation* and the 'divinity' which emerges in Shelley's later work. The movement toward divinity and away from natural law is toward a more consistent humanism. Regardless of nature's laws, it is finally people who must create the social utopia if a utopia is to exist."

BIBLIOGRAPHY

Sources

Pulos, C.E. *The Deep Truth: A Study of Shelley's Scepticism.* Lincoln: U of Nebraska P, 1962. Print.

Scrivener, Michael Henry. *Radical Shelley: The Philosophical Anarchism and Utopian Thought of Percy Bysshe Shelley.* Princeton, NJ: Princeton UP, 1982. Print.

Shelley, Percy Bysshe. *The Prose Works of Percy Bysshe Shelley.* Ed. E. B. Murray. New York: Oxford UP, 1993. Print.

Further Reading

Bernard, Ellsworth. *Shelley's Religion.* New York: Russel & Russel, 1964. Print.

Cameron, Kenneth Neill. *The Young Shelley: Genesis of a Radical.* New York: Macmillan, 1950. Print.

Kuhn, Albert J. "English Deism and the Development of Romantic Mythological Syncretism." *PMLA* 71.5 (1956): 1094-16. Print.

Shelley, Percy Bysshe. *The Complete Poetical Works of Percy Bysshe Shelley.* Ed. Thomas Hutchinson. Oxford: Oxford UP, 1970. Print.

Williams, Merle. "Contemplating Facts, Studying Ourselves: Aspects of Shelley's Philosophical and Religious Prose." *The Unfamiliar Shelley.* Ed. Alan M. Weinberg and Timothy Webb. Burlington, VT: Ashgate, 2009. 199-220. Print.

of *A Refutation of Deism* is sound, we must reject its traditional interpretation. The dialogue is ironical in a philosophical rather than in a satirical manner; it is ironical in the manner of Cicero's *De natura deorum*, not in the manner of [Jonathan] Swift's *A Modest Proposal*." As one of Shelley's most ambiguous works, *A Refutation of Deism* has continued to provoke scholarly argument into the twenty-first century.

Much scholarship has focused on how Shelley's prose works later influenced his poetry and on

Craig Barnes

ROSICRUCIAN MANIFESTOS

Anonymous

OVERVIEW

First published in Germany, the Rosicrucian manifestos—*Fama Fraternitatis* (1614) and *Confessio Fraternitatis R.C. ad Eruditos Europae* (1615)—concern the existence of a quasi-monastic order founded by Christian Rosenkreutz, or Brother C.R.C., as he is called in the texts. Written by an unknown author or group of authors, the pamphlets promise the dawn of a new age of truth and light but warn that the new age is threatened by skeptics, jealous intellectuals, and especially the Catholic Church. The *Fama* purports to give the history of the Rosy Cross, a fifteenth-century order whose members are said to possess secret and magical knowledge, including superior healing skills and a method of making gold. Both works call for religious reform and urge the abandonment of the Aristotelian orthodoxy of the Church in favor of the teachings of Paracelsus. Although the pamphlets, addressed to the European public, state that Rosicrucians are Christian, the *Fama* and *Confessio* draw on a variety of intellectual undercurrents popular at the time, including esotericism, kabbalism, hermeticism, and alchemy.

Upon publication, the pamphlets incited immediate and far-reaching furor. Controversy over authorship and authenticity abounded, and the elusive members of the Rosicrucian order were accused of practicing dark arts. Literature responding to the texts flooded northern Europe. Skeptics attributed the works to pranksters, while others saw them as divinely inspired. Still others believed them to be allegories. During the seventeenth century, many famous thinkers and prominent members of society took an interest in the pamphlets, and some contend that Rosicrucianism came to have a strong influence on science, politics, and culture in Protestant Europe. Centuries later, questions of authorship and authenticity continue to be sources of speculation. Many state that there is no evidence that the Rosicrucian order, supposedly founded in 1484, existed before 1614. However, the Rosicrucian manifestos continue to inspire and inform a variety of philanthropic, quasi-scientific, and mystical societies around the world.

HISTORICAL AND LITERARY CONTEXT

Appearing at the onset of the Scientific Revolution in Europe, the Rosicrucian manifestos tapped into popular expectations that major social changes were imminent. The explosion in scientific knowledge and two spectacular celestial events, the Fiery Trigon in 1603 and a supernova in 1604, led many Europeans to believe they were witnessing the dawn of a new age. At the same time, reform-minded Germans were distraught at the Catholic Church's attempts to extinguish advances in knowledge. Although a century had passed since Martin Luther had sparked the Protestant Reformation in Germany in 1517, it was still unsafe for Europeans to express opinions that might be construed as unorthodox. Thus, the *Fama* and the *Confessio* object strenuously, but anonymously, to the Church's continued chokehold on Europe's spiritual, intellectual, and political affairs.

Four years before the *Fama* appeared in print, the Church had accused astronomer Galileo and others of heresy for rejecting Aristotle's view of an earth-centered universe. By the time the *Confessio* was printed in 1615, the Church had subjected the astronomer to interrogation before the Roman Inquisition. Although many Europeans were attracted to the Rosicrucian manifestos' promises of material, physical, and spiritual benefits and wished to join the Rosicrucian order, none of the members identified themselves, leaving Europeans to wonder who authored the pamphlets. Skeptics have attributed the works to a person or persons affiliated with Tübingen University, where a small subset of the faculty and students cultivated an interest in mysticism. Others, including science fiction scholar Everett Bleiler, have dubbed the manifestos one of the most successful hoaxes in history.

The combination of instruction and storytelling in the Rosicrucian manifestos has invited comparisons to the Bible. Just as the Bible derives part of its authority from historical accounts of the lives of prophets and the Messiah, the pamphlets establish the authority of the Rosicrucian order by giving a historical account of Brother C.R.C., a German of noble birth, and his followers. In addition, the sections of the texts that call for reform owe a literary debt to the political proclamations of Martin Luther in his *95 Theses* (1517). Although the mystical references that appear in both works may seem at odds with the teachings of the Bible and the writings of Luther, the juxtaposition and interweaving of Christian concepts with eclectic schools of thought such as kabbalism, hermeticism,

✛ *Key Facts*

Time Period:
Early 17th Century

Movement/Issue:
Rosicrucianism; Reform of the Catholic Church

Place of Publication:
Germany

Language of Publication:
Latin

JOHANN VALENTIN ANDREAE: ROSICRUCIAN AUTHOR

Johann Valentin Andreae (1586-1654) was a Lutheran pastor in Germany and the author of the third piece of seventeenth-century Rosicrucian literature, *The Chemical Wedding of Christian Rosenkreutz* (1616). Andreae was believed by several of his contemporaries, in addition to some modern scholars, to also have participated in writing the *Fama* and the *Confessio*. Although he initially published *The Chemical Wedding* anonymously, he later acknowledged authorship in his autobiography. However, he never claimed authorship of the manifestos, and his references to the Rosicrucians as a fictitious fraternity cast doubt on his authorship.

Sometimes referred to as the third Rosicrucian manifesto, *The Chemical Wedding* is an allegorical text that differs dramatically from the *Fama* and the *Confessio* in tone, content, and style. Modeled on the alchemical fiction popular during the Italian Renaissance, the text relates the story, narrated by aged hermit Christian Rosenkreutz, of a group of royals who volunteer to undergo decapitation in order to be resurrected through an alchemical operation. Whereas in the manifestos, Rosenkreutz is a learned man who has traveled to the East, in the *Chemical Wedding* the narrator is a simple man whose primary occupation is prayer. Therefore, it is unclear whether the narrator is intended to be the same Rosenkreutz of the pamphlets.

and esotericism was nevertheless characteristic of early seventeenth-century Europe.

The Rosicrucian manifestos have inspired a wealth of fictional, philosophical, religious, and scientific works, starting with Johann Valentine Andreae's *The Chemical Wedding* in 1616 and Sir Francis Bacon's novel the *New Atlantis* in 1623. Treatments of the pamphlets have spread as far afield as Ben Jonson's satirical play in which one of the characters goes in search of the Rosicrucian brothers. During the Enlightenment era, esotericism and the occult experienced a resurgence of popularity in France, Britain, and America, and Rosicrucianism once again captured the popular imagination. Percy Bysshe Shelley's 1810 novel *The Rosicrucian* and the poetry of Emily Dickinson are among the best known examples of Rosicrucian-inspired works from the nineteenth century. Today, Rosicrucian images continue to fascinate readers. For example, the Rosy Cross is central to the wildly popular 2003 novel by Dan Brown, *The Da Vinci Code*.

THEMES AND STYLE

The central theme of the Rosicrucian manifestos is the coming of a new age of truth and light, which God has already begun to reveal to the Rosicrucians. The *Fama* states, "He hath also made manifest unto us many wonderful, and never-heretofore seen works and

Rosicrucian Symbol of the Hermetic Order of the Golden Dawn, anonymous, nineteenth century. © THE ART GALLERY COLLECTION/ALAMY

creatures of Nature, and, moreover, hath raised men, imbued with great wisdom, who might partly renew and reduce all arts (in this our spotted and imperfect age) to perfection." The pamphlets instructs learned men who wish to receive this new wisdom to become a member of the Rosicrucians, to work quietly for the betterment of the world, and to ignore the Church and others for whom the acquisition of wealth and power have become paramount.

The Rosicrucian manifestos' rhetorical success relies in part on the elements of history and biography included in the text. For example, the *Fama* provides the biography of Brother C.R.C., including his credentials as a prophet, and claims that although he was of noble birth, he eschewed wealth to become a humble monk and to devote his life to travel, study, and healing. In addition, both pamphlets trace the origin of the Rosicrucian philosophy to the Old Testament, laying claim to a tradition that predates the Catholic Church. The *Confessio* states, "Our Philosophy also is not a new invention, but as Adam after his fall hath received it, and as Moses and Solomon used it, also it ought not much to be doubted of, or contradicted by other opinions, or meanings." Also effective in attracting readers are repeated promises of wonders and worldly benefits that will accrue to learned men who join the cause. However, although the works are ostensibly recruiting tools for the Rosicrucian order, they use initials in place of the members' real names to shroud the order in mystery.

The dominant tone of the Rosicrucian manifestos is one of candor and severity with respect to the criticisms of the Catholic Church. The language goes further than earlier Protestant calls for reform, including Luther's *95 Theses*. Aimed at exposing the ecclesiastical fraud that the author(s) perceive to be rampant at the time, the pamphlets use the official language of the Church, borrowed from the Bible and other spiritual writings, to undermine the Church's own actions and orthodoxies. For example, the *Confessio* states, "[W]e hereby do condemn the East and the West (meaning the Pope and Mahomet) for their blasphemies against our Lord Jesus Christ, and offer to the chief head of the Roman Empire our prayers, secrets, and great treasures of gold."

CRITICAL DISCUSSION

The publication of the *Fama* and the *Confessio* aroused intense reactions in Europe. Within three years, both pamphlets had been reprinted seven times in German and had been translated into French, Latin, and English. Prominent men such as physician Robert Fludd came out in defense of the Rosicrucians, as did Count Michael Maier, an imperial physician, in his book *Themis Aurea: The Laws of the Fraternity of the Rosie Cross* (1618). By 1623 at least four hundred publications had been devoted to the Brethren. For the Catholic Church, the unorthodox views and antipapal rhetoric of the Rosicrucian manifestos represented a disturbing trend. For

reformers, the pamphlets provided a public expression of hidden beliefs during a time of fear and repression.

Although interest in the Rosicrucian manifestos waned in the eighteenth century, the documents gained popularity again in the nineteenth century as new Rosicrucian orders were formed and claimed a connection to the original group. The pamphlets and the work of Robert Fludd influenced twentieth-century thought as well, in particular psychologist Carl Jung's ideas about alchemy and the development of archetypal/depth psychology. Today, groups such as the Rosicrucian Fellowship and the Lectorium Rosicrucianum claim spiritual affiliation with the Rosicrucians, while the American Order of Rosicrucians and the Hermetic Order of the Golden Dawn claim to be direct descendants of the seventeenth-century organization.

Debate among modern scholars has focused on whether or not the Rosicrucian manifestos and Rosicrucianism had a significant impact on the politics, science, and culture of seventeenth-century Europe. In *The Rosicrucian Enlightenment* (1972), Frances Yates posits that the pamphlets were deliberate propaganda in support of German imperialism. However, other scholars have cast doubt on Yates's thesis. For example, C. Webster in a 1974 article in the *English Historical Review* writes, "The Rosicrucian literature has great literary interest, but the movement itself never occupied more than the extreme fringe of European thought. The capacity of Rosicrucianism to arouse curiosity must not be mistaken for proof of its permeating influence." According to another scholar, given the upheaval at the time of publication and the dearth of solid evidence tracing the influence of Rosicrucianism, it is impossible to measure the actual impact of the Rosicrucian manifestos and their apologists on the Scientific Revolution. Other branches of scholarly inquiry concern the influence of Rosicrucian ideas and imagery on literature. Literary scholars have identified Rosicrucian influences in the works of a wide range of authors, from William Shakespeare and William Butler Yeats to Emily Dickinson and Marion Zimmer Bradley.

BIBLIOGRAPHY

Sources

Bleiler, Everett F. "Johann Valentin Andreae, Fantasist and Utopist." *Science Fiction Studies* 35.1 (2008): 1-30. *JSTOR*. Web. 25 Aug. 2012.

Lewis, H. Spencer. *Rosicrucian Questions and Answers with Complete History.* San Jose: AMORC, 1979. Print.

Ormsby-Lennon, Hugh. "Rosicrucian Linguistics: Twilight of a Renaissance Tradition." *Hermeticism and the Renaissance. Intellectual History and the Occult in Early Modern Europe.* Ed. Ingrid Merkel and Allen G. Debus. Washington: Folger, 1988. 311-41. Print.

Webster, C. Rev. of *The Rosicrucian Enlightenment,* by Frances Yates. *English Historical Review* 89.351 (1974): 435-36. *JSTOR*. Web. 25 Aug. 2012.

Yates, Frances A. *The Rosicrucian Enlightenment.* London: Routledge and Kegan Paul, 1972. Print.

Further Reading

Andrea, Raymond. *The Technique of the Master*. San Jose: AMORC, 1979. Print.

Brown, Dan. *The Da Vinci Code*. New York: Doubleday, 2003. Print.

McIntosh, Christopher. *The Rose Cross and the Age of Reason: Eighteenth Century Rosicrucianism in Central Europe, and Its Relationship to the Enlightenment*. Leiden: Brill, 1999. Print.

———. *The Rosicrucians: The History, Mythology and Rituals of an Esoteric Order*. Weiser Books, 1988. Print.

Metzger, Bruce M. "Literary Forms in the Bible." *The New Oxford Annotated Bible*. Ed. Bruce M. Metzger and Roland E. Murphy. New York: Oxford UP, 1991. 397-400. Print.

"Rosicrucian." *The Oxford Companion to English Literature*. Ed. Margaret Drabble. Oxford: Oxford UP, 1995. 885. Print.

St. Armand, Barton Levi. "Emily Dickinson and the Occult: The Rosicrucian Connection." *Prairie Schooner* 51.4 (1977). 345-57. *JSTOR*. Web. 25 Aug. 2012.

Kristin King-Ries

TAMWORTH MANIFESTO

Sir Robert Peel

OVERVIEW

Written by Sir Robert Peel after he had accepted the appointment to the office of British prime minister by King William IV, the *Tamworth Manifesto* (1834) is an open letter to Peel's former constituency of Tamworth expressing a vision of a more modernized conservative party and announcing his departure from Parliament at the request of the king. Although Parliament had not yet been dissolved—and although Peel presents his letter as an effort to bid farewell to Tamworth as its member of Parliament—the *Tamworth Manifesto* was very much an electioneering document. As a member of the Tory Party, Peel sought to appeal to popular demand for reform by counteracting the staunch Ultra Tory faction while dealing delicately with the more moderate Tories who had opposed the Whig-sponsored 1832 Reform Act. To stress his nonpartisanship, Peel emphasizes King William IV's request for his premiership rather than the efforts of the Tory Party, promising that the spirit of reform will continue under his leadership. Although he addresses his letter to "the Electors of the Borough of Tamworth," the document was widely published to reach a national audience.

The letter immediately angered some Tories, who perceived it as an expression of Peel's overly liberal principles. Others saw it as a selfish ploy to make a power grab within the party. Peel's conservative platform appealed to certain voters, yet a series of political defeats in the House of Commons led the prime minister to resign his post in 1835. Despite the Conservative Party winning more than 100 seats by using the principles of the *Tamworth Manifesto* as a platform in the 1835 general election, Peel's government began and ended in a minority. The tumultuous political environment signaled a coming split among conservatives, leading to a Peelite faction that combined with Whigs and radicals in the second half of the nineteenth century to form the Liberal Party. Today, many view Peel's manifesto as a foundational document articulating the principles of the modern Conservative Party, which embraces the Peelite philosophy of conservative reforms through a political contract with the public.

HISTORICAL AND LITERARY CONTEXT

The *Tamworth Manifesto* clarifies Peel's opinion on the current and future direction of the Tory Party, which had suffered several high-profile defeats in the early 1830s. The 1832 Reform Act had enfranchised a significant portion of middle-class society, despite Tory opposition, resulting in a sound defeat of Tory politicians at the polls. Despite the triumph of Whig politicians and the growing popularity of liberal ideas, many Tories refused to permit further reforms and even planned to challenge, resist, or reverse existing ones. However, Peel and his supporters, perceiving the changing tide of political opinion and the popular desire for reform, concluded that, in order to survive, the Tories must seem receptive to change. With the 1835 general election imminent, Peel and other moderate conservatives desired to depict their party as conciliatory rather than as staunchly opposed to reform. On a personal level, Peel feared facing a short tenure as prime minister if his party failed in the general election.

On December 17, 1834, Peel sent a draft of the *Tamworth Manifesto* to his ministerial cabinet in order to aid cabinet members in drafting a statement of Tory Party principles. After much discussion, the document was sent to the three London morning papers—the *Times, Morning Herald,* and *Morning Post*—for publication on December 18. Although tactfully packaged as a letter to the constituency of Tamworth, the document was transparent in terms of its effort to reach a national audience. Such an open letter from the prime minister to the public was unprecedented, and moderate conservatives hoped its publication would be notable as an innovative political act.

The *Tamworth Manifesto* joins Edmund Burke's *Reflections on the Revolution in France* (1790) as part of the canon of important works of conservative British political thought. Written as a letter to a Parisian aristocrat, Burke's attack on the revolutionary climate of the late eighteenth century was later published for a wider audience, much like Peel's manifesto. However, unlike Burke's staunch condemnation of the rapid political change in revolutionary France, the *Tamworth Manifesto* takes a moderate view of British politics, incorporating the liberal call for reform into the author's vision for a new conservative ideology.

Peel's manifesto caused a stir among politicians and the voting public and prompted other candidates to publish open letters to constituents as a declaration of their principles and intentions. Although the

Key Facts

Time Period:
Mid-19th Century

Movement/Issue:
Political conservatism

Place of Publication:
England

Language of Publication:
English

SIR ROBERT PEEL AND THE CATHOLIC QUESTION

Sir Robert Peel's reversal of position on the Reform Bill of 1832 was not the first time he had angered members of his party. The statesmen began his political career at age twenty-one, when he joined his father, a wealthy textile manufacturer, as a member of Parliament. The young Peel quickly earned a post as undersecretary for war and in 1812 was named chief secretary of Ireland. He became popular among Tories for his staunch opposition to Roman Catholic emancipation. In addition to preventing representation of Catholics in Parliament, he attempted to suppress Irish dissent by establishing an Irish police force, members of which were dubbed "peelers."

Although he went so far as to resign his post as home secretary in 1827 due to prime minister George Canning's congenial attitude toward Catholic rights, Peel reversed his position less than two years later, helping to draft and pass the Catholic Emancipation Act, which allowed Catholics to work in government and to be elected to Parliament. The reversal outraged many in Peel's party who had once commended him on his hard-line approach to the question of Catholic representation. Others called the change of heart an act of statesmanship. Peel resigned his post following the controversy, and in 1830, after the death of his father, inherited a baronetcy and the patronage of the Borough of Tamworth.

Tamworth Manifesto failed to help the Tories gain ground in the 1835 elections, and Peel resigned only months after taking office, British politicians saw the value in publishing a statement to distance themselves from their opponents and to clarify the positions of the factions within their own party. A decade later, conservative party member and future prime minister Benjamin Disraeli devoted an entire chapter of his novel *Coningsby* (1844) to criticism of Peel's manifesto. By the early twentieth century, general election manifestos became common practice, and British political parties have continued the tradition into the present day, publishing comprehensive policy statements in newspapers and online.

THEMES AND STYLE

The main theme of the *Tamworth Manifesto* is Peel's promise to be moderate as prime minister and to serve, before his party or his own self-interest, the good of the people and of the state. He assures his constituents that he will not seek to reverse the recent reforms, primarily those passed in the 1832 Reform Act, but instead will support and accept the laws as "a final and irrevocable settlement of a great constitutional question—a settlement which no friend to the peace and welfare of this country would attempt to disturb, either by direct or by insidious means." He illustrates his dedication to reform by describing his policy positions and by referencing issues "in order to be more explicit" and to

directly address "some of those questions which have of late attracted the greater share of public interest and attention."

Rather than echoing the stubborn, dictatorial language of the old Tory government, Peel centers his rhetorical strategy on appeals to moderation and reconciliation. He begins the letter by bidding farewell to Tamworth in order to cast his departure as a new beginning for England (and for conservatives). He describes himself as a public servant bound to "enter into a declaration of my views of public policy, as full and unreserved as I can make it, consistently with my duty as a Minister of the Crown." He deflects focus from his personal aspirations by repeatedly appealing to the authority of the King to demonstrate that his motives are to serve the state and not a particular party.

Stylistically, as an open letter to his former constituency, the *Tamworth Manifesto* strikes an affable tone while maintaining the formality expected of a British prime minister. In introducing his policy positions, Peel tells his constituency, "You are entitled to this, from the nature of the trust which I again solicit, from the long habits of friendly intercourse in which we have lived, and from your tried adherence to me in times of difficulty, when the demonstration of unabated confidence was of peculiar value." He lauds his constituents as members of "that great and intelligent class of society"—an allusion to the rest of the British electorate. In plain, unadorned language he vows that he "is much less interested in the contentions of party, than in the maintenance of order and the cause of good government." Thus, through his direct, calm tone, he models the openness and moderation that will characterize his tenure as prime minister.

CRITICAL DISCUSSION

Initial reaction to the *Tamworth Manifesto* varied from staunch opposition to strong support. Donald Read writes in *Peel and the Victorians* (1987) that Peel's letter "came under immediate discussion throughout the country" and was "the basis for innumerable Conservative election speeches." George Kitson Clark notes in *Peel and the Conservative Party* (1929) that the statesman effectively tapped into the notion that "the country wished the reforms to continue, [and] the country would not stand an old Tory Government." Ultra Tories were disappointed by the manifesto's open appeal to reformism, but the manifesto gained traction among moderates in all political parties. Although conservatives managed to make inroads in rural areas during the 1835 general elections, the majority of urban dwellers ended up casting their votes for liberal Whigs.

Despite these defeats, the *Tamworth Manifesto* succeeded in inspiring a new breed of political thinkers who would reignite British conservatism—and Peel's career. In *Peel* (1976) Norman Gash argues that the manifesto "enabled a 'Conservative Party' in a real sense to come into existence." New conservatives had largely replaced members of the old Tory Party by the time Peel resumed the office of prime minister in 1841. In *The American Historical Review* (1995), John A. Phillips and Charles Wetherell write that Peel's manifesto "reflected the new world of popular politics that had been created by the reform" and the modern need for "a set of clear principles that voters could support or reject." Today scholars consider the *Tamworth Manifesto* to be a foundational document for modern conservatives and the inspiration for the modern-day tradition of drafting political manifestos.

The majority of scholarship based on the *Tamworth Manifesto* takes a biographical focus on Peel and the effect that the manifesto had on his political career. The most extensive text about Peel—and by extension the *Tamworth Manifesto*—discusses his lack of interest in using the document to create a legacy. Gash argues in *Sir Robert Peel* (1972) that the statesman wrote his manifesto "at short notice not for posterity but for the public and the electorate of 1834." Although Peel's purpose may have been immediate, T.A. Jenkins argues in *Sir Robert Peel* (1999) that the manifesto "was the key document in the evolution of Conservative ideas," showing the importance of reconciling Conservative interests "with the values and expectations of a society experiencing rapid and profound change."

BIBLIOGRAPHY

Sources

Clark, George Kitson. *Peel and the Conservative Party: A Study in Party Politics 1832-1841.* London: G. Bell & Sons, 1929. Print.

Gash, Norman. *Sir Robert Peel: The Life of Sir Robert Peel after 1830.* London: Longman, 1972. Print.

———. *Peel.* New York: Longman, 1976. Print.

Jenkins, T.A. *Sir Robert Peel.* New York: St. Martin's, 1999. Print.

Newbould, Ian. "Sir Robert Peel and the Conservative Party, 1832-1841: A Study in Failure?" *English Historical Review* 98.388 (1983): 529-57. Print.

Peel, Sir Robert. "The Tamworth Manifesto." *English Historical Documents.* Ed. W.D. Handcock. New York: Routledge, 1996.126-29. Web. 21 June 2012.

Phillips, John A., and Charles Wetherell. "The Great Reform Act of 1832 and the Political Modernization of England." *American Historical Review* 100.2 (1995): 411-36. Print.

Read, Donald. *Peel and the Victorians.* Oxford: Basil Blackwell, 1987. Print.

Further Reading

Davis, Richard W. "Toryism to Tamworth: The Triumph of Reform, 1827-1835." *Quarterly Journal Concerned with British Studies* 12.2 (1980): 132-46. Print.

Gash, Norman. *The Age of Peel.* London: Edward Arnold, 1968. Print.

———. *Politics in the Age of Peel.* London: Norton, 1971. Print.

Ramsay, Anna Augustus Whittall. *Sir Robert Peel.* Freeport: Books for Libraries, 1928. Print.

Shannon, Richard. "Peel, Gladstone and Party." *Parliamentary History* 18.3 (1999): 317-52. Print.

Cameron Dodworth

Sir Robert Peel in an 1838 portrait by John Linnell. NATIONAL PORTRAIT GALLERY, LONDON, UK/ THE BRIDGEMAN ART LIBRARY

TESTAMENT

Memoir of the Thoughts and Sentiments of Jean Meslier

Jean Meslier

❖ **Key Facts**

Time Period:
Early 18th Century

Movement/Issue:
Atheism; Enlightenment
rationalism; Democratic
reform

Place of Publication:
France

**Language of
Publication:**
French

OVERVIEW

Written by Jean Meslier, *Testament: Memoir of the Thoughts and Sentiments of Jean Meslier* (1729) argues for the nonexistence of God; the invalidity of all religions; and the necessity of political and social reform to promote justice, equality, and general happiness. For forty years Meslier served as a Roman Catholic priest in the Ardennes Parish of Étrépigny in France, all the while disguising his atheistic views out of fear of persecution and a wish to live a "tranquil" life. In the document, he appeals to popular dissatisfaction with the excesses of the Catholic Church and the French monarchy. Essentially a journal of the private religious and political convictions of Meslier, the work was published shortly after his death, when several copies of his original manuscript—some of them varying to significant degree from the original text—were released in Paris.

Testament had a muted impact on the French intellectual community of the eighteenth century. Although the work influenced several famous Enlightenment writers, its radicalism was diluted by numerous revisions and republications. The most famous version of the text, published by Voltaire in 1761 under the title *Extrait,* significantly varies from the original work and argues for deism, largely obscuring Meslier's atheistic thesis. Finally, in 1970 the text was published in its original form in French, though it was not translated into English until 2009. Today scholars agree that *Testament* is one of the first defenses of modern atheism—if not the first—and represents a pivotal work of the early eighteenth-century Enlightenment rationalist movement.

HISTORICAL AND LITERARY CONTEXT

Testament speaks to popular dissatisfaction with the French monarchy and the Catholic Church, which can be traced back to the sixteenth-century French Wars of Religion (1562-98), a violent domestic conflict between factions of Roman Catholics and Protestant Huguenots in which both sides committed many atrocities. Although the Edict of Nantes in 1598 ostensibly allowed for mutual toleration, the violence continued, culminating in Louis XIV's issuance of the Edict of Fontainebleau in 1685, which officially sanctioned Catholic persecution of Huguenots. The decree resulted in renewed violence and a mass migration of French Protestants to other more tolerant European nations, resulting in further disruption of French domestic life.

Testament foreshadows many of the popular grievances that would lead to the French Revolution in 1789, specifically the view that the French clergy and nobility were working in conjunction to enrich themselves by oppressing the French people. Meslier makes numerous references in his manuscript to the ways in which French religious and political authorities perpetuated the myth of their superiority in order to maintain power. His calls for a more just and equal society would later be echoed by numerous French eighteenth-century historical figures—notably Jean-Jacques Rousseau and Voltaire—and by the French *Declaration of the Rights of Man and of the Citizen* in 1789.

In *Testament,* Meslier draws on several contemporary and classical sources. Having read the works of René Descartes as a seminary student, he uses Cartesian assertions as a foil for his arguments for God's nonexistence. He also expresses admiration for writer

JEAN MESLIER: REBELLIOUS PRIEST

From what is known of his professional life, Jean Meslier was a competent if mildly rebellious priest. He lived modestly and distributed his excess wealth to his parishioners at the end of every year. He did not charge to perform marriage ceremonies (which was unusual at the time), and his church superiors twice reprimanded him for hiring cleaning maids under the age of forty.

Meslier had a contentious relationship with a local nobleman named Antoine de Toully, whom he believed was mistreating the peasants of Étrépigny. Meslier once barred the nobleman from entering the church to worship, prompting Toully to complain to the bishop. Although Meslier complied with the bishop's order to admit Toully to the church, he also asked, in Toully's presence, that the congregation pray for the nobleman to be a better Christian. When Toully complained to the bishop again, the bishop ordered Meslier to cease antagonizing him. Nevertheless, upon Toully's death, Meslier asked his congregation to pray that Toully's soul might one day reach heaven.

Michel de Montaigne and demonstrates the influence of thinkers Lucilio Vanini, Jean de La Bruyère, and Étienne de la Boétie, as well as Richard Simon, a Norman priest who wrote a critical history of the New Testament. Finally, Meslier draws on the works of classical writers Seneca and Tacitus, making numerous antagonistic references to biblical scripture. Along with *Testament,* he left behind detailed annotations refuting *The Demonstration of the Existence of God* (1688) by François Fenelon and the writings of the Jesuit intellectual Jean de Touinemire.

Testament, particularly Voltaire's version, influenced a number of subsequent publications, many of which obscured Meslier's original thesis or departed from it altogether. (A notable example is *The Good Sense of Curé Meslier* (1772) by Baron d'Holbach.) Despite these unfaithful republications, several well-known French intellectuals, including Denis Diderot, were clearly familiar with the work—although even Voltaire admitted he was uncertain of Meslier's authorship in a private letter. A more faithful edition of *Testament* was republished by a Dutch humanist in 1864. The definitive 1970 French edition established Meslier's legacy as a founding figure of modern atheism.

THEMES AND STYLE

The central theme of *Testament* is the nonexistence of God and the invalidity of all religious beliefs. A strict materialist, Meslier argues, "All the productions of Nature are really made by necessary and accidental causes, which are blind and completely deprived of reason." This central atheistic truth leads to all the "contrasts, absurdities, and palpable contradictions" entailed by a belief in God. A secondary theme is the magnitude of pain and injustice that religious beliefs cause in the world. He writes that religion is responsible for the "huge disproportion" of wealth and happiness in all societies. He calls this disproportion "totally unjust and detestable" because it is not based on the merit of individuals. Following this line of reasoning, he cites "love … for justice and truth, which I see so indignantly oppressed" as the inspiration for his writing. He declares that he stands against Christianity—and by extension all religion—because religion "allows and approves and even authorizes the tyranny of the princes and kings." He therefore proposes an alternative, secular communalist social and political organization in which individuals live and work together for their mutual benefit.

Rhetorically, *Testament* takes the form of a long sermon or soliloquy, which allows Meslier to repeatedly illustrate his argument for the nonexistence of God and the necessity of political and social reform. The original manuscript is more than one thousand pages long and contains ninety-seven chapters. Many sections of the work overlap, allowing the author to accumulate evidence in support of his position. Written in the first person, the text repeatedly asserts that Meslier has no interest in gaining an intellectual

reputation in his lifetime. Such declarations lend credibility to his more radical assertions by convincing the reader of the sincerity of his cause.

Stylistically, the prose in *Testament* tends to ramble, sometimes causing "the essential" to vanish "under the incidental," according to noted Meslier scholar Michael Onfray in a 2006 essay in *New Politics.* Some of the wording of the attacks on the church and government are shrill, including the declaration that Jesus Christ was "a vile and despicable man who had no mind, talent or knowledge … a fool, a madman, a wretched fanatic, and a miserable scoundrel." Meslier is even the original author of a famous quote often falsely attributed to Diderot concerning the common man's wish "that all the rulers of the earth and all the nobles be hanged and strangled with the guts of priests."

CRITICAL DISCUSSION

There is much scholarly debate as to how Meslier's *Testament* was first disseminated upon his death. Voltaire claims that of the three original manuscripts, one was seized by the grand-vicaire of Rheims, one was sent to the garde des sceaux Germain Louis

Portrait of Voltaire by Carle Van Loo. Jean Meslier's manuscript profoundly influenced Voltaire; however, Voltaire produced edited abstracts of the *Testament* that softened Meslier's atheism. KHARBINE-TAPABOR/THE ART ARCHIVE AT ART RESOURCE, NY

Chauvelin, and one was deposited with the clerk of court of Mézières. At some point, the manuscript sent to Chauvelin reached Anne Claude de Caylus, who distributed one hundred copies in Paris between 1742 and 1747. However, mentions of the original manuscript are rare in eighteenth-century writing, and its existence is often only noted in passing. While some French intellectuals were clearly familiar with the work, it is unclear if they knew Meslier's identity as the original author. Voltaire's 1761 deistic version of the work, *Extrait,* quickly overshadowed the atheistic original. Voltaire's edition was far less radical than Meslier's and minimized what would presumably have been a larger critical reaction. Ira O. Wade argues in a 1933 essay for *Modern Philology* that if more were known about the dissemination of *Testament,* "interesting light would be thrown upon the diffusion of ideas contained in unpublished eighteenth century works of a philosophical nature."

In the nineteenth century, *Testament* became better known because of its association with the French Revolution but mainly though the continued popularity of Voltaire's *Extrait,* which minimized Meslier's reputation as an intellectual founder of modern atheism. Various apocryphal versions of the original manuscript continued to circulate into the twentieth century, with some bearing almost no resemblance to Meslier's original. One of these versions influenced the early Bolsheviks, which prompted the inscription of Meslier's name on a Soviet monument in the early twentieth century. Until Michael Shreve's 2009 translation of *Testament,* Meslier's text was the subject of only a few scholarly treatments, such as Margaret Knight's *Humanist Anthology* (1961).

In the late twentieth and early twenty-first centuries, *Testament* has received greater critical attention. Onfray writes that Meslier was a "priest with no reputation and without any memorial" who "furnishes an ideological arsenal of the thought of the Enlightenment's radical function." Onfray also argues that *Testament* represents an attempt at rococo art and can be analyzed as the psychologically cathartic efforts of a man caught in the divide between public belief and private conviction. According to Onfray, the author's position as the first modern atheist has assured him a place in the history of the Enlightenment rationalist movement.

BIBLIOGRAPHY

Sources

Brewer, Colin. "Thinker: Jean Meslier." *New Humanist* 122.4 (2007): n. pag. Web. 25 Sept. 2012.

Onfray, Michel. "Jean Meslier and 'The Gentle Inclination of Nature.'" *New Politics* 10.4 (2006): 53-75.

Pailin, David A. Rev. of *Testament: Memoir of the Thoughts and Sentiments of Jean Meslier,* by Jean Meslier. *Journal of Theological Studies* 61.2 (2010): 857-62. Print.

Wade, Ira O. "The Manuscripts of Jean Meslier's *Testament* and Voltaire's *Extrait.*" *Modern Philology* 30.4 (1933): 381-98. *JSTOR.* Web. 25 Sept. 2012.

Further Reading

Gliozzo, Charles A. "The Philosophes and Religion: Intellectual Origins of the Dechristianization Movement in the French Revolution." *Church History* 40.3 (1971): 273-83. Print.

Kors, Alan Charles. *Atheism in France, 1650-1729: The Orthodox Sources of Disbelief.* Vol. 1. Princeton: Princeton UP, 1990. Print.

Meslier, Jean. *Le Testament de Jean Meslier.* Charleston: Nabu, 2010. Print.

———. *Testament: Memoir of the Thoughts and Sentiments of Jean Meslier.* Trans. Michael Shreve. Amherst: Prometheus, 2009. Print.

Moene, Genevieve. "Jean Meslier, prêtreathée et révolutionnaire." *French Review* 77.1 (2003): 114-25. Print.

Craig Barnes

THEOLOGICO-POLITICAL TREATISE

Benedict de Spinoza

OVERVIEW

Benedict de Spinoza's *Theologico-Political Treatise* (1670) challenges the supernatural interpretation of scripture by Christian and Jewish theologians, defends the supremacy of rational analysis of the natural world, and encourages individual freedom of expression as necessary to the maintenance of a healthy political state. The manifesto also emphasizes Spinoza's conception of God's existence and encourages the rational study of religious scripture. While the manifesto was intended to serve as a defense of Spinoza's personal views, it was published anonymously in Latin—as opposed to Spinoza's vernacular Dutch—in order to limit its readership during a tumultuous period of Dutch Protestant religious upheaval. The *Theologico-Political Treatise* is divided into twenty chapters, with the first fifteen chapters exploring a rational approach to analyzing scripture and the final five applying that approach to the religious and political relationship between individual and state.

The *Theologico-Political Treatise* provoked an immediate and severe backlash from religious and government officials. Chief among the charges leveled against Spinoza—whose authorship was revealed shortly after publication—was the label of atheist. Despite his rejection of the label and the religious nature of his work, many continental religious scholars and natural philosophers were quick to distance themselves from him, fearing he might suffer harsh legal consequences. One of his close intellectual contemporaries, Adriaan Koerbagh, was imprisoned and then banished from Holland after he wrote *Een ligt* (1698), which voiced similar but more-direct challenges to the religious establishment. The *Theologico-Political Treatise* proved to be a watershed moment in the development of Spinoza's reputation as a free-thinking religious and political scholar and in the Enlightenment rationalist movement as a whole, with the manifesto's unique emphasis on setting aside popular superstition in favor of rational analysis serving as an important precursor to the values of nineteenth-century European modernity.

HISTORICAL AND LITERARY CONTEXT

The *Theologico-Political Treatise* speaks to a crisis regarding the theological and political legitimacy of liberal and conservative religious factions in Holland and Northern Europe in the late seventeenth century. Spinoza alludes to one of these conflicts, the discord between the liberal Remonstrants and the conservative Contra-Remonstrants, in the treatise, entreating his readers to consider, "What … can be more hurtful than that men who have committed no crime or wickedness should because they are enlightened, be treated as enemies and put to death." More generally, the *Theologico-Political Treatise* was published at a time of economic hardship and political strife in Holland. In Spinoza's view, his native Amsterdam represented a relative oasis of calm and intellectual toleration, but it is questionable whether this was still the case at the time of the publication of the *Theologico-Political Treatise*.

The publication of the *Theologico-Political Treatise* shortly preceded a political revolution in which Holland's liberal ruler, Jan de Witt, a friend and intellectual protector of Spinoza, was forcibly removed from power by invading French and German armies in 1672. He was replaced by the more conservative Prince William III, giving Spinoza increasing reason to fear that the publication of the treatise would have harmful consequences on his personal life. Already fearing the ire of popular sentiment, Spinoza attempted to stall the translation of the *Theologico-Political Treatise* into Dutch in 1671. He was unsuccessful and, partially because of the political climate of the time, became a notorious and polarizing symbol for both sides of the religious legitimacy debate.

The *Theologico-Political Treatise* draws on several literary sources, most notably Thomas Hobbes's *Leviathan* (1651), which features multiple references to the necessity of individuals ceding certain rights to the state for their mutual benefit. To a lesser extent, the manifesto also echoes the views of Niccolò Machiavelli on the inherent amorality of the exercise of political power. In addition to Koerbagh, contemporary influences include prominent Enlightenment rationalist thinkers René Descartes—whose philosophy, form, and method greatly influenced Spinoza's conception of religion and nature as a whole—and Gottfried Leibniz. The *Theologico-Political Treatise* also bears degrees of influence by Abe Eera, Issac La Peyreve, Samuel Fisher, and the Socinians.

In the immediate aftermath of its publication, the *Theologico-Political Treatise* was used mainly by more-conservative intellectuals as the basis of their counter

+ *Key Facts*

Time Period:
Mid-17th Century

Movement/Issue:
Enlightenment;
Protestant reformation;
Liberalism

Place of Publication:
Netherlands

Language of Publication:
Latin

BENEDICT DE SPINOZA: LENS GRINDER

Throughout his professional life, Spinoza also worked as a lens grinder and made several notable contributions to the science of optics on both the theoretical and practical level. He constructed numerous microscopes and telescopes that were highly praised by his scientific contemporaries and advised other scientists on how to produce the best observation lenses. Spinoza also used his lenses to conduct his own studies, most notably a study of blood under a microscope. He later referred to this study in a philosophical analogy relating the harmony in the infinite world to a worm living in the blood.

Gottfried Leibniz praised Spinoza's work, writing in a letter that "he would not easily find somebody who in this field of studies could judge better." Another scientific contemporary, Theordor Kerckringh, wrote, "I own a first class microscope made by Benedictus Spinoza, that noble mathematician and philosopher." Spinoza's scientific endeavors also earned him the displeasure of the Dutch Reformed Church and prompted him to emphasize the importance of scientific freedom of expression in the *Theologico-Political Treatise*. In this regard, it can be argued that Spinoza's scientific career had considerable influence upon his work as a philosopher.

arguments—Pierre Bayle's *Dictionnaire historique et critique* (1697) being a prominent example. In the mid-eighteenth century, the treatise served as a constructive influence on Denis Diderot's *La promenade du sceptique* (1747) and later as a crucial inspiration for nineteenth-century German intellectuals, including Goethe,

Engraved portrait of Benedict de Spinoza. The *Theologico-Political Treatise* was intended to deflect charges of atheism and defend Spinoza's right to philosophize. © AISA/ EVERETT COLLECTION

Hegel, Schopenhauer, Nietzsche, and Marx. Numerous twentieth-century intellectuals also have cited Spinoza's *Theologico-Political Treatise* as a key influence.

THEMES AND STYLE

The central theme of the *Theologico-Political Treatise* is the importance of accurate, rational knowledge of scripture—and by extension human nature—in understanding divine law. For Spinoza this understanding allows for true happiness. He writes, "A man's true happiness and blessedness lies simply in his wisdom and knowledge of truth," as opposed to in a superstitious faith in miracles or divine revelation. Regarding the relative importance of religious rights outlined in scripture, Spinoza writes, "the divine law which makes men truly blessed, and teaches them true living, is common to all men; indeed, I derived it from human nature in such a way that it must be regarded as innate in the human mind and, so to speak, engraved upon it." A close secondary theme is the importance of freedom of expression, especially religious freedom. On this subject, Spinoza writes, "Thus, since everyone has a perfect right to think freely, even about religion, and cannot conceivably surrender this right, everyone will also have a perfect right and authority to judge freely about religion, and hence to explain and interpret it for himself." From this postulate, Spinoza proceeds to analyze Biblical scripture at length and to offer his own rational, nonmetaphysical interpretations, for example his assertion that God's promise to Noah to "set His bow in the cloud" in Genesis 9:13 is "another way of expressing the refraction and reflection which the rays of the sun are subjected to in water."

The *Theologico-Political Treatise* achieves its rhetorical effect through its systematic, almost scientific address first of explicitly religious and then of more politically salient questions. Each question is raised and answered within its own chapter, and the result is an accruing sense of inevitability regarding Spinoza's reasoning. Chapter title examples include "Of Prophecy," "Of Prophets," "Of the Authorship of the Pentateuch and the Other Historical Books of the Old Testament," and "Theology Is Shown Not to Be Subservient to Reason, Nor Reason to Theology: A Definition of the Reason Which Enables Us to Accept the Authority of the Bible." The arguments in each chapter build upon themselves along the lines of a logical proof. Most chapters refer to material from preceding chapters at the outset and finish with a summary conclusion.

Stylistically, the language of *Theologico-Political Treatise* is conservative and similar to that of classical texts. Much of this classical influence can be traced to the manifesto's original publication in Latin and the stylistic influence of Descartes. Spinoza occasionally makes use of the collective pronoun "we" in his direct address to the reader ("We have shown the following to be true"), a device must notably reminiscent of Socratic dialogue. Some scholars have argued that the language of the treatise is intentionally conservative in

PRIMARY SOURCE

THEOLOGICO-POLITICAL TREATISE

(20) Now, seeing that we have the rare happiness of living in a republic, where everyone's judgment is free and unshackled, where each may worship God as his conscience dictates, and where freedom is esteemed before all things dear and precious, I have believed that I should be undertaking no ungrateful or unprofitable task, in demonstrating that not only can such freedom be granted without prejudice to the public peace, but also, that without such freedom, piety cannot flourish nor the public peace be secure.

(21) Such is the chief conclusion I seek to establish in this treatise; but, in order to reach it, I must first point out the misconceptions which, like scars of our former bondage, still disfigure our notion of religion, and must expose the false views about the civil authority which many have most impudently advocated, endeavouring to turn the mind of the people, still prone to heathen superstition, away from its legitimate rulers, and so bring us again into slavery. (22) As to the order of my treatise I will speak presently, but first I will recount the causes which led me to write....

(29) Piety, great God! and religion are become a tissue of ridiculous mysteries; men, who flatly despise reason, who reject and turn away from understanding as naturally corrupt, these, I say, these of all men, are thought, 0 lie most horrible! to possess light from on High. (30) Verily, if they had but one spark of light from on High, they would not insolently rave, but would learn to worship God more wisely, and would be as marked among their fellows for mercy as they now are for malice; if they were concerned for their opponents' souls, instead of for their own reputations, they would no longer fiercely persecute, but rather be filled with pity and compassion....

[...] I constructed a method of Scriptural interpretation, and thus equipped proceeded to inquire—what is prophecy? (37) In what sense did God reveal himself to the prophets, and why were these particular men—chosen by him? (38) Was it on account of the sublimity of their thoughts about the Deity and nature, or was it solely on account of their piety? (39) These questions being answered, I was easily able to conclude, that the authority of the prophets has weight only in matters of morality, and that their speculative doctrines affect us little....

(42) Now, as in the whole course of my investigation I found nothing taught expressly by Scripture, which does not agree with our understanding, or which is repugnant thereto, and as I saw that the prophets taught nothing, which is not very simple and easily to be grasped by all, and further, that they clothed their leaching in the style, and confirmed it with the reasons, which would most deeply move the mind of the masses to devotion towards God, I became thoroughly convinced, that the Bible leaves reason absolutely free, that it has nothing in common with philosophy, in fact, that Revelation and Philosophy stand on different footings. In order to set this forth categorically and exhaust the whole question, I point out the way in which the Bible should be interpreted, and show that all of spiritual questions should be sought from it alone, and not from the objects of ordinary knowledge.

SOURCE: Translated by R.H.M. Elwes, 1670.

---

order to mitigate the effect of its radical content. It is also possible that Spinoza's scientific career influenced the procedural nature of the prose.

CRITICAL DISCUSSION

The initial critical reaction to the *Theologico-Political Treatise* was overwhelmingly negative; intellectuals and church authorities alike rushed to condemn the work. Even ostensibly liberal philosophers such as Lambent von Velthuysen dismissed the manifesto as atheistic, or at best a thin veneer of religious argument intended to promote atheism. Dutch church authorities went further in their condemnation, referring to the treatise as "a harmful book," "idolatry and superstition," and the "vilest and most sacrilegious book the world has ever seen." One theologian, Thomas J. Melchior, issued a refutation in which Spinoza was characterized as a freak. In 1674 the Supreme Court of Holland banned the book and declared punishments for anyone caught printing or distributing it.

Despite this negative critical reaction, the *Theologico-Political Treatise* was a commercial success for its original publisher, Jan Rieuwertsz, who oversaw the printing of several reissues under different titles. In the following decades, the treatise also enjoyed critical acceptance among small circles of like-minded intellectuals and political officials in London, Paris, Florence, Rome, and Stockholm. Spinoza had occasion to turn down several offers from admirers across the continent to visit and discuss the work. However, the treatise did not enjoy substantial critical praise until the mid-eighteenth century—long after Spinoza's death in 1677—or widespread acclaim until the nineteenth century, when it became a foundational text for German romantics and idealists, especially Hegel, who argued that all philosophers have a choice between Spinozism and no philosophy at all.

Contemporary scholarship on the *Theologico-Political Treatise* has focused on the seeming contradictions within the text, on comparisons to other

Enlightenment rationalist philosophers, especially Hobbes and Descartes, and on the status of the treatise as a document foreshadowing the nineteenth-century European transition to modernity and grudging religious plurality. Regarding the transition to modernity, Willi Goetschel notes in *Spinoza's Modernity: Mendelssohn, Lessing, and Heine* (2004) that Spinoza's apparent attack on Judaism as a superstitious belief system in the treatise is nuanced by his recognition of the faith's role as a political entity. Goetschel writes, "The *Theological-Political Treatise* has traditionally been read as a relentless attack on Judaism and its institutions, and consequently as a blanket rejection of theological claims to power and authority. However, for Spinoza, the theocracy of the state of the Hebrews serves as the only historical model of true democracy." Other notable Spinoza scholars include Edwin Curley, Leo Strauss, Don Garret, and Carl Gebhardt.

BIBLIOGRAPHY

Sources

Curley, Edwin. "Kissinger, Spinoza, and Genghis Khan." *The Cambridge Companion to Spinoza*. Ed. Don Garrett. New York: Cambridge UP, 1996. 315-42. Print.

Garret, Don. "Introduction." *The Cambridge Companion to Spinoza*. Ed. Don Garrett. New York: Cambridge UP, 1996. 1-12. Print.

Goetschel, Willi. *Spinoza's Modernity: Mendelssohn, Lessing, and Heine*. Madison: U of Wisconsin P, 2004. Print.

Moreau, Pierre-Francois. "Spinoza's Reception and Influence." Trans. Roger Ariew. *The Cambridge Companion to Spinoza*. Ed. Don Garrett. New York: Cambridge UP, 1996. 408-33. Print.

The Political Works: The Tractatus Theologico-Politicus in Part and the Tractatus Politicus in Full. Trans. and Ed. A. G. Wernham. London: Oxford UP, 1958. Print.

Further Reading

Garrett, Aaron. "Knowing the Essence of the State in Spinoza's *Tractatus Theologico-Politicus*." *European Journal of Philosophy* 20.1 (2012): 50-73. *Wiley Online Library*. Web. 21 Sept. 2012.

Gildin, Hilail. "Spinoza and the Political Problem." *Spinoza: A Collection of Critical Essays*. Ed. Marjorie Grene. Notre Dame: U of Notre Dame P, 1979. 377-87. Print.

Levene, Nancy. "Ethics and Interpretation, or How to Study Spinoza's *Tractatus Theologico-Politicus* without Strauss." *Journal of Jewish Thought & Philosophy* 10.1 (2000): 57-110.

Nadler, Steven M. *A Book Forged in Hell: Spinoza's Scandalous Treatise and the Birth of the Secular Age*. Princeton: Princeton UP, 2011. Print.

Spinoza, Baruch. *Tractatus Theologico-Politicus*. Trans. Samuel Shirley. Indianapolis: Hackett, 1998. Print.

Strauss, Leo. *Persecution and the Art of Writing*. Glencoe: Free Press, 1952. Print.

———. *Spinoza's Critique of Religion*. New York: Schocken Books, 1965. Print.

Craig Barnes

THE THEORY OF MORAL SENTIMENTS

Adam Smith

OVERVIEW

Written by Scottish social philosopher and economist Adam Smith, *The Theory of Moral Sentiments* (1759) represents a philosophical attempt to develop an understanding of the process by which individuals develop moral worldviews and make moral judgments. Ultimately, he argues, individuals choose to behave morally out of sympathy for the imagined sensory experience of others rather than out of an internal moral sense. As a result, sympathy for others, and the moral behavior it encourages, leads to a love of self resulting from the imagined joy of others. Smith's argument represents a crucial break with most of the moral philosophical positions of his day in that it inverts the process by which most moral philosophers believed individual moral judgments were made. Rather than looking inward for moral guidance, he maintains that individuals must first look to the world for exemplary illustrations in order to shape their moral imagination. Only then can an individual internalize moral behavior and thus experience the joy of self-love through behaving morally.

Widely read in mid-eighteenth-century English intellectual circles, *The Theory of Moral Sentiments* was heavily praised and established Smith's early reputation as a scholar and moral philosopher. While some contemporary intellectuals disagreed with parts of his argument, most accepted it as groundbreaking and worthy of consideration. *The Theory of Moral Sentiments* continues to be one of Smith's best-known works, second only to *An Inquiry into the Nature and Causes of the Wealth of Nations* (1776), upon which his modern reputation as an economist is based. *The Theory of Moral Sentiments* remains a frequent subject of academic study and has enjoyed a resurgence of critical attention in the late twentieth and early twenty-first centuries.

HISTORICAL AND LITERARY CONTEXT

The Theory of Moral Sentiments falls into a long English moral philosophical tradition of skepticism and questioning of the individual's role in society dating back to the political and religious tumult of the English Civil Wars (1642-51). Writing in the mid-eighteenth century, Smith occupies an important position in this tradition, with England and northern Europe on the cusp of political and economic modernity. The

individual's role in society—and, conversely, society's role in shaping the individual—is central to this transition, with the consequences ranging from general social ferment to potential revolution. The waning power of organized religion to impose a moral order on society was also crucial to this formulation. Discredited by the anxieties of the Reformation and the subsequent Enlightenment rationalist movement, many of Smith's contemporaries believed that the Church of England and other religious sectarian groups no longer held moral authority. The absence of this authority called for a new understanding of morality as a function of the science of human nature.

Smith's text was published at the height of the Seven Years' War (1756-63) between Britain and France. While he held a qualified admiration for several contemporary French philosophers—especially Denis Diderot, Jean-Jacques Rousseau, and Voltaire—and urged his students to read French philosophy, his work was interpreted by his contemporaries to be in the British camp of competing Anglo-Franco moral philosophical perspectives. The British viewed man's experience in society with relative optimism, while French intellectuals were more pessimistic. However, it is debatable to what extent these competing generalizations of the historical moment influenced Smith's writing.

In the British literary tradition, *The Theory of Moral Sentiments* draws on a number of philosophical writings, including the Enlightenment works of Thomas Hobbes and John Locke. As one of the foremost members of the Scottish Enlightenment intellectual movement, Smith was greatly influenced by his mentor at the University of Glasgow, Francis Hutcheson, and by the works of his close contemporary, David Hume, especially Hume's *Treatise of Human Nature* (1739), *Enquiry Concerning the Principles of Morals* (1751), and *Political Discourses* (1752). In the French literary tradition, Rousseau's *Discourse on Inequality* (1754) and Bernard Mandeville's *The Fable of the Bees* (1714) influenced *The Theory of Moral Sentiments* and provided intellectual positions for Smith to rebut. In the broader classical tradition, both the Epicurean and Stoic schools of philosophy—the former advocating emotional serenity and pleasures of the intellect and the latter supporting a tranquil mind and moral worth—influenced Smith's

✥ Key Facts

Time Period:
Mid-18th Century

Movement/Issue:
Ethics; Moral philosophy

Place of Publication:
England and Scotland

Language of Publication:
English

THE CAREER OF ADAM SMITH

In the decade after the publication of *The Theory of Moral Sentiments* (1759), Adam Smith resigned from his university post and took a position as the private tutor of the son of a British aristocrat. Not an uncommon career move, it allowed Smith to travel the European continent and to devote his energy to writing *An Inquiry into the Nature and Causes of the Wealth of Nations* in Kirkcaldy, Scotland, and London upon his return. The position, which his friend David Hume helped him secure, also included a lifetime pension.

Later in his life, Smith would advise the British government on the conflict with the North American colonies—he recommended allowing the colonies to become independent—and on the subject of Irish-British union. He also held public office as the British commissioner for customs from 1778 to his death in 1790.

text. Some scholars argue that the work represents an attempt to reconcile the two schools, with Hume's influence representing the Epicurean and Hutcheson's representing the Stoic.

Along with establishing Smith's intellectual reputation, *The Theory of Moral Sentiments* influenced much of his later work, including *The Wealth of Nations* (1776), *Essays on Philosophical Subjects* (1795), and *Lectures on Justice, Police, Revenue, and Arms,* published posthumously in 1896. *The Theory of Moral Sentiments* also influenced nineteenth-century European intellectuals, including English naturalist Charles Darwin in his 1871 work *The Descent of Man* and German philosopher Immanuel Kant. The work continues to have an effect on modern literary explorations of moral-social function and the psychological underpinnings of human behavior.

THEMES AND STYLE

The central theme of *The Theory of Moral Sentiments* is the importance of sympathy and the sympathetic imagination to individuals who engage in moral behavior. Smith begins the text by writing, "How selfish soever man may be supposed, there are evidently some principles in his nature, which interest him in the fortune of others, and render their happiness necessary to him, though he derives nothing from it except the pleasure of seeing it." This central idea is echoed in the subsidiary theme of the desire to please the "Impartial Spectator," an abstract viewpoint representing society's holistic judgment of an individual's morality. By pleasing the Impartial Spectator, an individual can hope "to be loved and to know that we deserve to be loved." Both of these themes work in conjunction to explain the harmonious interaction between human minds that allows for a moral society.

Smith makes his argument for the importance of sympathy through logical induction and the use

of vivid hypothetical illustrations that exemplify the function of the sympathetic imagination. One example of these vivid illustrations is Smith's invitation to readers to imagine being in a torture chamber watching their brother on the rack. He writes, "His agonies, when they are brought home to ourselves [through sympathetic imagination] ... begin at last to affect us, and we then tremble and shudder at the thought of what he feels." These illustrations and related analysis and argument are divided into a seven-part exploration of various moral issues, with each part divided into sections and chapters. The result is a systematic study of various moral philosophical categories drawn from Smith's academic background, with each part, section, and chapter completing a separate line of reasoning.

The language of *The Theory of Moral Sentiments* is academic in nature and—aside from the occasional vivid hypothetical scenario—is staid and even abstract. Smith writes, for example, "The propriety of every passion excited by objects peculiarly related to ourselves ... must lie ... in a certain mediocrity." Nonetheless, for the academic standard of the time, Smith's peers considered the prose of *The Theory of Moral Sentiments* to be exceptionally lucid and accessible. Some scholars have argued that Smith's easily understood prose resulted from his teaching experience, both at the university and as a private tutor.

CRITICAL DISCUSSION

Initial critical reception to *The Theory of Moral Sentiments* was largely positive. The work sold well both in England and in Scotland and was in demand immediately upon its publication in influential Scottish Enlightenment intellectual circles. Some of this demand is attributable to the efforts of Hume, who did much to promote his friend's work despite some differences of opinion with certain points of Smith's argument. Early reviews included a 1759 piece by British political thinker Edmund Burke and an influential, complimentary, anonymous review in the *Critical Review,* also published in 1759 and most likely written by Hume. John Home, Hume's cousin, also celebrated the publication of *The Theory of Moral Sentiments* in London. However, not all critical reaction to Smith's work was positive. Some conservative critics, such as Gilbert Elliot, were concerned about Smith's skeptical position regarding the role of natural religion in the formation of morality in relation to the shifting standards of society.

Smith revised *The Theory of Moral Sentiments* several times over his lifetime and ultimately produced six editions of the work, including a second edition in 1761 that addressed some of Hume's privately expressed concerns. With his intellectual future secured, Smith could focus on the composition of *The Wealth of Nations,* which—with the rise of the political economy in the Victorian Age—would eventually overshadow *The Theory of Moral Sentiments* and Smith's reputation as a moral philosopher. Taken together, the two works would give rise to the academically infamous "Adam Smith Problem," which concerned the seemingly fundamental contradiction between the emphasis on sympathy in *The Theory of Moral Sentiments* and that of self-interest in *The Wealth of Nations*. Academic debate over this issue has continued into the twenty-first century, with some scholars arguing that the resolution lies in recognizing that sympathy and self-interest are not mutually exclusive pursuits.

Recent scholarship has focused on exploring the full range of Smith's intellectual scope, beyond the study of political economy for which he is best known in the modern era. Study of *The Theory of Moral Sentiments* has been crucial to this exploration, and the work has enjoyed a resurgence of critical attention as an example of early modern moral philosophy. James Buchan argues in his 2006 book *The Authentic Adam Smith: His Life and Ideas* that in *The Theory of Moral Sentiments*, "[s]ociety itself appears in entirely modern guise as a sort of immense network of stimulation and reaction that need neither direction from above or maintenance from below." Also of note is Smith's description of society as a mirror for one's own self-conception, an important concept in postmodern identity studies.

BIBLIOGRAPHY

Sources

Broadie, Alexander. "Sympathy and the Impartial Spectator." *The Cambridge Companion to Adam Smith.* Ed. Knud Haakonssen. Cambridge: Cambridge UP, 2006. Print.

Buchan, James. *The Authentic Adam Smith: His Life and Ideas.* New York: Norton, 2006. Print.

Haakonssen, Knud. Introduction. *The Cambridge Companion to Adam Smith.* Ed. Knud Haakonssen. Cambridge: Cambridge UP, 2006. Print.

Lindgren, J. Ralph. *The Social Philosophy of Adam Smith.* The Hague: Nijhoff, 1973. Print.

Phillipson, Nicholas. *Adam Smith: An Enlightened Life.* New Haven: Yale UP, 2010. Print.

Ross, Ian Simpson. *The Life of Adam Smith.* Oxford: Clarendon, 1995. Print.

Further Reading

Jenkins, Arthur Hugh. *Adam Smith Today: An Inquiry into the Nature and Causes of the Wealth of Nations: Simplified, Shortened and Modernized.* Port Washington: Kennikat, 1948. Print.

Keppler, Jan Horst. *Adam Smith and the Economy of the Passions.* New York: Routledge, 2010. Print.

Lux, Kenneth. *Adam Smith's Mistake: How a Moral Philosopher Invented Economics and Ended Morality.* Boston: Shambhala, 1990. Print.

Shapiro, Michael J. *Reading "Adam Smith": Desire, History and Value, Modern Political Thought.* Vol. 4. Newbury Park: Sage, 1993. Print.

Smith, Adam. *The Theory of Moral Sentiments.* New York: Cosmo Classics, 2007. Print.

West, E.G. *Adam Smith.* New Rochelle: Arlington, 1969. Print.

Craig Barnes

Profile portrait of Adam Smith, whose *Theory of Moral Sentiments* attempts to explain the nature and motives of human morality. © BETTMANN/CORBIS

TRACT 90

John Henry Newman

OVERVIEW

Tract 90, the common name of a pamphlet titled *Remarks on Certain Passages in the Thirty-Nine Articles* written by John Henry Newman and published in 1841, attempts to prove that the Thirty-Nine Articles, the tenets of Anglicanism, are not in opposition to Roman Catholicism. It also aims to establish the Anglican religion as a branch of Roman Catholicism and thus a direct descendant of "true Christianity." *Tract 90* is the last of ninety pamphlets, or tracts, published in a series called Tracts for the Times. The pamphlets, written by different members of the Oxford movement, reached a broad audience, in part, because of their inexpensive price. The leaders of the Oxford movement hoped to convince England to return to a more traditional church, both in its rituals and ceremonies and in its role as the highest moral authority, superseding the power of the government.

When *Tract 90* was published in 1841, it was greeted with an immediate outcry by readers who saw it as justifying the practice of Roman Catholicism, a religion viewed with deep distrust by the British at the time. Newman retired from an active role in the Anglican ministry that year and converted to Roman Catholicism four years later. His conversion almost destroyed the Oxford movement. However, the movement had far-reaching religious effects, including the incorporation of more ritual and ceremony into the services of Anglican and Episcopal churches. The Oxford movement's emphasis on tradition and roots also had a far-ranging artistic effect: the Pre-Raphaelite Brotherhood, which included writers such as Dante Gabriel Rossetti and painters such as William Holman Hunt and John Everett Millais, was deeply influenced by the Oxford movement's emphasis on tradition and symbolism. In turn, the Pre-Raphaelite Brotherhood inspired many later art movements.

HISTORICAL AND LITERARY CONTEXT

The roots of the concerns that Newman addresses in *Tract 90* rested in the church's decreasing power in everyday life. Members of the Oxford movement viewed the increasing religious fragmentation of Victorian England, with radical evangelists on one side and atheists and agnostics on the other, as morally problematic. Tracing Anglicanism back to the earliest forms of Christianity, Oxford movement practitioners believed, would reaffirm its moral and political primacy.

In 1833 Parliament proposed that Ireland, a predominantly Roman Catholic country, should not have to support Anglicanism through taxation. In a sermon titled "National Apostasy," Rev. John Keble argues against this Erastianism, or the subordination of the power of the church to that of the state. This sermon sparked the Oxford movement, also known as the Tractarian movement, because Newman, as well as other members, such as Keble and Edward Pusey, published multiple pamphlets to argue for the Anglicanism's greater power. *Tract 90* is Newman's own attempt to work through an issue that was a mainstay of the Oxford movement—the concept, known as "via media," that Anglicanism served as middle way between Roman Catholicism and Protestantism. In *Tract 90* Newman goes a step further by suggesting that the Thirty-Nine Articles, which define the doctrine of Anglicanism in 1563, were not anti-Catholic but a means of correcting misunderstandings about the Roman Catholic Church.

Tract 90 follows a long tradition of religious writing by including excerpts from earlier theologians. Newman relies heavily on writings about the Thirty-Nine Articles, including those by the sixteenth-century Father Francis of Saint Clare and, perhaps that of his contemporary, William Palmer, although Newman denied having read his work.

Tract 90's primary influence was the social furor that it raised. However, the Tractarian movement, which widely distributed scholarly arguments about religious practices, can be seen as the inspiration for later organizations, such as the Jehovah's Witnesses, that operate by distributing religious pamphlets. Earlier in the century, the Oxford movement's success with tracts inspired foreign missionaries to produce reams of such pamphlets, and as a result this style of writing was the primary introduction to English literary output for many readers in countries around the world.

THEMES AND STYLE

Tract 90 focuses on proving that the Thirty-Nine Articles should not be seen as a break with the Catholic Church, but rather as a way of correcting errors and exaggerations into which it had fallen. In essence,

Newman presents arguments to show that the writers of the articles do not intend to leave behind the Catholic Church but rather to return to a truer Christianity. While the framers of the articles write against the Catholicism of the time, Newman writes in *Tract 90* that "it is a duty which we owe both to the Catholic Church and to our own, to take our reformed confessions in the most Catholic sense they will admit; we have no duties toward their framers." In short, he argues that Anglicanism's loyalty must be toward true Catholicism rather than the misinterpretations of either Roman Catholics or the founders of Anglicanism.

Newman presents his arguments for Anglicanism's lineage in a highly rational manner, which gives them persuasive force. He emphasizes the logical sense of his points, as in this excerpt from the introduction: "Here then we have to inquire, first, what is meant by Holy Scripture; next, what is meant by the Church; and then, what their respective offices are in teaching revealed truth, and how these are adjusted with one another in their actual exercise." Newman also employs concession, presenting his arguments in an accessible manner that does not seem overly dogmatic. Rather than vehemently insisting on his points, he admits that "no one can deny" that "there are real difficulties to a Catholic Christian in the Ecclesiastical position of our Church at this day," but adds that "the statements of the Articles are not in the number" of these difficulties.

Newman and others in the Oxford movement believed in "personal holiness," an ideal that requires modesty in expression, and this is reflected in the measured tone of *Tract 90*. Newman explicitly argues personal holiness in the text, pointing out that "religious changes, to be beneficial, should be the act of the whole body; they are worth little if they are the mere act of a majority. No good can come of any change which is not heartfelt, a development of feelings springing up freely and calmly within the bosom of the whole body itself." To foster this free, calm change, Newman stays away from rhetorical flourishes and showy language, and his sentences are often complex and indirect. For example, he writes,

> But these remarks are beyond our present scope, which is merely to show that, while our Prayer Book is acknowledged on all hands to be of Catholic origin, our articles also, the offspring of an uncatholic age, are, through GOD'S good providence, to say the least, not uncatholic, and may be subscribed by those who aim at being catholic in heart and doctrine.

CRITICAL DISCUSSION

The publication of *Tract 90* was met primarily with fear and suspicion, because it seemed to justify Roman Catholicism. Frederick Beasley, in *An*

NEWMAN AND EDUCATION

While John Henry Newman was an effective Anglican chaplain, who worked to support the rights of Catholic students at Oxford University (although politics prevented him from establishing a Catholic chaplaincy), his greatest link with education is his book, *Discourses on the Scope and Nature of University Education,* a collection of his lectures that was first published in 1852. In it he outlines the ideals of a liberal arts education in terms still used by many educators in the twenty-first century. He argues, "The purpose of higher education is neither to make men good, nor to make men employable, although it tends to make them both. Rather, its main purpose is to produce a habit of mind, which is free, equitable, moderate, calm, and wise." Universities, he states, must view knowledge as an end in and of itself, encourage interdisciplinary interaction, and foster active learning. Further, Newman argues that a university education creates ethical people (or, in Newman's formulation, "gentlemen," because university students were still exclusively male at the time), since the "clear-headedness" encouraged by a liberal arts education means that a college graduate is "too clear-headed to be unjust."

Pope Benedict XVI conducting the beatification mass for the nineteenth-century Anglican convert John Henry Newman in 2010; behind the Pope is Newman's image.
AP PHOTO/MATT DUNHAM

Examination of No. 90 of The Tracts for the Times (1842), attacks the "popish complexion and tendencies" of the Oxford movement's tracts and "the

Tractists," who he sees as involved "in an attempt stealthily and insidiously to vitiate the pure system of our faith with heretical doctrines, and defile our sanctuary with foul superstitions." In *Apologia Pro Vita Sua* (*A Defense of One's Life*), which was published in 1864, Newman writes, "I saw indeed clearly that my place in the Movement was lost; public confidence was at an end; my occupation was gone … I was denounced as a traitor who had laid his train and was detected in the very act of firing it against the time-honoured Establishment."

Newman's persuasiveness in *Tract 90* created a schism in English religious life. Over time, however, the view of Newman and *Tract 90* gradually grew closer to that given in church histories, with Catholics viewing Newman as one of the most important figures in modern Catholicism and contemporary Anglicans pointing to the ways in which Newman's writings allowed Anglicanism to understand itself as a direct descendant of the Roman Catholic Church. Critics remain split as to the ingenuousness of Newman's argument. Newman himself converted to Roman Catholicism after writing *Tract* 90, and in the 1860s Charles Kingsley, a prominent Anglican churchman, accused Newman of already having converted by the time he wrote the work. Walter E. Houghton, a Victorian scholar, tackled the same question in his 1945 book, *The Art of Newman's Apologia,* and others insist that *Tract 90* chronicles a genuine evolution in Newman's thoughts. In 2010 the Catholic Church clearly communicated its position by beatifying Newman.

For many years, Newman's work was primarily studied by ecclesiastical writers rather than literary critics. In the twentieth century, literary scholars saw *Tract 90* as an interesting window into several larger Victorian cultural philosophical quandaries. Gauri Viswanathan, author of *Outside the Fold: Conversion, Modernity, and Belief* (1998), argues that Newman's conversion can be read as a complex form of dissent; understanding it this way, she says, links Newman's conversion to those of colonized subjects around the world. Other critics point to Newman's dense writing style and emphasis on debate as indicative of his radical doubts about language's ability to shape belief, a concern echoed by many Victorian philosophers.

BIBLIOGRAPHY

Sources

Beasley, Frederick. *An Examination of No. 90 of the Tracts for the Times. Project Canterbury.* 1842. Web. 24 Aug. 2012.

Houghton, Walter E. *The Art of Newman's Apologia.* New Haven: Yale UP, 1945. Print.

Newman, John Henry. *Apologia Pro Vita Sua. Newman Reader.* National Institute for Newman Studies. 1864. Web. 28 Aug. 2012.

Newman, John Henry. *Discourses on the Scope and Nature of University Education: Addressed to the Catholics of Dublin.* Dublin: Duffy, 1852. Print.

Newman, John Henry, and William G. Ward. *A Collection of Tracts Regarding Tract No. 90 of Newman's Tracts for the Times: Including the Text of Tract 90.* Oxford: Parker, 1841. Print.

Viswanathan, Gauri. *Outside the Fold: Conversion, Modernity, and Belief.* Princeton: Princeton UP, 1998. Print.

Further Reading

Gates, Lewis E. *Three Studies in Literature.* New York: Macmillan, 1899. 75-82. Print.

Hammond, David. "The Interplay of Hermeneutics and Heresy in the Process of Newman's Conversion from 1830-1845." *Authority, Dogma, and History: The Role of the Oxford Movement Converts in the Papal Infallibility Debates.* Eds. Kenneth L. Parker and Michael J. G. Pahls. Palo Alto: Academica, 2009. 45-76. Print.

Newman, John Henry. "A Letter Addressed to the Rev. R. W. Jelf, DD., Canon of Christ Church, in Explanation of the Ninetieth Tract in the Series Called the Tracts for the Times." *Newman Reader.* National Institute for Newman Studies. 1841. Web. 14 Sept. 2012.

Pattison, Robert. *The Great Dissent: John Henry Newman and the Liberal Heresy.* New York: Oxford UP, 1991. Print.

Poston, Lawrence. "Newman's Tractarian Homiletics." *Anglican Theological Review* 87 (2005): 399-421. Print.

Tillotson, Geoffrey. Introduction. *Newman: Selected Prose and Poetry.* Cambridge: Harvard UP, 1970. 7-26. Print.

Turner, Frank. *John Henry Newman: The Challenge to Evangelical Religion.* New Haven: Yale UP, 2002. Print.

Abigail Mann

WADE-DAVIS MANIFESTO

Benjamin Wade, Henry Winter Davis

OVERVIEW

The "Wade-Davis Manifesto," composed by the Radical Republicans Senator Benjamin Wade of Ohio and Representative Henry Winter Davis of Maryland, first appeared on August 4, 1864, only months prior to the 1864 U.S. presidential election. The manifesto charged President Abraham Lincoln with adhering to a lenient Reconstruction policy and not signing the Wade-Davis Bill into law for political reasons. They claimed that "the President, by preventing this bill from becoming law, holds the electoral votes of the Rebel States at the dictation of his personal ambition." As with the Wade-Davis Bill that had preceded it, the manifesto had the support of a majority of the congressional Radical Republicans, who tended to be less willing to compromise on issues such as abolition and other domestic policies. Conservative or moderate Republicans such as Lincoln held to the Whig Party view that Southern states could not legally leave the Union and that the process to restore the states should therefore be simple and straightforward. Republicans controlled both the legislative and executive branches of the federal government, and they were beginning to establish a course of action, generally called Reconstruction, that would be followed for Southern states to be readmitted to the Union.

The "Wade-Davis Manifesto" had wide-ranging support in the U.S. Congress, and it initially stirred debate on Reconstruction. Ultimately, a majority of Republicans believed it went too far, and they refused to embrace the manifesto or the third-party challenge associated with it, choosing instead to side with President Lincoln. As abolitionist Gerrit Smith, a former congressman from New York, wrote in a letter to an editor of the *New York Times,* "I have read your protest. It is a strongly reasoned and instructive paper. Nevertheless I regret its appearance." In the end, the manifesto failed to unseat the incumbent president. The manifesto did influence, however, the future direction of congressional Reconstruction, providing a basis upon which congressional Republicans would later build during the administration of President Andrew Johnson.

HISTORICAL AND LITERARY CONTEXT

The "Wade-Davis Manifesto" was a response to the pocket veto by President Lincoln of the Wade-Davis Bill, which Congress had passed on July 2, 1864, in an attempt to reassert its authority over Reconstruction. The basic issue was that Radical Republicans such as Wade and Davis and moderate Republicans such as Lincoln held different views about how to reconcile the South into the Union after the war. Although President Lincoln had instituted the "Ten Percent Plan," which allowed states to apply to rejoin the Union once ten percent of its eligible voters, based on the 1860 census, took an oath of allegiance, the Wade-Davis Bill called for fifty percent of the voters to take an "ironclad" oath swearing that they had never taken up arms against the Union and had never supported the Confederacy. The bill exposed a schism between conservative and moderate Republicans on one hand and Radical Republicans on the other. Radical Republicans argued that the states in the Confederacy had in fact left the Union. Furthermore, they contended that once those states were conquered militarily, Congress had the authority to determine which restrictions and requirements must be met for readmission.

The manifesto appeared during the Civil War at a time of heightened opposition to the Lincoln administration both from within the Republican Party and from the Democratic Party. Although the Wade-Davis Bill had garnered votes from a majority of Congress, the ensuing manifesto lost support quickly. Victories on the battlefield and fear of a Democratic victory assisted Lincoln in maintaining wide Republican support. In the end, Davis (who had become an outspoken critic of Lincoln) was not reelected to Congress. However, the "Wade-Davis Manifesto" helped articulate the congressional position on Reconstruction. Ultimately, the Republican Party united behind Lincoln, but it did not develop a unified position on Reconstruction, and Radicals continued to block the readmission of Louisiana and Arkansas under the president's plan. This congressional Republican position would become dominant following the assassination of President Lincoln.

The "Wade-Davis Manifesto" drew on a history of opposition and political disagreement over the powers of the federal government. The manifesto raised a question over the approach that the federal government would take with rebel states. Radicals believed that the Confederate states had in fact left the Union, while moderates held the view that a state could not leave the Union.

❖ *Key Facts*

Time Period:
Mid-19th Century

Movement/Issue:
Reconstruction; Post-Civil War reform

Place of Publication:
United States

Language of Publication:
English

BENJAMIN WADE

Benjamin Wade, a native of Massachusetts, represented Ohio in the U.S. Senate from March 15, 1851, until March 4, 1869. Early in his career as a lawyer, Wade formed a law partnership with Joshua Giddings, a noteworthy antislavery figure. Wade, a Whig, was elected to the U.S. Senate in 1851. He joined the Republican Party after the Whig party fell apart. He was a close associate of northern Radical Republicans Thaddeus Stevens and Charles Sumner. He was an outspoken critic of the Kansas-Nebraska Act, because it allowed slavery to expand into new territories based on a popular majority vote. He supported women's suffrage, trade unions, and equality for African Americans.

During the Civil War, Wade harshly criticized President Lincoln, even referring to him as "white trash" for what he considered to be the slow pace at which Lincoln embraced the concepts of racial equality and permitting African American soldiers in the army. He also sharply criticized Lincoln's Reconstruction plan. Together with Henry Winter Davis of Maryland, Wade sponsored a bill that would have set a stricter Reconstruction policy. Following Lincoln's pocket veto of the Wade-Davis bill, the two issued the "Wade-Davis Manifesto." Wade became a leading Radical Republican and was instrumental in the implementation of congressional Reconstruction, the incorporation of the first black troops into the regular army, and the impeachment of President Andrew Johnson.

The "Wade-Davis Manifesto" assisted in shaping future debates concerning Reconstruction and the eventual supremacy of Congress when it came to the question of readmitting former Confederate states to the Union. Eventually, following the death of Lincoln, Congress and not the president would control the direction of Reconstruction and, as such, the future of Southern states. The manifesto presented a case for a strong legislative branch—"that the authority of Congress is paramount and must be respected." This influence was seen in the impeachment trial of President Johnson in 1868 following his violation of the Tenure in Office Act and his introduction of even weaker Reconstruction measures.

THEMES AND STYLE

The main theme of the "Wade-Davis Manifesto" is the Radical Republicans' argument that the legislative branch held the authority to devise a plan for the readmission of Southern states. Congressional Republicans feared the lax policies of presidential Reconstruction. "Seriously impressed with these dangers, Congress, the proper constitutional authority, formally declared that there are no State Governments in the Rebel States, and provided for their erection at a proper time; both the Senate and the House of Representatives rejected the Senators and Representatives chosen under the authority of what the President calls the Free Constitution

and Government of Arkansas." Toward this end, the manifesto outlines areas in which it claims the president was acting outside his constitutional authority. For example, the manifesto asserts that the president's Ten Percent Plan ignores the U.S. Supreme Court and that only Congress has the constitutional authority to determine what constitutes a state government. In addition, the manifesto states that President Lincoln had appointed, with no authority, military governors of the Southern states. The manifesto called on the supporters of the Republican Party to insist that these "usurpations" end.

The manifesto achieved its rhetorical goal through appeals against tyranny and assertions of unconstitutional presidential acts. First, Wade and Davis laid the groundwork for reclaiming power from the executive branch. They asserted that Lincoln was rushing to readmit Southern states to shore up his electoral prospects in the coming election. Next, they appealed to the voters of the North who had stood by their government during the Civil War to stand firm and vote against Lincoln if necessary. They questioned what the war was fought for if Southern states could simply send unrepentant Southerners to Congress and resume their place in the Union. Lastly, Wade and Davis asserted their belief that President Lincoln was claiming powers that belonged to the legislative branch.

Stylistically, the "Wade-Davis Manifesto" is distinguished by its forcefulness; it reads as a call to action. Written as an appeal to voters and Republican Party elites, it served as a list of grievances against the administration, and served as a rallying petition for party members. The manifesto was not an official bill or document. Rather, it appeared in the *New York Tribune*. The manifesto, while it did not lead to the defeat of Lincoln, did rally Republicans to the idea of legislative supremacy on the question of Reconstruction following the assassination of Lincoln, and this view prevailed in part because of the leadership of Andrew Johnson, Lincoln's successor to the presidency.

CRITICAL DISCUSSION

The Wade-Davis Bill enjoyed wide Republican support, but the manifesto, which appeared later, did not enjoy as broad support, even though it expressed the fears and beliefs of many Republicans. Letters such as the one from Gerrit Smith demonstrate that individual Republicans did not always agree with Lincoln or support his decisions but were unwilling to chance the loss of the Republican Party's control of the government or make a governmental change during the continuing military conflict. In many ways the "Wade-Davis Manifesto" backfired. Davis was defeated for reelection in the 1864 election and Lincoln was victorious. In other ways the manifesto foreshadowed policies that would become part of Reconstruction policy following the war. Congress became the dominant force in Reconstruction policy following the death of Lincoln.

Following the 1864 election, Congress continued in its refusal to seat the congressional delegations from Louisiana, Arkansas, and Tennessee. Further, Congress began to assert itself in Reconstruction more forcefully. Following the assassination of President Lincoln and the assumption of office by Johnson in 1865, the battle between the legislative and executive branches of government reached new heights. This and other issues helped lead to the passage of the Reconstruction Acts and the Tenure in Office Act, both in 1867, as well as to the impeachment of President Johnson in 1868. Following these actions Congress became the dominant force in Reconstruction politics.

Scholarship has focused on the battle between the legislative and executive branches regarding Reconstruction. Historian Eric Foner noted in *Reconstruction: America's Unfinished Revolution, 1863-1877* that the Wade-Davis Bill was "not the work of a narrow faction," but rather it was supported by a majority in Congress. Foner went on to assert that this battle was fought over constitutional authority. James M. McPherson offered a somewhat different analysis. While agreeing with Foner about the battle over constitutional authority and supremacy, he argued in *Ordeal by Fire: The Civil War and Reconstruction* that "the Wade-Davis Manifesto formed part of an ill-coordinated scheme for a new convention to nominate General Benjamin Butler for president." W.R. Brock provided yet another perspective in *An American Crisis: Congress and Reconstruction, 1865-1867.* Brock argued that the Wade-Davis Bill and ultimately the manifesto sought to do three things: first, to require an ironclad oath from Southerners; second, to force each Southern state to hold a convention of loyal white males who could take the ironclad oath; and third, the eventual readmission of the states to the Union. According to Brock, this was all part of a strategy to strengthen the powers of Congress.

BIBLIOGRAPHY

Sources

Brock, W.R. *An American Crisis: Congress and Reconstruction, 1865-1867.* New York: Harper Torchbooks, 1963. Print.

Foner, Eric. *Reconstruction: America's Unfinished Revolution, 1863-1877.* New York: Harper, 1988. Print.

McPherson, James M. *Ordeal by Fire: The Civil War and Reconstruction.* Boston: McGraw, 2001. Print.

Smith, Gerrit. *New York Times,* 16 Aug. 1864. Web. 31 Aug. 2012.

Wade, Benjamin, and Henry Winter Davis. "1864 The Wade-Davis Manifesto." *cclc.org.* Connecticut Consortium for Law & Citizenship Education. Web. 31 Aug. 2012.

Further Reading

Bogue, Allan G. "Historians and Radical Republicans: A Meaning for Today." *The Journal of American History* 70:1 (1983): 7-34. Print.

Currie, David P. "The Civil War Congress." *The University of Chicago Law Review* 73:4 (2006): 1131-26. Print.

George, Joseph, Jr. "A Long-Neglected Lincoln Speech: An 1864 Preliminary." *Journal of the Abraham Lincoln Association* 16:2 (1995): 23-28. Print.

Guelzo, Allen C. *Fateful Lightning: A New History of the Civil War and Reconstruction.* Oxford: Oxford UP, 2012. Print.

Robinson, Armstead L. "The Politics of Reconstruction." *The Wilson Quarterly* 2:2 (1978): 106-23. Print.

Rodney Harris

A Currier and Ives print of a Union soldier returning home at the end of the American Civil War. The "Wade-Davis Manifesto" set forth harsh repercussions for Southern states at the war's end. © HERITAGE IMAGES/ CORBIS

CITIZENS AND
REVOLUTIONARIES

ANARCHIST MANIFESTO

Anselme Bellegarrigue

OVERVIEW

One of the earliest explicitly anarchist manifestos, Anselme Bellegarrigue's 1850 *Anarchist Manifesto,* which the author self-published in his journal *l'Anarchie: Journal de l'Ordre* (Anarchy: A Journal of Order), states that authority is the source of all social disorder; therefore the absence of central authority promotes social harmony. Written during a period of intense political upheaval in France, the manifesto was published in Paris after the establishment of the Second Republic in 1848 but before the 1851 coup that ushered in the Second Empire. Chiefly an attack on all forms of government, the manifesto takes a staunchly individualist stance against socialism. As such, it most explicitly addresses "socialist and moderate" readers, whom Bellegarrigue calls "deluded bourgeois, ruined gentlemen and sacrificed proletarians." The manifesto is characterized by an intense skepticism of revolution and reform, and it calls on readers to abstain from participation in government, especially voting in elections.

Although Bellegarrigue's manifesto was not widely discussed or circulated (*l'Anarchie* went bankrupt after the second issue), it is remembered as an important contribution to the diversity of early anarchist voices. The treatise synthesizes ideas present in the works of anarchists such as Pierre-Joseph Proudhon and Max Stirner, and it provides an individualist counterpoint, if not a response, to *The Communist Manifesto* by Karl Marx, which was published just two years earlier. Bellegarrigue's work outlines the ideological differences between individualist and socialist anarchism, both of which gained a significant following during the late-nineteenth and early-twentieth centuries. Today, Bellegarrigue's *Anarchist Manifesto* is recognized as an important addition to the spectrum of French radical political thought.

HISTORICAL AND LITERARY CONTEXT

Bellegarrigue's manifesto might be read as a response to the frequent regime changes in France following the 1789 Revolution. Between 1789 and 1850 the French government was reinvented as many as nine times, with varying degrees of success. The short-lived Second Republic, which grew out of the 1848 Revolution, began with great optimism but quickly ended in disillusionment. Although the government set up public works projects, called national workshops, to employ more than one hundred thousand workers, it closed the workshops after only a few months. The action, popularly perceived as a betrayal, led to the June Days Uprising, which left more than one thousand dead and more than ten thousand imprisoned. It did not seem that the republic—or the monarchy it replaced—could solve the economic crisis that descended on France in the 1840s.

By the time *l'Anarchie* was published in 1850, popular disillusionment with the French government had intensified. Class divisions, especially between the working classes and the republican petit bourgeoisie, had become more pronounced (which Marx describes at length in his monograph *The Eighteenth Brumaire of Louis Bonaparte* [1852]). Although Bellegarrigue wrote his manifesto at the nadir of confidence in the republic, shortly after its publication Louis-Napoléon Bonaparte, nephew of former emperor Napoléon

❖ *Key Facts*

Time Period:
Mid-19th Century

Movement/Issue:
Anarchism

Place of Publication:
France

Language of Publication:
French

ANSELME BELLEGARRIGUE: EARLY ANARCHIST

History preserves very little biographical information about Anselme Bellegarrigue. The French political writer was born in Montfort, near Toulouse, on March 23, 1813, to John Joseph, a merchant, and Therèze Goulard. Prior to 1848 he traveled to the Caribbean and the United States, where he met President James K. Polk on a Mississippi steamboat. He would later write a book of essays about his experiences on the North American continent, *Les Femmes d'Amérique* (The Women of America) (1853).

Upon his return to France, Bellegarrigue participated in the 1848 Revolution and moved to Toulouse, where he edited the influential and widely circulated social democratic newspaper *La Civilisation*. In addition to his short-lived journal *l'Anarchie: Journal de l'Ordre* (Anarchy: A Journal of Order), he published *Au Fait! Au Fait! Interprétation de l'Idée Démocratique* (To the Point! To the Point! Interpretation of the Democratic Idea) in 1849 and *l'Almanach de la Vile Multitude* (Almanac of the Vile Multitude) in 1850. After the rise of the Second Empire under Louis-Napoléon Bonaparte, he emigrated to Honduras and later to El Salvador, where he reportedly lived the rest of his life as a government official.

PRIMARY SOURCE

ANARCHIST MANIFESTO

If I were to heed the meaning vulgarly attributed to certain words then, since vulgar error has taken "anarchy" to be synonymous with "civil war", I should be horrified by the title with which I have headed this publication, in that I have a horror of civil strife.

At the same time I account it a pleasure and an honour that I have never been party to a band of conspirators nor any revolutionary battalion; a pleasure and an honour because it furnishes the basis upon which I can establish, for one thing, that I have been enough of an honest man not to pull the wool over the people's eyes, and, for another, that I have been astute enough not to let the wool be pulled over my own eyes by the ambitious. I have watched—I cannot claim unmoved but at any rate with the utmost serenity—the passage of fanatics and charlatans, moved to pity for some and to utter contempt for the rest. And when, in the wake of these bloody struggles—having forced my enthusiasm not to overstep the narrow confines of syllogism—I have sought to draw up a balance-sheet of the benefits that each corpse has bought, the sum has added up to zero, and zero means nothing.

That nothing horrifies me; civil war horrifies me also.

Consequently, if I have inscribed ANARCHY on the mast-head of this newspaper, it cannot have been because I take that word in the sense attributed to it—much mistakenly, as I shall be explaining anon—by the governmentalist factions, but rather to ensure that it receives the etymological rights it deserves in a democracy.

Anarchy is the negation of governments. Governments, whose pupils we are, have naturally found nothing better to devise than to school us in fear and horror of their destruction. But as governments in turn are the negations of individuals or of the people, it is reasonable that the latter, waking up to essential truths, should gradually come to feel a greater horror at its own annihilation than that of its masters.

Anarchy is an ancient word, but, for us that word articulates a modem notion, or rather, a modern interest, the idea being daughter to the interest. History has described as "anarchic" the condition of a people wherein there are several governments in contention one with another, but the condition of a people desirous of being governed but bereft of government precisely because it has too many is

France experienced yet another regime change when the Second Republic took power following the 1848 Revolution. © EVERETT COLLECTION INC/ALAMY

one thing and the condition of a people desirous of governing itself and bereft of government precisely because it wishes none quite another. In ancient times, indeed, anarchy was civil war, not because it meant absence of governments but, rather, because it meant a multiplicity of them and competition and strife among the governing classes. The modern notion of absolute social truth or pure democracy has ushered in an entire series of discoveries or interests which have turned the terms of the traditional equation upside down. Thus anarchy, which, when contrasted with the term monarchy, means civil war, is, from the vantage point of absolute or democratic truth, nothing less than the true expression of social order.

Indeed:

- Who says anarchy, says negation of government;
- Who says negation of government says affirmation of the people;
- Who says affirmation of the people, says individual liberty;
- Who says individual liberty, says sovereignty of each;

- 'Who says sovereignty of each, says equality;
- Who says equality, says solidarity or fraternity;
- Who says fraternity, says social order;

By contrast:

- Who says government, says negation of the people;
- Who says negation of the people, says affirmation of political authority;
- Who says affirmation of political authority, says individual dependency;
- Who says individual dependency, says class supremacy;
- Who says class supremacy, says inequality;
- Who says inequality, says antagonism;
- Who says antagonism, says civil war,
- From which it follows that who says government, says civil war.

SOURCE: *l'Anarchie: Journal de l'Ordre,* 1850. Translated by Kate Sharpley.

Bonaparte, seized power in the coup d'état of December 1851 and dissolved the National Assembly, later declaring himself Emperor Napoleon III of the Second French Empire.

Bellegarrigue, unlike other French critics of the period, worked in relative isolation, self-publishing his journal to promote his brand of individualist anarchism. However, his journal owes much to the political journalism of its day. Leftist newspapers were highly influential in many of the social transformations of the mid-nineteenth century. The journal *La Reforme,* for instance, was an important forum for revolutionaries and was essential to the 1848 Revolution. Bellegarrigue's *l'Anarchie* was one of many radical newspapers—including those run by the anarchist Pierre-Joseph Proudhon, such as *La Voix du Peuple* (The Voice of the People)—to begin publishing during the Second Republic. In his manifesto Bellegarrigue is highly critical of these publications, even those published by fellow anarchists: "there is not one French newspaper that I can read without being moved either to great pity or profound contempt for the writer." He also argues that the partisan nature of French journalism makes it a disservice to the people it purports to serve.

In the decades following the collapse of the Second Republic, anarchist writings, including Bellegarrigue's manifesto, provided the central philosophies of anarchist-led political movements. Anarchist thought was especially influential in workers movements, particularly in the Paris Commune of 1871. However, rifts between anarchists and Marxists caused the dissolution of the united International Workingmen's Association (also known as the First International) in the 1870s. More recently, student revolts in Paris in May 1968, which exhibited characteristics of the Paris Commune, owed much of their theoretical basis to anarchist thought.

THEMES AND STYLE

The primary theme of Bellegarrigue's manifesto is that authority is the source of social disorder; therefore, anarchy, or lack of central governmental authority, produces social order. Bellegarrigue argues for abstention from cooperation with authority in favor of organic, voluntary social organization. He encapsulates his argument in the assertion that "anarchy is order, whereas government is civil war." The secondary concern of the manifesto is promoting individualism over socialism, part of a continuing debate that began as early as 1834 with the publication of Pierre Leroux's essay "Individualism and Socialism." Bellegarrigue argues that "collective interest" and Rousseau's "social contract" are fictions, and he instead aligns himself with German anarchist Max Stirner, author of *The Ego and Its Own* (1845), claiming that "every man is an egoist; anyone ceasing to be such becomes an object."

Bellegarrigue commences his argument through a chain of equivalences similar to those used by Plato. To explain his paradoxical contention that "anarchy is order," he leads the reader through a series of associations: "Who says anarchy, says negation of government; who says negation of government says affirmation of the people." Conversely, to prove that "who says government says civil war," he provides a sequence that begins, "who says government, says negation of the people," and ends, "who says antagonism, says civil war." Using a similar technique, he declares that individualism is paradoxically "the only fraternal dogma." He reinterprets "collective interest" as an accumulation of individual interests. This synthesis of seemingly contradictory terms culminates in his rhetorical blurring of the author and reader: "I am an anarchist," he claims, though he qualifies the statement by adding, "*I* represents, not so much the author, as the reader and listener: *I* stands for man."

The style of the manifesto is poignant, unwavering, and steeped in the politics of its day. As Sharif Gemie notes in the introduction to the 2002 edition of the manifesto, Bellegarrigue's rhetorical style recalls the language of the "banquet campaign," an 1846 political movement in which speakers at political banquets "used the after-dinner speech as a device to avoid government censorship." At times Bellegarrigue's conviction is compelling; occasionally it is antagonistic, even excessively so. To support his argument that elections are "a fraud and a robbery," for instance, he attacks the individual voter as a "bad citizen." His tone intensifies the immediacy of his claims, making the latter half of his manifesto more of a call to action—or, rather, a call to inaction—than the abstract political treatise in the former half.

CRITICAL DISCUSSION

Very little is known about the initial reaction to the manifesto, perhaps owing to Bellegarrigue's political independence. He ceased publication of the journal after its second issue because of a lack of funds. The coup d'état of 1851 caused him to curtail further publishing projects. As the paper's only writer, editor, and publisher, he was an outlier who, according to George Woodcock in *Anarchism: A History of Libertarian Ideas and Movements* (2004), "dissociated himself from all the political revolutionaries of 1848." As such, few other political writings of the time reference Bellegarrigue or his writings. However, a second French individualist anarchist journal named *l'Anarchie*—perhaps an homage to Bellegarrigue—began in 1905 and ran until 1914.

From the second half of the nineteenth century through the early twentieth century, anarchism as a political philosophy experienced relatively strong growth throughout Europe and the United States. Individualist anarchism expanded, especially in the United States; however socialist forms of the political doctrine proved to be more sustained. Anarcho-syndicalists, who organized and supported labor unions, made up some of the largest factions that fought in the Spanish Civil War. Bellegarrigue's contribution to anarchism, although not directly or obviously influential, might be interpreted as solidifying the competing philosophies of individualist and socialist anarchism.

In recent years historians of radical politics have rediscovered and discussed the *Anarchist Manifesto*. Many have celebrated it as the first anarchist manifesto in recorded history. Woodcock argues that *l'Anarchie* was the "the first periodical … to adopt the anarchist label." He suggests that Bellegarrigue's "refusal to cooperate" exhibits ideological similarity with the philosophy of Thoreau, who is sometimes cited as an individualist anarchist. Indeed, Bellegarrigue had traveled to the United States as a young man and had written extensively and enthusiastically about American democracy. Max Nettlau in *A Short History of Anarchism* (1996) even faults Bellegarrigue for his "exaggerated admiration of American liberties." Laurent Lemire, in a 2011 review of a Québecois edition, *Manifeste de l'anarchisme,* argues for the continuing relevance of Bellegarrigue's work and finds commonality between the 1848 Spring of Nations and the recent Arab Spring uprisings.

BIBLIOGRAPHY

Sources

Bellegarrigue, Alselme. *Anarchist Manifesto.* Berkeley: Kate Sharpley Library, 2002. Print.

Lemire, Laurent. "La Volunté du Peuple." March 2011. Rev. of *Manifeste de l'anarchisme.* Montreal: Lux Éditions, 2011. Web. 29 June 2012.

Nettlau, Max. *A Short History of Anarchism.* London: Freedom Press, 1996. Web. 29 June 2012.

Rapport, Mike. *1848: Year of Revolution.* New York: Basic Books, 2008. Print.

Woodcock, George. *Anarchism: A History of Libertarian Ideas and Movements.* Orchard Park: Broadview, 2004. Print.

Further Reading

Bellegarrigue, Anselme. *Les Femmes d'Amérique.* Paris: Blanchard, Libraire-Éditeur, 1855. Print.

Marx, Karl. *The Eighteenth Brumaire of Louis Bonaparte.* Chicago: Charles H. Kerr & Co., 1913. Web. 29 June 2012.

Maitron, Jean. *Le Mouvement Anarchiste en France.* Paris: François Maspero, 1975. Print.

Pilbeam, Pamela. "Upheaval and Continuity, 1814-1880." *Revolutionary France: 1788-1880.* Ed. Malcolm Crook. Oxford: Oxford UP, 2002. 36-62. Print.

Jonathan Reeve

AN ANSWER TO THE QUESTION

What Is Enlightenment?

Immanuel Kant

OVERVIEW

Immanuel Kant, in response to a December 1783 article by Johann Friedrich Zöllner, wrote "Beantwortung der Frage: Was ist Aufklärung?" ("An Answer to the Question: What Is Enlightenment?"), an essay that seeks to define what it means to be enlightened and also what constitutes a lack of enlightenment. The essay originally appeared in print in a December 1784 edition of the *Berlinische Monatsschrift,* the same publication in which Zöllner's 1783 article had appeared. As a manifesto, Kant's essay articulates enlightenment in relation to politics and religion, while constantly placing importance on reason and freedom as key factors in determining enlightenment. Kant's essay is meant for the general public, but the subject matter is more specifically oriented to governors, clergy, and also scholars. Even more specifically, Kant directs his message to King Frederick II of Prussia, or Frederick the Great, whose name he even equivocates with enlightenment in the essay.

Several leading intellectuals of the time replied to Zöllner's article with their own essays. Among them was Moses Mendelssohn, whose essay Kant acknowledges at the end of "What Is Enlightenment?" by stating that he had not read it. Kant relies on an argument that freedom of thought and expression, rather than knowledge, defines enlightenment, which differentiates his definition of enlightenment from that of many others. As a result, not everyone agreed with Kant's answer to Zöllner. Despite being received with skepticism and disagreement, Kant's essay created the most impact among the responses made to Zöllner's 1783 article, and it has most effectively withstood the test of time.

HISTORICAL AND LITERARY CONTEXT

Written at a time when monarchical governments were being challenged across Europe—as a direct result of the social and political questions raised by the Enlightenment, the very movement Kant seeks to define in his essay—"What Is Enlightenment?" straddles the political spectrum, revealing elements supportive of the Prussian monarch Frederick II as well as liberal elements relating to freedom of thought and expression independent from authority. Zöllner equates defining enlightenment to the task of defining truth, and, by claiming that enlightenment had never been

successfully defined, he seems to present a challenge for someone to do so. In his answer to what enlightenment is, Kant typically focuses on reason—reason that is compatible with an emphasis on governmental and ecclesiastical authority. This approach transcends other responses that mainly focused on the role of knowledge in enlightenment.

The political situation in Prussia played a key role in how Kant defines enlightenment. Kant's definition is a philosophical and theoretical one, but it also displays practical elements in relation to government, church, and the subjects of those political and religious governing bodies. By naming Frederick II in his essay and by including princes, clergymen, scholars, citizens, and military officers as practical examples in his application of enlightenment, Kant presents a definition of enlightenment that goes beyond the role of knowledge and even the role of despotism, relying instead on the role of reason in the public and private senses. These aspects differentiate Kant's definition from that of Mendelssohn.

Kant draws on several earlier philosophers and works in relation to the social and political views he presents. Elements of the idea of the social contract in Thomas Hobbes's *Leviathan* (1651), John Locke's *Second Treatise of Government* (1689), and Jean-Jacques Rousseau's *The Social Contract* (1762) are evident in Kant's presentation of the role of governmental authority. Furthermore, Kant's emphasis on how enlightenment necessitates an emergence from the guardianship of authority is reminiscent of Plato's allegory of the cave from the *Republic.*

Kant's articulation of his conception of human history and the role of government in this essay and in his *Critique of Pure Reason* (1782) influenced the development of German idealism. Kant's "What Is Enlightenment?"—in its philosophical, theoretical, and practical elements—has been consistently cited and quoted as a definitive text regarding the Enlightenment. More recently, the work of Jürgen Habermas has dealt with Kant and the Enlightenment, and Michel Foucault's "Qu'est-ce que les Lumières?" ("What Is Enlightenment?") (1984) deals more directly with Kant's namesake essay. Though it is read less and less as an articulation of the political and social climate of eighteenth-century Prussia, even today Kant's essay is looked to in efforts to conceive

✣ Key Facts

Time Period:
Late 18th Century

Movement/Issue:
Enlightenment; Liberalism

Place of Publication:
Germany

Language of Publication:
German

"WHAT IS ENLIGHTENMENT?"— A RESULT OF EVOLUTION, NOT REVOLUTION

In the years preceding the 1784 publication of Kant's "An Answer to the Question: What Is Enlightenment?" the American Revolutionary War (1775-1783) had been fought by the United States to become an independent country. Some five years later, Parisians stormed the Bastille early in the French Revolution. Despite the threat of revolution against monarchical European states, Kant's essay is carefully inconsistent regarding the role of revolution in the enlightenment of a state's citizens. Kant argues that "a public can achieve enlightenment only slowly. A revolution may well bring about a falling off of personal despotism and of avaricious or tyrannical oppression, but never a true reform in one's way of thinking."

Though Kant admits that tyranny and despotism are detrimental to the social health of a state, it is clear he advocates a state-sanctioned form of enlightenment that falls within the parameters of a monarchical government. For Kant, the responsibility of tolerance falls on the monarch, while the citizens must remain dutiful toward—but also take initiative to reason independently from—their ruler, particularly regarding religious thought. Consistent with scientific naturalism and the advancement of natural science contemporary to the Age of Enlightenment, Kant illustrates a symbiotic relationship between citizen and government, based on reason, tolerance, and duty.

Portrait of German philosopher Immanuel Kant. © THE ART GALLERY COLLECTION/ALAMY

and define the Enlightenment as a philosophical movement.

THEMES AND STYLE

While the attempt to articulate and define enlightenment is naturally at the forefront of the essay's discussion, Kant's differentiation between public and private reason is also a major theme in "What Is Enlightenment?" as well as the relationship between the church and state and the governed. For Kant, enlightenment can only be achieved if the public is able to reason freely and openly, independent from the guidance of authority. With that in mind, Kant also makes it clear that private reason is less effective in achieving enlightenment, as even an enlightened individual is not better than a single figure of authority in relation to the public. The public must be free to emerge from their "self-incurred minority" to use reason "without direction from another." Related to the requirement that the public must emerge from the dictated reason of authority to achieve enlightenment is Kant's stipulation that the state must not force a particular religion or religious point of view upon the public. For Kant, a monarch who does not prescribe a religion or religious way of thinking upon his people "is himself enlightened and deserves to be praised by a grateful world and by posterity."

Kant wrote his essay from Prussia, which was ruled by the monarchical government of Frederick II. Appealing both to Frederick's sense of tolerance but also authority, Kant writes, "Only one ruler in the world says: *Argue* as much as you will and about whatever you will, *but obey*!" Kant also flatters his ruler, remarking in the essay that "this age is the age of enlightenment or the century of Frederick" and that this king is a "shining example" as "no monarch has yet surpassed the one whom we honor." Conversely, Kant is far less flattering in his depiction of yet unenlightened humanity in the opening of his essay, claiming that the "laziness and cowardice" of humankind has prevented enlightenment, even using animalistic and juvenile imagery to describe the human condition in the absence of enlightenment.

The style of Kant's essay is eclectic—initially condescending and insulting but consistently well-reasoned and optimistic on the basis of a belief in the inevitability of humankind's enlightenment. Though brief, its attempt to define the multifaceted concept of enlightenment and provide a tactful discussion of freedom of thought and religion in relation to government is an ambitious, concise exploration of the subject. Even though Kant initially accuses humankind of complacency, he ambitiously argues that the human race cannot be denied enlightenment, saying, "One age cannot bind itself and conspire to put the following one into such a condition that it would be impossible for it to enlarge its cognitions." Essentially, human progress toward enlightenment must not be impeded.

CRITICAL DISCUSSION

Kant's depiction of enlightenment as an ideal state that humanity should strive for and eventually realize differed from that of more practical thinkers—including Karl Leonheld Reinhold and Johann Fichte—who viewed enlightenment as less abstract and only achievable through practical political, religious, social, and moral reforms. John R. Betz, translating Oswald Bayer's 2002 study of Johann Georg Hamann's critique of Kant, writes in 2004 that Hamann complained that Kant "unwittingly employs a metaphor" regarding the dependent-guardian relationship, making the mistake of discussing enlightenment "in aesthetic terms," and that Kant overemphasized the "tiresome" and "self-imposed guardian," since, for Hamann, *true enlightenment consists in a departure of the dependent* from the guardian. Disagreement with Kant's essay has typically been in the form of a philosophical conflict with his articulation and thinking rather than with the essay itself. Its brevity, its position as an answer to Zöllner, and others' practical focus in answering have combined to temper direct criticism of Kant's essay.

Although philosophers and critics such as Hegel, Heidegger, Nietzsche, and Max Weber have often returned to Zöllner's question, Foucault's "What Is Enlightenment?" focuses directly on Kant's essay, arguing that it "marks the discreet entrance into the history of thought of a question that modern philosophy has not been capable of answering, but that it has never managed to get rid of." James Schmidt addressed both Foucault's reading and the enlightenment debate contemporary to Kant in a 1989 article that attempts to look past how the "endless invocation of Kant's definition has dulled our sense of its peculiarity and its novelty." Few philosophical texts seeking to define enlightenment are cited as often as Kant's, which has come to thoroughly symbolize the Enlightenment in its intent and content.

Further scholarly discussion of Kant's "What Is Enlightenment?" has questioned his concepts of public and private reason. As Onora O'Neill remarks in "Vindicating Reason" (1992), "the essay is too vague about the social conditions for fully 'public' reasoning." In "Kant's Politics of Enlightenment" (2003), Ciaran Cronin discusses ambiguities in Kant's text, pointing out his "indecision over whether the failure of individuals to make independent use of their reason is due to lack of courage on their part or whether it is because they have been prevented from doing so by constraining social authorities." Although Cronin and Schmidt explore historical context and the political climate of eighteenth-century Prussia, most critical

approaches are consistent with Antoon Braeckman's claim in a 2008 article that Kant's essay "figures as a model text for the Enlightenment" because it seeks to promote enlightenment as part of the natural order of human development and also enacts the very principles it promotes: self-reflection, self-justification, and a "plea for the emancipation of thinking and the insistence on the importance of thinking *for oneself.*"

BIBLIOGRAPHY

Sources

Bayer, Oswald. *Vernunft ist Sprache: Hamanns Metakritik Kants.* Stuttgart: Frommann-Holzboog Verlag, 2002. Print.

Betz, John R. "Enlightenment Revisited: Hamann as the First and Best Critic of Kant's Philosophy." *Modern Theology* 20.2 (2004): 291-301. Print.

Braeckman, Antoon. "The Moral Inevitability of Enlightenment and the Precariousness of the Moment: Reading Kant's *What Is Enlightenment?*" *The Review of Metaphysics* 62.2 (2008): 285-306. Print.

Cronin, Ciaran. "Kant's Politics of Enlightenment." *Journal of the History of Philosophy* 41.1 (2003): 51-80. Print.

Foucault, Michel. "What Is Enlightenment?" ("Qu'est-ce que les Lumières?"). *The Foucault Reader.* Ed. Paul Rainbow. New York: Pantheon, 1984. 32-50. Print.

Kant, Immanuel. "An Answer to the Question: What Is Enlightenment?" (1784). *Immanuel Kant: Practical Philosophy.* Trans. Mary J. Gregor. New York: Cambridge UP, 1996. 17-22. Print.

O'Neill, Onora. "Vindicating Reason." *The Cambridge Companion to Kant.* Ed. Paul Guyer. New York: Cambridge UP, 1992. 280-308. Print.

Schmidt, James. "The Question of Enlightenment: Kant, Mendelssohn, and the *Mittwochsgesellschaft.*" *Journal of the History of Ideas* 50.2 (1989): 269-91. Print.

Further Reading

Cassirer, Ernst. *Kant's Life and Thought.* Trans. James Haden. New Haven, CT: Yale UP, 1981. Print.

Clarke, Michael. "Kant's Rhetoric of Enlightenment." *Review of Politics* 59.1 (1997): 53-73. Print.

Kuehn, Manfred. *Kant: A Biography.* New York: Cambridge UP, 2001. Print.

Strum, Arthur. "What Enlightenment Is." *New German Critique* 79 (2000): 106-36. Print.

Wood, Allen W. *Kant.* Malden, MA: Blackwell, 2005. Print.

Zöllner, Johann Friedrich. "Etwas von Vorurteilen und Aberglauben." *Berlinische Monatsschrift* 1 (1783): 468-75. Print.

Cameron Dodworth

ANTIRENTERS' DECLARATION OF INDEPENDENCE

Anonymous

✤ *Key Facts*

Time Period:
Mid-19th Century

Movement/Issue:
Land reform;
Anti-feudalism

Place of Publication:
United States

**Language of
Publication:**
English

OVERVIEW

The "Antirenters' Declaration of Independence," issued by the attendees of an Independence Day political rally held at Berne, New York, in 1839, announces the beginning of organized resistance by tenant farmers in upstate New York to a form of feudalism practiced there. For two centuries much of the farmland along the Hudson River had been owned by a few wealthy families who rented land to tenant farmers but denied tenants the right to own the land. The protestors, dubbed Antirenters, rejected the Dutch patroon system of landownership, whereby the landed aristocracy subjugated tenants to a condition of "voluntary slavery." Therefore, the declaration, addressed to landowners, warns that tenants will no longer tolerate an undemocratic system of property rights at odds with American values.

The publication of the declaration inspired many other New York tenant farmers to resist the traditional demands of landlords, which led to the Antirent Wars of the 1840s. During this conflict, many tenants refused to pay rents and sometimes used violent tactics to combat landlords' efforts to remove Antirenters from the land. The protestors even fought guerrilla battles with local sheriffs who were charged with enforcing the landlords' traditional legal rights. The Antirent conflict quickly became one of the most important problems in New York state politics, dividing both of the major political parties of the time. Eventually, the movement helped bring about the end of feudal land ownership in New York when a new state constitution was written in 1846. Today the Antirent declaration is seen as helping to shape ideas of individual property rights emerging in the early American republic and as influencing future decisions about homesteaders' rights as the nation's western frontier was settled.

HISTORICAL AND LITERARY CONTEXT

The "Antirenters Declaration of Independence" challenges property laws dating to the seventeenth century, when present-day upstate New York was ruled by the Dutch. At the time, the colonial administration had granted large tracts of land to individuals who promised to bring settlers to the colony in order to develop an agricultural economy. These grantees, known as patroons, retained ownership of the land even after the British acquired the colony from the Dutch and after the American colonies won independence from the British. Under the terms of the original land grants from the Dutch, the patroons enjoyed many of the same rights as feudal lords in Europe: in addition to having the right to receive rent payments from the tenants who farmed their large estates, the patroons could also demand that the tenants perform unpaid labor and make payment in the form of crops.

Around the time when the declaration was issued, the patroons owned estates that were between 3,000 and 750,000 acres each. One-twelfth of New York's population lived on these lands as tenants. Several factors contributed to the tenants' revolt against the old system. One was the death of prominent landlord Stephen Van Rensselaer III, known as the "Good Patroon" because he allowed his tenants to fall behind on rent payments. After his death, however, his heirs found that he was $400,000 in debt; thus, they tried to force tenants to pay what they owed. In addition, a stock market crash in 1837 left many landlords in financial straits, prompting them to pressure their own tenants for money.

The Antirenters attempted to position their declaration within the tradition of founding U.S. documents, especially the Declaration of Independence, which is invoked by the title of the Antirenters' document and by the date when it was issued. The Antirenters wanted to present their struggle as a new chapter in the struggle for freedom that the Declaration of Independence began. Claiming the symbolic mantle of the revolutionary period is an important part of the Antirenters' efforts to present themselves as a legitimate political movement by responsible citizens rather than as a group of dangerous rebels.

The "Antirenters' Declaration of Independence" launched a struggle that consumed New York for most of the 1840s. The Antirent War dominated the state's newspapers and shaped oral popular culture. Newspaper editors wrote a flurry of opinion pieces for or against the Antirenters, while the Antirenters used ballads as another method of spreading their ideas among the populace, which often lacked formal education and literacy, leaving behind a substantial body of protest songs. As a statement of opposition to the concentration of wealth and power in the hands of the elite, the declaration anticipates later movements that made similar critiques of U.S. society, from the Socialist Party of Eugene V. Debs to Occupy Wall Street.

THEMES AND STYLE

The "Antirenters' Declaration of Independence" rejects the demands made by landholder Stephen Van Rensselaer IV and affirms the values of freedom and equality of the American Revolution. The Antirenters assert that they are "inhabitants of a land of liberty and legitimate heirs of all its rights and privileges guaranteed by its Constitution." They present their position as balanced and fair: they deny "intending to ask anything unreasonable" but are unwilling "to submit to any wrong." By contrast, Van Rensselaer's resistance to negotiating shows that he is a tyrant who requires "unconditional submission to the will of one man, elevated by an aristocratic law." To support their decision to defy Van Rensselaer, the Antirenters state, "Honor, justice, and humanity forbid that we should any longer tamely surrender that freedom which we have most freely inherited from our gallant ancestors." They argue that their natural freedom as men and as Americans trumps Van Rensselaer's customary legal rights as landlord.

Rhetorically, the Antirenters develop their argument by invoking the memory of the American Revolution and by presenting detailed demands for Van Rensselaer to consider. The declaration

THE CALICO INDIAN DISGUISE

During the Antirent Wars in the 1840s, protestors often disguised themselves as Native Americans; men who hid their true identities in this way were known as calico Indians. The Antirenters had a number of reasons for adopting such disguises: the Antirenters had a practical need to conceal their identities since their protest tactics included illegal acts such as vandalizing the tools of farmers who took the side of the landlords and interfering (sometimes with violent force) with evictions of farmers who refused to pay rent.

The calico Indian disguises also served symbolic purposes: the Native American costumes represented a symbolic rejection of the landlords' claims as the original, inalienable owners of the land. Moreover, because the Antirenters were eager to lay claim to the memory of the American Revolution, their calico Indian disguises served as a powerful reminder of similar costumes used by the Sons of Liberty in the original Boston Tea Party. However, the calico Indians' acts were not merely symbolic: many of the disguised Antirenters participated in violent reprisals, such as tarring and feathering sheriffs who attempted to evict tenants.

repeatedly refers to events and people of the revolutionary period, such as the Stamp Act, one of the British acts that enraged the American colonists in

A nineteenth-century woodcut depicting an armed farmer during the American Revolution. The framers of the *Anti-Renters' Declaration of Independence* invoked the American Revolution while discussing the unfairness of land distribution. © NORTH WIND PICTURE ARCHIVES

the 1770s, and Benjamin Franklin's associate Charles Thomson. The Antirenters also attempt to demonstrate their suitability to engage in political debate by stating clear demands for reform, which they express in a technically proficient legal vocabulary. For example, in the second paragraph, they request Van Rensselaer to show a valid title to the land, to abolish the traditional feudal rents of labor services and payments in goods rather than in cash, and to allow tenants the opportunity to purchase the land they live on.

Dispassionate, legalistic language characterizes much of the declaration's style and tone. It begins with the formulaic legal term "Resolved," a rhetorical strategy that assists in the Antirenters' effort to cast themselves as the equals of educated and politically well-connected landlords like Van Rensselaer. However, the authors strike a more emotionally charged tone in their emphasis on the natural freedoms of all people and the honor that compels them to defend their freedom. Thus, the declaration combines legal and emotional arguments to appeal to a sense of patriotism and the Founding Fathers' resistance to similar injustices.

CRITICAL DISCUSSION

Initial reaction to the declaration from Van Rensselaer and other landlords was hostile. They used their powerful position in local politics to intensify pressure on rebellious tenants, sending sheriffs to serve eviction papers to those who refused to pay rents. Tenants, often disguised as Native Americans, fought back against the sheriffs, engaging in often violent reprisals. By 1840 the violence had forced New York governor William Seward (better known as president Abraham Lincoln's secretary of state during the Civil War) to declare martial law in several counties and to dispatch the state militia in order to maintain order. The conflict continued for nearly a decade, as the declaration fueled the protests of other Antirenters. Collectively, the Antirenters insisted that the opportunity to own the land they tilled was their natural right as human beings and their constitutional right as Americans.

As the Antirent War continued into the 1840s, the conflict generated a significant body of oral and print responses from both sides. The Antirenters composed many songs about their struggle, which they sang at Independence Day celebrations, political rallies, and other events. The Antirenters' songs addressed many of the same themes as the declaration. For example, Henry Christman in *Tin Horns and Calico: A Decisive Episode in the Emergence of Democracy* (1945) recalls the ballad "We Will Be Free" (1845), which states, "The time is past, when we'll consent / To pay for land, a yearly rent, / To you, whose title is at best, / One which you dare not now contest." Authors of popular fiction were also influenced by the Antirent War, a struggle in which some were personally interested. Writer James Fenimore Cooper,

himself a minor landlord, expressed the landlords' views on their traditional rights and obligations in his three Littlepage novels, while Herman Melville offers a critique of the landlords in *Pierre* (1852). Today the declaration remains an important text for understanding emerging American ideas on property rights.

Contemporary scholars typically emphasize that the declaration is an example of a trend toward wider participation in U.S. democracy. Reeve Huston, in a 2000 essay for *Journal of the Early Republic*, points out that in the decades just before the appearance of the declaration, tenants had become more involved in local politics as voters and as delegates to political party conventions and town meetings. Moreover, the ideas about individual liberty and property rights that characterized the language of both major political parties of the era (the Whigs and the Democrats) influenced the Antirenters' decision to resist a form of property ownership that they viewed as out of step with U.S. values. Finally, the Antirent struggle is recognized as a movement that increased the political influence of the middle class, the background from which most Antirenters came.

BIBLIOGRAPHY

Sources

"Anti-Renters' Declaration of Independence." *We, the Other People: Alternative Declarations of Independence by Labor Groups, Farmers, Woman's Rights Advocates, Socialists, and Blacks, 1829-1975.* Ed. Philip S. Foner. Urbana: U of Illinois P, 1976. 59-63. Print.

Christman, Henry. *Tin Horns and Calico: A Decisive Episode in the Emergence of Democracy.* New York: Henry Holt, 1945. Print.

Hecht, Roger. "Rents in the Landscape: The Anti-Rent War in Melville's *Pierre.*" *American Transcendental Quarterly* 19.1 (2005): 37-50. *360 Link.* Web. 3 Oct. 2012.

Huston, Reeve. "The Parties and 'The People': The New York Anti-Rent Wars and the Contours of Jacksonian Politics." *Journal of the Early Republic* 20.2 (2000): 241-71. *JSTOR.* Web. 3 Oct. 2012.

Pisani, Donald J. "The Squatter and Natural Law in Nineteenth-Century America." *Agricultural History* 81.4 (2007): 443-63. *JSTOR.* Web. 3 Oct. 2012.

Summerhill, Thomas. *Harvest of Dissent: Agrarianism in Nineteenth-Century New York.* Urbana: U of Illinois P, 2005. Print.

Further Reading

Bruegel, Martin. "Unrest: Manorial Society and the Market in the Hudson Valley, 1780-1850." *Journal of American History* 82.4 (1996): 1393-1424. *JSTOR.* Web. 3 Oct. 2012.

Earle, Jonathan H. *Jacksonian Antislavery & the Politics of Free Soil, 1824-1854.* Chapel Hill: U of North Carolina P, 2004. Print.

French, Florence H. "Cooper's Use of Proverbs in the Anti-Rent Novels." *New York Folklore Quarterly* 26 (1970): 42-49. Print.

Huston, Reeve. *Land and Freedom: Rural Society, Popular Protest, and Party Politics in Antebellum New York.* New York: Oxford UP, 2000. Print.

McCurdy, Charles W. *The Anti-Rent Era in New York Law and Politics, 1839-1865.* Chapel Hill: U of North Carolina P, 2001. Print.

Schachterle, Lance. "The Themes of Land and Leadership in 'The Littlepage Manuscripts.'" *Literature in the Early American Republic: Annual Studies on Cooper and His Contemporaries* 1 (2009): 89-131. Print.

John Walters

CATECHISM OF THE REVOLUTIONIST

Sergei Nechaev

✣ **Key Facts**

Time Period:
Mid-19th Century

Movement/Issue:
Anarchism; Terrorism;
Russian students'
Revolutionary movement

Place of Publication:
Russia

**Language of
Publication:**
Russian

OVERVIEW

Written by Sergei Nechaev in 1869, the *Catechism of the Revolutionist* prescribes a ruthless, amoral code of conduct for members of such secret societies as Nechaev's the People's Justice. Though historians have suggested that Nechaev wrote the *Catechism* in cooperation with his mentor and fellow anarchist Mikhail Bakunin, its ideas have become synonymous with Nechaevism, a cold-blooded brand of Russian Jacobinism that Nechaev promoted. Divided into two major sections, the *Catechism* first charts the hierarchy of a terrorist organization and then describes the ideal revolutionary character. Guided by the principle that the end justifies the means, the *Catechism* focuses solely on how to achieve the total destruction of the existing social order and excludes any vision of the new society that might take its place.

SERGEI NECHAEV: A RUTHLESS REVOLUTIONARY

Born to a family of Russian serfs in 1847, Sergei Nechaev was among the first student revolutionaries to emerge from the peasantry whom the movement sought to liberate. However, Nechaev's career was cut short after he brutally murdered his fellow revolutionary Ivan Ivanovich Ivanov. An effort to consolidate power, the murder was a chilling enactment of the principles set forth in the *Catechism of the Revolutionist* and continues to define Nechaev's legacy.

Ivanov, a member of Nechaev's secret society the People's Justice, made the fatal mistake of questioning the group's legitimacy. He convinced several other members of the organization that Ivanov was an informant; on November 21, 1869, they brutally attacked him and submerged his body in an icy pond. Authorities soon learned of the murder, for which hundreds of revolutionaries were arrested and dozens tried. Nechaev himself eluded arrest until 1872. Convicted and imprisoned, he nonetheless gained enough influence over his guards to obtain their help in exchanging letters with the People's Will, the group responsible for the assassination of Tsar Alexander II. Once his dealings were discovered, however, Nechaev was subjected to harsh treatment, which contributed to his death, at the age of thirty-five, of consumption and scurvy.

First published in 1871 in the *Government Herald,* the *Catechism* served as a blueprint for the People's Justice and influenced similar groups, such as the People's Will, which orchestrated the assassination of Tsar Alexander II in 1881. Nechaev and his *Catechism* became infamous following the murder of his fellow revolutionary Ivan Ivanovich Ivanov, for which Nechaev was ultimately convicted and imprisoned. While the *Catechism* is a seminal document in the history of Russian anarchism, its endorsement of revolutionary authoritarianism puts it at the fringes of a movement that tended to be dominated by libertarian socialists. Still, it holds a significant place in the political and intellectual trajectory leading to the Bolshevik revolution, influencing both Vladimir Lenin and Joseph Stalin. While the Bolsheviks argued against the terrorism and assassination campaigns of the Narodniks, the Bolsheviks nevertheless shared Nechaev's vanguardist orientation.

HISTORICAL AND LITERARY CONTEXT

The *Catechism* was written in the context of Russia's student revolutionary movement, which was spurred by the abolition of serfdom and erupted in a series of attempts on the tsar's life. Although the tsar granted the serfs their freedom in 1861, their economic situation became so dire that they were arguably in a worse position after emancipation than before. Unrest and class inequality bred revolutionary sentiment in an emerging generation influenced by both Marxism and Russian anarchists. In the late 1860s tensions increased following the first attempt on Tsar Alexander II's life. The would-be assassin, Dmitry Karakozov, had connections to Nicholas Ishutin's terrorist organization, Hell, a subset of the secret society called simply the Organization.

The Karakozov incident sparked the "white terror," a reactionary wave of patriotic sentiment and government suppression of revolutionary activity. Pushed further underground, student revolutionary circles became fertile ground for secret organizations to form. The *Catechism* reflects this movement toward a model of revolution orchestrated by small, centralized groups and away from the populist notion of a spontaneous mass uprising. However, anarchists and libertarian socialists—including Bakunin, Nechaev's onetime mentor, who sent a letter to Nechaev in 1870 disavowing the philosophies expressed in the

Painting by Jean-Baptiste Carpeaux (1827-1875) depicting the 1867 assassination attempt by Antoni Berezowski, Polish anarchist, against Alexander II, Tsar of Russia. Sergei Nechaev also plotted to kill the tsar during the 1860s. Alexander was ultimately assassinated in 1881 by the revolutionary group the People's Will. GIANNI DAGLI ORTI/THE ART ARCHIVE AT ART RESOURCE, NY

Catechism—largely repudiated Nechaev's ideas as excessively authoritarian and immoral. Still, within a decade of the *Catechism*'s appearance, Russia's first major professional terrorist organization, the People's Will, was formed; in 1881 the group succeeded in assassinating the tsar.

Broadly speaking, the *Catechism* follows in the tradition of Jacobinism, and Nechaev was influenced by such thinkers as Jean-Jacques Rousseau and Maximilien Robespierre. A closer antecedent is Peter Zaichnevsky, whose leaflet *Young Russia* (1862) calls for a bloody eradication of the tsar and his circle by any means necessary. Pytor Tkachev, a contemporary of Nechaev and a Russian Jacobin who was later dubbed the first Bolshevik, also influenced Nechaev's intellectual development; the pair eventually collaborated on *A Program of Revolutionary Action* (1869), a direct forerunner of the *Catechism* in both style and substance. Like many revolutionaries of his day, Nechaev was also inspired by the character Rakhmetov from Nikolay Chernyshevsky's novel *What Is to Be Done?* (1864); Rakhmetov is an extreme ascetic who practices such behavior as eating uncooked meat and sleeping on a bed of nails.

Nechaev became notorious for embodying the ruthlessness his *Catechism* describes, and the document's literary afterlife frequently centers on its author's biography. Most famously, Fyodor Dostoevsky's novel *The Possessed* (1872) critiques revolutionary terrorism in its portrayal of events inspired by the Ivanov murder; the character Pyotr Verkhovensky is based on Nechaev. Nechaev-like figures also appear in twentieth-century fiction. For example, *The Master of St. Petersburg* (1994) by J. M. Coetzee is a reimagining of *The Possessed*, in which Dostoevsky and Nechaev become acquainted in the aftermath of a mysterious death. Nechaev's legacy can also be seen in *Impressions of Lenin* (1964) by Angelica Balabanoff, in which the author grapples with the ethics of revolution, questioning whether actions performed in service of the cause are morally exempt.

THEMES AND STYLE

The *Catechism*'s guiding theme is that revolution is possible only if its proponents devote every effort and action to achieving it, with no regard to morality or decency. For Nechaev, revolution requires a single-minded, self-negating intent to abolish the existing order. The *Catechism*'s well-known second section is divided into four categories that dictate a revolutionary's personal characteristics, behavior toward fellow revolutionaries, and attitude toward society at large, as well as the secret society's obligations to the masses. A "doomed" man, the revolutionary himself is

PRIMARY SOURCE

CATECHISM OF THE REVOLUTIONIST

1. The revolutionary is a doomed man. He has no personal interests, no business affairs, no emotions, no attachments, no property, and no name. Everything in him is wholly absorbed in the single thought and the single passion for revolution.

2. The revolutionary knows that in the very depths of his being, not only in words but also in deeds, he has broken all the bonds which tie him to the social order and the civilized world with all its laws, moralities, and customs, and with all its generally accepted conventions. He is their implacable enemy, and if he continues to live with them it is only in order to destroy them more speedily.

3. The revolutionary despises all doctrines and refuses to accept the mundane sciences, leaving them for future generations. He knows only one science: the science of destruction. For this reason, but only for this reason, he will study mechanics, physics, chemistry, and perhaps medicine. But all day and all night he studies the vital science of human beings, their characteristics and circumstances, and all the phenomena of the present social order. The object is perpetually the same: the surest and quickest way of destroying the whole filthy order....

8. The revolutionary can have no friendship or attachment, except for those who have proved by their actions that they, like him, are dedicated to revolution. The degree of friendship, devotion and obligation toward such a comrade is determined solely by the degree of his usefulness to the cause of total revolutionary destruction....

13. The revolutionary enters the world of the State, of the privileged classes, of the so-called civilization, and he lives in this world only for the purpose of bringing about its speedy and total destruction. He is not a revolutionary if he has any sympathy for this world. *He should not hesitate to destroy any position, any place, or any man in this world.* He must hate everyone and everything in it with an equal hatred. All the worse for him if he has any relations with parents, friends, or lovers; *he is no longer a revolutionary if he is swayed by these relationships.*

among that which will be sacrificed to achieve revolution. Because the revolutionary's ultimate task is total destruction, he is not responsible for putting in place or even imagining a new order; instead, this task is left to future generations.

The *Catechism*'s rhetorical strategy is to assume that readers already possess the necessary characteristics of a revolutionary. Because a revolutionary has already broken every tie to society, through both speech and action, he cannot decide to return to it. In this way, the *Catechism* constructs an indoctrinated audience with no choice but to give themselves entirely to the cause of revolution. Thus, the *Catechism* makes no effort to convince the reader that revolution is right but instead focuses on the most effective means of achieving it, thereby precluding any alternative course of action. By maintaining that a revolutionary has already forfeited his personal identity—he owns nothing, cares for nothing, and is connected to no one— the *Catechism* leaves him no option but to surrender his pure, untethered existence to the revolution. The document further cautions him to sever ties with family, friends, and lovers, insisting that these relationships are entirely incompatible with his new role.

Composed as a series of injunctions, the *Catechism* methodically prescribes the behaviors and mind-set of the ideal revolutionary. These injunctions, couched in a language of unrelenting extremes, appeal only to a reader predisposed to ruthlessness, one who wholly rejects the existing order as something literally revolting to him. In celebrating the revolutionary's fanaticism, the *Catechism* suggests that he is both set apart from and above a corrupt society. It thus reinforces the revolutionary's sense of his own exceptionality at the same time that it requires him to forsake his individuality. Furthermore, by failing either to reference any particular historical moment or to personalize its interlocutor, the *Catechism* reinforces the need for uniformity among revolutionaries while claiming its universal authority as a primer for any revolution.

CRITICAL DISCUSSION

Critics and intellectuals have alternatively rejected and embraced the *Catechism* since its publication. Its legacy remains entwined with the Ivanov murder, which, in the words of Randall Law in *Terrorism: A History* (2009), "was a humiliating blow" to the revolutionary movement. According to Paul Avrich in his *Anarchist Portraits* (1988), libertarian socialists charged that Nechaev's authoritarian principles "could not inspire a true socialist revolution because they lacked a true socialist morality." Still, the *Catechism* served as a stimulus both to the People's Will and to Lenin, who reportedly admired its code of self-abnegation and organizational discipline.

14. Aiming at implacable revolution, the revolutionary may and frequently must live within society will pretending to be completely different from what he really is, for he must penetrate everywhere, into all the higher and middle-classes, into the houses of commerce, the churches, and the palaces of the aristocracy, and into the worlds of the bureaucracy and literature and the military, and also into the Third Division and the Winter Palace of the Czar....

23. By a revolution, the Society does not mean an orderly revolt according to the classic western model – a revolt which always stops short of attacking the rights of property and the traditional social systems of so-called civilization and morality. Until now, such a revolution has always limited itself to the overthrow of one political form in order to replace it by another, thereby attempting to bring about a so-called revolutionary state. The only form of revolution beneficial to the people is one which destroys the entire State to the roots and exterminated all the state traditions, institutions, and classes in Russia.

24. With this end in view, the Society therefore refuses to impose any new organization from above. Any future organization will doubtless work its way through the movement and life of the people; but this is a matter for future generations to decide. Our task is terrible, total, universal, and merciless destruction.

25. Therefore, in drawing closer to the people, we must above all make common cause with those elements of the masses which, since the foundation of the state of Muscovy, have never ceased to protest, not only in words but in deeds, against everything directly or indirectly connected with the state: against the nobility, the bureaucracy, the clergy, the traders, and the parasitic kulaks. We must unite with the adventurous tribes of brigands, who are the only genuine revolutionaries in Russia.

26. To weld the people into one single unconquerable and all-destructive force – this is our aim, our conspiracy, and our task.

This view was shared by radical revolutionary leaders of the twentieth century, including Eldridge Cleaver of the Black Panther Party, who acknowledges the *Catechism*'s influence in *Soul on Ice* (1968).

Much modern critical debate centers on whether the *Catechism* advanced the revolutionary cause or represents a significant strain of thought in the history of Russian anarchism. According to Adam Ulam in *The Bolsheviks* (1965), "the *Catechism* is not really a political manifesto; it is much more an expression of the misanthropic Machiavellianism of a perverse and criminal youth." Ulam goes on to call Nechaev "an exception among the revolutionaries, a maverick" and suggests that the *Catechism* "belongs to what might be called the psychopathology of revolution." Avrich takes a more nuanced view. While arguing that "in Nechaev's hands, anarchism ... was soiled, debased, and finally distorted beyond recognition," Avrich acknowledges that Nechaev's capacity for self-abnegation inspired the revolutionaries of 1905 and 1917. Abbott Gleason, in *Young Russia: The Genesis of Russian Radicalism in the 1860s* (1980), concurs, remarking that "Nechaev left his footprints in Russia's radical political culture."

Most critics agree that Nechaev was a harbinger of post-revolution Russia's darkest chapters. Avrich claims that the *Catechism*'s revolutionary authoritarianism "ultimately foreshadows, on however small a scale, the mass murders of Stalin in the name of revolutionary necessity." Many critics also conclude that its legacy extends beyond totalitarianism to modern-day terrorism. In *How Russia Shaped the Modern World* (2003), Steven Marks suggests that the *Catechism* had a "major impact on modern politics, by providing rudimentary principles for the world's first organized terror movements." Ana Siljak corroborates this view in *Angel of Vengeance* (2008), proposing that the *Catechism* offered Russia its "first glimpse into the mind of a terrorist" and "described a perfectly constructed terrorist network."

BIBLIOGRAPHY

Sources

Avrich, Paul. *Anarchist Portraits*. Princeton, NJ: Princeton UP, 1988. Print.

Gleason, Abbott. *Young Russia: The Genesis of Russian Radicalism in the 1860s*. New York: Viking, 1980. Print.

Law, Randall. *Terrorism: A History*. Malden: Polity, 2009. Print.

Marks, Steven. *How Russia Shaped the Modern World: From Art to Anti-Semitism, Ballet to Bolshevism*. Princeton: Princeton UP, 2003. Print.

Nechaev, Sergei Gennadievich. *Catechism of the Revolutionist.* Stirling: Violette Nozieres and A.K., 1989. Print.

Siljak, Ana. *Angel of Vengeance: The "Girl Assassin," the Governor of St. Petersburg, and Russia's Revolutionary World.* New York: St. Martin's, 2008. Print.

Ulam, Adam. *The Bolsheviks: The Intellectual and Political History of the Triumph of Communism in Russia.* New York: Macmillan, 1965. Print.

Further Reading

Chaliand, Gerard, and Arnaud Blin, eds. *The History of Terrorism: From Antiquity to Al Qaeda.* Berkeley: U of California P, 2007. Print.

Crenshaw, Martha, ed. *Terrorism in Context.* University Park: Pennsylvania State UP, 1995. Print.

Gillespie, Michael. *Nihilism before Nietzsche.* Chicago: U of Chicago P, 1995. Print.

Laqueur, Walter, ed. *Voices of Terror: Manifestos, Writings, and Manuals of Al Qaeda, Hamas, and Other Terrorists from around the World and throughout the Ages.* New York: Reed, 2004. Print.

Marshall, Peter. *Demanding the Impossible: A History of Anarchism.* London: HarperCollins, 1992. Print.

McLaughlin, Paul. *Anarchism and Authority: A Philosophical Introduction to Classical Anarchism.* Aldershot: Ashgate, 2007. Print.

Pomper, Philip. *Sergei Nechaev.* New Brunswick: Rutgers UP, 1979. Print.

Rees, E.A. *Political Thought from Machiavelli to Stalin: Revolutionary Machiavellism.* New York: Palgrave Macmillan, 2004. Print.

Melanie Brezniak

CIVIL DISOBEDIENCE

Henry David Thoreau

OVERVIEW

Henry David Thoreau's "Civil Disobedience" (1849) asserts the supremacy of the individual conscience and argues for nonparticipation as a means to resist unjust government. An abolitionist and transcendentalist, Thoreau designed his essay as a model for political protest on an individual scale. Composed during the Mexican-American War (1846-48), which abolitionists viewed as an unjust conflict waged to expand slavery, the essay draws on Thoreau's experience of being jailed for refusing to pay a poll tax in order to affirm the power of transcendental principles and acts of civil disobedience. His goal was to persuade reform-minded abolitionists in the North to act on their antislavery convictions by refusing to support a government that accommodated slavery. "Civil Disobedience" gained popularity with political and civil rights movements of the twentieth century, and its powerful rhetoric, which urges readers to halt the machinery of unjust government through individual acts of resistance, remains influential today.

"Civil Disobedience" initially received little recognition outside of Thoreau's immediate circle of Massachusetts transcendentalists. First delivered as a lecture in 1848 and revised for publication in 1849, the essay was then published in the posthumous collection *A Yankee in Canada, with Antislavery and Reform Papers* (1866). Scholars continue to debate whether Thoreau himself would have chosen this title. Regardless, the publication of the collection brought his antislavery writings wider exposure and recognition, though his primary literary reputation was as a nature writer. In the early twentieth century, the British Labour party and Fabians began to recognize the applicability of civil disobedience to political causes. Today Thoreau's brand of political resistance is credited with inspiring civil rights leaders including Mohandas Gandhi and Martin Luther King, Jr.

HISTORICAL AND LITERARY CONTEXT

"Civil Disobedience" was written as a response to abolitionist fears that the Mexican-American War would lead to the expansion of slavery. Although Thoreau says in the essay that he was jailed for refusing to pay a poll tax to fund the Mexican-American War, the levy was, in fact, a local one, and he had stopped paying it years before the war began. This inconsistency demonstrates how Thoreau tailored his facts to address the immediate political concerns of his audience. Later essays, such as "Slavery in Massachusetts" (1854) and "A Plea for Captain John Brown" (1859), reveal that he continued developing his antislavery stance, adjusting his views as events in the 1850s deepened the slavery crisis.

"Civil Disobedience" illustrates the tension between individualism and political action within transcendentalism. Ralph Waldo Emerson, Thoreau's mentor and friend, first popularized transcendentalism in the 1830s with his emphasis on self-reliance, at times poking fun at various reform societies. As the controversy over slavery grew, however, transcendentalists struggled to defend their individualism against allegations of political complacency. Throughout the 1840s, figures such as Bronson Alcott, Margaret Fuller, and Elizabeth Peabody rejected individualism by joining various reform projects, and even Emerson began to contribute to antislavery causes. Thoreau's text attempts to maintain the integrity of transcendental individualism while enacting political change.

"Civil Disobedience" reflects transcendental and abolitionist discourse of the period. Emerson's essays "The American Scholar" (1837) and "Politics" (1844) develop similar stances on the sovereignty of individual conscience and resistance based on "fit action." While Emerson influenced Thoreau's thinking, many scholars note that Thoreau acted upon convictions that Emerson merely theorized. Thoreau's essay also reveals his changing political positions. His 1848 lecture refers explicitly to "non-resistance," a tenet of radical abolitionist William Lloyd Garrison. Garrisonian nonresistance rejected all violence on individual or government levels. It also rejected the Constitution as a proslavery document and advocated disunion. Thoreau's 1849 revision of his lecture, "Resistance to Civil Government," breaks with nonresistance, as evidenced by its title. Emphasizing a need for "better government" instead of "no government," Thoreau develops ideas that are in step with those of Frederick Douglass, a former Garrisonian who argued for immediate abolition within the framework of the U.S. Constitution. While "Civil Disobedience" focuses on nonviolent resistance, Thoreau never outright rejected violent means to end slavery.

First conceived as "The Rights and Duties of the Individual in Relation to Government," the essay

✣ *Key Facts*

Time Period:
Mid-19th Century

Movement/Issue:
Abolitionism;
Transcendentalism;
Civil Rights Movement

Place of Publication:
United States

Language of Publication:
English

HENRY DAVID THOREAU: THE HERMIT OF WALDEN POND

Henry David Thoreau was born on July 12, 1817. A graduate of Harvard College, he was expected to enter a professional career. Instead, he took a position as a public school teacher, quitting two weeks later after refusing to use corporal punishment. To earn money, he worked at his father's pencil manufacturing business and picked up small manual labor and land surveying jobs.

Thoreau also was a frequent houseguest of Ralph Waldo Emerson, and this relationship influenced his beliefs and provided access to an inner circle of transcendentalists. Even so, there was tension between Emerson's genteel persona and Thoreau's radical nonconformity. Many contemporaries found Thoreau to be a contrarian who lacked ambition. His decision to build a cabin at Walden Pond in Massachusetts and to live there alone earned him the nickname "The Hermit of Walden Pond." *Walden* (1854), which recounts his experiences and reflections while living in nature, sold only modestly at first but eventually became a seminal work of American literature. On May 6, 1862, Thoreau died of tuberculosis. It would be several more decades until readers fully appreciated his brand of nonconformity.

reached a limited audience of lyceum attendees in his native Concord, Massachusetts. The second version of the essay, published a year later in Peabody's periodical, *Aesthetic Papers,* found a wider readership in Boston. Yet it is unlikely that Thoreau's ideas received much attention even in this venue, as the publication did not gain enough subscribers to continue beyond the first issue. Its publication under the title "Civil Disobedience" sold modestly, partially because the

Portrait of Henry David Thoreau. © NORTH WIND PICTURE ARCHIVES/ALAMY

1866 volume in which it appeared emphasized his nature writing rather than his political essays. By the turn of the nineteenth century, however, the essay began to garner worldwide attention.

THEMES AND STYLE

The central theme of "Civil Disobedience" is that there is no higher duty than to live according to one's conscience; when an individual's conscience is at odds with the government, breaking the law is justified. Thoreau rejects the traditional political process as a means of change, arguing that representative government gives the individual conscience away to a legislative body operating by majority rule. An individual, writes Thoreau, needs to take action when asked to participate in an injustice put forth by the government: "If [the injustice] is of such a nature that it requires you to be the agent of injustice to another, then, I say break the law. Let your life be a counter friction to stop the machine." Withdrawing support, both personal and financial, from an unjust government "clogs" its mechanism, creating the possibility of a "peaceable revolution" through individual resistance. Absent in Thoreau's discussion are women, who besides having no role in the official political process of the time, are often depicted as negative symbols of domesticity in Thoreau's works.

The essay achieves its rhetorical effect through the American homiletic tradition, as well as the use of figurative language. "Civil Disobedience" operates within the framework of the jeremiad, which reminds people of their sins, emphasizes their past glory, and references possible redemption. Thoreau alludes to the American Revolution and to the Bible to contrast the nation's past with its current state, enhancing his message of the need for redemption. The essay's central metaphor, which casts the government as a machine and individual resistance as a counter friction against its injustices, creates a strong image of one's ability to stop injustice. Metaphor also is used to a powerful effect when Thoreau describes his imprisonment: "I saw that, if there was a wall of stone between me and my townsmen, there was a still more difficult one to climb or break through, before they were as free as I was." Here Thoreau emphasizes his transcendental belief in the human mind, arguing that walls may confine his body but not his thoughts. In addition, "Civil Disobedience" utilizes classical rhetoric, such as a series of rhetorical questions leading to logical conclusions, repetition, anaphora, and chiasmus.

Stylistically, the text represents the formal didactic tone of many transcendental works, but it also shifts between irreverent and prophetic voices. The logical appeals ask a largely abolitionist audience to reconsider the ends of its relationship with the government and to redefine its understanding of political participation. The irreverent tone regarding social customs and institutions likewise encourages readers to consider if they are not mere machines living under the tyranny of majority rule. The essay ends with a transcendental vision of a "still more perfect and glorious State" that may be achieved when the individual is recognized "as a higher and independent power." As a whole, the work guides readers through a logical consideration of the state, appealing to emotions of indignation, patriotism, and hope.

CRITICAL DISCUSSION

Initially, "Civil Disobedience" received little critical attention. According to Lawrence Rosenwald in *A Historical Guide to Henry David Thoreau* (2000), Alcott, an attendee at Thoreau's lecture, noted that the audience was "attentive," and he found the speech "an admirable statement." Initial reaction to Thoreau's published essay suggests his ideas were considered extreme. A critic for *The New Englander* in 1849 claimed, "Of all the odd things in the collection, the queerest is the Essay on Resistance to Civil Government." The critic balked at Thoreau's refusal to pay taxes and speculated how many times he had been jailed, concluding, "He writes straight on what he thinks, and it is no slight matter, to be able to know by actual inspection, that such a man as this breathes and lives in New England." Thoreau was known primarily as a nature writer from the 1860s onward until Henry Salt, a British social reformer, published a volume of his political writings in 1890. The Labour Party in Britain, as well as writer Leo Tolstoy, began to take inspiration from "Civil Disobedience" and republish it in various forums.

The lasting legacy of "Civil Disobedience" was formed in the twentieth century. Gandhi first read the essay in 1907, and he published it in paraphrased form in South Africa. Eventually, the essay was included in the reading list for his followers. In *A Political Companion to Henry David Thoreau* (2009), Anthony J. Parel points out that Gandhi's campaign for social justice began before he read "Civil Disobedience" but that Thoreau's work "confirmed and morally supported" his cause. Political movements in the mid-twentieth century solidified the essay's influence. King claimed that reading Thoreau in college shaped his methods of nonviolent resistance, making "Civil Disobedience" an important text in the civil rights movement. It also influenced protests against the Vietnam War in the 1960s. As Michael Meyer asserts in his introduction to *Walden and Civil Disobedience* (1986), it is "very likely the most famous essay in American literature."

Current scholarship focuses on the work's relationship to reform movements of the antebellum era and on philosophical influences on Thoreau's thought. Shannon L. Mariotti's *Thoreau's Democratic Withdrawal: Alienation, Participation, and Modernity* argues that Thoreau withdrew from social and political spaces in order to "engage in an alternative form of democratic politics." Deak Nabors has explored the connections between "Civil Disobedience" and natural law, and both James J. Donahue and Lawrence Rosenwald have traced how Thoreau's views on slavery developed after "Civil Disobedience." Most recently interest has centered on eco-critical analysis of his nature writings as scholars examine the "green" Thoreau.

BIBLIOGRAPHY

Sources

"Literary Notices." *New Englander* 7.28 (1849): 634-35. Cornell University Library. Web. 12 Oct. 2012.

Meyer, Michael. Introduction. *Walden and Civil Disobedience.* New York: Penguin, 1986. 7-36. Print.

Mariotti, Shannon L. *Thoreau's Democratic Withdrawal: Alienation, Participation, and Modernity.* Madison: U of Wisconsin P, 2010. Print.

Packer, Barbara. *The Transcendentalists.* Athens: U of Georgia P, 2007. Print.

Parel, Anthony J. "Thoreau, Gandhi, and Comparative Political Thought." *A Political Companion to Henry David Thoreau.* Ed Jack Turner. Lexington: U of Kentucky P, 2009. 372-92. Print.

Rosenwald, Lawrence. "The Theory, Practice, and Influence of Thoreau's 'Civil Disobedience.'" *A Historical Guide to Henry David Thoreau.* Ed. William Cain. Oxford: Oxford UP, 2000. 153-80. Print.

Further Reading

Donahue, James T. "'Hardly the Same Man': 'Civil Disobedience' and Thoreau's Response to John Brown." *Midwest Quarterly* 48.2 (2007): 247-65. Print.

Fink, Steven. *Prophet in the Marketplace: Thoreau's Development as a Professional Writer.* Princeton: Princeton UP, 1992. Print.

Glick, Wendell. *The Recognition of Henry David Thoreau: Selected Criticism since 1848.* Ann Arbor: U of Michigan P, 1969. Print.

Hodder, Alan D. *Thoreau's Ecstatic Witness.* New Haven: Yale UP, 2001. Print.

Lysanker, John T., and William Rossi, eds. *Emerson and Thoreau: Figures of Friendship.* Bloomington: U of Indiana P, 2010. Print.

Myerson, Joel, ed. *The Cambridge Companion to Henry David Thoreau.* Cambridge: Cambridge UP, 1995. Print.

Nabers, Deak. "Thoreau's Natural Constitution." *American Literary History* 19.4 (2007): 824-48. Print.

Petrulionis, Sandra Harbert. *Thoreau in His Own Time: A Biographical Chronicle of His Life, Drawn from Recollections, Interviews, and Memoirs by Family, Friends, and Associates.* Iowa City: U of Iowa P, 2012. Print.

Schneider, Richard J., ed. *Henry David Thoreau: A Documentary Volume.* Detroit: Gale, 2004. Print.

Kim Banion

DECLARATION OF THE RIGHTS OF MAN AND OF THE CITIZEN

National Assembly of France

❖ *Key Facts*

Time Period:
Late 17th Century

Movement/Issue:
French civil rights

Place of Publication:
France

Language of Publication:
French

OVERVIEW

The *Declaration of the Rights of Man and of the Citizen* (*Déclaration des droits de l'homme et du citoyen*) was presented by the National Assembly of France on August 20, 1789, in order to define the natural rights of French citizens. The document sought to establish legislated protection for the lower classes in France from the rule of the aristocracy and religious leaders. It was composed during the early stages of the French Revolution (1789-99) and is heralded as the key document in the uprising that ultimately brought down the French monarchy and overturned the governing structure of the nation.

Upon its appearance, the declaration elicited both praise and criticism from the French people. Although it succeeded in defining the idea of universal human rights for all citizens, it excluded all social minorities from the definition of "citizen," thus creating a very limiting and patriarchal view of human rights. The document was highly influential in changing attitudes about the relationship between citizen and state during the French Revolution, but this exclusion of women, people of color, slaves, Jews, and other demographics was met with disapproval by theorists in other countries and by some French revolutionists. Today, the text continues to be regarded with mixed emotions among scholars: it is an undeniably powerful piece of writing that ultimately altered the way human rights were observed in the eighteenth century—in both France and elsewhere—but its focus solely on white men as citizens is too narrow to ignore when discussing the inherent natural rights of all humans.

HISTORICAL AND LITERARY CONTEXT

The main concern of the *Declaration of the Rights of Man and of the Citizen* is the establishment of the rights of men based on the developing theories of natural science. The notion that society was a result of human interaction with the natural world—as opposed to being based on the hierarchical structure of the monarchy or the doctrine imposed by the Catholic Church—had developed from scientific exploration. This viewpoint had become publicly accessible through mediums such as scientific journals and newspapers, and formal essay competitions arose to encourage questions about the natural world. With the development of this scientific worldview—and, in turn, ideas of natural freedoms and inherent civil rights—the governing structures of the church and monarchy began to appear contrived and restricting.

The *Declaration of the Rights of Man and of the Citizen* was released at the beginning of the French Revolution, when ideas of natural science and intrinsic human rights began to take on political significance. The concept of basic social freedom was based on the ideas of natural philosophy proposed by leading theorists such as Jean-Jacques Rousseau and the Comte de Buffon. These scholars equated the birth of humans with the processes of nature and reasoned that the development of society was a natural result of the interaction of citizens. In other words, universal rights and freedoms were constructed by these theorists as natural extensions of human birth and development. The declaration, which was written in reaction to the prevailing relationship between the French people and the governing bodies of the state, incorporates the theories from these key thinkers in order to define human rights and spur change to the concepts of citizenship in France.

The text fits within a growing number of revolutionary documents that emerged in Europe and America during the eighteenth century. It primarily draws on the *Declaration of Independence* in creating a collective identity of citizens. Despite the influence of this document, however, the *Declaration of the Rights of Man and of the Citizen* is regarded as a unique work that ultimately led to a new view of the relationship between citizens and the state.

After the initial presentation of the declaration, other documents expressing the universality of human rights appeared in France and other nations, including numerous amendments to the French constitution and the highly influential work *Rights of Man* by English writer Thomas Paine. Though it garnered popular and political support, the *Declaration of the Rights of Man and of the Citizen* was criticized for its exclusion of everyone except white men from the definition of "citizen." The *Declaration of the Rights of Woman*, written by Olympe de Gouges in 1791, was released in response to the National Assembly's blatant (though not surprising at the time) exclusion of women from its discussions of civil rights and freedoms. Today, the *Declaration of the Rights of Man and of the Citizen* is seen both as the catalyst of French democracy and the ironic herald of human rights because of its restrictive correlation between man and citizen.

THEMES AND STYLE

The document's main theme is that the governing systems of eighteenth-century France are outdated and causing considerable harm to the French people because of their disregard for basic rights and freedoms. The text begins: "The representatives of the French people, organized as a National Assembly, believ[e] that the ignorance, neglect, or contempt of the rights of man are the sole cause of public calamities and of the corruption of governments." After identifying the violation of human rights as the primary source of social unrest, the document lists seventeen articles of basic human rights and insists that these be enforced to prevent the government from taking advantage of non-aristocratic citizens. The writers of the declaration contend that the recognition of their proposed rights will result in a more contented and functional country.

The *Declaration of the Rights of Man and of the Citizen* achieves its rhetorical effect by evoking the ideas of natural science and applying them to the political situation in France at the beginning of the French Revolution. The first article states, "Men are born and remain free and equal in rights," while the second claims, "The aim of all political association is the preservation of the natural and imprescriptible rights of man." With these two opening articles, the National Assembly effectively proposes that civil rights and freedoms are a product of the natural world and that governing systems of society should protect them. Such actions, according to the National Assembly, will prevent the type of infringement of which the French monarchy and Catholic Church are guilty.

The document is formally written, employing the theoretical language of the day in order to present its view, which is that human rights are "natural, unalienable, and sacred" and, therefore, must be protected within the legal and political structures of France. The later articles focus on freedom of speech and the right to hold property, stating that "free communication of ideas and opinions is one of the most precious of the rights of man" and "property is an inviolable and sacred right." These inclusions suggest the extent to which the governing forces of eighteenth-century France were taking advantage of the non-aristocratic people. The text applies simple reason to right these perceived wrongs and inspire a change in the very essence of French citizenship.

CRITICAL DISCUSSION

The *Declaration of the Rights of Man and of the Citizen* initially stirred strong emotional responses—both positive and negative—that focused on the concepts

DECLARATION OF THE RIGHTS OF WOMAN

The National Assembly's *Declaration of the Rights of Man and of the Citizen* faced contemporary criticism for its limited definition of "citizen." Among the many written responses to this document is the *Declaration of the Rights of Woman,* written by Olympe de Gouges (1748-93) in 1791. De Gouges plays off the ideas and language in the National Assembly's work, claiming in her opening that the "ignorance, neglect, or contempt for the rights of women are the sole causes of public misfortunes and governmental corruption." This opening suggests that women's rights are ignored by the state and by the revolutionary movement, which is supposed to represent collective freedoms.

The *Declaration of the Rights of Woman* was intended to be read alongside the National Assembly's document in order to add to the discussion of human rights and reveal the flawed notion of natural rights being applicable only to certain men. The document ultimately failed to generate a serious feminist movement after it was published, partially because it played into stereotypes about women while trying to claim social and political equality for them.

of inherent and universal human rights and how they should be applied to the politics of a society. Some contemporary thinkers were critical of the document because of its groundbreaking nature and the societal upheaval it created. In *Reflections on the Revolution in France* (1790), Edmund Burke calls the declaration "a mine that will blow up, at one grand explosion, all examples of antiquity, all precedents, charters, and acts of parliament." Other thinkers, such as Count Antoine Destutt de Tracy and Louis-Sébastien Mercier, thought it was a beacon of light that would liberate the French from their current political situation. Lynn Hunt discusses these differing opinions in *The French Revolution and Human Rights* (1996), stating, "Many considered such a declaration a necessary preliminary to any constitution," while others "resisted the idea of a declaration as dangerous because it would raise popular expectations of massive changes."

Despite the criticism it generated, the declaration influenced political and philosophical writings and changed the relationship between people and society in the eighteenth century. In *The Evolution of International Human Rights* (2003), Gordon Lauren notes that the declaration made a "profound" impact because "it demonstrated a level of success and attention that others sought to emulate." Mary Ashburn Miller, writing in *A Natural History of Evolution* (2011), claims the declaration "brought changes in the atmosphere of Paris, so that the air was purer, the people more virtuous, and the nation more jubilant." Modern historians and philosophers view the document as instrumental in catalyzing the development

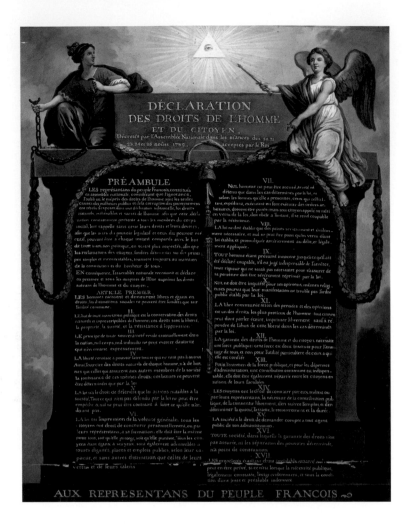

The ideals of the French Revolution spawned the 1789 *Déclaration des Droits de l'Homme et du Citoyen (Declaration of the Rights of Man and Citizen).* GIANNI DAGLI ORTI/THE ART ARCHIVE AT ART RESOURCE, NY

of human rights and altering theoretical discourse so that it equated the universal rights of citizens with the natural world.

Current trends in scholarship treat the *Declaration of the Rights of Man and of the Citizen* in a mixed manner, recognizing its importance in the evolution of human-rights discourse but criticizing its exclusionary definition of "citizen." In *Between the Queen and the Cabby* (2011), John Cole writes, "'Race, class and gender' may be a mantra for us, but it was not one for the deputies who proclaimed equal rights for all men without apparent awareness of effective exclusions." Lauren acknowledges this standpoint but also writes that the text "through its actions and its ideology proved to be one of the most profound revolutions in history."

BIBLIOGRAPHY

Sources

Burke, Edmund. *Reflections on the Revolution in France.* 1790. Ed. Frank M. Turner. New Haven: Yale UP, 2003. Print.

Cole, John R. *Between the Queen and the Cabby: Olympe de Gouges's Rights of Woman.* Montreal: McGill-Queen's UP, 2011. Print.

"Declaration of the Rights of Man and of the Citizen (1789)." *Encyclopedia of Emancipation and Abolition in the Transatlantic World.* Ed. Junius Rodriguez. Vol. 3. Armonk: Sharpe Reference, 2007. 677-78. *Gale Virtual Reference Library.* Web. 21 Sept. 2012.

Hunt, Lynn, ed. and trans. *The French Revolution and Human Rights: A Brief Documentary History.* Boston: Bedford Books, 1996. Print.

Lauren, Paul Gordon. *The Evolution of International Human Rights: Visions Seen.* 2nd ed. Philadelphia: U of Pennsylvania P, 2003. Print.

Miller, Mary Ashburn. *A Natural History of Revolution: Violence and Nature in the French Revolutionary Imagination, 1789-1794.* Ithaca: Cornell UP, 2011. Print.

Further Reading

Cohen, Yehuda. *The French: Myths of Revolution.* Brighton: Sussex Academic, 2011. Print.

De Gouges, Olympe. "Declaration of the Rights of Woman (September 1791)." *The French Revolution and Human Rights: A Brief Documentary History.* Ed. and trans. Lynn Hunt. Boston: Bedford Books, 1996. 124-29. Print.

Hancock, Ralph C., and L. Gary Lambert, eds. *The Legacy of the French Revolution.* Lanham, MD: Rowman & Littlefield, 1996. Print.

Israel, Jonathon I. *Democratic Enlightenment: Philosophy, Revolution, and Human Rights 1750-1790.* Oxford: Oxford UP, 2011. Print.

Montfort-Howard, Catherine. *Literate Women and the French Revolution of 1798.* Birmingham: Summa, 1994. Print.

Paine, Thomas. "Rights of Man." *Peter Linebaugh Presents Thomas Paine: Common Sense, Rights of Man and Agrarian Justice.* Ed. Jessica Kimpell. New York: Verso, 2009. Print.

Scott, Joan. "French Feminists and the Rights of Man: Olympe de Gouges's Declarations." *History Workshop* 28 (1989): 1-21. Print.

Steger, Manfred B. *The Rise of the Global Imaginary: Political Ideologies from the French Revolution to the Global War on Terror.* Oxford: Oxford UP, 2008. Print.

Katherine Barker

THE DECLARATION, RESOLUTIONS, AND CONSTITUTION OF THE SOCIETIES OF THE UNITED IRISHMEN

Theobald Wolfe Tone

OVERVIEW

In 1791 Theobald Wolfe Tone wrote *The Declaration, Resolutions, and Constitution of the Societies of the United Irishmen,* the founding charter for a republican organization demanding equal representation for Ireland in British Parliament. Drawing on the philosophical foundations of recent revolutions in the American colonies and France, the document outlines three resolutions by which the organization will attempt to secure Irish liberty: the presentation of a united front against British transgressions; active pursuit by that front of substantial reform in parliamentary representation; and selection thereafter of delegates representing all religious populations equally (one British tactic in controlling the Irish was to agitate preexisting conflicts between Catholics and Protestants). At the *Declaration*'s heart is Tone's insistence that Ireland's first steps toward sovereignty be constitutional not militant.

Though some Catholic supporters of the parliamentary reform movement were wary of the predominantly Protestant United Irishmen, the *Declaration* was largely supported among nationalists. French constitutional republicans, who had staged a successful revolution of their own just two years prior, publicly praised Tone and his ideals, and the organization enjoyed a period of rapid growth until it was outlawed and forced underground following the French declaration of war on Britain in 1793. Tone himself was captured by British forces and committed suicide in 1798 before he could be executed, but his contributions helped to forge a new direction—indeed, a new identity—for Irish nationalism. Today, it is commonly held that a direct line can be drawn between Tone's manifesto in 1791 and the inception of an independent Republic of Ireland in 1948.

HISTORICAL AND LITERARY CONTEXT

The late eighteenth century was an age of intellectual and political revolution. The British colonies in America had declared their independence in 1776 and waged a successful war to ensure the acknowledgement thereof. Their greatest intellectual champion, Thomas Paine, then took his ideas about human rights and civil liberties to France, where he became immensely influential in the French Revolution beginning in 1789. It was in the combination of the two successful revolutions that Tone and the Irish republicans found their inspiration. The latter revolution represented a more general separation from old structures of monarchy, aristocracy, and religious authority, while the former was a separation specifically from British rule.

Through the Americans and particularly the French, the Irish had come to understand both the importance of unity in mounting successful campaigns for sovereignty and the tendency of monarchical governments to use religion as a tool to disrupt unity. Seeing the total separation of church and state as a near-impossibility in Ireland, Tone modified their examples when drafting the *Declaration,* proposing instead that Catholics and Protestants be equally represented among Irish members of Parliament. This, in Tone's estimation, was the most agreeable way to eliminate religion from the political equation, a measure he felt was crucial in promoting unity among Irish nationalists.

All three revolutions drew heavily from the writings of Paine, a British-born American author and political theorist. American revolutionaries had been galvanized by *Common Sense* and *The American Crisis,* a pair of pamphlets published by Paine in 1776 decrying monarchical and aristocratic tyranny (particularly as enacted by Britain) and extolling the virtue of the American independence movement. Then, in March 1791, responding to Edmund Burke's conservative tract denouncing the French Revolution, Paine released the first part of *Rights of Man,* which submits that revolution is not only acceptable but necessary when a government neglects its people's safety, denies them their rights, and acts against their national interests.

The *Declaration* was composed just a few months after *Rights of Man* and builds on Paine's visions of civil liberty. Recognizing that Irish independence would likely be a slower, subtler process, Tone saw the first step as being radical parliamentary reform. Only through equal representation, Tone argued, could

❖ *Key Facts*

Time Period:
Late 18th Century

Movement/Issue:
Irish nationalism

Place of Publication:
Ireland

Language of Publication:
English

PRIMARY SOURCE

THE DECLARATION, RESOLUTIONS, AND CONSTITUTION OF THE SOCIETIES OF THE UNITED IRISHMEN

In the present great era of reform, when unjust Governments are falling in every quarter of Europe; when religious persecution is compelled to abjure her tyranny over conscience; when the rights of man are ascertained in theory, and that theory substantiated by practice; when antiquity can no longer defend absurd and oppressive forms against the common sense and common interests of mankind; when all Government is acknowledged to originate from the people, and to be so far only obligatory as it protects their rights and promotes their welfare; we think it our duty, as Irishmen, to come forward, and state what we feel to be our heavy grievance, and what we know to be its effectual remedy. We have no national Government—we are ruled by Englishmen, and the servants of Englishmen whose object is the interest of another country, whose instrument is corruption, and whose strength is the weakness of Ireland; and these men have the whole of the power and patronage of the country as means to seduce and subdue the honesty and spirit of her representatives in the legislature.

Such an extrinsic power, acting with uniform force, in a direction too frequently opposite to the true line of our obvious interests, can be resisted with effect solely by unanimity, decision and spirit in the people—qualities which may be exerted most legally, constitutionally, and efficaciously by that great measure essential to the prosperity, and freedom of Ireland—an equal representation of all the people in Parliament. We do not here mention as grievances the rejection of a place-bill, of a pension bill, of a responsibility-bill, the sale of peerages in one house, the corruption publicly avowed in the other, nor the notorious infamy of borough traffic between both, not that we are insensible to their enormity, but that we consider them as but symptoms of that mortal disease which corrodes the vitals of our constitution, and leaves to the people in thier own government but the shadow of a name.

Impressed with these sentiments, we have agreed to form an association to be called "The

Ireland ensure its people's safety, secure and guarantee their rights, and serve its national interests. Though the United Irishmen strayed more and more toward militarism, with failed rebellions in 1798 and 1803 effectively collapsing the organization, Tone's original declaration would later be echoed in the republican efforts that led to the Easter Rising of 1916, Irish Free State status in 1922, and the Republic of Ireland in 1948. For his contributions with the United Irishmen, Tone is often referred to as the "father of Irish republicanism."

THEMES AND STYLE

The central theme of the *Declaration* is the right of Irish citizens to at least equal representation in Parliament, if not to sovereignty. "In the present great era of reform, when unjust Governments are falling in every quarter of Europe," Tone argues, British transgressions against the Irish can no longer be tolerated. Recognizing, however, that the single most effective means of suppression employed by the British is division, he insists that such transgressions "can be resisted with effect solely by unanimity, decision, and spirit in the people." He maintains that this spirit of unity is the surest means by which to secure "equal representation of all the people in Parliament," which would, in turn, provide a legal, legitimized, and public venue in which to address Irish interests. To that end, the Society of United Irishmen set as its objectives to "pledge ourselves to our country, and mutually to each other, that we will steadily support and endeavour, by all due means," to serve the interests of the Irish people.

For his rhetorical strategies, Tone turned most clearly to Paine. Drawing on Paine's vision of government's civic duties—namely to serve the interests of its constituents—Tone submits that the Irish "are ruled by Englishmen, and the servants of Englishmen whose object is the interest of another country." Those servants, Tone contends, are "acting with uniform force, in a direction too frequently opposite to the true line of [Ireland's] obvious interests." In so locating Ireland's grievances, Tone declares on behalf of the United Irishmen, "We have gone to what we conceive to be the root of the evil." Parliamentary reform, he argues, is the only remedy—"without it, nothing can be done."

The emotional tenor of the document can also be traced to Paine, as the *Declaration* eschews impassioned pleas in favor of appeals to "common sense." Tone posits unity in pursuit of justice and liberty as the natural disposition of all nation-states—particularly the type of republic many nationalists were hoping would manifest in a free

Society of United Irishmen", and we do pledge ourselves to our country, and mutually to each other, that we will steadily support and endeavour, by all due means, to carry into effect the following resolutions:

FIRST RESOLVED—That the weight of English influence on the Government of this country is so great as to require a cordial union among *all the people of Ireland,* to maintain that balance which is essential to the preservation of our liberties and the extension of our commerce.

SECOND—That the sole constitutional mode by which this influence can be opposed is by a complete and radical reform of the representation of the people in Parliament.

THIRD—That no reform is practicable, efficacious, or just, which shall not include Irishmen of every religious persuasion.

Satisfied, as we are, that the intestine divisions among Irishmen have too often given encouragement and impunity to profligate, audacious and corrupt ad-ministrations, in measure which, but for these divisions, they durst not have attempted, we submit our resolutions to the nation as the basis of our political faith. We have gone to what we conceive to be the root of the evil. We have stated what we conceive to be the remedy. With a Parliament thus reformed, everything is easy; without it, nothing can be done. And we do call on, and most earnestly exhort, our countrymen in general to follow our example, and to form similar societies in every quarter of the kingdom for the promotion of constitutional knowledge, the abolition of bigotry in religion and politics, and the equal distribution of the rights of men through all sects and denominations of Irishmen. The people, when thus collected, will feel their own weight, and secure that power which theory has already admitted to be their portion, and to which, if they be not aroused by their present provocation to vindicate it, they deserve to forfeit their pretensions for ever.

SOURCE: *Journals of the House of Commons of the Kingdom of Ireland, 1613-1800,* ed. xvii, pp. 888–889 in original.

Ireland—contending, "The people, when thus collected, will feel their own weight, and secure that power which theory has already admitted to be their portion." The only hint of an emotional undertone in the *Declaration* is an implication of guilt in the closing sentiment, when Tone warns that any Irish citizens who are "not aroused by their present provocation to vindicate it … deserve to forfeit their pretensions" of patriotism.

CRITICAL DISCUSSION

The *Declaration*—and for that matter, the United Irishmen themselves—was afforded little attention outside the Irish nationalist political scene. While no substantial print responses have survived, Thomas Bartlett's biography *Theobald Wolfe Tone* surmises from the letters and journals of various men that there were "unwelcome signs among the Presbyterians that the idea of an alliance of creeds in pursuit of parliamentary reform might prove difficult to attain" and that Catholics also received the United Irishmen's doctrines with "something less than rapture." Bartlett further suggests that, despite this fact, United Irish members seemed unaware that they would "encounter sustained resistance and opposition." This very opposition produced the only other significant response to the group and its declaration when, in 1793, the British government outlawed the organization for colluding with the French, who had just declared war on the empire.

Tone had been appointed to a paid position as secretary for the Roman Catholic Committee in 1792, and following the criminalization of the United Irishmen, his efforts on behalf of the group were conducted clandestinely through that post. From 1793 to 1798, he became increasingly displeased with the growing militancy of the group's activities. Yet Andrew Boyd notes in his article "Wolfe Tone: Republican Hero or Whig Opportunist?" that despite Tone's disassociation with the group—and his lack of interaction with the Irish general public during his active period—he has remained "the most venerated among all those who lost their lives in the cause of Irish independence." Tone's constitutional approach to reform also fell by the wayside, as the United Irishmen emerged from hiding to stage the unsuccessful Irish Rebellion of 1798. While the group dissolved shortly thereafter, its brand of republicanism became the presiding platform for Irish nationalist movements all the way up to the acknowledgement of Irish sovereignty in 1922.

Contemporary scholarship is characterized by a readiness to reassess Tone's political motivations, placing his contributions in tension with the more

Theobald Wolfe
35 / Tone

Born June 20. 1764
Died Nov. 19. 1798

THE IRISH STORE, NEW YORK

Irish Revo-
lutionist

Portrait of Theobald
Wolfe Tone.
© BETTMANN/CORBIS

ambiguous nature of his personal politics. Here again, Boyd provides insight into the "marked hostility to the Catholic Church as an international institution, and [the] ingenuous and ill-informed admiration for the revolutionary French," evident in Tone's journals and letters. Boyd sees these sentiments as countering the anti-sectarian and anti-militant philosophies Tone espoused in public forums. Addressing Tone's continued veneration among Irish nationalists, Boyd concludes that contemporary scholars sympathetic to the nationalist cause "explain away what is clearly Tone's early political ambiguity on the grounds that republicanism is itself an ambiguous philosophy."

BIBLIOGRAPHY

Sources

Bartlett, Thomas. *Theobald Wolfe Tone.* Dublin: Historical Association of Ireland, 1997. Print.

Boyd, Andrew. "Wolfe Tone: Republican Hero or Whig opportunist?" *History Today* 48.6 (1998): 14+. *Academic OneFile.* Web. 21 Aug. 2012.

Smyth, Jim. "Wolfe Tone's Library: The United Irishmen and Enlightenment." *Eighteenth-Century Studies* 45.3 (2012): 423-35. *Academic Search Complete.* Web. 21 Aug. 2012.

Society of United Irishmen of Dublin. *The Declaration, Resolutions, and Constitution, of the Societies of United Irishmen.* Dublin, 1791. *Eighteenth Century Collections Online.* Web. 21 Aug. 2012.

Further Reading

Curtin, Nancy J. *The United Irishmen: Popular Politics in Ulster and Dublin, 1791-1798.* Oxford: Clarendon Press, 1994. Print.

Elliott, Marianne. *Partners in Revolution: The United Irishmen and France.* New Haven: Yale UP, 1982. Print.

"The Irish Rising of 1798." *History Today* 48.6 (1998): 12. *Academic Search Complete.* Web. 21 Aug. 2012.

Thuente, Mary H. *The Harp Re-Strung: The United Irishmen and the Rise of Irish Literary Nationalism.* Syracuse: Syracuse UP, 1994. Print.

Clint Garner

THE END OF THE OLD WORLD

Claude Fauchet

OVERVIEW

The Abbé Claude Fauchet's 1793 journal article "The End of the Old World" chastises the repressive and radical measures of the French revolutionary government and argues for a brighter, religiously informed future. This short article incorporates the language of biblical prophecy and of an impassioned sermon to make its points. Fauchet, a prominent religious and political leader, published the text in *Journal des Amis* ("Journal of Friends"), which he had cofounded earlier in 1793. The article presented readers with a political alternative to the powerful anticlerical and repressive currents of the revolutionary government.

The political situation in France in 1793 was dire. The king had been beheaded in January, and radical Jacobins had come to power and were casting moderate Girondins as enemies of the revolution. Fauchet himself fell out of favor because of his association with Girondin moderates. This fall from political grace, propelled largely by his polemical writings in *Journal des Amis,* proved fatal. The Committee of Public Safety—the government institution in charge of the 1793-94 Reign of Terror against counterrevolutionary opposition—arrested Fauchet, and he was guillotined on October 31, 1793. Thus, "The End of the Old World" did little to sway the revolutionary government from the reactionary violence of the Terror policies that continued and intensified into 1794.

HISTORICAL AND LITERARY CONTEXT

The eighteenth century brought major shifts in political and philosophical thinking to France, culminating with the explosive, rapid changes ushered in by the revolution of 1789. Over the course of the eighteenth century, enlightenment philosophy tore away at institutionalized injustice and inequality. The bourgeois class gained economic power and grew dissatisfied with archaic forms of privilege and exclusion that denied it political power. The situation came to a head during the economic crisis of the late 1780s and with the ensuing political fights over representative government and the origins of power when King Louis XVI convened the Estates-General. Political dissidents stormed the Bastille prison on July 14, 1789, marking the symbolic beginning of revolution and France's near-century-long fight over becoming a modern republic.

"The End of the Old World" appeared as the revolution was moving toward the bloody and repressive period of the Terror. Though only four years removed from relatively moderate demands for equal representation and a constitution based on popular sovereignty that surrounded the meeting of Estates-General, the political situation in France had changed drastically. The revolutionary government had confiscated all church property and then restructured the church with the 1790 *Civil Constitution of the Clergy.* This controversial new law also required members of the clergy to swear a loyalty oath to the new national government, a practice that rendered the church subordinate to that government. The new government still stood on a precarious footing by 1793. Counterrevolutionary loyalists, known popularly as *chouans,* were waging a vicious war in the west of France, and Prussian forces were attacking from the east. In the unstable atmosphere, a divide developed between the radical Jacobin and more moderate Girondin leaders. In 1793 the Jacobins, led by Maximillien Robespierre, took over the government, suspended the new constitution, and began enacting repressive measures to protect the infant republic. These measures included the arrest and execution of those perceived to be a danger to the country. Fauchet's presentation of the apocalypse in "The End of the Old World" responds to the Jacobin rise to power and the repressive measures they enacted.

Fauchet's major influences were the Catholic Church and ethical ideas of enlightenment philosophy. Born into a wealthy provincial family, Fauchet benefited from aristocratic support and rose to prominence in the clergy. A skilled rhetorician, he became a popular clergyman, at one point serving as the king's preacher at Versailles. Revolution brought internal rift to the church in France. Papal leadership condemned revolutionary freedom and equality as threats to church authority, but Fauchet and many other clergy members saw revolution as an opportunity to realign French society with Christ's teachings. Catholic response to enlightenment philosophy was also ambivalent. Again, Rome often officially condemned philosophers such as Jean-Jacques Rousseau and Montesquieu, but Fauchet broke from doctrine and embraced them. He delivered a series of lectures on Rousseau, wrote a eulogy honoring Benjamin

✤ *Key Facts*

Time Period:
Late 18th Century

Movement/Issue:
Counter-French Revolution; Revolutionary Christianity

Place of Publication:
France

Language of Publication:
French

THE SOCIÉTÉ DES AMIS DES NOIRS

Like many of the major European powers and like the newly created United States, France played a major role in the international slave trade of the eighteenth century. Slavery obviously ran counter to the political and ethical thinking of the revolutionary leaders. It was far from consistent for a new government based on liberty, fraternity, and equality to condone the buying and selling of human beings. During the revolutionary years, a group of antislavery leaders formed an abolitionist movement called the *Société des Amis des Noirs* (Society of Friends of Black People) with the aim of ending the slave trade. Fauchet, General Lafayette, the Abbé Grégoire, and the philosopher Nicolas de Condorcet were members.

The abolitionist movement of the 1790s was briefly successful in obtaining an emancipation decree in 1794, but Napoleon Bonaparte reintroduced slavery eight years later after taking control of the French government. Following Napoleon, slavery would remain legal in France for nearly another half-century. In 1848 France underwent another revolution that established what is known as the Second Republic. Though this second attempt at republican government in France was short-lived (1848-52), France abolished slavery again, this time permanently, in 1848.

Franklin, and cited Montesquieu when he equated revolutionary fraternity with the Gospel. In her essay "The Revolutionary Bishops and the Philosophes," Ruth Graham writes, "Fauchet praised philosophy for recalling men to the principles of religion."

Fauchet's writing ignited vehement Jacobin resistance. He had walked a tenuous line between the Jacobins and Girondins, and in 1792 he broke with the Jacobins. This invited charges that he sided with the moderate Girondins, so he was already a target of Jacobin suspicion when he cofounded *Journal des Amis*. "The End of the Old World" and his other writings in the journal intensified scrutiny and ultimately led to his arrest and execution. His aspiration of uniting church teachings with republican government bears little resemblance to modern France's insistent and fundamental separation of church and state.

THEMES AND STYLE

For having a title that is so clearly apocalyptic, "The End of the Old World" offers a surprisingly optimistic vision of the future. It does so even as it states that "we are in the most terrible crisis of humanity." Fauchet presents this crisis as a "second travail of nature." As terribly painful as this second birth was, Fauchet reassures readers that the coming days will redeem the current difficulties: "Yes, the universe will be free … the age of reason for humanity draws near." Fauchet returns frequently to this message of hope. In the final paragraph, he also displays his desire that philosophy and religion work in tandem as he brazenly accuses the

revolutionary government of incompetence: "Nothing is more opposed to philosophy than those domineering and pretentious legislative heads, who have not even the elements of morality and the principles of common sense."

Stylistically, "The End of the Old World" resembles biblical prophecy in many ways. The majority of its sentences are in the future tense: "Society *will* embrace nature … we *shall* be happy with all things. Fraternity *will* unite the human family, and equality of rights *will* finally make man king of earth." This prophetic style creates a tone of biblical authority, as Fauchet speaks as if he knows definitively what the future holds. His assertive voice and his message about a better future provide reassurance in the midst of the national uncertainty. It is difficult, however, to gauge whether readers were responsive to this message of hope while living through such difficult and frightening times.

Fauchet's language is charged with the urgent vehemence of revolutionary leadership and passionate preaching. The content alone already carries a high emotional charge that Fauchet's rhetoric intensifies. There are few simple descriptive sentences. Fauchet is either promising ideal conditions in the future ("It is universal war that is going to bring to birth the peace of the universe") or accusing the Jacobin leaders of incompetence and challenging their revolutionary character ("with irreligion, you have the very breakdown of social values: with habitual failure to think, comes inability to make stable laws and form a government"). This combination of prophetic promise and dangerous political polemic creates an emotional force perhaps intended to galvanize resistance to the extreme Jacobin positions.

CRITICAL DISCUSSION

Initial response to Fauchet took place in the political sphere, the result of his talk of the disasters of war, the fate of the republic, and the schism between moderate and radical aspirations for the revolutionary. Fauchet had been a visible player in revolutionary debates. He had cofounded the debate society called the *Cercle Social des Amis de la Vérité* (Social Circle of the Friends of Truth) and had developed associations with members of the Girondins. His inflammatory writings, such as "The End of the Old World" in *Journal des Amis*, reinforced this label and allowed Jacobin enemies to depict him as an enemy and a threat to the nation. Executed for his association with the rival faction in October 1793, Fauchet failed to unify Christian religion and enlightenment ethics as he had hoped. The Jacobins remained in power well into 1794, and the explicitly Christian form of democracy Fauchet envisioned was never realized in France.

Because it was part of a wave of similar writing and because it has remained relatively obscure, gauging the long-term impact of "The End of the Old World" is methodologically difficult. With the

torrent of the new political press in the early 1790s, it is nearly impossible to determine exactly how this one-page article influenced the millions of hearts and minds involved in the revolution. It is certain, however, that Fauchet's ideal version of a religiously informed democracy did not come to pass in the 1790s. France would not establish a stable republic until the period following the Franco-Prussian War of 1870-71. Furthermore, the modern French republic has moved away from the comingling of religion and politics that Fauchet foresaw and sought to create in 1793. In 1905 France adopted a law on the separation of church and state that remains in effect today. Still, "The End of the Old World" retains its historical pertinence because of the perspective it provides into the complex relationship between the church and the revolutionary government.

Current scholarship on "The End of the Old World" generally appears as part of more general projects. A handful of article-length studies on religion during the revolution examine the work as an element of a broader question, and Norman Ravitch discusses it in his essay in *Journal of the American Academy of Religion*. Such studies delve into the complex relationship between the church and the dramatic political shifts in France in the early 1790s and challenge simplistic historical understandings of politics and religion. Not all priests opposed the revolution, just as today it is impossible to neatly align an individual's religious affiliation with a set of automatically corresponding political positions.

BIBLIOGRAPHY

Sources

Fauchet, Claude. "The End of the Old World." *The Press in the French Revolution: A Selection of Documents Taken from the Press of the Revolution for the Years 1789-1794.* Ed. John Gilchrist and W. J. Murray. New York: St. Martin's, 1971. 262-63. Print.

Graham, Ruth. "The Revolutionary Bishops and the Philosophes." *Eighteenth-Century Studies* 16.2 (1982-83). 117-40. Print.

Langois, Claude. "Religion, culte ou opinion religieuse: La politique des révolutionaires." *Revue Française de Sociologie* 30.3-4 (1989): 471-96. *JSTOR.* 19 Oct. 2012. Web.

Lyon, Janet. *Manifestos: Provocations of the Modern.* Ithaca: Cornell UP, 1999. Print.

Ravitch, Norman. "The Abbé Fauchet: Romantic Religion during the French Revolution." *Journal of the American Academy of Religion* 42.2 (1974): 247-62. Print.

Further Reading

Fauchet, Claude. *Oeuvres.* Geneva: Slatkine, 1969. Print.

———. "A Discourse by M. L'Abbe Fauchet, on the Liberty of France." Trans. William Harvey. London: W. Chalken, 1790. *Eighteenth Century Collections Online.* 19 Oct. 2012. Web.

Huet, Marie-Hélène. "Twilight of the Gods." *A New History of French Literature.* Ed. Denis Hollier. Cambridge: Harvard UP, 2001. Print.

Jones, Colin. *The Cambridge Illustrated History of France.* 2nd ed. Cambridge: Cambridge UP, 1999. Print.

Robinson, J.H., ed. *The Civil Constitution of the Clergy: July 12, 1790.* Hanover Historical Texts. 19 Oct. 2012. Web.

Nicholas Snead

POLITICS OF OBEDIENCE

The Discourse of Voluntary Servitude

Étienne de la Boétie

OVERVIEW

Composed between 1552 and 1553 by French writer Étienne de la Boétie, *Politics of Obedience: The Discourse of Voluntary Servitude* (*Discours de la servitude volontaire*) theorizes that individuals permit themselves to be ruled by tyrants out of habit and due to the hope for personal gain. La Boétie argues that this permission can be revoked through collective non-violent refusal to acquiesce to the tyrant's demands, which will then result in the tyrant's fall. For La Boétie, such refusal is born of the embrace of reason and personal liberty, as well as of a clear vision of how the pageantry of the state is designed to reinforce the individual's habit of subjugation. Written at a time of political and religious upheaval in French history, *The Discourse of Voluntary Servitude* indirectly addresses the concerns of Huguenot Protestant groups frustrated by oppression from the Catholic-dominated government but is primarily a more generalized analysis of the nature of civil obedience throughout Western political history. For this reason, the work enjoyed several resurgences of popular interest in the centuries that followed—most notably during the French Revolution.

Although not widely distributed during La Boétie's lifetime, *The Discourse of Voluntary Servitude* circulated in sympathetic French intellectual circles and earned the author a strong intellectual reputation at a young age, especially in his native Périgord region of southern France. Scholars speculate that he never officially published *The Discourse of Voluntary Servitude* because of its radical nature and out of interest for his professional career. It was anonymously distributed in pamphlet form as a piece of Huguenot propaganda, and many scholars consider it to be a foundational text of French political thought, various civil disobedience movements, and pacifist anarchism. A portion of the text was first published anonymously in the Huguenot journal *Reveille-Matin des Francois* (1574). The first full version, under the title *Against One,* appeared in a collection of Huguenot essays in 1576. In his first edition of *Essays* (1580), Michel de Montaigne included *The Discourse of Voluntary Servitude* and declared La Boétie its author.

HISTORICAL AND LITERARY CONTEXT

The Discourse of Voluntary Servitude responds to a buildup of political and religious strife on the eve of the French Wars of Religion (1562-98). The strife was primarily due to the growing strength of Calvinist French groups, known collectively as the Huguenots, who opposed Roman Catholicism as the official state religion. Fearing the social and political upheaval gripping other European nations with similar religious conflicts, the French government moved to suppress the Huguenots by declaring them to be radicals and heretics and by blocking them from government office. The Huguenots responded by launching a propaganda campaign against what they perceived to be tyrannical action by the French government. In 1562 the conflict turned violent in the Massacre of Vassy.

Liberal French universities were a crucial intellectual source for the Huguenot movement, influencing noted Protestant intellectuals such as John Calvin. As a student at the University of Orleans from 1548 to

LA BOÉTIE'S DEATH, MONTAIGNE'S LEGACY

Étienne de la Boétie died unexpectedly at the age of thirty-two in 1563. Prior to his death, he named Michel de Montaigne the executer of his estate and left all of his works—including *The Discourse of Voluntary Servitude,* which had yet to be published—to Montaigne to do with as he pleased. Some scholars argue that Montaigne intended to publish *The Discourse of Voluntary Servitude* with his own essays in 1571 but held back because of the work's problematic association with the radical Huguenot cause. Other scholars speculate that *The Discourse of Voluntary Servitude* was actually written by Montaigne but published in La Boétie's name to preserve Montaigne's political reputation. In any case, Montaigne repeatedly lowered the age at which he claimed La Boétie had first written *The Discourse of Voluntary Servitude* from eighteen—resulting in the long-believed 1548 composition date—to sixteen in an effort to portray the work as representative of La Boétie's renounced radical youth.

Key Facts

Time Period:
Mid-16th Century

Movement/Issue:
Civil disobedience;
French Revolution;
Huguenot Protantism

Place of Publication:
France

Language of Publication:
French

PRIMARY SOURCE

POLITICS OF OBEDIENCE: THE DISCOURSE OF VOLUNTARY SERVITUDE

...The fundamental political question is why do people obey a government. The answer is that they tend to enslave themselves, to let themselves be governed by tyrants. Freedom from servitude comes not from violent action, but from the refusal to serve. Tyrants fall when the people withdraw their support.

...Our nature is such that the common duties of human relationship occupy a great part of the course of our life. It is reasonable to love virtue, to esteem good deeds, to be grateful for good from whatever source we may receive it, and, often, to give up some of our comfort in order to increase the honor and advantage of some man whom we love and who deserves it. Therefore, if the inhabitants of a country have found some great personage who has shown rare foresight in protecting them in an emergency, rare boldness in defending them, rare solicitude in governing them, and if, from that point on, they contract the habit of obeying him and depending on him to such an extent that they grant him certain prerogatives, I fear that such a procedure is not prudent, inasmuch as they remove him from a position in which he was doing good and advance him to a dignity in which he may do evil. Certainly while he continues to manifest good will one need fear no harm from a man who seems to be generally well disposed.

But O good Lord! What strange phenomenon is this? What name shall we give it? What is the nature of this misfortune? What vice is it, or, rather, what degradation? To see an endless multitude of people not merely obeying, but driven to servility? Not ruled, but tyrannized over? These wretches have no wealth, no kin, nor wife nor children, not even life itself that they can call their own. They suffer plundering, wantonness, cruelty, not from an army, not from a barbarian horde, on account of whom they must shed their blood and sacrifice their lives, but from a single man;

1553, La Boétie was exposed to Huguenot ideas and participated in liberal dialogues concerning Huguenot subjects in his training as a law student. Although he never converted to Protestantism, he urged toleration for the Huguenots and supported the Edict of January issued by Michel de L'Hopital, then chancellor of France, granting Protestants certain freedoms in 1562. He almost certainly wrote *The Discourse of Voluntary Servitude* in his time at the University of Orleans, not, as was long believed, at the age of eighteen in 1548. He never publically acknowledged his authorship in his subsequent professional life as a judge and a member of the Bordeaux Parliament.

The Discourse of Voluntary Servitude draws primarily on works of classical antiquity for inspiration, notably Homer's *Iliad* (c. 750 BCE) and various Greek and Roman classics, including the works of Xenophon and Plutarch (which La Boétie translated as a student) and Tacitus. The text was also heavily influenced by the works of Niccolo Machiavelli, including *The Prince* (1532), in its treatment of the social and political relationship between governments and the governed. La Boétie was also inspired by the contemporary Pléiade poets—Pierre de Ronsard, Jean Dorat, and Jean-Antoine de Baïf—and by his instructor at the University of Orleans, Anneda Bourg, a future Huguenot martyr.

The Discourse of Voluntary Servitude had a significant impact on La Boétie's contemporaries and has influenced centuries of political intellectuals. Most notably, Michel de Montaigne's essay *On Friendship* (1588) concerns Montaigne's relationship with La Boétie, a connection founded upon Montaigne's appreciation of *The Discourse of Voluntary Servitude*. La Boétie himself also drew on the work in his later, more conservative writings concerning the Edict of January. Numerous intellectual figures of the French Revolution referenced *The Discourse of Voluntary Servitude*, as did nineteenth-century advocates of civil disobedience such as Leo Tolstoy and Henry David Thoreau. In the twentieth century, German anarchist Gustav Landauer referred to *The Discourse of Voluntary Servitude* in his work *Die Revolution* (1919), and Dutch pacifist-anarchist Barthelemy de Ligt translated the work into Dutch in 1933. Many of the themes in *The Discourse of Voluntary Servitude* are present in Jean-Jacques Rousseau's *Social Contract* (1767), the *Preamble* to the U.S. Constitution (1783), and the work of political philosopher Hannah Arendt.

THEMES AND STYLE

The central theme of *The Discourse of Voluntary Servitude* is that individuals voluntarily submit to the will of tyrants through their continued support of tyrannical regimes and that this support can be voluntarily and nonviolently withdrawn. La Boétie writes, "I should like merely to understand how it happens that so many men ... suffer under a single tyrant who has no other power than the power they give him ... who could do them absolutely no injury unless they preferred to put

not from a Hercules nor from a Samson, but from a single little man. Too frequently this same little man is the most cowardly and effeminate in the nation, a stranger to the powder of battle and hesitant on the sands of the tournament; not only without energy to direct men by force, but with hardly enough virility to bed with a common woman! Shall we call subjection to such a leader cowardice? Shall we say that those who serve him are cowardly and faint-hearted? If two, if three, if four, do not defend themselves from the one, we might call that circumstance surprising but nevertheless conceivable. In such a case one might be justified in suspecting a lack of courage. But if a hundred, if a thousand endure the caprice of a single man, should we not rather say that they lack not the courage but the desire to rise against him, and that such an attitude indicates indifference rather than cowardice? When not a hundred, not a thousand men, but a hundred provinces, a thousand cities, a million men, refuse to assail a single man from whom the kindest treatment received is the infliction of serfdom and slavery, what shall we call that? Is it cowardice? Of course there is in every vice inevitably some limit beyond which one cannot go. Two, possibly ten, may fear one; but when a thousand, a million men, a thousand cities, fail to protect themselves against the domination of one man, this cannot be called cowardly, for cowardice does not sink to such a depth, any more than valor can be termed the effort of one individual to scale a fortress, to attack an army, or to conquer a kingdom. What monstrous vice, then, is this which does not even deserve to be called cowardice, a vice for which no term can be found vile enough, which nature herself disavows and our tongues refuse to name?

SOURCE: *Politics of Obedience: The Discourse of Voluntary Servitude.* Trans. Harry Kurz. Auburn, AL: Ludwig von Mises Institute, 2008. 39, 41–43. Copyright © 2008 by Ludwig von Mises Institute. All rights reserved. Reproduced by permission.

up with him rather than contradict him." Regarding the nonviolent withdrawal of this support, he suggests, "But if not one thing is yielded to [the tyrants], if, without any violence they are singly not obeyed, they become naked and undone and as nothing." Despite the apparent ease of this voluntary withdrawal of support, La Boétie acknowledges that few individuals are capable of exercising it because of their habitual familiarity with a state of subjugation or their hopes of personal gain under the regime. For the author, this state of subjugation is "quite natural the condition into which [the individuals] are born" and can only be overcome by the triumph of individual reason through the exercise of personal liberty. *The Discourse of Voluntary Servitude* largely avoids commenting on the contemporary political-religious situation in France and only makes one direct reference to the French government, an arguably satirical statement expressing awe for the pageantry of the French monarchy.

La Boétie's rhetorical strategy in *The Discourse of Voluntary Servitude* hinges on the use of rhetorical questions (e.g., "Who could believe the following...?") and powerful, sometimes graphic analogies to illustrate his points. One example is his description of the state of individuals who do not realize they are voluntarily consenting to tyranny: "A people enslaves itself, cuts its own throat, when, having a choice between being vassals and being free men, it deserts its liberties and takes on the yoke." La Boétie also makes use of numerous classical allusions to contextualize his points, such as the assertion that Marcus Junius Brutus and Gauis Cassius Longinus were successful in eliminating servitude with the murder of Julius Caesar in their attempt to restore liberty.

On the whole, the language in *The Discourse of Voluntary Servitude* is speculative, abstract, and deductive—qualities that set it apart from other works primarily concerned with advancing the Huguenot cause. Scholars suggest that this academic-style prose reflects La Boétie's experience as a law student at the University of Orleans. The lack of stridency in the language of *The Discourse of Voluntary Servitude* has contributed to the work's reputation as a timeless milestone in the history of political discourse, with the prose seemingly more comparable to a work from the eighteenth or nineteenth century.

CRITICAL DISCUSSION

Already well-known in influential French intellectual circles by the time of its attributed publication in 1576, *The Discourse of Voluntary Servitude* provoked a strong reactionary backlash from French conservatives and the pro-Catholic factions of the French government. Even the Huguenots responsible for its distribution were careful to distance themselves from La Boétie's more radical assertions concerning the limits of government authority. In an effort to protect his friend's reputation in the midst of the French Wars of Religion, Montaigne claimed *The Discourse of Voluntary Servitude* was only a rhetorical exercise on La Boétie's part,

Detail of the St. Bartholomew's Day Massacre by François Dubois. Pirated editions of *The Discourse of Voluntary Servitude* were used to foment Huguenot resistance after the massacre in 1572. ALFREDO DAGLI ORTI/ THE ART ARCHIVE AT ART RESOURCE, NY

Huguenot monarchomach works, such as Francois Hotman's *Franco-Gallia* (1573).

Scholarship on *The Discourse of Voluntary Servitude* continues to focus on La Boétie's relationship to Montaigne and also to Machiavelli, with Émile Bréhier arguing in *Histoire de la Philosophie* (1967) the importance of distinguishing between Machiavelli's "cynical realism" and La Boétie's "juridical idealism." Rothbard also points out how La Boétie's emphasis on the role of voluntary consent to governance has failed to influence U.S. foreign policy in its analysis of popular domestic resistance to communist regimes. *The Discourse of Voluntary Servitude* continues to be a foundational text in the study of modern political science.

BIBLIOGRAPHY

Sources

Allen, J.W. *A History of Political Thought in the Sixteenth Century.* New York: Barnes and Noble, 1960. Print.

Bizer, Marc. *Homer and the Politics of Authority in Renaissance France.* Oxford: Oxford UP, 2011. Print.

Bréhier, Émile. *Histoire de la Philosophie: Moyen Age et Renaissance.* Paris: PUF, 1967. Print.

Kurz, Harry. "The Actuality of Étienne de la Boétie." *Books Abroad* 23.2 (1949): 127-28. *JSTOR.* Web. 21 Sept. 2012.

Montaigne, Michel de. *The Complete Essays.* Trans. M. A. Screech. London: Penguin, 1991. Print.

Rothbard, Murray N. Introduction. *The Politics of Obedience: The Discourse of Voluntary Servitude.* By Étienne de la Boétie. Trans. Harry Kurz. New York: Free Life Editions, 1975. Print.

Sibley, Mulford Q., ed. "Étienne de la Boétie: Voluntary Servitude." *The Quiet Battle: Writings on the Theory and Practice of Non-violent Resistance.* Chicago: Quadrangle Books, 1963. Print.

Further Reading

Boétie, Étienne de la. *Anti-Dictator.* Trans. Harry Kurz. New York: Columbia UP, 1942. Print.

Gunn, Richard, and Adrian Wilding. "Holloway, La Boétie, Hegel." *Journal of Classical Sociology* 12.2 (2012): 173-90. Print.

Imbruglia, Giroiamo. "Two Principles of Despotism: Diderot between Machiavelli and de la Boétie." *History of European Ideas* 34.4 (2008): 490-99. Print.

Keokane, Nannerl O. "The Radical Humanism of Étienne de la Boétie." *Journal of the History of Ideas* 38.1 (1977): 119-30. *JSTOR.* Web. 21 Sept. 2012.

Moser, Patrick. "Montaigne's Literary Patrons: The Case of La Boétie." *Sixteenth Century Journal* 31.2 (2000): 381-97. *JSTOR.* Web. 21 Sept. 2012.

Schaefer, David Lewis, ed. *Freedom over Servitude: Montaigne, La Boétie, and On Voluntary Servitude.* Westport: Greenwood, 1998. Print.

and, in practice, the author complied with all laws under which he was born. Montaigne also later criticized *The Discourse of Voluntary Servitude* for encouraging a tyranny "of the individual" in which competing individual arrogances lead to general political chaos, the only solution to which is an absolute monarchy.

Many scholars have argued that *The Discourse of Voluntary Servitude* foreshadows many of the prominent political themes of the eighteenth-century Enlightenment rationalist movement, specifically, according to J.W. Allen in *A History of Political Thought in the Sixteenth Century* (1960), with its emphasis on "the natural liberty, equality and fraternity of man." The work was not widely disseminated until the close of the eighteenth century with the onset of the French Revolution, and then again in 1852 during the regime of Napoleon III. In this regard, Murray N. Rothbard argues in the introduction to the 1975 Free Life Edition of *The Politics of Obedience* that La Boétie was "a founder of modern political philosophy in France" and that *The Discourse of Voluntary Servitude* should be separated from other

Craig Barnes

THE REBEL MANIFESTO

Jabez L. M. Curry

OVERVIEW

Composed by Jabez L.M. Curry and issued as a joint resolution of the Confederate Congress, *The Rebel Manifesto* (1864), or *Address of Congress to the People of the Confederate States,* defends the Confederate cause in the U.S. Civil War, condemns the United States for aggression, and encourages the southern populace to remain united in their support of the Confederacy. Drafted in December 1863 by the provisional Confederate Congress, *The Rebel Manifesto* was distributed throughout the American South in early 1864. The resolution was also published in some northern newspapers and sent overseas to France, Belgium, and Great Britain. While essentially a reiteration of the original southern case for secession and a catalog of further grievances against the North, the timing of the distribution of *The Rebel Manifesto* speaks to the Confederate government's interest in influencing the 1864 U.S. presidential election and ongoing efforts to win diplomatic recognition from Europe. Confederate President Jefferson Davis and Confederate Congress members hoped the resolution would reinvigorate the Confederate war effort and convince the northern public that the South was determined to fight on in the face of losses, thereby increasing support for peace negotiations and diplomatic recognition.

The Rebel Manifesto had little effect on public or governmental opinion in the North or in Europe. Abraham Lincoln defeated Democratic presidential nominee and presumed peace advocate George B. McClellan in the 1864 presidential election, and European governments continued to withhold official recognition of the Confederate States of America. A subsequent and similar work, *Manifesto of the Confederate Congress,* published in June of 1864, received some editorial attention from northern newspapers but only garnered strong rebuttals. *The Rebel Manifesto* remains an important historical document for its lucid presentation of the southern case for secession.

HISTORICAL AND LITERARY CONTEXT

The roots of *The Rebel Manifesto* lay in the Confederate government's political understanding of states' rights in the context of U.S. history. In the Confederate view, each state retains the right to withdraw from the United States if it is no longer in that state's best interest to remain a part of the Union. With the election of Republican Abraham Lincoln, southern political officials no longer believed their political, social, and economic interests would be sufficiently respected by the U.S. government. They cited the doctrine of states' rights as grounds for their secession and united to form the Confederate States of America in 1861. Lincoln declared the secession to be illegal and threatened to take military action to reunite the states. This conflict led to the outbreak of the U.S. Civil War.

By the time *The Rebel Manifesto* was drafted in late 1863, the war had caused great loss of life on both sides. The South appeared to be in the weaker position after military defeats at the battles of Gettysburg, Vicksburg, and Chattanooga and with the Confederate capital, Richmond, threatened by Union forces. Confederate leaders remained hopeful of a negotiated peace that might preserve the Confederacy but believed they would have to convince the northern public that the South could continue the war for

✣ **Key Facts**

Time Period:
Mid-19th Century

Movement/Issue:
Secession; U.S. Civil War; Foreign recognition of the Confederacy

Place of Publication:
United States (Confederate States of America)

Language of Publication:
English

CONFEDERATE DIPLOMACY IN FRANCE

In addition to sending *The Rebel Manifesto* to France and Belgium early in 1864, the Confederate government shifted the focus of its propaganda efforts in Europe away from Britain and toward France after officials came to believe the British government was too fundamentally devoted to the abolitionist cause. At this time, several Confederate naval ships were undergoing repairs in French ports, and the Confederate government hoped to buy more ships for the upcoming year.

The French government of Napoleon III had initially expressed support for the Confederacy, but when faced with the threat of war with the United States and the refusal of the British government to recognize the Confederacy, Napoleon III ultimately chose to keep France neutral. However, he did keep Confederate diplomatic hopes for French recognition alive through 1865. This refusal proved to be not only disappointing but damaging to the Confederate cause, with anecdotal scholarly evidence pointing toward a Confederate hope that the French navy might intervene on behalf of the Confederate Army against the U.S. Navy, much as it had on behalf of the Continental Army against the British navy during the American Revolution.

PRIMARY SOURCE

THE REBEL MANIFESTO

CAUSE OF THE WAR.

Compelled by a long series of oppressive and tyrannical acts, culminating at last in the selection of a President and Vice-President by a party confessedly sectional and hostile to the South and her institutions, these States withdrew from the former Union, and formed a new Confederate alliance, as an independent Government, based on the proper relations of labor and capital. This step was taken reluctantly, by constraint, and after the exhaustion of every measure that was likely to secure us from interference with our property, equality in the Union, or exemption from submission to an alien Government. The Southern States claimed only the unrestricted enjoyment of the rights guaranteed by the Constitution. Finding, by painful and protracted experience, that this was persistently denied, we determined to separate from those enemies, who had manifested the inclination and ability to impoverish and destroy us; we fell back upon the right for which the colonies maintained the war of the revolution, and which our heroic forefathers asserted to be clear and inalienable. The unanimity and zeal with which the separation was undertaken and perfected, finds no parallel in history. The people rose en masse to assert their liberties and protect their menaced rights. There never was before such universality of conviction among any people on any question involving so serious and so thorough a change of political and international relations. This grew out of the clearness of the right so to act, and the certainty of the perils of further association with the North. The change was so wonderful, so rapid, so contrary to universal history, that many fail to see that all has been done in the logical consequence of principles, which are the highest testimony to the wisdom of our fathers, and the best illustration of the correctness of those principles. This Government is a child of law instead of

years at huge cost to the North. The candidacy of McClellan seemed to offer the most hope for a negotiated peace, as Lincoln was adamant during previous negotiations that the Confederate states must unconditionally return to the Union to end hostilities. Confederate leaders also hoped that a European power such as Britain or France might still be willing to recognize the Confederate States of America and mediate a peace between the North and the South, if not intervene militarily in the South's favor. *The Rebel Manifesto* was drafted and distributed in the interest of these concerns and to further motivate Confederates to continue the war.

The Rebel Manifesto includes many themes present in John C. Calhoun's *Southern Address* (1850) and in the speeches of Alexander H. Stephens. The work falls into a tradition of Confederate propaganda efforts, including presidential proclamations, newspaper editorials, schoolbook publications, political sermons, and women's patriotic societies. This tradition also includes European propagandist publication efforts such as Henry Hotze's *Index*.

The Rebel Manifesto's subsequent literary influence was minor, with the most direct influence in the subsequent and similar *Manifesto of the Confederate Congress* by Virginia Confederate Congressman William C. River. The themes of the document are also echoed in President Davis's *Address to the Soldiers* (1864). *The Rebel Manifesto* played a small role in the literary history of the Civil War and is today largely unknown outside of academic circles.

THEMES AND STYLE

The central themes of *The Rebel Manifesto* are northern fault for the war, the righteousness of the Confederate cause, the U.S. government's refusal to engage in negotiations, and exhortations to Confederates to continue fighting. The address claims that secession was "compelled by a long series of oppressive and tyrannical acts, culminating at last in the selection of a President … hostile to the South and her institutions." Curry goes on to state that "the war in which we are engaged was wickedly, and against all our protests and most earnest efforts to the contrary, forced upon us." The work charges that "the course of the Federal Government has proved that it did not desire peace, and would not consent to it on any terms that we could possibly concede" and repeatedly exhorts "our fellow-citizens to be of good cheer, and spare no labor nor sacrifices that may be necessary to enable us to win the campaign." Curry also emphasizes that, despite military setbacks, the Confederate cause is not lost and includes an extensive list of crimes committed by the U.S. government.

The rhetorical strategy of *The Rebel Manifesto* relies on emotional appeals to history, fear, and solidarity in the face of a cruel enemy. Composed in

sedition, of right instead of violence, of deliberation instead of insurrection. Its early life was attended by no anarchy, no rebellion, no suspension of authority, no social disorders, no lawless disturbances. Sovereignty was not for one moment in abeyance. The utmost conservatism marked every proceeding and public act. The object was "to do what was necessary, and no more; and to do that with the utmost temperance and prudence."

...

WE HAVE NO ALTERNATIVE

but to do our duty. We combat for property, homes, the honor of our wives, the future of our children, the preservation of our fair land from pollution, and to avert a doom which we can read, both in the threats of our enemies and the acts of oppression we have alluded to in this address.

The situation is grave, but furnishes no just excuse for despondency. Instead of harsh criticisms on the Government and our Generals; instead of bewailing the failure to accomplish impossibilities, we should rather be grateful, humbly and profoundly, to a benignant Providence, for the results that have rewarded our labors. Remembering the disproportion in population in military and naval resources, and the deficiency of skilled labor in the South, our accomplishments have surpassed those recorded of any people in the annals of the world. There is no just reason for hopelessness or fear. Since the outbreak of the war the South has lost the nominal possession of the Mississippi River and fragments of her territory, but Federal occupancy is not conquest. The fires of patriotism still burn unquenchably in the breasts of those who are subject to foreign domination. We yet have in our uninterrupted control a territory which, according to past progress, will require the enemy ten years to overrun....

SOURCE: *New York Times,* February 25, 1864.

the first-person collective, the "we" of the work is intended to engage the southern audience in the Confederate struggle. Historical appeals, such as an account of past U.S. government condemnations of British abolitionist activities, are intended to show the U.S. government as hypocritical. In an attempt to unite the white populace against a common threat, Curry repeatedly invokes the fear of an emancipated slave population, claiming, "President Lincoln has sought to convert the South into a St. Domingo, by appealing to the Cupidity, lusts, ambition and ferocity of the slave" and that a "cruel foe seeks to reduce our fathers and mothers, our wives and children to abject slavery." The text offers a grim portrayal of southern life in the aftermath of a Confederate defeat, speculating, "We would be made the slaves of our slaves— hewers ... [on] whom God has stamped indelibly the marks of physical and intellectual inferiority."

In keeping with its emotional rhetorical appeals, the language of *The Rebel Manifesto* is often hyperbolic and contains numerous allusions to wounded sentiment. For example, "We charge the responsibility of this war upon the United States. They are accountable for the blood and havoc and ruin it has caused. For such a war we were not prepared." The Confederates accuse the Union Army of being a "hireling soldiery" of "paupers, criminals or emigrants" and assures all "fellow-citizens" that "nothing short of your utter subjugation ... will satisfy the demands of the North." In contrast, the efforts of the Confederate government are presented in a reasonable tone: "We can only repeat the desire of the people for peace, and our readiness to accept terms consistent with the honor and integrity and independence of the States."

CRITICAL DISCUSSION

Critical reception to *The Rebel Manifesto* was minimal domestically and abroad. As a joint resolution of the Confederate Congress, it was signed by nearly all of its members but was completed at the close of the congressional term, with Curry having lost his reelection bid. It was reprinted in southern newspapers as well as the *New York Times.* The closely related *Manifesto of the Confederate Congress* received more attention, appearing in the *Richmond Whig* and the *Daily Dispatch* in June 1864. The *New York Times* printed a rebuttal to the *Manifesto of the Confederate Congress* on June 3, 1864, claiming, "Its literary character is contemptible" and "They cannot expect us ... to put this construction upon their acts.... We have no fear of the verdict of the future."

The Rebel Manifesto and the *Manifesto of the Confederate Congress* received little scholarly attention in the decades following the war. E. Merton Coulter notes in *The Confederate States of America, 1861-1865* (1950) that the June manifesto was notable because it "still seemed to prize the good opinion of Europe

and to desire that European nations understand how determined the Confederates were to win their independence." He refers to the work as a "manly peace manifesto" passed in the face of Lincoln's reelection and notes how the Confederate Congress made "ringing speeches" in addition to issuing *The Rebel Manifesto* in February 1864. Another scholar noted *The Rebel Manifesto*'s emphasis on encouraging Confederates who had tired of the war to continue supporting the cause—especially voters who had chosen not to reelect Curry.

Contemporary scholarship on *The Rebel Manifesto* increased with the publication of Wilfred Buck Yearns's *The Confederate Congress* (1960). Regarding the 1864 U.S. presidential election, Yearns asserts that the Confederate Congress misinterpreted the peace platform aspect of McClellan's candidacy and "failed to realize that it presupposed reunion and was not a declaration of peace at any price." He writes that the Confederates "rationalized" Lincoln's reelection "as a triumph of political chicanery rather than any positive expression of public opinion." As a result, Yearns

argues, the Confederate government believed the North was closer to seeking peace than was actually the case. Yearns also explores how the various peace-seeking elements of the Confederate Congress were unable to achieve their goals. He asserts that *The Rebel Manifesto* represented a compromise between these groups and other, more hawkish elements of the Confederate government.

BIBLIOGRAPHY

Sources

"Address of Congress to the People of the Confederate States, Joint Resolution in Relation to the War." *Southern Historical Society Papers* 1.1 (1876): 23. *American Periodicals Series.* Web. 31 Oct. 2012.

Coulter, E. Merton. *The Confederate States of America, 1861-1865.* Baton Rouge: Louisiana State UP, 1950. Print.

"Curry, Jabez L.M." *Encyclopedia of the Confederacy.* Vol. 1. Ed. Richard N. Currant. New York: Simon & Schuster, 1993. Print.

"Manifesto of the Confederate Congress." *Daily Dispatch* 15 June 1864. *Perseus Digital Library.* Web. 31 Oct. 2012.

"*The Rebel Manifesto* and the *Declaration of Independence*." *New York Times* 3 July 1864. *ProQuest.* Web. 1 Nov. 2012.

Yearns, Wilfred Buck. *The Confederate Congress.* Athens: Georgia UP, 2010. Print.

Further Reading

Davis, William C. *Look Away! A History of the Confederate States of America.* New York: Free Press, 2002. Print.

Dumond, Dwight Lowell, ed. *Southern Editorials on Secession.* Gloucester: American Historical Association, 1964. Print.

Eaton, Clement. *A History of the Southern Confederacy.* New York: Macmillan, 1954. Print.

Harwell, Richard B., ed. "President Davis' Address to the Soldiers." *The Confederate Reader.* New York: Longman's, Green, 1957. 249-52. Print.

Hubbard, Charles M. *The Burden of Confederate Diplomacy.* Knoxville: Tennessee UP, 1998. Print.

Vandiver, Frank E., and Jon L. Wakelyn, eds. *Biographical Dictionary of the Confederacy.* London: Greenwood, 1977. Print.

Craig Barnes

THE RED MAN'S REBUKE

Simon Pokagon

✥ **Key Facts**

Time Period:
Late 19th Century

Movement/Issue:
Native American rights;
Colonialism

Place of Publication:
United States

**Language of
Publication:**
English

OVERVIEW

At the 1893 World's Fair Columbian Exposition in Chicago, Potawatomi Indian Simon Pokagon sold a booklet titled *The Red Man's Rebuke* (later printed as *The Red Man's Greeting*), which decries what the author describes as white America's violent and deceitful treatment of American Indians. The theme of the fair was to celebrate the four-hundredth anniversary of Christopher Columbus's arrival in the Americas as well as to demonstrate American civilization and technological advancement. Pokagon's *Rebuke* is a reply to both the anniversary of "discovery" and to America's self-satisfied narrative of progress, which was in evidence in many ways at the exposition. Letter press printed on birch bark, the sixteen-page tract condemns the negative treatment of Native Americans by Europeans, primarily offering a lament for the irremediable loss of native culture and life. Pokagon closes with a call to American Indians to renounce the white man's ways.

SIMON POKAGON: BUREAUCRATIC HUSTLER

Simon Pokagon represented the Catholic Potawatomi community in Michigan until the early 1880s, mostly in its legal claims against the U.S. government. As the first chair of the Business Committee of the Michigan and Indiana Potawatomi tribes, he advocated hiring private lawyers, a move that earned the Potawatomis $39,000 compensation as back payment from an unfavorable 1866 congressional resolution. Unsatisfied with even that decision, Pokagon pushed Congress for several more years—despite no longer being a member of the Business Committee—until, in 1892, the federal government awarded the tribe almost $105,000 in back annuities.

Pokagon became a near prankster in finding new avenues by which to claim redress from federal and local institutions. In 1897 he instigated what has since been dubbed the "Sand Bar Claim," wherein he asserted that nearly all of Chicago's reclaimed lakefront was situated on submerged land parcels that the Potawatomi never ceded to the government. A federal district court in 1914 summarily dismissed the claim.

Pokagon became quite famous upon the booklet's release, though that fame would prove fleeting. *The Red Man's Rebuke* gained favor among native populations and non-native supporters of the resistance against assimilation, and as a result Pokagon was invited to ring the Liberty Bell and deliver a speech at Chicago Day proceedings during the World's Fair. Instead of reflecting the sentiments expressed in the booklet, however, Pokagon presented a case *for* assimilation, a contradiction that gained him the favor of mainstream white America but alienated him from his supporters. Despite this falling out, *The Red Man's Rebuke* remained an influential text for native peoples' resistance movements, with Pokagon's proposal, made at the fair, for a congregation of Native American leaders foretelling the formation of the Society of American Indians just eighteen years later.

HISTORICAL AND LITERARY CONTEXT

The last decades of the nineteenth century were generally known as the Gilded Age of the United States, the age of the incorporation of businesses—an event that, with the advent of the railroad, the telegraph, and other innovations, made the vast expanse of the United States more manageable. National corporations, such as Rockefeller's Standard Oil, emerged, and organized labor grew rapidly and became increasingly more political. In 1893 Chicago hosted the Columbian Exposition World's Fair to honor the four-hundredth anniversary of Columbus's discovery of the Americas and to present a new, industrial vision of America's future. The fair and its White City—an area around the Court of Honor at the fair—were marketed by the organizers as "the first expression of American thought as unity."

Not all Americans, however, shared in this vision of unity. The experience of the Native Americans in this period was defined by the passing of the Dawes Severalty or General Allotment Act (1887), which gave Native Americans the choice to assimilate or submit to what amounted to government-sanctioned extinction. Tensions arising from implementation of the Dawes Act led to the assassination and imprisonment of tribal leaders such as Crazy Horse and Geronimo and the massacre of hundreds at Wounded Knee Creek, South Dakota. Chief Simon Pokagon, whose family had been granted the section of Chicago upon which the White City was built in the 1833 Treaty of Chicago, wrote *The Red Man's Rebuke* to vent his frustration at the lack of representation accorded to native populations in the fair's vision of a unified America.

Although Native Americans were increasingly marginalized, the waning years of the nineteenth century saw an unprecedented level of representation of native peoples in the published word. The voices and opinions represented by these works were as divergent as their authors' backgrounds. In 1881 Susette LaFlesche Tibbles, also called Insta Theamba (Bright Eyes), published "Nedawi: An Indian Story from Real Life," one of the first short stories by an American Indian that was not based on American Indian mythology. Sarah Winnemucca Hopkins, among the few members of the Piute Nation able to read and write in English, turned a series of lectures denouncing the reservation system into a wildly successful autobiography, *Life among the Piutes: Their Wrongs and Claims* (1883).

Building on the success of his predecessors, Pokagon was in a unique position among Native American writers. The public knew Pokagon as a highly educated man and a poet, as "the Longfellow of his race," or the "Red Man's Longfellow." As such, he was able to imbue *The Red Man's Rebuke* with a lyricism and emotional resonance unprecedented in early Native American publications. He would later use this same capacity in crafting *O-gi-wam-kwe Miti-gwa-ki, Queen of the Woods* (1899), the second novel published by a Native American and the first to deal directly with Native American culture.

THEMES AND STYLE

The central theme of *The Red Man's Rebuke* is protestation against the forced assimilation of Native Americans by Europeans. Pokagon opens by declaring to "the pale-faced race that has usurped our lands and homes that we have no spirit to celebrate with you the great Columbian Fair now being held." He reminds readers that when European settlers "came by chance to our shores, many times very needy and hungry," Native Americans welcomed and fed them. After several lyrical passages chronicling the white man's offenses against native peoples, Pokagon closes by imagining a version of Judgment Day wherein white men answer to the Great Spirit rather than the God of European religions. In his vision, those who smoke, drink, letch, and act violently against other humans (all intended to implicate white men) are cast out of Paradise.

The booklet's rhetorical power derives from Pokagon's ability to temper his hostility with lyricism. In decrying American violence and wastefulness in sport hunting, Pokagon says of the hunted animals: "their bleaching bones now, scattered far and near, in shame declare the wanton cruelty of the pale-faced men." He likens westward-pushing settlers to a storm that "unsatisfied on land, swept our lakes and streams while before its clouds" resources dwindled. Being an educated man, Pokagon knew that imbuing his

admonishments with a lyrical quality would lull some readers into a more receptive state and win others over by sheer force of his aptitude.

Owing again to Pokagon's awareness of his audience, the booklet eschews militant derision in favor of an almost biblical tone. In addition to quoting Old Testament passages, he employs lyrical descriptions and passages reminiscent of the poems of the Book of Psalms. In the closing passages, which envision the Great Spirit's chastisement of the white man for his wrongs against Native Americans, Pokagon repeats the imperative "neither shall you" to evoke the Ten Commandments. The desire to ensure a greater readership within the white American population guided Pokagon's literary decisions.

CRITICAL DISCUSSION

The booklet received little to no critical response. Benjamin (B.O.) Flower, in an 1896 article for the *Arena,* chose to ignore the more hostile booklet, gushing

Chief Simon Pokagon, author of *Red Man's Rebuke,* in an 1898 portrait by Elbridge Ayer Burbank. NEWBERRY LIBRARY, CHICAGO, ILLINOIS, USA/THE BRIDGEMAN ART LIBRARY

instead about his surprise at Pokagon's attire (a navy wool suit with a traditional Potawatomi headdress) and the poet's eloquence during the Chicago Day proceedings, marveling at the "breadth of thought and innate spirituality which permeate[d]" the address. Many journalists seem to have made the same choice, as critical treatments of the speech far outnumber those of the booklet.

Presenting at an event as large as the World's Fair afforded Pokagon a wider audience than he might have otherwise had. As a result, he enjoyed a modest career as a public speaker and author, traveling around the country delivering speeches that addressed the "Indian problem" and publishing a dozen or so articles, five birch-bark booklets, and two hymns prior to his death on January 28, 1899. His novel was published posthumously, and while it was successful upon its release, the polished nature of its prose contrasted with the unpolished diction and syntax of his letters, which have led some to doubt his authorship.

Contemporary scholarship tends to reconsider the booklet, typically examining Pokagon's rhetorical complexity. Both Bernd Peyer and Jonathan Berliner have observed that his decision to print the booklet on birch bark is the most fundamentally effective strategy employed. In *The Thinking Indian* (2007), Peyer declares that the decision to print on birch "establishes a symbolic as well as material link between [the writing of the book's author] and traditional Native American uses of birch-bark as a creative medium." Berliner, writing for *PMLA,* seconds Peyer's notion, adding that Pokagon was likely aware that "the use of birch bark in the United States was nostalgically linked with American Indian curiosities in the popular imagination" and used this knowledge to maximize the booklet's marketability. For its lyrical register and its rhetorical prowess, *The Red Man's Rebuke* remains a landmark subversive, and not merely critical, exploration of the Native American relationship to the dominant late-nineteenth-century discourses of civilization/savagery and American imperialism.

BIBLIOGRAPHY

Sources

Berliner, Jonathan. "Written in Birch Bark: The Linguistic-Material Worldmaking of Simon Pokagon." *PMLA* 125.1 (2010): 73-91. Print.

Flower, B.O. "An Interesting Representative of a Vanishing Race." *Arena* 16.2 (1896): 240-50. *EText Center, UVA Library.* Web. 19 July 2012.

Peyer, Bernd. *American Indian Nonfiction: An Anthology of Writings, 1760s-1930s.* Norman: U of Oklahoma P, 2007. 233-43. Print.

———. *The Thinking Indian: Native American Writers, 1850s-1920s.* New York: Peter Lang, 2007. Print.

Further Reading

Dockstader, Frederick J. *Great North American Indians: Profiles in Life and Leadership.* New York: Van Nostrand Reinhold, 1977. Print.

Hopkins, Sarah W., and Mary T. P. Mann. *Life among the Piutes: Their Wrongs and Claims.* Boston: Cupples, Upham, 1883. Print.

Marcus, Greil, and Werner Sollors. *A New Literary History of America.* Cambridge: Belknap Press of Harvard UP, 2009. Print.

Pokagon, Simon. *Queen of the Woods.* Hartford: Engle. 1899. Print.

Rydell, Robert. *All the World's a Fair.* Chicago: U of Chicago P, 1984. Print.

Walker, Cheryl. *Indian Nation: Native American Literature and Nineteenth-Century Nationalisms.* Durham: Duke UP, 1997. Print.

Witalec, Janet, Jeffery Chapman, and Christopher Giroux. *Native North American Literature: Biographical and Critical Information on Native Writers and Orators from the United States and Canada from Historical Times to the Present.* New York: Gale Research, 1994. Print.

Clint Garner

REPORT ON THE PRINCIPLES OF POLITICAL MORALITY

Maximilien Robespierre

OVERVIEW

Maximilien Robespierre, the architect of the French Revolution's Reign of Terror, delivered his speech "Sur les principes de morale politique" ("Report on the Principles of Political Morality") in Paris on February 5, 1794, at a meeting of the revolutionary legislature, the National Convention. The speech is an arresting statement of Robespierre's political vision that seeks to justify the so-called Terror, the violent repression of any person suspected of disloyalty to the revolution, often by means of the guillotine. The immediate occasion for Robespierre's speech was the mounting dissension among the leaders of the revolution. Robespierre intended his "Report" to silence his opponents—those who believed the Terror had accomplished its aims and should be dismantled. Robespierre postulated an inextricable relationship between "virtue," the fundamental principle of democracy, and "terror," prompt and unforgiving justice. As Katharine J. Lualdi characterizes the "Report," "Robespierre met his critics head on, holding up terror as the sword of liberty."

By the time Robespierre spoke, the revolution had succeeded in overthrowing the monarchy and establishing a constitutional republic, but civil war, military losses on the frontiers, and bitter political rivalries threatened the foundations of the fledgling government. With Robespierre and his associates, the Jacobins, in control of the executive body of the Convention (the twelve-member Committee of Public Safety), a bloody campaign against counterrevolutionaries was progressing unchecked. Robespierre's "Report" met with thunderous applause at the Convention. The speech was printed and widely distributed, and there followed the arrests and executions of former committee member Georges Danton and his circle of vocal critics of the committee's tactics and policies. However, the tide of opinion quickly turned against Robespierre amid growing evidence of his tyranny. Less than six months after delivering his speech, he was arrested and beheaded, bringing an end to the Terror. Robespierre remains one of the most controversial figures in history, remembered by some as a champion of liberty and democracy but by others as a bloodthirsty despot. His "Report," offered in evidence of both opinions, has taken a prominent place in the study of his legacy as a seminal text in the justification of political violence.

HISTORICAL AND LITERARY CONTEXT

The French Revolution (1787-99) was a massive popular insurrection that brought about a period of unprecedented social, political, and economic change to France. It replaced the old ideals of aristocracy, monarchy, and religious authority with the Enlightenment ideals of liberty and equality and government by the citizenry, with profound implications for the future course of European and world civilization. In the spring of 1789, King Louis XVI convened a meeting of the Estates-General to address the country's fiscal crisis. The Estates-General was an assembly of representatives of the three orders of the realm: the clergy (First Estate), the nobility (Second Estate), and the commoners (Third Estate). When the deputies of the Third Estate—among them Robespierre—were left unsatisfied, they promptly reconvened separately and redefined themselves as an independent parliamentary body, the National Assembly. The country was ripe for revolution: the government of Louis XVI was bankrupt; there was rioting over food shortages and skyrocketing prices; and the poor and starving of the Third Estate, heavily burdened by unequal taxation, were appalled by the luxurious existence of Louis and his court. The people moved quickly, storming the Bastille on July 14, 1789, and the Palace of Versailles less than three months later. The Republic of France was founded in September 1792, and Louis XVI and his wife, Marie Antoinette, were executed by guillotine the following year by order of the renamed legislature, the National Convention.

Robespierre, a provincial lawyer from Arras, quickly rose to positions of influence in the new government, partly based on his talent for oratory and an unerring devotion to republican principles. He amassed a large popular following as the leader of the radical political club the Jacobins. Once the Jacobins had quashed the moderates and assumed a majority in the National Convention, a government emerged that derived its authority from the Committee of Public Safety. Thousands were killed in the Terror, which targeted not only dissenters but also anyone whose

❖ Key Facts

Time Period:
Late 18th Century

Movement/Issue:
French Revolution; Jacobinism; Reign of Terror

Place of Publication:
France

Language of Publication:
French

A RELIGION OF VIRTUE

The Roman Catholic religion was attacked during the French Revolution, a process that involved the destruction of churches throughout the country. As a disciple of the Enlightenment philosopher Jean-Jacques Rousseau, Robespierre was a deist, though he had little objection to the antichurch laws passed by the revolutionary government. On June 8, 1794, just four days after his election as president of the national legislature, Robespierre staged a spectacular festival to introduce a new civic religion, the Cult of the Supreme Being. The festival was orchestrated with the help of the painter Jacques-Louis David and included a lavish procession led by Robespierre that made its way through the Tuileries Gardens and up to the top of a man-made mountain on the Champ de Mars. Robespierre decreed that the new godhead, the Supreme Being, symbol of Virtue, would be honored with regular holidays scheduled according to the new republican calendar, which divided each month into three ten-day weeks so as to eliminate any old associations with the Sabbath. Spectators reported that Robespierre appeared to fashion himself a latter-day Moses as he came down from the mountaintop. The festival turned public opinion against Robespierre, who was now widely thought to have lost touch with reality. He was sent to the guillotine on July 28, 1794.

commitment to the revolution was deemed unsatisfactory or who actively opposed the revolutionary government. Robespierre's "Report" of February 5, 1794, helped to convince the National Convention of the purity of his motives, and he was elected its president just months later on June 4. Robespierre's power base, however, quickly dissolved with the growing perception that his influence had devolved into fanatical autocracy. Mass paranoia, even among his longtime supporters, gripped the nation in response to a rapid increase in executions. On July 27, 1794, Robespierre was arrested by some of his own allies and beheaded the following day.

Like many of the educated of his generation, Robespierre had been swept up in the excitement of the Enlightenment and the example of the American colonies. His study of the writings of the Enlightenment philosophers Voltaire, Montesquieu, and Jean-Jacques Rousseau had taught him to question the sanctity of all inherited social and cultural institutions. He embraced the Enlightenment ideals of liberty, equality, and reason; believed in democracy and the natural goodness of man; and, before the onset of the Terror, called for freedom of the press and an end to the death penalty. Robespierre found his greatest inspiration in Rousseau's social contract theory, which held that government is a contract entered into by the people and that any form of legal and social privilege is subservient to the will of the citizenry. As evidenced in his "Report," Robespierre adopted Rousseau's idea of virtue as the informing principle of responsible

citizenship; he defended the Terror as virtuous because he was convinced that it was the only rational way to protect the revolution against its enemies.

To many of Robespierre's contemporaries, both at home and abroad, his conjunction of terror with virtue rang hollow in the face of the kangaroo courts and mass executions ordered by the Jacobins. The executions claimed more than 1,300 victims in Paris in one six-week period of 1794 alone. In total, including the peasants slaughtered in regional uprisings, an estimated 250,000 persons were killed. The question that has puzzled scholars for more than 200 years is how Robespierre—a man so committed to humanitarian reform that he was rumored to have slept with a copy of Rousseau's *The Social Contract* under his pillow—could have sanctioned so violent an assault on individual liberties as the Terror.

THEMES AND STYLE

In his "Report on the Principles of Political Morality," Robespierre argues that the political revolution must be accompanied by a moral revolution. He begins by reasserting the Enlightenment aims of the Revolution—love of country, equality, and liberty—and then proceeds to defend the legitimacy and systematization of the Terror as necessary to safeguarding these ideals. He defines virtue as "nothing other than the love of country and of its laws" and reminds his audience that, though a virtuous citizenry is guided by reason, its enemies are not. It is therefore necessary, Robespierre continues, that these enemies be eliminated through terror: "If virtue be the spring of popular government at times of peace, the spring of that government during a revolution is virtue combined with terror: virtue without which terror is destructive; terror, without which virtue is impotent."

Robespierre's exhortation is carefully developed through a series of persuasive strategies appealing to both the intellect and the emotions. The speech is peppered with rhetorical questions meant to enlist audience identification with Robespierre's argument: "What is the goal toward which we are heading?" he asks early in the oration. A few sentences later, after having extolled the merits of the republican form of government, he poses a question to his listeners he has just answered, thereby directing their response: "What kind of government can realize these wonders?" Expanding upon the revolutionary language of binaries—patriot and traitor, aristocrat and citizen—Robespierre devotes an entire paragraph to establishing an opposition between behavior that is revolutionary and virtuous and that which is counterrevolutionary and self-serving. The paragraph begins, "[We] want to substitute morality for egotism, integrity for formal codes of honor, principles for customs, a sense of duty for one of mere propriety, the rule of reason for the tyranny of fashion…." He casts any form of hesitation in endorsing the Terror and its urgency as itself an act of counterrevolution. He

LA NUIT DU 9 AU 10 THERMIDOR AN II.

coaxes his audience into accepting the sincerity of his intentions with nautical metaphors that image him as captain of the "ship of the Republic" steering France through a "tempest" to "calmer waters."

The whole of Robespierre's appeal is couched in language that is utopian, calling on the people to participate in the making of a regenerated France that will be the glory of all free peoples. As Hilary Mantel observes of this utopian scheme, "Virtue and Terror became inseparable, a single Janus-faced god who guarded the gate to a better world." Robespierre invokes the memory of the great classical civilizations: "I speak of the public virtue which worked so many wonders in Greece and Rome and which ought to produce even more astonishing things in republican France." Matthew S. Buckley, in a 2006 book on the tragic drama of the French Revolution, cites Marc Blanchard's *Saint-Just & Cie: La revolution et les mots* (1980) in underscoring the power of the classical metaphor:

Blanchard has argued that this sort of oratory did more than simply offer a figurative context in which the historical process of the revolution became comprehensible; rather, it installed revolutionary action with an imaginary stage setting, producing "the illusion of playing *History* in a magically summoned scene, in which men no longer keep their names but

take, like actors in the theatre, the traditional names of the heroes of Greece and Rome."

CRITICAL DISCUSSION

Following Robespierre's death, he was made a scapegoat for the Terror and its aftermath. He was reviled as Maximilien the Exterminator, Mad Max, and the Drinker of Blood and held solely accountable by many for the very murder of the revolution itself, paving the way for the rise of Napoleon Bonaparte and the subsequent return of the Bourbon dynasty to the throne of France. In such a climate, Robespierre's oratory became an integral part of his crazed and inflexible will to power.

Because of the momentousness of the French Revolution, Robespierre's leading role in it has been a subject of extensive study for some of the world's most prominent historians, beginning in the nineteenth century. Robespierre remains one of history's most polarizing figures. The puzzle of Robespierre's legacy that has consumed scholars is summarized by his biographer Peter McPhee:

Was Robespierre the first modern dictator, inhuman and fanatical, an obsessive who used his political power to try to impose his rigid ideal of a land of Spartan "virtue"? Or was he a principled, self-abnegating visionary ... Were the controls on individual liberties and the mass arrests and executions of "the Terror" … the necessary price to pay to save the Revolution? Or was this … a time of horror, of unnecessary death, incarceration, and privation?

A number of twenty-first-century scholars have looked to the "Report" in seeking to explain where Robespierre found the justification for condemning so many people to death. Some have argued that Robespierre's faith in his own righteousness led him to believe that men could be forced into the virtue and goodness that Rousseau had ascribed to them. Others have suggested that Robespierre felt compelled to point the finger at others when it became clear that his Utopian aspirations for the Revolution were unattainable. Still others have emphasized that Robespierre did not act alone. Marisa Linton writes in a 2006 *History Today* article that

> [Robespierre] would never have been so influential had he not spoken for a wide swath of society and government. When he spoke of conspiracies against the Revolution, of the threats to 'the *patrie* in danger', and the need for extreme measures, he voiced the fears of many at that time that France was about to be overwhelmed by foreign and internal enemies.

The issues that Robespierre addressed in his "Report" have deep resonance for twenty-first-century students of revolutions worldwide. As historian Lynn Hunt observes in the DVD *The French Revolution* (2005), "The question raised by the French Revolution is how much violence is justified in achieving the better society? Do people have the right to overthrow what they see as an unjust system to replace it with what they are convinced in their hearts is a more just system? … We still have this question today."

BIBLIOGRAPHY

Sources

Buckley, Matthew S. "The Drama of the Revolution." *Tragedy Walks the Streets: The French Revolution in the Making of Modern Drama.* Baltimore: Johns Hopkins, 2006. 34-68. Print.

The French Revolution. Dir. Doug Shultz. Narr. Edward Hermann. Partisan Pictures, 2005. DVD.

Linton, Marisa. "Robespierre and the Terror." *History Today* 56.8 (2006): 23-29. Web. 15 Aug. 2012.

Lualdi, Katharine J. "The Cataclysm of Revolution, 1789-99: Defending Terror." *Sources of the Making of the West. Vol. II. Since 1500: Peoples and Cultures.* Boston: Bedford/St. Martin's, 2012. 124-27. Print.

Mantel, Hilary. Rev. of *Robespierre,* Ed. Colin Haydon and William Doyle. *London Review of Books* 30 Mar. 2000: 3-8. Web. 16 Aug. 2012.

McPhee, Peter. *Robespierre: A Revolutionary Life.* New Haven, CT: Yale UP, 2012. Print.

Robespierre, Maximilien Marie Isidore. "The Principles of Political Morality." *Infamous Speeches: From Robespierre to Osama bin Laden,* ed. Bob Blaisdell. Mineola, NY: Dover, 2011. 1-17. Print.

Further Reading

Johnson, Paul. "From Robespierre to al-Qa'eda: Categorical Extermination." *Spectator* 10 (Sept. 2005): 31. *Gale Biography in Context.* Web. 16 Aug. 2012.

Johnson, Timothy. "Humanist Terrorism in the Political Thought of Robespierre and Sartre." *Engaging Terror: A Critical and Interdisciplinary Approach.* Ed. M. Vardalos et al. Boca Raton, FL: Brown Walker, 2009. 387-96. Print.

Popkin, Jeremy. *A Short History of the French Revolution.* 5th ed. Boston: Prentice, 2010. Print.

Rudé, George. *Great Lives Observed: Robespierre.* Englewood Cliffs, NJ: Prentice, 1967. Print.

Thompson, J.M. *Robespierre and the French Revolution.* London: English Universities, 1952. Print.

Žižek, Slavoj. *Virtue and Terror.* New York: Verso, 2007. Print.

Janet Mullane

RIGHTS OF MAN

Thomas Paine

OVERVIEW

Although author Thomas Paine claims in *Rights of Man* (1791) to endorse no particular form of government, he nonetheless extols the virtues of a republican political system that respects the natural rights of men and firmly locates sovereignty in the nation as a whole rather than in a particular individual or family. Paine's pamphlet was one of at least fifty that repudiated Edmund Burke's *Reflections on the Revolution in France* (1790), a vitriolic assault on the French uprising and a defense of monarchy. A staunch supporter of American independence, as expressed in his work *Common Sense* (1776), Paine in *Rights of Man* extends his Enlightenment ideals of equality to revolutionary France and advocates for progressive political and economic policies in Britain. Addressed to a broad citizenry, from political leaders to commoners, *Rights of Man* was published in two parts, the first appearing in 1791 and the second in 1792.

Paine's book, titled *The Rights of Man, Being an Answer to Mr. Burke's Attack on the French Revolution,* was an immediate sensation in both England and the United States; an estimated 1.5 million copies were sold in England alone. The second part, which was especially popular among the laboring classes, proved even more successful than the first. However, the work's overt criticism of the British government, coupled with its extraordinary popularity, angered British authorities. They banned the publication of the work and in 1792 tried Paine in absentia for seditious libel. Nevertheless, the philosophy expressed in *Rights of Man* continued to fuel the growth of radical political movements and political consciousness, especially among segments of the population where it had previously been lacking, such as the working classes.

HISTORICAL AND LITERARY CONTEXT

Written at a time of revolutionary fervor (both the American Revolution and French Revolution had taken place within the previous two decades), the *Rights of Man* articulates many of the radical political principles behind these events, such as the rejection of hereditary government, the right of the people to choose their government, and the importance and primacy of man's natural rights. Many were frustrated by the hereditary government of England because the succession of monarchs had no direct input from the people. As nations cast off the dominion of the past, some English citizens saw the inequality between a king and his subjects and between the aristocracy and the working classes as an outrageous insult to the belief that all men are created equal.

By the time Paine published *Rights of Man* in 1791, concern about the influence of revolution in France on England was of particular concern for English citizens. Whereas some feared that the violent revolutionary energies unleashed on the continent might spread to England and ignite chaos, others applauded the republican struggle for liberty. The polarization of the British populace was reflected in the press, which published writers in support of and opposed to the French Revolution. Paine's role in the political print culture of the 1790s, and the success and popularity of the *Rights of Man,* made him synonymous with supporters of the French Revolution, whereas Burke represented the side of the opponents.

Although the *Rights of Man* resembles Paine's earlier pamphlet defending American independence from British rule, *Common Sense* (1776), it also shares similarities with the many responses to Burke's *Reflections,* including Mary Wollstonecraft's *Vindication of the Rights of Men* (1790) and Joseph Priestley's *Letters to the Right Honourable Edmund Burke* (1791). Paine's work also owes much to the American *Declaration of Independence* and the French *Declaration of the Rights of Man and of Citizens,* both of which prominently feature the idea that all men are created equal.

The *Rights of Man* significantly influenced political writing, both radical and conservative, in the 1790s and facilitated the development and rejuvenation of radical political societies. William Cobbett and Thomas Spence, inspired by Paine's work, explored their own brand of Painism in, respectively, *The Soldier's Friend* (1792) and *The Meridian Sun of Liberty; or the Whole Rights of Man Displayed and Most Accurately Defined* (1796). Conservative works, such as Hannah More's *Village Politics* (1793), also imitated Paine's plain style and attempted to reach the same, partially literate audience in order to counteract his infectious influence. Although Paine's authority waned after 1850, his work is today recognized as a foundational document of modern political writing and thinking.

❖ Key Facts

Time Period:
Late 18th Century

Movement/Issue:
Democratic reform; French Revolution

Place of Publication:
England

Language of Publication:
English

THE SALES PRICE OF THE *RIGHTS OF MAN*

The first part of the *Rights of Man* sold for three shillings, the standard price for materials of the sort (Edmund Burke's *Reflections* sold for the same price). The second part of the *Rights of Man,* however, sold for the much lower price of six pence. When Paine published the second part, he reissued the first part for the new, lower price. At twelve pence per shilling, Paine reduced the price by more than eight percent so that lower-income citizens could afford to buy it.

The purposeful reduction in price angered authorities perhaps more than the work's "seditious" content. The attorney general who prosecuted Paine in the 1792 sedition trial characterized the work's price as the proverbial last straw: "when I found that it was printed at a very low price, for the express purpose of its being read by the lowest classes of people ... I did not hesitate one moment in putting the very reprehensible transaction in a judicial process." In 1790s England the prospect of the "very lowest classes of people" reading about politics alarmed many. Thus, Paine's willingness to make his work accessible and affordable to these classes was seen as even more radical and seditious than the ideas he advanced.

THEMES AND STYLE

The main theme of the *Rights of Man* is that any government not formulated by the consent of the people—including the "monarchical and hereditary systems of government" in prerevolutionary France and England—lacks political legitimacy and flirts with despotism. "Sovereignty, as a matter of right," Paine argues, "appertains to the nation only and not to any individual." The nation has "at all times an inherent, indefeasible right to abolish any form of government it finds inconvenient, and establish such as accords with its interest, disposition, and happiness." According to Paine, the United States and France are extraordinary and commendable examples of nations exercising their natural right to establish a government of their choosing that is commensurate with their interest. For Paine, the revolutions of the United States and France mark the beginning of a new era in the world's history, the Age of Reason.

The *Rights of Man,* especially part one, is structured as a series of loosely connected responses to Burke's *Reflections* rather than as a "coherent and sustained argument." In order to refute Burke, Paine borrows Burke's language and steers it in another direction. For example, Burke brands the ideas that motivated the French Revolution as a "barbarous philosophy," whereas Paine contends that the real atrocity is the monarchical system that Burke defends: "The romantic and barbarous distinction of men into kings and subjects, though it may suit the condition of courtiers, cannot that of citizens ... Every citizen is a member of the Sovereignty, and ... his obedience can be only to the laws." Whereas Burke criticizes the revolution for its brutal treatment of the French royal family (he describes how two bodyguards were "cruelly and publicly dragged to the block and beheaded"), Paine counters by arguing that the monarchical system has treated many citizens the same way: "When we survey the wretched condition of man, under the monarchical and hereditary systems of Government, *dragged* from his home by one power, or driven by another ... it becomes evident that those systems are bad, and that a general revolution ... is necessary." Such rhetorical borrowings make the *Rights of Man* an effective and insidious weapon against the antirevolutionary position.

Although the *Rights of Man* borrows some of its language from *Reflections,* the two texts are stylistically distinct. Whereas Burke writes in an elaborate, excessive rhetorical mode (which Paine calls a "dramatic performance"), Paine's text is marked by concision and economy, making it popular among semiliterate, working-class readers. In addition to his stylistic simplicity, his gestures of commiseration are another reason for his success among the lower classes: "In taking up this subject I seek no recompense—I fear no consequence. Fortified with that proud integrity, that disdains to triumph or to yield, I will advocate the Rights of Man." Paine's comparatively plain style and expression of sympathy for the poor demonstrate his commitment to the equality he so passionately defends.

CRITICAL DISCUSSION

The radicalism of the *Rights of Man* met with a mixed reception upon the work's publication. Although political radicals and commoners admired the work, others were outraged by its seditious content. Many of the nearly eighty published responses to Paine's book were hostile and criticized the author for his plainspoken prose. Paul Keen notes in *The Crisis of Literature in the 1790s: Print Culture and the Public Sphere* (1999) that many British citizens felt that the lower classes were not intelligent enough to "exchange ideas rationally." During Paine's sedition trial in 1792, the jury was instructed to mind both the work's content and the "phrase, act, and manner of this author. He dealt in short sentences." Still, revolutionaries such as Thomas Jefferson praised Paine for his "ease and familiarity of style," which helped account for the work's astonishing sales figures.

The book's popularity among the working classes and among political radicals contributed to what Marilyn Butler in *Burke, Paine, Godwin, and the Revolution Controversy* (1984) calls a "steady pressure" by the British government to curtail the publication and spread of Paine's ideas. However, the increasing violence and despotism of the French Revolution led to the decline in popularity of *Rights of Man* in the late 1790s. Despite the lull in readership, the document, and Paine more generally, experienced renewed popularity and interest throughout the first half of the nineteenth century, especially at points of political upheaval. Although Paine's reputation declined after 1850, scholars continue to recognize the modernity of his political ideas and his significant influence on politics and literature.

Critics have focused on the quality of Paine's writing and its effectiveness in communicating his revolutionary message. He has come to be regarded, in Butler's words, as a "master of prose," and the sophisticated clarity of his writing lent itself to what Keen calls the "democratization of reading." Scholars are particularly interested in how the ease and familiarity of Paine's style made the *Rights of Man* accessible to a working-class audience that lacked the educational credentials to read more-elaborate works of political theory. Historically minded scholars, such as Gregory Claeys in *Thomas Paine: Social and Political Thought* (1989), have focused on how the writer's "demand for universal recognition of certain inviolable principles of freedom of thought, speech, and association" has become "one of the defining characteristics of modern politics."

BIBLIOGRAPHY

Sources

Burke, Edmund. *Reflections on the Revolution in France.* Ed. L. G. Mitchell. Oxford: Oxford UP, 2009. Print.

Butler, Marilyn, ed. *Burke, Paine, Godwin, and the Revolution Controversy.* Cambridge: Cambridge UP, 1984. Print.

Claeys, Gregory. *Thomas Paine: Social and Political Thought.* Boston: Unwin Hyman, 1989. Print.

Clemit, Pamela, ed. *The Cambridge Companion to British Literature of the French Revolution in the 1790s.* Cambridge: Cambridge UP, 2011. Print.

Keen, Paul. *The Crisis of Literature in the 1790s: Print Culture and the Public Sphere.* Cambridge: Cambridge UP, 1999. Print.

Paine, Thomas. *Rights of Man, Common Sense, and Other Political Writings.* Ed. Mark Philp. Oxford: Oxford UP, 2008. Print.

Further Reading

Behrendt, Stephen C., ed. *Romanticism, Radicalism, and the Press.* Detroit: Wayne State UP, 1997. Print.

Boulton, James. *The Language of Politics in the Age of Wilkes and Burke.* London: Routledge and Kegan Paul, 1963. Print.

Fruchtman, Jack, Jr. *The Political Philosophy of Thomas Paine.* Baltimore: Johns Hopkins UP, 2009. Print.

Kates, Gary. "From Liberalism to Radicalism: Tom Paine's Rights of Man." *Journal of the History of Ideas* 50.4 (1989): 569-87. Print.

Larkin, Edward. *Thomas Paine and the Literature of Revolution.* New York: Cambridge UP, 2005. Print.

Whatmore, Richard. "'A Gigantic Manliness': Thomas Paine's Republicanism in the 1790s." *Economy, Polity and Society: British Intellectual History, 1750-1950.* Ed. Stefan Collini, Richard Whatmore, and Brian Young. Cambridge: Cambridge UP, 2000. 135-57. Print.

Alexander Covalciuc

A 1792 British cartoon satirizing Thomas Paine's support of the French Revolution. He is depicted holding his *Rights of Man* while carrying torture devices on his back and trampling on scrolls with labels such as "Religion" and "Morality." EVERETT COLLECTION

SCIENCE OF REVOLUTIONARY WARFARE

A Handbook of Instruction Regarding the Use and Manufacture of Nitroglycerine, Dynamite, Gun-Cotton, Fulminating Mercury, Bombs, Arsons, Poisons, etc.

Johann Most

✣ **Key Facts**

Time Period:
Late 19th Century

Movement/Issue:
Anarchism; Terrorism

Place of Publication:
United States

Language of Publication:
English

OVERVIEW

Originally titled *Military Science for Revolutionaries* after the newspaper columns Johann Most wrote, his 1885 *Science of Revolutionary Warfare: A Handbook of Instruction Regarding the Use and Manufacture of Nitroglycerine, Dynamite, Gun-Cotton, Fulminating Mercury, Bombs, Arsons, Poisons, etc.* gestures toward the problems of economic and social oppression while detailing active strategies to overcome them. While most of the pamphlet provides technical instructions for successful intrigues and violent actions, these instructions support Most's creed of "propaganda by deed," or "*attentat.*" Propaganda by deed is the idea of spreading ideals through actions and is often associated with violence. First written in German, *Science of Revolutionary Warfare* appealed to a working-class group of U.S. immigrants who felt muted by the conditions surrounding them and who found the "voice of dynamite" alluring.

Science of Revolutionary Warfare became immediately popular with Most's followers and significantly cohered the anarchist movement in the United States. Some copies of *Science* were shared, passing from hand to hand, but more were sold at gatherings of like-minded thinkers already attuned to Most's fiery spleen. Published at a time when numerous laborers and immigrants felt particularly powerless, many welcomed *Science of Revolutionary Warfare* and its violent means of communication. Concomitantly, the police quickly recognized its dangerous potential. Law enforcement and the Pinkerton Detective Agency increased their infiltration and surveillance of anarchist organizations. Although interest in Most's pamphlet lost momentum following the 1886 Haymarket affair, with which it is linked, his arguments are considered key to nineteenth-century anarchist activity and have resurged time and again in radical political movements.

HISTORICAL AND LITERARY CONTEXT

Science of Revolutionary Warfare responds to the mounting friction over working conditions and wages in the United States in the second half of the nineteenth century and gives voice to those who felt powerless in the oppressive political climate. The Bavarian-born Most, disappointed by Marxist socialism, expelled by the Social-Democratic Party for his dangerous writings, and inspired by the tactics of Russian Nihilists, immigrated to the United States to observe its labor struggles and industrial disputes. He had long fought against what he perceived as an unfair allocation of resources and a broken system. Prior to writing *Science of Revolutionary Warfare,* he was well known for joining conversations increasingly held in print, making his speeches, and writing articles in his newspaper *Freiheit* (Freedom).

The anarchist movement was growing but disorganized, and its discourse was largely theoretical before Most published *Science of Revolutionary Warfare.* Dissidents Peter Kropotkin, Albert and Lucy Parsons, and Mikhail Bakunin, among others, headed sects with varied approaches until Most's electrifying text crystallized and directed the movement, giving it a central axis for a time. Although not all branches of anarchism followed Most's insurrectionary ideals, his influential pamphlet has forever altered the public's understanding of anarchism. Shifting Errico Malatesta's term "propaganda by deed" from theory to practice, Most urges his followers to commit to action by taking recourse in explosives and saving their energy for evading capture and reorganizing the structures of society.

Science of Revolutionary Warfare draws on other calls to arms such as Karl Marx and Friedrich Engels's *Communist Manifesto* (1848) and Sergey Nechayev's *Catechism of a Revolutionary* (1869). The former's anticapitalist precepts and focus on class struggle, and the authoritarian dictates for ruthlessness of the latter influenced Most's writing, shaping his long-running newspaper *Freiheit* and *Science of Revolutionary Warfare.* Aptly nicknamed "Dynamost" by his peers, Most believed that a more egalitarian society could only be achieved by literally destroying the current system and its foundations. He states in his 1884 speech "The Beast of Property" that "if the people do not crush [the foundations of society], they will crush the people, drown the revolution in the blood of the best, and rivet the chains of slavery more firmly than ever. Kill or be killed is the alternative. Therefore massacres of the people's enemies must be instituted." Similar beliefs filtered into many of his texts and speeches.

In 1886 a protest for an eight-hour working day in Chicago's Haymarket Square turned violent when an unidentified perpetrator—widely assumed to have been an anarchist—exploded a bomb at the event. The incident, known as the Haymarket affair, launched the popular stereotype of anarchists as bomb-clutching madmen bent on chaos. Leading to a backlash against Most and the anarchist movement, the affair had long-ranging effects. For example, the first libertarian movement sputtered out, in part, because of its ties to anarchism. Public reaction to the Haymarket affair led anarchists to tone down their polemics, and voices such as Benjamin Tucker, the "gentleman anarchist," became more prominent. Nevertheless, Most's later writings such as "To The Proletariat" and "The Social Monster" clearly reflect his continued anticapitalist stance. Although anarchism has taken many forms since the publication of *Science of Revolutionary Warfare,* the period between the World War I until after the Cold War saw a decrease of interest in anarchism as labor conditions improved and because Communist suppression spread. Not until the *Anarchist Cookbook* was published in 1971 did another manifesto that mixed recipes and anarchist rhetoric reach the notoriety of *Science of Revolutionary Warfare.*

THEMES AND STYLE

Science of Revolutionary Warfare suggests that the masses should fight to bring equilibrium back to society through explosive demonstrations and spectacles against illegitimate and oppressive authority, referring to their struggle as "war" and labeling inaction a "fiasco." Underscoring the idea of social polarization central to *Science of Revolutionary Warfare,* Most lumps his targets under the general heading of a "Property Monster" composed of "capitalist privilege," a dehumanized adversary that he breaks into categories such as "exploiters," "oppressors," "riff-raff of the upper-class variety," "law-in-order hounds," and "uniformed murderers." Most distances his readers from their shared, demonized "enemies," whom he discards as a faceless "Other," reminding his audience to take every precaution when following his directives as "the real plan is for *others* to lose *their* lives." In such ways, he mimics the rhetoric of war, stressing the difference between murder and killing "targets" for a cause.

The rhetoric of *Science of Revolutionary Warfare* is steeped in solidarity-infused, rather than individualistic, language. The authorial "we," which addresses the audience ("you"), invites the reader to join the writerly "we" by taking up the mantle of "propaganda by

SCIENCE OF REVOLUTIONARY WARFARE AS EVIDENCE IN THE HAYMARKET TRIAL

Science of Revolutionary Warfare became a central piece of evidence against eight anarchists who were arrested and tried for their alleged involvement in the Haymarket affair, the 1886 protest-turned-bombing. At the conclusion of the trial, the defendants were convicted of murder. Four were subsequently hanged, and a fifth took his own life while awaiting execution. The book's incendiary language was read aloud at the trial as an indictment of those present in Haymarket Square who possessed the pamphlet and Most, who had authored it, despite his alibi and lack of further connection to the protestors. After he realized how his words were being used against his comrades, he refused to reprint his pamphlet and urged his fellow anarchists to temper their language to prevent another such witch hunt.

In the aftermath of the Haymarket trial, widespread opinion was that it had had been flawed and unduly harsh. William Dean Howells was notably inspired, protesting the outcome in *A Hazard of New Fortunes* (1889). Even Most's rival Benjamin Tucker supported Most during and after the trial. Although Tucker used the brouhaha surrounding the Haymarket affair to promote his own school of anarchy, he wrote in solidarity with Most, decrying the state as a monster, which "among the victims of these authority-ridden maniacs is John [*sic*] Most. Toward him as a social reformer *Liberty*'s attitude has been and will be hostile in the extreme, but toward him as a human being deprived of his fundamental rights it can be nothing but sympathetic."

deed." Writing for and of the masses as a political and intellectual authority, Most uses pronouns to elevate his voice, and by extension his audience's. Further, by using a fallacious "we" when not writing strictly declarative prose, he suggests that *Science of Revolutionary Warfare* was produced by a team of experts who double as the head of their anarchist movement. Phrases such as "we carried out tests with these bombs ... and the results were always satisfactory" merge with warnings such as "you must be extremely careful when screwing in the plug in the bomb casing" to underscore Most's technical expertise. His use of "we" also lends political gravitas to declarations such as "we are exposing those who are disarming the people" and gives added weight to motivational phrases such as "we don't want to hear any more excuses!" This powerful "we" is set up as a foil to the "enemy" and suggests his readers are either with him or against him and all he represents.

When not slipping into technical descriptions of how to build bombs or use invisible ink, Most alternatively bullies and cajoles his readers, speaking

Assassination of Czar Alexander II, 1881. Johann Most expressed his pleasure at the assassination of Alexander II in his newspaper *Freiheit* and was subsequently imprisoned. © DIZ MUENCHEN GMBH, SUEDDEUTSCHE ZEITUNG PHOTO/ALAMY

vehemently against his detractors while crediting his supporters with patriotism, intelligence, and heroism. He couches his pamphlet as a scientific handbook for freedom fighters who are engaged in "patriotic warfare" by referring to documents such as the *Declaration of Independence.* Writing that his directions are "for the people," and aligning the right to use dynamite with the "right to bear arms" against "tyrants" and "oppressors," Most strongly invokes the ideals upon which the United States was built, declaring that those ideals and his readers' rights are in imminent danger and that only his methods can save them.

CRITICAL DISCUSSION

Just after it was published, *Science of Revolutionary Warfare* was received less as a handbook for active revolutionaries than as a manual for people seeking to cash in on insurance policies, as through arson, for personal gain or for the advancement of anarchism. Most approved of such rebellious moves against the inner workings of the state and regularly accepted funds raised through insurance fraud. Historian Max Nomad deems identification with arsonists to have been an exercise in bad judgment. Likewise, Most's contemporary Benjamin Tucker decried Most's complicity with insurance fires. Further, Tucker, publisher of the rival anarchist paper *Liberty,* took exception to Most's screed to violence, condemning his use of the term "anarchist." He declared Most's ideology a "tyranny worse than any that now exists." Nevertheless, *Science* sold well and its contents were widely serialized in other anarchist publications circulated in Chicago such as August Spies's *Arbeiter-Zeitung* (Worker's Newspaper) and the Parsons' *The Alarm.*

Almost immediately after the publication of *Science of Revolutionary Warfare,* mainstream periodicals and prominent citizens began to indict it. Moreover, the widespread attention the manifesto received

after the Haymarket affair spread Most's message of empowerment through violence and propaganda by deed beyond his circle of anarchists and laborers and drew it to the public eye. It became known well enough to influence more than radical activists and terrorists, making its way into popular American culture. Moreover, its eruptive admixture of science, propaganda by deed, and revolutionary rhetoric still reverberates in literature, from Joseph Conrad's denunciatory *The Secret Agent* (1907) to sympathetic novels such as William Dean Howells' *A Hazard of New Fortunes* (1889) and more modern works that valorize anarchist protagonists such as Thomas Pynchon's *Against the Day* (2006) and Alan Moore and David Lloyd's *V for Vendetta* (1982-89).

As the United States continues its War on Terror, Most's pamphlet has enjoyed a resurgence of critical attention. *Science of Revolutionary Warfare* has become a much-cited text on the birth and development of terrorism. Criminal justice scholars such as Arthur Garrison cite the text when trying to understand terrorists' inner workings, deeming Most's pamphlet foundational to the justification of the use of explosives in subsequent terrorist actions. Others, such as historian Mark Sedgwick, spend more time on how *Science of Revolutionary Warfare*'s central idea, propaganda by deed, and Most's innovations such as the letter bomb have moved from political anarchists to religious radicals such as al-Qaeda.

BIBLIOGRAPHY

Sources

Garrison, Arthur, H. "Defining Terrorism: Philosophy of the Bomb, Propaganda by Deed and Change Through Fear and Violence." *Criminal Justice Studies* 17.3 (2004): 259-79. Print.

Nomad, Max. *Apostles of Revolution.* Boston: Little, Brown, 1939. Print.

Sedgwick, Mark. "Al-Qaeda and the Nature of Religious Terrorism." *Terrorism and Political Violence* 16.4 (2004): 795-814. Print.

Tucker, Benjamin. "The Beast of Communism." *Liberty* 27 Mar. 1886: 1. *Libertarian Labyrinth.* Web. 24 Sept. 2012.

Further Reading

Avrich, Paul. *The Haymarket Tragedy.* Princeton: Princeton UP, 1984. Print.

Cole, Sarah. "Dynamite Violence and Literary Culture." *Modernism/modernity* 16.2 (2009): 301-328. *Project Muse.* Web. 16 Sept. 2012.

Goyens, Tom. "Most, Johann." *Germany and the Americas: Culture, Politics, and History.* Vol. 1. Ed. Thomas Adam. Santa Barbara: ABC-CLIO, 2005. 777-79. Print.

McElroy, Wendy. "The Schism Between Individualism and Communist Anarchism in the Nineteenth Century." *Journal of Libertarian Studies* 15.1 (2000): 97-123. *Ludwig von Mises Institute.* Web. 24 Sept. 2012.

Merriman, John M. *The Dynamite Club: How a Bombing in Fin-de-Siècle Paris Ignited the Age of Modern Terror.* New York: Houghton Mifflin Harcourt, 2009. Print.

Schaack, Michael J. *Anarchy and Anarchists: A History of the Red Terror and the Social Revolution in American and Europe: Communism, Socialism, and Nihilism in Doctrine and in Deed: The Chicago Haymarket Conspiracy, and the Detection and Trial of the Conspirators.* Chicago: Shulte, 1889. Print.

Trautmann, Frédéric. *The Voice of Terror: A Biography of Johann Most.* Westport: Greenwood Press, 1980. Print.

Katherine Bishop

EMANCIPATION AND INDEPENDENCE

ACT OF ABJURATION

Anonymous

OVERVIEW

Written by members of the States General (the central legislative body of the United Provinces of the Netherlands) and signed on July 26, 1581, the *Act of Abjuration* (in Dutch, *Plakkaat van Verlatinghe*) served as the formal document by which the United Provinces ended its loyalty to King Philip II of Spain, its erstwhile ruler. Composed amid widespread religious disharmony and Spanish military activity in the Low Countries, the act puts forth a lengthy justification of the decision to sever allegiance with Philip. The document cites the king's failure to honor traditional civic and provincial rights and privileges, his vicious persecution of dissenters, and the destruction wrought by his military forces. Asserting that through his tyrannical behavior he has betrayed the responsibility of his position and forfeited his right to sovereignty, the act makes official Philip's deposition and instates Francis, duke of Anjou, as the new sovereign.

Unsurprisingly, Philip did not accept the act's legitimacy, and it was not until after decades of warfare, in 1648, that the Dutch Republic was recognized by Spain. The act served to delineate the split between the mostly Protestant United Provinces and the mostly Catholic provinces of the Spanish Netherlands, which retained loyalty to Spain and today largely comprises parts of Belgium, Luxembourg, and northern France. The *Act of Abjuration* presaged the eventual republicanism of the United Provinces, notwithstanding the appointment of Anjou, who, dismayed by his limited power, was forced to flee the Netherlands after an unsuccessful attempt at a coup at Antwerp. The act now stands as a seminal early instance of a declaration of independence from a tyrannical oppressor, serving as an important precursor to future declarations both formally and through its specific rhetoric.

HISTORICAL AND LITERARY CONTEXT

The *Act of Abjuration* is largely a response to the political oppression and social upheaval that beset the Netherlands after Philip had inherited its rule in 1555. Philip had attempted to establish a much greater degree of control over the Dutch provinces than they had traditionally endured, and his sovereignty was marked by the imposition of various religious edicts intended to suppress the spread of Calvinist Protestant doctrines. Dutch resentment of Philip was exacerbated

in 1567, when, in response to extremist Protestant demonstrations in protest of heresy laws, he sent over a large army along with the Duke of Alva, who brutally persecuted heretics and dissenters, and attempted to levy substantial taxes to fund the army. A low point in the occupation came in 1576, when unpaid Spanish soldiers mutinied and ransacked Antwerp, killing hundreds in a brutal rampage now remembered as the Spanish Fury.

By the time the act was written in 1581, the northern and southern Dutch provinces had reached an impasse with regard to Spanish rule. An uprising against the Spanish army, led by William, Prince of Orange, had been ongoing since 1568, and in the wake of the Spanish Fury the Dutch provinces signed the Pacification of Ghent, a short-lived pledge of allegiance against the occupying forces. In 1579, however, the predominantly Catholic southern provinces were persuaded to affirm loyalty to Philip in exchange for the restoration of local privileges and the suspension of foreign troop garrisons. The more-Protestant northern provinces formed their own alliance, the Union of Utrecht, and continued their rebellion before formally breaking with Philip when they signed the *Act of Abjuration*.

The act largely draws upon the ideological points expressed in the political literature—especially the pamphlets—of the Dutch Revolt. The act's opposition to absolute monarchy, along with its assertion that through tyranny the king had abandoned his right to the loyalty of his subjects, can be discerned in various polemical writings justifying the rebellion, including William's 1580 *Apology*. The rebellious Dutch ideology was itself probably influenced by that of the French Huguenots, who also endured anti-Protestant persecution and often opposed absolute rule. The 1579 Huguenot tract *Vindiciae contra Tyrannos* (A defense of liberty against tyrants) strongly prefigures the arguments of the *Act of Abjuration*.

As a pioneering declaration of political independence from an oppressive ruler, the *Act of Abjuration* was an important antecedent for various similar declarations. The ultimate success of the Dutch Revolt easily could have been regarded as a vindication of the act itself, and although the extent to which it served as a consciously imitated model for future writers is debatable, it may nonetheless be seen, for example,

✣ **Key Facts**

Time Period:
Late 16th Century

Movement/Issue:
Dutch independence
from Spain

Place of Publication:
The Netherlands

**Language of
Publication:**
Dutch

THE DUKE OF ALVA

Apart from King Philip II of Spain, the Spanish oppressor who receives the greatest amount of condemnation within the *Act of Abjuration* is probably Don Fernando Álvarez de Toledo, the third duke of Alva. Sent by Philip to the Netherlands in 1567 for the purpose of crushing dissent and consolidating royal control over the Dutch provinces, Alva arrived in August accompanied by a 10,000-person army. Deeply intolerant of Protestantism and thoroughly contemptuous of his Dutch subjects, the duke soon established a tribunal, known as the Council of Troubles, to try to punish suspected political and religious dissidents.

Around 9,000 people were convicted of treason or heresy. Of these, more than a thousand were executed, most prominently the Counts Egmont and Hoorn, a pair of conciliatory Catholic nobles who subsequently became martyrs for the rebellious cause (their deaths are mentioned among the grievances enumerated in the act). Alva's commission came to be popularly known as the Council of Blood, and many early writings of the Dutch Revolt cited his tyranny, rather than that of Philip, as the cause for rebellion. The duke was unable to effectively combat the open insurrection, which he partially inspired, and in 1573 he left the Netherlands so Philip could send in a replacement.

as a significant ideological precursor to the American *Declaration of Independence* (1776), particularly given the generally acknowledged impact of the Dutch Revolt itself on the ideology of the American Revolution. The influence of the act on subsequent political writing remains a subject of interest in contemporary scholarship.

THEMES AND STYLE

The primary theme of the *Act of Abjuration* is that King Philip, in oppressing the people of the Netherlands, has effectively violated the duties that he had sworn to uphold and therefore no longer deserves to be treated as king. Prior to a lengthy elaboration of Philip's various abuses, the Act states, "[T]he prince of a country is appointed by God to be the head of his subjects to protect and shield them from all iniquity … if he acts differently and instead of protecting his subjects endeavors to oppress and molest them … he must be regarded not as a prince but as a tyrant." The act states that such a tyrant should be repudiated by his subjects, especially if "these subjects have been unable to soften their prince's heart through explanations humbly made." The act asserts that such attempts at swaying Philip have failed and that the king responded to them by having the spokesmen arrested and killed, violating "all fundamental rights, always strictly maintained by even the most cruel and tyrannical princes."

The act's rhetoric is largely based on appeals to traditional political customs and privileges rather than on new and radical assertions. Despite its renown as the Dutch declaration of independence (a phrase that only came to describe the act several centuries later), the act scrupulously avoids outright expression of revolutionary sentiments. Indeed, its censure of Philip for violating traditional provincial rights casts him as a nontraditional party, flouting the rules by which his father, Charles V, had always been willing to abide. Likewise, the act calls not for the rejection of any single ruler but for the specific rejection of a bad ruler: "[A]ll this has given us more than enough legitimate reasons for abandoning the king of Spain and for asking another powerful and merciful prince to protect and defend these provinces." The act's designation of the Duke of Anjou as Philip's replacement underlines this sentiment and demonstrates the act's preoccupation with maintaining consistency with existing protocols, even though the new ruler's tenure later turned out to be quite abbreviated.

The language of the act is stylistically earnest and straightforward, adamant but not intemperate. As befits its status as a formal document, it avoids excessive emotionality and presents the United Provinces' break with Philip as a natural consequence of the king's actions. The act's elaboration of the proper conduct of a ruler is prefaced by the phrase "it is common knowledge," contributing to the act's overriding portrayal of Philip as a criminal transgressing against the known laws of the land. To that end, the few instances of relatively impassioned diction discuss the outrageousness of Philip's conduct, as when his treatment of his subjects is described as an attempt to "deprive these countries of their ancient freedom and to bring them into slavery under Spanish rule." Likewise, the act's measured and reasonable tone is in keeping with its presentation of its signatories' actions as eminently lawful and proper.

CRITICAL DISCUSSION

The act was controversial even among the provinces that signed it, aside from the Dutch provinces outside the Union of Utrecht. In *The Dutch Republic: Its Rise, Greatness, and Fall, 1477-1806* (1995), Jonathan Israel observes, "[R]esistance theories were now in vogue. But there were still many who abhorred such doctrines and rejected the *Act of Abjuration*." This had concrete political ramifications: "[N]umerous officeholders resigned their positions especially in Gelderland, Overijssel, and Friesland. The States of Overijssel accepted the Act only with great reluctance." The act thus served as a divisive text not just between the Netherlands and Spain, or between the United Provinces and the Spanish Netherlands, but also within the Low Countries.

Since the act functioned as a kind of manifesto and as a political action, its legacy can arguably be felt throughout the subsequent history of the Netherlands. A landmark event in the Dutch Revolt, it was also a crucial step in the United Provinces' transition to explicit republicanism, which culminated in December 1587 when the Earl of Leicester, Anjou's eventual successor as the appointed (and frustrated) ruler of the United Provinces, departed. Likewise, the eventual success of the Dutch Republic as an independent state made it an inspirational model for future revolutionary endeavors. In a 1997 essay in *Royal and Republican Sovereignty in Early Modern Europe: Essays in Memory of Ragnhild Hatton*, G. C. Gibbs observes, "[T]he Dutch Revolt appeared to Americans and, indeed, to many Europeans, as the most obvious point of comparison in recent European history for the Anglo-American crisis." Scholarship on the act often focuses on its role in this legacy and on its place in the ideological firmament of the Revolt.

Contemporary scholarship is often devoted to contextualizing the act's ideas within the historical milieu of the seventeen provinces of the Low Countries. To that end, Martin van Gelderen's 1992 study *The Political Thought of the Dutch Revolt, 1555-1590*, describes the act as "a sober, prudent, and not highly original document. Essentially the preamble reiterated views which had become commonplace in the political literature of the Revolt." Meanwhile, other scholars have sought to draw connections between the act and subsequent political writing, a trend exemplified by Stephen E. Lucas's 1994 essay in *Connecting Cultures: The Netherlands in Five Centuries of Transatlantic Exchange*, which puts forth the argument—accepted by some, contested by others—that the act directly served as a model for the composition of the American *Declaration of Independence*.

BIBLIOGRAPHY

Sources

"Edict of the States General of the United Netherlands by Which They Declare That the King of Spain Has Forfeited the Sovereignty …" *Texts Concerning the Revolt of the Netherlands.* Ed. E. H. Kossman and A. F. Mellink. London: Cambridge UP, 1974. 216-28. Print.

Gelderen, Martin van. *The Political Thought of the Dutch Revolt, 1555-1590.* Cambridge: Cambridge UP, 1992. Print.

Gibbs, G. C. "The Dutch Revolt and the American Revolution." *Royal and Republican Sovereignty in Early Modern Europe: Essays in Memory of Ragnhild Hatton.* Ed. Robert Oresko, G. C. Gibbs, and H. M. Scott. Cambridge: Cambridge UP, 1997. 609-37. Print.

Israel, Jonathan I. *The Dutch Republic: Its Rise, Greatness, and Fall, 1477-1806.* Oxford: Clarendon, 1995. Print.

Lucas, Stephen E. "The Plakkaat van Verlatinge: A Neglected Model for the American *Declaration of Independence*." *Connecting Cultures: The Netherlands in Five Centuries of Transatlantic Exchange.* Ed. Rosemarijn Hoefte and Johanna C. Kardux. Amsterdam: VU UP, 1994. 187-207. Print.

Further Reading

Arnade, Peter. *Beggars, Iconoclasts, and Civic Patriots: The Political Culture of the Dutch Revolt.* Ithaca: Cornell UP, 2008. Print.

Boone, Marc. "The Dutch Revolt and the Medieval Tradition of Urban Dissent." *Journal of Early Modern History* 11.4-5 (2007): 351-75. Print.

Gelderen, Martin van, ed. and trans. *The Dutch Revolt.* Cambridge: Cambridge UP, 1993. Print.

Nierop, Henk van. *Treason in the Northern Quarter: War, Terror, and the Rule of Law in the Dutch Revolt.* Trans. J. C. Grayson. Princeton: Princeton UP, 2009. Print.

Tanis, James R. "The Dutch-American Connection: The Impact of the Dutch Example on American Constitutional Beginnings." *New York and the Union: Contributions to the American Constitutional Experience.* Ed. Stephen L. Schechter and Richard B. Bernstein. Albany: New York State Commission on the Bicentennial of the United States Constitution, 1990. 22-28. Print.

Tracy, James D. *The Founding of the Dutch Republic: War, Finance, and Politics in Holland, 1572-1588.* Oxford: Oxford UP, 2008. Print.

James Overholtzer

The *Act of Abjuration* formally declared the Dutch Low Countries independent from their overlord, King Philip II of Spain, depicted here in a painting by Sofonisba Anguiscola (1581). THE ART ARCHIVE AT ART RESOURCE, NY

APPEAL IN FOUR ARTICLES

David Walker

✢ *Key Facts*

Time Period:
Mid-20th Century

Movement/Issue:
Abolitionism

Place of Publication:
United States

Language of Publication:
English

OVERVIEW

Composed by David Walker, *Appeal in Four Articles* (1829) describes the unjust suffering of enslaved black people in an effort to bring to the attention of white people the inherent cruelty and inhumanity of the institution of slavery and to encourage rebellion and resistance among slaves. The manifesto was written in response to the conditions endured by slaves, which Walker had witnessed firsthand in the early nineteenth-century southern United States. Born free in Wilmington, North Carolina, c. 1797, to an enslaved father and a free mother, Walker witnessed the harsh reality of slavery during extensive travels throughout the South. After moving to Boston 1825, he began to develop the argument made in his *Appeal.* Addressed to "my dearly beloved Brethren and Fellow Citizens," the *Appeal in Four Articles* makes a religious and historical argument that slavery is immoral. Central to the manifesto are its four articles, which outline the causes of the "wretched" state of blacks in the United States.

The initial reaction to Walker's *Appeal in Four Articles* was strongly divided. White southerners denounced and banned the manifesto, and many blacks and abolitionists, white and black, were concerned that the plan was too radical; but others were inspired by the document's denunciation of slavery and argument for racial equality. Walker's manifesto relied on the precepts in the Bible and the *Declaration of Independence* to make the case for liberating blacks from the bondage of slavery. The *Appeal* marked a new urgency in the long antislavery movement, which grew in strength over the next several decades until slaves were emancipated near the end of the American Civil War in 1865. Today, the *Appeal in Four Articles* is widely considered the first thorough polemic against slavery to appear in the United States and a key document in the history of abolitionism.

HISTORICAL AND LITERARY CONTEXT

Appeal in Four Articles responds to the abject suffering of slaves in the early nineteenth century. One of many pockets of localized resistance to slavery was in Charleston, South Carolina, where Walker lived in the late 1810s and early 1820s. A branch of the African Methodist Episcopal (AME) Church—which was founded in Philadelphia, Pennsylvania, in 1816 by free blacks—was formed in Charleston in 1818. Through his involvement in the AME Church, Denmark Vesey, a free black man, attempted to organize a rebellion in Charleston. When the plot was uncovered in 1822, it was brutally put down by the city's white authorities. The violent suppression of Vesey's uprising fueled the longstanding rebellion while simultaneously pushing it further underground.

When Walker was writing *Appeal in Four Articles,* political activity by free blacks in the North was increasingly well organized and assertive. As a resident of Boston, Walker was at a nerve center of the movement for black solidarity and against racial oppression. Organizations such as the Massachusetts General Colored Association, to which Walker belonged, provided the mechanism for blacks to achieve political progress. The AME Church and other black churches increased their presence and served as sites for the development of a black political consciousness, united by a desire to end racial oppression and enslavement and to engage with whites to mount a challenge for equal citizenship. When the *Appeal* appeared in 1829, it provided a platform around which the various elements of the growing black reform movement could coalesce.

In addition to drawing on a long tradition of extemporaneous black oratory, Walker's *Appeal in Four Articles* responded to contemporary antislavery journalism, particularly that of *Freedom's Journal.* Established in 1827, *Freedom's Journal* was the first newspaper in the United States owned and operated by African Americans. The origins of many of Walker's arguments can be traced to the paper, to which Walker contributed. For example, his historical argument for the African, rather than European, origin of civilization appeared first in *Freedom's Journal.* In composing his manifesto, Walker also drew significantly from the tradition of black preaching. This influence can be seen in the text's structure and tone, which function to incite its audience to action in the cause of freedom for slaves.

Appeal in Four Articles is a seminal work from the beginning of a long tradition of African American writings on race and oppression. The legacy of

Walker's *Appeal* is apparent in works of political journalism in abolitionist newspapers such as *The Liberator* (founded in 1831) and can be seen in many antislavery texts and speeches that were produced before the Civil War. In his 1852 speech "The Meaning of the Fourth of July for the Negro," for example, black abolitionist Frederick Douglass echoed many of Walker's arguments. The influence of the *Appeal in Four Articles* carried well into the twentieth century and can be found in *The Autobiography of Malcolm X* (1965), a controversial work that advocates for a philosophy of black nationalism that has roots in Walker's manifesto.

THEMES AND STYLE

The central theme of *Appeal in Four Articles* is that slavery inflicts inexpressible suffering and that resistance to the institution is imperative. The manifesto opens by bluntly declaring "that we (coloured people of the United States) are the most degraded, wretched, and abject set of being that ever lived since the world began." In Article I, Walker refutes the argument that whites are superior to blacks and are therefore justified in their barbarity. In Article II, he argues that whites have kept slaves servile by denying them knowledge and that blacks must therefore pursue education in order to become free. In Article III, he describes whites' failure to fight slavery as a failure of their Christian duty to heed the word of God. In Article IV, Walker portrays efforts to send blacks "back to Africa" as misguided and unjust.

The manifesto achieves its rhetorical effect through appeals to the infallible and omnipresent authority of God, which transcends the laws and arguments of men. Throughout his *Appeal in Four Articles,* Walker invokes God and Jesus Christ and refers to biblical stories and figures as a means not only to dignify blacks and their struggles but to reinforce the idea that Christianity itself is a humanizing common factor between blacks and whites. "Did our creator make us to be slave to dust and ashes like ourselves?" Walker asks his reader. He also links the effort against American slavery to the biblical story of the Israelites' successful effort to escape enslavement in Egypt, arguing that the Egyptians, "having got possession of the Lord's people, treated them *nearly* as cruel as *Christian Americans* do us, at the present day."

Stylistically, *Appeal in Four Articles* is distinguished by its emphatic simplicity. Written to appeal primarily to slaves and free blacks in the North who gathered in secret, Walker's manifesto was designed to be read aloud to large (and largely illiterate) audiences and aimed to incite them to action. It was written, in Walker's words, "in language so very simple, that the most ignorant, who can read at all, may easily understand." It is also written in the first person and alludes throughout to the author's direct observation of the

DAVID WALKER: REVILED AND REVERED

David Walker is remembered as the author of a radically forward-thinking essay that laid the foundation for nearly two centuries of African American thinking about the path of liberation from racial oppression. This vaunted reputation would have been inconceivable to those who knew him as a child in North Carolina. Though Walker was born "free," he lived in a deeply racist society. Walker's experience motivated him not only to flee for the greater opportunity of the North but to work to gain freedom for his bonded brethren. His efforts to do so made him a reviled figure throughout the slaveholding South.

Officials in the South responded to the *Appeal* by passing laws to ban abolitionist literature and to prohibit education for blacks. Louisiana even made reading *Appeal in Four Articles* punishable by life imprisonment or death. Then, in 1830, less than a year after the publication of the manifesto, Walker died. Rumors of foul play flared. Some claimed that Walker had been poisoned. Others claimed he had been murdered by someone hoping to a collect a reward issued by proponents of slavery. However, no evidence of foul play ever turned up, and the likely cause of Walker's death was far more mundane: tuberculosis.

In his *Appeal in Four Articles,* David Walker speaks out against the racist sentiments of Thomas Jefferson, depicted here in an 1800 portrait.
© BETTMANN/CORBIS

PRIMARY SOURCE

APPEAL IN FOUR ARTICLES

My dearly beloved Brethren and Fellow Citizens.

Having travelled over a considerable portion of these United States, and having, in the course of my travels, taken the most accurate observations of things as they exist—the result of my observations has warranted the full and unshaken conviction, that we (coloured people of these United States) are the most degraded, wretched, and abject set of beings that ever lived since the world began; and I pray God that none like us ever may live again until time shall be no more. They tell us of the Israelites in Egypt, the Helots in Sparta, and of the Roman Slaves, which last were made up from almost every nation under heaven, whose sufferings under those ancient and heathen nations, were, in comparison with ours, under this enlightened and Christian nation, no more than a cipher—or, in other words, those heathen nations of antiquity, had but little more among them than the name and form of slavery; while wretchedness and endless miseries were reserved, apparently in a phial, to be poured out upon our fathers, ourselves and our children, by *Christian* Americans!

These positions I shall endeavour, by the help of the Lord, to demonstrate in the course of this *Appeal,* to the satisfaction of the most incredulous mind—and may God Almighty, who is the Father of our Lord Jesus Christ, open your hearts to understand and believe the truth.

The *causes,* my brethren, which produce our wretchedness and miseries, are so very numerous and aggravating, that I believe the pen only of a Josephus or a Plutarch, can well enumerate and explain them. Upon subjects, then, of such incomprehensible magnitude, so impenetrable, and so notorious, I shall be obliged to omit a large class of, and content myself with giving you an exposition of a few of those, which do indeed rage to such an alarming pitch, that

indignities he describes. In so doing, Walker illustrates not only his knowledge of slavery but his compassion for the institution's victims. With its oratorical form, hortatory style, prophetic tone, and religious allusions, the manifesto assumes the style of a church sermon, thereby paralleling the struggle to escape slavery with the struggle to achieve salvation.

CRITICAL DISCUSSION

When *Appeal in Four Articles* first appeared, proslavery Americans were alarmed but the response within antislavery circles was mixed. When it surfaced in the South, the manifesto was confiscated and banned; some states even passed laws that tightened restrictions on the education of slaves. In the North, the black response was enthusiastic. According to the *Boston Daily Evening Transcript,* "It is evident they [black Bostonians] have read this pamphlet … and that they glory in its principles, as if it were a star in the east, guiding them to freedom and emancipation." Some who were impressed with the document's erudition questioned whether a black man was capable of writing it. In the Boston newspaper *The Liberator,* a letter writer sympathetic to the manifesto's claims argued in 1831 that the "pamphlet is the result of more reading than could have fallen to the lot of that man [Walker]." Some antislavery whites and free blacks rejected the manifesto because of its call for violence.

In the years following its publication, the *Appeal* remained an important source of inspiration for those working to end slavery. It exerted decided influence on Boston abolitionist William Lloyd Garrison's founding of *The Liberator,* a powerful abolitionist newspaper that ran from 1831 through the Civil War. Also in 1831, Nat Turner, a Virginia slave, led a slave rebellion that resulted in the death of fifty-five white people. According to scholar Amy Reynolds, "A large number of slaveholders, newspaper editors and public officials in the South directly attributed the August 1831 slave insurrection led by Nat Turner to Walker, Garrison and other abolitionists."

Much of the extensive body of criticism that has been written on the manifesto has focused on its influence on later strategies for black resistance to white oppression. According to historian Sterling Stuckey in *Slave Culture: Black Nationalist Theory & Foundations of Black America* (1972), Walker "is the father of black nationalist theory in America because much of the substance of that ideology is found in his writings, despite the sometimes disjointed way in which he presented his views." Commentators have also drawn attention to the "culturally embedded rhetorical strategies of the *Appeal,*" as scholar Ian Finseth describes them in a 2001 piece for *Mississippi Quarterly.* Finseth further examines "the ways in which antislavery representations of the relationship between racial and national history drew upon scientific and quasi-scientific concepts of human and nonhuman 'nature.'"

they cannot but be a perpetual source of terror and dismay to every reflecting mind.

I am fully aware, in making this appeal to my much afflicted and suffering brethren, that I shall not only be assailed by those whose greatest earthly desires are, to keep us in abject ignorance and wretchedness, and who are of the firm conviction that Heaven has designed us and our children to be slaves and *beasts of burden* to them and their children. I say, I do not only expect to be held up to the public as an ignorant, impudent and restless disturber of the public peace, by such avaricious creatures, as well as a mover of insubordination— and perhaps put in prison or to death, for giving a superficial exposition of our miseries, and exposing tyrants. But I am persuaded, that many of my brethren, particularly those who are ignorantly in league with slave-holders or tyrants, who acquire their daily bread by the blood and sweat of their more ignorant brethren—and not a few of those too, who are

too ignorant to see an inch beyond their noses, will rise up and call me cursed—Yea, the jealous ones among us will perhaps use more abject subtlety, by affirming that this work is not worth perusing, that we are well situated, and there is no use in trying to better our condition, for we cannot. I will ask one question here.—Can our condition be any worse?—Can it be more mean and abject? If there are any changes, will they not be for the better, though they may appear for the worst at first? Can they get us any lower? Where can they get us? They are afraid to treat us worse, for they know well, the day they do it they are gone. But against all accusations which may or can be preferred against me, I appeal to Heaven for my motive in writing—who knows that my object is, if possible, to awaken in the breasts of my afflicted, degraded and slumbering brethren, a spirit of inquiry and investigation respecting our miseries and wretchedness in this *Republican Land of Liberty! ! ! ! ! !*

BIBLIOGRAPHY

Sources

Asukile, Thabiti. "Embracing Black Nationalist Theories of David Walker's *Appeal.*" *Black Scholar* 29.4 (1999): 16-25. Web. 11 July 2012.

Finseth, Ian. "David Walker, Nature's Nation, and Early African-American Separatism." *Mississippi Quarterly* 54.3 (2001): 337-63. Web. 12 July 2012.

Hinks, Peter P. *To Awaken My Afflicted Brotherhood: David Walker and the Problem of Antebellum Slave Resistance.* University Park: Pennsylvania State UP, 1997. Print.

Reynolds, Amy. "The Impact of Walker's *Appeal* on Northern and Southern Conceptions of Free Speech in the Nineteenth Century." *Communication Law and Policy* 9.1 (2010): 73-100. Web. 12 July 2012.

Seraile, William. "David Walker and Malcolm X: Brothers in Radical Thought." *Black World* 22.12 (1973): 68-73. Print.

Stuckey, Sterling. *The Ideological Origins of Black Nationalism.* Boston: Beacon Press, 1972. Print.

Further Reading

Alford, Terry. *Prince Among Slaves.* New York: Harcourt Brace Jovanovich, 1977. Print.

Berlin, Ira. *Generations of Captivity: A History of African-American Slaves.* Cambridge: Belknap of Harvard UP, 2003. Print.

Cornelius, Janet Duitsman. *"When I Can Read My Title Clear": Literacy, Slavery, and Religion in the Antebellum South.* Columbia: U of South Carolina P, 1991. Print.

Davis, David B. *The Problem of Slavery in the Age of Revolution, 1770-1823.* Ithaca: Cornell UP, 1975. Print

Frey, Sylvia. *Water from the Rock: Black Resistance in a Revolutionary Age.* Princeton: Princeton UP, 1991.

Jacobs, Donald M. "David Walker and William Lloyd Garrison: Racial Cooperation and the Shaping of Boston Abolition." *Courage and Conscience: Black and White Abolitionists in Boston.* Ed. Donald M. Jacobs. Bloomington: Indiana UP, 1993. 9-17. Print.

Theodore McDermott

BASEL PROGRAM
Theodor Herzl

✣ *Key Facts*

Time Period:
Late 19th Century

Movement/Issue:
Zionism

Place of Publication:
Switzerland

Language of Publication:
German

OVERVIEW

Formulated by the First Zionist Congress in Basel, Switzerland, in 1897 under the aegis of Theodor Herzl, the Basel Program established the foundation of political Zionism, which sought to create an internationally recognized Jewish state in Palestine. The program, also known as the Basel Declaration, sets forth four ways to achieve this goal. Prior to the congress, a number of groups, such as Hovevei Zion, had engaged in Zionist activities, though with no central doctrine or clear organizing principles. At Basel, Herzl founded the Zionist Organization (now called the World Zionist Organization) to move on the program's action points.

"THE PROTOCOLS OF THE ELDERS OF ZION"

First published in 1903 and widely disseminated in the early twentieth century, "The Protocols of the Elders of Zion" (also known as "The Protocols of the Meetings of Learned/Sage Elders") is purportedly the minutes from a late-nineteenth-century meeting of Jewish leaders elaborating a secret plot to take over the world. The document is made up of twenty-four "protocols" that treat basic philosophy, methods of conquest, and the ultimate aims of "The Jewish Ruler." Though it was widely debunked, it is still presented as a legitimate document in certain print and online sources and has been used to promote anti-Semitism and to justify crimes against Jews.

"The Protocols of the Elders of Zion" first appeared in September 1903 in the far-right-wing St. Petersburg daily *Znamja* under the headline "The Jewish Program for the Conquest of the World." Several versions of the document were published in Russia in the years following its initial appearance, largely as a way of explaining Russia's defeat in the Russo-Japanese War, as well as the Russian Revolution of 1905. "The Protocols" remained relatively unknown outside of Russia until its export to Europe with "white Russians" fleeing the Bolshevik Revolution of 1917. Within Russia, "The Protocols" had been used to enact widespread slaughter of Jews in the civil wars following the revolution. Abroad, anticommunist Russians immigrating to the West denounced the Bolsheviks as Jews who were enacting the plan set forth in the "The Protocols." This allegation would be used to demonize Jews and other groups throughout the twentieth century, most notably in Adolf Hitler's Nazi Germany.

While many European Jews, especially more secular members of the intelligentsia, agreed with Herzl's platform, there was opposition to Zionism—in particular, to political Zionism—from both Orthodox and Reform leaders in the Jewish community. Indeed, the congress was originally planned for Munich but had to be moved to Switzerland because of protests from Jews in Germany. Some settlement Zionists, who focused on settling Palestine and working the land, thought that Herzl's agitation would be harmful to the Jews, particularly the laboring classes already on the ground in Palestine. The congress also attracted attention from anti-Semitic elements in Europe; for example, "The Protocols of the Elders of Zion," a fabricated anti-Semitic document, has falsely been attributed to the First Zionist Congress. Herzl summarized the impact of the 1897 gathering in Switzerland as such: "At Basel I founded the Jewish state." Though this assessment is subject to debate, the First Congress and the Basel Program are widely considered foundational to the Zionist movement.

HISTORICAL AND LITERARY CONTEXT

The Basel Program responds to the failure of emancipation in the nineteenth century to create truly equal and just conditions for assimilated Jews in Europe. The Jewish diaspora following the conquest of the Kingdom of Judah in the sixth century BCE and the first century CE destruction by the Romans of the rebuilt state of Judea led to widespread migration and settlement of Jews across Europe. Through much of this history, Jews, particularly those in cities, were segregated from the Christian majority and had limited ability to participate in economic and political life. With the rise of Enlightenment ideals and increasing liberalization in many countries, Jews throughout Europe were gradually awarded more rights and freedom. However, anti-Semitism also grew, as both nationalist and racist arguments were made against Jewish participation in society.

Herzl was deeply influenced by the Dreyfus affair, in which a Jewish man in the French army, Alfred Dreyfus, was wrongfully convicted of treason in 1894. Ironically, France was one of the most liberal of the European nations regarding the treatment of Jews in the late nineteenth century. Assimilated Jews participated freely in French society, including joining the country's army, which was considered, as Adam Gopnik notes in his 2009 article in the *New Yorker,* "the sword and shield of the nation." As the Paris correspondent for a Viennese paper, Herzl bore witness to the Dreyfus affair. He was present for Dreyfus's degradation ceremony, when the soldier was publicly stripped of his rank in front of jeering crowds following a secret military trial. While anti-Semitism did not drive the persecution of Dreyfus, it was likely a strong factor in his subsequent incarceration, which lasted until 1900, even though it was obvious early on that he was not guilty of the charges. The case led Herzl to believe that if assimilation could not work in France, it could not work at all. Jews, he concluded, must have their own state.

The Basel Program reflects the ideas developed in Herzl's 1896 book *The Jewish State,* as well as a more lengthy tradition of writings dealing with dilemmas facing Jews in an increasingly secular world. Moses Hess, famous for his *Rom und Jerusalem* (1862), called on Jews to sacrifice the benefits of emancipation in the name of a nationalist identity. In the 1880s Moshe Lilienblum wrote extensively about the necessity of a Jewish state, most notably in *O Vozrozhdenii Yevreiskavo Naroda* (1883).

In the decades after the Basel Program appeared, there were a number of other calls for the establishment of a Jewish state in Palestine. The Balfour Declaration of 1917 declared Britain's support for such a state and was later included in the Sèvres Peace Treaty with Turkey (1920) and the Mandate for Palestine (1922). The United Nations Partition Plan for Palestine (1947) sought to partition Palestine along Jewish/Arab lines, creating territory for each and protections for minorities living in contested areas. This resulted in civil war that lasted into 1948, and conflict in the region has continued to the present day.

THEMES AND STYLE

Foremost among the Basel Program's themes is the necessity of establishing a permanent and legally recognized homeland for the Jewish people. Herzl presents this as a goal of the Zionist movement as expressed through the First Congress, underlining its importance to a large body of Jews and cementing his conception of Zionism as explicitly political. Further, he elaborates practical steps Jews can take to reach this goal, such as establishing farms and businesses in Palestine. With a growing Jewish presence in Palestine, civic institutions could be established, providing a sense of community and identity. Finally, Herzl says, Jews should lay the foundation for a Jewish state by beginning the process of seeking legal recognition in Palestine.

The Basel Program achieves its effect by appealing to the almost universally felt Jewish yearning for a

"home" after two thousand years in exile. This appeal is followed by a list of practical steps to meet this end. Scholars have noted that a number of the delegates to the First Congress had sought to include the phrase "by international law," but Herzl chose instead to say "secured by public law," perhaps to avoid inciting anti-Semites, who had already begun to murmur about Jewish conspiracies. The use of the word "home" versus "state" may have been undertaken for similar reasons. Furthermore, the language of the program's action points is purposely vague, allowing for a variety of interpretations of "appropriate institutions" or the nature of the "national consciousness."

The clear and succinct tone of the Basel Program reflects Herzl's strongly held belief that the answer to the Jewish question is both straightforward and achievable. Through the application of simple, matter-of-fact language, the Basel Program's four action points attempt to rally the Jewish people around the goal of creating a state:

> Zionism seeks to establish a home for the
> Jewish people in Eretz-Israel secured under

A 1914 portrait of Theodor Herzl, founding figure of political Zionism and the First Zionist Congress. ERICH LESSING/ART RESOURCE, NY

public law. The Congress contemplates the following means to the attainment of this end:

1. The promotion by appropriate means of the settlement in Eretz-Israel of Jewish farmers, artisans, and manufacturers.

2. The organization and uniting of the whole of Jewry by means of appropriate institutions, both local and international, in accordance with the laws of each country.

3. The strengthening and fostering of Jewish national sentiment and national consciousness.

4. Preparatory steps toward obtaining the consent of governments, where necessary, in order to reach the goals of Zionism.

CRITICAL DISCUSSION

The First Zionist Congress and its Basel Program provoked a variety of reactions both inside and outside the Jewish community. In his book *The Iron Wall*, Avi Schlaim notes that "Herzl himself exemplified the Zionist tendency to indulge in wishful thinking." Some critics saw this trait in the Basel Program, pointing out that the text ignores the Arab presence in Palestine. Moreover, these critics claimed the Jewish state was a utopian vision that would most likely fail in practice.

Contemporary scholars such as Shlomo Avineri view Herzl not as a revolutionary thinker but as a transformative figure in Jewish history, one who reconfigured Zionism from "a parochial concern of some Jewish intellectuals" to an "issue of world politics." In the aftermath of the First Zionist Congress, meetings were held annually with the goal of establishing an infrastructure in Palestine; today such meetings take place every four years. Important organizations were founded during these meetings, such as the Jewish National Fund, created to purchase land in the future Israel, and the Zionist Commission, whose mission was to study Israeli social and economic conditions.

The Basel Program is not generally treated as an object of literary scholarship; instead, it is more often analyzed as an important historical moment in Jewish and European history or in the context of Herzl's biography. Additionally, after the declaration of Israel's independence in 1948, many Jews felt that the Zionist platform should be updated to reflect the new realities of the twentieth century. The first Zionist Congress to convene following the establishment of the State of Israel voted to maintain the Basel Program but to "complete" it to reflect a more modern conception of the "task of Zionism." This new formulation is commonly known as the Jerusalem Program and defines the mission of Zionism as "the consolidation of the state of Israel and the ingathering of the exiles in Eretz-Israel and the fostering of the unity of the Jewish people." Some elements of the congress did not support an entirely new program, especially since the majority of the world's Jews did not live in the homeland, thus leaving the Basel Program's objectives unfulfilled. The Jerusalem Program was revised in 1968 and again in 2004.

BIBLIOGRAPHY

Sources

Avineri, Shlomo. *The Making of Modern Zionism.* New York: Basic Books, 1981. Print.

Biasini, Nadia Guth, and Heidi Brunnschweiler. "The Jewish Museum of Switzerland." *European Judaism* 36.2 (2003): 74+. *General OneFile.* Web. 25 June 2012.

Gonen, Jay. *A Psycho-History of Zionism.* New York: Mason Charter, 1975. Print.

Gopnik, Adam. "Trial of the Century: Revisiting the Dreyfus Affair." *New Yorker.* 28 Sept. 2009. Web. 25 June 2012.

Shlaim, Avi. *The Iron Wall: Israel and the Arab World.* New York: W. W. Norton and Sons, 2001. Print.

Zwergbaum, Aharon. "Basel Program." *Encyclopaedia Judaica.* Ed. Michael Berenbaum and Fred Skolnik. 2nd ed. Vol. 3. Detroit: Macmillan Reference USA, 2007: 202-03. *Gale World History in Context.* Web. 26 June 2012.

Further Reading

Berkowitz, Michael. *Zionist Culture and West European Jewry before the First World War.* Cambridge: Cambridge UP, 1993. Print.

Boaz, Neumann. *Land and Desire in Early Zionism.* Waltham: Brandeis UP, 2011. Print.

Chowers, Eyal. *The Political Philosophy of Zionism: Trading Jewish Words for a Hebraic Land.* Cambridge: Cambridge UP, 2012. Print.

Halpern, B., and J. Reinharz. *Zionism and the Creation of a New Society.* Oxford: Oxford UP, 1998. Print.

Vital, D. "Zionism as Revolution? Zionism as Rebellion?" *Modern Judaism* 18.3 (2008): 205-15. Print.

Daisy Gard

CARTAGENA MANIFESTO

Simón Bolívar

OVERVIEW

The "Cartagena Manifesto," written by Simón Bolívar in Cartagena de Indias, New Granada (modern-day Colombia) on December 15, 1812, following the fall of the Venezuelan First Republic, is a call for New Granadans to join Venezuelans in a unified Latin American fight for independence from Spain. Having fled the chaos of the defeated First Republic in Venezuela, Bolívar entered a similar environment in Cartagena, where New Granadans were embroiled in their own civil war and were wary of listening to the pleas of this relatively unknown Venezuelan fugitive. The first of Bolívar's major political documents, the manifesto criticizes the individualist and federalist political leanings of his compatriots, analyzing the First Republic's 1811 Constitution in detail to reveal its lack of realism and reliance on abstract Enlightenment ideals. Bolívar addresses his manifesto specifically to the people of New Granada, enlisting their support for a renewed attempt at obtaining independence for his homeland.

The "Cartagena Manifesto" had an immediate impact in the region, winning Bolívar the support of New Granada and paving the way for the launch of his Admirable Campaign in February 1813. The manifesto is written as an explanation of the failures of Venezuela's initial attempt at independence and presents several of Bolívar's central political beliefs, which would become more apparent later in his career: his commitment to adapting Latin American laws to local cultural and economic conditions, his preference for a strong central government and rejection of federalism, and his intolerance for abstract theorists who were not grounded in the political reality of their surroundings. Today, the "Cartagena Manifesto" is regarded as one of Bolívar's major political writings and is included in many histories and courses on the Latin American independence period.

HISTORICAL AND LITERARY CONTEXT

The "Cartagena Manifesto" responds to the mounting unrest in Venezuela and New Granada over the unjust rule of the Spanish government. While the defeat of Venezuela, one of the first Spanish American colonies to have declared its independence from Spain, came as a blow to certain progressive-minded colonists, most of the region still worked within the Spanish system at the Cortes de Cádiz, Spain, which resulted in the liberal constitution of 1812. Nevertheless, many colonists were concerned by Spain's decision in the second half of the eighteenth century to open up the economy to free trade and to increase taxes. Within the region, neighboring Buenos Aires was one of the first cities to rebel against Spanish rule; it became the first legitimately independent area of South America.

When Bolívar was composing his manifesto, New Granada was divided into three blocs—the United Provinces, Cundinamarca, and the royalist provinces. Bolívar entered Cartagena in the aftermath of a rebellion headed by radical leaders whose central objective was to increase the civic and economic rights of Cartagena's colonists, though they also wanted to gain independence. This atmosphere of ideological and social feuds left New Granada politically divided.

❖ *Key Facts*

Time Period:
Early 19th Century

Movement/Issue:
Colonialism; Latin American independence

Place of Publication:
New Granada (modern-day Colombia)

Language of Publication:
Spanish

SIMÓN BOLÍVAR: THE LIBERATOR OF LATIN AMERICA

Simón José Antonio de la Santísima Trinidad Bolívar y Palacios, commonly known as Simón Bolívar, was a Venezuelan political and military leader. Born June 24, 1783, in Caracas, Venezuela, Bolívar became involved in the military at a young age. While spending time in Paris, he witnessed the coronation of Napoleon Bonaparte, which inspired him to bring similar glory and triumph to his own people in Venezuela. Today, Bolívar is regarded as a Latin American visionary and revolutionary hero and is considered one of the most influential politicians in the history of the Americas.

After assuming military command in Tunja, New Granada (modern-day Colombia), in 1813, Bolívar led the provinces of New Granada to independence from Spain, which was ultimately achieved in 1819. Bolívar then played a fundamental role in the establishment of Gran Colombia, the first union of independent nations in Latin America, in 1821. He served as president of Gran Colombia from 1819 to 1830, although he ruled as a dictator from 1828 until his resignation in early 1830. During his lifetime, Bolívar wrote many notable political documents, including the "Cartagena Manifesto" (1812), his "Carta de Jamaica" (Letter from Jamaica, 1815), and his "Angostura Address" (1819). Bolívar died of tuberculosis on December 17, 1830, at age forty-seven. He is often referred to as the "Liberator of Latin America" because of his monumental contributions to Latin American independence.

Camilo Torres, the president of the Cundinamarca legislative body at the center of the colony's political feuds, eventually came to support Bolívar's belief in a strong central government despite his initial federalist views.

The "Cartagena Manifesto" is a response to what Bolívar saw as the weakness of the First Republic's 1811 Constitution and reflects his reaction to contemporary politics, specifically the royalists' unwillingness to support his cause. Bolívar's political ideology was influenced by Montesquieu's "On the Spirit of Laws" (1748), particularly the idea that the success of a political system lies less in its abstract theory or mechanisms than in geographical and social conditions and its "appropriateness to the times." Bolívar responds to other works of the Enlightenment, challenging and rejecting many of the assumptions of the Age of Reason. He condemns the lofty philosophical thinking of the Enlightenment, promoting instead a concrete, realistic vision.

The "Cartagena Manifesto" influenced Bolívar's later writings—in which his advocacy for a central executive was strengthened and his political beliefs were solidified—and his body of work had a major impact on Latin American literature. After he wrote the "Cartagena Manifesto," Bolívar went into exile and moved toward a more autocratic vision, which is evidenced in the "Letter from Jamaica" (1815)

and is particularly prevalent in the 1826 Bolivian Constitution. Bolívar's work influenced much of the political writing during the era of Latin American independence, including the 1816 Declaration of Independence of the United Provinces of South America (modern-day Argentina), which discussed the ideal government for its new republic, and the 1833 Chilean Constitution, which structured the republic as a unitarian state with strong central leadership. Today, the "Cartagena Manifesto" in particular and the work of Bolívar in general continue to influence scholarship on the literature of revolution, as well as the ideology and writing of Latin American politicians.

THEMES AND STYLE

In the "Cartagena Manifesto," Bolívar's main goal was to summarize his experiences in Venezuela during the collapse of the First Republic in order to gain the support of the New Granadan people for a united independence movement and to help them avoid the same errors. Bolívar writes, "Allow me … to flatter myself that the terrible and exemplary lessons proffered by that extinct Republic will persuade America to improve her own conduct, correcting the failures … manifest in her several governments." The manifesto lays out several major flaws in the governance of the First Republic, including poor

This 1883 painting by Arturo Michelena depicts Simón Bolívar presenting the captured Spanish flag to a victorious battalion after the Battle of Carabobo in Venezuela, June 24, 1821. GIANNI DAGLI ORTI/THE ART ARCHIVE AT ART RESOURCE, NY

administration of state revenue, a weak federal system, the army's ineffectiveness, the opposition posed by the Catholic Church, and the response to the 1812 Caracas earthquake.

The manifesto achieves its rhetorical impact by voicing concern for the fate of New Granada and appealing to a Pan-Spanish American need for liberation from the Spanish Crown. "My purpose in writing this memorial is to spare New Granada the fate of Venezuela and to redeem Venezuela from the affliction it now suffers," Bolívar begins. The author emphasizes his personal investment in the future of New Granada in the opening line to gain the trust and attention of the people he directly addresses. Later in the manifesto, Bolívar relates his concern for New Granada with the need for the unity in Spanish America: "I am of the opinion that until we centralize our American governments, our enemies will gain irreversible advantages …. To this end I present as an indispensable measure for the security of New Granada the reconquest of Caracas." By emphasizing the shared struggles of Venezuela and New Granada, Bolívar attempts to gain support for his true cause: Venezuelan independence.

To achieve his goal, Bolívar adopts the personal tone of a memorial, conveying his individual experiences directly to his audience in a formal, highly educated fashion. The "Cartagena Manifesto" proves its authenticity through the firsthand testimony of a witness to the defeat of the First Republic, demanding respect from the New Granadans to whom it is addressed. "I am, Granadans, a son of unhappy Caracas, who miraculously escaped from amid her physical and political ruins and … now follow the banners of independence fluttering so gloriously in these States." The first-person perspective and words of praise for New Granada's zeal for independence strengthen Bolívar's message. Despite the lofty vocabulary employed by the author, his humble tone as "a son of unhappy Caracas" effectively appeals to the emotions of his audience.

CRITICAL DISCUSSION

The "Cartagena Manifesto" was enthusiastically embraced by New Granadans and other Spanish Americans involved in the fight for independence. The manifesto gained the political and financial support Bolívar needed to renew the independence movement in Venezuela. The literary response to the "Cartagena Manifesto" is difficult to trace since the Spanish government heavily censored publications during this period. It is likely that early newspapers carried news of the manifesto when it emerged in 1812, but no record of any such article exists today. Later publications that emerged in the early twentieth century, such as *Latin America: Its Rise and Progress* by Francisco Garcia Calderon (1912), praised

Bolívar for restoring a belief in the possibility of independence.

Above all, the "Cartagena Manifesto" has been influential in the revolutionary writing of Bolívar's political successors—José Martí, Che Guevara, even Hugo Chavez. During the era of Latin American independence, the manifesto had a profound impact on the political writings of Argentine general and revolutionary leader José de San Martín, including his proclamation of Peru's independence. Bolívar's manifesto also heavily influenced the political ideology of Chilean liberator Bernardo O'Higgins, which is reflected in the correspondence between O'Higgins and San Martín that is now housed in the University of Notre Dame's archival collection. Bolívar's influence is also apparent in the 1818 Chilean Declaration of Independence, drafted by O'Higgins, which establishes a strong central executive. The major works of Bolívar, including the "Cartagena Manifesto," have been the subject of much scholarly criticism in the two centuries since their publication.

Much scholarship on the "Cartagena Manifesto" focuses on Bolívar's detailed criticism of the First Republic. In his 2006 book *Simón Bolívar: A Life,* John Lynch explains, "In Bolívar's first major statement of his political ideas, the so-called 'Cartagena Manifesto' … he further analysed the failings of the first Venezuelan republic and probed its political assumptions, offering these 'terrible lessons' as an example and a warning." Lynch enumerates the specific points made by Bolívar in the manifesto. By contrast, Lester D. Langley has viewed the "Cartagena Manifesto" as "the first indicator of a temperament too accepting of strong executive power and even dictatorship, thus laying the foundation for his severe rule." While scholars and historians have been critical of Bolívar's totalitarian rule at the end of his career, he is generally remembered for his pivotal role in the liberation of Spanish America.

BIBLIOGRAPHY

Sources

Arismendi Posada, Ignacio. *Gobernantes Colombianos/ Colombian Presidents.* Bogotá: Interprint Editors, 1983. Print.

Bolívar, Simón. "The Cartagena Manifesto: Memorial Addressed to the Citizens of New Granada by a Citizen from Caracas." *El Libertador: Writings of Simón Bolívar.* Trans. F. Fornoff. New York: Oxford UP, 2003. 3-11. Print.

Bushnell, D., and L. Langley, eds. *Simón Bolívar: Essays on the Life and Legacy of the Liberator.* Lanham: Rowman & Littlefield, 2008. Print.

Gustafson, Sandra M. "Histories of Democracy and Empire." *American Quarterly* 59.1 (2007): 107-33. Print.

Langley, Lester D. *Simón Bolívar: Venezuelan Rebel, American Revolutionary.* Lanham: Rowman & Littlefield, 2009. Print.

Lynch, John. *Simón Bolívar: A Life.* New Haven: Yale UP, 2006. Print.

Further Reading

Bushnell, David. *Simón Bolívar: Liberation and Disappointment.* New York: Pearson Longman, 2004. Print.

Costeloe, Michael P. *Response to Revolution: Imperial Spain and the Spanish American Revolutions, 1810-1840.* New York: Cambridge UP, 1986. Print.

Cussen, Antonio. *Bello and Bolívar: Poetry and Politics in the Spanish American Revolution.* New York: Cambridge UP, 1992. Print.

Davies, Catherine. "Colonial Dependence and Sexual Difference: Reading for Gender in the Writings of Simón Bolívar (1783-1830). *Feminist Review* 79 (2005): 5-19. Print.

Lecuna, Vicente, and Harold Bierck, eds. *Selected Writings of Bolívar.* New York: Colonial, 1951. Print.

Lynch, John. "Bolívar and the Caudillos." *Hispanic American Historical Review* 63.1 (1983): 3-35. Print.

———. *Simón Bolívar and the Age of Revolution.* London: U of London Institute of Latin American Studies, 1983. Print.

Katrina White

CHAINS OF SLAVERY

Jean-Paul Marat

OVERVIEW

Jean-Paul Marat's *Chains of Slavery,* a pamphlet decrying political absolutism and the tyranny of kings, was first issued in London in the spring of 1774. Featuring the lengthy subtitle *A Work Wherein the Clandestine and Villainous Attempts of Princes to Ruin Liberty Are Pointed Out, and the Dreadful Scenes of Despotism Disclosed, to Which Is Prefixed an Address to the Electors of Great Britain, in Order to Draw Their Timely Attention to the Choice of Proper Representatives in the Next Parliament,* the work hints at the incendiary invective that would characterize Marat's famous radical republican newspaper of the French Revolution, *L'ami du peuple* (1789-93). Politically, however, *Chains of Slavery* is relatively conservative, preaching the merits of an enlightened constitutional monarchy. It was originally written to stir the English people to vigilant civic duty on the occasion of a parliamentary election. Nineteen years later, Marat reissued *Chains of Slavery* in French with a new preface and other additions meant to make the work more pertinent to the crisis in revolutionary France.

Marat's preface to the 1793 edition, *Chaînes de l'esclavage,* details an elaborate conspiracy spearheaded by English prime minister Frederick, Lord North, to suppress the original book before the parliamentary general election in the fall of 1774 so that it would not jeopardize his majority in the House of Commons. Marat claims in the preface to have sidestepped the plot by sending copies of the tract to patriotic societies in the north of England that secured its release in Newcastle-upon-Tyne. From there, Marat continues, the work enjoyed widespread circulation and caused a political ferment. Scholars have since discredited much of Marat's preface as a subterfuge calculated to enhance his reputation in France. In truth, the Newcastle reissue appeared in 1775 after the elections had already taken place. The first printing was little reviewed in the British press, and it sold poorly. By the time Marat brought out the French version, however, he was famous as the most violent extremist of the Revolution.

HISTORICAL AND LITERARY CONTEXT

Chains of Slavery warns of the dangers to liberty posed by despotic governments throughout Europe. Marat reduces many of the evils of contemporary society to the practices of tyrannical rulers and their ministers, but he also faults the people for allowing themselves to be so dominated. In the address to the British electorate prefixed to the volume, Marat urges constituencies to exercise great vigilance in the upcoming parliamentary elections to ensure that they select representatives who will work in the people's interest. The alternative, Marat writes, will be the debasement of the constitution of England, "a monument of political wisdom compared to others."

Born in Neuchâtel, Switzerland, and educated in Paris and Bordeaux, Marat moved to London in 1765, where he practiced medicine and observed firsthand the operation of the English constitution. Marat had written *Chains of Slavery* a few years before its 1774 publication during what has come to be known as the Wilkes controversy, the set of disputes between English radical politician and journalist John Wilkes and the government of King George III that had resulted in Wilkes's repeated arrests for libel and his expulsion from Parliament. The controversy reached its height in 1768 when government troops gunned down several people who had gathered in St. George's Fields to protest Wilkes's detention in King's Bench Prison, an incident that Marat in his 1793 preface claims to have witnessed. Wilkes was not alone in protesting monarchial abuses; after his reentry into politics, he succeeded in securing passage of legislation that protected the freedom of the press and prevented the issue of general warrants.

Chains of Slavery—like Wilkes's crusade against government corruption—contributed to the movement for reform of the English constitution that characterized the liberal British press of the period. In the 1793 preface, Marat attests that the Wilkes controversy had made him an apostle of liberty. Critics have disputed this claim, noting that Marat waited more than a decade before devoting himself to politics and had even served in the interim as the physician to the bodyguard of the comte d'Artois (later Charles X of France). Still, scholars have discerned in *Chains of Slavery* and some of Marat's other early writings seeds of the radicalism that would define his contribution to the French Revolution.

Modern historians study Marat's writings of the 1770s and 1780s to explain the profound shift in his thinking and behavior—from a man of science advocating reserved liberalism to a political reactionary

⁙ Key Facts

Time Period:
Mid-18th Century

Movement/Issue:
Liberalism; Enlightened constitutional monarchism

Place of Publication:
England

Language of Publication:
English

THE DEATH OF JEAN-PAUL MARAT

On July 13, 1793, Charlotte Corday, a royalist sympathizer from Caen, France, stabbed Jean-Paul Marat to death while he soaked in his bathtub at his home in Paris. Marat had been largely confined to medicinal baths due to a painful skin condition thought to have been contracted during the months he spent hiding from his enemies in the sewers of Paris. Corday gained access to Marat's apartment on the pretense of supplying him with a list of political moderates of the Girondin faction, which was planning an uprising against Marat and the radical Jacobins.

In truth, Corday allied herself with the Girondins, was horrified by the execution of King Louis XVI, and blamed Marat for the recent rash of killings of suspected traitors to the Revolution. Marat is thought to have died almost immediately, and Corday waited calmly for the police to come and arrest her. At her trial, Corday testified that she believed she could reverse the violence by assassinating Marat. Four days after killing Marat, Corday was executed by guillotine. The bathtub murder scene is depicted in one of the most famous images of the Revolution, Jacques-Louis David's painting *The Death of Marat*.

demanding the deaths of hundreds of royalist sympathizers and moderates in defense of the Revolution. Marat's lasting reputation rests on his diatribes in the *L'ami du peuple* exhorting the lower classes to mass rebellion, made all the more compelling by the dramatic circumstances of his stabbing death on July 13, 1793, by Charlotte Corday, a young woman of aristocratic heritage who believed she could put an end to the horrific violence destroying her country by killing its chief instigator, Marat. In both its original and revised editions, *Chains of Slavery* has taken a place in revisionist histories arguing that Marat's polarized legacy—a martyr for liberty to some, a monstrous madmen to others—demands more objective treatment.

THEMES AND STYLE

Chains of Slavery postulates an elaborate conspiracy throughout history on the part of rulers—who are in league with armies, the clergy, and legislative bodies—to hoodwink the people into subjection. The conspiracy succeeds, Marat contends, because the people are complacent and fail to detect the self-serving deceptions behind the words and displays of seeming benevolence: "Seduced by such artifices, the people rush to servitude, confirm to the Prince his usurpation." Marat's ideas on despotism and civic responsibility, as they were formulated in 1774, preach vigilance rather than rebellion. He writes, "The greatest misfortune that could happen to a free state, where the Prince is powerful and clever, is to not have public discussion, rallies, and groups."

Marat's principal strategy in convincing citizens of their responsibilities is to point to the authority of history. He illustrates the horrific consequences of not heeding his advice by surveying a range of despotic governments from classical times to the present, with special emphasis on the seventeenth-century English kings Charles I and Charles II. In the 1793 preface, Marat refers to his success in agitating against special political appointments in England. However, R.C.H. Catterall details the spurious content of the preface in his essay "The Credibility of Marat" and notes that no such bill outlawing the buying of political favors was passed in 1775 on Marat's recommendation. Further, Catterall points out, this suggestion for parliamentary reform was not even made part of the text until its appearance in a new section appended to the French version.

The declamatory style and urgent tone of *Chains of Slavery* is established at the outset in the address to the British electorate: "Gentlemen … Is the age of liberty passed away? Shall your children, bathing their chains with tears, one day say, 'These are the fruits of the venality of our fathers?'" Marat applies his characteristically inflammatory rhetoric to contemporary political ideology, both French and English. Critic Pasi Ihalainen credits Marat with helping to introduce English readers to French Enlightenment ideals of democracy and popular sovereignty, as does Stephen Miller, who writes in *Three Deaths and Enlightenment Thought: Hume, Johnson, Marat* (2001), "Sounding like [Jean-Jacques] Rousseau, [Marat] says that liberty is in danger everywhere in modern Europe … Many passages in *Chains of Slavery,* especially the attacks on luxury, seem to be taken almost directly from Rousseau's *Discourse on the Arts and Sciences.*" In a 2005 article for *The Historical Journal,* however, Rachel Hammersley argues for the opposite transcultural effect, describing how the text popularized in France the language of reform that had evolved out of the English revolution (1640-60): "It … constitutes one of the means by which English republican ideas made their way across the Channel."

CRITICAL DISCUSSION

Scholars concur that Marat greatly exaggerated the influence of *Chains of Slavery* in England in his 1793 preface to the French edition. According to Miller, "[T]he book sank without a trace." The French version appeared less than four months before Marat's assassination. Louis R. Gottschalk records in *Jean-Paul Marat: A Study in Radicalism* (1967) that immediately following Marat's death, plans were made by his left-wing supporters to distribute copies of *Chaînes de l'esclavage* among the sectional assemblies of Paris as "an infallible antidote to despotism." *Chaînes de l'esclavage* was reissued in 1833 in the aftermath of the French Revolution of 1830, with an introduction by Adolphe Havard stressing its antimonarchial implications.

Since the early twentieth century, scholars have emphasized the importance of *Chains of Slavery* as a source of information about Marat's political theories before and during the French Revolution. They have traced his revolutionary campaigns on behalf of the poor and needy back to ideas he first articulated in *Chains of Slavery,* as well as such other early works as the novel *Les lettres polonaises,* believed to have been written when Marat was in his thirties, and the treatise *Plan de legislation criminelle* (1780). In the opinion of Gottschalk, "[W]hat is most important in the education of the Marat of the Revolution is that the writing of [*Chains of Slavery*] caused him to reflect seriously upon the sovereignty of the people." Other critics, including Hammersley, have illustrated that Marat drew on *Chains of Slavery,* and on his knowledge of the defects of the English constitution, in his contributions to the debate surrounding the drafting of a new French constitution in 1789.

Scholars have also looked to *Chains of Slavery* to explain Marat's conspiratorial sensibility. The 1793 preface, with its account of Lord North's suppression plot, is cited as one of many examples of Marat's efforts at self-glorification. The most sympathetic treatments of the preface have argued that the invented conspiracy plot is an ingenious device supporting the theme of aristocratic treachery that occupies so much space in the text. Gottschalk offers the following explanation for Marat's much-maligned fanaticism: "[H]is one-track mind could grasp but one side to any question, because he was always absolutely convinced of his own sincerity and infallibility and, therefore, of the insincerity and fallibility of those who disagreed with him."

BIBLIOGRAPHY

Sources

Bax, Ernest Belfort. *Jean-Paul Marat: The People's Friend.* 2nd ed. London: Grant Richards, 1901. Print.

Gottschalk, Louis R. *Jean-Paul Marat: A Study in Radicalism.* Chicago: U of Chicago P, 1967. Print.

Hammersley, Rachel. "Jean-Paul Marat's *The Chains of Slavery* in Britain and France, 1774-1833." *Historical Journal* 48.3 (2005): 641-60. *Cambridge Journals Online.* Web. 29 Aug. 2012.

Marat, Jean-Paul. *Chains of Slavery.* Farmington Hills: Gale ECCO, 2010. Print.

———. *Les chaines de l'esclavage.* Ed. Adolphe Havard. Paris: Editions Complexe, 1988. Print.

Miller, Stephen. "The Death of Marat." *Three Deaths and Enlightenment Thought: Hume, Johnson, Marat.* Lewisburg: Bucknell, 2001. 123-61. Print.

The Murder of Marat, a 1794 painting by Jean-Jacques Hauer, depicts Jean-Paul Marat's assassination by Charlotte Corday. © RMN-GRAND PALAIS/ART RESOURCE, NY

Further Reading

Beebee, Thomas O. "A Revolution in Letters." *Epistolary Fiction in Europe: 1500-1850.* Cambridge: Cambridge UP, 1999. 137-65. Print.

Bernstein, Samuel. "Marat, Friend of the People." *Essays in Political and Intellectual History.* Freeport: Books for Libraries, 1955. 9-25. Print.

Catterall, R.C.H. "The Credibility of Marat." *American Historical Review* 16.1 (1910): 24-35. *JSTOR.* Web. 29 Aug. 2012.

Ihalainen, Pasi. "The American Crisis, Representation and the British People, 1772-1780." *Agents of the People: Democracy and Popular Sovereignty in British and Swedish Parliamentary and Public Debates, 1734-1800.* Leiden: Brill, 2012. 246-69. Print.

Sonenscher, Michael. "A Limitless Love of Self: Marat's Grim View of Human Nature." *Times Literary Supplement* 6 Oct. 1995: 3. Print.

Janet Mullane

DECLARATION OF INDEPENDENCE

Thomas Jefferson

✥ *Key Facts*

Time Period:
Late 18th Century

Movement/Issue:
National independence

Place of Publication:
United States

Language of Publication:
English

OVERVIEW

Drafted by Thomas Jefferson, the *Declaration of Independence* (1776) lists various violations committed by King George III and proclaims the independence of the thirteen American colonies from the British Empire. Originally titled the *Declaration by the Representatives of the United States in General Congress Assembled,* the final version of the document was adopted by the Continental Congress on July 4, 1776. The *Declaration* reflects American colonists' opposition to the British Empire's tyrannical policies, including martial law in Massachusetts, immunity extended to British officials, mandated quartering of British troops, and taxes levied on the colonies. This opposition is what had incited the American Revolution in 1775, and it eventually grew into a desire for independence as a sovereign nation. Addressed to the world at large, the *Declaration* endorses the premise that all people are inherently independent and, thus, have the right to redress violations of their independence through revolution.

The document was published and read aloud to audiences throughout the colonies, although only about one-third of the American population supported independence. Britain responded to the *Declaration* by attacking its wording, pointing out the hypocrisy of the statement that "all men are created equal" because the writers owned slaves. Despite this incongruity, the document's preamble is considered one of the most foundational assertions of individual freedom in history, and its language and moral standards influenced the French Revolution (1789) and struggles for independence such as those of the Confederate States of America (1860) and Vietnam (1945). The preamble's insistence that every individual has the inalienable right to life, liberty, and the pursuit of happiness has helped to inspire many groups seeking equality, from nineteenth-century abolitionist and women's suffrage movements to the United Nations' Universal Declaration of Human Rights (1948).

HISTORICAL AND LITERARY CONTEXT

In addition to offering a rebuttal to the various taxes levied by the British government on the American colonies, the *Declaration* criticizes the British Empire for inhibiting American commerce, fomenting domestic war between the multiple Native American tribes and the colonists, and depriving the colonists of trial by jury and direct representation in Parliament. Following the Seven Years' War (1756-63), Britain attempted to alleviate its debt and pay for its continued maintenance of troops in North America by assessing taxes such as the Sugar Act (1764) and the Stamp Act (1765). Although Parliament regarded the taxes as legal, the colonists, who were not represented in Parliament, argued that they alone had the right to impose levies upon themselves. In 1767 Parliament again established a series of taxes on colonial imports and sent troops to Boston in 1768. In March 1770 British troops fired into a crowd of protesters, killing five civilians. Known as the Boston Massacre, this incident helped solidify the colonists' resentment toward British rule. By 1773 Parliament had enacted multiple revenue acts, including the tax on tea from the East India Company. Each measure was passed without the colonists' consent, leading to more public protests, including the Boston Tea Party (1773). Parliament responded to the unruly colonists by imposing a series of measures known as the Intolerable Acts, which closed the Boston port, reorganized the Massachusetts government, and quartered British soldiers in private homes. Stemming from the frayed relationship between the colonies and the British crown, the colonists organized the First Continental Congress in September 1774, which hoped to persuade the crown to reinstitute self-rule to the colonies.

In the spring of 1775, prior to the drafting of the *Declaration of Independence,* tensions had escalated to the point where the colonists were at war with Great Britain. The Second Continental Congress convened in May 1775 and petitioned King George III to reconcile with the colonies. The king rejected the petition, declaring that the colonies were in rebellion. As the war raged on, the Continental Congress appointed a committee of five—John Adams, Roger Sherman, Robert Livingston, Benjamin Franklin, and Jefferson—to draft a document detailing America's reasons for declaring independence. The committee appointed Jefferson as the primary author. The *Declaration* itemizes the various violations committed by King George III and follows with a brief lamentation that a compromise could not be reached. The writers conclude by asserting that, given the conditions produced by Great Britain's policies, the colonies had no choice but to abolish all ties with the British government.

The *Declaration of Independence* draws heavily from Enlightenment-era thinkers, particularly John Locke, whose *Second Treatise of Government* (1689) argues for representative government, private property, and the right to revolution. Jefferson also borrows language and ideas from the *Constitution of Virginia* (1776) and the *Virginia Declaration of Rights* (1776), both of which champion the natural, inherent rights of man and call revolution a necessary response to tyranny.

The *Declaration of Independence* sparked numerous responses. In *The Rights of Great Britain Asserted against the Claims of America: Being an Answer to the Declaration of the General Congress* (1776), Sir John Dalrymple criticizes the soundness of the *Declaration*'s premises. On the other hand, subsequent revolutions utilized the document's language in their own declarations of independence, including the French *Declaration of the Rights of Man and Citizen* (1789), the *Venezuelan Declaration of Independence* (1811), and the *Declaration of Independence of Lower Canada* (1838). In his book, *The* Declaration of Independence: *A Global History,* David Armitage suggests that since the *Declaration*'s publication, "more than one hundred such documents have been issued on behalf of regional or nationalist groups."

THEMES AND STYLE

The thrust of the *Declaration* is its refusal to accept the tyrannical policies instituted by the British government. Finding its foundation in natural law, it opens with the following statement: "When in the Course of human events, it becomes necessary for one people to dissolve the political bands which have connected them with another, and to assume among the powers of the earth, the separate and equal station to which the Laws of Nature and of Nature's God entitle them." The document then proclaims the universal idea that "all men are created equal" and have certain rights that governments are responsible to maintain. Moreover, if the people find that the government violates these rights, it is justifiable for citizens "to throw off such Government, and to provide new Guards for their future security." The *Declaration* makes its case by detailing the ways in which King George III has violated the colonists' rights, including failing to pass reasonable laws, quartering military troops, and establishing taxes without consent. In conclusion, the manifesto reaffirms the colonists' duty to protect their security through establishing their sovereignty as an independent nation.

Addressed to not only the British government but also to the colonists and the world at large, the *Declaration* situates the American Revolution within the entire "course of human events." The introduction sets the tone, identifying the dispute with Britain as a

ABRAHAM LINCOLN: EXTENDING THE *DECLARATION OF INDEPENDENCE*

The *Declaration of Independence* had a resounding influence on the abolishment of slavery. In his "Peoria Speech" in 1854, Abraham Lincoln articulated the widely held belief that the founding fathers had intended for slavery to eventually fade away. For Lincoln, declaring that all men are created equal was meant to be a universal statement and not one that merely pertained to white, property-owning men. Thus, the *Declaration* was a living document, one that was open to interpretation and offered a profound way to assess the Constitution. Lincoln asserted that the Founding Fathers envisioned a nation based upon the principles of liberty and justice and framed the Constitution around universal equality.

Lincoln's views reinvigorated the *Declaration,* changing how people perceived the document. It became a guide on how to interpret the Constitution since it offered moral standards by which to judge the laws of the country. The ideals of the *Declaration of Independence* animated many of Lincoln's addresses, and his rereading of the Constitution through its lens provided ample support for the various human rights movements that followed after the Civil War. In addition to the abolitionist movements, women's rights activists in the nineteenth and twentieth centuries modeled their appeals for equality on the *Declaration*'s assertion of universal equality. Similarly, leaders of the civil rights movement of the 1960s demanded that the principles of equality and justice be extended to minority groups. In the late twentieth and early twenty-first centuries, GLBT (gay, lesbian, bisexual, and transgender) groups, immigrants, and Americans with disabilities advocated for equal protection and equal rights guaranteed under the Constitution.

major event in history and postulating that revolution is a logical and necessary occurrence within the present conditions. By outlining its terms, the manifesto assumes a more objective tenor and offers descriptions rather than prescriptions. Moreover, the *Declaration* progresses in a logical manner, suggesting that the assertion of revolution follows from its premises.

Stylistically, the *Declaration* resembles a legal defense. The writers assert, "The history of the present King of Great Britain is a history of repeated injuries and usurpations, all having in direct object the establishment of an absolute Tyranny over these states. To prove this, let Facts be submitted to a candid world." The general scope of the document indicates that the grievances outlined by Jefferson will convince unbiased readers that King George is indeed a tyrant. If readers fail to be swayed, it is not due to the demonstration; rather, it is because they failed to remain impartial. Thus, the language subtly pushes the audience away from contesting the conclusion and forces the interlocutor to establish that the facts are not true. In a rhetorical sleight of hand, the "proof" is offered

John Trumbull's 1832 painting *The Declaration of Independence, July 4, 1776.* WADSWORTH ATHENEUM MUSEUM OF ART/ART RESOURCE, NY

by an anonymous author. The document relies upon an empirical foundation that holds up its observations as coming directly from experience and without interpretation.

CRITICAL DISCUSSION

When the *Declaration of Independence,* with its fifty-six signatories, was first circulated, most people within the colonies either opposed independence or did not care enough to form an opinion on the matter. Furthermore, its language and claims were highly contested by British authors. Most notably, Thomas Hutchinson openly challenged the *Declaration*'s contention that the colonists had attempted all other avenues of reconciliation. As Armitage remarks in "The *Declaration of Independence* in World Context," opponents "deplored the presumptuousness of the colonists or took comfort from the fact that a long-mediated conspiracy for independence had been flushed out into the open." Other detractors pointed to the hypocrisy in the *Declaration,* whose writers relied heavily on the trope of slavery but were still slaveholders themselves.

Considered a performative document, the *Declaration* fell into obscurity during the drafting of the Constitution and thereafter. Eventually, however, attention moved away from its specific grievances and turned to the manifesto's sweeping claims concerning equality and unalienable rights. James Stoner notes in "Is There a Political Philosophy in the *Declaration of Independence?*" that Abraham Lincoln's use of the *Declaration*'s principles in his arguments against slavery "set a precedent for its use to reform the regime from within." Throughout the nineteenth and twentieth centuries, scholars debated the political force underlying its legacy. Its greatest, most undeniable influence has stemmed from its concept of unalienable rights and equality. Abolitionist writers such as Frederick Douglass, Harriet Beecher Stowe, Sojourner Truth, and Harriett Tubman drew on the *Declaration* to illustrate the evils of slavery, and Dr. Martin Luther King Jr. invoked its language during the civil rights movement in the 1960s. Furthermore, women suffragists extended the *Declaration*'s principles to their own cause.

Contemporary scholarship surrounding the *Declaration of Independence* has focused primarily on the preamble. Discussing the legacy of the document, Armitage surmises that the *Declaration* is more concerned with affirming "before world opinion the rights of a group of states to enter the international realm as equals with other such states than asserting the rights of individuals. Despite the initial controversy concerning its effacement of women and minorities, historians and activists alike have celebrated its articulation of a robust freedom. For example, William Pencak writes in "The *Declaration of Independence*: Changing Interpretations and a New Hypothesis" that the *Declaration* offers "a continuing inspiration in the United States and throughout the world to eliminate oppression and to ensure that all groups of people enjoy adequate self-government and representation of both their collective interests and their personal freedom."

BIBLIOGRAPHY

Sources

Armitage, David. *The* Declaration of Independence*: A Global History.* Cambridge: Harvard UP, 2007. Print.

———. "The *Declaration of Independence* in World Context." *OAH Magazine of History* 18.3 (2004): 61-66. *JSTOR*. Web. 21 May 2012.

Pencak, William. "The *Declaration of Independence*: Changing Interpretations and a New Hypothesis." *Pennsylvania History* 57.3 (1990): 225-35. *JSTOR* Web. 21 May 2012.

Stoner, James. "Is There a Political Philosophy in the *Declaration of Independence*?" *Intercollegiate Review* (2005): 3-11. Print.

Tyler, Moses Coit. "The *Declaration of Independence* in the Light of Modern Criticism." *North American Review* 163.476 (1896): 1-16. *JSTOR*. Web. 19 May 2012.

Further Reading

Burgan, Michael. *Declaration of Independence.* Minneapolis: Compass Point, 2001. Print.

McCabe, J.P. "The *Declaration of Independence* and the Frailties of Historical Method." *Historian* 57.4 (1995): 859-72. Print.

Morsink, Johannes. *Inherent Human Rights. Philosophical Roots of the Universal Declaration.* Philadelphia: U of Pennsylvania P, 2009. Print.

Rackove, Jack. "The Patriot Who Refused to Sign the *Declaration of Independence*." *American History* 4 (2010): 59-63. Print.

Viegas, Jennifer. *The* Declaration of Independence*: A Primary Source Investigation into the Action of the Second Continental Congress.* New York: Rosen, 2003. Print.

Joshua Harteis

DECLARATION OF SENTIMENTS OF THE AMERICAN ANTI-SLAVERY SOCIETY

William Lloyd Garrison

❖ *Key Facts*

Time Period:
Mid-19th Century

Movement/Issue:
Abolitionism; Opposition
to "recolonization"
of Africa by black
Americans

Place of Publication:
United States

**Language of
Publication:**
English

OVERVIEW

Drafted by abolitionist and journalist William Lloyd Garrison in December of 1833, the *Declaration of Sentiments of the American Anti-Slavery Society* outlines the founding principles of what would become the nation's premiere abolitionist organization. Affirming American values such as "life, LIBERTY, and the pursuit of happiness," the text calls for the immediate abolition of slavery without financial consideration to slave owners, rejects the efforts of the American Colonization Society to relocate freed slaves to Africa, and outlines a plan for the society's work. Borrowing language from both the *Declaration of Independence* and scripture, the document presents abolition as a moral imperative and as the only course in keeping with the religious and philosophical principles on which the nation was founded.

After its drafting, the *Declaration of Sentiments* was widely reprinted in northern newspapers. Although it found a sympathetic audience among those already predisposed to support abolition, the declaration also provoked controversy and violence. In 1834 the New York City homes and businesses of abolitionists were attacked during four days of rioting. Opponents feared that abolition would lead to intermarriage between the races, the possible breakup of the Federal Union, and competition for jobs if blacks were granted equal rights with whites. In actuality the text was pacifist in nature, and the American Anti-Slavery Society eventually issued a statement explaining that they did not intend to promote intermarriage, disunion, or congressional action. Despite the early confusion and controversy surrounding it, the *Declaration of Sentiments* is remembered today as an important text of the anti-slavery movement, and the efforts of the American Anti-Slavery Society are widely credited with helping to bring an end to slavery in the United States.

HISTORICAL AND LITERARY CONTEXT

The *Declaration of Sentiments* enters into ongoing debate over the future of slavery in the United States. In the years leading up to its writing, slavery had become an increasingly divisive economic, political, and moral issue. Public thinking about slavery had begun to shift early in the nineteenth century. In 1807 the U.S. banned the international slave trade, while allowing the domestic slave trade and the practice of slavery to continue. In 1820 the Missouri Compromise banned slavery in all states carved from the Louisiana Territory apart from Missouri, largely preventing the practice from spreading westward. In the early 1830s, as anti-slavery sentiment was growing in the North, southern agriculture, transitioning from tobacco to cotton, was becoming increasingly dependent on slave labor to fuel its economy. Pro-slavery sentiment was fueled in the South in 1831, when Nat Turner, a Virginia slave, led a rebellion that left sixty white citizens dead. Turner's rebellion convinced many, including some northerners, of the already prevalent myth that African Americans were dangerous and could not be freed. Desperate to expose the humanity of enslaved peoples and the horrors and hypocrisies of slavery, Garrison began publishing his groundbreaking abolitionist newspaper, the *Liberator,* in 1831.

When the American Anti-Slavery Society was first formed and its *Declaration of Sentiments* written, Americans remained deeply divided over the practice of slavery. Although state and local organizations were growing in strength, no cohesive national abolitionist movement existed. Moreover, there was no national consensus, even among anti-slavery activists, as to the course abolition should take. Many northern Christians opposed slavery but rejected calls for its immediate abolition, instead advocating a gradual phasing out of the institution. The American Colonization Society supported abolition but believed freed slaves ought to be resettled in Africa. Calling for immediate abolition and rejecting colonization, the American Anti-Slavery Society and its founding declaration provided a platform around which the abolitionist movement could organize. Among its influential members were writer and speaker Theodore Dwight Weld; writer and social reformer Lydia Marie Child; and escaped slave Frederick Douglass, who was a frequent speaker at events sponsored by the society. The work of the society is widely credited alongside Garrison's *Liberator* with rallying northerners behind abolition.

In writing the *Declaration of Sentiments,* Garrison drew on both a tradition of European abolition writings as well as the founding documents of the

United States. He borrowed liberally from the *Declaration of Independence* in making the case that if all men are created equal, "no man has a right to enslave or imbrute his brother—to hold or acknowledge him, for one moment, as a piece of merchandise—to keep back his hire by fraud—or to brutalize his mind by denying him the means of intellectual, social, or moral improvement." He also quotes heavily from the Bible in making his argument, asserting, for example that "every American citizen, who detains a human being in involuntary bondage as his property, is, according to Scripture ... a man-stealer."

The American Anti-Slavery Society and its declaration inspired a large body of work about slavery, ranging from songs and broadsides to books, all of which helped shine a critical light on human bondage. These works include *The Anti-Slavery Picknick*, an anthology of songs, poems, and stories from 1842; *The Anti-Slavery Almanac*, composed by Child in 1843 for the American Anti-Slavery Society; and "The Negro Woman's Appeal to Her White Sisters," published in the 1850s. The society also published Weld's collection *American Slavery As It Is* (1838), which brings together first-person slave testimonies.

THEMES AND STYLE

The main theme of the *Declaration of Sentiments of the American Anti-Slavery Society* is that slavery is a sinful institution that runs counter to American values. In

THE AMERICAN COLONIZATION SOCIETY AND LIBERIA

African American Quaker Paul Cuffee financed a successful expedition by former American slaves to Sierra Leone in 1811. In part due to his success, a group of white organizers formed the American Colonization Society (ACS), which attracted esteemed members such as politician Henry Clay and Bushrod Washington, nephew of President George Washington. Many free African Americans were skeptical of the ACS due to its connections with so many prominent southerners. In 1820 the ACS sent its first immigrants to Liberia, where they settled on Shebro Island in Sierra Leone. In 1821, after the area proved ill-suited for a colony, the ACS purchased land north of Sierra Leone and began building a settlement there in 1822.

In the United States, the idea of colonization appealed to many in the North who favored abolition but did not see a future for freed slaves in America. Colonization societies were formed to encourage and fund the immigration of freed slaves to Africa, despite the fact that most had been born in the United States and had never been to Africa. In 1838 Liberian colonies established by competing colonization societies formed a commonwealth and adopted a constitution. In 1847 the Liberian Declaration of Independence was adopted, stating their independence from the United States. Shortly after, Britain recognized Liberia as an independent nation.

Practical Illustration of the Fugitive Slave Law, a satirical illustration of William Lloyd Garrison and other northern abolitionists facing off against Secretary of State Daniel Webster (depicted with a slave catcher on his back) and other proponents of the Fugitive Slave Act of 1850. F&A ARCHIVE/ THE ART ARCHIVE AT ART RESOURCE, NY

the first paragraph Garrison evokes the memory of the American Revolution and founding of the republic, writing, "the corner-stone upon which is founded the Temple of Freedom was broadly this—'that all men are created equal; that they are endowed by their Creator with certain inalienable rights; that among these are life, liberty, and the pursuit of happiness.'" Garrison questions why African American men were not born with the same rights, pointing out that one-sixth of the population was held in captivity as "commodities—as goods and chattels." The declaration makes it clear that Garrison considered slavery a sin not only for slave owners but also for the nation that allowed it to continue. Consequently, Garrison calls on the nation to "repent," stating that "no man has a right to enslave or imbrute his brother."

The *Declaration of Sentiments* achieves much of its rhetorical force through its appeals to the familiar conventions of Evangelical Christianity and to those political ideals foundational to America. Calling on the nation to repent of its sin and to fight for the abolition of slavery in the same manner an evangelical minister would call on a congregation or individual congregate to stop sinning, the declaration is clearly intended as a call to action. Garrison addresses northerners as well as southerners, exhorting listeners to act out of Christian duty and questioning their Christianity if they fail to respond:

> That all those laws which are now in force, admitting the right of slavery, are therefore before God utterly null and void; being an audacious usurpation of the Divine prerogative, a daring infringement on the law of nature, a base overthrow of the very foundations of the social compact, a complete extinction of all relations, endearments and obligations of mankind, and a presumptuous transgression of all the holy commandments—and that therefore they ought to be instantly abrogated.

At the same time, in borrowing language from the *Declaration of Independence,* Garrison seeks to invest the society's agenda with the spirit of the American Revolution, drawing parallels between the abolitionists' goals and early American patriots' quest for "Truth, Justice, and Right." In the opening paragraphs of the declaration, Garrison calls on his readers to complete the work begun by their forefathers, noting that "we have met together for the achievement of an enterprise, without which that of our fathers is incomplete."

Stylistically, the declaration alternates between impassioned rhetoric and carefully crafted plans for action. Garrison describes the horrors of slavery in the language of melodrama, relating, for example, how slaves "are ruthlessly torn asunder—the tender babe from the arms of its frantic mother—the heart-broken wife from her weeping husband—at the caprice or pleasure of irresponsible tyrants." In other passages, however, he resorts to the formal language more commonly associated with public documents: "We regard as delusive, cruel and dangerous, any scheme of expatriation which pretends to aid, either directly or indirectly, in the emancipation of the slaves, or to be a substitute for the immediate and total abolition of slavery." In this manner he is able to appeal to his readers both emotionally and intellectually.

CRITICAL DISCUSSION

The initial response to the *Declaration of Sentiments* was mixed. Although northern newspapers printed the text, they often qualified their support in commentary accompanying it. Others expressed concern about document's potential for inciting violence. The *Vermont Chronicle,* for example, worried that the declaration would signal to slaves that "they have much better reasons for taking up arms against us, than our fathers had for taking up arms against Great Britain." Over time, however, the text provided a rallying cry for abolitionist groups and expanded the number as well as types of people involved in the political process. Women, despite their lack of suffrage, became politically involved, creating their own anti-slavery organizations and going door to door with abolitionist petitions to Congress. These activities brought women into the forefront of the movement, but their participation was controversial and eventually led to a schism among the abolitionists.

The Anti-Slavery Society and its declaration had broad-ranging effects on the political culture of the United States from the 1830s through the 1860s. Following the Civil War, the society formally disbanded, and its members went on to pursue other political causes. The abolitionist movement opened new doors for women and was also part of a broader social movement. Over time, the *Declaration of Sentiments* ceased to be controversial, but it has remained of interest to historians, who have viewed it not only as an important early statement against slavery but also as a document that helped to shape the future of American politics and political parties.

Recent scholarship has focused generally on the effects of the abolition movement. In *Free Soil, Free Labor, and Free Men* (1995), historian Eric Foner examines at length the role played by the Anti-Slavery Society in the development of America's political parties. In *Bearing Witness against Sin* (2006), Michael Young traces many aspects of modern social movements back to the founding of the Anti-Slavery Society. Politically, the anti-slavery movement helped launch new political parties, including the Liberty Party, the Free Soil Party, and ultimately the Republican Party. Young suggests that the temperance movement and anti-slavery movement should be viewed as the starting point for modern social and political movements and sees them as evangelical in their reliance on the power of confession and forgiveness to approach social problems.

BIBLIOGRAPHY

Sources

"American Anti Slavery Society." *Vermont Chronicle* 20 Dec. 1833: 202. Print.

Garrison, William Lloyd. "Declaration of the National Anti-Slavery Convention, 1833." *Selections from the Writings and Speeches of William Lloyd Garrison.* 1852. New York: Negro UP, 1968. 66-71. Print.

Foner, Eric. *Free Soil, Free Labor, Free Men: The Ideology of the Republican Party before the Civil War.* New York: Oxford UP, 1995. Print.

Mayer, Henry. *All on Fire: William Lloyd Garrison and the Abolition of Slavery.* New York: W.W. Norton, 2008. Print.

Muelder, Owen W. *Theodore Dwight Weld and the American Anti-Slavery Society.* Jefferson: McFarland, 2011. Print.

Young, Michael. *Bearing Witness against Sin: The Evangelical Birth of the American Social Movement.* Chicago: U of Chicago P, 2006. Print.

Further Reading

Brewer, James Stewart. *William Lloyd Garrison and the Challenge of Emancipation.* Arlington Heights: Harlan Davidson, 1992. Print.

Farrow, Anne, Joel Long, and Jenifer Frank. *Complicity: How the North Promoted, Prolonged, and Profited from Slavery.* New York: Ballantine, 2006. Print.

Petrulionis, Sandra Harbert. *To Set This World Right: The Antislavery Movement in Thoreau's Concord.* Ithaca: Cornell UP, 2006. Print.

Watson, Harry L. *Liberty and Power: The Politics of Jacksonian America.* New York: Hill and Wang, 1990. Print.

Rodney Harris

ELECTION MANIFESTO

Daniel O'Connell

✥ *Key Facts*

Time Period:
Mid-19th Century

Movement/Issue:
Discrimination against
Irish Catholics;
Catholicism

Place of Publication:
England

**Language of
Publication:**
English

OVERVIEW

In 1828, while campaigning for a seat in the British Parliament, Irish politician Daniel O'Connell delivered his Election Manifesto, a speech promising to end discrimination against Irish Catholics by the British government. Although several relief acts had been passed in Parliament during the late eighteenth and early nineteenth centuries to restore property rights and religious freedoms to Catholics, full emancipation, including rights of representation, had not been granted to Catholics. Because O'Connell was by law not allowed to hold the office for which he was running, his speech, and his campaign more generally, served to foster popular support for Catholic emancipation and to force the British government's hand. Addressed to the voters of County Clare, the speech contains several promises, including pledges to vote for the equitable distribution of church funds to the needy, the easement of unfair tax rates, the repeal of unjust laws restricting Catholic land ownership, and radical reform of the parliamentary representative system.

The speech elicited praise from the Catholic majority in Ireland and fear from the British government. O'Connell, through his work with the Catholic Association and his subsequent political campaign, had succeeded in organizing hundreds of thousands of Irish Catholics in support of emancipation. Fear of an uprising led Parliament to pass the Catholic Relief Act of 1829, overturning the harshest limitations levied against Catholics in Britain—including the restriction against Catholics holding seats in Parliament. O'Connell became the first Irish Catholic to stand in Parliament and earned the nickname "the Great Liberator." Today, scholars see him not as a lone force for liberation but as the man who turned demand for Catholic emancipation into a popular movement too large to be ignored.

HISTORICAL AND LITERARY CONTEXT

In England, Catholics had not been allowed to hold office in Parliament since the 1662 Act of Uniformity, which restricted many of Catholics' rights and freedoms. Most of Ireland's land was owned by the affluent Protestant minority, who often used their power to manipulate tenants' votes, effectively forcing the Irish to participate in their own subjugation. Thus, in the late eighteenth century, sympathetic Protestant members of Parliament lent support to emancipation by pursuing it constitutionally. However, opposition from conservative Irish Protestants, the British public, and the British monarchy stifled progress at every turn. Irish radicals disliked the notion of gradual emancipation and preferred a violent struggle for independence from Britain.

In 1823, O'Connell founded the Catholic Association with aims of promoting Catholic interests and winning emancipation. His efforts with the Catholic Association gained him great favor among the predominantly Catholic Irish public, for whom opposition to emancipation symbolized the injustice of British rule in Ireland. O'Connell argued that Catholic interests could only be served by Catholic representatives, much as Irish revolutionary Theobald Wolfe Tone had argued in the 1790s that Irish interests could only be served by Irish representatives in Parliament.

In fact, the Election Manifesto is modeled on Tone's early Irish nationalist writings and orations, which are themselves modeled on American writer Thomas Paine's nationalist rhetoric. Tone posits in his writings that the interests and needs of the Irish would always be overshadowed by those of the English as long as Englishmen held the parliamentary seats for Irish counties. Thus, from Tone's works, such as *Declaration of the Society of United Irishmen* (1791), O'Connell inherited a focus on parliamentary reform, particularly with regard to the question of direct representation for neglected demographics. Because O'Connell had witnessed the failure of militancy in gaining equal rights, he beseeched the Irish public to return to Tone's principles, insisting that lasting freedom could only come about as the result of constitutional action—namely, the constitutional repeal of the Act of Union of 1800, which united Ireland under British rule.

By the time he delivered his Election Manifesto in 1828, O'Connell had organized a Catholic emancipation movement that was hundreds of thousands strong. Taking advantage of his popularity, and building on the promise of emancipation set forth in his Election Manifesto, O'Connell won the popular vote in the 1828 election and filled a recently vacated seat in Parliament. Aware of his popularity, and fearful of a violent uprising if O'Connell was not allowed to take office after his victory, the British government was pressured into passing the Catholic Relief Act of 1829, which eliminated a large number of the restrictions on Roman Catholics in the United Kingdom.

THEMES AND STYLE

The central theme of O'Connell's Election Manifesto is that Catholic emancipation, particularly as it concerns the admission of Irish Catholics to Parliament, is possible. At the time in which the manifesto was written, any land-owning male could stand for election, but if elected, he would have to swear oaths to the royal crown and the Protestant church. O'Connell states, "[A]s a Catholic I cannot, and of course never will, take the oaths … but the authority which created these oaths can abrogate them." He insists to the Irish public, "if you elect me, the most bigoted of our enemies will see the necessity of removing from the chosen representative of the people an obstacle which would prevent him from doing his duty to his King and to his country." To emphasize his unwavering commitment to the idea of emancipation, he asserts that he "has ever lived, and is ready to die, for the integrity, the honor, the purity of the Catholic faith."

O'Connell's primary rhetorical strategy is to emphasize the inadequacy of non-Irish, non-Catholic representatives in serving Irish Catholic interests. He characterizes his opponent, Vesey Fitzgerald, an English Protestant, as Catholics' "worst and most unrelenting enemy … who has so long cultivated his own interest." He challenges Fitzgerald's claim that Fitzgerald is a "friend to the Catholics," pointing out that electing a non-Catholic representative to serve Catholic interests is ludicrous: "Why, I am a Catholic myself; and if he be sincerely our friend, let him vote for me, and raise before the British empire the Catholic question in my humble person." O'Connell concludes his manifesto by exhorting voters to choose between himself, "one who has devoted his early life to your cause [and] who has consumed his manhood in a struggle for your liberties," and Fitzgerald, a "sworn libeller of the Catholic faith."

The speech's tone is both ardent and ingratiating. Although O'Connell paints himself in sharp contrast to his opponent, he addresses the constituency of County Clare with humbleness and respect: "Of my qualifications … I leave you to judge. The habits of my public speaking … render me, perhaps, equally suited with most men to attend to the interests of Ireland in parliament." However, he asserts, what sets him apart from other politicians are his passion and powerful vision for political revolution. He asserts that "the attempt to exclude your representative from the house of commons … will create a sensation all over Europe, and produce such a burst of contemptuous indignation against British bigotry, in every enlightened country in the world." The contrast between his humble assertion of personal qualifications and

O'CONNELL AND THE ACT OF UNION OF 1800

One of Daniel O'Connell's primary goals as a member of British Parliament was to repeal the Act of Union of 1800, which made Ireland part of Great Britain. Although his efforts ultimately proved unsuccessful, he enjoyed widespread support for his call for Irish independence. In 1843 he began holding public rallies, delivering rousing addresses to crowds so large that the rallies became known as "monster meetings." The first such rally, held in Limerick, Ireland, on April 19, was reported to have drawn a crowd of 30,000 to 40,000. Subsequent crowds grew exponentially: 150,000 at Mullingar; 400,000 at Mallow and at Lismore; and between 800,000 and one million at Tara.

However, the MP soon became disenchanted by calls for violent revolution among his audiences. He publicly denounced the emerging militant nationalist group Young Ireland, a move that some historians have linked to the ultimate failure of the repeal movement. The symbolic end of the movement came in 1843 when Prime Minister Robert Peel, fearing the collapse of the British Empire, cancelled the last of the monster meetings to be held at Clontarf, outside Dublin. Peel not only broke up the assembly but also imprisoned O'Connell for conspiracy, thereby signaling the end of the MP's influence in British government.

his passionate endorsement of broad political reform demonstrates his unwavering commitment to Irish Catholic interests.

CRITICAL DISCUSSION

Until the election results were announced, there was no significant critical response to O'Connell's manifesto. After O'Connell's victory, an 1828 article in the *Northern Whig,* a Belfast periodical, conveyed the significance of the election results. Given Fitzgerald's personal and financial connections with local aristocracy, the support that O'Connell enjoyed was unprecedented. The overwhelming margin by which O'Connell won succeeded in persuading MP George Dawson—brother-in-law of staunch anti-emancipation MP Robert Peel—to support Catholic emancipation. During a subsequent speech, Dawson asked, "Is it possible I can look with apathy upon the degraded state of my Catholic fellow countrymen?" These responses, and others like them, alarmed the British government and signaled a turning point in the fight for emancipation.

The victory helped augment O'Connell's already immense popularity, gained through his work with the Catholic Association. Intimidated by his substantial following, British officials passed the Catholic Relief Act of 1829, which allowed Catholics to become members of Parliament, largely as a

Portrait of Daniel
O'Connell. © HOLMES
GARDEN PHOTOS/ALAMY

a 1975 article for *Studies: An Irish Quarterly Review* agrees that the Great Liberator "is the principal folk-hero in modern Irish history," he acknowledges that O'Connell's reputation has suffered during periods of increased militancy in the Irish nationalist movement. O'Connell and his efforts to support Catholic emancipation have also appeared in popular art, including Irish scholar and dramatist Brian Friel's 1980 play *Translations,* which explores language in the context of Irish nationalism. Friel's drama takes place in Ireland in 1833 and features characters who occasionally paraphrase or mention O'Connell while engaging in their clandestine nationalist activities.

BIBLIOGRAPHY

Sources

Bew, Paul. *Ireland: The Politics of Enmity, 1789-2006.* Oxford: Oxford UP, 2007. Print.

Friel, Brian. *Translations.* London: Faber, 1981. Print.

McGraw, Sean, and Kevin Whelan. "Daniel O'Connell in Comparative Perspective, 1800-50." *Eire-Ireland: A Journal of Irish Studies* 40.1-2 (2005): 60-89. *Academic OneFile.* Web. 27 Aug. 2012.

O'Connell, Daniel. "Election Manifesto." *The Age of Peel.* Ed. Norman Gash. London: Edward Arnold, 1968. 22-24. Web. 27 Aug. 2012.

O'Connell, Maurice. "O'Connell Reconsidered." *Studies: An Irish Quarterly Review* 64.254 (1975): 107-19. *JSTOR.* Web. 27 Aug. 2012.

Further Reading

Eversley, George Shaw-Lefevre. *Peel and O'Connell: A Review of the Irish Policy of Parliament from the Act of Union to the Death of Sir Robert Peel.* Port Washington: Kennikat, 1970. Print.

Finnegan, Richard B., and Edward T. McCarron. *Ireland: Historical Echoes, Contemporary Politics.* Boulder: Westview, 2000. Print.

McCaffrey, Lawrence J. *The Irish Question: Two Centuries of Conflict.* Lexington: UP of Kentucky, 1995. Print.

Moody, T.W., and F.X. Martin, eds. *The Course of Irish History.* Lanham: Roberts Rinehart, 2001. Print.

O'Ferrall, Fergus. *Catholic Emancipation: Daniel O'Connell and the Birth of Irish Democracy, 1820-30.* Dublin: Gill, 1985. Print.

Clint Garner

conciliatory gesture to avoid large-scale civil war. After O'Connell's death in 1847, his legacy helped to galvanize a generation in working toward disestablishing the Protestant Church of Ireland and securing the passage of the Land Acts in the 1880s, which focused on Irish property rights. Shortly after Ireland gained its independence in 1922, Sackville Street, Dublin's high street, was renamed O'Connell Street in honor of the country's Great Liberator.

Today, many scholars consider O'Connell's contributions within the historical context of early nineteenth-century Great Britain. Sean McGraw, writing for *Eire-Ireland* in 2012, sees O'Connell not just as an important Irish political figure but "arguably the most influential Catholic activist in nineteenth-century European politics." Although Maurice O'Connell in

EMANCIPATION PROCLAMATION

Abraham Lincoln

OVERVIEW

On January 1, 1863, U.S. president Abraham Lincoln issued the Emancipation Proclamation as an executive order freeing slaves in Union-occupied areas of Confederate states that had not yet returned to the Union. The declaration came less than two years after the start of the U.S. Civil War, which erupted after several Southern states seceded from the Union, dissatisfied with the election of a president whom they saw as hostile to slavery. Although the proclamation committed the Union to abolishing slavery, a controversial decision even in the North, it did not immediately outlaw slavery or grant newly freed slaves citizenship. Instead, the proclamation, addressed primarily to the states engaged in rebellion against the Union, defined limited terms of emancipation and allowed for the enrollment of freed slaves in the Union army.

The proclamation was intensely unpopular even in its conceptual stages. Political resistance to abolition made it necessary for Lincoln to declare emancipation as an executive order under his authority as commander in chief, because emancipation legislation would have been summarily rejected by Congress. Lincoln's political allies thought the proclamation went too far; abolitionists thought it did not go far enough. Most abolitionists felt that the provisions of the order were weak; however, its enactment reassured them that the federal government recognized and supported their efforts to some extent. The order effectively weakened the Southern economy—and by extension Southern resistance—and undermined European efforts to support the Confederacy. In December 1865, eight months after the Confederacy surrendered to the Union army and the Civil War ended, the states ratified the Thirteenth Amendment, completing the process of abolition begun by Lincoln's order. Today, the proclamation is widely considered one of the most pivotal documents in U.S. history.

HISTORICAL AND LITERARY CONTEXT

Before the proclamation was issued, efforts to abolish slavery had largely been hampered by U.S. constitutional law, particularly by the Fifth Amendment, which prevented the government from seizing private property without just compensation. Attempts at compensated emancipation failed in several states, and the First Confiscation Act (1861) and Second Confiscation Act (1862), which allowed for the seizure of slaves of Confederate forces and made it illegal for Union officers to return fugitive slaves to their owners, were severely limited in scope.

By 1863, Lincoln had come to realize that, in order to win the war, he would have to issue an executive order of emancipation using his powers as commander in chief. He drafted the order to allow for the gradual freeing of slaves as Union armies advanced and issued it in two steps. The first part, released on September 22, 1862, announced his intention to order the emancipation of all slaves in any state of the Confederacy that did not lay down arms and return to the Union by the end of the year. The executive order itself, issued January 1, 1863, allowed for the enrollment of freed slaves in the Union Army. Unlike the Confederate army, which did not allow any of the South's roughly three millions slaves into its ranks, the Union army succeeded in enlisting nearly 200,000 black soldiers, mostly ex-slaves, as a result of the proclamation.

The Emancipation Proclamation builds on a tradition of executive direct action that has played a key role in American history since the nation's founding. Perhaps the most significant of these orders was the Proclamation of Neutrality, issued by president George Washington on April 22, 1793, in response to escalating violence on American soil between French and British forces. Released in an effort to solidify the new nation's independence, the proclamation threatened legal proceedings against Americans who provided assistance to either side, a stance made non-negotiable in 1794 after the passing of the Neutrality Act. As was the case with many such proclamations, Washington's order was widely opposed; it even prompted the resignation of Washington's secretary of state, Thomas Jefferson.

Perhaps no presidential proclamation since the Emancipation Proclamation has had such a powerful impact on American history. The majority of modern presidential proclamations are ceremonial in nature or are used to recognize certain groups of Americans. However, several have made profound statements about human rights, such as John F. Kennedy's 1962 proclamation that U.S. marshals and federal troops would ensure the safety of James Meredith, the first black man allowed to register as a student at the University of Mississippi. Other significant proclamations include President Gerald Ford's pardon of Richard M.

❖ Key Facts

Time Period:
Mid-19th Century

Movement/Issue:
American Civil War; Slavery; Abolitionism

Place of Publication:
United States

Language of Publication:
English

ABRAHAM LINCOLN: THE GREAT DEBATER

The Lincoln-Douglas Debates of 1858 became one of the most famous series of political debates in U.S. history. In all, seven debates were held between U.S. Senate candidates Abraham Lincoln and Stephen A. Douglas. The debates effectively presaged the issues Lincoln would face in his 1860 presidential campaign, foremost among them slavery. Lincoln argued against expansion of slavery in the West, while Douglas emphasized his Freeport Doctrine, which held that individual states had the authority to grant slave-owning rights to local settlers.

The debates drew thousands of spectators. Although Lincoln was seen as an awkward man, in both appearance and mannerism, most saw in his debate performances a great deal of leadership potential. Nevertheless, the legislature reelected Douglas to the Senate (at the time U.S. senators were elected by their state's legislature, not by popular vote). Lincoln was disappointed by the result. The power of his orations, however, had won him a national reputation. When asked shortly after his loss about the possibility of running for president, Lincoln simply said, "The taste is in my mouth a little."

Nixon and President George W. Bush's declaration of disaster areas in the aftermath of Hurricane Katrina.

THEMES AND STYLE

The overriding theme of the Emancipation Proclamation is the legal basis for the gradual emancipation of slaves. The order does not immediately free all slaves; rather, it sets the conditions for their release, listing "designated States, and parts of States" in which emancipation must immediately take effect. The document further declares that "the Executive government of the United States, including the military and naval authorities thereof, will recognize and maintain the freedom of said persons." To ensure the document's legal validity, Lincoln enacts the proclamation "by virtue of the power in me vested as Commander-in-Chief, of the Army and Navy of the United States in time of actual armed rebellion against the authority and government of the United States, and as a fit and necessary war measure for suppressing said rebellion." By invoking his power as commander in chief and declaring the domestic armed rebellion a state of war, Lincoln argues his legal right to order emancipation.

The document's legal rigidity is perhaps not only its greatest rhetorical strength but also its greatest weakness. Whereas the proclamation's predecessors, such as the Declaration of Independence, employ impassioned appeals to humanity, freedom, and equality, Lincoln's order is pragmatic in its approach. Instead of referring to emancipation as a matter of human rights, he calls it "an act of justice, warranted by the Constitution, upon military necessity." The repetition of clauses, a formulation usually reserved for legal documents, reinforces the proclamation's legitimacy as a binding order. However, the document's form and content failed to appeal to abolitionists who desired an impassioned moral argument for emancipation.

The overall tone of the proclamation is firm and dispassionate. The document makes no provisions for the future of freed men and women beyond encouraging them to "abstain from all violence" and to "labor faithfully for reasonable wages" and permitting them "to be received into the armed service of the United States." The only time in which Lincoln betrays a hint of emotion is when he "invoke[s] the considerate judgment of mankind, and the gracious favor of Almighty God." Ironically, and perhaps tellingly, the inclusion of these statements was not Lincoln's idea. Hesitant to betray any personal investment in the matter for fear that the opposition would capitalize on his vulnerability and overturn the order, the president was eventually persuaded by Secretary of Treasury Salmon P. Chase to include a small signal of humanity in order to ensure the proclamation's viability among abolitionists.

CRITICAL DISCUSSION

The Emancipation Proclamation met with immediate and almost unanimous denunciation. Democrats, whether they supported the war or not, were outraged. Jennifer L. Weber, in *Copperheads: The Rise and Fall of Lincoln's Opponents in the North* (2006), quotes the words of Democratic representative Henry A. Reeves on the Proclamation: "In the name of freedom of Negroes, it imperils the liberty of white men ... it overturns the Constitution and Civil Laws and sets up Military Usurpation in their Stead." Even Lincoln's political and intellectual allies were unhappy with the provisions of the order. Republican representative Thaddeus Stevens called them the "most diluted milk-and-water-gruel ... ever given to the American nation." Revolutionary socialist Karl Marx added that they were reminiscent of the "trite summonses that one lawyer sends to an opposing lawyer, the legal chicaneries and pettifogging stipulations" of a court case. As Lincoln's friend and ally Frederick Douglass would later observe, the president could not hope to satisfy everyone.

Abolitionists within the Republican Party, despite their criticisms of Lincoln and his order, redoubled their support for the president and vowed not to block his renomination. What small strides the proclamation made invigorated the cause and eventually led to the complete abolition of slavery in December 1865, in a series of events scholars have called a second American Revolution. The U.S. Civil Rights Movement in the 1960s would give rise to a second wave of ambivalence regarding the proclamation, as black intellectuals voiced disenchantment with Lincoln's lack of support for abolition and freed men and women. Indeed, President Lyndon B. Johnson, in a 1963 Memorial Day address, invoked the proclamation as a series of promises not yet fulfilled. Nevertheless, the document is

remembered for its profound impact on the U.S. Civil War in particular and American history in general.

Modern scholarship tends to hold the document, and Lincoln, in high regard. In *Emancipating Lincoln: The Proclamation in Text, Context, and Memory* (2012), Harold Holzer offers a concise view of this trend, pointing out that the document is often seen as "forgoing ringing poetry for rigorous and uninspiring prose" in order to foster political support for a growing cause. Holzer points out that historians have recast Lincoln "more as orator than emancipator," perhaps contributing to the Emancipation Proclamation's two divergent, yet parallel, legacies: one as beacon of freedom, the other as a rhetorical debacle.

BIBLIOGRAPHY

Sources

The Emancipation Proclamation: The National Archives Experience. Washington, DC : National Archives and Records Admin., 2010. Print.

Finkelman, Paul. "Lincoln and Emancipation: Constitutional Theory, Practical Politics, and the Basic Practice of Law." *Journal of Supreme Court History* Nov. 2010: 243-66. *Academic OneFile.* Web. 31 July 2012.

Holzer, Harold. "A Promise Fulfilled: The Emancipation Proclamation All but Guaranteed the Death of Slavery, but Exactly What That Document Did—and Did Not—Do Remains the Subject of Heated Debate."

Civil War Times 48.6 (2009): 28-35. *Academic One-File.* Web. 31 July 2012.

———. *Emancipating Lincoln: The Proclamation in Text, Context, and Memory.* Cambridge: Harvard UP, 2012. Print.

Marx, Karl. "On Events in North America." *Karl Marx on America and the Civil War.* Ed. Saul K. Padover. New York: McGraw-Hill, 1972. 221-22. Print.

Morel, Lucas E. "Lincoln's Proclamation: Emancipation Reconsidered." *Civil War History* 57.2 (2011): 188-90. *Academic OneFile.* Web. 31 July 2012.

Weber, Jennifer L. *Copperheads: The Rise and Fall of Lincoln's Opponents in the North.* New York: Oxford UP, 2006. Print.

Further Reading

Berlin, Ira. *Generations of Captivity: A History of African-American Slaves.* Cambridge: Harvard UP, 2003. Print.

Cooper, Phillip J. *By Order of the President: The Use and Abuse of Executive Direct Action.* Lawrence: UP of Kansas, 2002. Print.

Foner, Eric. *The Fiery Trial: Abraham Lincoln and American Slavery.* New York: Norton, 2010. Print.

Klingaman, William K. *Abraham Lincoln and the Road to Emancipation, 1861-1865.* New York: Viking, 2001. Print.

McPherson, James. *Battle Cry of Freedom: The Civil War Era.* Oxford: Oxford UP, 1988. Print.

Clint Garner

Depiction of Abraham Lincoln reading the Emancipation Proclamation to members of his Cabinet. From an engraving by Alexander Hay Ritchie after a painting by Francis Carpenter. © BETTMANN/CORBIS

ETHIOPIAN MANIFESTO

Issued in Defense of the Black Man's Rights in the Scale of Universal Freedom

Robert Alexander Young

❖ *Key Facts*

Time Period:
Early 19th Century

Movement/Issue:
Black nationalism;
Abolitionism

Place of Publication:
United States

**Language of
Publication:**
English

OVERVIEW

Written by a free black man in New York City named Robert Alexander Young, the pamphlet *The Ethiopian Manifesto, Issued in Defence of the Blackman's Rights, in the Scale of Universal Freedom* (1829) was one of the earliest expressions of black nationalist ideology. In his document, Young predicted the coming of a black Messiah to bring about the freedom of slaves, warning white slave owners of God's judgment against them. *The Ethiopian Manifesto* was published at a time when northern educators were renewing their abolitionist efforts after a period of inaction, arousing increasingly virulent hostility from southern slaveholders who blamed them for growing unrest among slaves. The pamphlet directly addresses all people of African descent with an inspirational tenor aimed at bringing hope to the oppressed black masses, while it simultaneously warns slaveholding whites of the wrath of a God disapproving of their endeavors.

Although Young's pamphlet received scant response, many southern slave owners immediately rejected the text as a direct threat to their livelihood and feared the rebellion of their slaves. It was received in a favorable light by the few free blacks who responded to it, however, contributing to an emerging pan-African and black nationalist discourse that would soon be taken up by many other African Americans. *The Ethiopian Manifesto* adopted the Ethiopian prophecy of the Bible that presented slaves—and all people of African descent—as the chosen ones whom God would deliver from the bonds of slavery. The word "Ethiopian" used in this context refers to all Africans, and the prophecy predicted the emergence of an African prophet, or Messiah, who would lead the Africans to salvation. The Christian rhetoric employed by Young throughout the pamphlet appealed to the religious sentiment of abolitionists and slaveholders alike, forging allies while it signaled to the enemies whose evil nature would be judged by a higher power. Today, Young's pamphlet is regarded by many scholars as an important early piece of African American literature and expression of the notion of a black nation that significantly influenced the abolitionist and pan-African movements of the nineteenth century.

HISTORICAL AND LITERARY CONTEXT

The Ethiopian Manifesto is a direct response to the perpetual bondage of blacks in the New World under slavery. It was written during a time of growing unrest among free blacks and pro-abolition whites, who forged the beginning of the abolitionist movement. There had already been a number of significant slave revolts in North Carolina (as well as other states) by 1796, when a grand jury directly blamed the influence of the Quakers for sparking the revolts. A rebellion on the outskirts of Richmond, Virginia, in 1800—known as Gabriel's Rebellion because of the leadership of a slave named Gabriel Prosser—also evidenced the increasing discontent among slaves at the turn of the nineteenth century. Continued efforts on the part of abolitionist and religious groups during the early nineteenth century to educate slaves in the South led to increased hostility among many slaveholders.

By the time Young published *The Ethiopian Manifesto* in 1829, the abolitionist movement was beginning to take shape in the United States. Although the gradual abolition of slavery in states north of the Mason-Dixon Line (dividing Pennsylvania and Maryland) beginning around 1804 only further threatened the southern plantation economies dependent on slave labor, it simultaneously spurred the action of abolitionist groups whose main target was now the South. By 1808 both the United States and Britain had outlawed the international import or export of slaves, legislation that was perhaps paradoxically embraced by American slaveholders who saw the value of their slaves increase exponentially. Free blacks such as Young were important advocates of the abolitionist movement; enslaved blacks contributed to the abolitionist movement to the best of their abilities—while many were illiterate, the few educated slaves kept their peers informed of the abolitionist developments.

The Ethiopian Manifesto follows the examples of early African American writers as well as the tradition of abolitionist literature from both Britain and the United States. African American writer Jupiter Hammon, in his poem "An Evening Thought: Salvation by Christ with Penitential Cries" (1761), employed Christian rhetoric and biblical references, an approach adopted by Young decades later. In 1786 Hammon—who remained a slave until his death—gave the "Address to the Negroes of the State of New York," in which he promoted emancipation and stressed the idea that all humans were equal in the eyes of God. It is very likely that the work of contemporary free black writers such as David Walker, Peter Williams Jr., and John Russwurm—all of whom contributed to the first black abolitionist newspaper in the United States, *Freedom's Journal*—directly influenced Young. The work of other abolitionist groups, such as the London-based Sons of Africa, may also have impacted him, specifically the book *Thoughts and Sentiments on the Evil of Slavery* (1791) by Quobna Ottobah Cugoano.

In the years immediately following the publication of *The Ethiopian Manifesto*, other works of a similar abolitionist vein appeared rather quickly. The most notable of these is Walker's *An Appeal ... to the Coloured Citizens of the World*, published later in 1829, which applied the Ethiopian prophecy in an approach similar to Young's but in a more incendiary manner by calling for slaves to rebel against their masters as proof of their manhood. Slave narratives written by former slaves championing the abolitionist cause also emerged around this period. These narratives often employed Christian rhetoric in a manner similar to Young's to explain their logic. An example of this approach can be seen in *Narrative of the Life of Frederick Douglass*, written by freed slave Douglass in 1845. Today, *The Ethiopian Manifesto* is regarded as an important early expression of black abolitionism and formulation of the idea of a black nation and continues to be studied alongside other notable abolitionist literature from the period.

THEMES AND STYLE

Central to *The Ethiopian Manifesto* was a condemnation of the institution of slavery and the prediction of the coming of a black Messiah to emancipate slaves and punish slaveholders. Young laments, "Fallen, sadly, sadly low indeed, hath become our race, when we behold it reduced but to an enslaved state, to raise it from its degenerate sphere, and instill into it the rights of men, are the ends intended of these our words." With this goal in mind—emancipating the black race from its current state of bondage—Young invokes God and his own Christian values to legitimate the task at hand, using the words of that God to denounce the white slave owners. "Your God, the great and mighty God, hath seen your degradation of your fellow brother, and mortal man," warns Young, using all the power behind the threat of God's wrath to strengthen his message.

The Ethiopian Manifesto achieves its message by employing biblical passages that draw on the Ethiopian prophecy, which stated that blacks throughout

THE FIGHT FOR EMANCIPATION: ABOLITIONISM IN THE UNITED STATES

The first tentative steps taken on the path to abolition began in the United States even before the end of the Revolutionary War. The first known champions of the cause were Quakers, who formed the Society for the Relief of Free Negroes Unlawfully Held in Bondage, in Philadelphia in 1775—the first abolitionist organization in the North American colonies. One of the earliest writings to advocate abolition was Thomas Paine's article "African Slavery in America," which appeared in *Pennsylvania Magazine* in March 1775. The first federal legislative efforts addressing slavery, although not yet fully abolitionist, began in the early nineteenth century when President Thomas Jefferson signed the "Act to Prohibit the Importation of Slaves," which outlawed the international trade of slaves and went into effect in 1808. However, the federal government did little to address slavery following this act until the events surrounding the Civil War in the 1860s.

Both abolitionist whites and free blacks led the growing abolitionist movement in the North; their combined efforts brought about widespread attention for the cause by the mid-nineteenth century. Notable white social reformers included William Lloyd Garrison, who founded the American Anti-Slavery Society; Wendell Philips; and writers such as Harriet Beecher Stowe. More than 300 black abolitionists were actively involved in the antislavery movement, including Frederick Douglass, Robert Purvis, and Sojourner Truth, as well as the brothers Charles Henry Langston and John Mercer Langston, who were pivotal in the founding of the Ohio Anti-Slavery Society. The efforts of abolitionists throughout the country—not only those in the North—combined with the seditious acts of the southern states that prompted the Civil War in 1861, led to Abraham Lincoln's 1863 Emancipation Proclamation, an executive order that proclaimed the freedom of all slaves in Confederate states. In 1865 the Thirteenth Amendment followed up Lincoln's proclamation, which rendered slavery illegal throughout the United States.

the world would convert to Christianity and that God would deliver black slaves in the New World from slavery. Young emphasizes unity among blacks across the continents, reflecting a type of pan-African ideology. "We here speak of the whole of the Ethiopian people, as we admit not even those in their state of native simplicity, to be in an enjoyment of their rights, as bestowed to them of the great bequest of God to man." The author's use of the collective "we" further emphasizes that he speaks for an entire group, not just for himself, reinforcing a sense of solidarity among people of African descent across the globe. According to Young, even those "Ethiopians" who were not enslaved still endured a common experience

PRIMARY SOURCE

ETHIOPIAN MANIFESTO: ISSUED IN DEFENSE OF THE BLACK MAN'S RIGHTS IN THE SCALE OF UNIVERSAL FREEDOM

Ethiopians! the power of Divinity having within us, as man, implanted a sense of the due and prerogatives belonging to you, a people, of whom we were of your race, in part born, as a mirror we trust, to reflect to you from a review of ourselves, the dread condition in which you do at this day stand. We do, therefore, to the accomplishment of our purpose, issue this but a brief of our grand manifesto, herefrom requiring the attention towards us of every native, or those proceeding in descent from the Ethiopian or African people; a regard to your welfare being the great and inspiring motive which leads us to this our undertaking. We do therefore strictly enjoin your attention to these the dictates from our sense of justice, held forth and produced to your notice, but with the most pure intention.

Ethiopians! open your minds to reason; let therein weigh the effects of truth, wisdom, and justice (and a regard to your individual as general good),

and the spirit of these our words we know full well, cannot but produce the effect for which they are by us herefrom intended. –Know, then, in your present state or standing, in your sphere of government in any nation within which you reside, we hold and contend you enjoy but few of your rights of government within them. We here speak of the whole of the Ethiopian people, as we admit not even those in their state of native simplicity, to be in an enjoyment of their rights, as bestowed to them of the great bequest of God to man.

...

We find we possess in ourselves an understanding; of this we are taught to know the ends of right and wrong, that depression should come upon us or any of our race of the wrongs inflicted on us of men. We know in ourselves we possess a right to see ourselves justified therefrom, of the right of God; knowing, but of his power hath he decreed to man, that either in himself he stands, or by himself he falls. Fallen, sadly, sadly low indeed, hath become our race, when we behold it reduced but to an enslaved state, to raise it from its degenerate sphere,

of oppression and subordination and were unable to exercise all of the rights God bestowed on all humans.

Writing in an impassioned tone and employing morality to make his point, Young presents himself as a religious prophet who has received a revelation that it was time for the suffering of his fellow blacks to end. His message reads as one of encouragement and strength for the slaves. Describing the coming Messiah in detail, Young writes, "the man we proclaim ordained of God, [is summoned] to call together the black people as a nation in themselves." The very idea of a black nation is one of inspiration and hope for the enslaved blacks and reflects the nascent ideology of black nationalism, which would take shape much more clearly over the next century. "To him, thou poor black Ethiopian or African slave, do thou, from henceforth, place a firm reliance thereon, as trusting in him to prove thy liberator from the infernal state of bondage." Young emphasizes the fact that the decree for slave's delivery from bondage has already been issued from heaven through the ordainment of their coming savior.

CRITICAL DISCUSSION

Although *The Ethiopian Manifesto* received little initial critical response when it was published in early 1829, certain historians have concluded that white slave owners viewed it with a mixture of open hostility

and rejection, while literate blacks and many abolitionists embraced it with hope and enthusiasm. Unfortunately, little is known about the author, partially due to the lack of critical responses to the pamphlet during his lifetime. Although later scholars were quick to draw connections between the work of Young and his contemporaries such as Walker and Nathaniel Paul, there is no evidence of any relationship between the author and these individuals. As Peter Hinks notes in *To Awaken My Afflicted Brethren* (1997), "No reference to Robert Alexander Young or his work exists in *Freedom's Journal, The Rights of All* [an abolitionist newspaper], or any other black writings or oratory from that time, including the *Appeal.*" Walker's incredibly incendiary *Appeal* of the same year sparked many critical responses, mostly from whites condemning his approach, while Young's more cautious approach did not incite such a vehement reaction from the slaveholding population, although they most likely still found its antislavery message troubling.

The emergence of *The Ethiopian Manifesto* immediately following the publication of Young's text, as well as Nat Turner's historic slave revolt of 1831, only further evoked the wrath of white slaveholders. The pamphlet would be taken up by later black nationalists, including Martin Delany in the 1850s and Marcus Garvey in the twentieth century. Thomas

and instill into it the rights of men, are the ends intended of these our words; here we are met in ourselves, we constitute but one, aided as we trust, by the effulgent light of wisdom to a discernment of the path which shall lead up to the collecting together of people, rendered disobedient to the great dictates of nature, by the barbarity that hath been practices upon them from generation to generation of the will of their more cruel fellow-men. Am I, because I am a descendent of a mixed race of men, whose shade hath stamped them with a hue of black, to deem myself less eligible to the attainment of the great gift allotted of God to man, than are any other of whatsoever cast you please, deemed from being white as being more exalted than the black?

…

I speak for no man, understanding but in myself my rights, that from myself shall be made known to a people, rights, which I, of the divine will of God, to them establish. Man – white man – black man – or, more properly, ye monsters incarnate, in human shape, who claim the horrid right to hold nature's untutored son, the Ethiopian, in bondage, to you I do herefrom speak. Mark me, and regard well these my words; be assured, they convey the voice of reason, dictated to you through a prophetic sense of truth. The time is at hand when many signs shall appear to you, to denote that Almighty God regards the affairs of afflicted men: –for know, the cries of bitter servitude, from those unhappy sons of men, whom ye have so long unjustly oppressed with the goading shafts of an accursed slavery, hath ascended to Deity. Your God, the great and mighty God, hath seen your degradation of your fellow brother, and mortal man; he bath long looked down with mercy on your suffering slave; his cries have called for a vindication of his rights, and know ye they have been heard of the Majesty of Heaven, whose dignity have you not offended by deeming a mortal man, in your own likeness, as but worthy of being your slave, degraded to your brute? The voice of intuitive justice speaks aloud to you, and bids you to release your slave; otherwise stings, eternal stings, of an outraged and goading conscience will, ere long, hold all them in subjection who pay not due attention to this, its admonition.

Emancipated slaves holding church services in Washington, D.C., in the 1870s. © NORTH WIND PICTURE ARCHIVES/ALAMY

Poole acknowledges the pamphlet's importance, stating, "The call for an Ethiopian body politic and the prediction of a black messiah came together in 'The Ethiopian Manifesto' to form, not only one of the earliest black analyses of American society, but one of the first expressions of black nationalist ideology as well." Since its publication, *The Ethiopian Manifesto* has been analyzed and discussed by numerous scholars for its historical importance and influence on the abolitionist and black nationalist movements.

Much scholarship has focused on a comparison between Walker's *Appeal* and *The Ethiopian Manifesto,* as both emerged in the same time period. Bruce Dain writes in *A Hideous Monster of the Mind* (2002), "Interesting as Young's manifesto is, it could not compare with Walker's fiery *Appeal* in impact and notoriety. Young relied upon an avenging messiah. Walker, prominent in the black community, called upon the oppressed themselves and issued a warning to the oppressors." Many other scholars are interested in Young's text as an early expression of black nationalism. In *Going through the Storm* (1994), Sterling Stuckey writes, "Brief as [Young's] document is, it contains essential elements of black nationalism.... The *Ethiopian Manifesto* contains one of the earliest extant calls for the reassembling of the African race, one of the first formulations of the imperative need for Africans, severely oppressed and locked in degradation, *to become a people.*"

BIBLIOGRAPHY

Sources

Dain, Bruce. *A Hideous Monster of the Mind: American Race Theory in the Early Republic.* Cambridge: Harvard UP, 2002. Print.

Hinks, Peter. *To Awaken My Afflicted Brethren: David Walker and the Problem of Antebellum Slave Resistance.* University Park: Penn State UP, 1997. Print.

Poole, Thomas. "What Country Have I? Nineteenth-Century African-American Theological Critiques of the Nation's Birth and Destiny." *Journal of Religion* 72.4 (1992): 533-48. Print.

Stuckey, Sterling. *Going through the Storm: The Influence of African American Art in History.* Cambridge: Harvard UP, 1994. Print.

Young, Robert A. *The Ethiopian Manifesto, Issued in Defence of the Blackman's Rights, in the Scale of Universal Freedom.* February 1829. *Classical Black Nationalism: From the American Revolution to Marcus Garvey.* Ed. W. Moses. New York: New York UP, 1996. 60-67. Print.

Further Reading

Aptheker, H., ed. *A Documentary History of the Negro People in the United States: Volume 1.* Secaucus: Citadel, 1973. Print.

Berlin, Ira. *Many Thousands Gone: The First Two Centuries of Slavery in North America.* Cambridge: Belknap Press of Harvard UP, 1998. Print.

———. *Generations of Captivity: A History of African-American Slaves.* Cambridge: Belknap Press of Harvard UP 2003. Print.

Crockett, Hasan. "The Incendiary Pamphlet: David Walker's Appeal in Georgia." *Journal of Negro History* 86.3 (2001): 305-18. Print.

Fredrickson, George M. *Black Liberation: A Comparative History of Black Ideologies in the United States and South Africa.* Oxford: Oxford UP, 1996. Print.

Gordon, Dexter. *Black Identity: Rhetoric, Ideology, and Nineteenth-Century Black Nationalism.* Carbondale: Southern Illinois UP, 2006.

Jeynes, William H. *American Educational History: School, Society, and the Common Good.* Thousand Oaks: Sage, 2007. Print.

Rodriguez, Junius P. *Slavery in the United States: A Social, Political, and Historical Encyclopedia, Volume 2.* Santa Barbara: ABC-CLIO, 2007. Print.

Walker, Clarence E. *We Can't Go Home Again: An Argument about Afrocentrism.* Oxford: Oxford UP, 2001. Print.

Katrina White

THE JEWISH STATE

Theodor Herzl

OVERVIEW

Der Judenstaat (*The Jewish State*, 1896) by Theodore Herzl argues for the establishment of an independent nation-state for the Jewish people. Herzl cites the prevalence of anti-Semitism in Europe, the failure of the European Jewish population to assimilate into greater society, and the need for the Jewish people to take on the role of nation builders. He proposes practical steps for organizing Jewish immigration to this new state—suggesting Argentina and Palestine as possible locations—and political and social reforms to be enshrined into law. *The Jewish State* was published in pamphlet form in Vienna and was widely disseminated in part because of Herzl's career as a prominent journalist. While the pamphlet was ostensibly addressed to wealthy Jewish community leaders and European political officials, it was also widely read by the European Jewish community at large. *The Jewish State* earned Herzl a reputation as one of the principal members of the Zionist movement and led to the founding of the World Zionist Organization and the First Zionist Congress in 1897.

While the individuals Herzl targeted rejected his proposals, *The Jewish State* was popular with leftist segments of the European Jewish lower classes. More conservative Jews rejected his suggestion that powers traditionally granted to religious authorities should be transferred to a secular national government; some even argued that his views were an attempt to usurp God's authority to decide when and if a Jewish state should be created. Herzl negotiated with the Ottoman, German, and British governments on the basis of the proposals outlined in *The Jewish State*, but these negotiations were ultimately unsuccessful. Despite the failure of *The Jewish State* to convince the European community to establish an independent Jewish state during this period, Herzl's plan is now recognized as a catalyst in the advancement of the Zionist cause.

HISTORICAL AND LITERARY CONTEXT

The Jewish State was written in reaction to a thousand-year history of anti-Semitism in European society and the resulting cycles of Jewish persecution. These cycles repeatedly divided and dispersed European Jewish populations through multiple diasporas; by the late nineteenth century, many European Jewish communities existed in segregated ghettos within cities. Their

physical isolation encouraged the development of insular Jewish social and economic systems and further defined the Jews against other European populations. The rise of nationalist sentiment in Europe exacerbated this tension, with Jews increasingly being viewed as an alien group within national borders and as a threat to ethno-nationalist solidarity.

By the time *The Jewish State* was published, there had long been a trickle of Jewish immigrants to Palestine in response to a rise in racist ideology in Western Europe. Already targeted for religious persecution, European Jews came increasingly under attack as a supposedly inferior ethnic minority weakening the ethno-nationalist makeup of the nations they inhabited. This was especially the case in France and Austria, with Vienna becoming a focal point of racially motivated anti-Semitism in the 1890s. In his work as a foreign correspondent, Herzl witnessed the French populist anti-Semitic response to the Dreyfus Affair in 1895, the same year Karl Lueger's anti-Semitic

✣ *Key Facts*

Time Period:
Late 19th Century

Movement/Issue:
Zionism

Place of Publication:
Austria

Language of Publication:
German

THEODOR HERZL AND THE TECHNOLOGY OF THE FUTURE

In addition to his efforts to establish a Jewish state, Theodor Herzl was a committed futurist with a strong interest in the technological possibilities of the twentieth century. He makes frequent reference in his writings to modern technologies such as the airplane (which had yet to be tested successfully for most of his life), dirigibles, automobiles, railways, steamships, electricity, and photography, as well as futuristic novels. He repeatedly noted that these new technologies had made the most recent Jewish diaspora at the end of the nineteenth century possible and emphasized the ways they would be of service in the formation of a Jewish state.

Herzl further explored the role of technology in society in his journalism and in his utopian novel, *Altneuland* (*The Old New Land*, 1902), which featured a new Jewish society built using the latest scientific methods, including a monorail to link different regions of the new Jewish nation. He also championed many modern social reforms, such as the development of organized labor, the seven-hour workday, and the rights of small firms and entrepreneurs.

A knotted wool carpet with a depiction of Theodor Herzl, early twentieth century. THE JEWISH MUSEUM, NEW YORK/ART RESOURCE, NY

and was disturbed by the rise of Édouard Drumont's anti-Semitic newspaper *Libre Parole* in France. Herzl was familiar with the work of French writers Ernest Renan, Drumont, and Maurice Barrès; he described himself as a Spinozist after seventeenth-century Jewish philosopher Benedict (Baruch) de Spinoza.

The literary legacy of *The Jewish State* is varied and far-reaching. *Altneuland* (1902), Herzl's utopian novel about a multilingual Jewish society, was heavily influenced by *The Jewish State,* and two-thirds of his feuilleton essays in *Neue Freie Presse* appeared after the pamphlet's publication, although the paper did not officially support the Zionist cause. Herzl also helped oversee the founding of the Zionist movement newspaper *Die Welt* and influenced numerous other pro-Zionist writings in the decades leading up to World War II. *The Jewish State* established Herzl's intellectual reputation and served as the basis for his subsequent role as a leader of the Zionist movement.

THEMES AND STYLE

The central theme of *The Jewish State* is the need for an autonomous Jewish state to protect and preserve the Jewish people. To this end, Herzl writes, "No one can deny the gravity of the situation of the Jews. Wherever they live in perceptible numbers, they are more or less persecuted. Their equality before the law … has become a dead letter." In order to protect the Jewish population, Herzl asks that "sovereignty be granted us over a portion of the globe large enough to satisfy the rightful requirements of a nation; the rest we shall manage for ourselves." The assertion that Jews will "manage" for themselves in their new state, is crucial to Herzl, who writes that ghetto culture had deprived Jews of the skills necessary to support themselves. Herzl also claims that European governments would be receptive to the idea: "The Governments of all countries scourged by Anti-Semitism will be keenly interested in assisting us to obtain the sovereignty we want." Throughout *The Jewish State,* he emphasizes the resilience of the Jewish people, asserting that "the distinctive nationality of Jews neither can, will, nor must be destroyed…. This is shown during two thousand years of appalling suffering."

Herzl's rhetorical strategy in *The Jewish State* centers on moralistic appeals, practical specificity, and preemptive rebuttals. To encourage a sense of moral agreement in the reader, Herzl often begins his assertions with a rhetorical question ("Is what I am saying not yet true?") and invites the reader to follow his train of reasoning in a methodical progression ending with the assertion of the necessity of a Jewish state. He emphasizes the concrete steps that must be taken to ensure a successful Jewish migration, laying them out in six comprehensive chapters with titles such as "The Jewish Question" and "The Jewish Company." He also repeatedly assures the reader that these steps—such as establishing a Jewish joint-stock company to fund immigration to the new state—are not only

Christian Social Party won the Vienna municipal election. Scholars point to both events as galvanizing forces behind Herzl's publication of *The Jewish State.*

The Jewish State was influenced by several earlier publications, including Moses Hess's *Rom und Jerusalem* (1862), which had already proposed the possibility of a Jewish state. Conversely, Eugen Duhring's *The Jewish Question as a Problem of Race, Custom and Culture* (1879), along with many similar anti-Semitic works, convinced Herzl that virulent anti-Semitism was on the rise in the European intellectual community. Herzl's own play, *The New Ghetto* (1894), portrayed the failures of the Jewish assimilation effort and was blocked from the stage by anti-Semitic forces. He sometimes argued for the Zionist cause in his work as the feuilleton editor with the Vienna *Neue Freie Presse*

possible but can be straightforwardly accomplished. He explicitly defends himself against the charge that his proposal is unworkable and utopian by emphasizing its practical points.

The tone of *The Jewish State* varies between emotionally strident and eminently practical. At one point, Herzl exhorts the reader in feuilleton style, claiming, "The men who inaugurate this movement will hardly live to see its glorious conclusion. But the very inauguration will bring a lofty pride and the happiness of inner freedom into their lives." He also includes three technical paragraphs concerning how the Jewish Company will handle the issue of nontransferable goods. In this sense, the language of *The Jewish State* can be divided into one part stirring editorial and one part business proposition. He also includes several pithy turns of phrase, such as when he poses the question, "Will there thus be no payment of wages in the initial period of settlement?" and answers himself in the following paragraph in two words: "Certainly: Overtime."

CRITICAL DISCUSSION

Reaction to *The Jewish State* in the Jewish community was mixed along lines of economic and religious stratification. Despite Herzl's appeals, the majority of the wealthy Jewish elite chose not to join the Zionist cause, and some Jewish religious authorities rejected his proposals as a secular threat to their traditional position in society. However, *The Jewish State* found populist favor with the Jewish poor and Eastern European socialist and Marxist supporters. This support was substantial enough to convene the First Zionist Congress in Basel, Switzerland, in 1897 and to earn Herzl audiences with the sultan of Turkey and Kaiser Wilhelm II of Germany, the latter despite a largely negative reaction to *The Jewish State* from the German press. Herzl was able to convene six Zionist Congresses in his lifetime, including one in which he achieved symbolic passage of a resolution to open British Uganda to Jewish settlement after the Russian pogroms (riots) of 1903. The Russian Jewish contingent of the congress chose not to act on this resolution.

The outbreak of World War II and the devastation of the Holocaust dramatically reshaped the legacy of *The Jewish State*, with some commentators pointing to Herzl's prescience in declaring the need for a Jewish homeland and others attacking him for underestimating anti-Semitic zeal and overestimating the power of international diplomacy. In the decades following the establishment of Israel, Herzl has been attacked for his assertion that the establishment of a Jewish state would end anti-Semitism in Europe and for his initial failure to account for the Arab population of Palestine. Kalman Sultanik of the World Jewish Congress also notes that Herzl's attacks of "pusillanimity" and "lack of dignity" against his Jewish contemporaries who worked in finance were probably not valid in his time.

PRIMARY SOURCE

THE JEWISH STATE

The Jewish question still exists. It would be foolish to deny it. It is a remnant of the Middle Ages, which civilized nations do not: even yet seem able to shake off, try as they will. They certainly showed a generous desire to do so when they emancipated us. The Jewish question exists wherever Jews live in perceptible numbers. Where it does not exist, it is carried by Jews in the course of their migrations. We naturally move to those places where we are not persecuted, and there our presence produces persecution. This is the case in every country, and will remain so, even in those highly civilized—for instance, France—until the Jewish question finds a solution on a political basis. The unfortunate Jews are now carrying the seeds of Anti-Semitism into England; they have already introduced it into America.

I believe that I understand Anti-Semitism, which is really a highly complex movement. I consider it from a Jewish standpoint, yet without fear or hatred. I believe that I can see what elements there are in it of vulgar sport, of common trade jealousy, of inherited prejudice, of religious intolerance, and also of pretended self-defense. I think the Jewish question is no more a social than a religious one, notwithstanding that it sometimes takes these and other forms. It is a national question, which can only be solved by making it a political world-question to be discussed and settled by the civilized nations of the world in council.

We are a people—one people.

We have honestly endeavored everywhere to merge ourselves in the social life of surrounding communities and to preserve the faith of our fathers. We are not permitted to do so. In vain are we loyal patriots, our loyalty in some places running to extremes; in vain do we make the same sacrifices of life and property as our fellow-citizens; in vain do we strive to increase the fame of our native land in science and art, or her wealth by trade and commerce. In countries where we have lived for centuries we are still cried down as strangers. and often by those whose ancestors were not yet domiciled in the land where Jews had already had experience of suffering. The majority may decide which are the strangers; for this, as indeed every point which arises in the relations between nations, is a question of might. I do not here surrender any portion of our prescriptive right, when I make this statement merely in my own name as an individual. In the world as it now is and for an indefinite period wilt probably remain, might precedes right. It is useless, therefore, for us to be loyal patriots, as were the Huguenots who were forced to emigrate. If we would only be left in peace....

But I think we shall not be left in peace.

SOURCE: *Essential Texts of Zionism,* translated by Sylvie D'Avigdor. American Zionist Emergency Council, 1946.

Analysis of Herzl's identity as a Zionist leader continues, with scholar Shmuel Almog questioning whether Herzl was truly a Jewish nationalist or only using the idea of Jewish nationalism to appeal to European nationalist sentiment. Others have noted that the seemingly paradoxical inclusion of anti-Semitic language in *The Jewish State* is not a categorical phenomenon unique to Herzl but can also be found in the occasionally self-depreciatory writings of some Czech and Irish national leaders. Despite this ongoing critical reevaluation, Sultanik maintains that while Herzl "did not invent Zionism," he "remains a figure of gigantic stature in Jewish history."

BIBLIOGRAPHY

Sources

Friedman, Isaiah. "Theodor Herzl: Political Activity and Achievements." *Israel Studies* 9.3 (2004): 46-79. Print.

Herzl, Theodor. "Theodor Herzl: On the Jewish State, 1896." *Modern History Sourcebook.* Fordham University, 1997. Web. 8 Oct. 2012.

Isseroff, Ami. "Herzl's 'The Jewish State.'" *MidEastWeb.* MidEastWeb, 2002-03. Web. 8 Oct. 2012.

Loewenberg, Peter. "Between Fantasy and Reality." *Theodor Herzl: Visionary of the Jewish State.* Ed. Gideon Shimoni and Robert S. Wistrich. New York: Herzl, 1999. 3-14. Print.

Shimoni, Gideon, and Robert S. Wistrich. Introduction. *Theodore Herzl: Visionary of the Jewish State.* Ed. Shimoni and Wistrich. New York: Herzl, 1999. xiii-xxiii. Print.

Timms, Edward. "Ambassador Herzl and the Blueprint for a Modern State." *Theodor Herzl and the Origins of Zionism.* Ed. Ritchie Robertson and Edward Timms. Edinburgh: Edinburgh UP, 1997. 12-26. Print.

Further Reading

Chertok, Haim. "Herzl at 150: Mulling It Over." *Midstream* 56.4 (2010): 5. Print.

Cohn-Sherbok, Dan. *Introduction to Zionism and Israel, From Ideology to History.* New York: Continuum, 2012. Print.

Elon, Amos. *Herzl.* New York: Holt, Rinehart, and Winston, 1975. Print.

Herman, David. "Zionism as Utopian Discourse." *CLIO* 23.3 (1994): 235. *Academic One File.* Web. 8 Oct. 2012.

Zilbersheid, Uri. "The Utopia of Theodor Herzl." *Israel Studies* 9.3 (2004): 80-114. *ProQuest.* Web. 8 Oct. 2012.

Craig Barnes

LIBERTY OR DEATH: PROCLAMATION TO THE PEOPLE OF HAITI

Jean-Jacques Dessalines

OVERVIEW

"Liberty or Death: Proclamation to the People of Haiti" was first delivered as a speech by black military commander Jean-Jacques Dessalines on January 1, 1804, to the recently liberated people of the former French colony of Saint-Domingue. Most scholars have attributed the proclamation's authorship to Dessalines's secretary, Louis-Félix Boisrond-Tonnerre, although some have contested the attribution. The proclamation, also known as Haiti's Declaration of Independence, came less than two months after Dessalines's victory in the Battle of Vertières, the final battle of the Haitian Revolution. Because the French army had attempted to reestablish slavery and the rule of the white planter class in Saint-Domingue (as it had done successfully in Guadeloupe), many believed that expelling the French was the only way to ensure that former African slaves and their descendants would remain free. Addressed to the citizens of the newly formed republic of Haiti, the speech proclaims the country's independence and declares that the Haitian people will die before allowing their freedom to be taken from them.

The proclamation, later published in local newspapers and by the government, was initially ridiculed by many French citizens and politicians. Racial prejudice led many to believe it was impossible for a person of African descent to compose such a coherent proclamation. Dessalines's speech, however, was embraced and applauded by the predominantly black Haitian population. White Haitians reacted with anger and fear at the prospect of losing their wealth, their livelihood, and—after the Haitian government gave orders to kill all French people remaining on the island—their lives. Today, the proclamation is recognized as the new government's official declaration of Haitian independence and as a marker of the victory of the most successful slave rebellion in history.

HISTORICAL AND LITERARY CONTEXT

In the years leading up to the Haitian Revolution, worsening conditions and extremely high mortality rates led to mounting unrest in the enslaved black community. The growing population of runaway slaves formed maroon (*mawon* in Haitian) communities in the inhospitable island mountains, and *mawon* leaders aided plantation slaves in escaping or plotting revenge against their masters. Among the most famous *mawon* leaders were Francois Mackandal, who led an unsuccessful slave revolt in the 1750s, and Dutty Boukman, who sparked the 1791 slave rebellion that started the Haitian Revolution. The 1791 revolt was a response to white plantation owners' refusal to recognize the new rights granted by the French revolutionary government to the *gens de couleur,* a class of free people of African or mixed African and European ancestry.

The revolution came just two years after the French Revolution of 1789, which demonstrated the power of the lower classes to confront and overthrow a repressive government. While such generals as Jean-François Papillon, Georges Biassou, and Toussaint Louverture played pivotal roles in the war, Dessalines, who assumed full command of the troops after Louverture's forced departure, led Haiti to victory in 1803. The 1804 declaration followed earlier proclamations made by Dessalines regarding the revolutionary army's fight for independence, including "I Have Avenged America" (April 28, 1803) and a proclamation made on November 29, 1803, with Henri Christophe and Philippe Clerveaux following the defeat of France in the Battle of Vertières.

"Liberty or Death" takes its cue from late-eighteenth-century declarations of independence, specifically that of the newly formed United States, and from the proclamations of the French revolutionary government. The French National Constituent Assembly's *Declaration of the Rights of Man and of the Citizen* (1789), which declares all men free and equal, particularly influenced Dessalines's condemnation of the old French colonial structuring of society, which violated the rights of free and enslaved blacks. Dessalines's proclamation of independence and condemnation of the French government also mirrors the U.S. Declaration of Independence, which presents a list of grievances based on the assertion of certain natural and legal rights. "Liberty or Death" differs, however, in its open animosity toward France and in its attention to the abolition of slavery.

Among white Europeans, the publication of Dessalines's 1804 proclamation primarily inspired disparaging accounts of the Haitian Revolution and of Dessalines's despotic and "barbaric" rule. Nineteenth-century literary responses to the document

Time Period:
Early 19th Century

Movement/Issue:
Haitian independence;
Colonialism

Place of Publication:
Haiti

**Language of
Publication:**
French

THE HAITIAN REVOLUTION: FROM SLAVE REBELLION TO REPUBLIC

The Haitian Revolution, which lasted from 1791 to 1804, is known as the most successful slave rebellion in the world and the only slave uprising to lead to the establishment of a state. The revolution began in August 1791 with the massive revolt of Saint-Domingue slaves against their French masters. Within the first ten days, the slaves gained control of the entire northern region of the island. In 1793 Great Britain and Spain entered into war against France and aided Haitian revolutionary forces in compelling French commissioner Léger-Félicité Sonthonax to free the colony's slaves. The French government quickly abolished slavery and granted political and civil rights to all black men in the French colonies.

Nevertheless, the revolution continued, and Toussaint Louverture became a central leader of the Haitian revolutionary army, which expelled the Spanish and ruled the colony until 1802, when Louverture was deceived by the French and imprisoned. Jean-Jacques Dessalines became the new leader of the black Haitian army, winning the final battle of the revolution in November 1803. Following independence, however, the social and economic structures of the former colony changed little, and a two-class system persisted. Much of the power of French plantation owners passed to their mixed-race descendants, who employed most of Haiti's former slaves as rural subsistence farmers.

and Dessalines's leadership draw on the conventions of gothic literature in alluding to indescribable acts of violence and Haitian leaders' rejection of Enlightenment-era rationality. Two such historiographies, which purposefully vilify Dessalines and his revolutionary cause, are James Barskett's *History of the Island of St. Domingo: From Its First Discovery by Columbus to the Present Period* (1818) and Peter Stephen Chazotte's *Historical Sketches of the Revolutions, and the Foreign and Civil Wars in the Island of St. Domingo* (1840).

THEMES AND STYLE

The central theme of "Liberty or Death" is that, because of the atrocities carried out by the French against their former slaves, strong national unity and total rejection of France are the only means by which Haitians can maintain their independence. For Dessalines, liberty means cleansing the Haitian republic of the French: "let this be our cry: 'Anathema to the French name! Eternal hatred of France!'" He chastises Haitian citizens for not having sought revenge of their own accord, declaring, "It is not enough to have expelled the barbarians who have bloodied our land for two centuries ... We must, with one last act of national authority, forever assure the empire of liberty in the country of our birth." Although many Haitians had been born in Africa, Dessalines insists that all share a common origin—another way in which he appeals to national unity in the face of possible re-enslavement.

In expressing his belief that Haitians must vigorously defend their liberty, Dessalines employs extremist rhetoric that reinforces his reputation as a stern and brutal leader. Although he directly addresses the citizens of Haiti, his message also is aimed at potential opponents of Haitian liberty, whom he wishes to intimidate into respecting Haiti's autonomy. He tells Haitians, "know that you have done nothing if you do not give the nations a terrible, but just example of the vengeance that must be wrought by a people proud to have recovered its liberty and jealous to maintain it. Let us frighten all those who would dare try to take it from us again; let us begin with the French." To justify his call for revenge, he repeatedly alludes to the cruel, inhumane acts carried out by the French, whom he refers to as "tigers still dripping with ... blood." Recalling the violent acts of the French during the revolutions in Haiti and in France, he asks, "What do we have in common with this nation of executioners? ... if they find refuge among us, they will plot again to trouble and divide us."

The formal style of late-eighteenth-century political declarations and speeches that is used in "Liberty or Death" tempers the extremism of Dessalines's ideas. The document lends credibility to the new country—and eases the worries of neighboring islands and colonies that feared the spread of abolitionist ideas—by calling upon the Haitian masses to be responsible in exercising their liberty: "let us not, as revolutionary firebrands, declare ourselves the lawgivers of the Caribbean, nor let our glory consist in troubling the peace of the neighboring islands." Thus, even as the proclamation achieves its aim of instilling fear in and demanding respect from the would-be enemies of Haiti—specifically France—it also appeals to potential allies of the fledgling nation.

CRITICAL DISCUSSION

When "Liberty or Death" was published, the international community and local white and mixed-race Haitian plantation owners reacted with shock and fear. The majority of Haitian citizens, who were predominantly former slaves, celebrated their newly acquired independence and fully embraced Dessalines's message—including his later order to kill any French who remained on the island. White European intellectuals reacted with vehemently racist sentiment. According to Deborah Jenson in a 2009 essay for the *Journal of Haitian Studies,* the authors of the French *Journal des débats et lois pouvoir législatif: et des actes de gouvernement* responded to the proclamation in an editorial in March 1804, stating, "the above proclamation is not the work of Dessalines, who is unable to sign his own name, nor of any other individual of his color." A similar tendency to defame and demonize Dessalines is exemplified in Marcus Rainford's 1805 *An Historical Account of the Black Empire of Hayti.*

After Haiti was recognized as an independent state, "Liberty or Death" was recognized and reprinted as one of the central documents of the Haitian Revolution. In particular, scholars demonstrated renewed interest in the proclamation when an original government-printed version of the document was rediscovered in the British Archives in 2010. (The Haitian government did not have an original copy.) Jenson calls the proclamation "one of the most remarkable monuments of Black Atlantic textual history." In *The Declaration of Independence: A Global History* (2008), David Armitage writes that the Haitian proclamation is significant for revealing that "the common possession of declarations of independence was no guarantee of kinship between new states." (The United States did not officially recognize Haiti until 1862.)

Contemporary scholarship has focused on Dessalines's treatment of race in the proclamation and in the 1805 Haitian constitution. As Sibylle Fischer notes in *Modernity Disavowed: Haiti and the Cultures of Slavery in the Age of Revolution* (2004), "At a time when eighteenth-century racial taxonomies were beginning to mutate into racist biology and scientific racism, the Haitian constitutions take the opposite direction and infuse distinctions of skin color with political meaning." Other scholars, including David Nicholls and Alex Dupuy, have asserted that Dessalines's desire for unity, as expressed in his proclamation, and his specificity in the constitution about racial differences are contradictory. Scholars also have explored the influence of racial ideologies promoted by white European colonizers in the Caribbean.

BIBLIOGRAPHY

Sources

Armitage, David. *The Declaration of Independence: A Global History.* Cambridge: Harvard UP, 2008. Print.

Clavin, Matt. "Race, Rebellion, and the Gothic: Inventing the Haitian Revolution." *Early American Studies* 5.1 (2007): 1-29. Print.

Dessalines, Jean Jacques. "The Haitian Declaration of Independence." *Slave Revolution in the Caribbean 1789-1804: A Brief History with Documents.* Ed. Laurent Dubois and John D. Garrigus. Boston: Bedford / St. Martin's, 2006. Print.

Fischer, Sybille. *Modernity Disavowed: Haiti and the Cultures of Slavery in the Age of Revolution.* Durham: Duke UP, 2004. Print.

Jenson, Deborah. "Dessalines' American Proclamations of the Haitian Independence." *Journal of Haitian Studies* 15.1-2 (2009): 72-102. Print.

Munro, Martin. "Avenging History in the Former French Colonies." *Transition* July 2008: 18-39. Print.

Nicholls, David. *From Dessalines to Duvalier: Race, Colour and National Independence in Haiti.* Cambridge: Cambridge UP, 1979. Print.

Twa, Lindsay. "Jean-Jacques Dessalines: Demon, Demigod, and Everything in Between." *Circulations: Romanticism and the Black Atlantic.* University of Maryland, 2011. Web. 7 Aug. 2012.

Further Reading

Dayan, Joan. *Haiti, History and the Gods.* Berkeley: U of California P, 1995. Print.

Fick, Carolyn E. "Dilemmas of Emancipation: From the Saint Domingue Insurrections of 1791 to the Emerging Haitian State." *History Workshop Journal* 46 (1998): 1-15. Print.

Geggus, David. *The Impact of the Haitian Revolution in the Atlantic World.* Columbia: U of South Carolina P, 2001. Print.

Ghachem, Malick. *The Old Regime and the Haitian Revolution.* Cambridge: Cambridge UP, 2012. Print.

Girard, Philippe R. "Caribbean Genocide: Racial War in Haiti, 1802-4." *Patterns of Prejudice* 39.2 (2005): 138-61. Print.

Pons, Frank Moya. *The Dominican Republic: A National History.* Princeton: Markus Weiner, 1998. Print.

Katrina White

Painting of Jean-Jacques Dessalines, author of "Liberty or Death: Proclamation to the Inhabitants of Haiti."
© MIKE GREENSLADE/ ALAMY

THE MANIFESTO OF MONTECRISTI

Máximo Gómez, José Martí

❖ **Key Facts**

Time Period:
Late 19th Century

Movement/Issue:
Cuban independence

Place of Publication:
Dominican Republic

Language of Publication:
Spanish

OVERVIEW

The Manifesto of Montecristi, also known as *The Montecristi Manifesto,* was written by José Martí and Máximo Gómez in March 1895 in Montecristi, Dominican Republic, as a declaration of the goals for and ideology behind Cuba's war of independence. Originally written in Spanish as a direct message to the Cuban people, the manifesto envisions Cuba as an independent republic and proclaims the end of the colony's economic and political repression. Furthermore, it denounces racial discrimination and celebrates Cuba's African roots. The manifesto followed Martí and Gómez's founding of the Partido Revolucionario Cubano, or the Cuban Revolutionary Party, and marked the culmination of years of planning and fundraising for the Cuban revolutionary movement. In addition to declaring the objectives of the movement, the manifesto outlines five central rules of fighting for the revolutionary forces.

As a revolutionary call to arms published during a period of heightened political tension in the Spanish colony of Cuba, *The Manifesto of Montecristi* had a polarizing effect: it was embraced and celebrated by pro-independence Cubans and derided and scorned by colonial authorities and colonists who backed Spain. The document served as the ideological foundation for the Cuban War of Independence, which was already underway, and its central tenets of privileging human rights over all else have been referenced over the past century in the composition of legislation in Cuba and elsewhere. *The Manifesto of Montecristi* was even incorporated into the Cuban educational system as an example of the revolutionary ideals upon which the nation was founded.

HISTORICAL AND LITERARY CONTEXT

The Manifesto of Montecristi imposed policy on the Cuban War of Independence, which had begun on February 24, 1895—a month before the document appeared—with the Grito de Baire uprising. The document's antecedents include Martí's own earlier political writings, including *Resoluciones* (1891) and *Bases y Estatutos Secretos del Partido Revolucionario Cubano* (1892). Martí also adopted ideals espoused by Carlos Manuel de Céspedes in the *Grito de Yara,* a document produced at the beginning of the Ten Years' War (1868-78) that calls for Cuba's complete independence from Spain and the abolition of slavery. The outrage among Cuban colonists had grown during the Ten Years' War, as numerous atrocities were committed by Spanish authorities against the revolutionary forces and their sympathizers. The revolutionary movement organized by Martí and Gómez took up the cause of their predecessors, including Céspedes and Antonio Maceo, who had fought against Spain in the Ten Years' War and the Little War (1879-80).

When *The Manifesto of Montecristi* appeared in 1895, the third and final chapter of the fight for Cuban independence was underway. While Martí, living in exile in New York, acted as the revolutionaries' intellectual advocate abroad, Gómez stayed in the Caribbean region, serving as an active military leader in the Cuban revolutionary army. Having served as a major general in the Ten Years' War, Gómez had assumed the role of military commander by the time the War of Independence began in 1895. Maceo and Flor Crombet were also high-ranking military officers who had participated in the two earlier wars and were key figures in the revolutionary movement forged by Martí. The actions of Gómez, Maceo, and Crombet, among others, in the Cuban War of Independence exemplified the ideals set forth in the 1895 manifesto.

The Manifesto of Montecristi falls within the tradition and ideology of the early nineteenth-century Latin American independence movements led by such revolutionaries as Simón Bolívar. In fact, the text that perhaps most influenced Martí when composing his manifesto was Bolívar's *Cartagena Manifesto* (1812), which advocates for the independence of all Latin American countries from Spanish rule. Martí's 1895 manifesto adopts a similar ideology but applies it specifically to Cuba. In addition, there is clear continuity between *The Manifesto of Montecristi* and Céspedes's *Grito de Yara*; the two documents focus on many of the same issues, including Spain's excessive taxation of Cubans, the colonial power's corrupt government, and the violation of colonists' political and religious rights. While *The Manifesto of Montecristi*'s five central elements of war policy were new, the text's proclamation of independence and denunciation of the Spanish crown echo the revolutionary tone of earlier Latin American manifestos.

Following Cuban independence from Spain in 1898, *The Manifesto of Montecristi* continued to reverberate. It played a particularly strong role in framing the ideology of Fidel Castro's revolutionary movement in the 1950s, which culminated in the Cuban revolution of 1959. In 1953, Castro, along with other leaders of the movement, released the *Manifesto to the Nation*. This document functioned similarly to Martí's, directly addressing the Cuban people and calling them to arms against their oppressor—in this case, Cuban dictator Fulgencio Batista. In 1957, five leaders of the revolution published a joint statement, the *Manifesto of the Five* (*Manifiesto de los Cinco*), which advocates national unity and emphasizes the need to respect human rights, themes that hark back to *The Manifesto of Montecristi*.

THEMES AND STYLE

The central theme of *The Manifesto of Montecristi* is that the War of Independence is necessary in order to form a Cuban republic and, as Luz Elena Ramírez writes in the *Encyclopedia of Postcolonial Studies*, "to create order from Cuba's confused historical origins." The manifesto opens with a reaffirmation of the revolutionary ideals that the forces fighting for independence will uphold: "The elected representatives of the revolution that is reaffirmed today recognize and respect their duty to repeat before the patria … the precise aims [that lead] … all elements of Cuban society into combat." *The Manifesto of Montecristi* proceeds to outline the five main policies of the war, which, above all, stress respect for human rights and racial equality on the battlefield.

Through lofty, formal, and expansive rhetoric, Martí's manifesto appeals to the intelligence and progressive ideals of the Cuban public. Martí praises the evolution of the Cuban people following conflicts such as the Ten Years' War and solicits their support for and loyalty to the revolutionary cause: "This war is … the solemn demonstration of the will of a country that endured far too much in the previous war to plunge lightly into a conflict that can end only in victory or the grave, … without a determination so estimable—for it is certified by death—that it must silence those less fortunate Cubans who do not have equal faith in the capacities of their nation." Martí seeks to draw a line in the sand, gathering in the pro-independence sector of the population while marginalizing the segment that is opposed to the movement. Although *The Manifesto of Montecristi* cautions revolutionary supporters against regarding individual Spaniards as their enemies, its oppositional rhetoric had a polarizing effect.

The manifesto personalizes the independence movement, thereby enabling Cubans to identify with the revolution in an intimate way. Martí makes the reader feel invested in the cause with such passages as "Cuba is embarking upon this war in the full certainty … of the ability of its sons to win a victory through the energy of the thoughtful and magnanimous revolution." The employment of an impassioned, inspiring tone further draws in the reader. Martí's formal

JOSE MARTÍ: EARLY CUBAN REVOLUTIONARY

Jose Martí was an anticolonial Cuban activist and revolutionary, as well as a renowned writer of prose, poetry, and political and philosophical essays. He is remembered as an early proponent of Cuban independence from Spain and a thinker with a central role in the formation of a Cuban nation.

Born in Havana in 1853 to a working-class family, Martí became involved in anticolonial activities at an early age, publishing essays and pamphlets calling for Cuban independence. Largely influenced by his liberal mentor and schoolteacher Rafael Maria de Mendive, Martí moved within Havana's politically progressive intellectual groups, which were often the target of persecution by police. Martí was sentenced to forced labor in 1870 and exiled to Spain the following year for his opposition to colonial rule. While in Spain, he published *El Presidio Politico en Cuba,* one of his first significant political works, which exposed the horrors of political imprisonment in Cuba. After reuniting with his family in Mexico, he married Cuban national Carmen Zayas Bazan.

Martí returned to Cuba in 1878 but was quickly exiled to Spain again after organizing against the Spanish crown. In 1880, he fled to the United States and devoted his energies to organizing a revolutionary movement in Cuba. After founding the Partido Revolucionario Cubano (Cuban Revolutionary Party), he traveled in 1895 to Montecristi, Dominican Republic, where he wrote the manifesto that defined the party's movement, *The Manifesto of Montecristi.* Martí did not live to see the fruits of his labor, dying in a battle against Spanish troops in 1895.

language and structure, geared toward an educated, intellectual audience, may have alienated the Cuban working class. Nevertheless, the manifesto resonated with the large middle- and upper-class, liberal segment of the population that supported the independence movement.

CRITICAL DISCUSSION

The Manifesto of Montecristi met with a mixed response. Pro-Spain readers and colonial authorities were quick to condemn the manifesto's independence-minded rhetoric, whereas liberal Cuban colonists were inspired by the work and rallied around the War of Independence. The vast majority of responses to the manifesto were local and written in Spanish. In addition, few intellectuals reacted directly to the manifesto, preferring to focus on the concrete developments of the war itself. Nevertheless, many of Martí's contemporaries regarded the manifesto as the ultimate expression of the war's revolutionary ideals, referring to it for help in defining the movement's goals for themselves.

Following the War of Independence, *The Manifesto of Montecristi* influenced the revolutionary undertones of Cuban life during the dictatorial

An illustration depicting Cuban independence fighter José Martí. ALBUM/ART RESOURCE, NY

broader scale, *The Manifesto of Montecristi* has been used as a source for international legislation, including the Universal Declaration of Human Rights (1948), a document adopted by the United Nations that focuses on the right to resist acts of tyranny and oppression.

Contemporary scholarship continues to view Martí's manifesto as being central to the ideology of the Cuban independence movement. In "Jose Martí and Social Revolution in Cuba," Richard B. Gray calls *The Manifesto of Montecristi* "the expression of the need to establish governmental forms that could be derived from native foundations." Experts on Cuban history often place the manifesto alongside Martí's other prominent political works, including *Resoluciones* (1891) and *Bases y Estatutos Secretos del Partido Revolucionario Cubano* (1892). Additionally, much scholarship, including that of Jaime Suchlicki, focuses on the five main points of the manifesto's war policy. Suchlicki writes in "The Political Ideology of Jose Martí" that the document "advocated a war without hate, with mutual respect for the honest Spaniard, pious with those who repented, but inflexible with vice, crime or inhuman actions."

BIBLIOGRAPHY

Sources

Gray, Richard B. "Jose Martí and Social Revolution in Cuba." *Journal of Inter-American Studies* 5.2. (April 1963): 249-56. Print.

Miller, Nicola. "The Absolution of History: Uses of the Past in Castro's Cuba." *Journal of Contemporary History* 38.1 (2003): 147-62. Print.

Morsink, Johannes. *The Universal Declaration of Human Rights: Origins, Drafting, and Intent.* Philadelphia: U of Pennsylvania P, 1999. Print.

Ramírez, Luz Elena. "Biography: Jose Martí." *Encyclopedia of Postcolonial Studies.* Ed. John C. Hawley. Westport: Greenwood, 2001. 292-93. Print.

Suchlicki, Jaime. "The Political Ideology of Jose Martí." *Caribbean Studies* 6.1 (1966): 25-36. Print.

Further Reading

Abel, Christopher, and Nissa Torrents, eds. *José Martí: Revolutionary Democrat.* Durham: Duke UP, 1986. Print.

Carr, Aviva, et al., eds. *The Cuba Reader: History, Culture, Politics.* Durham: Duke UP, 2003. Print.

Castro, Fidel. *Fidel Castro: My Life: A Spoken Autobiography.* London: Allen Lane, 2007. Print.

Guerra, Lillian. *The Myth of José Martí: Conflicting Nationalisms in Early Twentieth-century Cuba.* Chapel Hill: U of North Carolina P, 2005. Print.

Ferrer, Ada. *Insurgent Cuba: Race, Nation, and Revolution, 1868-1898.* Chapel Hill: U of North Carolina P, 1999. Print.

Helg, Aline. *Our Rightful Share: The Afro-Cuban Struggle for Equality, 1886-1912.* Chapel Hill: U of North Carolina P, 1995. Print.

administrations of Gerardo Machado and Fulgencio Batista. It had a notable and direct effect on several manifestos that emerged from the revolutionary movement of the 1950s. Additionally, the manifesto was incorporated into the mandatory curriculum of the Cuban educational system following the resolutions of the country's first congress in 1942. In "The Absolution of History: Uses of the Past in Castro's Cuba," Nicola Miller writes that the government declared that Martí's manifesto "should be [the] 'basis of Cuban ideology' because it brought together 'a profound sense of nationality, an embrace of the whole American continent and a universal inspiration and reach.'" Cuba's ministry of education reproduced the manifesto for use in schools, and it remained part of the curriculum until well into the 1960s. On a

Miller, Nicola. *In the Shadow of the State: Intellectuals and the Quest for National Identity in Twentieth-Century Spanish America.* New York: Verso, 1999. Print.

Ripoll, Carlos. *José Martí, the United States, and the Marxist Interpretation of Cuban History.* New Brunswick: Transaction, 1984. Print.

———. "José Martí." *Florida International University, Free Cuba Foundation.* Web. 1 July 2012.

Rojas, Rafael. "'Otro Gallo Cantaria': Essay on the First Cuban Republicanism." *The Cuban Republic and José Martí: Reception and Use of a National Symbol.* Ed. Mauricio Font and Alfonso Quiroz. Lanham: Lexington, 2006. 7-17. Print.

Torres-Saillant, Silvio. *An Intellectual History of the Caribbean.* New York: Palgrave Macmillan, 2006. Print.

Wolf, Donna Marie. "Double Diplomacy: Ulises Heureaux and the Cuban Independence Movement." *Caribbean Studies* 14.1 (1974): 75-103. Print.

Katrina White

THE NECESSITY FOR DE-ANGLICIZING IRELAND

Douglas Hyde

✥ *Key Facts*

Time Period:
Late 19th Century

Movement/Issue:
Irish cultural revival; Irish nationalism

Place of Publication:
Ireland

Language of Publication:
English

OVERVIEW

Composed by Douglas Hyde in December 1892, "The Necessity for De-Anglicizing Ireland" describes a history of a colonial people in the process of losing their indigenous Irish culture and exhorts the revival of the Irish language throughout Irish society. He wrote the address as the newly appointed president of Dublin's National Literary Society, a cultural group established by writer William Butler Yeats, patriot and feminist Maud Gonne, and others in order to create "a living literature for a living Ireland." As the diverse membership of the National Literary Society attests, "The Necessity for De-Anglicizing Ireland" was crafted to generate support from all Irish citizens, regardless of their nationalist or unionist sympathies. Delivered before this literary society, the speech calls on Irish citizens to revive the cultural prosperity of their nation by reviving its language.

Hyde's address drew a large audience and met with immediate approval in literary and journalistic circles. Though the speech suggested wide-ranging approaches to reviving the Irish language, the changes were apolitical and inspired many Irish people to learn, speak, and write in Irish. Furthermore, Hyde's words led to the formation of the Gaelic League in 1893, which became the leading organization in the promotion of Irish. The Gaelic League, following suggestions put forth in Hyde's essay, published Irish language newspapers, including *An Claidheamh Soluis* ("The Sword of Light") edited by nationalist Patrick Pearse. In the twenty-first century, "The Necessity for De-Anglicizing Ireland" is recognized as among the most significant political documents of the emerging Irish nation and is considered to be an influence on later postcolonial movements around the world.

HISTORICAL AND LITERARY CONTEXT

"The Necessity for De-Anglicizing Ireland" responds to the cultural and political crises facing Ireland at the end of the nineteenth century, when the possibility for Home Rule (the movement to ensure Irish political autonomy within the British Empire) was a tantalizing but uncertain hope. In 1870 activists had formed the Irish Land League, a group that organized boycotts and resistance to assist Irish tenant farmers. The violence of the Land League's tactics escalated to the point that the government suppressed the organization. In an attempt to restore an Irish parliament, Liberal Party Prime Minister William Gladstone attempted a first Home Rule bill, but it was defeated in London's Parliament in 1886. The anti-Home Rule government instead offered the Plan of Campaign, which intended to turn the Irish away from their desire for Home Rule by reducing high rents for overwhelmed tenant farmers. The Plan of Campaign was supplemented by the Irish Coercion (or Crimes) Act of 1887, which prevented organizing or assembly by tenants. Arrests made under the act intensified a feeling of injustice that increased sympathy for the Home Rule movement.

By the time "The Necessity for De-Anglicizing Ireland" was written in 1892, Irish political opposition to British rule had experienced multiple setbacks. Even before the fall of Home Rule leader Charles Stewart Parnell, Irish nationalists had begun forming cultural groups to foster a sense of Irish national spirit. Chief among them was the Gaelic Athletic Association, formed in 1884 by Michael Cusack, Maurice Davin, and others to "foster a spirit of earnest nationality" by promoting the cultural native pastimes of Ireland. Irish writers and academics formed their own clubs: in London, England, Yeats organized the Irish Literary Society and then in Dublin, Ireland, the National Literary Society. When Hyde delivered his speech to the National Literary Society in 1892 and reminded Ireland of the significance of its native language, he provided a platform around which nationalists and unionists could initially gather. The central idea of Hyde's essay—the revival of Ireland's native language—was taken on by the Irish separatist movement. Later, in independent Ireland, Irish became a compulsory subject in schools and became a cultural signifier.

"The Necessity for De-Anglicizing Ireland" draws on a history of Irish resistance through cultural assembly that can be traced back to the Young Ireland movement of the 1840s. When they created the Literary Society, Yeats, Gonne, and the others announced their intentions in the *Freeman's Journal* to continue the projects of the Young Ireland movement and to produce an Irish literature and improve the distribution of Irish works. Hyde, an academic, also had much to learn from the cultural preservation exemplified in Standish O'Grady's collections of Irish folklore. Called the father of the Irish Literary

Revival, O'Grady connected "the revival of Irish literary energy and the return of Irish self-esteem." In his essay, Hyde called upon these ideas as well as his own earlier speech "A Plea for the Irish Language" and the work of his colleague Eugene O'Growney's "The National Language."

In the decades following the speech, "The Necessity for De-Anglicizing Ireland" inspired a body of literature and cultural dialogue in response to its key ideas of language revival. Beginning with political journalism in papers such as the *United Irishmen* and the *Weekly Freeman,* Irish writers and intellectuals at the beginning of the twentieth century considered their work in relation to their cultural heritage. For some, Irish writing could be an interplay of the Irish and English languages. Others, such as Patrick Pearse, urged a cultural revival that would take place exclusively in Irish. Hyde himself had already published Irish verse and went on to write Irish-language dramas, notably *Casadh an tSugáin,* translated by Lady Gregory as "The Twisting of the Rope" for the Irish Literary Theatre. Though Hyde advocated the teaching and use of Irish, perhaps his greatest contribution to literature were his books of folklore, which collected Irish songs and stories and conveyed them in the rhythms of Hiberno-English. These renderings of Irish speech inspired Yeats, Lady Gregory, and dramatist John Millington Synge in their creation of a subsequent major movement of letters—the Irish literary revival.

THEMES AND STYLE

The central theme of "The Necessity for De-Anglicizing Ireland" is that the Irish people have failed themselves in allowing the loss of their native culture even as they refuse to become totally assimilated citizens of Britain. Recognizing the potentially divisive message imparted by its title, the essay opens with an appeal to the responsibilities of all: "This is a question which most Irishmen will naturally look at from a National point of view, but it is one which ought also to claim the sympathies of every intelligent Unionist." To this end, Hyde enumerates the many ways in which all Irish people suffer at the loss of their culture ("one of the most classically learned and cultured nations in Europe, is now one of the least so"). In order that the Irish will no longer suffer the indignity of a British cultural identity, Hyde states how all Irish people can restore Irish to the center of their cultural worlds, starting with the instruction of the Irish language and the promotion of Irish books and publishing.

Hyde's speech achieves its rhetorical effect through appeals to an Irish unity that transcends political divisions according to unionist or nationalist sentiment. This sense of unity is achieved primarily through Hyde's use of the inclusive pronoun "we." His essay was written to address the National Literary Society, but his speech envisions an even more inclusive public body, whose interests and well-being hinge

DOUGLAS HYDE—SCHOLAR, POET, PRESIDENT

Douglas Hyde's life and career were distinguished by his nonpartisan work on behalf of the Irish language. Hyde, an Anglo-Irish Protestant, was born in 1860 in County Sligo. He spent his childhood in western Ireland, where he was introduced to Irish through servants. Hyde attended Trinity College in Dublin and studied languages, including French, German, Greek, Hebrew, and Latin.

Hyde's true passion was the Irish language. While an academic—in 1909 he became the first professor of Modern Irish in University College, Dublin—Hyde wrote verse in the Irish language under the pseudonym An Craoibhin Aoibhinn, collected and translated Irish folklore (notably *Love Songs of Connacht*), and gave lectures. In the United States, he told audiences that the only way to revive the Irish spirit was through the advent of Home Rule and by putting the Irish language in all the country's institutions and schools. Hyde avoided political extremism in his statements: "I do not want to be an impossible visionary or rabid partisan." When the Gaelic League became a thriving organization in Irish life, Hyde was invited to seek a seat in the British Parliament, but he refused. As the Irish language revival was co-opted by the political, nationalist Sinn Féin movement, apolitical Hyde was eventually forced out of the Gaelic League. His astute observations about Irish cultural preservation served him well: Hyde was appointed the first president of the Irish Free State, in part as an acknowledgement of his role in Irish independence through the revival of the Irish language.

on the health of a heritage that creates a sense of personal and national Irishness. For the support and benefit of this nation of Ireland—"one of the quickest, most sensitive, and most artistic races on earth" but also one of the quickest to assimilate—Hyde urges the excavation and promotion of their Irish birthright. Notably, Hyde names Ireland's foreign detractors (for example, Italian activist Giuseppe Mazzini, who dismissed Irish nationhood in part because of its loss of language) and addresses their criticisms in order to inspire his audience. Hyde, however, is careful to avoid taking political sides within his country and uses his essay to rouse both sides of the political divide: "every one … who wishes to see Ireland do its best."

Stylistically, "The Necessity for De-Anglicizing Ireland" is distinguished by its inclusiveness and its conversational tone. Written as a public speech that would both inform and inspire, Hyde's essay generates goodwill and credibility as it attempts to make a balanced assessment of the Irish people in relation to their language. The essay addresses the criticisms of Ireland's people as a way to emphasize the consequences of having "lost the notes of nationality, our

Irish/English bilingual street signs in Lisdoonvarna, Ireland. SPENCER GRANT/PHOTO RESEARCHERS/GETTY IMAGES

language and customs." At the same time, by offering the Irish-language revival as a solution to valid criticisms, Hyde offers a useful approach to a hopeful and autonomous future. Although its informality renders "The Necessity for De-Anglicizing Ireland" a pleasant, even humorous talk, the speech gains rhetorical force through its careful examination of Irish weaknesses and elevation of Ireland's notable cultural heritage.

CRITICAL DISCUSSION

When Hyde first delivered his lecture in 1892, it received much attention and praise within literary and nationalist circles. He spoke to a large crowd for more than an hour. Two years later, the critic W.P. Ryan described the address as "sensational" in his book *The Irish Literary Revival.* Yeats overheard someone say that "it was the most important utterance of its kind" since 1848, the year of the Young Irelander Rebellion. Many unionists were wary of cultural revival groups as a form of nationalist resistance. However even the unionist *Irish Times* praised Hyde as "an able, well-educated man." Meanwhile, *United Ireland* published an editorial, describing the speech as "one of the most practical lectures on a National topic I have heard in a long time." Given the noble and apolitical aims of Hyde's lecture, many rallied to his exhortations, and Hyde was to give the lecture several more times throughout Ireland.

Hyde's lecture became a significant force in the Irish language and literary revival and led to the formation of the Gaelic League, the leading institution and forum for discourse in the country's movement for cultural preservation. At the time, the matter of language preservation and a literary revival became a matter of political dispute, something Hyde sought to avoid. By 1904 the Gaelic League was so popular that Hyde was wooed by the Parliamentary Party, but he refused a seat in government. He managed to keep politics out of the league until 1915, when an increasingly ideological agenda forced him to resign the presidency. Since its composition, Hyde's essay has been the subject of extensive criticism that has considered its influence in historical, political, and postcolonial terms.

Much scholarship has been focused on the specific controversies between Irish and Anglo-Irish writers: Synge, for example, argued against the Gaelic League's intention of restoring Irish as the vernacular of Ireland. For him, the Anglo-Irish dialect was "an expression of Irish mentality through the English language, a miraculous growth without which the Irish Literary Revival could not have taken place." Other scholars have offered comparative descriptions of ideological polemics (as in D. P. Moran's early twentieth-century work *The Philosophy of Irish-Ireland*). Still others have traced the careers of the revivalists who gained prominence in public affairs or have examined the demographics of the Gaelic League (as in Timothy McMahon's study 'All creeds and all classes'? Just who made up the Gaelic League?" in the journal *Eire-Ireland*).

BIBLIOGRAPHY

Sources

Dunleavy, Gareth W., and Janet Egleson. *Douglas Hyde: A Maker of Modern Ireland.* Berkeley and Los Angeles: U of California P, 1991. Print.

Hyde, Douglas. "The Necessity for De-Anglicizing Ireland." *Poetry and Ireland since 1800: A Source Book.* Ed. Mark Storey. London: Routledge, 1988. Print.

Kiberd, Declan. *Inventing Ireland.* London: Jonathan Cape, 1995. Print.

———. *The Irish Writer and the World.* Cambridge: Cambridge UP, 2005. Print.

Mathews, P.J. *Revival The Abbey Theatre, Sinn Féin, the Gaelic League and the Co-Operative Movement.* Cork, Ireland: Cork UP, 2003. Print.

Pierce, David. *Light, Freedom and Song: A Cultural History of Modern Irish Writing.* New Haven, CT: Yale UP, 2005. Print.

Ryan, W.P. *The Irish Literary Revival: Its History, Pioneers and Possibilities.* New York: Lemma, 1970. Print.

Further Reading

Bhabha, Homi K. *The Location of Culture.* New York: Routledge, 1994. Print.

Delaney, Paul. "D. P. Moran and the Leader: Writing an Irish Ireland through Partition." *Eire-Ireland: A Journal of Irish Studies* 38.3-4 (2003): 189+. *Literature Resource Center.* Web. 3 Aug. 2012.

Lanters, Jose. "The Irish Language Movement." Review of *Grand Opportunity* by Timothy G. McMahon. *English Literature in Transition 1880-1920* 52.3 (2009): 361+. *Literature Resource Center.* Web. 2 Aug. 2012.

McMahon, Timothy G. "'All Creeda and All Classes'? Just Who Made Up the Gaelic League?" *Eire-Ireland:*

A Journal of Irish Studies (2002): 118+. *Literature Resource Center.* Web. 2 Aug. 2012.

Reynolds, Lorna. "The Irish Literary Revival: Preparation and Personalities." *The Celtic Consciousness.* Ed. Robert O'Driscoll. Portlaoise, Ireland: Dolmen, 1981. 383-99. Rpt. in *Twentieth-Century Literary Criticism.* Vol. 222. Detroit: Gale, 2010. *Literature Resource Center.* Web. 2 Aug. 2012.

Karen Bender

NEGRO DECLARATION OF INDEPENDENCE

National Independent Political Union

✢ *Key Facts*

Time Period:
Late 19th Century

Movement/Issue:
Civil rights;
Reconstruction

Place of Publication:
United States

**Language of
Publication:**
English

OVERVIEW

Issued by the Committee on Resolutions of the National Independent Political Union (NIPU), a group composed of African American representatives from most U.S. states, the *Negro Declaration of Independence* stems from a meeting held February 28, 1876, in Washington, D.C. The document expresses its authors' and signatories' frustrations with corruption in the Republican Party and their determination to support candidates who genuinely work for their interests regardless of party affiliation. Written toward the end of the post-Civil War period known as Reconstruction (1863-77), the *Negro Declaration of Independence* responds to the reemergence of white rule despite African Americans' best efforts to exercise their newly won political rights. Like its model, the U.S. Declaration of Independence, the statement contains a long list of grievances and a pledge to cooperate in throwing off the yoke of the oppressor—in this case, the Republican Party.

The *Negro Declaration of Independence,* which may have been either a genuine expression of political independence or a first step toward support of the Democratic Party in the election of 1876, garnered relatively little attention. Prominent African American leaders, meeting a few months later, reaffirmed their support for the Republican Party. The results of the election itself were politically mixed but uniformly disastrous for African American civil and political rights. Nevertheless, the declaration provides valuable insight into the development of African American political thinking in the immediate post-emancipation period and serves as an example of how U.S. citizens in the nation's centennial year adapted the form and rhetoric of the country's founding document to contemporary purposes.

HISTORICAL AND LITERARY CONTEXT

The *Negro Declaration of Independence* reflects concerns of African Americans at the end of Reconstruction. While the years immediately after the Civil War brought reason to expect full legal and social equality through the Thirteenth, Fourteenth, and Fifteenth Amendments to the U.S. Constitution, by 1876 African Americans were concerned that the Republican Party was abandoning their interests in favor of renewed alliances with southern whites. Corruption

and profiteering associated with key institutions originally designed to support former slaves—notably the Freedmen's Bank, which failed in June 1874—further fed some African Americans' belief that the Republican Party was not effectively representing their interests.

In this context, a group of African American leaders from northern and southern states decided to publicly renounce their allegiance to the Republican Party and form an independent political body. Little is known about most of the signatories of the *Negro Declaration of Independence*; the exception is Rev. Garland H. White, a former slave whose acquaintance with Secretary of State William Seward—who served under Abraham Lincoln—and whose role in recruiting members of the U.S. Colored Troops are chronicled in records in the National Archives. It seems likely that many participants in the meeting, like White, were disillusioned Republican loyalists.

The committee members' decision to model their text on the U.S. Declaration of Independence was no doubt influenced by a long tradition of borrowing the form of the nation's founding documents for other purposes and by the centennial year in which they were writing. The most famous earlier document modeled on the U.S. Declaration of Independence is the *Declaration of Sentiments and Resolutions* issued by the Women's Rights Convention held at Seneca Falls, New York, in July 1848. By 1876 a number of groups representing laborers had also issued declarations asserting their rights and especially their independence from various powerful individuals and groups. For instance, in 1829 George Henry Evans, an advocate of a separate Working Man's Party, wrote the *Working Men's Declaration of Independence* as a recruiting tool, and in 1834 the Boston Trades' Union issued a *Declaration of Rights*. In 1874 socialists issued a *Declaration of Principles and Bill of Grievances,* which, like the *Negro Declaration of Independence,* accused the U.S. party system of failing to protect the interests of voting citizens.

While the *Negro Declaration of Independence* was circulated as a pamphlet, there is little evidence that it achieved its aim of preserving and strengthening African Americans' political power. Whether the declaration was genuinely intended to herald the founding of an independent political entity representing the interests of African Americans, by August 1876, according to a report in the *Georgia Weekly Telegraph,* White was campaigning for Samuel J. Tilden, a Democratic presidential candidate with a history of supporting reform. White remained convinced that this was a wise choice; in 1894, toward the end of his life, he proudly reminded listeners of his support for Tilden in a eulogy for Democratic South Carolina Governor Zebulon B. Vance, who was part of Tilden's 1876 slate.

THEMES AND STYLE

Most of the *Negro Declaration of Independence* is dedicated to providing examples of the faithlessness of the Republican Party to its African American constituents. A long section details problems with the Freedmen's Bank, described as a "*pseudo philanthropic,* but ruinous receptacle," established "ostensibly for the benefit of the Freedmen, but actually for the pecuniary advancement of knavish bankrupts, favorites of the administration," and trusted by the former slaves "only because of its Republican character." By contrast, the authors argue, Republicans "ignor[ed] intelligent colored men, of undoubted character, in the distribution of the patronage." The declaration also blames Republicans for the country's economic woes and accuses them of violating their own labor standards. Another ongoing theme is the accusation that Republicans deliberately created conflict between black and white southerners for personal and political benefit, "banding ignorant colored men against their fellow white citizens in order that greedy and unscrupulous cormorants from the North might ride into office and then leave them, after

GARLAND H. WHITE

Born into slavery in Virginia, Garland H. White was sold as a child to Robert Toombs, a lawyer from Georgia who served in the U.S. Congress between 1852 and 1858. While living in the District of Columbia and working as Toombs's body servant, White escaped to Canada, where he was able to make use of the credentials he had earned while in slavery and find work as an African Methodist Episcopal pastor.

After Abraham Lincoln approved the participation of African American troops in the Civil War in 1863, White volunteered to help with the recruitment effort. He eventually served as a chaplain with the 28th U.S. Colored Infantry and participated in the liberation of Richmond, Virginia, reuniting with his mother, whom he had not seen for twenty years, in the process. During the war White reported regularly to the *Christian Recorder,* a black Methodist newspaper, and afterward he served as a pastor in Ohio and North Carolina despite poor health caused at least in part by his Civil War service. When he died, probably in late 1894, he was once again living in Washington, D.C., and working as a messenger, despite illness and advanced age.

amassing fortunes and attaining honor and fame, the enemies of those who would otherwise have befriended and protected them."

The accumulated examples serve as justification for the decision announced at the end of the first paragraph and elaborated upon in the final

The Colored National Convention in Session, Nashville, Tennessee, April 5-7, 1876, engraving from Frank Leslie's *Illustrated Newspaper.* PRIVATE COLLECTION/THE BRIDGEMAN ART LIBRARY

three: renunciation of the "self-imposed party yoke" that the authors have assumed "since [they] became citizens." "For these and other reasons too numerous for enumeration," the authors write at the beginning of the final section of the document, "we feel justified in severing all connection with this profligate party," and "pledging our hearty support, zeal and devotion" to anyone who will support their goals of "FULL AND EQUAL JUSTICE BEFORE THE LAW, PROTECTION FOR OUR LIVES AND PROPERTY AGAINST LAWLESSNESS AND MOB VIOLENCE, AND EQUITABLE RECOGNITION IN THE SEVERAL DEPARTMENTS OF THE GOVERNMENT, BASED UPON OUR INTELLIGENCE AND OUR INTEGRITY" (emphasis in original). Rather than vote in a solid bloc, as heretofore, the authors write, they "propose to stand by *principles,* and support only the men *who will do the most for us.*" In addition to securing their own rights, they hope that their stance will bring "a speedy return to good feeling between the late master and now FREE CITIZEN."

In contrast to the conciliatory tone they adopt toward the southern whites with whom they hope to ally, the declaration's authors are scathing in their descriptions of what they see as Republican betrayal and corruption. The party is "profligate, teeming with the most loathsome corruption," it is "flagrant" in its "violations of the Constitution," it "trample[s] local self government" and insults "brave and well-disposed fellow citizens of the South." The final paragraph adopts a calmer and more hopeful tone, describing the "departure" from the Republican Party as "*carefully considered*" and based on "well grounded complaint," "invit[ing] the hearty and cordial co-operation of the colored people of the whole country" and offering a final wish for the "prosperity and unification of all the sections of our indivisible republic."

CRITICAL DISCUSSION

Beyond the presence of the *Negro Declaration of Independence* in several repositories, including the Library of Congress and the Huntington Library, there is little evidence of reaction to the NIPU's work. As Tundu Adeleke notes in *Without Regard to Race* (2003), a National Colored Convention held in April 1876 in Nashville, possibly convened "in response to the NIPU," voted down a resolution calling for "the immediate severance of all ties with the Republican Party" and instead "reaffirmed strong support for the Republican Party and likened support for the Democrats to 'supporting the devil against God.'" The resolution of the disputed presidential election of 1876, which placed Tilden's opponent, Rutherford P. Hayes, in office and cemented Democratic control of the southern states, help explain this view. Democrats' "redemption" of the South led to the effective loss of voting rights for African Americans in the region, a situation that was not remedied until the 1960s.

The political philosophy underlying White's decision to stump for Tilden and Vance—a belief that alliances between former slaveholders and former slaves in the South could better serve southern African Americans' political interests than association with the Republicans, a party mostly identified with the northern states—nevertheless remained influential. Most notably, it shaped the thinking of Booker T. Washington, who, like White, sought to cooperate with white southern leaders as a means of advancing the economic welfare of African Americans in the South, albeit at the expense of the political rights the NIPU had striven effectively to exercise.

Today, the *Negro Declaration of Independence* is of interest primarily as a document capturing a time in history when it still seemed possible that the political influence former slaves had exercised in the immediate postwar era might continue and as an example of the adoption of the form of the U.S. Declaration of Independence to other uses. In 1976, the U.S. bicentennial, Philip S. Foner reprinted the declaration in the collection *We, the Other People: Alternative Declarations of Rights by Labor Groups, Farmers, Woman's Rights Advocates, Socialists, and Blacks, 1829-1975.* Adeleke also considers the NIPU's activities an example of "a developing trend, albeit a minority one, within the black struggle that was associated with calls for 'a new departure'" and a potential influence on the thought of African American leader Martin Delany, whom the NIPU appointed its leader for a group of states "south of North Carolina."

BIBLIOGRAPHY

Sources

Adeleke, Tunde. *Without Regard to Race: The Other Martin Robison Delany.* Jackson: UP of Mississippi, 2003. Print.

"A New Development." *Georgia Weekly Telegraph and Georgia Journal & Messenger* 8 Aug. 1876: 1. *19th-Century U.S. Newspapers.* Web. 5 Oct. 2012.

Foner, Philip S. *We, the Other People: Alternative Declarations of Rights by Labor Groups, Farmers, Woman's Rights Advocates, Socialists, and Blacks, 1829-1975.* Urbana: U of Illinois P, 1976. Print.

National Independent Political Union. "Negro Declaration of Independence." *We, the Other People: Alternative Declarations of Rights by Labor Groups, Farmers, Woman's Rights Advocates, Socialists, and Blacks, 1829-1975.* Ed. Philip S. Foner. Urbana: U of Illinois P, 1976. 90-94. Print.

White, Garland H. "The Colored Men Praise Vance." *News Observer Chronicle* 1 May 1894: 1. *19th-Century U.S. Newspapers.* Web. 5 Oct. 2012.

Further Reading

Blight, David W. *Race and Reunion: The Civil War in American Memory.* Cambridge: Harvard UP, 2002. Print.

Foner, Eric. *Reconstruction: America's Unfinished Revolution, 1863-1877.* New York: Harper & Row, 1988. Print.

Foner, Eric, and Joshua Brown. *Forever Free: The Story of Emancipation & Reconstruction.* New York: Vintage, 2005. Print.

Hahn, Steven. *A Nation under Our Feet: Black Political Struggles in the Rural South from Slavery to the Great Migration.* Cambridge: Harvard UP, 2005. Print.

Hendrick, George, and Willene Hendrick. *Black Refugees in Canada: Accounts of Escape during the Era of Slavery.* Jefferson: McFarland, 2010. Print.

Litwack, Leon F. *Been in the Storm So Long: The Aftermath of Slavery.* New York: Vintage, 1980. Print.

Miller, Edward A. "Garland H. White, Black Army Chaplain." *Civil War History* 43:3 (1997): 201-18. *Project MUSE.* Web. 6 Oct. 2012.

Weidman, Budge. "Preserving the Legacy of the United States Colored Troops." *Teachers' Resources.* National Archives. Web. 5 Oct. 2012.

Catherine E. Saunders

PROLETARIANS

AN AGREEMENT OF THE FREE PEOPLE OF ENGLAND

John Lilburne, William Walwyn, Thomas Prince, Richard Overton

OVERVIEW

An Agreement of the Free People of England (1649), authored by Lt. Col. John Lilburne, William Walwyn, Thomas Prince, and Richard Overton, contains proposals for a new constitution of Great Britain and for the reconciliation of various contentious factions of the parliamentary side of the English Civil Wars (1638-51). It was written to appeal to the rank and file of Parliament's New Model Army and to civilians who felt they should have a larger stake in the new government. Lilburne and his colleagues had become known as Levellers, although Lilburne rejected the term because it implied an attack on the rights of private property while his concern was with what are now called the civil rights of individuals. The final draft of the manifesto was smuggled out of the Tower of London, where the authors had been imprisoned by the revolutionary government. Earlier drafts, chiefly the work of Lilburne and Overton, had been produced in October 1647 and December 1648.

The 1647 draft was embraced by the common soldiers of the New Model Army (as were all subsequent versions) and reviled by the high officers (known as Grandees). Alarmed by the egalitarian nature of the document, Oliver Cromwell and the other Grandees were untiring in their efforts to suppress the manifesto and the Levellers. Although the Levellers themselves ceased to exist a few months after the publication of the final draft, *Agreement* continued to inspire people in the succeeding centuries. Its language of equality is found in the writings of Thomas Paine, the *Declaration of Independence,* the U.S. Constitution (especially in the Bill of Rights), and the *People's Charter* of nineteenth-century England. Left-wing socialists and right-wing libertarians alike claim *Agreement* as an influence.

HISTORICAL AND LITERARY CONTEXT

Historically, *An Agreement of the Free People of England* marks the first detailed assertion of what its principal author, Lilburne, calls "freeborn rights," or rights that are inborn and are not bestowed upon an individual by the state. The manifesto proposes a government that protects and guarantees these rights. The work's provisions—such as equality of all persons before the law, the abolition of imprisonment for debt, the freedom from self-recrimination in a criminal trial, the abolition of military conscription, the right of all men aged twenty-one and older to vote, and the separation of church and state—reflect the personal experiences of the authors and seek to fashion a society in which people are free from the abuses of arbitrary power.

The final version of *Agreement* was published four months after the victorious parliamentary forces had beheaded King Charles I and established a commonwealth and a few months before the final suppression of the Levellers. During this time the Civil Wars were being fought on both religious and political grounds. On one side, the Stuart kings aspired to be absolute monarchs over the kingdoms of England, ruling with the "divine right of kings." As heads of the Church of England, they wanted an exclusive church organized from the top down. Parliament, meanwhile, sought exclusive control of the legislative and financial functions of government. It was of primary concern to Lilburne and the Levellers that an absolute monarch not be succeeded by an absolute dictator, but four years after *Agreement* was published, Cromwell appointed himself Lord Protector, a position that came with dictatorial powers.

Lilburne and his *Agreement* coauthors were not concerned with literature as such and did not view themselves as writers or intellectuals. For them, writing was simply a means for political action. There is no significant literary precedent for *Agreement,* in which the idea of the "rights of the people" makes its first appearance on the historical stage. The *Agreement* authors saw themselves, literally, as the voice of the people, as opposed to being a mouthpiece for some specific institution or creed. Pious men themselves, Lilburne and the Levellers represent the secularization of the Protestant Reformation, although Martin Luther would not have approved. When Luther had urged a "priesthood of all believers" and for every Christian to read the Bible for himself or herself, he meant for only a religious application of the principles.

Their lack of literary ambition notwithstanding, Lilburne and his fellow Levellers had an immense impact on the field of democratic political theory.

Key Facts

Time Period:
Mid-17th Century

Movement/Issue:
Human rights;
Democratic reform

Place of Publication:
England

Language of Publication:
English

THE ENGLISH BIBLE

The Levellers learned to read using the Bible, and both their syntax and ideas were shaped by the scriptures, especially the New Testament. The notion that all Christians should be able to read the Bible in their own language came from Martin Luther, who completed the German translation himself. However, it was nearly a century before the British monarchy sanctioned an English translation of the Bible. Even when he broke with Rome in 1529 to marry a woman who could produce a male heir, Henry VIII forbade English translations of the Bible as propagating heresies, and his children—Edward IV, Mary, and Elizabeth I—followed suit.

Shortly after King James I ascended the throne, at the Hampton Court conference of 1604, it was proposed that an official translation be prepared. The king agreed, and the King James Bible, technically the "Authorised Version (AV)," was published in 1611. To be sure, it was the age of William Shakespeare and Ben Jonson, Christopher Marlowe and John Webster, but John Lilburne and his fellow Levellers were Puritans, and they did not go to the theater. The epigraph to *An Agreement of the Free People of England* is from the Sermon on the Mount: "Blessed are the Peace-makers for they shall be called the children of God" (Matthew 5:9).

Paine's *The Crisis, The Rights of Man,* and *The Age of Reason* are steeped in the Levellers' doctrines of innate rights and religious freedom and are written in the same spirit and style. The notion of "unalienable rights" in the *Declaration of Independence* can be traced back to Lilburne's "freeborn rights." Further, *Agreement*'s influence is seen in the articles of the U.S. Constitution, such as Article VI, which reads: "There shall be no religious test for any public office under the United States."

THEMES AND STYLE

The two main themes of the *Agreement of the Free People of England* are (1) the safeguarding of the individual conscience and individual rights from the encroachments of arbitrary power and factional partisanship, and (2) that peace and domestic harmony are the essential preconditions to a better state. Relating to this second point, the subtitle of the work reads, "Tendered as a *Peace-Offering* to this distressed *Nation*." The authors frequently utilize a rhetorical device known as "the Lesson," pointing out ways that the English can learn from their mistakes. They begin by suggesting that the English treat the recent upheavals as opportunities for making the country better: "If afflictions make men wise, and wisdom direct to happinesse, then certainly this Nation is not far from such a degree." From there, the authors outline, clause by clause, the legal framework that can be built from the upheavals and deprivations the people have recently endured.

The principal strategy of the authors is to first articulate, as fellow sufferers, the dreadful problems their country has created through incompetence and abuse of power. In the provisions that follow, each suggested constitutional article aims to prevent a specific abuse. For example, on the matter of conflict of interest among elected representatives, the authors write:

> And to the end all publick Officers may be certainly accountable, and no Factions made to maintain corrupt Interests, no Officers of any salary Forces in Army or Garison, nor any Treasurer or Receiver of publick monies, shall (while such) be elected a Member for any Representative; and if any Lawyer shall at any time be chosen, he shall be uncapable of practice as a Lawyer, during the whole time of that Trust. And for the same reason, all persons may be capable of subjection as well as rule.

The language in *Agreement* is both passionate and idiosyncratic. It represents an outpouring by independent thinkers who are surer of their opinions than of spelling or grammar, who were raised on religious tracts and the King James Bible, and who desperately want to persuade other independent-minded people to follow their vision of a free future. Their principal potential readership was the New Model Army, and seldom has an organized body of men been so aptly named. Before the English Civil Wars, there had never been an army in which every soldier felt entitled to political opinions and had intellectual and philosophical motives for fighting. In *Agreement,* the Levellers are speaking to soldiers who have learned to read and to think for themselves: "We the free People of *England* ... [a]gree to ascertain our Government, to abolish all arbitrary Power, and to set bounds and limits both to our Supreme, and all Subordinate Authority, and remove all known Grievances."

CRITICAL DISCUSSION

Upon its publication, *An Agreement of the Free People of England* was viewed as a partisan political document. Royalist London newspapers such as *Mercurius Pragmaticus* predictably denounced it. The work was also received negatively by Presbyterians and Puritans such as Edward Winslow (1595-1655), who fought in the Civil Wars and then served in Cromwell's government. Groups such as the Diggers, even more radical than the Levellers, rejected the *Agreement* because it said nothing about abolishing private property. Civilians who sympathized with the Levellers adopted *Agreement* as their creed, and common soldiers marched into battle with folded copies of the manifesto placed in their hatbands.

The immediate impact of *Agreement* was virtually nil. The Levellers were decisively suppressed a few months after the final draft was published and ceased to exist as an organized political entity. Indeed, the ideas contained in the manifesto made no contribution to the Revolutionary Settlement of 1689 and ran underground in English discourse until they resurfaced in 1838 in the *People's Charter*. The concepts in *Agreement* had considerably more influence in America of the 1760s, France of 1789, and Russia of 1917. The most threatening aspect of *Agreement* to the established order was the simple proposition that all citizens or subjects are equal before the law. This remains true today. However widely such equality has been accepted in theory by civilized nations, it has yet to take complete hold in practice.

Since the 1960s, the Levellers have been among the most widely studied and chronicled groups from the English Civil Wars. Although libertarians call *Agreement* a seminal document, most of the scholarly interest in the Levellers and their manifesto has come from the Left. Marxists such as Christopher Hill rank Lilburne's radicalism with the rebellion of Spartacus as a pivotal episode in the evolution of class consciousness. In *The World Turned Upside Down: Radical Ideas during the English Revolution,* Hill writes, "Just as the Levellers elevated the jury over the judge, so the radical sectaries no longer looked up to the specialized, educated priest as the arbiter of precedent." Feminist historians have not been so kind, noting that the Levellers *could* have proposed extending the franchise to adult women but did not. Consequently, feminists have looked elsewhere for early champions of their cause.

BIBLIOGRAPHY

Sources

Gregg, Pauline. *Free-born John: A Biography of John Lilburne.* London: Harrap, 1961. Print.

Grob-Fitzgibbon, Benjamin. "'Whatsoever Yee Would That Men Should Doe unto You, Even So Doe Yee to Them': An Analysis of the Effect of Religious Consciousness on the Origins of the Leveller Movement." *Historian* 65.4 (2003): 901+. General OneFile. Web. 6 Aug. 2012.

Haller, William, ed. *The Leveller Tracts, 1647-1653.* Gloucester: P. Smith, 1964. Print.

Hill, Christopher. *The World Turned Upside Down: Radical Ideas during the English Revolution.* Harmondsworth: Penguin, 1975. Print.

Lilburne, John, et al. *An Agreement of the Free People of England*: Tendered as a *Peace-Offering to This Distressed* Nation. London: Gilbert Mabbot, 1649. Print.

Mendle, Michael, ed. *The Putney Debates of 1647: The Army, the Levellers, and the English State.* Cambridge: Cambridge UP, 2001. Print.

Further Reading

Aylmer, G. E., ed. *The Levellers in the English Revolution.* Ithaca: Cornell UP, 1975. Print.

Butt, J. J. Rev. of *Radical Religion in Cromwell's England: A Concise History from the English Civil War to the End of the Commonwealth,* by Andrew Bradstock. *CHOICE: Current Reviews for Academic Libraries* Oct. 2011: 382+. General OneFile. Web. 6 Aug. 2012.

Corns, Thomas N. *John Milton: The Prose Works.* Twayne's English Authors Series 546. New York: Twayne, 1998. Print.

Chadwick, Owen. *The Protestant Reformation.* The Pelican History of the Church: 3. Harmondsworth: Penguin, 1964. Print.

Loxley, James. "Literature, Gender and Politics during the English Civil War." *Renaissance Quarterly* 59.3 (2006): 982+. General OneFile. Web. 6 Aug. 2012.

Wedgwood, C. V. *The King's Peace: 1637-1641.* London: Deborah Owen, 1955. Print.

Young, Michael B. "The Constitutionalist Revolution: An Essay on the History of England." *Journal of Church and State* Autumn 2007: 768+. General OneFile. Web. 6 Aug. 2012.

Gerald Carpenter

A plaque commemmorating the Levellers on the south wall of Burford Church, Burford, Oxfordshire. The Levellers were imprisoned and sometimes killed for protesting the English government in the seventeenth century. © EEIL/HIP/THE IMAGE WORKS

ANTI-PLEBISCITE MANIFESTO

International Workingmen's Association and the Federal Chamber of Labor Societies

❖ **Key Facts**

Time Period:
Late 19th Century

Movement/Issue:
Revolutionary socialism;
Marxism

Place of Publication:
France

Language of Publication:
French

OVERVIEW

Composed by members of the International Workingmen's Association and the Federal Chamber of Labor Societies, the *Anti-Plebiscite Manifesto* (1870) urges French workers to abstain from participating in a popular vote (or plebiscite) on proposed parliamentary reforms and thereby reject the rule of Napoleon III, the French emperor. The manifesto was issued during a time of mounting unrest, particularly among the Parisian working class. In response to this growing dissatisfaction and the threat of revolution, Emperor Napoleon III had proposed a plebiscite that allegedly aimed to increase the people's democratic power. Members of the increasingly prominent communist movement in France considered this vote a deliberate attempt to diffuse the growing revolutionary fervor. Addressed to

"All French Workingmen," the *Anti-Plebiscite Manifesto* argued that the realization of a socialist republic was in reach and that participation in the impending vote would only undermine its fruition.

Although the *Anti-Plebiscite Manifesto* did not prevent the passage of the measure, it did help to consolidate the socialist movement in Paris. In 1870, the same year that the manifesto was issued, Napoleon III entered into a war against Prussia and surrendered during the battle of Sedan; he was deposed shortly thereafter. The next year, a socialist government known as the Paris Commune was established that opposed the return of a conservative, monarchist majority to the National Assembly. Although the Paris Commune lasted only two months before it was toppled, it is considered the first proletarian-led communist government in Europe. In the twenty-first century, the *Anti-Plebiscite Manifesto* is recognized as a significant influence on the revolution of 1871 and is considered a vital document in the history of communism.

HISTORICAL AND LITERARY CONTEXT

The *Anti-Plebiscite Manifesto* responds to the political unrest facing France in the late 1860s and early 1870s, when rapid modernization brought economic and social change and instability that required new political solutions. At the end of the eighteenth century, the French Revolution brought down the country's long-standing absolute monarchy. France, however, struggled during the early nineteenth century to find a stable replacement for the old order. After a series of revolutions, counterrevolutions, and coups d'état that resulted in continuous upheaval, Napoleon III wrested control in the early 1850s and established the Second Empire. The first decade of his reign was characterized by its authoritarianism, but he instituted increasingly liberal reforms during the 1860s in order to quell the mounting opposition to his rule. The result was democratic reform, economic growth, and increasing industrialization. Despite these gains, left-wing opposition continued to rise in the form of republican, anarchist, and communist movements.

By the time the *Anti-Plebiscite Manifesto* was issued in 1870, opposition to Napoleon III was strong and increasingly well organized. Among the most

MARX AND THE INTERNATIONAL

In 1864 Karl Marx was living in London. Sixteen years before, he had published the *Communist Manifesto,* which went on to become perhaps one of the most important communist texts ever authored. At the time, however, it was obscure and rarely read—and Marx himself was a minor figure. The socialist movement, though, was growing in Europe and becoming increasingly well organized. Therefore, when a small congress of workers was scheduled to convene at St. Martin's Hall in London, Marx was only invited at the last minute and was not asked to speak. Even so, he attended and, as his biographer Robert Payne writes, "was merely tolerated." Along with Marx, about two thousand people attended the meeting, most of them English laborers. It was decided at the meeting that a charter for the group was needed. Though Marx was one of thirty-four people appointed to draft the document, he surreptitiously authored the entire text himself. The document was accepted, and the International was born.

Over the next several years, the group spread throughout Europe and attracted up to a million members. Marx remained in control of the International and worked to foment a revolution that would take over the entire continent. With the collapse of the Paris Commune in 1871, however, the International effectively ended, too. Marx continued to agitate for the communist cause until his death in 1883.

vocal advocates for revolution was the International Workingmen's Association. Better known simply as the International, the group was founded in Paris in 1864 and aimed to organize the European working class into a revolutionary movement that would bring communism to the entire continent and beyond. The group was led by Karl Marx, a German who was the world's foremost communist thinker and leader. Though the exact size of the group is unknown, it is estimated that up to a million workers were members of the International by the 1860s. As a result, the group was important in leading the left-wing opposition to Napoleon III. This opposition came not only from communists but also from less radical liberals and republicans. In response, Napoleon III proposed major constitutional changes that would shift power to the French citizenry. A plebiscite—through which Napoleon III hoped to consolidate his position—was issued in 1870 to allow the people a chance to ratify these changes and to express their support for Napoleon's reign. In response, the International issued the *Anti-Plebiscite Manifesto*, urging workers to abstain from the vote so as not to legitimize the monarchy.

The *Anti-Plebiscite Manifesto* draws from other documents issued by the International Workingmen's Association beginning in the 1860s. Delivered in 1864, Marx's inaugural address to the International outlined the group's mission and its ideology. As Marx declared there, the capitalist system could not be improved or reformed. It was "a truth," he argued, that none of the economic advances of the system "will do away with the miseries of the industrious masses; but that, on the present false base, every fresh development of productive powers of labour must tend to deepen social contrasts and point social antagonisms." This argument against compromise and for entrenched opposition provides the framework for the *Anti-Plebiscite Manifesto*.

Upon its publication, the *Anti-Plebiscite Manifesto* was followed by a number of communist manifestos and polemics that elaborated the aims of the International and, later, of the Paris Commune. In July 1870, the Paris section of the International issued the *Manifesto against War* in response to Napoleon III's declaration of war against Prussia. In it, the group reiterated its argument that "societies can have no legitimate basis other than that of production and the equitable distribution of its fruits." Over the next two years, as revolution erupted and the Paris Commune was established, the International and other communist groups continued to issue polemics, declarations, and manifestos. These writings continue to command significant scholarly interest.

THEMES AND STYLE

The central theme of the *Anti-Plebiscite Manifesto* is that participation in the 1870 plebiscite will undermine the realization of a socialist republic in France. The manifesto opens by declaring that "the

sovereignty of labor is the only constitutive basis upon which modern society should rest." It is the worker, then, who "is called upon to regenerate the old order," and working people must band together to reject the rule of the reigning empire. The manifesto states that "it is not enough to answer by a purely negative vote this plebiscite that they have the audacity to thrust upon us.... Out of the ballot-box must come the most absolute condemnation of the monarchic régime, the complete, the radical affirmation of the only form of the government that can give scope to our legitimate aspirations—the *Social and Democratic Republic*." For the manifesto's authors, consenting to the vote is tantamount to consenting to the despotic rule of France's Second Empire. By abstaining, the reader can aid in the realization of a socialist reinvention of society.

The manifesto makes its case for abstention by offering a lofty vision of the socialist system that awaits the oppressed worker who helps bring down the empire. The text describes a social republic that will "assure" such benefits, among many others, as "integral, free, and obligatory instruction for all!" As the manifesto proceeds, it describes the decision of

In the *Anti-Plebiscite Manifesto*, author Karl Marx reminds his audience of the importance of labor after events like the French Revolution of 1789. This painting depicts the storming of the Bastille at the start of that revolution. ERICH LESSING/ART RESOURCE, NY

PRIMARY SOURCE

ANTI-PLEBISCITE MANIFESTO

To All French Workingmen:

Citizens—After the Revolution of 1789 and the Declaration of Rights of 1793, the sovereignty of labor is the only constitutive basis upon which modem society should rest.

Labor is, in effect, the supreme law of humanity, the source of public wealth, and the most efficient cause of individual well-being.

The workingman alone is entitled to the esteem of his fellow-citizens; he imposes even upon those who exploit him a sense of his honesty; he is called upon to regenerate the old order.

This is why we say to the urban and rural workers, to the small manufacturers, to the small business men, and to all those who sincerely desire the reign of liberty founded upon equality: It is not enough to answer by a purely negative vote this plebis-cite that they have the audacity to thrust upon us; not enough to prefer the constitution of 1870 to that of 1852—a parliamentary government to a personal one. Out of the ballot-box must come the most absolute condemnation of the monarchic regime, the complete, the radical affirmation of the only form of government that can give scope to our Intimate aspirations—the Social and Democratic Republic.

Insensate is he who would believe that the constitution of 1S70 would enable him, any more than that of 1852, to assure to his children the benefits of integral, free, and obligatory instruction for all!

That it would allow the reformation and the reorganization of the great public services (mines, canals, railroads, banks, etc) for the benefit of all, instead of being as they are to-day, a means of exploitation for the feudality of capital!

The complete changing of the mode of levying taxes, which until now have been progressive in the direction of poverty I

The restoration to the public domain of the properties which the clergy, secular and regular, have seized upon by subreption in defiance of the laws of 1789 and 1790!

The putting an end to the abuse of power by all the governmental functionaries great and small (constables, juges d'tnstruction, commissaires de police, etc.), whose arbitrary conduct is to-day covered by article 75 of the Constitution of the year VIII!

whether or not to participate in the coming vote as a grand opportunity "to put an end to all defilements of the past" and to assure for all "peace and liberty, equality and work." To participate, on the other hand, is to affirm an empire intent on war and founded on injustice.

Stylistically, the *Anti-Plebiscite Manifesto* is distinguished by its effusiveness. Throughout the brief document, the authors exclaim the possibilities of socialism and the indignities of despotism. In long sentences, they imbue their argument with momentum and energy. In short sentences, they make staccato calls for the reader's attention. By alternating the two, the manifesto captures its audience and compels its interest. "Workers of the country districts!" they write. "Like your city brothers you bear the crushing burdens of the present social system; you produce without ceasing, and most of the time you lack the necessaries of life, while the *fisc*, the usurer, and the proprietors thrive at your expense." The manifesto also directly addresses its audience and employs vivid imagery to striking effect. The empire drafts young men—"your sons"—into the army only to "strew their abandoned corpses over the desert plains of Syria, Cochin-China and Mexico" to fight Napoleon III's imperial wars.

CRITICAL DISCUSSION

When the *Anti-Plebiscite Manifesto* was issued in 1870, it was received enthusiastically within the Parisian communist movement while being largely overlooked outside it. Endorsed not only by the Federated Parisian Sections of the International Workingmen's Association but also by the Federal Chamber of Labor Societies, the manifesto provided a cohesive and organized response to the plebiscite from the French communist community. Other groups also opposed the plebiscite. Among those voting against the measure or abstaining from voting stood the liberal, reformist Republicans; the conservative, monarchist Bonapartists; and the ultraconservative Legitimists, who supported a return to Bourbon rule. Nevertheless, the constitutional reforms won overwhelming approval, with 7,358,786 votes in favor and 1,571,939 against. Despite this seeming victory for Napoleon III, his regime was toppled a year after the plebiscite was passed.

Following the issuance of the *Anti-Plebiscite Manifesto*, the International gained in prominence. The group's opposition to the Franco-Prussian War, as expressed in the *Manifesto against War* (1870) and other writings and speeches, proved popular. After Napoleon III and the French army surrendered in September 1870, revolution erupted in Paris.

And finally, the suppression of the blood-tax (the standing anny) by abolishing the conscription!

No! Citizens, such could not be the case. Despotism has the fatal quality of being able to engender only despotism. The test has been made.

And, moreover, we refuse to recognize in the executive the right to question us. This right would imply on our part a subjection against which the very name of the power that arrogates It protests when that power indicates that he is not the master, but only and nothing more than the executor of the sovereign will of the nation.

If then, with us, you desire to put an end to all the defilements of the past; if you desire that the new social compact, consented to by citizens, equals in rights as in duties, shall assure to each of you peace and liberty, equality and work; if you want to affirm the Social and Democratic Republic, the best means as we see it is either to refuse to vote or else vote against the constitution—and this without excluding the other modes of protestation.

Workers of all crafts, remember the massacres at Aubin and at la Ricamarie, the convictions at Autun and the acquittal at Tours; and, while you take your ballots to show that you are not indifferent to your civic duties, remember to abstain from voting.

Workers of the country districts ! Like your city brothers you bear the crushing burdens of the present social system; you produce without ceasing, and the most of the time you lack the necessaries of life, while the fisc, the usurer, and the proprietors thrive at your expense.

The Empire, not satisfied at crushing you with taxes, takes from you your sons, your only support, to make papal soldiers of them, or to strew their abandoned corpses over the desert plains of Syria, Cochin-China and Mexico.

We likewise advise you to abstain from voting, because abstention is the protest that the author of the coup d'état fears the most; but if you are compelled to cast your ballot, let it either remain blank or bear the words: Radical change in taxation! No more conscription! The Social and Democratic Republic!

SOURCE: *The Paris Commune,* Socialist Labor Party, 2005, pp. 107, 108, 109.

A moderate provisional government—the Government of National Defense—was established, but political unrest continued to spread. The International led the formation of a "vigilance committee" that aimed to monitor the government in the interest of the working class. After Paris was besieged by the Prussians and unrest within the city continued to mount, the provisional government lost control of the city in 1871. Various radical, left-wing groups took control and organized elections for a communal council, which became known as the Paris Commune. Influenced in part by the International, the city's new government instituted numerous liberal and socialist reforms, but it lasted only two months. Although the *Anti-Plebiscite Manifesto* has attracted little critical attention in English, some scholars have considered the document's legacy in historical and political terms.

Of the limited scholarship on the manifesto, much of it has considered the text within the context of the various opposition movements that were active in Paris in 1870. In *The First International in France, 1864-1872* (1997), historian Julian P. W. Archer writes that the manifesto "was to date the boldest public statement of the Republican sentiments that were surfacing within the International and the labor movement." Archer also notes that the manifesto triggered suppression from the Second Empire, which was alarmed by the International's efforts against the plebiscite: "From the Imperial government's viewpoint the leadership of the International clearly had overstepped the bounds of tolerable behavior, and so it decided to decapitate the organization in Paris once again." Commentators also have viewed the manifesto within the context of communist ideology. Lucien Sanial, in his notes to the English translation of Marx's *The Paris Commune,* argues that the manifesto's authors "understood the nature of the class struggle; hence the class character of their manifesto, which was obviously intended, not for 'the people,' so called in bourgeois parlance, but for the working people...."

BIBLIOGRAPHY

Sources

Archer, Julian P. W. *The First International in France, 1864-1872.* New York: UP of America, 1997. Print.

Lozovsky, A. [Solomon Abramovich Dridzo]. *Marx and the Trade Unions.* Westport, CT: Greenwood, 1935. Print.

Marx, Karl. *The Paris Commune.* New York: New York Labor News, 1960. Print.

Payne, Robert. *Marx.* New York: Simon, 1968. Print.

Schulkind, Eugene, ed. *The Paris Commune of 1871: The View from the Left*. New York: Grove, 1974. Print.

Further Reading

Bernstein, Samuel. "The First International on the Eve of the Paris Commune." *Science & Society* 5.1 (1941): 24-42. *JSTOR.* Web. 21 Sept. 2012.

Christiansen, Peter. *Paris Babylon: The Story of the Paris Commune.* New York: Penguin, 1994. Print.

Devreese, Daisy E. "The International Working Men's Association (1864-1876) and Workers' Education: An Historical Approach." *Paedagogica Historica: International Journal of the History of Education* 35.1 (2006): 15-21. Print.

Starr, Peter. *Commemorating Trauma: The Paris Commune and Its Cultural Aftermath.* New York: Fordham UP, 2006. Print.

Williams, Roger L. *The French Revolution of 1870-1871.* New York: Norton, 1969. Print.

Theodore McDermott

A DECLARATION FROM THE POOR OPPRESSED PEOPLE OF ENGLAND

Gerrard Winstanley

OVERVIEW

A Declaration from the Poor Oppressed People of England, published on June 1, 1649, and signed by Gerrard Winstanley and 44 others (the precise authors are unclear, though Winstanley is generally credited as the primary author), is a political pamphlet explaining and justifying the actions of members of the agrarian socialist Digger movement on the common land of England. Written partly in response to the hostility of landowners who disapproved of the Diggers' practice of digging and planting crops on parts of the commons, the *Declaration* attacks both the legitimacy of the landowners' holdings and the legitimacy of private property. Using biblical doctrine as support, the pamphlet lays out an argument for the Diggers' use of common land in the creation of small, communistic societies free from the covetousness and rapacity that characterized mainstream English life.

The *Declaration* likely served as a communal affirmation for members of the Digger movement and may have helped propagate the Digger cause among the populace at large (though the movement never achieved great popularity). However, the document was not at all well received by its ostensible target audience, the landowners of England, who continued their attempts to combat the Diggers and eventually stamped out the movement altogether. The pamphlet is nonetheless noteworthy as an artifact of one of the most radical of several dissenting social reform groups that came to relative prominence in England during the upheaval of the English Civil Wars. Considered together with the various other Digger tracts published around the same time, the *Declaration* may be seen as a significant prefiguration of later utopian social experiments.

HISTORICAL AND LITERARY CONTEXT

The *Declaration* is largely a response to the widespread economic inequality that characterized English society in the seventeenth century. In addition to asserting that wealthy English landowners' claim to their property was historically founded on theft and murder, the pamphlet attacks the very legitimacy of private property as an institution, declaring it to be a fundamentally corrupt and irreligious system that inevitably leads to inequality and oppression. The document condemns the practice of enclosure, whereby open fields, traditionally designated as common land, are fenced off and reserved for the exclusive use of the landholder, often resulting in the displacement of peasants and other poor laborers who had previously relied on the use of the land in question.

When the *Declaration* appeared in June 1649, England was in a state of profound civil unrest and ideological disunity. Just a few months before, in the wake of several years of civil war, the English king Charles I had been beheaded, marking the first time an English monarch was legally executed by his subjects. Revolutionary and reform-oriented rhetoric, both within England's fractious new republican government and outside it, was common during this period, and the Diggers—particularly as represented by the writings of Gerrard Winstanley, the movement's primary spokesperson—were among the most radical products of this environment. Although the Diggers were one of the smallest nonconformist groups of mid-seventeenth-century England, their rejection of private property made them one of the most notorious.

One of a large number of Digger tracts published during the movement's short-lived existence, the *Declaration* emerged from a crowded and diverse literary milieu of English sociopolitical activism. An important predecessor was *An Agreement of the People,* an influential manifesto published in several successive versions from 1647 to 1649. This major document of Civil War-era English egalitarian writing served as a rallying point for numerous reform-minded English activists, especially members of the influential Leveller movement, which was similar to the Diggers in that it advocated political equality. However, unlike the Diggers, the Levellers stopped short of challenging property rights. The Diggers therefore referred to themselves as True Levellers, hence the title of Winstanley's *The True Levellers Standard Advanced* (1649), the first major Digger manifesto and the *Declaration*'s most immediate antecedent.

The *Declaration*'s influence on subsequent writing is difficult to gauge, although its sociopolitical ideas may be seen as prefiguring those of later texts. Walter F. Murphy, in a 1957 essay for *The Review of Politics,* observes that although Winstanley's writings may well have had a profound influence on theorists

❖ *Key Facts*

Time Period:
Mid-17th Century

Movement/Issue:
Property rights reform

Place of Publication:
England

Language of Publication:
English

GERRARD WINSTANLEY: RELIGIOUS MYSTIC AND POLITICAL ACTIVIST

Gerrard Winstanley, the principal author of *A Declaration from the Poor Oppressed People of England,* was one of the most noteworthy—though not the most influential—political ideologues of mid-seventeenth-century England. Born in 1609, he developed his communistic political philosophy largely as a result of his religious convictions, which in their emphasis on intuition and mysticism diverged widely from the Puritan beliefs characteristic of many radicals in revolutionary England, particularly those who had deposed the late king. Following an intense spiritual experience, described in the pamphlet *The New Law of Righteousness* (1649), during which he felt himself to be the recipient of a divine revelation, he immediately set about propagating a doctrine of collectivist societal organization. This ethos formed the theological core of the Digger movement.

After the Digger movement was defeated, Winstanley continued to write, and in 1652 he composed *The Law of Freedom,* a rather totalitarian utopian portrait of an ideal English commonwealth, which he addressed to Oliver Cromwell, the military commander, member of Parliament, and future lord protector of England. However, Cromwell ignored it. *The Law of Freedom* would be the last of Winstanley's polemical writings, and in his later years he became a corn chandler. Upon his death in 1676, he received a Quaker burial.

such as James Harrington, John Bellers, Robert Owen, and various Marxists, "it is probable that people who later employed the same political and economic ideas as Winstanley were drawing from a common background of discontented rumbling rather than borrowing directly." Regardless of the extent of its direct influence, the *Declaration* (considered part of Digger literature in general) is now regarded by many contemporary historians as an important early manifestation of English communist thought.

THEMES AND STYLE

The principal theme of the *Declaration* is that the earth was created for the common use of all of humanity and that the activities of the Diggers represent an attempt to live by this belief in the face of landowners' proprietary rapacity. The text advances a fundamentally communistic view of natural resources, asserting that "the Earth … was made to be a common Store-house of Livelihood to all Mankinde, friend and foe, without exception." The institution of private property is therefore not just wrongheaded but evil, as is the practice of monetary exchange: "Money must not any longer … be the great god, that hedges in some, and hedges out others; for Money is but part of the Earth." The *Declaration* emphasizes that despite the enormity of the landholders' iniquities, the Diggers are not actively causing trouble for them but merely attempting to carve out their own communities in a way consistent with their

principles. Therefore, any legal action against them would be wholly unjustified: "and so your Selves, your Judges, Lawyers, and Justices, shall be found to be the greatest Transgressors, in and over Mankinde."

The *Declaration*'s rhetorical approach is characterized by frequent appeals to scripture and traditional views of history. The Bible is frequently invoked as a means of support, both by way of allusion and through direct citation, as when the societal change envisioned by the Diggers' practices is seen as a fulfillment of biblical prophecy. The text asserts that people "shall buy Wine and Milk, without Money, or without price, as *Isaiah* speaks." Likewise, the pamphlet situates its condemnation of private property within a mid-seventeenth-century tendency to equate contemporary English oppression with the legacy of the Norman conquest of Britain in 1066. This conquest is alluded to when the *Declaration* asserts that "the power of inclosing Land, and owning Propriety, was brought into the Creation by your Ancestors by the Sword." This passage delegitimizes landowners' holdings by associating them with violent plunder while simultaneously implying a pre-Norman historical precedent for the Diggers' seemingly radical ideas.

The *Declaration* takes an adamant tone commensurate with the comprehensive expression of firmly held beliefs to a hostile audience. The long-winded text is characterized by extremely lengthy sentences and is unapologetically antagonistic toward the landowners it addresses. For instance, the landowners' unwillingness to share their resources communally informs the *Declaration*'s complaint that they "will offer up nothing to this publike Treasury; but will rather see your fellow-Creatures starve for want of Bread, that have an equal right to it with your selves, by the Law of Creation." Nonetheless, the *Declaration* refrains from indulging in virulent invective against its targets, attacking landowners' practices and institutions rather than the landowners themselves. Although its language befits this rhetorical intent, the *Declaration* exhibits the writing style of a vigorous, impassioned—but not intemperate—screed.

CRITICAL DISCUSSION

The ideas expressed in the *Declaration,* which was published roughly contemporaneously with a number of other Digger texts by Winstanley and others, received some sympathy among English nonconformists, though the work's reception among landowners, wealthy and otherwise, was often hostile. Some of the more radical members of the Leveller movement agreed with the Diggers' views on private property, and *The True Levellers Standard Advanced* (1649) was reprinted in the Leveller newspaper *The Moderate.* Christopher Hill, in his 1972 study of radical thought, *The World Turned Upside Down: Radical Ideas during the English Revolution,* says of Winstanley's pamphlets, "some at least seem to have borne fruit," citing the appearance of various other Digger colonies apart from Winstanley's commune in

Surrey. Local landowners, meanwhile, responded aggressively to Digger rhetoric and activities with litigation, appeals to armed forces, and brutal suppression, eventually forcing the nascent communities to disband.

Beyond its immediate impact on the formation of short-lived Digger communities, the *Declaration*'s main social legacy lies in its status as an artifact of an early agrarian communist ideology. C.H. George asserts in a 1975 essay in *The Dissenting Tradition: Essays for Leland H. Carlson,* "the most enduring excitement for the student of Winstanley is [the] knowledge that he is the *original* socialist." While not all scholars agree with this statement, it may certainly be said that the ideas expressed in the *Declaration* stand as a significant precursor to much of the collectivist political thought that came to prominence in later eras. The use of the Digger name by the San Francisco Diggers, a radical anticapitalist theatrical collective active during the 1960s, testifies to the movement's enduring association with utopian socialism. Scholarship of the *Declaration* often emphasizes this association, as well as the relationship between Digger ideology and the ideology of its era in general.

The *Declaration* is rarely discussed as a work in itself but is often incorporated (sometimes without being explicitly named) into analyses of Winstanley's politics or the Digger movement as a whole. These analyses often place Digger political beliefs in a wider context of idealistic socioeconomic discourse, as in J.C. Davis's 1981 study *Utopia and the Ideal Society,* which situates the Diggers within a long history of English utopianism. Geoff Kennedy's *Diggers, Levellers, and Agrarian Capitalism* (2008) is similarly devoted to historical contextualization, providing a detailed elaboration of how the Digger movement fits into the ideological firmament of seventeenth-century England and discussing how this intellectual climate developed from historical conditions.

BIBLIOGRAPHY

Sources

Davis, J.C. *Utopia and the Ideal Society: A Study of English Utopian Writing, 1516-1700.* Cambridge: Cambridge UP, 1981. Print.

George, C.H. "Gerrard Winstanley: A Critical Retrospect." *The Dissenting Tradition: Essays for Leland H. Carlson.* Ed. C. Robert Cole and Michael E. Moody. Athens: Ohio UP, 1975. 191-225. Print.

Hill, Christopher. *The World Turned Upside Down: Radical Ideas during the English Revolution.* New York: Viking, 1972. Print.

Kennedy, Geoff. *Diggers, Levellers, and Agrarian Capitalism: Radical Political Thought in Seventeenth Century England.* Lanham: Lexington, 2008. Print.

Murphy, Walter F. "The Political Philosophy of Gerrard Winstanley." *Review of Politics* 19.2 (1957): 214-38. *JSTOR.* Web. 19 Sept. 2012.

Winstanley, Gerrard. *The Works of Gerrard Winstanley.* Ed. George H. Sabine. New York: Russell & Russell, 1965. Print.

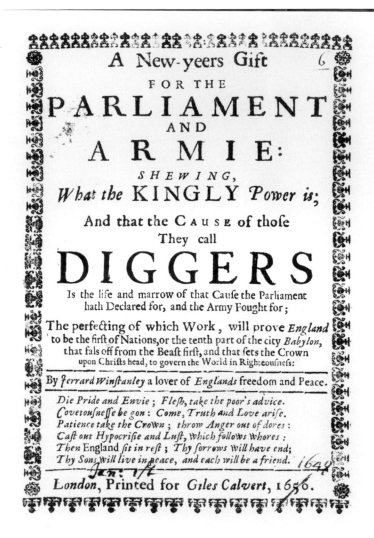

Further Reading

Appelbaum, Robert. "'O Power …': Gerrard Winstanley and the Limits of Communist Poetics." *Prose Studies* 22.1 (1999): 39-58. Print.

Bradstock, Andrew, ed. *Winstanley and the Diggers, 1649-1999.* London: Frank Cass, 2000. Print.

Cherniak, Warren. "Civil Liberty in Milton, the Levellers and Winstanley." *Prose Studies* 22.2 (1999): 101-20. Print.

Gurney, John. "Gerrard Winstanley and the Digger Movement in Walton and Cobham." *Historical Journal* 37.4 (1994): 775-802. Print.

McDowell, Nicholas. *The English Radical Imagination: Culture, Religion, and Revolution, 1630-1660.* Oxford: Oxford UP, 2003. Print.

Mulder, David. *The Alchemy of Revolution: Gerrard Winstanley's Occultism and Seventeenth-Century English Communism.* New York: Lang, 1990. Print.

Shulman, George M. *Radicalism and Reverence: The Political Thought of Gerrard Winstanley.* Berkeley: U of California P, 1989. Print.

James Overholtzer

A document from Gerrard Winstanley and the Diggers, a group promoting land distribution for the poor in seventeenth-century England. PRIVATE COLLECTION/THE BRIDGEMAN ART LIBRARY

DIGGER'S SONG

Anonymous

❖ *Key Facts*

Time Period:
Mid-17th Century

Movement/Issue:
Property rights reform;
Agrarian socialism

Place of Publication:
England

**Language of
Publication:**
English

OVERVIEW

The "Digger's Song" (1649) is an anonymous musical composition that presents the complaints and aims of the Diggers, an English property-rights reform society active during the short-lived Commonwealth of England (1649-1653). The creation of the commonwealth, following the overthrow of Charles I, led many to believe a new age for England was dawning. The Diggers, a group of reformers seeking to democratize the system of land ownership in England, decried the tyranny of the English ruling classes and claimed that property was granted to all men and women by God, not just to select noblemen by the state. Their song, addressed to fellow Diggers and often chanted while plowing or planting crops on vacant state land, was intended to force the issue of equitable redistribution of land. Although the original two-and-a-half page lyric sheet is unsigned, authorship is often attributed to the Diggers' founder, Gerrard Winstanley, because it echoes Winstanley's declarative manifestoes from the same period, namely *The New Law of Righteousness* (1649) and *A Declaration from the Poor Oppressed People of England* (1649).

The Diggers' tactics met with hostility from both the government and local landowners, many of whom hired mercenaries to drive the Diggers off the land. As the Council of State had been vocal about its disapproval of the Diggers, the government allowed the aggression to continue. The Diggers disbanded shortly thereafter, having effected little to no change in English property law. Nevertheless, the short-lived group created a legacy as the first example of organized communism in England, and their declarations and songs are considered early prototypes of the modern manifesto.

HISTORICAL AND LITERARY CONTEXT

Parliamentarian supporters fought Royalists in the English Civil Wars (1642-1651). After King Charles I was deposed, tried, and executed for treason in January 1649, a republican government, the Commonwealth of England, was established in place of the monarchy, a change that many hoped would usher in an era of radical reform. Seeing little change in English laws, however, small bands of passive reformers began to appear. The first such group, called the Levellers, was led by John Lilburne. Their primary aim was to secure citizenship and equal (or level) representation under the law for all inhabitants, regardless of class. Although their proposed reforms ensured any man with the funds to make land purchases could do so, they did not provide for any change to the current state of land ownership in England.

Protestant reformer Gerrard Winstanley saw the Levellers' refusal to implement a new land-distribution system as an affront to the English lower classes, because he believed that ownership of land represented the only means by which the underclass could improve its circumstances (taxation and food costs were at all-time highs). As such, he set about organizing a society of his own, and on April 1, 1649, he and a group of twenty to thirty others formed a small, egalitarian rural community on public land at St. George's Hill near Cobham, Surrey. By digging on common land, the group hoped to show the public the merits of the social restructuring they proposed. Arguing for the immediate and equal redistribution of land, the group called themselves the True Levellers—though as a result of their unauthorized farming, they became known to both opponents and supporters as Diggers.

The "Digger's Song" draws heavily on the English folk tradition. Although the original lyric sheet does not indicate the tune to which the song was to be sung, E.A. White in a 1940 article for the *Journal of the English Folk Dance and Song Society* suggested that it might have taken its tune from the Scottish folk song "My lufe is lyand sick, send him joy, send him joy." The song appears in *The Complaynt of Scotland*, an anonymous 1549 collection of political stories and songs celebrating Scottish culture and denouncing the proposed union with England. The book was released as part of a war of words in which numerous books were written on the subject of the union by both English and Scottish figures, usually in response to one another.

Written during a period rife with political publications, the "Digger's Song" was one of many pamphlets and declarations that the Diggers and Levellers produced to invoke a collective "we" in their demands for equity. Although the song itself had little impact, its meter and tune continued to be employed in English and Scottish political folk songs for several decades. The song reemerged in the papers of Charles W. Clark in the 1890s, enjoying perhaps its first period of widespread popularity. Nearly one century later, the Leon Rosselson song "The World Turned Upside Down" (1974) told the story of the St. George's Hill occupation, though it was not an adaptation of the Diggers' anthem.

THEMES AND STYLE

The central theme of the "Digger's Song" is to call for the equal distribution of parishes, estates, and manors under the new republic as a mandate from God. The landless classes are enjoined by the refrain to "stand up now, stand up now" to act in defiance "gainst lawyers and gainst priests ... for tyrants they are both." Because the Diggers are a fundamentally religious group, they argue that God provides the earth for all humans to sustain themselves equally. Therefore, the song promotes peaceful protest, urging followers "to conquer them by love ... for hee is King above, noe power is like to love." The lyrics encourage the Diggers to conduct themselves peaceably not only because they are Christian but also because peaceful action places them on higher moral ground than the ruling class, for whom "the club is all their law."

The song's primary rhetorical strategy is to unite Diggers against the ruling classes by depicting priests, lawyers, and the gentry as equally corrupt and tyrannical. The song begins by reminding the Diggers of the abuses they have suffered at the hands of the Cavaliers, a name for the Royalists who had supported King Charles: "Theire self-will is theire law.... Since tyranny came in they count it now no sin ... to sterve poor men therein." The clergy perpetuate these abuses by "say[ing] it is a sin / That we should now begin, our freedom for to win." The song also indicts the lawyers, who "conjoyne ... to arrest." The solution, the song concludes, is to invert the social order such that the ruling classes "come down, and the poor shall wear the crown."

The tone of the song is one of passionate defiance against a corrupt and tyrannical enemy. The repetition of "stand up now ... Stand up, Diggers all" urges solidarity against enemies who would "kill ... if they could." The priests and lawyers are cast as "tyrants ... both even flat against their oath"; the latter are even equated with the devil, who "in them lies and hath blinded both their eyes." By contrast, the Diggers are Christian soldiers who will "conquer ... by love," united by their dedication to peaceful resistance. Their weapons are simple "spades and hoes and plowes," but their digging is the best method of defying the landed classes.

CRITICAL DISCUSSION

Little is known about the immediate response to the "Digger's Song." Most published responses to the Diggers focused on the group's declarations and pamphlets and their unauthorized farming tactics. Although Oliver Cromwell had yet to become the commonwealth's

first Lord Protectorate, his influence on, and his role as advisor to, the presiding Council of State was significant. His advice to local landowners who complained about the vagrant farmers occupying nearby lands was to pursue eviction through the courts. In turn, the land owners' response was to hire thugs to evict the Diggers. On June 11, 1649, four Diggers at the colony at St. George's Hill were savagely beaten with clubs and staffs by men dressed as women, and an arson attack followed shortly thereafter. By August, in the face of continued harassment and the threat of military involvement, the Diggers had voluntarily disbanded.

The Diggers advocated an agrarian society like the one depicted in Walter Crane's illustration *The Ploughman.* PRIVATE COLLECTION/THE BRIDGEMAN ART LIBRARY

LEVELLERS AND DIGGERS: INVOCATIONS OF "WE"

Although John Lilburne of the Levellers and Gerrard Winstanley of the Diggers had a contentious relationship, they shared a desire to eliminate socioeconomic class divisions and to form an egalitarian nation state. Before Lilburne and Winstanley published their pamphlets and declarations, most political tracts and orations referred to the public in the third person—simply as "the people." However, Lilburne, to some extent in *England's New Chains Discovered* (1649), and Winstanley, most notably in *A Declaration from the Poor Oppressed People of England* (1649), pioneered the invocation of the collective "we." Winstanley's *Declaration* begins, "We whose names are subscribed ... declare unto you that call yourselves Lords of Manors and Lords of the Land." This invocation can be seen as a direct forebear of the ubiquitous "We the people" first popularized in the U.S. Constitution.

Also recognized as pioneering concepts were Lilburne's concept of "freeborn rights" and Winstanley's invocation of Providence in matters of property law. Their ideas were so influential that Thomas Paine's *Rights of Man* and Thomas Jefferson's invocation of "self-evident truths" picked up and expanded on in Lilburne's and Winstanley's ideas. Thus, the Diggers and Levellers became the forefathers of modern civil liberties and the concept of inherent rights.

PRIMARY SOURCE

"DIGGERS SONG"

"You noble Diggers all, stand up now, stand up now,
  You noble Diggers all, stand up now,
  The waste land to maintain, seeing Cavaliers by name
  Your digging do disdain and persons all defame.
  Stand up now, stand up now.

Your houses they pull down, stand up now, stand up now,
  Your houses they pull down, stand up now;
  Your houses they pull down to fright poor men in town,
  But the Gentry must come down, and the poor shall wear the crown.
  Stand up now, Diggers all!

With spades and hoes and plowes, stand up now, stand up now,
  With spades and hoes and plowes, stand up now;
  Your freedom to uphold, seeing Cavaliers are bold
  To kill you if they could, and rights from you withhold.
  Stand up now, Diggers all!

Their self-will is their law, stand up now, stand up now,
  Their self-will is their law, stand up now;
  Since tyranny came in, they count it now no sin
  To make a goal a gin, to starve poor men therein.
  Stand up now, stand up now.

The Gentry are all round, stand up now, stand up now,
  The Gentry are all round, stand up now;
  The Gentry are all round, on each side they are found,
  Their wisdom's so profound to cheat us of our ground.
  Stand up now, stand up now.

The Lawyers they conjoin, stand up now, stand up now,
  The Lawyers they conjoin, stand up now;
  To arrest you they advise, such fury they devise,
  The devil in them lies, and hath blinded both their eyes.
  Stand up now, stand up now.

The Clergy they come in, stand up now, stand up now,
  The Clergy they come in, stand up now;
  The Clergy they come in, and say it is a sin
  That we should now begin our freedom for to win.
  Stand up now, Diggers all!

The tithes they yet will have, stand up now, stand up now,
  The tithes they yet will have, stand up now;
  The tithes they yet will have, and Lawyers their fees crave,
  And this they say is brave, to make the poor their slave.
  Stand up now, Diggers all!

'Gainst Lawyers and 'gainst Priests, stand up now, stand up now,'
  Gainst Lawyers and 'gainst Priests, stand up now;
  For tyrants they are both, even flat against their oath,
  To grant us they are loath, free meat and drink and cloth.
  Stand up now, Diggers all!

The club is all their law, stand up now, stand up now,
  The club is all their law, stand up now;
  The club is all their law, to keep poor men in awe;
  But they no vision saw to maintain such a law.
  Stand up now, Diggers all!

The Cavaliers are foes, stand up now, stand up now,
  The Cavaliers are foes, stand up now;
  The Cavaliers are foes, themselves they do disclose
  By verses, not in prose, to please the singing boys.
  Stand up now, Diggers all!

To conquer them by love, come in now, come in now,
  To conquer them by love, come in now;
  To conquer them by love, as it does you behove,
  For He is King above, no Power is like to Love.
  Glory here, Diggers all!"

Although the group's actions effected no real property reform, their tactics—and those of the Levellers—were eventually seen as pioneering. Janet Lyon asserts in *Manifestoes: Provocations of the Modern* (1999) that the Diggers represented a prototypical "form of agrarian communism," and the distinctions they and the Levellers made in their pamphlets and declarations "between petition on the one hand and self-proclamation or anthem, as it were, on the other" signaled the emergence of the public "we" at the rhetorical center of the modern manifesto. A resurgence in interest surrounding the Diggers in the twenty-first century gave rise to an annual festival in Wigan commemorating the group's short-lived occupation of St. George's Hill.

Some modern scholars disagree with Lyon's assessment of Digger society as a prototype for communism. Ben Sandell, in a 2011 article for *History Review,* writes, "The idea that Winstanley was a forerunner of modern communism is a hard one to support, for he was a deeply religious man." He points to the general tendency of communist societies toward secularism, adding that "the world in which [Winstanley] lived cannot be understood simply in terms of a class struggle." Nevertheless, there seems to be little argument over Lyon's assessment of the Diggers as forebears of the modern manifesto. She suggests that the period following the English Civil Wars marked the first major confluence of "political crises" involving "definitions of citizenship and political subjecthood" in the modern world, necessitating a new form in which to voice "demands for active citizenship."

BIBLIOGRAPHY

Sources

Berens, Lewis Henry. *The Digger Movement in the Days of the Commonwealth*. London: Simpkin, Marshall,

Hamilton, Kent, 1906. *Project Gutenberg.* Web. 5 Sept. 2012.

Gurney, John. "Gerrard Winstanley and the Digger Movement in Walton and Cobham." *Historical Journal* 37.4 (1994): 775-802. *JSTOR.* Web. 3 Sept. 2012.

Lyon, Janet. *Manifestoes: Provocations of the Modern.* Ithaca: Cornell UP, 1999. Print.

Sandell, Ben. "Gerrard Winstanley and the Diggers." *History Review* 70 (2011): 9-13. *Academic Search Complete.* Web. 3 Sept. 2012.

White, E.A. "The Digger's Song." *Journal of the English Folk Dance and Song Society* 4.1 (1940): 23-30. *JSTOR.* Web. 3 Sept. 2012.

Further Reading

Davidson, J.M. *Concerning Four Precursors of Henry George and the Single Tax, as Also the Land Gospel according to Winstanley "the Digger."* Port Washington: Kennikat, 1971. Print.

Hopton, Andrew. *Digger Tracts, 1649-50.* London: Aporia, 1989. Print.

Kenyon, Timothy. *Utopian Communism and Political Thought in Early Modern England.* London: Pinter, 1989. Print.

Purkiss, Diane. *The English Civil War: Papists, Gentlewomen, Soldiers, and Witchfinders in the Birth of Modern Britain.* New York: Basic, 2006. Print.

Webb, Darren. "The Bitter Product of Defeat? Reflections on Winstanley's Law of Freedom." *Political Studies* 52.2 (2004): 199-215. *Academic Search Complete.* Web. 3 Sept. 2012.

Winstanley, Gerrard, Thomas N. Corns, Ann Hughes, and David Loewenstein. *The Complete Works of Gerrard Winstanley.* Oxford: Oxford UP, 2009. Print.

Clint Garner

ENGLAND'S NEW CHAINS DISCOVERED

John Lilburne

❖ *Key Facts*

Time Period:
Mid-17th Century

Movement/Issue:
Leveller movement;
Democratic reform

Place of Publication:
England

**Language of
Publication:**
English

OVERVIEW

England's New Chains Discovered (1649) by John Lilburne is one of the most celebrated pamphlets from the seventeenth-century Leveller movement. In this work, Lilburne examines the shortcomings of the recently empowered "Rump" Parliament, catalogs its continued oppression of citizens, and itemizes a series of proposals for parliamentary reform. The execution of King Charles I and subsequent ascendancy of Parliament had been expected to bring dramatic improvements to representation and voting policies. When those changes were not realized, several reform organizations emerged. Foremost among these were the Diggers and Levellers, the former advocating land reform and the latter parliamentary reform. Pamphleteering was the medium of choice for both groups, and *England's New Chains Discovered* represents one of the final and most comprehensive proclamations by the Levellers prior to their dissolution.

England's New Chains Discovered was well received by radical factions and even a small number of royalists, albeit for very different reasons. The Levellers and their supporters considered the document to be a comprehensive statement of the movement's vision for England and a castigation of the Rump Parliament's inaction; meanwhile, the royalists who backed the document did so only because it weakened the Rump's authority, a circumstance they hoped to turn to their own advantage. *England's New Chains Discovered* accuses the new government of being just as tyrannical as the monarchy it had replaced. The charge proved to be accurate, as Lilburne and several other prominent Levellers were soon incarcerated, effectively ending the movement. Today the document is seen as a landmark text in the rise of both English republicanism and the manifesto as a form.

HISTORICAL AND LITERARY CONTEXT

The Parliament that, with the aid of the New Model Army, executed King Charles in January 1649 was far from united. In December 1648 members of Parliament opposing the trial and execution of Charles I (243 in all) had been prevented from entering the chambers. Those allowed to enter (46 men) were sympathetic to the republican cause and formed what became known as the Rump Parliament. The Rump then tried and executed King Charles, abolished the

monarchy, and dissolved the House of Lords in short order. In the estimation of the Rump members, English interests were best served by the House of Commons, representatives of the citizenry from whom they proposed all power should originate. The Rump's policies and actions, however, did not fulfill the promise of its rhetoric.

In the backlash against Rump policies, the Diggers movement, made up primarily of the rural poor, proved to be the least effectual. The Levellers, in contrast, were members of the emerging middle class—they were literate, metropolitan people whose opinions, while often aligned with those of the rural poor, were more acceptable to the gentry. As the unofficial leader of the Levellers, Lilburne articulated an unprecedentedly secular, rationalist argument for increased individual rights, which was exactly the position the new Rump claimed to espouse. In *England's New Chains Discovered,* Lilburne posits that in its restriction of voting rights and denial of people's right to petition, the Rump's proposed constitution did not deliver on the group's promises.

England's New Chains Discovered fit comfortably within a burgeoning form of public discourse. In 1611 the tone of public dialogue had been indelibly changed by the publication of the King James Bible, which for the first time presented holy scripture in conversational English. These terms were later developed further in the works of English scholar and philosopher Thomas Hobbes. His *De Cive* (1642) presents early iterations of principles of popular sovereignty, the notion that government's legitimacy originates in and is sustained by the consent of the governed. Lilburne tapped into this same idea in *England's New Chains Discovered.*

However, the influence of Lilburne's document extended beyond the specifics of its arguments. In the emerging political climate of the 1640s, a new popular literary genre emerged: the manifesto, embodied first by the pamphlets and declarations of the Levellers, including *England's New Chains Discovered.* Born in the nascent stages of English republicanism, the manifesto, as noted by Janet Lyon in *Manifestoes: Provocations of the Modern* (1999), "drew its power from ... the emergent languages of the republic itself, that is, the languages of contestation, debate, and liberal freedoms." Lilburne's *England's New Chains Discovered* employs these "emergent languages" in cataloging the unfulfilled promises of the Rump Parliament and enumerating a host of reforms aimed at rectifying what he perceived to be a dereliction of duty. Lilburne's and the Levellers' invocation of a public "we" would be emulated by the Diggers and expanded on by the architects of the French, American, and Irish revolutions at the end of the eighteenth century.

THEMES AND STYLE

England's New Chains Discovered focuses on the continued tyranny of the parliamentarian government and the Rump's failure to acknowledge, let alone advance, the ideas of popular sovereignty and civil liberties. The document's opening passage recalls Parliament's own declaration "that the People (under God) are the original of all just Powers," leveling the accusation that in its failure to adhere to that principle, it has subjected the people to "a condition neerest to bondage." Responding to the recently produced *An Agreement of the People* (variations of which represented drafts of a new constitution), *England's New Chains Discovered* holds that "many particulars in the Agreement before you are, upon serious examination thereof, dis-satisfactory to most of those who are very earnestly desirous of an Agreement." The pamphlet then outlines those "particulars" and proposes reforms.

Lilburne's primary rhetorical strategy in *England's New Chains Discovered* is to explain the interests and concerns of the English commoner in legal, constitutional language. He submits to Parliament that the people "hope for and expect what protection is in you and the Army to afford." Speaking on the people's behalf, he declares that "we ... do earnestly desire, that you will publikely declare your resolution" in the form of a universally agreeable constitution. The Parliament is then qualified as hypocritical, its members having "freighted their former promises, and renewed them with such appellations as they knew did most distaste the People." Lilburne warns Parliament that in the people's efforts to secure justice, they are unified and resolved: "prosperity we doubt not shall reap the benefit of our endeavours," he writes, "what ever shall become of us."

Although Lilburne favored logical and rhetorical soundness over emotional charge, *England's New Chains Discovered* is punctuated by moments of fervent candor. Lilburne acknowledges Parliament's intentions as honorable but classifies its performance in the advancement of civil liberties as a categorical failure. "Since woeful experience has manifested this to be a truth," he writes, "there seems no small reason that you should seriously lay to heart what at present we have to offer for discovery and prevention of so great a danger" in the enactment of policy hereafter. If the enumerated deficiencies are addressed, he tells the members of Parliament, it will "fasten you in the affections of the people and of the honest officers and soldiers" so completely as to not only provide

JOHN LILBURNE AND CONTEMPORARY CIVIL LIBERTIES

Though some of John Lilburne's reform proposals went unrealized (England still does not elect its judiciary), many Leveller ideas were folded into England's increasingly republican political infrastructure. Having been shuffled in and out of courtrooms and the prison system as a public agitator, Lilburne took a special interest in the legal rights of the nation's citizens, and it was during his 1638 trial for bringing a Puritan pamphlet into England that his popularity increased.

During the trial, he refused to answer any questions until he was told what charges were being leveled against him. He further insisted that the court's method of questioning was more akin to entrapment than investigation; therefore, he refused to respond for fear of self-incrimination. Protection against self-incrimination was one of many rights Lilburne claimed God had granted all people. The idea passed into law in England less than a century later and eventually in the United States via the Fifth Amendment to the Constitution. In the case of *Miranda v. Arizona* in 1966, the U.S. Supreme Court cited Lilburne's case when establishing the legal requirement for law enforcement officers to inform all citizens of their rights before taking them into custody.

political stability in the present but also ensure that the people "bend all [their] studies and endeavours to render [Parliament] honourable to all future generations."

CRITICAL DISCUSSION

England's New Chains Discovered received support from radical parliamentarians (early republicans) and some royalists, but it was understandably received poorly by members of Parliament. For his accusations in the pamphlet, Parliament's leaders had Lilburne arrested. Amos Tubb reports in a 2004 article for the *Huntington Library Quarterly* that "Lilburne's followers presented a petition to Parliament, allegedly containing eighty thousand signatures, demanding his release." Parliament's reaction, according to Tubbs, was to expedite his indictment and immediately imprison him. The royalist publications *Mercurius Elencticus* and *Pragmaticus* openly praised the pamphlet in their pages shortly thereafter. However, their praise was motivated less by agreement with the Leveller position and more by the fact that the pamphlet, as well as the public reaction to Lilburne's incarceration, visibly weakened the authority and stability of the Rump.

Although a new Parliament—again including the House of Lords—was eventually reestablished, followed in 1660 by the reestablishment of the monarchy of King Charles II, the philosophies espoused by the Levellers helped to alter the discourse of

Coll. John Lilborne.

Contemporary scholarship of *England's New Chains Discovered,* and the Levellers in general, is represented by Lyon's assessment. Rachel Foxley, writing in the *Historical Journal,* maintains that "while it would be wrong to see the Levellers' writings ... as an early flowering of the classical republicanism of the 1650s, Lilburne's remaking of the English materials surely marks one stage in this transformation." For Foxley, Lilburne's most important contribution was in the reshaping of the language of English politics—in his willingness to place himself among the ranks of English citizens of all classes to "establish that Englishmen, as Englishmen, had political status" and the right to all the liberties that accompanied it.

BIBLIOGRAPHY

Sources

Brailsford, Henry N. *The Levellers and the English Revolution.* Stanford: Stanford UP, 1961. Print.

Haller, William, and Godfrey Davies. *The Leveller Tracts, 1647-1653.* New York: Columbia UP, in cooperation with Henry E. Huntington Library and Art Gallery, 1944. Print.

Foxley, Rachel. "John Lilburne and the Citizenship of 'Free-born Englishmen.'" *Historical Journal* 47.4 (2004): 849+. *Academic OneFile.* Web. 7 Sept. 2012.

Lyon, Janet. *Manifestoes: Provocations of the Modern.* Ithaca: Cornell UP, 1999. Print.

Tubb, Amos. "Mixed Messages: Royalist Newsbook Reports of Charles I's Execution and of the Leveller Uprising." *Huntington Library Quarterly* 67.1 (2004): 59-74. *Academic OneFile.* Web. 7 Sept. 2012.

Further Reading

Corns, Thomas N. *Uncloistered Virtue: English Political Literature, 1640-1660.* Oxford: Clarendon, 1992. Print.

Frank, Joseph. *The Levellers: A History of the Writings of Three Seventeenth-Century Social Democrats: John Lilburne, Richard Overton, William Walwyn.* Cambridge: Harvard UP, 1955. Print.

Grob-Fitzgibbon, Benjamin. "'Whatsoever Yee Would That Men Should Doe unto Uou, Even So Doe Yee to Them': An Analysis of the Effect of Religious Consciousness on the Origins of the Leveller Movement." *Historian* 65.4 (2003): 901+. *Academic OneFile.* Web. 7 Sept. 2012.

Hibbert, Christopher. *Cavaliers & Roundheads: The English Civil War, 1642-1649.* New York: C. Scribner's Sons, 1993. Print.

Peacey, J. T. "John Lilburne and the Long Parliament." *Historical Journal* 43.3 (2000): 625+. *Academic OneFile.* Web. 7 Sept. 2012.

Purkiss, Diane. *The English Civil War: Papists, Gentlewomen, Soldiers, and Witchfinders in the Birth of Modern Britain.* New York: Basic Books, 2006. Print.

Vallance, Edward. *A Radical History of Britain: Visionaries, Rebels and Revolutionarie—the Men and Women Who Fought for Our Freedoms.* London: Little, Brown, 2009. Print.

English politics. The existence of an elected representative leader (known as the prime minister) and the reduced influence of the House of Lords as agreed upon in the Revolutionary Settlements (1688-1720) may be seen as direct results of the Levellers' contributions to English republicanism and its language. Lyon asserts that "the force of [*England's New Chains Discovered*]—indeed, of all the Levellers' tracts—derived not just from their collective status as the expression" of a unified English public "but especially from the political dilemma into which [that unity] forced Parliament." She argues that the Levellers' writings forced political discourse away from the "rhetoric of passive obedience" and toward the language of empowered, inherent liberty that persists in today's understandings of democracy.

Clint Garner

First and Second Manifestos of the General Council of the International Workingmen's Association on the Franco-Prussian War

Karl Marx

OVERVIEW

Composed by Karl Marx, the *First Manifesto of the General Council of the International Workingmen's Association on the Franco-Prussian War* and the *Second Manifesto of the General Council of the International Workingmen's Association on the Franco-Prussian War* were addressed to members of the association on July 23, 1870, and September 9, 1870, respectively. The first manifesto calls for the working class in all countries to unite against wars perpetrated by states with imperial ambitions. The second manifesto reacts with cautious optimism to France's establishment of the Third Republic, which was declared on September 4, 1870. Both manifestos are examples of Marx's application of his economic theories to political events and document the socialist response to the rapid expansion of European empires in the nineteenth century.

Composed as a call to action for the International Workingmen's Association (IWA), known also as the First International, the manifestos did not have a lasting impact on the outcome of the Franco-Prussian War itself. Following a brutal four-month siege of Paris by Prussian forces, in January 1871 the government of the newly formed Third Republic was forced to cede control of the disputed Alsace and Lorraine territories to Germany, leading to the unification of the German states and the establishment of the German Empire under Kaiser Wilhelm II. Yet the manifestos did prove influential in rallying the working class in the immediate aftermath of France's defeat, as workers briefly seized control of Paris and established a socialist regime from March 18 to May 28, 1871, in what came to be known as the Paris Commune. Originally published as pamphlets aimed at the IWA in Europe and America, the manifestos embody Marx's opposition to nationalism, imperialism, and the manipulation of the working class by power-hungry elites.

HISTORICAL AND LITERARY CONTEXT

In exile with Friedrich Engels and other revolutionaries, Marx found a home in London, where he arrived in 1849. The IWA, a loose confederation of socialist groups that included anarchist, socialist, and reformist strands, was founded in 1864 and held significant influence in the late 1860s. As a member of the General Council of the IWA, Marx provided leadership for the organization, and it bolstered Marx's hope of transforming his economic philosophy into political reality. The two manifestos on the Franco-Prussian War were written in response to the political situation created by the Franco-Prussian War in the early 1870s. Examining the belligerent tangle between Prussia, France, and Germany, Marx held all three states guilty for inflicting their expansionist aims on the proletariat. In Marx's analysis, their warfare only causes proletarians to suffer and fight unnecessarily against their brothers in other countries.

The first manifesto was written in opposition to France's declaration of war on Prussia on July 15, 1870, and the second was written following a tumultuous series of political events in France: the surrender of Napoleon III, the subsequent collapse of the Second French Empire, and the establishment of the Third Republic. The manifestos responded to the position of workingmen in France during the war. In the first manifesto Marx had called on the proletariat to stand against the war in which France and Prussia were engaged, and in the second he advises the French proletarians that they should be skeptical of the new government's aims but should nevertheless work to "improve the opportunities of Republican liberty" within the framework of the Third Republic lest they contribute to the demise of the French state and further consolidate power into the hands of imperialists.

These manifestos bear the hallmarks of Marx's activist goals and approach, best known from his *Communist Manifesto* (1848). In them, Marx applies the economic thought that he developed in the *Communist Manifesto* to the political situation in Europe. In the first manifesto on the Franco-Prussian War, Marx rallies French workers, reminding them that workingmen's associations in Berlin, Brunswick, and Chemnitz have all issued declarations in which they

✣ *Key Facts*

Time Period:
Late 19th Century

Movement/Issue:
Franco-Prussian War; Establishment of the Third Republic

Place of Publication:
England

Language of Publication:
French

MARX AND THE INTERNATIONAL WORKINGMEN'S ASSOCIATION

Although Karl Marx was the effective leader of the IWA, the organization actually owed only part of its existence to his work. Labor movements had been gathering strength in Europe and the United States in the late 1850s and 1860s. Growing from an existing British labor coalition, the London Trades Council, the IWA held its first public meeting, in London, on September 28, 1864. The secretary of the council, George Odger, had composed a manifesto that provided the initial document for the IWA, or First International, as it was also called.

Expelled from France, Marx arrived in London in 1849. Although he had been aloof from the English labor movement, Marx attended the first meeting of the IWA through an invitation extended by an acquaintance from France. Marx was elected to the association's General Council and soon after delivered an *Inaugural Address,* in which he attempted to combine the IWA's moral concerns with his own economic arguments. Becoming politically active, Marx soon realized that despite its solid organizational foundation the English labor movement did not have the international vision he wished. As a result, the two manifestos on the Franco-Prussian War may be an example of Marx's attempt to rouse a reluctant British audience to exercise political force.

condemn the Franco-Prussian War and proclaim their solidarity with French proletarians. In the second manifesto, Marx mocks middle-class German rhetoric, declaring that bourgeois Germans who support the annexation of Alsace and Lorraine and the unification of Germany are simply being used by Prussia's leader, Bismarck, to achieve his expansionist goals.

Although the manifestos are a rare written record of an explicitly political agenda by Marx, they have been largely overshadowed by his more famous works. In addition to the *Communist Manifesto, Das Capital,* published in three volumes between 1867 and 1894, has dominated Marx's reputation. *Das Capital* remains the foundation of Marx's impact on subsequent social movements. By contrast, the two manifestos on the Franco-Prussian War have been overlooked, both as literary works and as activist documents. The lack of attention was also partly a result of the fact that the manifestos' audience, the IWA, dissolved shortly after the Paris Commune's demise in 1871.

THEMES AND STYLE

The two manifestos on the Franco-Prussian War proclaim a theme that is common in Marx's writing: proletarians everywhere are brothers, and—united against "dynastic" wars—they can resist the expansionist aims of their governments and establish a peaceful international order. To support the image of working-class

solidarity, Marx quotes a resolution from a German labor organization that declares, "Mindful of the watchword of the International Workingmen's Association: *Proletarians of all countries unite,* we shall never forget that the workmen of *all* countries are our *friends* and the despots of *all* countries our *enemies.*" Marx expands on this by reminding the IWA that the English workingmen are pressuring the British government to recognize the Third Republic as the legitimate government of France. In both manifestos he warns that continued inactivity by the IWA will only result in more war, leading "to a renewed triumph over the workman by the lords of the sword, of the soil, and of capital." Thus, Marx pleads for an active, determined IWA that will succeed in its battle for international peace under the banner of working-class freedom.

The two manifestos use the rhetoric of grievance, disgust, and irony to foreground the absurdity of the Franco-Prussian War and to underscore the brotherhood of the proletariat. In particular, Marx emphasizes the IWA's balance between unity and diversity by naming the various European chapters that oppose any war of imperial expansion. He does not ignore national differences but uses them to bolster a sense of essential equality. Centered on a desire for freedom from capitalism and war, this equality leads "the English working class [to] stretch the hand of fellowship to the French and German working people. They feel deeply convinced that whatever turn the impending horrid war may take, the alliance of the working classes of all countries will ultimately kill war." For Marx, capitalism necessarily results in war; a new system based on labor must bring international peace, and the "pioneer of that new society is the International Workingmen's Association." Even as he concludes both manifestos with the claim that the IWA is the flagship of a new political order, Marx demands that his followers take definite political action.

In keeping with their purpose, both manifestos use highly emotional language. In the first manifesto, Marx uses rhetorical questions to indict Bismarck for the evils he has perpetrated: "On the German side, the war is a war of defense; but who put Germany to the necessity of defending herself? Who enabled France's Napolean III to wage war upon her? *Prussia!*" He condemns Napoleon III's government as a "ferocious farce," and he calls German intellectuals to account for being "sycophants of the powers that be" who "poison the popular mind by the incense of mendacious self-praise." Far from dispassionate, Marx's tone in both manifestos is impassioned by the sufferings of his working brothers in Europe. By adopting this incendiary stance, Marx attempts to leverage the weight of the IWA to stop the war, and when that effort fails, to redouble their efforts on "our common task—the emancipation of labor."

CRITICAL DISCUSSION

As Samuel Bernstein notes in "The First International on the Eve of the Paris Commune," the first manifesto was "circulated widely" and "was received with commendation, even by [British philosopher] John Stuart Mill." The second manifesto, he continues, "was largely instrumental in initiating a drive in England for the recognition of the French republic and an international protest against the German annexation of Alsace-Lorraine." Some members of the French contingent of the IWA found inspiration in the two manifestos as they attempted to overthrow the new government of France, establishing the Paris Commune. This action was something that Marx in the second manifesto had warned would be "a desperate folly," but he later praised it in a pamphlet titled *The Civil War in France* [1871]). For its agitation under the leadership of Marx, the IWA was vilified by the government of the Third Republic, and the IWA largely disappeared after 1872.

Despite the IWA's disappearance, the sentiments that Marx had expressed in the two manifestos continued to inspire working-class rhetoric. An article written in 1872 by E. Gryzanovski describes the IWA's importance to trade unions. In 1902 the New York Labor News Company published *The Paris Commune,* which included both manifestos on the Franco-Prussian War along with *The Civil War in France.* In the preface, Lucien Sanial, editor of the publication, attributes some of the obscurity of the manifestos to a distortion of history by "capitalist mouthpieces." Echoing Marx's style, Sanial writes that the Paris Commune "is conquered; the Commune is murdered. Is its spirit dead? Read the manifesto. The class war has only begun…." This air of unquenchable proletarian energy resembles Marx's tone in the manifestos.

Very little modern scholarship has dealt directly with Marx's manifestos on the Franco-Prussian War. Studies concerning Marx and this period in France focus more on the Paris Commune and the international responses to it, partly because of Marx's efforts to associate the IWA with the Commune in *The Civil War in France.* David Felix, noting the conflict between Marx's rejection of hasty revolutionary uprisings in the second manifesto and his later embrace of it, writes in a 1983 article in *The Review of Politics* that "the association of the International and the Commune will remain one of the wonders of modern history." Another strand in modern scholarship focuses on Marx's impact on labor unions in Britain and the United States. Henry Collins, in a 1962 article in *Science & Society,* traces Marx's involvement in the British labor movement, mentioning that "at first sight it seems surprising" that Marx was involved with the founding of the IWA since nearly "all his energy during this period went into his work on *Capital.*" Finally, another strand discusses Marx's international influence, but very little of this scholarship

directly address the relationship between the manifestos, Marx's thought, and contemporary political situations. In the end, the two manifestos remain an important but largely overlooked moment in Marx's political career.

BIBLIOGRAPHY

Sources

Bernstein, Samuel. "The First International on the Eve of the Paris Commune." *Science & Society* 5.1 (1941): 24-42. *JSTOR.* Web. 18 October 2012.

Collins, Henry. "Karl Marx, the International and the British Trade Union Movement." *Science & Society,* 26.4 (1962): 400-21. *JSTOR.* Web. 4 October 2012.

Felix, David. "The Dialectic of the First International and Nationalism." *The Review of Politics* 45.1 (1983): 20-44. *JSTOR.* Web. 18 October 2012.

Gryzanovski, E. "On the International Workingmen's Association; Its Origin, Doctrines, and Ethics." *The North American Review,* 114.235 (1872): 309-76. *JSTOR.* Web. 4 Oct. 2012.

NAPOLÉON LE PETIT.

SAILLANT, Edit. r du Croissant, 5 à 10

AU BAGNE !.. MISÉRABLE !..

In the manifestos on the Franco-Prussian War, author Karl Marx speaks out against Louis Napoleon, also known as Napoleon III, as a foe of the International Workingmen's Association. This caricature, drawn by Charles Frondat, dates from the first manifesto and shows the widespread displeasure with the French leader. MUSÉE D'ART ET D'HISTOIRE, SAINT-DENIS, FRANCE/GIRAUDON/THE BRIDGEMAN ART LIBRARY

Marx, Karl. *The Paris Commune.* Ed. Lucien Sanial. New York: New York Labor News, 1902. *Open Library.* Web. 4 Oct. 2012.

Sanial, Lucien. Preface. *The Paris Commune.* By Karl Marx. Ed. Sanial. New York: New York Labor News, 1902. ix-xxxv. *Open Library.* Web. 4 Oct. 2012.

Further Reading

Bernstein, Samuel. "American Labor and the Paris Commune." *Science & Society,* 15.2 (1951): 144-62. *JSTOR.* Web. 4 October 2012.

Engels, Frederich. Introduction. *The Paris Commune.* By Karl Marx. Ed. Lucian Sanial. New York: New York Labor News, 1902. 1-20. *Open Library.* Web. 4 Oct. 2012.

Gilbert, Alan. "Social Theory and Revolutionary Activity in Marx." *The American Political Science Review,* 73.2 (1979): 521-38. *JSTOR.* Web. 4 October 2012.

Gouldner, Alvin W. "Marx's Last Battle: Bakunin and the First International." *Theory and Society,* 11.6 (1982): 853-84. *JSTOR.* Web. 4 October 2012.

Harison, Casey. "The Paris Commune of 1871, the Russian Revolution of 1905, and the Shifting of the Revolutionary Tradition." *History and Memory,* 19.2 (2007): 5-42. *JSTOR.* Web. 4 Oct. 2012.

Harrison, Royden. "Marx, Engels, and the British Response to the Commune." *The Massachusetts Review,* 12.3 (1971): 463-77. *JSTOR.* Web. 4 Oct. 2012.

Lissagaray, Prosper Olivier. *History of the Paris Commune of 1871.* Trans. Eleanor Marx. St. Petersburg, FL: Red and Black, 2007. Print.

Evelyn Reynolds

THE MANIFESTO OF THE COMMUNIST PARTY

Karl Marx, Friedrich Engels

OVERVIEW

The Manifesto of the Communist Party by Karl Marx and Friedrich Engels was originally published anonymously in German in 1848. It proclaims the triumph of the bourgeoisie through capitalism's absolute transformation of economy and society, to be followed inevitably by the bourgeoisie's supercession by the proletariat it has created, leading to the abolition of private property and the institution of a communist society in which "the free development of each is the condition for the free development of all." The *Manifesto* was commissioned by the London-based Communist League, an outgrowth of several other small groupings composed of middle-class radicals, artisans, exiles, and intellectuals. It was written by Marx, then living in Brussels, on the basis of a draft by Engels in the form of a catechism. It appeared on the cusp of the roiling upheaval that became known as the Revolution of 1848, which broke out in Paris in the following weeks and spread to envelop much of the European continent. The *Manifesto* is notable for its purportedly scientific character—arguing for inevitable change based on its objective analysis of history and society—and by its uncompromising nature.

Although it was reprinted several times within a few months, the *Manifesto* then practically disappeared from public view for more than two decades. Marx himself disbanded the Communist League later in 1848, deciding after the failure of the revolutionary efforts that it was premature to advocate for the communist transition. He returned to Germany to help along the bourgeois revolution that he considered its necessary precondition there. However, by the early 1870s it experienced a revival of interest, and in the next forty years, as Marxist influence and socialist parties spread, it was published in hundreds of editions in about thirty languages. The 1917 Soviet revolution institutionalized the *Manifesto* as the founding text of "real existing socialism," producing print runs in the millions. Although the collapse of the Soviet Union and associated communist regimes in 1989-1991 has thrown into doubt the validity of the communist project, Jeffrey C. Isaac's introduction to a 2012 edition still calls the *Manifesto* "perhaps the most extensively published and widely read text in the history of political thought."

HISTORICAL AND LITERARY CONTEXT

The *Communist Manifesto* is in part a response to the frustration of mid-nineteenth century radicals who saw the dynamism and exhilaration of the French Revolution channeled into war, empire, and the stultifying reaction of the post-Napoleonic era, as well as to the mind-boggling economic changes brought on by the Industrial Revolution. Marx himself stated that his system was a synthesis of British political economy, French socialism, and German philosophy. Study of the works of figures such as Adam Smith and David Ricardo confronted him with the power and scope of the capitalist system in formation, with its assumption that liberal economic principles and free trade would bring prosperity and liberty to all. The failure of the 1830 July Revolution and a subsequent 1839 attempted revolt in France made the optimistic predictions of the British thinkers ring false. In Germany, philosopher Georg Wilhelm Friedrich Hegel had provided a view of history powered forward by dialectics. Marx, searching for a motor of history that lent itself to political action rather than a mystical search for Hegel's philosophy of Absolute Spirit, "turned Hegel on his head" in his formulation of dialectical materialism, the idea that history moves forward based on the resolution of contradictions, but powered by economic rather than spiritual forces or ideas.

By the time Marx arrived in his Paris exile in late 1843, the city was a boiling pot of ideas about socialism, communism, national liberation, and radical action of all varieties. He both profited from the ideas of and vehemently disagreed with figures such as Russian anarchist Mikhail Bakunin (1814-1876) and Pierre Joseph Proudhon (1809-1865), in whose *What Is Property* (1840) he found an effective critique of the bourgeois concept of private property. Marx's synthesis allowed him to sharply differentiate his and his fellow communists' position from the many other ideas and groups jostling for influence in the struggle for democracy, equality, and freedom.

Marx and Engels' text, in its universalism and self-certainty, lies firmly in the trajectory of the Enlightenment and especially the French Revolution it spawned. Ironically, numerous commentators have also pointed out a sense of religiosity in the *Manifesto,* in its faith and conviction that the proletariat will coalesce, rise, and inherit the earth.

+ *Key Facts*

Time Period:
Mid-19th Century

Movement/Issue:
Communism; French revolutionary activity; Hegelian philosophy

Place of Publication:
Germany

Language of Publication:
German

(This resonates with analyses of the subsequent communist movement, generally from opponents, which see it as a 'secular religion,' replacing religion while doing away with none of its trappings or habits of mind.) Isaac's analysis mentions the Bible, William Shakespeare, and Johann Wolfgang von Goethe as literary influences and the source of allusions in the text.

Although it is difficult to disentangle the effects of the *Manifesto* itself from those of Marx's subsequent organizing and scholarly activities, by the end of the nineteenth century both the document and the man served as totemic symbols to the growing workers' movements across Europe and beyond. Positions for or against Marxism, as either political tendency or analytical method, have defined practically all of the major intellectual and political conflicts of the twentieth century, at least until the collapse of communism at the beginning of the century's last decade. Since then, the man and the manifesto have spawned accusation and ridicule by supporters of the now-hegemonic capitalist system, while opponents, including "critical Marxists," have engaged in much soul-searching. Nevertheless, the appearance of numerous new editions, particularly on the occasion of the manifesto's hundred and fiftieth anniversary and, in 1998, the first

new translation into English since the 1888 edition by Samuel Moore, attest to its literary vitality and political interest, if not viability.

THEMES AND STYLE

The central theme of the *Manifesto* is expressed in the famous first sentence of its first section, "Bourgeois and Proletarians": "The history of all hitherto existing society is the history of class struggles." There follows a *tour de force* of historical exposition, explaining the whole history of human civilization in terms of dialectical materialism, with systems based on different "relations of production" (ancient slavery, feudalism, capitalism) succeeding each other when the contradictions between their technology and productive power on the one hand and their property and class relationships on the other forced crises that led to the replacement of the old by the new. The emerging bourgeoisie has accelerated and globalized this process, and is on its way to simplifying the class landscape into the two great classes of the section title—bourgeois and proletarians—thus "produc[ing] … its own gravediggers." Since the proletarians, ultimately forming the vast majority of society, will have been stripped of all illusions and attachments by the ruthless logic of capital, they will inexorably unite to overthrow bourgeois rule and capitalist economic organization, leading to communism, in which everyone will be free to pursue his or her own potential.

The second section, "Proletarians and Communists," lays out the principles and roles of the communists, "the most advanced and resolute section of the working-class parties ... [who] have over the great mass ... the advantage of clearly understanding the lines of march." Their conclusions stem not from invented ideas but "merely express ... actual relations"; thus, in contrast to the myriad other (false) socialist movements and principles—each in turn dispatched with merciless invective in the third section—the *Manifesto* purports to represent a "scientific" approach. The second section continues with the airing of various "bourgeois" charges—such as that the communists want to abolish the family—with dismissive, sarcastic responses, and closes with a list of surprisingly reformist general policy prescriptions, including free universal education, state control of credit, and a graduated income tax. A fourth and final section—generally held to have been dashed off quickly, as Marx was behind on the League's deadline and had been given an ultimatum—aligns the communists in terms of the struggles in various countries.

While commentators on all sides have argued ceaselessly about the wisdom and relevance of the *Manifesto,* they are practically unified on the power of its writing. Gareth Stedman Jones (a sympathizer with Marxism), in his book-length introduction to the 2002 Penguin edition, lauds its "rhetorical force" expressed through its "caustic and apparently undeviating logic"—giving the impression that no counterargument is even possible. Vladimir Tismaneanu (a critic), in an essay in the 2012 Yale edition, calls it "perhaps the most inflammatory and impassioned text ever written by a philosopher" and "scathing, vitriolic and incandescent," but also "revolutionary poetry." Martin Puchner, in his book *Poetry of the Revolution: Marx, Manifestos, and the Avant-Gardes,* cites the text's "impatience" and "pose of authority." An often perplexing aspect has been the fulsomeness of the praise of the bourgeoisie in the first section, which "has created more massive and more colossal productive power than have all previous generations put together." All this adds up to a sense in which history, economic forces, and unchallengeable deduction render any opposition to or even slight deviation from the *Manifesto*'s program—or any attachment to the past—illegitimate or impossible.

CRITICAL DISCUSSION

The *Manifesto* did not reach a wide public audience until its "second wave" appearance a quarter-century after its initial, anonymous publication. At that point, Marx's prominent status in the broader field of radical politics to a large extent conditioned responses to the text. The 1871 Paris Commune—in which a truly radical workers' movement succeeded in seizing power, if only for two months—and Marx's account of it in his *The Civil War in France* (1871) made him a *bête noire* in the conservative press and a hero across the Left. Marx and Engels wrote prefaces for seven different editions, which performed a protective function by both admitting shortcomings and asserting the inviolability of the original as a "historical document." As the Marxist movement matured and began to fracture at the end of the nineteenth century, a more substantive criticism emerged. Eduard Bernstein set it in motion in 1988 by asserting the vagueness of the promised communist future and that "this goal ... is nothing to me, the movement is everything." In his article "Revising the Communist Manifesto," he also questioned the "imminent collapse of the bourgeois economy," and advocated a gradualist, as opposed to a revolutionary, approach. His critics, including Karl Kautsky and Lenin, defended the *Manifesto*'s integrity while acknowledging that the past half-century's history had not proceeded as envisioned. With the 1917 victory of Lenin's Bolsheviks, the status of the *Manifesto* within the communist movement became largely ossified and effectively immune from any criticism.

Through the twentieth century, and especially after the commencement of the Cold War, the *Communist Manifesto* was subject to the strictures of the grand ideological and geopolitical struggle. Outside the communist world, this generally boiled down to the question of whether the authoritarian distortions of the free and stateless communist ideal under Stalin could be traced to aspects of the "founding document" itself. Martin Malia, in his introduction to the 1998 Signet Classic edition, states that "the Communist failure stems from the perverse logic of Marx's project itself": reformist and not revolutionary proletarian consciousness is the inevitable outcome of capitalist industrial development (as Bernstein recognized), and thus revolution can only be forced by a Leninist "professional bearer of revolutionary consciousness." Post-*Manifesto* development has in this sense "turned Marx on his head," in that revolution has only succeeded in the least-developed countries, rather than in the most advanced, as Marx's historical schema would have it; and nowhere has the proletariat played a leading role. Another criticism is the underestimation of the power of non-material motivations such as nationalism and, more recently, fundamentalist religion.

More scholarly, less politically invested criticism, however, has examined the *Manifesto* not as prognosis but as literature. Marshall Berman pioneered this approach in his 1982 book *All That Is Solid Melts into Air: The Experience of Modernity,* which, juxtaposing Marx's work with that of Goethe, French poet Charles Baudelaire, the literary denizens of St. Petersburg, and Robert Moses, finds in his anxious, fervent paean to capitalist modernity and "the tension between [his] critical insights and his radical hopes" the essence of the (artistic) modernist impulse. Puchner finds the *Manifesto* "addressed to a recipient [the proletariat] who does not fully exist," thus

PRIMARY SOURCE

THE MANIFESTO OF THE COMMUNIST PARTY

The history of all hitherto existing society is the history of class struggles.

Freeman and slave, patrician and plebeian, lord and serf, guild-master and journeyman, in a word, oppressor and oppressed, stood in constant opposition to one another, carried on an uninterrupted, now hidden, now open fight, a fight that each time ended, either in a revolutionary reconstitution of society at large, or in the common ruin of the contending classes.

In the earlier epochs of history, we find almost everywhere a complicated arrangement of society into various orders, a manifold gradation of social rank. In ancient Rome we have patricians, knights, plebeians, slaves; in the Middle Ages, feudal lords, vassals, guild-masters, journeymen, apprentices, serfs; in almost all of these classes, again, subordinate gradations.

The modern bourgeois society that has sprouted from the ruins of feudal society has not done away with class antagonisms. It has but established new classes, new conditions of oppression, new forms of struggle in place of the old ones.

Our epoch, the epoch of the bourgeoisie, possesses, however, this distinct feature: it has simplified class antagonisms. Society as a whole is more and more splitting up into two great hostile camps, into two great classes directly facing each other—Bourgeoisie and Proletariat.

…

This organisation of the proletarians into a class, and, consequently into a political party, is continually being upset again by the competition between the workers themselves. But it ever rises up again, stronger, firmer, mightier. It compels legislative recognition of particular interests of the workers, by taking advantage of the divisions among the bourgeoisie itself. Thus, the ten-hours' bill in England was carried.

Altogether collisions between the classes of the old society further, in many ways, the course of development of the proletariat. The bourgeoisie finds itself involved in a constant battle. At first with the aristocracy; later on, with those portions of the bourgeoisie itself, whose interests have become antagonistic to the progress of industry; at all time with the bourgeoisie of foreign countries. In all these battles, it sees itself compelled to appeal to the proletariat, to ask for help, and thus, to drag it into the political arena. The bourgeoisie itself, therefore, supplies the proletariat with its own elements of political and general education, in other words, it furnishes the proletariat with weapons for fighting the bourgeoisie.

Further, as we have already seen, entire sections of the ruling class are, by the advance of

establishing a "performative" aspect (both addressing and calling into being its audience) that was part of Marx and Engels's creation of the "distinct genre" of the manifesto. Deconstructionist theorist Jacques Derrida, in his 1994 essay "Spectres of Marx," brings together both approaches to the *Manifesto,* as literature and as politics, invoking its famous opening sentence ("A spectre is haunting Europe—the spectre of communism") to postulate a "spirit of Marx" that still haunts our understandings of philosophy, history, and a triumphalist political and economic system that proclaims (ever more anxiously) that there is no alternative to it. Students of globalization in the twenty-first century have observed the eerie prescience of the *Manifesto*'s description of capitalist globalization, and the dizzying change and misery that globalization spawns seems today a more concrete indication of the manifesto's continuing relevance.

BIBLIOGRAPHY

Sources

Berman, Marshall. "All That Is Solid Melts into Air: Marx, Modernism and Modernization." *All That Is Solid Melts into Air: The Experience of Modernity.* New York: Penguin, 1988. 87-129. Print.

Bernstein, Eduard. "Revising the Communist Manifesto." *The Communist Manifesto.* Ed. Frederic L. Bender. New York: Norton, 1988. 125-27. Print.

Derrida, Jacques. "Spectres of Marx." *New Left Review* 205 (May/June 1994). 31-58. Print.

Isaac, Jeffrey C. "Introduction: Rethinking the Communist Manifesto." *The Communist Manifesto.* By Karl Marx and Friedrich Engels. Ed. Jeffrey C. Isaac. New Haven: Yale UP, 2012. 1-42. Print.

Malia, Martin. Introduction. *The Communist Manifesto.* By Karl Marx and Friedrich Engels. New York: Signet Classic, 1998. vii-xxviii. Print.

industry, precipitated into the proletariat, or are at least threatened in their conditions of existence. These also supply the proletariat with fresh elements of enlightenment and progress.

Finally, in times when the class struggle nears the decisive hour, the progress of dissolution going on within the ruling class, in fact within the whole range of old society, assumes such a violent, glaring character, that a small section of the ruling class cuts itself adrift, and joins the revolutionary class, the class that holds the future in its hands. Just as, therefore, at an earlier period, a section of the nobility went over to the bourgeoisie, so now a portion of the bourgeoisie goes over to the proletariat, and in particular, a portion of the bourgeois ideologists, who have raised themselves to the level of comprehending theoretically the historical movement as a whole.

Of all the classes that stand face to face with the bourgeoisie today, the proletariat alone is a really revolutionary class. The other classes decay and finally disappear in the face of Modern Industry; the proletariat is its special and essential product.

The lower middle class, the small manufacturer, the shopkeeper, the artisan, the peasant, all these fight against the bourgeoisie, to save from extinction their existence as fractions of the middle class. They are therefore not revolutionary, but conservative. Nay more, they are reactionary, for they try to roll back the wheel of history. If by chance, they are revolutionary, they are only so in view of their impending transfer into the proletariat; they thus defend not their present, but their future interests, they desert their own standpoint to place themselves at that of the proletariat.

…

The essential conditions for the existence and for the sway of the bourgeois class is the formation and augmentation of capital; the condition for capital is wage-labour. Wage-labour rests exclusively on competition between the labourers. The advance of industry, whose involuntary promoter is the bourgeoisie, replaces the isolation of the labourers, due to competition, by the revolutionary combination, due to association. The development of Modern Industry, therefore, cuts from under its feet the very foundation on which the bourgeoisie produces and appropriates products. What the bourgeoisie therefore produces, above all, are its own grave-diggers. Its fall and the victory of the proletariat are equally inevitable.

SOURCE: *Marx/Engels Selected Works,* edited Andy Bluden. Progress Publishers with cooperation of International Publishers, 1969. Pp. 98-137. Copyright © 1969 by the International Publishers. All rights reserved. Reproduced by permission.

Puchner, Martin. *Poetry of the Revolution: Marx, Manifestos, and the Avant-Gardes.* Princeton, NJ: Princeton UP, 2006. Print.

Stedman Jones, Gareth. Introduction. *The Communist Manifesto.* By Karl Marx and Friedrich Engels. London: Penguin, 2002. 3-187. Print.

Tismaneanu, Vladimir. "Reflections on the Fate of Marxism in Eastern Europe: Fulfillment or Bastardization?" *The Communist Manifesto.* By Karl Marx and Friedrich Engels. Ed. Jeffrey C. Isaac. New Haven: Yale UP, 2012. 166-86. Print.

Further Reading

Berlin, Isaiah. *Karl Marx: His Life and Environment.* New York: Time, 1963. Print.

Bronner, Stephen Eric. "The *Communist Manifesto*: Between Past and Present." *The Communist Manifesto.* Karl Marx and Friedrich Engels. Ed. Jeffrey C. Isaac. New Haven: Yale UP, 2012. 144-65. Print.

Cowling, Mark, ed. *The Communist Manifesto: New Interpretations*: *Including, in Full, The Manifesto of the Communist Party,* translated by Terrell Carver. NY: New York UP, 1998. Print.

Eagleton, Terry. *Why Marx Was Right.* New Haven: Yale UP, 2011.

Sassen, Saskia. "Marxism and Globalization: Revisiting the Political in the *Communist Manifesto. The Communist Manifesto.* Karl Marx and Friedrich Engels. Ed. Jeffrey C. Isaac. New Haven: Yale UP, 2012. 187-203. Print.

Sweezy, Paul M., and Leo Huberman. "The Communist Manifesto after 100 Years." New York: Monthly Review, 1964. 87-113. Print.

Trotsky, Leon. "The Communist Manifesto Today." *The Communist Manifesto.* By Karl Marx and Friedrich Engels. New York: Pathfinder, 1970. 3-11. Print.

Richard Esbenshade

MANIFESTO OF THE EQUALS

Sylvain Maréchal

OVERVIEW

Sylvain Maréchal's "Manifeste des égaux" (April 1796; "Manifesto of the Equals") is a condensed exposition of the political and economic agenda of a group of Paris radicals who joined together to protest the corruption of the republican ideals of the French Revolution of 1789 by the bourgeois regime of the Directory (1795-99). The tract draws on the theories of Enlightenment philosopher Jean-Jacques Rousseau in calling for a new revolution that will recognize the people's natural right to social equality and abolish all discrepancies of wealth and privilege. The seven members of the group, which called itself the Secret Directory of Public Safety, were so committed to the idea of absolute equality that they plotted an armed uprising of the masses to overthrow the government. The plot, known as the Conspiracy of the Equals, was discovered and suppressed in May 1796 before it ever erupted.

Originally planned for mass distribution, "Manifesto of the Equals" was going to serve as the rallying cry of the new revolution, but certain members of the Secret Directory thought some of its language too extreme. In its stead, the Secret Directory drafted a declaration of twelve articles of equality, "Analyse de la doctrine de Babeuf," which was placarded about the city of Paris. Maréchal, long known as an agent of the Revolution through his poems, plays, and journalism, had composed the "Manifesto of the Equals" while serving as one of the top aides to François Noël (Gracchus) Babeuf, the founder of the Secret Directory and the inspiration behind the failed Conspiracy of the Equals. At the trial of the conspirators, two men were sentenced to death, including Babeuf, and seven were deported, among them Maréchal. The stillborn insurrection was largely forgotten until 1828, when Philippe Buonarroti, a revolutionary originally from Italy, also deported for his role in the plot, published an eyewitness account, *Histoire de la conspiration pour l'égalité, dite de Babeuf* (History of the Conspiracy of the Equals), that explained Babeuf's doctrine as it had been formulated in the "Manifesto of the Equals" and other tracts. Buonarroti's book sold extremely well, was translated into several languages, and was a source of inspiration to French revolutionary socialist Louis-Auguste Blanqui (1805-81), some of whose ideas ("Blanquism") are thought to have been adapted by Karl Marx and Friedrich Engels in their

Communist Manifesto (1848). Maréchal's "Manifesto of the Equals" has since come to be recognized as an important influence on the formation of socialist and anarchist groupings throughout the nineteenth century and beyond.

HISTORICAL AND LITERARY CONTEXT

Babeuf and his group, commonly known as the Babouvists, aimed to replace the Directory with a government that more closely resembled the uncompromising republicanism of Maximilien de Robespierre and his allies, the Jacobins, who controlled the national legislature for much of 1793 and 1794. During this period, through the authority of an executive body called the Committee of Public Safety, the Jacobins enforced a violent campaign of repression against any person even remotely suspected of disloyalty, the so-called Terror, during which thousands were sent to the guillotine. After Robespierre was himself guillotined in July 1794, the Terror ceased, and with it the Jacobin ascendancy. The Babouvists, however, denied the validity of the 1795 constitution, which placed power firmly in the hands of property owners and an executive committee of five "directors" from the upper classes. The Babouvists demanded a restoration of the Constitution of 1793, which had been ratified by public referendum but never adopted, as a preliminary to establishing a collectivist state. The ultimate aim of the Conspiracy of the Equals was to reestablish a state of nature in society, much as Rousseau had described in *The Social Contract*. Maréchal writes at the beginning of "Manifesto of the Equals," "Equality! The first wish of nature, the first need of man. …We intend from now on to live and die as equals, just as we were born. We want true equality or death."

Maréchal wrote his tract during a time of high inflation and massive food shortages, largely the result of the Directory's elimination of the price controls of the Robespierre years. "We declare that we can no longer put up with the fact that the great majority work and sweat for the smallest of minorities," Maréchal proclaimed. The Directory had also passed new censorship legislation that safeguarded the individual's right to free expression but effectively criminalized political difference by banning all printing presses and political clubs representative of collective opinion. The immediate occasion for the formation of the Secret Directory was in fact the government's shutdown of Babeuf's earlier club, the Society of the Pantheon, as well as his newspaper, *Tribun du Peuple.*

Critics have cited the "Manifesto of the Equals" as a seminal text in the transformation of the genre of the manifesto that occurred late in the French Revolution. It was around this time that subversion first came to be identified as one of the constitutive traits of the manifesto, as distinct from its previous conception as a forum for official government proclamations or statements of public policy. According to Benedikt Hjartarson in his essay in *Modernism, Vol. 1* (2007), "[Fundamental] changes can be seen in the use of the term in the second phase of the French Revolution. Radical groups of Jacobins start publishing 'manifestoes' in which they present their demands for radical social change, the two primary examples being Gracchus Babeuf's '*Manifesto des plébéiens*' …and Sylvain Maréchal's '*Manifeste des égaux.*'" (Babeuf's *Manifesto of the Plebeians* was a precursor tract to Maréchal's that appeared in the *Tribun du Peuple* in 1795.) Hjartarson defines the subversive manifesto as one that "manifest[s] the will of 'the people' … as opposed to the bourgeois 'citizen' … in order to demonstrate the exclusion of the lower classes from revolutionary discourse and articulate its demands to participate in it." Drawing on Jürgen Habermas, Janet Lyon, in *Manifestoes: Provocations of the Modern* (1999), similarly discusses the revolutionary manifesto as a new outlet of expression for the "plebeian public sphere." Yet she emphasizes that however much these plebian manifestos were reputedly dedicated to all oppressed peoples, they were in fact almost always gendered in conception. She cites from the "Manifesto of the Equals" to clarify her point about the limitations to equality: "Let there no longer be any difference between people than that of age and sex." In an 2010 essay on print culture during the French Revolution, Sanja Perovic also argues that the "Manifesto of the Equals" marked a turning point in the history of the genre of the manifesto, noting that Maréchal extrapolated from Rousseau's theory of the state of nature—a prehistoric condition where humans enjoyed complete freedom uncorrupted by society—in calling for the elimination of political representation altogether. Perovic then quotes from Maréchal's text: "Let these revolting distinctions between rich and poor, great and small, masters and servants, *governors and the governed* finally disappear!"

While scholars debate the exact relationship between Babeuf's doctrine and the "Manifesto of the Equals," and the relationship between both of these and Buonarroti's text, most view the rabid egalitarianism of the "Manifesto of the Equals" as a progenitor of a wide array of socialist, communist, and nationalist revolutionary movements that followed. The document, with its concept of social upheaval as the harbinger of a second, more sweeping revolution, has

also been judged a forerunner of radical conceptions of modernity built upon the notion of historical rupture and rebirth.

THEMES AND STYLE

The main ideas of the "Manifesto of the Equals" are the fight for equality—through insurrection and class warfare—and the establishment of a society in an organic state of harmony. The equality it promotes as the future condition of the human race is unlike any articulated or experienced before. The tract takes as its motto a phrase drawn on the writings of revolutionary philosopher and mathematician the Marquis de Condorcet: "Real equality, the final end of the social art." In line with Condorcet's thinking, Maréchal proceeds to lay bare the distinction between the equality allowed by political codes and the equality to which humans are actually entitled, that which existed in nature before the advent of civilization. Praising the Constitution of 1793 as "a great de facto step toward real equality," Maréchal declares that it yet failed to achieve the "common good." The "common good" for the Babouvists is nothing less than a socialist interpretation of the original motto of the French Revolution: "liberty, equality, fraternity." Maréchal demands "the *community of goods.* No more individual property inland: *the land belongs to no one.*" Thus, for Maréchal and his associates, "real equality" could only be achieved through a plan of sweeping social reorganization that not only created direct democracy but also eliminated private property. Their critique of property was extremely radical, taking the idea of agrarian reform—the equal distribution of land to all individuals—to a new level.

Maréchal uses strategies of comparison to stress the urgent need for "another revolution, one that will be bigger, more solemn, and which will be the last." He opposes the "conditional equality" of the present, which has made of the people "filthy rabble," with the "real equality" of the future, which will break the chains of slavery. He invites the people to envision a

PRIMARY SOURCE

"MANIFESTO OF THE EQUALS"

People of France!

For fifteen centuries you lived as a slave and, consequently, unhappy. For the last six years you barely breathe, waiting for independence, freedom and equality.

EQUALITY! The first wish of nature, the first need of man, the first knot of all legitimate association! People of France! You were not more blessed than the other nations that vegetate on this unfortunate globe! Everywhere and at all times the poor human race, handed over to more or less deft cannibals, served as an object for all ambitions, as feed for all tyrannies. Everywhere and at all times men were lulled with beautiful words; at no time and in no place was the thing itself ever obtained through the word. From time immemorial they hypocritically repeat; *all men are equal;* and from time immemorial the most degrading and monstrous inequality insolently weighs upon the human race. As long as there have been human societies the most beautiful of humanity's rights is recognized without contra-

diction, but was only able to be put in practice one time: equality was nothing but a beautiful and sterile legal fiction. And now that it is called for with an even stronger voice we are answered: be quiet, you wretches! Real equality is nothing but a chimera; be satisfied with conditional equality; you're all equal before the law. What more do you want, filthy rabble? Legislators, you who hold power, rich landowners, it is now your turn to listen.

Are we not all equal? This principle remains uncontested, because unless touched by insanity, you can't say it's night when it's day.

Well then! We claim to live and die equal, the way we were born: we want this *real* equality or death; *that's* what we need.

And we'll have this real equality, at whatever price. Unhappy will be those who stand between it and us! Unhappy will be those who resist a wish so firmly expressed.

The French Revolution was nothing but a precursor of another revolution, one that will be bigger, more solemn, and which will be the last.

future more prosperous than the degraded present: "Groaning families, come sit at the common table set by nature for all its children." Maréchal casts the government of the Directory as "the enemies of the most natural order of things," political tyrants no less evil than the deposed monarchy intent on stalling the inevitable progress of democracy. In her essay in *Legitimating the Artist: Manifesto Writing and European Modernism* (2003), Luca Somigli notes that Maréchal repeatedly addresses the "People of France!" as a unitary body but makes clear that the people are actually divided. The critic writes, "There are in fact two addressees in the manifesto. Initially, using the familiar 'tous' [all], the text addresses 'the people,' the subjects of an unequal, unjust, and repressive social order. …Quickly, however, another addressee—the bourgeoisie whose counter-revolution has trampled over the aspirations of the first 'tous'— emerges."

The language of the "Manifesto of the Equals" is both reasoned and rousing. Maréchal undermines the intellectual foundations of the Directory government: "Are we not all equal? This principle remains uncontested, because unless touched by insanity, you can't say it's night when it's day." More stirring is his enlistment of the people in a noble project, a "holy enterprise" "more sublime and more just." As a call to action, Maréchal reminds the people that history

has bequeathed to them a lofty enterprise: "The purest of all glories was thus reserved for you! Yes it is you who first should offer the world this touching spectacle."

CRITICAL DISCUSSION

The "Manifesto of the Equals" was not authorized for publication because it did not receive unanimous acceptance among the Secret Directory, some of whom believed Maréchal had gone too far in advocating the destruction of existing institutions and culture with his declaration, "We consent to everything for [equality], *to make a clean slate so that we hold to it alone.* Let all the arts perish, if need be, as long as real equality remains!" The Conspiracy of the Equals had acquired 17,000 recruits by the time an army informant leaked the scheme to the government, quashing all plans for insurrection. Maréchal died in 1803 at the age of fifty-two, but Buonarroti lived into old age attempting to spearhead popular revolutions throughout Europe. When his *History of the Conspiracy of the Equals* appeared in 1828, the radical left lionized him as the high priest of socialism.

The "Manifesto of the Equals" and the Conspiracy of the Equals played only a small part in the French Revolution, but, thanks to Buonarroti's *History of the Conspiracy of the Equals,* their legacy has

The people marched over the bodies of kings and priests who were in league against it: it will do the same to the new tyrants, the new political Tartuffes seated in the place of the old.

What do we need besides equality of rights?

We need not only that equality of rights written into the Declaration of the Rights of Man and Citizen; we want it in our midst, under the roofs of our houses. We consent to everything for it, *to make a clean slate so that we hold to it alone.* Let all the arts perish, if need be, as long as real equality remains!

Legislators and politicians, you have no more genius than you do good faith; gutless and rich landowners, in vain you attempt to neutralize our holy enterprise by saying: They do nothing but reproduce that agrarian law asked for more than once in the past.

Slanderers, be silent: and in the silence of your confusion listen to our demands, dictated by nature and based on justice.

The Agrarian law, or the partitioning of land, was the spontaneous demand of some unprincipled soldiers, of some towns moved more by their instinct than by reason. We reach for something more sublime and more just: *the common good* or the *community of goods!* No more individual property in land: *the land belongs to no one.* We demand, we want, the common enjoyment of the fruits of the land: *the fruits belong to all.*

We declare that we can no longer put up with the fact that the great majority work and sweat for the smallest of minorities.

Long enough, and for too long, less than a million individuals have disposed of that which belongs to 20 million of their like, their equals.

Let it at last end, this great scandal that our descendants will never believe existed! Disappear at last, revolting distinctions between rich and poor, great and small, masters and servants, *rulers* and *ruled.*

SOURCE: Translated by Mitchell Abidor. Ph. Buonarroti. *La conspiration pour l'égalité*, Editions Sociales, Paris. 1957; translated for www.marxist.org. Copyright © marxists.org 2004 under the Creative Commons Attribute.

---

endured. Yet, given that this legacy has in large part resided in the interpretation and dissemination of the ideas presented by Buonarroti, a known partisan, scholars have found it difficult to exactly define the separate contributions of the three men. Despite this blurred background, the "Manifesto of the Equals" is judged the single most important summary statement of the Secret Directory's criticisms of the Directory. Political theorists and historians continue to debate whether the document adopts a position that is anarchic or libertarian, but its influence on the future course of social and political thought is overwhelmingly acknowledged. As one of the earliest subversive political manifestos, the "Manifesto of the Equals" foreshadowed socialist manifestos emanating from a variety of groups in the nineteenth and twentieth centuries, "texts," according to Hjartarson, "ranging from utopian socialists, through Marx and Engels to the Russian Bolsheviks."

Much discussion has been given over to Maréchal's call for the erasure of historical memory. This idea of a radical break with the past as the only possible avenue to a better future has been the basis for comparisons among Maréchal, the Romantics, and avant-garde movements of the nineteenth and early twentieth centuries. Perovic argues that Maréchal's gesture toward radical discontinuity was also a strategy devised to sidestep the new censorship laws. According to Perovic, Maréchal placed himself outside traditional legal mechanisms first by transferring the aim of political organization to a future revolution and then by claiming that this revolution would give birth to a society governed by universal reason, obviating the need for the mediation of political representation. The critic explains further, "[The] revolutionary transgressed all boundaries only in order to affirm that transgression was no longer possible because there was no authority higher than the naked truth. This, then, was the true meaning of a manifesto: it was written against all constitutions and all laws."

BIBLIOGRAPHY

Sources

Hjartarson, Benedikt. "Myths of Rupture: The Manifesto and the Concept of the Avant-Garde." *Modernism, Vol. 1.* Ed. Astradur Eysteinsson and Vivian Liska. Amsterdam: Benjamins, 2007. 173-94. Print.

Lyon, Janet. *Manifestoes: Provocations of the Modern.* Ithaca, NY: Cornell, 1999. Print.

Maréchal, Sylvain. *Manifesto of the Equals. The Communist Manifesto and Other Revolutionary Writings: Marx, Marat, Mao, Gandhi, and Others.* Ed. Bob Blaisdell. New York: Dover, 2003. 92-95. Print.

Perovic, Sanja. "Mediating Print Culture: Censorship, Revolutionary Journalism and the *Manifesto of Equals*." *Romanticism and Victorianism on the Net* 57-58 (2010). *érudit.org*. Web. 20 Aug. 2012.

Somigli, Luca. "Strategies of Legitimation: The Manifesto from Politics to Aesthetics." *Legitimating the Artist: Manifesto Writing and European Modernism, 1885-1915*. Toronto: U of Toronto, 2003. 29-92. Print.

Further Reading

Bernstein, Samuel. "Babeuf and Babouvism." *Science & Society* 2.1 (1937): 29-57. *JSTOR*. Web. 27 Aug. 2012.

Di Luchetti, Marco. "Appendix Q: Sylvain Maréchal's Corrective to Revolution." *Illuminati Manifesto of World Revolution*. By Nicholas Bonneville. Ed. and trans. Marco Di Luchetti. Charleston, SC: BookSurge, 2011. 313-32. Print.

Furet, François. "Babeuf." *A Critical Dictionary of the French Revolution*. Ed. François Furet and Mono Ozouf. Cambridge, MA: Belknap, 1989. 179-85. Print.

Palmer, R.R. "The French Directory between Extremes." *The Age of the Democratic Revolution. II, The Struggle*. Princeton, NJ: Princeton UP, 1964. 231-62. Print.

Rothbard, Murray N. "The Conspiracy of Equals." Ludwig von Mises Institute. *mises.org*. Web.27 Aug. 2012.

Janet Mullane

MANIFESTO OF THE PARIS COMMUNE OF 1871

Anonymous

OVERVIEW

Published in the short-lived communard newspaper *Paris Libre* on April 21, 1871, by leaders of the Paris Commune, the "Manifesto of the Paris Commune of 1871" demanded the resignation of the French government at Versailles and called for a return to a true republic in the aftermath of France's humiliating defeat in the Franco-Prussian War. The essay was part of an attempt by a loose conglomeration of elected French socialists in Paris to wrest power from the moderate provisional government seated in Versailles led by Adolph Thiers and to urge Parisians to fight against any of Thiers's further attempts to overthrow the commune. The text achieved its goals in the short term, but the Paris Commune was ultimately crushed by the French army with the massacre of 25,000 Parisians in May 1871 during the *Semaine Sanglante* (bloody week). Though the end of the commune devastated the workers' movement in France in the decade that followed, the essay and the commune would go on to inspire Karl Marx and Vladimir Lenin and would remain a general touchstone of labor politics well into the twentieth century.

The publication of the "Manifesto of the Paris Commune" marked the beginning of the end for the Paris Commune, but its demands for reforms to improve the lives of the French working class have proven more enduring. The essay's major demands were for basic social reforms such as the separation of church and state, the right to peaceful assembly, and the right to popular vote on public policy matters. Written after several skirmishes between commune forces and the French army, the text summarized once more the commune's goals, which had become increasingly difficult to narrow down given the lack of a clear leader in the commune. Nevertheless Parisians did succeed in the creation of workers' cooperatives and free, secular public education in working-class districts of Paris. Ironically, most contemporary scholars note that many of the reforms carried out in response to the essay were not socialist; for example, the commune made no move to nationalize the Bank of France or to seize private property. Communards did cause physical damage, such as demolishing the Vendome column and the Tuileries—both symbols of the military and the monarchy—but such destruction was not explicitly part of the commune's platform as it is outlined in the text. The commune ended within five weeks of the essay's publication. As an assertion of the will of the people, however, the "Manifesto of the Paris Commune" remained a source of inspiration to socialists worldwide.

HISTORICAL AND LITERARY CONTEXT

The "Manifesto of the Paris Commune of 1871" responds directly to the power vacuum created by the disastrous Franco-Prussian War, in which the French found themselves quickly overwhelmed by the forces of Otto von Bismarck and forced to accept a humiliating peace treaty at Versailles in January 1871. Parisians were still suffering the after effects caused by five months of siege by 200,000 Prussian soldiers in the winter of 1870-71 and felt increasingly marginalized by the new government at Versailles. The fact that Bismarck had demanded a victory parade through Paris as part of the treaty—and that Thiers had agreed to it—further inflamed Parisians who felt that the new Third Republic was far too moderate.

Furthermore, under the Second Empire of Napoleon III, workers had seen their rights increasingly eroded as a result of his authoritarian efforts to consolidate economic and political power. The commune and its subsequent essay represented a concerted effort by the Parisian population to restore basic rights lost during the empire and advance social reforms benefiting the middle and lower classes. Thirty-five of the ninety-two elected members of the communal council were manual laborers and craftspeople. Among their chief reforms were the elimination of back rent payments that had accumulated during the siege and the creation of cooperatives to take over abandoned workshops.

The Paris Commune was actually the second major worker uprising in the nineteenth century. The 1848 insurrection in Paris had set the precedent for such revolts, and that earlier uprising had greatly influenced the publication of Marx and Friedrich Engels's *Communist Manifesto* in 1848. The *Manifesto of the 60*, written by French socialist Henri Tolain in 1864, was another inspiration to the communards. Tolain's document demanded reforms for the proletariat, including the right to unionize and the right to strike.

❖ *Key Facts*

Time Period:
Late 19th Century

Movement/Issue:
Socialism

Place of Publication:
France

Language of Publication:
French

WHAT IS A COMMUNE?

Despite its historical association with radical workers' movements, a commune in France is quite simply the smallest administrative subdivision within the French republic (the others are *cantons, arrondissements, départements,* and *régions*). The rough equivalent of a municipality in the United States, a commune may be as large as that of Paris, with more than two million inhabitants, or a small village with only dozens. The modern French commune was established after the French Revolution, and its function and general organization remains much the same today as it was then. The mayor, who is elected, acts as the executive of the commune, managing the budget, hiring staff, and handling local responsibilities related to schools, waste removal, transportation, and general functioning of public services within the commune. In 2010 the French National Institute for Statistical and Economic Studies counted 36,682 communes in France. That the commune is such an integral part of modern French civic life is but further evidence of the disparity between the mythic status of the Paris Commune of 1871 and the reality of the event as a failed attempt to overthrow the more moderate Third Republic.

The "Manifesto of the Paris Commune of 1871" is most often discussed relative to the *Communist Manifesto.* Indeed, Marx wrote extensively about the 1871 commune in subsequent writings. In literature, many well-known French writers of the period immediately drew upon the disastrous events of the Paris Commune. Arthur Rimbaud's collection of poetry *Une Saison en enfer* (1873; *A Season in Hell*) contains poems filled with the violent imagery of siege and destruction, while Victor Hugo, who had witnessed the 1848 revolution as well, was critical of both sides and wrote a collection of poetry, *L'Année terrible* (1872; "The Terrible Year"), about the event.

THEMES AND STYLE

The central theme of the "Manifesto of the Paris Commune of 1871" is that the provisional government in Versailles has failed to follow the will of the people and that it therefore falls to the Paris Commune to create and govern the Third Republic according to the demands of the French. The communards are thus asserting their role as representatives of all the people of France. The text also places the blame for any deaths as a result of this struggle squarely on the shoulders of the Versailles government as a way to unite the broader populace against the provisional government in the event that civil war begins. The document asserts that "it is up to France"—that is, the commune and its allies—"to disarm Versailles through the solemn manifestation of its irresistible will."

The essay achieves its rhetorical tone by retelling the events that have led to its publication in simple terms. The writers juxtapose the lofty heritage and noble suffering of "France" and "Paris" against the "onerous centralization" and the "old governmental and clerical world" of "Versailles." The commune is positioned as the rightful heir to the ideals first laid out by the 1789 and 1848 revolutions, which called for a "new era of experimental, scientific politics." In both tone and content the text is a more lucid version of many of the editorials that appeared in *Paris Libre* during April and May 1871.

The "Manifesto of the Paris Commune of 1871" is organized into three parts and references previous French revolts in order to assert its legacy as the incarnation of the "modern" revolution. It opens with a stinging rejection of the Thiers government that has "delivered Paris to the foreigners," which is a "treason." The essay then lists the "inherent rights" of the commune, chief among these the "voluntary association of all local initiatives." It closes with a warning that civil war will surely come if the commune is threatened, for "victory, pursued with an indomitable energy by the National Guard, will go to the idea and to right." The text thus demands credibility as an official document and intentionally evokes the *Declaration of the Rights of Man and Citizen,* especially Article 2: "The aim of all political association is the preservation of the natural and imprescriptible rights of man. These rights are liberty, property, security, and resistance to oppression." By widening its scope to include all French people, the essay reached out to other cities in France that were sympathetic to the Paris Commune, most notably those in Lyons and Marseilles.

CRITICAL DISCUSSION

While Marx and Lenin wrote at length about the commune and the essay, the "Manifesto of the Paris Commune of 1871" also struck a chord with French historians in the nascent Third Republic. French critic and historian Hippolyte Taine viewed the insurrection as a chance to suppress the "bourgeois" and to "establish a Republic where workers like [him] are ministers and presidents." Historian and sociologist Ernest Renan was less enamored, believing that the communards were out of their depth and that "it is more essential to produce enlightened masses than it is to produce great geniuses and a public capable of understanding them."

After the commune, the essay remained an important reference for social and political revolutions worldwide, especially the intellectuals who hoped to lead them. Marx called the commune a "glorious harbinger of a new society" and a test of his ideas outlined in the *Communist Manifesto.* For Lenin, "the history of the Commune offered still timely rules for how workers might seize control of the state and then hold onto it." In the century and a half since the "Manifesto of the Paris Commune of 1871" was written, historians in particular continue to reevaluate its social and political legacy. In a 2007 essay in *Yale French Studies,* Tyler Stovall observes that with the end of the commune "revolutionary republicanism gave way to socialism as the principal utopian vision of social justice." Thus the 1871 manifesto has come to be viewed as a turning point in which the more radical French republican model outlined in the document was finally rejected in favor of the more moderate French socialist state that still exists today.

Contemporary scholars continue to study the commune largely in terms of its role within the broader discussion of the development of the modern French nation based on a shared, if somewhat embellished, past. Along with other historians, Stovall points out that the events of the commune and subsequent republic ironically "created the second greatest national empire of the modern era" in fin-de-siècle France. They also point to its significance as a text about the near-mythical role of courageous Parisians and the commune as a further crystallization of French national identity. Since the importance of the commune itself was largely inflated by subsequent generations (perhaps most importantly during the mass antigovernment protests students and workers started in May 1968), the "Manifesto of the Paris Commune of 1871" best represents the enduring disconnect between French republican goals for social welfare and the political reality of governing a modern Western nation whose economy is anchored by free trade.

BIBLIOGRAPHY

Sources

Gould, Roger V. *Insurgent Identities: Class, Community and Protest in Paris from 1848 to the Commune.* Chicago: U of Chicago P, 1995. Print.

Harison, Casey. "The Paris Commune of 1871, the Russian Revolution of 1905, and the Shifting of the Revolutionary Tradition." *History and Memory* 19.2 (2007): 5-42. Print.

Marx, Karl, and V.I. Lenin. *Civil War in France: The Paris Commune.* 1871. New York: International Publishers, 1988. Print.

Parsons, George. "The Politics of Paris." *AQ: Australian Quarterly* 80.2 (2008): 13-17. Print.

Stovall, Tyler. "The Myth of the Liberatory Republic and the Political Culture of Freedom in Imperial France." *Yale French Studies* 111 (2007): 89-103. Print.

Further Reading

Anderson, Benedict. *Imagined Communities: Reflections on the Origin and Spread of Nationalism.* 1983. London: Verso, 2006. Print.

Fermer, Douglas. *France at Bay, 1870-1871: The Struggle for Paris.* Barnsley: Pen and Sword, 2011. Print.

Greenman, Richard. "The Permanence of the Commune." *Massachusetts Review* 12.3 (1971): 388-96. Print.

Horne, Alistair. *The Fall of Paris: The Siege and the Commune 1870-71.* 1965. London: Penguin, 2007. Print.

Nora, Pierre. *Realms of Memory: Rethinking the French Past, Vol. 1—Conflicts and Divisions.* 1992. Trans. Arthur Goldhammer. New York: Columbia UP, 1996. Print.

Elizabeth Vitanza

Cover of the sheet music (circa 1900) for "La Communarde," a song glorifying the Paris Commune. "The Manifesto of the Paris Commune" clarified the ideas of the Commune's defenders. CCI/THE ART ARCHIVE AT ART RESOURCE, NY

THE MANIFESTO OF THE SOCIALIST LEAGUE

Ernest Belfort Bax, William Morris

❖ *Key Facts*

Time Period:
Late 19th Century

Movement/Issue:
Socialism

Place of Publication:
England

Language of Publication:
English

OVERVIEW

The Manifesto of the Socialist League (1885), primarily authored by William Morris and Ernest Belfort Bax, enumerates the positions and beliefs of the Socialist League as a whole, articulating broad rationales for socialist government and positioning the newly formed Socialist League within the complex socio-political landscape of late Victorian radicalism. The manifesto explains the reasons for the group's formation and specifies its positions on common property, redistribution of wealth, the replacement of "economical slavery" with "obligations to the community," the transformation of "modern bourgeois property-marriage" into more equal relations between the sexes, and the detachment of education from "commercialism on the one hand and superstition on the other." Morris and Bax then address other strategies for social transformation, including "Absolutism, Constitutionalism, Republicanism … Co-operation … [and] Nationalisation," identifying the drawbacks of each method before declaring that only a socialist revolution can solve the problems of class inequality and struggle. The manifesto is short, simple, and direct, presenting socialism as a rational solution to widespread social problems.

Because the Socialist League was small in both membership and influence, the publication of its manifesto did not have much impact. Although the members of the Socialist League included major figures of nineteenth-century socialism, such as Eleanor Marx (daughter of Karl Marx) and Morris himself, the league dissolved in 1901, having become a primarily anarchist organization and having lost the support of its founding socialist members. While the effect of the Socialist League as an individual organization was relatively small, the larger conversation about communalist social structures in which the Socialist League participated had major impacts on political history in the nineteenth and twentieth centuries.

HISTORICAL AND LITERARY CONTEXT

The highly stratified nature of Victorian society, in which social classes were separated by vast gulfs of wealth, education, and opportunity, created an environment in which socialist and democratic reforms were a perennial political hot topic. In the early Victorian era, Chartist reformers agitated for suffrage rights to be extended to working-class men and attempted to create a place for working-class voices in British government. Although the Chartist movement had largely collapsed by 1848, awareness of class struggle and inequality continued to be a significant force shaping Victorian leftist and radical politics. Toward the end of the century, a number of socialist societies and organizations focused on transforming class structures in Britain. These groups included the Democratic Federation (1881), the Fabian Society (1884), and the Social Democratic Foundation (SDF, 1884).

The 1885 publication of *The Manifesto of the Socialist League* marked the culmination of a year of particular dissention in the ranks of socialists. The Socialist League was founded in 1884 as a splinter group of the SDF. Writer and politician Henry Hyndman, the founder and leader of the SDF, was a controversial figure; Friedrich Engels, co-author of the *Communist Manifesto* (1848), repudiated Hyndman's work, and in 1885, Morris, Bax, Eleanor Marx, Edward Aveling, and others led a revolt against what they saw as Hyndman's involvement with parliamentary politics, which Morris characterized as a palliative that did little to aid the working poor. Abandoning the SDF as, in Eleanor Marx's words, "not *worth having*," these activists formed the Socialist League to advance the adoption of socialist principles in Britain without relying on parliamentary politics as a strategy.

The Manifesto of the Socialist League is most obviously indebted to the writings of Marx and Engels, quoting directly from the *Communist Manifesto* (which was written after an 1847 meeting of the Congress of the Communist League in London) and utilizing Marxist terminology to decry the alienation of the working classes from the means of production with which they worked. Morris and Bax were well positioned to be aware of socialist art and writing; they were the co-editors of the Socialist League's paper *The Commonweal,* a weekly publication financed privately by Morris. *The Commonweal* printed both poetry and polemics, and several of Morris's significant writings were originally published there.

Communist and socialist movements and manifestos such as that of the Socialist League had a profound effect on literature, influencing authors such as George Bernard Shaw, who was a member of and writer for the Fabian Society; H. G. Wells, who attended socialist lectures at Morris's Kelmscott

House and later explored extremes of social stratification in his speculative science fiction; children's novelist Edith Nesbit, who worked as an activist and lecturer for the Fabian Society and other socialist concerns; and Virginia Woolf, who combined socialist ideas with feminist and antiwar concerns in her work. In the mid-twentieth century, Marxist theory revolutionized literary criticism and the social sciences, giving scholars new language with which to discuss the impact of economic and social class systems on cultures and societies.

THEMES AND STYLE

The Manifesto of the Socialist League insists on the ubiquity of class struggle. In doing so, Morris and Bax resist being positioned as provocateurs; as their rhetoric seeks to make clear, although they are dedicated to struggling against class inequality, they are not the creators or originators of the struggle. Rather, they position their socialist activism as a counterblow in an ongoing war between rich and poor: "The profit-grinding system is maintained by competition, or veiled war, not only between the conflicting classes, but also within the classes themselves: there is always war among the workers for bare subsistence, and among their masters, the employers and middle-men, for the share of the profit wrung out of the workers." Morris and Bax identify many forms of class antagonism as part of a "ceaseless" overarching conflict, which on the workers' part can take the form of "open rebellion, sometimes of strikes, sometimes of mere widespread mendicancy and crime; but it is always going on in one form or other, though it may not always be obvious to the thoughtless looker-on." The manifesto seeks to recognize and name an extant conflict, rather than to create one from nothing.

The second half of the document furthers these aims by providing a list of socialist goals, innovations, and improvements. In clearly demarcated paragraphs, Morris and Bax briefly summarize the Socialist League's positions; they critique other proposed solutions to problems of social inequality with equal brevity. These points of argument and critique are presented in the style of a logical proof, with each point delivered in a simple, boiled-down form. Unlike longer and more complex communalist documents of the era, such as the *Communist Manifesto*, *The Manifesto of the Socialist League* presents the argument for class revolution in a minimalist and simplified fashion, relying on pointed clarity rather than complexity.

In style, the manifesto is clear, rational, and succinct. The authors employ a third-person-plural form of address, yoking them to their readers in a universalizing "we." It is noteworthy that this device conceals Morris and Bax's own upper-class origins, instead creating a sense of socialist solidarity in the face of class conflict that disregards the class background of its participants. Perhaps because of Morris and Bax's lack of direct experience of poverty or class oppression,

THE DESIGN OF THE MANIFESTO

Among his many other creative skills, William Morris was known for his work as a designer, printer, and binder of exceptionally beautiful books; his 1896 Kelmscott Press edition of the works of Geoffrey Chaucer is still admired as a masterpiece of book-making and illumination. The design of *The Manifesto of the Socialist League* balances Morris's characteristic concern for beauty with an awareness of the economic constraints of the work's audience. The manifesto was priced at a single penny, allowing it to be purchased, read, and circulated by the working people that the socialist activists aimed to aid.

The cover of the printed manifesto includes an illustration by Morris, which features the central figure of an angel, wings spread, holding a banner reading "The Socialist League"; around her head is a stylized halo reading "Educate." Workmen in the lower corners also bear banners, reading "Organize" and "Agitate," respectively. They are surrounded by twining oak branches laden with leaves and acorns—a nod, perhaps, to Morris's environmentalism. Universal access to art and beauty was a central tenet of Morris's socialism, and the manifesto reflects this by combining elegant design and decoration with a low price and a clear, straightforward text.

The Manifesto of the Socialist League avoids melodramatic descriptions of impoverished suffering, instead dwelling on the reasonable nature of socialist reform.

CRITICAL DISCUSSION

The political impact of the Socialist League was relatively small—both figuratively and literally, as membership in the group six months after its foundation totaled only 230 people across eight branches.

English designer, artist, writer, and socialist William Morris created this banner for the Socialist League he founded. PRIVATE COLLECTION/THE STAPLETON COLLECTION/ THE BRIDGEMAN ART

Although Morris and Bax followed the manifesto with a number of other pieces of socialist commentary, all published in *The Commonweal,* the league itself was relatively short-lived. In a March 1886 letter to a friend, Engels lamented that "Our good Bax and Morris, craving to do something (if only they knew what?), are restrained only by the fact that there is absolutely nothing to do … prospects are [by] no means bright." By 1887, tensions between activist and anarchist factions of the Socialist League were running high, and by 1889, the group had come to be dominated by anarchist interests. Morris was replaced as editor of *The Commonweal* in 1889, and by the autumn of 1890, he had left the Socialist League altogether. Bax rejoined the SDF, going on to edit its paper, *Justice.*

The history and the manifesto of the Socialist League have been largely forgotten outside of historical circles. Morris's fictional works on socialism, such as *The Dream of John Ball* (1888) and *News from Nowhere* (1890), are more widely remembered, and he had a major impact on a number of other fields, including historical preservation and interior design. However, the broader philosophy of socialism flourished in Britain before and after World War I, leading to the adoption of a number of socialist policies, including the institution of voting reforms, the establishment of a minimum legal wage, and the institution of socialized health care and education.

Scholarship on *The Manifesto of the Socialist League* tends to place it in one of two contexts: as part of the history of British socialism, as in the work of H. Tudor, who in *Marxism and Social Democracy* (1988) places Morris and Bax's manifesto in an ongoing multinational conversation about social revolution in the nineteenth century; or as part of Morris's massive creative oeuvre, which is so broad and wide-ranging that it has often posed a problem for critics trying to piece his medievalism, aestheticism, and socialism into a coherent whole. Recent criticism has investigated the peculiar connection between Bax's socialism and his vehement antifeminism; in *Equivocal Feminists: The Social Democratic Federation and the Woman Question, 1882-1911* (1996), Karen Hunt studies Bax as a representative of a larger complication in Victorian radicalism located at the intersection of class and gender concerns.

BIBLIOGRAPHY

Sources

Glasier, J. Bruce. *William Morris and the Early Days of the Socialist Movement.* London: Longmans, Green, 1921. Print.

Hunt, Karen. *Equivocal Feminists: The Social Democratic Federation and the Woman Question, 1882-1911.* New York: Cambridge UP, 1996. Print.

Kapp, Yvonne. *Eleanor Marx: Family Life (1855-1883).* London: Lawrence, 1972. Print.

Marx, Karl, and Friedrich Engels. *Karl Marx, Friedrich Engels: Collected Works.* Vol. 47. London: Lawrence, 1988. Print.

Morris, M. *William Morris: Writer, Artist, Socialist.* Vol. 2. New York: Russell, 1966. Print.

Morris, William, et al. "The Manifesto of the Socialist League." *The Victorian Age: An Anthology of Sources and Documents.* Ed. Josephine M. Guy. New York: Routledge, 1998. 193-98. Print.

Tudor, H., and J.M. Tudor, eds. *Marxism and Social Democracy: The Revisionist Debate, 1896-1898.* New York: Cambridge UP, 1988. Print.

Further Reading

Bevir, Mark. "Republicanism, Socialism, and Democracy in Britain: The Origins of the Radical Left." *Journal of Social History* 34.2 (2000): 351-68. Print.

Cowley, John. *The Victorian Encounter with Marx. A Study of Ernest Belfort Bax.* London: Tauris, 1993. Print.

Hale, Piers J. "Labor and the Human Relationship with Nature: The Naturalization of Politics in the Work of Thomas Henry Huxley, Herbert George Wells, and William Morris." *Journal of the History of Biology* 36.2 (2003): 249-84. Print.

Johnson, Graham. "'Making Reform the Instrument of Revolution': British Social Democracy, 1881-1911." *Historical Journal* 43.4 (2000): 977-1002. Print.

Laybourne, Keith. "The Failure of Socialist Unity in Britain c. 1893-1914." *Transactions of the Royal Historical Society* 6.4 (1994): 153-75. Print.

Livesay, Ruth. "Morris, Carpenter, Wilde, and the Political Aesthetics of Labor." *Victorian Literature and Culture* 32.2 (2004): 601-16. Print.

Salmon, Nicholas. *William Morris: Political Writings, Contributions to Justice and Commonweal 1883–1890.* Bristol: Thoemmes, 1994. Print.

Thompson, E.P. *William Morris: Romantic to Revolutionary.* London: Merlin, 1977. Print.

Carina Saxon

A MITE CAST INTO THE COMMON TREASURY

Robert Coster

OVERVIEW

Written by Robert Coster and published in December 1649, *A Mite Cast into the Common Treasury* is a political pamphlet written to vindicate the actions of the Diggers, a group of radical English activists who started farming and establishing small utopian communes on common land during a brief period from 1649 to 1650. Written after Coster's own Digger colony in Surrey was forced to relocate amid harassment and litigation from local landholders, the pamphlet impugns the legitimacy of those landholders' ownership of their land. In *A Mite Cast,* Coster decries the iniquity of economic social divisions and makes a case for the Diggers' actions as contributing to the breakdown of artificial socioeconomic barriers in order to bring about human equality. The text ends with a lengthy verse section that foresees a better future, despite the depredations the Diggers had suffered at the hands of England's entrenched societal institutions.

The pamphlet may well have validated and comforted Coster's fellow Diggers. It may also have popularized the movement to a very limited extent. The Diggers never gained a large number of adherents and remained a fringe group for their entire existence, failing to sway the attitudes of local landowners, who antagonized the Diggers until they ceased their social experiment. Despite its lack of impact in its own time, however, Coster's text is now seen, along with the numerous other Digger tracts published during the period, as an important and especially radical text of the populist ideology that came to the fore in public life during the English Civil Wars.

HISTORICAL AND LITERARY CONTEXT

A Mite Cast responds to the class-based exploitation prevalent in English society at the time, notwithstanding the revolutionary atmosphere and intragovernmental strife that attended the ongoing civil wars during the mid-seventeenth century. The pamphlet attacks the socioeconomic structure of England, which allowed wealthy landholders to amass huge amounts of money by charging large sums for rent, a situation exacerbated by the rising cost of living that accompanied the wars. Meanwhile, poor laborers hired to work on the land were paid very little, thus perpetuating society's unequal state. The situation was made even worse by

the church's tithing requirement, as well as by the gentry's frequent practice of enclosing common land for private use, thus cutting peasants off from an important source of livelihood.

When Coster's text was published in December 1649, the political climate was fractious and radical, although many of the nonconformist egalitarian movements had faded somewhat. The English Civil Wars, which resulted in the establishment of an English republic following the execution of King Charles I in January 1649, were accompanied by political agitation on behalf of the disenfranchised. Radicals included the reform-oriented Leveller movement, which enjoyed substantial influence for a while before the ideological atmosphere became more conservative and authoritarian by the end of 1649. Meanwhile, the eight-month-old Digger movement—never very popular—frequently endured harassment and legal prosecution from landowners, and it did not last through the following year.

Part of a large corpus of polemical Digger writing that appeared during the movement's brief history, *A Mite Cast* has several immediate predecessors in the work of Coster's own compatriots and is slightly more remotely descended from various writings within English egalitarian rhetoric in general. The pamphlet echoes the ideology and sentiments of other Digger tracts, especially those of Gerrard Winstanley (the primary leader and philosopher of the movement), whose *The True Levellers Standard Advanced* (1649) was the first major Digger text. A more distant precursor is the Leveller pamphlet *A Light Shining in Buckinghamshire* (1648), which adumbrates many of the Diggers' convictions about social inequality and oppression, although without suggesting the utopian activities central to the Digger movement.

Taken in isolation, *A Mite Cast* is not known to have had much influence on subsequent texts, but considered as a part of Digger writing in general, it may be seen as a noteworthy precursor to various future leftist polemics. Though it is generally Winstanley, rather than Coster, who is cited as the seminal figure in ideological history, *A Mite Cast* contains many of the same ideas as Winstanley's writings and may thus be plausibly grouped with them. Digger literature is now considered a foundational landmark of

❖ *Key Facts*

Time Period:
Mid-17th Century

Movement/Issue:
Land reform; Diggerism; Socialism

Place of Publication:
England

Language of Publication:
English

THE NORMAN YOKE

Robert Coster's assertion, found in many Digger tracts, that the institution of private property was founded on "Murther and Theft" is representative of a tendency in seventeenth-century English political writing to associate perceived tyranny and exploitation with the Norman Conquest of Britain in 1066. Many English believed that, prior to the Norman invasion, Britain existed as an idyllic and egalitarian Anglo-Saxon society, free from oppression and injustice. The Normans shattered this paradisiacal state, bringing war and slaughter, followed by autocracy and subjugation. Traditional British rights were lost but not forgotten.

Seventeenth-century social injustices were thus seen as the latest manifestation of this "Norman Yoke," a historical concept that allowed English reformers to combine their revolutionary ideas with an appeal to a mythical, idealized Anglo-Saxon past. The Diggers were neither the first nor the last group to make rhetorical use of this theory. In addition to its use by them and the Levellers, the Norman Yoke was drawn upon by the Whigs of the English Restoration period, as well as by individuals as varied as Thomas Jefferson, Catharine Macaulay, John Cartwright, and Thomas Paine, fading permanently from political eminence only in the nineteenth century, though it has remained an important part of England's national mythology.

English agrarian communism and thus holds a significant place in the history of political rhetoric, despite its relative lack of verifiable direct influence on later manifestos.

THEMES AND STYLE

Central to *A Mite Cast*'s themes is the conviction that the Diggers' activities represent a way to circumvent the tyrannous institution of private property and bring society closer to the free state intended by God, who bequeathed the earth to all people equally. Coster asks rhetorically "whether particular propriety was not brought into the roome of publick Community by Murther and Theft" and goes on to imply that, after the deposition of Charles I, whatever claim of ownership the "Lords of Mannors" have over England's common land is now invalid since their claim had been derived "meerly from the Kings Will, (which Will proving a Burthen to the Nation, caused the King to loose his head)." The Diggers' cultivation of common land is thus not merely legitimate but salutary to England as a whole, because it gives poor laborers a way to support themselves without contributing to the vast, ill-gotten income of wealthy landowners: "if the Lords of Mannors, and Other Gentlemen, had not those great bagges of mony brought into them … then there might be an acknowledgment of one another to be fellow-Creatures."

The text's rhetorical approach is marked by frequent invocations of scripture, combined with a thoroughgoing rejection of entrenched authority. The prose section of the pamphlet begins and ends with biblical justifications of Coster's assertions, with the very first sentence asking "whether all men (by the grant of God) are not alike free, and all to enjoy the Earth with the fulness thereof alike (Geneses)." However, the church, being a significant contributor to poverty through its collection of tithes, generally comes under fire, as when Coster indicates that cruelty and rapacity "lie lurking under fig-leave Clothing, such as Sabboth, Fasting, and Thanksgiving dayes, Doctrines, Formes, and Worships." Secular authority is likewise castigated when Coster asserts that if the oppressed poor are denied access to the earth, they "will be necessitated to make a breach of the Lawes of the Nation." Significantly, however, he nonetheless takes care to emphasize the legality of the Diggers' activities.

Stylistically, *A Mite Cast* is characterized by religiously impassioned prose and a beleaguered but ultimately optimistic tone. About half of the prose section consists of rhetorical questions, while the other half is devoted to confident declaration, as when Coster argues for the legitimacy of the Digger colonies by saying that "there is no Statute-Law in the Nation that doth hinder the common people from seizing upon their own Land (but onely the mercinary wills of men) and therefore where there is no Law, there is no transgression." Likewise, the verse section is essentially a paean to Digger fortitude and the rightness of the cause, asserting that "Though stripes we receive, / We do them forgive, / Which acts such cruelty" and looking forward to the realization of an egalitarian English society: "The glorious State / Which I do relate / Unspeakable comfort shall bring." The zealous confidence of the pamphlet's writing style reflects its rhetorical project of positioning the Diggers' actions as divinely sanctioned, despite society's intolerance and persecution.

CRITICAL DISCUSSION

A Mite Cast, considered in combination with similar Digger works published during the movement's brief duration, was received somewhat congenially among certain English reformers, though many landowners and less radical activists reacted negatively. Some of the more Left-leaning Levellers looked favorably upon the ideas propounded in Coster's pamphlet. Fenner Brockway observes in his 1980 study of Civil War-era English reformers that "despite [Leveller John] Lilburne's criticism of them, there was considerable sympathy with the Diggers among the Levellers." Many of the more moderate (and influential) Levellers, however, were anxious to dissociate themselves from the Diggers, with whom they were sometimes equated by conservatives. Many of those conservatives were landowners who reacted to the Diggers' actions and rhetoric with fierce suppression, a situation not helped by Coster's prose, which threatened the established order more explicitly than certain other Digger works.

The legacy of *A Mite Cast* is bound up with that of Digger literature as a whole, which stands as a significant early elaboration of English utopian communism. David W. Petegorsky's 1940 analysis of the Digger movement asserts that "the impact of the Diggers on the political thought of their period does not seem to have been much more significant than their influence on the course of events." Starting in the late nineteenth century, however, the movement increasingly came to be seen as a philosophically groundbreaking early instance of radical leftist ideology, hence the San Francisco Diggers, a collectivist theatrical group active in the 1960s who appropriated their name from the seventeenth-century movement. Contemporary scholarship continues to gauge the significance of the Diggers' legacy, as well as contextualize the work within the ideological climate of its historical milieu.

Scholarship rarely focuses specifically on *A Mite Cast,* which is generally subsumed into discussions of the Digger movement as a whole. These discussions tend to downplay Coster, a relatively unimportant figure about whom very little is known, in favor of Winstanley. J.C. Davis's *Utopia and the Ideal Society* (1981) discusses Winstanley at length but singles out Coster's pamphlet as containing "one of the best descriptions" of the economic revolution the Diggers hoped to bring about by withdrawing labor from the exploitative system. Likewise, Winthrop S. Hudson's 1946 essay differentiating Winstanley's thought (and hence that of the Diggers) from Marxism similarly treats Winstanley as the ideological representative of the movement, citing Coster—who largely echoed Winstanley's assertions—only in passing.

Robert Coster was affiliated with the Diggers, an agrarian movement promoting agrarian reform in seventeenth-century England. This mosaic is in Cobham, Surrey, England, an area that was the center of Digger activities. © HOMER SYKES/ALAMY

BIBLIOGRAPHY

Sources

Brockway, Fenner. *Britain's First Socialists: The Levellers, Agitators and Diggers of the English Revolution.* London: Quartet Books, 1980. Print.

Coster, Robert. "A Mite Cast into the Common Treasury." *The Works of Gerrard Winstanley.* 1941. Ed. George H. Sabine. New York: Russell & Russell, 1965. 655-61. Print.

Davis, J.C. *Utopia and the Ideal Society: A Study of English Utopian Writing, 1516-1700.* Cambridge: Cambridge UP, 1981. Print.

Hudson, Winthrop S. "Economic and Social Thought of Gerrard Winstanley: Was He a Seventeenth-Century Marxist?" *Journal of Modern History* 18.1 (1946): 1-21. *JSTOR.* Web. 25 Sept. 2012.

Petegorsky, David W. *Left-Wing Democracy in the English Civil War: A Study of the Social Philosophy of Gerrard Winstanley.* 1940. New York: Haskell House, 1972. Print.

Further Reading

Bradstock, Andrew, ed. *Winstanley and the Diggers, 1649-1999.* London: Frank Cass, 2000. Print.

Chakravarty, Prasanta. *"Like Parchment in the Fire": Literature and Radicalism in the English Civil War.* New York: Routledge, 2006. Print.

Cherniak, Warren. "Civil Liberty in Milton, the Levellers and Winstanley." *Prose Studies* 22.2 (1999): 101-20. Print.

Gurney, John. *Brave Community: The Digger Movement in the English Revolution.* Manchester: Manchester UP, 2007. Print.

Hill, Christopher. *The World Turned Upside Down: Radical Ideas during the English Revolution.* New York: Viking, 1972. Print.

Hopton, Andrew, ed. *Digger Tracts, 1649-50.* London: Aporia, 1989. Print.

Kennedy, Geoff. *Diggers, Levellers, and Agrarian Capitalism: Radical Political Thought in Seventeenth Century England.* Lanham: Lexington Books, 2008. Print.

McDowell, Nicholas. *The English Radical Imagination: Culture, Religion, and Revolution, 1630-1660.* Oxford: Oxford UP, 2003. Print.

James Overholtzer

A New Engagement, or, Manifesto

Levellers

✛ *Key Facts*

Time Period:
Mid-17th Century

Movement/Issue:
Leveller movement;
Political reform

Place of Publication:
England

Language of Publication:
English

OVERVIEW

A New Engagement, or, Manifesto is a declaration prepared by the Levellers in 1648 to set forth their grievances against English statesman Oliver Cromwell's Parliament and to make demands for a more equitable government. While *A New Engagement* declares the "sence and resolution of many thousands of well-affected people in and about London, and some adjacent counties," it owes most of its claims to the political philosophy of the three Leveller leaders: Richard Overton, John Lilburne, and William Walwyn. These men actively opposed Cromwell's government and banded together officially in 1647, one year before *A New Engagement* was composed, to form the Leveller party, which thereafter grew rapidly. Like the party's other pamphlets, the manifesto is an appeal for the unity of and a declaration from the common people, and a call for political and social justice. At the manifesto's heart are sixteen demands for political change.

As one of many Leveller manifestos, *A New Engagement* contributed to the Leveller influence in mid-seventeenth-century England. It captures several Leveller concerns, particularly that political power not be consolidated in the hands of any individual ruler or group of rulers and that the middle class be given power to elect its own representatives. Ultimately, the Levellers did not achieve these goals; however *A New Engagement* is part of the Levellers' contribution to political thought. For example, the manifesto's first half lists ills that are echoed in the American Declaration of Independence (1776)—such as the problem of government without representation—and suggests solutions that were finally included in the American political system. Thus, although the manifesto did not result in direct political reform, it helped to solidify the Levellers' place as a significant historical movement.

HISTORICAL AND LITERARY CONTEXT

A New Engagement exemplifies concerns predominant in England in the 1640s. In 1642 the first of the English Civil Wars began between King Charles I and Parliament; it ended in 1646 when the Parliamentarians captured the king. In 1648, the year *A New Engagement* was published, war resumed when King Charles escaped and joined forces with Scotland, though he was later defeated by Cromwell. During this turmoil, the Levellers organized to protect the interests of the middle class, particularly the rank and file in the English army. The Levellers feared King Charles, but when they perceived that Parliament inflicted its own privations, they began to call for general governmental decentralization.

Responding to unrest in the English army, the Levellers proposed that leaders should be held to strict account to ensure the people's religious and economic freedom. In *A New Engagement,* the authors call the army, at that time still under parliamentary authority, to join their side against Parliament in order to receive a good political and social reward for its service. More broadly, they appeal to the once-prosperous middle classes who had suffered through the civil wars and now wanted a government that would make those sacrifices worthwhile. Among other issues, the Levellers grapple with high taxes, religious intolerance, legal equality, and government without representation. Despite these general appeals, the Leveller program never came to political fruition. Their attempt at working together with the army fell apart on questions of religious tolerance and equal franchise. Although the Levellers continued to be advocates of peace and the sanctity of common law, they never gained full political power.

A New Engagement was one of many manifestos composed by the Levellers, who were some of the most prolific English pamphleteers in the mid-seventeenth century. Nostalgic for an ideal English past, they often used a style that echoed the Magna Carta, which, written in 1215, required the monarch to act within parameters established by the people. Since people's rights were central to the Leveller agenda, *A New Engagement* opens with the statement that it is a resolution from the people to their government. By employing this language, the Levellers adopt the stance of citizens fighting for their rights. This attitude pervades other Leveller documents, too. For example, among the party's most important manifestos is the *Agreement of the People,* a text that summarizes the resolutions of the English common people fighting for their rights against an oppressive government.

Although *A New Engagement* did not have a long lasting impact as an individual piece, it exemplifies the Levellers' political philosophy, which became foundational for the composition of documents by subsequent groups. The American Declaration of Independence, for example, written in 1776, opens as a statement from the common people to an oppressive English government. It draws upon the conventional language of last resort used in *A New Engagement*. It is also based on *A New Engagement*'s broadly humanistic philosophy. Therefore, while the Levellers may not be well known to twenty-first-century audiences, their literary tropes have shaped the rhetoric of freedom that persists in modern political systems.

THEMES AND STYLE

The foundational idea of *A New Engagement* is that government has failed to secure peace and prosperity for the common citizen and that England must be restored by decentralizing the political system. Drawing upon the rhetoric of natural freedom, the document opens by claiming that "THE freedom we were born to, is so justly due to every English man," and by reminding its readers that the English people have zealously fought for this freedom in the recent past. Thus, the document addresses both "thousands of well-affected people" and the standing army. Furthermore, *A New Engagement* states that instead of obtaining the peace and prosperity they had hoped for, the people have found themselves "more slaves every day" to Parliament's high taxes and arbitrary harshness. They have been made subject to "corruption," "tediousness," "changeableness," and "obscurity." To counteract these problems, the document outlines five particular concerns and then offers sixteen ways to achieve political, social, and economic rest.

A New Engagement maintains its rhetorical effect by appealing to a sense of united Englishness and a desire for national prosperity. It repeats "the people," "the English man," and "the people's good," and calls upon the commonwealth to emphasize its vision of a nation of independent, concerned citizens. The primary solution to England's problems is political: the manifesto's first demand is that "a period of time be set wherein this present Parliament shal certainly end." Subsequently, it demands that officeholders be restricted to one- or two-year appointments, that huge bodies of complex and restrictive laws be repealed, and that members of Parliament be forced to sign a promise to defend the people's freedoms. After listing these political changes, the manifesto appeals to the middle class in general and to the army in particular. It emphasizes the predations of the recent war, particularly high taxes and the decay of trade. Among other solutions, *A New Engagement* calls for an account to be rendered of government spending, for the excise tax to be abolished, and for "no less care taken for the growing wealth of the Nation, consisting principally in trade." The manifesto demands an end to slavery—not racial slavery but a form of indentured servitude.

A New Engagement relies on a tone of virtuous outrage. Its authors state in the first paragraphs that they "carry our lives in our hands" to make this plea

RICHARD OVERTON, JOHN LILBURNE, AND WILLIAM WALWYN: LEVELLER LEADERS

Among the Levellers' best-known leaders, Richard Overton, John Lilburne, and William Walwyn were integral to the movement. Before the Levellers became an organized party, each of the three men was already a notable pamphleteer. Much of their writing had been part of the struggle for religious freedom, in which each had taken part. On this point they were unusual for the times since they argued for religious freedom for all, including for Roman Catholics and Jews, two groups that were often persecuted. In addition to this shared experience, Lilburne and Overton had suffered imprisonment in 1647, after the Levellers became a formalized group in 1645. This political harassment only fueled their pamphleteering rhetoric.

Despite their similar backgrounds, however, the three men had different personal concerns, a fact that contributed to the Levellers' eventual demise. Lilburne, a charismatic leader, tended to focus on religious questions, whereas Overton preferred to place social issues first, particularly those most pressing in London. Walwyn, on the other hand, had a more philosophical bent. This disparity in interests and leadership styles prevented the group from having a consistent, unified platform from which to work. During their heyday, however, their pamphleteering experience allowed them to be highly successful at stirring up popular zeal for their cause.

since they have been previously unjustly imprisoned by Parliament. They defend their "irregular manner of prosecuting our un-doubted rights" by claiming to have exhausted all other means. Far from dispassionate, the authors say that tithes have been "rigorously and cruelly" exacted, call the commonwealth's state "deplorable," and use adjectives such as "barbarous" for Parliament. This highly charged emotional language clashes with the methodical list of changes presented, thereby heightening the manifesto's tension. Behind the carefully reasoned political suggestions, the authors claim, is a righteous wellspring of moral concern for the nation's welfare.

CRITICAL DISCUSSION

As a product of the Levellers, *A New Engagement* shares its authors' fate. In an essay in *Literature Criticism from 1400 to 1800* (2000), F.D. Dow summarizes their situation: "In their heyday ... the Levellers exhibited great flair in exciting the popular imagination and dramatizing public events," as *A New Engagement* successfully does with its emotionally charged rhetoric. Ultimately, though, Dow writes, they "alienated key groups above them," "failed to consolidate their appeal to the middling orders whose interests they especially represented," and "neglected or were actively hostile to

THE

Declaration and Standard

Of the *Levellers* of England;
Delivered in a Speech to his Excellency the Lord Gen. *Fairfax*,
on *Friday* last at White-Hall, by Mr. *Everard*, a late Member of the
Army, and his Prophesie in reference thereunto; shewing what will
befall the Nobility and Gentry of this Nation, by their submitting to
community; With their invitation and promise unto the people, and
their proceedings in *Windsor* Park, *Oatlands* Park, and severall other
places; also, the Examination and confession of the said Mr. *Everard*
before his Excellency, the manner of his deportment with his Hat on,
and his severall speeches and expressions, when he was commanded
to put it off. Together with a List of the severall Regiments of Horse
and Foot that have cast Lots to go for *Ireland*.

Imprinted at *London*, for *G. Laurenson*, *April 23. 1649.*

"The Declaration and Standard of the Levellers," a woodcut print dated April 23, 1649. The Levellers wrote prolifically to protest the English government of the seventeenth century. PRIVATE COLLECTION/THE BRIDGEMAN ART LIBRARY

those below them in the social scale." Even though *A New Engagement* seems to be aimed at the middle class, it does not address the upper or lower classes. Furthermore, despite their attempt at a common voice, the Levellers garnered criticism from contemporary thinkers for being irreligious. *A New Engagement* exemplifies this issue since it makes almost no direct religious claims. To counteract this accusation, in 1649 the Levellers wrote *A Manifestation,* which synthesizes Puritan ideology with their claims about natural law. By this time, however, the party's influence as a political movement was already declining. Attempts by supporters to stir up mutinies in the army had been repressed, and soon sectarian interests started to undermine the Levellers' general appeal. This division in their ranks, along with the death or imprisonment of their leaders, resulted in the Levellers' gradual disintegration as a political party.

Since *A New Engagement* never stood alone historically but was part of the anonymous work of the Leveller movement, most critical responses treat the party's philosophy and rhetoric as a whole but not the text alone. The appeal for decentralized government

made by *A New Engagement,* for example, was typical of Leveller philosophy and became a forerunner of late-eighteenth-century political thought. Indeed, the American Declaration of Independence rests on Leveller ideas. Recently critics such as Michael W. Spicer, in a 2004 article in *Administrative Theory & Praxis,* have discussed at length the similarities between Leveller philosophy and the American political system. In a review of Michael Mendle's *The Putney Debates of 1647: The Army, the Levellers, and the English State* (2003), Joyce Lee Malcolm describes the Levellers as "a group scarcely suffering from neglect," an accurate assessment of the Levellers and their writing, supported by an array of recent critical, literary, and historical works.

Much recent scholarship has considered the Levellers' political philosophy and rhetorical strategies. Christopher Hill's groundbreaking work *The World Turned Upside Down* (1972) establishes the scholarly foundation for debates surrounding the Levellers' influence. In response to Hill, Nicholas McDowell in *The English Radical Imagination* (2003) attempts to argue for a new analysis of the Levellers' "rhetorical strategies, stylistic devices, and discursive contexts." Other scholars have followed more specialized threads. For instance, in a 2005 article in *Huntington Library Quarterly,* Martin Dzelzainis considers the Levellers' ideology in relation to English poet John Milton's philosophy. Dzelzainis situates "Milton in relation to the radicalized vision of 'Anglobritannia' that developed in the late 1640s" as a consequence of Leveller influence. Thus, while some contemporary scholars pursue questions about the Levellers' role in shaping modern political structures, others consider the party's influence in its own historical moment, not only in politics but also in literature.

BIBLIOGRAPHY

Sources

Dow, F.D. "The Levellers." *Literature Criticism from 1400 to 1800.* Ed. Marie Lazzari. Vol. 51. Detroit: Gale Group, 2000. 200-313. *Literature Criticism Online.* Web. 30 Aug. 2012.

Dzelzainis, Martin. "History and Ideology: Milton, the Levellers, and the Council of State in 1649." *Huntington Library Quarterly* 68.1-2 (2005): 269-87. Web. 30 Aug. 2012.

Malcolm, Joyce Lee. Rev. of *The Putney Debates of 1647: The Army, the Levellers, and the English State,* by Michael Mendle. *The Journal of Interdisciplinary History* 33.4 (Spring 2003): 615-16. Web. 30 Aug. 2012.

McDowell, Nicholas. *The English Radical Imagination: Culture, Religion, and Revolution, 1630-1660.* Oxford: Oxford UP, 2003. Print.

A New Engagement, or, Manifesto. London: n.p., 1648. Web. 30 Aug. 2012.

Spicer, Michael W. "The English Levellers and American Public Administration." *Administrative Theory & Praxis* 26. 4 (2004): 566-87. *JSTOR.* Web. 30 Aug. 2012.

Further Reading

Chakravarty, Prasanta. *"Like Parchment in the Fire": Literature and Radicalism in the English Civil War.* New York: Routledge, 2006. Print.

Hawes, Clement. *Mania and Literary Style: The Rhetoric of Enthusiasm from the Ranters to Christopher Smart.* Cambridge: Cambridge UP, 1996. Print.

Hill, Christopher. *The World Turned Upside Down: Radical Ideas during the English Revolution.* New York: Viking, 1972. Print.

Lilburne, John. *A Manifestation from Lieutenant Col. John Lilburne, Mr. William Walwyn, Mr. Thomas Prince, and Mr. Richard Overton* … London: n.p., 1649. Print.

Mendle, Michael, ed. *The Putney Debates of 1647: The Army, the Levellers, and the English State.* Cambridge: Cambridge UP, 2001. Print.

Overton, Richard. *A Remonstrance of Many Thousand Citizens* … London: n.p., 1646. Print.

Robinson, Marsha S. "The English Radical Imagination: Culture, Religion, and Revolution, 1630-1660." *Renaissance Quarterly* 57.4 (2004): 1495-96+. *Literature Resource Center.* Web. 30 Aug. 2012.

Vallance, Edward Woodbridge. *Revolutionary England and the National Covenant: State Oaths, Protestantism, and the Political Nation, 1553-1682.* Rochester: Boydell, 2005. Print.

Walwyn, William. *The Writings of William Walwyn.* Athens: U of Georgia P, 1989. Print.

Evelyn Reynolds

PEOPLE'S CHARTER

William Lovett

✣ *Key Facts*

Time Period:
Mid-19th Century

Movement/Issue:
Workers' rights;
Democratic reform

Place of Publication:
England

**Language of
Publication:**
English

OVERVIEW

Composed primarily by William Lovett, the *People's Charter* (1838) describes a history of discrimination affecting Britain's working classes and demands electoral reforms aimed at remedying injustice. Although the manifesto, addressed to "the People of the United Kingdom," was composed primarily by Lovett, it purported to be the work of a twelve-member committee divided equally between Members of Parliament and members of the London Working Men's Association. Recent scholarship, however, has suggested that the committee was a fiction aimed at bolstering the manifesto's credibility and that Lovett drafted it in its entirety with input from social reformer Francis Pace and radical Member of Parliament John Roebuck. Lovett's collaboration with the more affluent Roebuck attests to the fact that the manifesto was designed to garner the support of citizens from all classes of society. Central to the manifesto are six demands aimed at extending suffrage and Parliamentary representation to members of the working classes.

Initially rejected by some radicals as too conservative, the *People's Charter* and its modest demands eventually achieved support that extended beyond the working classes. It engendered a political movement known as Chartism that was active for at least a decade. Although Parliament refused to take up the *People's Charter* on each of the three occasions when it was brought before the House of Commons (1839, 1842, and 1848), five of the manifesto's six points would be embraced by Parliament over the course of the next century (the only point not accepted was a call for annual Parliamentary elections). The *People's Charter* is considered among the most important political documents of the nineteenth century and is recognized as a significant influence on later labor movements around the globe.

HISTORICAL AND LITERARY CONTEXT

The *People's Charter* responds to the political and economic crises facing Britain in the late 1830s, when the struggles of the working classes were intensified by poor trade, low wages, and legal reforms aimed at reducing pauperism. In 1832 the First Reform Bill had extended voting rights to the middle classes and substantial tenant farmers. It had, however, pointedly excluded the working classes from the scope of its reform, a move that left many of its advocates feeling betrayed. The sense of economic injustice was heightened in 1834 with the passage of the Poor Law Amendment Act, or New Poor Law, which eliminated public charity other than austere workhouses. Unrest further intensified with the arrests, trials, and transportation of several high-profile trade unionists for their political activities.

By the time the *People's Charter* was written, working opposition to existing socioeconomic policies was strong but not well organized. Among the most vocal advocates for change was the London Working Men's Association, which had formed in 1836 in order to further the rights of the working classes. Lovett was one of the organization's founding members. When the *People's Charter* appeared in 1838, it provided a platform around which trade unions, working men's associations, and radical reading groups in both rural and urban areas could coalesce. Chartism, the movement that the manifesto engendered, would remain a strong force in England until 1848, and five of its six goals would come to fruition over the course of the next century.

The *People's Charter* draws on a history of declarations of the rights of English citizens that can be traced back to another charter, the Magna Carta. Written in 1215, the Magna Carta limited the powers of the English monarch by claiming rights for the English people. The writers of the *People's Charter* framed their work as a new Magna Carta that would rescue the working classes from the whims of a Parliament in which they had no representation, just as the earlier charter had protected citizens from the whims of kings. In composing their manifesto, Lovett drew extensively on John Cartwright's 1777 pamphlet *The Legislative Rights of Commonalty Vindicate; or, Take Your Choice,* which was known to him through its influence on a series of demands made in 1780 by citizens of Westminster.

In the decades following its publication, the *People's Charter* inspired a large body of literature supporting the manifesto and its key demands. Beginning with works of political journalism in radical working-class papers such as the *Northern Star,* Chartist writers quickly branched out to develop an extensive tradition of poetry, among the most notable works of which are

Thomas Cooper's *The Purgatory of Suicides* (1846) and Ernest Jones's *The New World* (1850). Although many Chartist writers initially eschewed fiction out of a fear that it would prevent their political concerns from being taken seriously, Chartist literature eventually grew to include the fiction of writers such as Cooper and Thomas Martin Wheeler, whose *Sunshine and Shadow* (1849-50) is among the best-known Chartist novels. Today Chartist literature, while not as well known as the industrial fiction of canonical middle-class novelists such as Charles Dickens and Elizabeth Gaskell, continues to command significant scholarly interest.

THEMES AND STYLE

The central theme of the *People's Charter* is that Britain's government has failed in its duty to all citizens by excluding the working classes from the electoral process. With the force of the Magna Carta echoing behind it, the manifesto opens with an appeal to the responsibilities of Britain's elected government: "Whereas, to insure, in as far as possible by human forethought and wisdom, the just government of the people, it is necessary to subject those who have the power of making the laws to a wholesome and strict responsibility to those whose duty it is to obey them when made." To this end, the manifesto outlines its six points: annual Parliamentary elections, universal male suffrage, equal voting districts, no property qualification for voting, voting by secret ballot, and payment for service in Parliament in order to make such service financially viable for members of the working classes.

The manifesto achieves its rhetorical effect through appeals to a British unity that transcends social class. This sense of unity is primarily accomplished through the repeated use of the term "the people." Addressing a broad audience of "the People of the United Kingdom," the *People's Charter* envisions a single, inclusive, public body, whose interests are unified and to whom the legislative body ought to be accountable. The best legislature, the opening paragraphs of the manifesto suggest, is one that "emanates directly from, and is immediately subject to, the whole people, and which completely represents their feelings and their interests." Notably absent from the manifesto, despite its appeals to unity and universal suffrage, is any reference to the voting rights of women. Although they were actively involved in the movement, women were excluded from proposed reforms out of a fear that a demand for female suffrage would be so controversial that it would guarantee the charter's defeat.

Stylistically, the *People's Charter* is distinguished by its formality. Modeled after the Magna Carta and employing the official language expected in a piece of legal writing, the manifesto demands credibility as an official document. It also uses Parliament's own tools to attack the legislature for its

WILLIAM LOVETT: SOCIAL REFORMER

Remembered for his role in writing the *People's Charter*, William Lovett was a social reformer who dedicated his life to reforms benefiting the working classes. Prior to his involvement with Chartism, Lovett was active in the movement that culminated in the Reform Bill in 1832. He was a committed trade unionist and an advocate of making reading materials accessible to workers. He partnered with other working-class radicals to fight for the repeal of taxes that made newspapers prohibitively expensive for laborers.

After the Reform Bill failed to extend benefits to the working classes, Lovett joined with Henry Hetherington and others to found the London Working Men's Association in 1836 and was a driving force in the production of the *People's Charter*. He was elected secretary of the Chartist Convention in February 1839. A few months later, however, he was arrested after he publicly berated police for using force to break up a Chartist gathering in Birmingham. He was convicted of seditious libel and sentenced to twelve months in prison. While incarcerated, Lovett composed "Chartism, a New Organisation of the People," outlining plans for improving the working classes through education. After his release from prison in 1840, he devoted the remainder of his life to efforts aimed at educating laborers and their children.

failure to respect "the people's wishes, feelings, and interests." Simultaneously, by framing the charter as a draft parliamentary act and petitioning Parliament to consider it as legislation, Lovett ostensibly demonstrates the fitness of the working classes for participation in the electoral activities from which they had been excluded. Although its legal pretense renders the *People's Charter* somewhat dispassionate in tone, the manifesto achieves its force through its careful manipulation of the conventions of the system it seeks to reform.

CRITICAL DISCUSSION

When the *People's Charter* was first published in 1838, it received mixed reactions both within and outside the working-class circles. Some working-class activists, including *Northern Star* proprietor Feargus O'Connor, initially felt that the demands outlined in the manifesto did not go far enough. For many in the middle and upper classes, working-class supporters of the charter were a threatening force. For others, particularly working-class citizens, the *People's Charter* offered hope in a bleak time. Frank F. Rosenblatt's 1916 book *The Chartist Movement* describes a situation in which "the masses were imbued with the hope that the People's Charter would bring about complete salvation." Even many middle-class intellectuals saw the power of the movement, even if they were not in complete agreement with its cause or its methods. In *Chartism* (1840) Thomas Carlyle recognized that "the matter of

Chartists enter Newport, Monmouthshire, Wales, to free Chartist prisoners held at the Westgate Hotel. © LEBRECHT MUSIC AND ARTS PHOTO LIBRARY/ ALAMY

Chartism is weighty, deep-rooted, far-extending; it did not begin yesterday; will by no means end this day or to-morrow."

After the Chartist movement died out following the final rejection of the *People's Charter* by Parliament in 1848, the manifesto remained an important source of working-class pride and political inspiration. In his introduction to *The Literature of Struggle* (1995), an anthology of fiction from the Chartist movement, Ian Haywood describes the manifesto as "the expression and symbol of a disenfranchised working class claiming their membership in the body politic." In the century and a half since the manifesto was first written, it has been the subject of an extensive body of criticism that has considered its legacy in historical, political, literary, and gendered terms.

Much scholarship has been focused on the political significance of the *People's Charter* despite its ostensible failure as a piece of legislation. Discussing the political impact of the manifesto, Malcolm Chase notes in his book *Chartism: A New History* (2007) that it "was truly the first nationwide political movement and even those who were unsympathetic to it were made to review and reflect on their attitudes to working people." Commentators have also drawn attention to the manifesto's failure to embrace women's suffrage as part of its platform. In her book *Women in the Chartist Movement* (1991), for example, Jutta Schwartzkopf explores the gender politics of the *People's Charter* and the political movement it brought

about. She argues that although men and women both contributed to the movement, they experienced its effects in radically different ways. She suggests that "the campaign for the Charter had bolstered male working-class stamina, enabling men to come to terms with industrial capitalism." At the same time, she says, "the definite defeat of Chartism left women doubly disempowered," a disappointment to which she attributes the withdrawal of women from working-class activism in the decades following the failure of the *People's Charter.*

BIBLIOGRAPHY

Sources

Carlyle, Thomas. *Chartism.* Boston: Charles C. Little and James Brown, 1840. 3-4. Print.

Chase, Malcolm. *Chartism: A New History.* Manchester: Manchester UP, 2007. Print.

Haywood, Ian. Introduction. *The Literature of Struggle: An Anthology of Chartist Fiction.* Ed. Haywood. Aldershot: Scolar, 1995. 1-25. Print.

Lovett, William. *The People's Charter: Being an Outline of an Act to Provide for the Just Representation of the People of Great Britain in the Commons House of Parliament.* London: H. Hetherington, 1838.

Rosenblatt, Frank F. *The Chartist Movement: Its Social and Economic Aspects.* London: Frank Cass and Company, 1916.

Schwartzkopf, Jutta. *Women in the Chartist Movement.* New York: St. Martin's, 1991. Print.

Further Reading

Charlton, John. *The Chartists: The First National Workers' Movement.* Chicago: Pluto Press, 1997. Print.

Ledger, Sally. "Chartist Aesthetics in the Mid Nineteenth Century: Ernest Jones, a Novelist of the People." *Nineteenth-Century Literature* 57.1 (2002): 31-63. Print.

Schnepf, Ariane. *Our Original Rights as a People: Representations of the Chartist Encyclopaedic Network and Political, Social and Cultural Change in Early Nineteenth Century Britain.* Bern: Peter Lang, 2006. Print.

Thompson, Dorothy. *The Chartists: Popular Politics in the Industrial Revolution.* New York: Pantheon, 1984. Print.

Wheeler, Thomas Martin. *Sunshine and Shadow. Chartist Fiction.* Ed. Ian Haywood. Aldershot: Ashgate, 1999. Print.

Greta Gard

PRINCIPLES OF SOCIALISM

Manifesto of Nineteenth Century Democracy

Victor Considerant

OVERVIEW

Composed by Victor Considerant in 1843, *Principles of Socialism: Manifesto of Nineteenth Century Democracy* (*Principes du socialisme, Manifeste de la démocratie au XIXe siècle*) describes the dehumanizing injustice of free-market capitalism and argues for social, political, and economic reform based upon collectivist principles. Like other early French socialists such as Charles Fourier, Pierre Leroux, Philippe Buchez, and Henri-Claude de Saint-Simon—who are known as utopian or romantic socialists—Considerant wrote in response to the failure of the French Revolution to live up to its promise of radical democratic change. With its call for peaceful rather than revolutionary change and its Christian undertones, Considerant's tract typifies utopian socialist writing. *Principles of Socialism* offers an indictment of the "cruel, stupid system" of capitalism and proposes in its stead "a rational, equitable, Christian industrial organization" based on socialist principles.

The piece originally appeared in 1843 as the introduction to a socialist newspaper published by Considerant. It was reprinted in book form as *Principles of Socialism: Manifesto of Nineteenth Century Democracy* in 1847, on the cusp of the French Revolution of 1848. The ideas of Considerant and other utopian socialists helped inspire the unrest, and the revolution's failure was widely viewed as an indictment of their collectivist ideas. While Considerant was forced into exile in 1849 for his continued agitation for reform, the ideas expressed in *Principles of Socialism* have been highly influential on the development of socialist thought. Today, Considerant's text is viewed as a foundational document in the history of socialism.

HISTORICAL AND LITERARY CONTEXT

Principles of Socialism responds to the political and economic crises facing France in the mid-nineteenth century. Guided by Enlightenment principles of inalienable human rights to freedom and equality, the French Revolution began in 1789 and resulted in the violent overthrow of the French monarchy. The revolution achieved limited reforms but failed to create a republican democracy. In the early nineteenth century, the nation's struggle to find a stable replacement for the old monarchical order continued. In this milieu utopian socialists emerged in the early 1830s. As scholar Jonathan Beecher writes of these socialists in *Victor Considerant and the Rise and Fall of French Romantic Socialism* (2000), "They believed that their great task was to reconstruct social and intellectual order in a world turned upside down by the Revolution."

By the time *Principles of Socialism* was written, utopian socialism was growing in prominence in France. Beginning in the early 1830s, during the reign of a liberal constitutional monarchy known as the July Monarchy, utopian socialist thought and activity proliferated in Paris. Saint-Simon and Fourier emerged as the movement's preeminent theorists and leaders. Considerant first came to intellectual prominence in the mid-1830s as an advocate of Fourierism, which envisioned a system of communal social organization based on scientific analysis and various idiosyncratic theories about religion and human nature. In 1834 Considerant published the first volume of *Destinée sociale,* a three-volume treatise on Fourierism. In 1836 he started a journal, *La Phalange. Journal de la science sociale,* devoted to the movement. Seven years later Considerant founded *La Démocratie pacifique,* one of the first socialist daily newspapers; his manifesto, which had not yet been given the title *Principles of Socialism,* appeared in the first issue.

Principles of Socialism draws from other utopian socialist writings, in particular from Fourier's *Théorie de l'unité universelle* (four volumes, 1841-43), a utopian vision of a society organized in *phalanges* (phalanxes), or small, harmonious groups. Considerant adapted many of Fourier's theories in *Principles of Socialism,* including ideas about the nature of economic production. Fourier writes, "Let us refute ... a strange sophism of the economists who claim that the unlimited increase of manufactured goods constitutes an increase in wealth." This critique of capitalist commerce is taken up in Considerant's tract, which declares, "The most developed nations are sinking under the deadly weight of overproductions, while in their midst legions of workers are wasting away because their low wages prevent them from consuming this overwhelming production!"

✣ Key Facts

Time Period:
Mid-19th Century

Movement/Issue:
Utopian socialism

Place of Publication:
France

Language of Publication:
French

LA RÉUNION: UTOPIA IN TEXAS

In 1852, after living in Belgium for several years, Victor Considerant arrived in New York and was immediately impressed with what he found. "Civilization here is still civilization, no doubt," he wrote to a correspondent in France, "but instead of stagnating it advances like a great river and does not present obstacles to real progress." He soon visited a Fourierist settlement in Red Bank, New Jersey, and was not nearly as impressed, calling it "cold, frozen, dead." Rather than being deterred from his socialist idealism by his visit, Considerant was motivated to establish his own communal experiment in the New World.

His plans for this colony were elaborately described in his book *Au Texas* (*The Great West* in its American edition). What he proposed was not a Fourierist utopia but a "colonizing company" that would raise funds, hire American recruits to lay the settlement's foundation, and transport settlers from Europe to a "great protected area freely open to all forms of progressive thought." In 1855 Considerant's company purchased land near Dallas and named it La Réunion. Some two hundred colonists came to settle before the colony had been adequately provisioned and organized. When Considerant arrived in June of that year, the colony was in a state of disorder from which it never recovered. In 1856 Considerant abandoned La Réunion and his hopes for a utopia in Texas.

Principles of Socialism influenced a number of communist and socialist writers, including Karl Marx and Friedrich Engels. Some even claim that the text is more than an influence. Joan Roelofs notes in her 2008 article in *Science and Society,* "There have been persistent rumors by scholars and activists that parts of the 1848 *Communist Manifesto* by Marx and Engels were plagiarized" from *Principles of Socialism.* Writing for *Social Science Quarterly,* Rondel Davidson argues that while it is "certain that Marx and Engels were thoroughly familiar with the activities and writings of Victor Considerant," charges of plagiarism are demonstrably false, as the texts differ in important ways, notably in Considerant's calls for peaceful, reformist change and for the preservation of private property.

THEMES AND STYLE

Principles of Socialism centers on the premise that the reforms brought about by the French Revolution had failed to create social and economic justice and, therefore, a new socialist order is needed to provide greater efficiency and equitability. The text begins with a lengthy description of the causes and outcomes of the French Revolution. Though Considerant acknowledges socialists' many victories, he argues that the revolution's true aim of establishing a "New Order" based on equality remained unfinished. "All the work

of organizing the New Order remains to be done," he emphatically declares. To that end, Considerant advocates "a rational, equitable, Christian industrial organization that rewards work with charity, justice, and liberality; holds Labor's rights to be at least as sacred as those of property; and gives to Labor and Talent, as to Capital, their legitimate shares of the returns from wealth Production."

The tract employs—to great effect—rhetoric that is at once lofty and plainly practical. Considerant maintains this balance by tempering utopian visions of French potential with careful economic and historical analysis. Rather than call for a complete overthrow of the entire social order, he makes a sober case for peaceful, gradual reform that builds on the democratic achievements of the French Revolution. Considerant argues that the revolution "marks the great division in humanity's history between the Old Order and New Order." Fulfilling this new order's potential, he writes, "is the problem and task of our era; it is the puzzle that Destiny's spirit charges us to resolve." There are two solutions, he argues. "One of these approaches is violent, destructive, revolutionary, and furthermore, illusory." Considerant's vision, on the other hand, is of capital, labor, and talent "wisely combined in industry and the three wheels of the machine harmoniously in gear."

Stylistically, *Principles of Socialism* takes a tone of passionate assurance. Throughout the essay, Considerant declaims his views in broad and certain terms. The essay begins, "Ancient societies had as their basic principle, Might makes right…" and ends, "Don't you see comfort and well-being spreading through all classes, your great, stopped-up, national markets expanding, your shrinking outlets growing, the legitimate rewards of Capital increasing incessantly, and those of Labor and Talent rising in corresponding proportion?" This confidence of tone serves Considerant's rhetorical aim of rallying readers to his agenda. The text's assured style allows him to make claims about the historical origins of the contemporary situation that are as strong and compelling as his vision of society's future.

CRITICAL DISCUSSION

Principles of Socialism immediately proved influential within socialist circles. When it first appeared in 1843 in *Démocratie pacifique,* which Beecher calls "the most ambitious and widely influential of all the Fourierist journals," the tract reached a large audience within the early French socialist movement. Many readers initially viewed Considerant's work as an elaboration of Fourier's thought. When it was reprinted in pamphlet form in 1847, it—along with Considerant's position as elected deputy and his service on the Constitutional Committee of the Constituent Assembly in 1848—helped bring his demand for the "right to work" to the forefront of protesters' concerns during the Revolution of 1848.

Though the Revolution of 1848 failed to bring about the fulfillment of Considerant's theories, *Principles of Socialism* remained an important source of socialist thought. Most notably, its critique of free markets influenced Marx and thereby helped shape the various Marxist revolutions that took place around the world in the late nineteenth and twentieth centuries. Considerant's argument for peaceful socialist reform can be detected in the social democratic movement that spread through Europe in the late nineteenth century. Considerant himself put his theory into practice when he was exiled from France in the mid-1850s. While living in Texas, he established a short-lived experimental colony based on his socialist principles of organization. The body of criticism about *Principles of Socialism* has only grown in the 150 years since it was written.

Much scholarship has been focused on the relationship between *Principles of Socialism* and the *Communist Manifesto*. Numerous commentators have noted the similarities and differences between the two documents. In her review of the English translation of Considerant's manifesto, Amy Buzby views the text's reformist prescriptions in light of Marx's and Engels' revolutionary message. "From the perspective of Marx and Engels," she writes, "Considerant's failure to make the logical move and develop a concrete basis for genuine resistance is an almost counter-revolutionary abdication." Commentators have also considered the tract in the context of Fourier. Roelofs notes their differing relations to religion, observing that "Fourier's religion had been his own version of deism: passionate attraction was God's plan for humanity's salvation. Considerant instead suggests a Christian socialist approach, one of his radical emendations of Fourier."

French social theorist Charles Fourier (1772-1837). Victor Considerant, author of *Principles of Socialism,* was a collaborator and disciple of Fourier. MUSÉE DU TEMPS, BESANCON, FRANCE/GIRAUDON/THE BRIDGEMAN ART LIBRARY

BIBLIOGRAPHY

Sources

Beecher, Jonathan. *Victor Considerant and the Rise and Fall of French Romantic Socialism.* Berkeley: U of California P, 2000. Print.

Buzby, Amy. Review of *Principles of Socialism: Manifesto of 19th Century Democracy,* by Victor Considerant. *Journal of the Research Group on Socialism and Democracy Online.* Socialism and Democracy, July 2009. Web. 4 Sept. 2012.

Davidson, Rondel. "Reform versus Revolution: Victor Considerant and *The Communist Manifesto.*" *Social Science Quarterly* 58.1 (1977): 74-85. *Academic Search Elite.* Web. 4 Sept. 2012.

Fourier, Charles. *The Utopian Vision of Charles Fourier: Selected Texts on Work, Love, and Passionate Attraction.* Ed. and trans. Jonathan Beecher and Richard Bienvenu. Boston: Beacon, 1971. Print.

Roelofs, Joan. "Considerant's 'Principe du Socialisme.'" *Science and Society* 72.1 (2008): 114-27. *UM-Missoula Article Linker.* Web. 4 Sept. 2012.

Further Reading

Considerant, Victor. *Principles of Socialism: A Manifesto of 19th Century Socialism.* Trans. Joan Roelofs. College Park: Maisounneuve, 2006. Print.

Crossley, Ceri. Review of *Victor Considerant and the Rise and Fall of French Romantic Socialism,* by Jonathan Beecher. *French Studies* 52.2 (2002): 250. *Oxford Journals Full Collection.* Web. 4 Sept. 2012.

Davidson, Rondel. "Victor Considerant and the Failure of La Réunion." *Southwestern Historical Quarterly* 76.3 (1973): 277-96. *JSTOR.* Web. 4 Sept. 2012.

———. *Did We Think Victory Great? The Life and Ideas of Victor Considerant.* Lanham: UP of America, 1988. Print.

Jones, Russell M. "Victor Considerant's American Experience (1852-1869)." *French-American Review* 1 (1976-77): 65-94, 124-50. Print.

Lovell, David W. "Early French Socialism and Politics: The Case of Victor Considerant." *History of Political Thought* 13.2 (1992): 257-79. Print.

Theodore McDermott

Reply to the Impertinent Question, "What Is a *Sans-Culotte?*"

Anonymous

❖ *Key Facts*

Time Period:
Late 18th Century

Movement/Issue:
French Revolution;
Jacobinism

Place of Publication:
France

**Language of
Publication:**
French

OVERVIEW

The anonymously published "Reply to the Impertinent Question: What Is a *Sans-Culotte?*" (April 1793) is a brief statement summarizing the defining characteristics of the *sans-culottes,* the radical partisans of the middle and lower classes who provided the manpower that brought down the monarchy during the French Revolution (1789-99) and were the principal support behind the rise to power of left-wing factions of the new government in 1792 through 1794. Representative of the fiery rhetoric the sans-culottes brought to revolutionary politics, the statement portrays the sans-culotte as the hero of the revolution, the common man of egalitarian sympathies fierce in his opposition to wealth and the aristocracy. The label *sans-culotte* (literally, "without culottes") is itself commentary on the group's republican ideals. Mostly composed of artisans and shopkeepers, the sans-culottes disdained the silk breeches of the upper echelons of society in favor of the ordinary long trousers worn by manual laborers.

Just under 300 words in length, the "Reply to the Impertinent Question" is known to have appeared in pamphlet form, but scant evident exists to document its mode of dissemination or its immediate reception. The text has been variously attributed to Jean-Baptiste Vingtergnier, a professional revolutionary soldier, and Antoine-François Momoro, a printer and politician of the people, but these assignations cannot be substantiated. Still, it is widely agreed that the sans-culotte piece was written by one of the revolutionaries' own, presumably to champion the purity of their motives in response to widespread negative publicity in the French and foreign press depicting them as uncivilized barbarians responsible for much of the extremist violence of the revolution. Among modern scholars of the French Revolution, "Reply to the Impertinent Question" is a frequently cited document of contemporary self-definition that figures in ongoing debates about the extent of the social cohesion of the sans-culottes and their relationship to the peasants and the bourgeoisie.

HISTORICAL AND LITERARY CONTEXT

In establishing a contrast between the industrious and militant sans-culottes and the idle rich, "Reply to an Impertinent Question" helps to clarify a transformation in the character of the French Revolution. At its inception, the French Revolution pitted the Third Estate (the commoners, including the peasants, laborers, and bourgeoisie) against the First and Second Estates, the clergy and the nobility, respectively. However, once the monarchy of King Louis XVI was overthrown and the Republic of France was proclaimed in late 1792, antagonisms developed among the various classes of the Third Estate over the direction of the revolutionary project. The sans-culottes were highly active in the forty-eight sectional assemblies that constituted Paris municipal politics. For them, the term "aristocracy" came to denote not only the former nobility but also anyone deemed to be insufficiently civic minded and committed to the principle of equality. As "Reply" indicates, the sans-culottes targeted as counterrevolutionary the "powdered, perfumed, and booted" of the upper tier of the Third Estate as well as the political moderates represented by the Girondin press, referenced in the statement as "the garbage of [Antoine-Louis] Gorsas with the *Chronique* and the *Patriot Française.*" The sans-culottes took part in all of the major early events of the revolution, including the storming of the Bastille and the Palace of Versailles, and they made up the bulk of the French army defending the provinces from invading Austrian and Prussian troops. By the spring of 1793, when "Reply" appeared, Spain, Britain, and the Dutch Republic had joined in the war against France, and royalists had mounted a full-scale rebellion in the Vendée. The crisis in the republican cause is reflected in the militant tone of "Reply."

Shortly after "Reply" was written, the left-wing Jacobins came to dominate the Convention, the national legislature of the Republic. It was only with the backing of the sans-culottes, who controlled the Paris sections, that the Jacobins were able to secure power. For the Jacobins, this meant acceding to some of the political and economic demands of the sans-culottes, who had managed to consolidate their influence through their association with the "Hébertists," a group led by pamphleteer and journalist Jacques Hébert, who also agitated for direct democracy, price controls, property redistribution, and the suppression of all enemies of the people.

"Reply" forms a contribution to the vitriolic series of attacks and counterattacks that characterized the revolutionary press of the day, giving shape and definition to the various factions that vied for control of the new government. The sans-culottes received some of their worst publicity for their role in the so-called September Massacre—the mass killings of royalist and other prisoners, including women, children, and the clergy—that took place in Paris in September 1792. The sans-culottes were caricatured in British cartoons eating the heads of their victims, and they were similarly reviled in moderate and conservative circles in France. In defense against these attacks—which included a poster issued by Gorsas questioning the sans-culottes' demagogic rise to power—stood the people's press of Jean-Paul Marat, *L'Ami du Peuple,* and that of Hébert, *Le Père Duchesne,* both of which valorized the rank and file of the revolutionary movement.

Revisionist historians of the French Revolution have often pointed to "Reply" in attempting to clarify the social characteristics of the sans-culottes. The renewed interest in the group stems from the conviction that earlier accounts homogenized their composition, either by failing to distinguish them from the rural peasants and urban poor or by ignoring the ramifications of their various alliances and disputes with the bourgeoisie. The legacy of the sans-culottes has undergone a series of transformations, as Hugh Gough explains in his review of Michael Sonenscher's *Sans-Culottes*:

> Historians once had a relatively straightforward view of the role of *sans-culottes* in the French Revolution, based on the conclusions of a generation of postwar social historians who dispelled the myth that they formed a protoproletarian movement and repositioned them as lower-middle-class activists, artisans, and skilled laborers who were bound together by a common commitment to the ideals of direct democracy and the "moral economy." That view was later modified by a new generation of social historians ... who pointed to the relative wealth of many *sans-culotte* activists and the localized roots of their power and prestige.

THEMES AND STYLE

"Reply to the Impertinent Question" addresses the question of the sans-culotte identity, an issue, then as now, of considerable debate. In his essay in *Fraternity and Politics* (1998), critic Fred E. Baumann offers a thumbnail summary of the piece: "The description is primarily ... not of tenets of belief but of characteristics of class, dress, manners and taste. They all mingle to reveal an identity, an inner disposition in turn equated with political righteousness." Though brief,

THE POPULAR IMAGE OF THE SANS-CULOTTE

The distinctive image of the sans-culotte—a ragged figure armed with a pike and clad in long pants, a short jacket, and the red cap of liberty embellished with the tricolor cockade—has entered history as an iconic symbol of the French Revolution. During the period of the revolution, the upper classes identified the sans-culottes with some of the most cruel and bloody violence of the period: the parading of decapitated heads on pikes, the castration of the Swiss guards at the Tuileries Gardens, the stringing up of bodies on lampposts, the grisly murders of half the Paris prison population in the September massacres of 1792. The street-mob violence of the sans-culottes was widely denounced in the press, most famously in cartoons depicting their cannibalism by the British caricaturist James Gillray.

Some of the most enduring images of the sans-culottes derive from English writer Charles Dickens's *A Tale of Two Cities* (1859). Among other atrocities depicted in the novel is a description of sans-culotte women impassively knitting red caps of liberty while watching a series of beheadings at the guillotine. French writer Victor Hugo was more sympathetic to the sans-culottes' cause. The following account comes from his novel *Les Misérables* (1862): "Savage. What was the aim of those bristling men who in ... revolutionary chaos, ragged, howling, wild, with tomahawk raised, and pike aloft, rushed over old over-turned Paris? They desired the end of oppressions, the end of tyrannies, the end of the sword, labour for man, instruction for children, social gentleness for woman, liberty, equality, fraternity, bread for all, ideas for all."

"Reply" establishes a sharp contrast between the virtuous political and social conduct of the sans-culottes and the vanities of the idle rich. By thus proclaiming the superior virtue of the group, the writer of the piece defends their militancy as a moral imperative. The theme of the purposeful work is central to the definition of the sans-culotte. As William H. Sewell, Jr. writes in his piece in *Work & Revolution in France* (1980), "Labor is an integral element in a whole network of moral and political identities that define the *sans-culotte* and distinguish him from the counterrevolutionary moderate."

The contrast between the revolutionary and the counterrevolutionary is developed through an accumulation of specific detail describing the everyday lives of the two groups. The sans-culotte deduces character from costume and habits. He disdains the frivolous trappings of the aristocracy. He "always goes on foot ... has no millions ... no castle, no valets to serve him." The sans-culotte "lives with his wife and children, if he has any, on the fourth or fifth floor." With this remark, the writer alludes to the fact that social distinctions in Paris were based on stories rather than section locale. The remark also stresses the

An eighteenth-century engraving depicting a sans-culotte killing a nobleman. GIANNI DAGLI ORTI/THE ART ARCHIVE AT ART RESOURCE, NY

of his attacks with topical references specifying exactly where the counterrevolutionary might be found—in reading rooms that supply the politically moderate newspapers of the Girondins, at the fancy restaurant Café des Chartres, or at a National Theater performance of *L'Ami des Lois,* a play challenging Jacobin extremism.

CRITICAL DISCUSSION

Contemporary response to "Reply" is little recorded, though modern critics are quick to point out that such statements of self-definition were common among the sans-culottes. In broad terms, sans-culotte militancy fell out of favor with the Convention's discrediting of Jacobin Maximilien Robespierre and the so-called Terror associated with his political influence—the violent campaign to hunt down and eliminate all traitors to the revolution. By the time Robespierre and other Jacobins were themselves sent to the guillotine and replaced with the conservative government of the Directory in 1795, the sans-culottes had lost all political influence.

The sans-culottes became the subject of growing scholarly attention with the increase in class-based analyses of the French Revolution beginning in the 1960s. These studies tended to stratify the bourgeois character of the revolt, emphasizing that the upper tier of the Third Estate—the politicians and large property owners—had concerns very different from those of the rural peasants and urban militants, classes themselves distinct in terms of political and economic demands. Documents such as "Reply" have proved useful to historians in establishing that the sans-culottes were not the poorest members of the Parisian population and that, while they objected to the accumulation of great wealth and ostentatious display, they were not opposed to ownership outright.

Scholars have explained the sans-culottes' notion of egalitarianism by pointing to their understanding of labor. The description of labor in "Reply" is considered particularly illuminating in this regard. The piece stresses the sanctity of labor, indicating that equality is more a moral than an economic or social category. In his essay in *The French and Their Revolution* (1998), Richard Cobb observes, "A *sans-culotte,* we often read, may have a comfortable income provided that it is the recompense of hard work. Property is sacred, so long as it is not excessive." The direct correspondence between labor and political virtue established in "Reply" is further delineated by an account of the type of labor that is most useful to the republic: that produced by those who work with their hands. The recourse to manual labor to make a living positioned the sans-culottes below the bourgeoisie on the social ladder but above the starving masses. Documents of the period reveal that a majority of the sans-culottes were artisans and shopkeepers, some of whom employed several workers and many of whom were ranking members of the Paris civil committees.

importance of raising children who will lead the revolution into the future. The sans-culotte performs useful work: "[He] knows how to plow a field, to forge, to saw, to file, to roof a building, to make shoes." The sans-culotte dutifully attends his section meetings at night. He is never found in the evil haunts of the wealthy—the cafés and theaters and "gambling dens where men conspire over a game of dice." It is because the sans-culotte commits all his daily activity in service to the republic that he is ready at a moment's notice to defend the nation in times of peril.

The tone of "Reply" is itself militant. It is addressed to the "rogues" who have asked, "What is a sans-culotte?" (in some English versions, "rogue" appears as "stuck-up bastards"). According to Baumann, "The question is of course highly pertinent to the *sans-culottes* themselves; it is called impertinent in the gruff style of Hébert's *Père Duchesne* to make it appear that the answer is self-evident, and this in turn because it is not." The pursuits of wealth and luxury are condemned as supercilious and depraved. The writer pulls no punches in exposing the targets

The problem of defining the sans-culottes is further complicated by the fact that the group included entrepreneurs and bourgeoisie with unearned incomes. In *The Sans-Culottes: The Popular Movement and Revolutionary Government, 1793-1794* (1980), author Albert Soboul writes of the misleading notion that the sansculottes represented a unified class: "[The] masses considered social characteristics insufficient to define a *sans-culotte*; a counterrevolutionary worker could not be a good *sans-culotte,* but a patriotic and republican bourgeois was willingly labeled one."

BIBLIOGRAPHY

Sources

"Anon., 'What Is a *Sans-Culotte?*', 1793." *From Enlightenment to Romanticism: Anthology I.* Ed. Ian Donnachie and Carmen Lavin. Manchester: Manchester UP, 2003. 92-3. Print.

Baumann, Fred E. "Fraternity and the *Sans-Culottes.*" *Fraternity and Politics: Choosing One's Brothers.* Westport: Praeger, 1998. 55-87. Print.

Cobb, Richard. "The Revolutionary Mentality in France." *The French and Their Revolution: Selected Writings.* Ed. David Gilmour. New York: New Press, 1998. Print.

Gough, Hugh. Rev. of *Sans-Culottes: An Eighteenth-Century Emblem in the French Revolution,* by Michael Sonenscher. *Historian* 73.4 (2011): 885-87. *Wiley Online Library.* Web. 1 Sept. 2012.

Sewell, William H., Jr. "Labor and Property in *Sans-Culotte* Ideology." *Work & Revolution in France: The Language of Labor from the Old Regime to 1848.* Cambridge: Cambridge UP, 1980. 109-13. Print.

Soboul, Albert. *The Sans-Culottes: The Popular Movement and Revolutionary Government, 1793-1794.* Trans. Rémy Inglis Hall. Princeton: Princeton UP, 1980. Print.

Further Reading

Karmel, Alex. *Guillotine in the Wings: A New Look at the French Revolution and Its Relevance to America Today.* New York: McGraw-Hill, 1972. Print.

Lewis, Gynne. *Life in Revolutionary France.* London: Batsford, 1972. Print.

McPhee, Peter. *The French Revolution 1789-1799.* Oxford: Oxford UP, 2002. Print.

Sonenscher, Michael. *Sans-Culottes: An Eighteenth-Century Emblem in the French Revolution.* Princeton: Princeton UP, 2008. Print.

Williams, Gwyn A. "*Sans-Culottes.*" *Artisans and Sans-Culottes: Popular Movements in France and Britain during the French Revolution.* New York: Norton, 1969. 20-38. Print.

Janet Mullane

THE RIGHT TO BE LAZY

Paul Lafargue

✥ *Key Facts*

Time Period:
Late 19th Century

Movement/Issue:
The Paris Commune;
Marxism

Place of Publication:
France

**Language of
Publication:**
French

OVERVIEW

French revolutionary journalist Paul Lafargue's *The Right to Be Lazy* (1883) is an assertion of the human right to leisure and a repudiation of "the religion of abstinence and the dogma of work." Finalized while Lafargue was incarcerated in the Sainte-Pelagie Prison in Paris, the pamphlet responds to the right to work reform movement instituted by the French Revolution of 1848. Lafargue develops his thesis in four chapters, concluding with a plea to "Laziness, mother of the arts and noble virtues" to soothe the pain inherent in modern life, a pain caused by "the vice of work." An appendix calls to account "three-for-a-cent philosophers" who prop up right-to-work dogma, directing them to consider the morality of canonizing work when the dream of ancient Greek philosopher Aristotle—that "the shuttles of weavers did their own weaving" and "the foreman of the workshop … have no more need of helpers, nor the master of slaves"—is "our reality."

Addressed to the French proletariat, *The Right to Be Lazy* was widely read following its publication, although Lafargue's ideas did little to change the political climate in France at the time. The work first appeared in 1880 as a series of articles in the newspaper *Equality* and was subsequently released as a short pamphlet. The revised version containing the preface appeared in 1883, with additional printings in the years that followed. Still widely available, *The Right to Be Lazy* remains interesting to modern readers, despite widespread changes in labor laws that have limited working hours in Western countries to well below the levels that so outraged Lafargue.

HISTORICAL AND LITERARY CONTEXT

In February 1848 revolts against the monarchy in France touched off a series of revolutions across Europe, most of which were led by some combination of political reformers and workers' organizations. The revolution in France had been brewing for some time. Only a small percentage of citizens were allowed to vote, and the suppression of political organization of the masses, combined with widespread poverty, resulted in growing unrest. In 1847 a "campaign of banquets" was instituted to circumvent the government's ban on organized political activities. The banquets gave the public a forum to air grievances against the government, and, when they were forcibly suppressed by the conservative government of Louis-Philippe I, unrest turned to revolution. The king fled, and a provisional government, the Second Republic, was instituted. Louis Blanc, a prominent socialist, was appointed director of the commission on labor, and he implemented a series of workshops designed to get the large number of unskilled and unemployed back to work. The socialist elements of the government were purged following the April elections, the results of which reflected a split between the working classes in Paris and the rural farmers, who had been forced to carry the tax burden of the New Right to work national workshops in the cities. While the workshops ended almost as soon as they had begun, the conception of work as a right, which the movement enshrined, remained a part of the French consciousness.

The Paris Commune (1871), a much revered but short-lived working-class government in power briefly at the close of the Franco-Prussian War, issued decrees reflecting the entrenched right-to-work mentality that Lafargue rejects. Pawn shops were ordered to return tools to the tradespeople forced to pawn them during the war, and workers were given leeway to operate businesses that had been abandoned by their war-fleeing owners. Ultimately, the decrees came to naught, as they were disregarded after the bloody end of the commune when leftist activities were again repressed. Still, the right-to-work impulse was very much present as the Third Republic became established.

Although Lafargue was influenced by Karl Marx (who, incidentally, was Lafargue's father-in-law) and Friedrich Engels's *Communist Manifesto* (1848) and viewed his own work as Marxist, continuing the analysis of the alienation of labor and problems of overproduction and consumption, *The Right to be Lazy* exhibits a utopian vision largely absent from Marx's and Engels's work. Some similarity has been detected between Lafargue's piece and artist and socialist William Morris's "Useful Work Versus Useless Toil," which, though less extravagant in its utopian imaginings, still offers a view of the "holiday our whole lives might be, if we were resolute to make all our labor reasonable and pleasant." Morris, who was a significant figure in the Arts and Crafts movement and the author of the utopian novel *News from Nowhere* (1890), believed with Lafargue that technology could be used to reduce working hours. It remains an open question how closely related

Lafargue's conception of "laziness" and Morris's ideas about "useful work" might be. While use of the word "lazy" suggests idleness, Lafargue writes admiringly of "the Greeks in the era of greatness," mentioning, for instance, Aristotle, whose conception of a good life free of work is filled with "exercises for the body and mind."

The Right to Be Lazy remains the most discussed of Lafargue's writings and has influenced contemporary thinkers such as anarchist Bob Black, whose "The Abolition of Work" asserts that to stop suffering, work should be replaced with "a new way of life based on play … festivity, creativity, conviviality, commensality, and maybe even art." Black, whose essay explicitly acknowledges his debt to Lafargue, has in turn influenced Bruce Sterling's cyberpunk fiction and *The Simpsons* television show creator Matt Groening's comic strip *Work Is Hell.*

THEMES AND STYLE

Chief among Lafargue's themes is that, in a capitalist society, the love of work amounts to bourgeois propaganda perpetrated against the proletariat, propaganda that has been internalized to the point that it is widely believed. Relaxation is a natural human state, but after relentless indoctrination, work is revered as a right to be defended, "the furious passion for work" to be "pushed even to the exhaustion of the vital force of the individual and his progeny." Chief among the problems that Lafargue cites as arising from these mistaken ideas is the vicious cycle of overwork and overproduction, which lines the pockets of the industrialists while lowering the value of labor and depriving workers of the means to support themselves and, even more importantly, depriving them of leisure. Leisure, for Lafargue, is the true right worth fighting for. As a solution, *The Right to Be Lazy* proposes that the workday be limited to no more than three hours, a reduction that would be supported by advances in labor-saving mechanization; this change would subsequently limit the amount of goods produced and, in eliminating surplus, would stop not only the false need to overconsume but also the necessity for France to enter into the international market.

Lafargue appeals to his audience with a utopian vision of days filled with "leisure and feasting," promising "juicy beefsteaks of a pound or two … broad and deep bumpers of Bordeaux and Burgundy," and a short workday guaranteeing time to enjoy this bounty. Further, he asserts that human misery will "vanish like hyenas and jackals at the approach of the lion, when the proletariat says 'I will,'" the assent they must offer a disavowal of the passion for work. If the "neighborly housewives" of folklore do not entice and the tales from "happy nations leafing in the sun smoking cigarettes" do not compel, Lafargue also buttresses his argument with reference to Jehovah, who "gave his worshipers the supreme example of ideal laziness; after six days of work, he rests for all eternity."

The Right to Be Lazy strikes an irreverent and sarcastic tone, beginning with the title. While some

BOB BLACK'S "THE ABOLITION OF WORK"

"The Abolition of Work," anarchist Bob Black's 1985 essay, begins with the startling declaration that "no one should ever work." Aligning his views with the surrealists, "except that I'm not kidding," Black rejects mainstream ideology regarding work. For Black, work is defined as "forced labor," *travail* dictated by the demands of the market, and most work is unnecessary, serving "unproductive purposes of commerce or social control" rather than meeting basic needs for food and shelter. "The Abolition of Work" advocates cessation of all unnecessary work, ranging from service work to production. With the elimination of paid work would come an attendant elimination of unpaid domestic labor, which would also eliminate the need for schools, which Black conceives as "youth concentration camps" instituted to keep children "out of Mom's hair but still under control."

Of course, Black acknowledges that some amount of work must still be done, some of it unpleasant. His solution is to imbue work with a spirit of play, suggesting that removing the necessity of tasks also removes the unpleasantness. For the work that is almost universally reviled, Black rather comically imagines exploiting "perversities," putting Roman emperor Nero to work in a slaughterhouse and organizing young children "who notoriously relish wallowing in filth" into "'Little Hordes' to clean toilets and empty the garbage, with medals awarded to the outstanding." Having described his utopian vision, Black, in a nod to Marx, exhorts, "Workers of the world … *relax!*"

translators have titled the work *The Right to Leisure,* the contemporary consensus supports the translation of the word *paresse* as "laziness," a usage that seems calculated to provoke and amuse. The tone continues in the first chapter, "A Disastrous Dogma," which begins with a parody of the opening of the *Communist Manifesto.* Rather than nations being "haunted" by "the specter of communism," "a strange delusion possesses the working classes." This discussion continues in the ironically titled second chapter, "The Blessings of Work." At the close of the piece, Lafargue describes the punishment of the bourgeoisie, imagining bourgeois politicians being forced to participate in a real "Electoral Farce" rather than in the farce he sees masquerading as electoral politics. His vision continues with a play, "The Theft of the Nation's Goods," which will open with "Capitalist France, an enormous female, hairy-faced and bald-headed, fat, flabby, puffy and pale," eventually overthrown by "Historic Destiny."

CRITICAL DISCUSSION

The Right to Be Lazy received mixed treatment in the press when it was first released. In *Paul Lafargue and the Founding of French Marxism 1842-1882* (1991), Leslie Derfler quotes journalist Édouard Drumont describing the pamphlet as "almost a masterpiece of irony," despite certain "useless blasphemies." Overall,

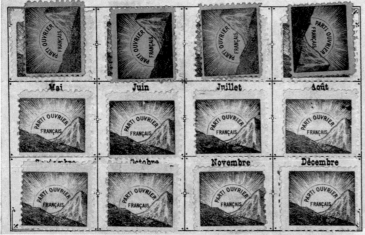

French Workers' Party membership card. Paul Lafargue helped found the party and wrote works such as *The Right to Be Lazy*. PRIVATE COLLECTION/ ARCHIVES CHARMET/THE BRIDGEMAN ART LIBRARY

the pamphlet sold well and was subject to numerous printings. Questions were occasionally raised, according to Derfler, about the originality of Lafargue's ideas. French economist Louis Moreau-Christophe's *The Right to Idleness and the Organization of Servile Labor in the Greek and Roman Republics* (1849), a book Lafargue was familiar with from Marx's library, is not only similarly titled but also contains a number of the same references to antiquity found in *The Right to Be Lazy*.

Lafargue's ideas have been referenced as influencing organized labor activities in France, such as in the Situationist revolutionary agitation tied to the 1968 strikes, as well as in contemporary movements to limit workweek hours, including the push to reduce the working week in France from thirty-nine to thirty-five hours. This proposal, which was originally one of the Socialist Party's "110 Propositions for France" advanced during the 1981 presidential election, was drafted into law under Socialist prime minister Lionel Jospin. Outside of France, such movements are likely influenced by other traditions, but interest in *The Right to Be Lazy* remains, particularly among anarchist and contemporary direct action groups.

Most recent critical interest in *The Right to Be Lazy* has focused on the work in the larger context of Lafargue's life and political activities. Derfler's pair of books on Lafargue explores his role in disseminating Marxist thought in France and the subsequent "flowering" of French socialism into a "significant political force." Derfler claims a status of continuing relevance for Lafargue, citing the numerous republications of *The Right to Be Lazy* and "their success with a more libertarian audience" as evidence of his remaining "in posthumous touch with later revolutionary aspirations." Gary Cross, on the other hand, in an article published in *Social Research* in 2005, implicates Lafargue's "archaic" conceptions of leisure in the failure of his theories to accurately predict the result of labor-saving technologies on the duration of work. Cross points out that "Lafargue's images of peasants frolicking around maypoles and miners lingering with friends over a beer … totally missed the new form of sociability: conversation through goods." Moreover, Cross suggests that a person's continued "busyness" may be only partially because of increasing consumption and that "strong cultural, technological, political, and even biological forces come together to make us busy and, even more, to make the virtues and rights of 'laziness' unintelligible."

BIBLIOGRAPHY

Sources

Black, Bob. "The Abolition of Work." *"The Abolition of Work" and other Essays*. Port Townsend, WA: Loompanics, 1985. Print.

Cross, Gary. "A Right to Be Lazy? Busyness in Retrospective." *Social Research* 72.2 (2005): 263+. *General One-File*. Web. 10 Aug. 2012.

Derfler, Leslie. *Paul Lafargue and the Founding of French Marxism 1842-1882*. Cambridge: Harvard UP, 1991. Print.

———. *Paul Lafargue and the Flowering of French Socialism 1882-1911*. Cambridge: Harvard UP, 1998. Print.

Lafargue, Paul. *The Right to Be Lazy*. Trans. Charles Kerr. Chicago: Kerr, 1989. Print.

Marx, Karl, and Frederick Engels. *The Communist Manifesto*. 1848. *Marxists Internet Archive*. Web. 12 Aug. 2012.

Morris, William. *Useful Work Versus Useless Toil*. London: Penguin, 2008. Print.

Further Reading

Jacoby, Russell. *The End of Utopia: Politics and Culture in an Age of Apathy*. New York: Basic, 1999. Print.

Judt, Tony. *Marxism and the French Left: Studies on Labor and Politics in France 1830-1981*. New York: New York UP, 2011. Print.

Kołakowski, Leszek. *Main Currents of Marxism*. New York: Norton, 2005. Print.

Stuart, Robert. *Marxism at Work: Ideology, Class and French Socialism during the Third Republic*. Cambridge: Cambridge UP, 1992. Print.

Daisy Gard

WHAT IS THE THIRD ESTATE?

Emmanuel-Joseph Sieyès

OVERVIEW

With pre-Revolutionary France on the cusp of economic collapse and with the country vehemently debating the nature of political representation, the Abbé Emmanuel-Joseph Sieyès's 1789 pamphlet *What Is the Third Estate?* argued for a drastic redistribution of political power within the French legislative system. The Third Estate was one of the three "orders," or chambers, in the Estates-General, France's pre-Revolutionary legislative body. It represented France's popular and bourgeois classes, while the other two orders represented the clergy and the aristocracy. King Louis XVI had called upon the Estates-General the previous year for help in finding new sources of state revenue. Many were angered by the traditional voting procedures at the Estates-General that effectively removed the influence of the Third Estate and those they represented. With the Estates-General set to convene in May 1789, *What Is the Third Estate?* argued for fundamental change to the way the people were represented at the Estates-General.

What Is the Third Estate? was instantly popular. The pamphlet was widely read, and three editions were printed in 1789. Many of the ideas Sieyès presents became central tenets in the modern French political system, and the pamphlet launched him into a prominent political career. He was involved in some of the major decisions that shaped the course of the French Revolution, such as the creation of the National Assembly and the 1799 coup that brought Napoleon Bonaparte to power. Though Sieyès did not advocate an overthrow of the monarchy, *What Is the Third Estate?* contributed to the political movement that exploded in the Revolution of 1789 and the subsequent political unrest and violence that plagued France in the 1790s and throughout the nineteenth century.

HISTORICAL AND LITERARY CONTEXT

What Is the Third Estate? challenged the institutionalized inequality that limited the legislative power of the Third Estate. Two thirds of the seats in the Estates-General belonged to the upper chambers, representing the clergy and aristocracy, but these "privileged orders" accounted for only a small fraction of France's population. Sieyès and other reformers were unhappy with this unequal representation and also with the traditional voting procedure of the Estates-General. Votes were tallied by order. The three orders voted separately, and the collective vote of each counted as a single voice toward final decisions. The aristocracy had one collective vote, the clergy one vote, and the Third Estate one vote. The Third Estate could not adopt any resolution without the support of at least one of the other orders, and the other orders could effectively veto the demands of the Third Estate. There had been legal deliberations about changing this voting procedure, but the Paris Parlement, France's most powerful court, advocated it in September 1788, enraging Sieyès and many other reformers who were sympathetic to the demands of the Third Estate.

The Estates-General differed from modern legislatures. It was not a regularly convening body. The king could call legislative sessions and theoretically needed members' approval for new tax measures. However, meetings of the Estates-General had become a nearly archaic concept in 1789. The legislature had last met in 1614. In the summer of 1786, finance minister Jacques Necker informed King Louis XVI that the state treasury was in trouble. The king feared that a meeting of the Estates-General would encourage political opposition and that members would demand that the Estates-General become a regularly standing body, such as the British Parliament. After several unsuccessful attempts to circumvent legislative procedure, he finally gave in and called the Estates-General in July 1788. Their meeting was set for the following May, and *What Is the Third Estate?* appeared in January.

During the months before the French Revolution, thousands of pamphlets appeared, many calling for legislative reforms. Legislative reformers had two common demands: (1) that the Third Estate have an equal number of representatives as the other two chambers, and (2) that a simple head count vote replace the vote by order. Sieyès's writing on the matter grew largely out of eighteenth-century Enlightenment philosophy. Rousseau's conception of the social contract was an ambiguous influence, and Adam Smith's description of the political economy was crucial to one of Sieyès's major tenets: that the Third Estate did most of the useful work of the nation and thus deserved greater legislative power.

❖ Key Facts

Time Period:
Late 18th Century

Movement/Issue:
Democratic reform

Place of Publication:
France

Language of Publication:
French

PRIMARY SOURCE

WHAT IS THE THIRD ESTATE?

The Third Estate is a Complete Nation

...

Public services can [...] at present, be divided into four known categories; the army, the law, the Church and the bureaucracy. It needs no detailed analysis to show that the Third Estate everywhere constitutes nineteen-twentieths of them, except that it is loaded with all the really arduous work, all the tasks which the privileged order refuses to perform. Only the well paid and honorific posts are filled by members of the privileged order. Are we to give them credit for this? We could do so only if the Third Estate was unable or unwilling to fill these posts. We know the answer. Nevertheless, the privileged have dared to preclude the Third Estate. "No matter how useful you are," they said, "no matter how able you are, you can go so far and no further. Honors are not for the like of you." The rare exceptions, noticeable as they are bound to be, are, mere mockery, and the sort of language allowed on such occasions is an additional insult.

If this exclusion is a social crime, a veritable act of war against the Third Estate, can it be said at least to be useful to the commonwealth? Ali!

Do we not understand the consequences of monopoly? While discouraging those it excludes, does it not destroy the skill of those it favors? Are we unaware that any work from which free competition is excluded will be performed less well and more expensively?

When any function is made the prerogative of a separate order among the citizens, has nobody remarked how a salary has to be paid not only to the man who actually does the work, but to all those of the same caste who do not, and also to the entire families of both the workers and the nonworkers? Has nobody observed that as soon as the government becomes the property of a separate class, it starts to grow out of all proportion and that posts are created not to meet the needs of the governed but of those who govern them? Has nobody noticed that while on the one hand, we basely and I dare say stupidly accept this situation of ours, on the other hand, when we read the, history of Egypt or stories of travels in India, we describe the same kind of conditions as despicable, monstrous, destructive of all industry, as inimical to social progress, and above all, as debasing to the human race in general and intolerable to Europeans in particular?

Historian William Sewell has called *What Is the Third Estate?* the most influential of the pamphlets that appeared during the winter of 1788 and 1789. Before its publication Sieyès was an unknown ecclesiastical scholar living in Chartres. Though he became the great advocate of the Third Estate, he was actually a member of the clerical order. By the time the Estates-General convened in May, he was known nationally as a major voice in the debate about legislative reform. His conception of representative government ultimately became the French model that is still in place today.

THEMES AND STYLE

What Is the Third Estate? explains the origins of executive power while arguing for a radical change to the French legislative system. Pushing his arguments further than the more reserved pamphleteers, Sieyès challenges the legitimacy of the other two estates and their right to represent the nation. His argument is based on principles of economic utility and the injustice of aristocratic privileges. According to Sieyès, the Third Estate does the overwhelming majority of France's useful work, while the other orders enjoy a privileged

status. For Sieyès, privilege set the other two estates apart and made them foreign to the national workforce. He believed they had forfeited their right to represent the nation by choosing to withdraw into a privileged and foreign state: "It is indisputable that [the privileged orders], having renounced the very charter of citizenship, ought, more certainly than a foreigner, to be denied the right to elect or to be eligible."

In *What Is the Third Estate?* Sieyès persuades with a series of rhetorical questions focused on social utility and privilege. He introduces questions and then answers them himself as he builds his argument for the rights of the Third Estate. The pamphlet begins with a general summary in three questions of the current status of the Third Estate:

> What is the third estate?—*Everything.*
>
> What, until now, has it been in the existing political order?—*Nothing.*
>
> What does it want to be?—*Something.*

From here, questions become more specific and support and develop upon these general ideas. For example, chapter 1 develops a monologue of questions and

What Has the Third Estate Been Until Now? Nothing

...

Let us pursue our theme. By Third Estate is meant all the citizens who belong to the common order. Anybody who holds a legal privilege of any kind deserts the common order, stands as an exception to the common laws and, consequently, does not belong to the Third Estate. As we have already said, a nation is made one by virtue of common laws and common representation. It is indisputably only too true that in France a man who is protected only by the common laws is a nobody, whoever is totally unprivileged must submit to every form of contempt, insult and humiliation. To avoid being completely crushed, what must the unlucky nonprivileged person do? He has to attach himself by all kinds of contemptible actions to some magnate; he prostitutes, his principles and human dignity for the possibility of claiming, in his need, the protection of a somebody.

What Ought to Have Been Done? Basic Principles

...

It is impossible to create a body for any purpose without giving it the organization, procedures and laws appropriate for it to fulfill its intended functions. This is called the constitution of this body. Obviously, the body cannot exist without it. Therefore, it is equally obvious that every government in general is true for each of its components. Thus the Assembly of Representatives which is entrusted with the legislative power, i.e. the exercise of the common will, exists only in the form which the nation has chosen to give it. It is nothing outside the articles of its constitution; only through its constitution can it act, conduct its proceedings and govern...

What ought to have been done amidst all the difficulties and disputes about the coming Estates General? Should we have convened Notables? No. Should we have let the nation and its interests languish? No. Should we have exercised diplomacy upon the interested parties to persuade them all to compromise? No. We should have resorted to the extreme measure of calling an extraordinary representative body. It is the nation that ought to have been consulted.

answers that explain why the Third Estate is "everything": "What does a nation need to survive and prosper? It needs *private* employments and *public* services." "Who undertakes [the activities that support] society? The Third Estate."

Sieyès is a veritable master of varying tone, and he often goes from a very neutral presentation of information to caustic sarcasm on a single page. In places, a question simply frames the discussion of the coming chapter. Elsewhere, drawn-out series of rhetorical questions hurl ridicule upon his political opposition. One example occurs when Sieyès responds to a compromise proposal that asked nobles to give up their tax-exempt status but that maintained the traditional structure of the Estates-General. Sieyès vehemently opposed this compromise and mocked it in his pamphlet:

> The privileged orders do not tire of saying that, from the moment that the three orders jointly surrender their purely monetary exemptions, everything will be equal between them. But if everything will be equal, why then should they be afraid of the [political] demands of the Third Estate? Is it to be supposed that the Third Estate would want to harm itself by attacking a common interest? If everything is to be equal, how can one explain all those efforts to prevent the Third Estate from escaping from its political nullity?

CRITICAL DISCUSSION

Initial reaction to *What Is the Third Estate?*—and the two other pamphlets Sieyès published in 1788 and 1789—was overwhelmingly favorable among reformers. Sieyès was viewed as a revolutionary oracle, and his newfound fame won him a seat at the Estates-General, where he became a respected leader during deliberations. Writer Madame de Staël saw him as the Isaac Newton of politics, and the philosopher and revolutionary political leader Benjamin Constant wrote two essays in homage to Sieyès in 1830. For the most part, however, Sieyès's ideas fell out of favor for much of the nineteenth century. Civil law scholars of the Third Republic, which was established in the years following the Franco-Prussian war of 1870-71, restored him as an important revolutionary figure.

The political impact of *What Is the Third Estate?* was profound and immediate during the debates over the makeup of the 1789 Estates-General. The pamphlet was one of many forces that steered reform efforts toward the more radical course that the French Revolution ultimately followed. Sieyès's argument about the "constitution" contributed to drastic changes in the fundamental structure of the French government. In the context of the 1789 debates, the term "constitution" can have two meanings. It refers to the fundamental structures of the government and also to the written document that establishes those fundamental structures. Sieyès asserted that only the will of the people could create a legitimate constitution in both senses of the word. Because the people had not chosen the constitution of the Estates-General, the Third Estate had the authority to draft a new national constitution based on the will of the people. Following this argument, the Third Estate voted on June 17, 1789, to declare itself a national assembly and begin the work of creating a new French constitution. Sieyès himself authored the resolution that created the modern French National Assembly. Since

the reestablishment of Sieyès as a revolutionary figure, *What Is the Third Estate?* has remained a central document for historians and students looking to understand the political, social, and economic atmosphere that led to revolution, the overthrow of the French monarchy, and nearly a century of political unrest that followed.

In the introduction to his translations of Sieyès's pamphlets, Michael Sonenscher forcefully explains why Sieyès and *What Is the Third Estate?* remain current more than two hundred years after the beginning of the French Revolution. Sieyès grapples with the uncertain and ambiguous "theoretical problems underlying modern democracy and the sometimes perplexing combination of sovereign states, majority rule, competitive markets, and individual liberty." Sewell has studied *What Is the Third Estate?* to better understand the relationship between rhetoric and social and political change. In addition, more philosophically focused scholars such as Keith Michael Baker and Stephanie Frank have worked on the tensions between Sieyès's and Rousseau's thinking on political representation and the general will.

BIBLIOGRAPHY

Sources

Baker, Keith Michael. *Inventing the French Revolution: Essays on French Political Culture in the Eighteenth Century.* Cambridge: Cambridge UP, 1990. Print.

Frank, Stephanie. "The General Will beyond Rousseau: Sieyès' Theological Arguments for the Sovereignty of the Revolutionary National Assembly." *History of European Ideas* 37.3 (2011): 337-43. *SciVerse.* Web. 22 Sept. 2012.

Sewell, William H. *Rhetoric of Bourgeois Revolution: The Abbé Sieyes and "What Is the Third Estate?"* Durham: Duke UP, 1994. *Google Book Search.* Web. 9 Oct. 2012.

Sonenscher, Michael, ed. and trans. *Sieyes: Political Writings.* Indianapolis: Hackett, 2003. *Google Book Search.* Web. 9 Oct. 2012.

Further Reading

Benrekassa, Georges. "Crise de l'ancien régime, crise des idéologies: Une année dans la vie de Sieyès." *Annales. Histoire, Sciences Sociales* 44:1 (1989): 25-46. *JSTOR.* Web. 9 Oct. 2012.

Bronislaw, Baczko. "The Social Contract of the French: Sieyès and Rousseau." *Journal of Modern History* 60 Supplement: *Rethinking French Politics in 1788* (1988). S98-S125. *JSTOR.* Web. 9 Oct. 2012.

Champion, Edme. Introduction. *Qu'est-ce que le tiers état?* Paris: Au siège de la sociéte, 1888. I-XIII. *Archive.org.* Web. 9 Oct. 2012.

Chisick, Harvey. "The Pamphlet Literature of the French Revolution: An Overview." *History of European Ideas* 17.2-3 (1993): 149-66. Print.

Forsyth, Murray. *Reason and Revolution: The Political Thought of the Abbé Sieyes.* New York: Leicester UP, 1987. Print.

Kaiser, Thomas, and Dale Van Kley, eds. *From Deficit to Deluge: The Origins of the French Revolution.* Stanford: Stanford UP, 2011. Print.

Laquièze, Alain. "La Réception de Sieyès par la doctrine publiciste française du XIXème et du XXème siècles." *Electronic Journal of Constitutional History* 6 (2005). *Rediris.es.* Web. 9 Oct. 2012.

Sieyès, Emmanuel-Joseph. *Qu'est-ce que le tiers état?* Paris: Au siège de la sociéte, 1888. *Internet Archive.* Web. 9 Oct. 2012.

Sonenscher, Michael. *Before the Deluge: Public Debt, Inequality, and the Intellectual Origins of the French Revolution.* Princeton: Princeton UP, 2007. Print.

Nicholas Snead

WOMEN

AN APPEAL AGAINST FEMALE SUFFRAGE

Mary Augusta Ward

OVERVIEW

Chiefly penned by British writer Mary Augusta Ward, *An Appeal against Female Suffrage* (1889) was a public declaration of the arguments (later called the Forward Policy) of the organized opposition to the nineteenth-century women's suffrage movement. The manifesto, published in the June 1889 issue of the journal the *Nineteenth Century,* was a textual response to essays in support of early women's suffrage bills, and it represents the paradoxical nature of the oppositional movement's endeavor to craft an intellectually sophisticated and politically persuasive argument for why women were unfit for political franchise. The arguments of the anti-suffragists were based on widely held beliefs about the biological and intellectual differences between the sexes and on the fear that political franchise would diminish women's moral character. Addressed to the "men and women of England," the document was signed by 104 prominent women in the antisuffrage movement distinguished by their class privilege and dedication to social causes such as women's education and the improvement of childcare. The appeal marked a major milestone in the movement, which to that point had been reluctant to make so public a political statement.

Ward's appeal touched off a debate in British magazines, with replies in the *Nineteenth Century,* the *Fortnightly,* and the *National Review.* In addition, the appeal was accompanied by a petition of support titled "Female Suffrage: A Women's Protest," which female readers were requested to sign; the resultant list of 1,500 names was published in the August 1889 issue. The women-led antisuffrage movement also attracted male supporters who agreed that parliamentary representation of women would undermine women's proper role of promoting social reform and safeguarding the family and community. Opposition to women's suffrage remained strong for the following three decades; British women did not gain the vote until 1918. Although the authors of the appeal ultimately lost the battle against women's suffrage, they are noteworthy for their promotion of active female citizenship and social welfare.

HISTORICAL AND LITERARY CONTEXT

An Appeal against Female Suffrage responds to late-nineteenth-century suffragists' demands for parliamentary franchise. Many suffragists rejected the socially accepted belief in intellectual differences between women and men, arguing that democracy demands that men and women share equal rights. By contrast, the upper-class men and women who opposed suffrage believed that women's abilities were different than men's and that women were best suited to care giving. Still, many antisuffragists believed that women's maternal instincts should be applied beyond the household in order to benefit the local community. However, when in April 1889 Parliament seemed likely to pass a bill enfranchising women, few women who opposed the extension of political franchise seemed willing to associate themselves with a public antisuffrage campaign.

More than any other text of the period, *An Appeal against Female Suffrage* fueled the growth of the antisuffrage movement. Although Ward is credited as the document's primary author, several other prominent antisuffragists contributed to its writing. One of the coauthors, Louise Creighton, a leading antisuffrage figure, later became founding president of the National Union of Women Workers, a middle-class social action organization. Ethel Harrison, another coauthor, took part in numerous social actions with the antisuffrage movement. All three had long been devoted to combining maternalistic views of femininity with their beliefs in social duty and education for women, subjects on which they wrote articles before and after the publication of the appeal.

The authors framed the appeal as a response to many of the issues raised in *Enfranchisement of Women* (1851), an essay by John Stuart Mill and his wife, Harriet Taylor. One of several texts responsible for launching the nineteenth-century suffrage debate, *Enfranchisement of Women* proposes that denial of political franchise subjects intellectually sophisticated women to the whims of their social inferiors. Such class distinctions related to social hierarchy were intrinsic to the suffrage debate and were to be found in equal measure in *An Appeal,* which argued that the enfranchisement of women would grant to immoral, uneducated women political rights they could not effectively wield. The Mills' essay, published in the *Westminster Review,* attacks arguments that there is a biological basis for women's inferiority, that women's "proper sphere" is the home, and that women can perform domestic duties and at the same time be

Key Facts

Time Period:
Late 19th Century

Movement/Issue:
Opposition to women's suffrage

Place of Publication:
England

Language of Publication:
English

MARY AUGUSTA WARD: ANTI-SUFFRAGIST AND WOMAN OF LETTERS

By the time *An Appeal against Women's Suffrage* was published in 1889, Mary Augusta Ward, referred to as Mrs. Humphry Ward, was an acclaimed novelist and campaigner for social causes. The wife of an Oxford academic and niece of poet Matthew Arnold, Ward financially supported her family through her writing and was a vocal advocate for women's education. Her first novel, *Robert Elsmere* (1888), dealt boldly with topics of loss of faith and disillusionment in the church. The book was so controversial that it prompted a reply from British prime minister William Gladstone, which drove sales of the novel even higher.

Ward traveled widely in order to raise funds for various charities, to exhaustively promote social reform, and to spread her personal belief in progress. In 1908 she helped found the Women's National Anti-Suffrage League in England, which also led to her meeting U.S. president Theodore Roosevelt. As one of the leading Edwardian female novelists, she was asked by Roosevelt to write for readers in the United States about England's contribution to the World War I effort. The articles served as an inspiration for several of her subsequent novels. Shortly before her death in 1920, she became one of England's first female magistrates.

politically active. Nevertheless, *Enfranchisement of Women* was not a plea for equity so much as a request that the higher-ranking women of the sort who were leading the debate on both sides should not be represented politically by those who were less knowledgeable or of a lower social position.

An Appeal against Female Suffrage influenced several subsequent antisuffrage texts, including the Women's National Anti-Suffrage League's formal constitution, which Ward helped to draft in 1908. In 1912 Violet Markham, one of the antisuffrage movement's key speakers, gave a speech at a rally at Albert Hall, echoing Ward's view that women play an important political role not through voting but through their commitment to social action. However, following the enfranchisement of women, antisuffrage literature became overshadowed by suffragist writing, which had proved crucial to inciting political and social change. Nevertheless, *An Appeal against Female Suffrage* remains significant for its role in pioneering the idea that although women and men should play different political and social roles, women's role is equally important as men's.

THEMES AND STYLE

The central theme of *An Appeal against Female Suffrage* is that men are better suited to national politics whereas women should focus on their local community. The appeal aims to convince readers that women's "work

for the State, and their responsibilities towards it, must always differ essentially from those of men, and that therefore their share in the working of the State machinery should be different from that assigned to men." The authors provide six points of support for their argument: women should not impinge on matters that require force or aggression, women's participation in politics impairs their morality, enfranchisement threatens the structure of the English family, enfranchisement is merely a political ploy to gain votes from women, Parliament is already attending to injustices toward women, and increased suffrage would not help to address women's needs.

The document's rhetorical strategy relies on its sophisticated appeals to the "common sense" of educated English men and women. It replies to specific arguments in the suffrage debate, defining citizenship as "participation of each individual in effort for the good of the community" and affirming women's social value as citizens. The appeal demonstrates the unity of the writers and signatories through use of the first-person plural: "We, the undersigned." Despite the fact that all of the signatories are women, however, the document refers to women in the third person: "we would give them their full share in the State of social effort and social mechanism ... but we protest against their admission to direct power in that State." In a society dominated by men, the implied distance between the authors as women and British women as a whole lends objectivity to the document and posits the question of suffrage as a political rather than an emotional issue.

The appeal is written in the style of a formal address. Its scholarly language highlights the gentility and intelligence of the authors and their supporters in order to gain the respect of readers from a similar economic class. The authors retain a respectable emotional distance from the text in order to impress upon the reader the "gravity of the question." Their appeal is phrased as a request rather than as an attack, demonstrating the sympathetic, peaceful nature that the authors' claim is inherent to all women. Still, the authors are firm in their criticism of enfranchisement as a selfish enterprise, which they claim is unbecoming of women and damaging to society as a whole: "the pursuit of a mere outward equality with men is for women not only vain but demoralizing ... It tends to personal struggle and rivalry, where the only effort of both the great divisions of the human family should be to contribute the characteristic labor and best gifts of each to the common stock."

CRITICAL DISCUSSION

Upon publication, Ward's appeal met with equally strong support and criticism. The editor of the publication in which it was printed observed that the petition could be taken as a sample of the good judgment of the educated women of the country. By contrast, leading suffragettes Millicent Garrett Fawcett and Mary Margaret Dilke criticized the document's definition of womanhood and the claim that

enfranchisement would damage the family. Fawcett observes in a reply published in the same journal that the signatories are all of similar class advantage and thus do not represent the concerns of the majority of their sex. However, she agrees with Ward's claims that there are important differences between the sexes: "Let this fact be frankly recognized and let due weight be given to it in the representative system of the country." In a reply printed in the same issue as Fawcett's, Dilke echoes the sentiment: "woman may never be intellectually fitted for the position of minister of the Crown or ambassador … but that does not affect one way or the other her right to vote, or the right of the nation to have her recorded opinion on every question with which she is familiar."

The debate ignited by *An Appeal against Women's Suffrage* shaped the discourse on enfranchisement for several decades, until the "woman question" was finally answered in 1918. Following the enfranchisement of women, the antisuffrage appeal retained importance as a significant early document in the suffrage debate and as a departure from the dominant view that women should abstain from all involvement in affairs of the state. In an essay in *Women's History Review,* Julia Bush (2002) writes that the appeal was "certainly encouraged and facilitated by male antisuffragists, including the editor of the journal, but the private correspondence of Mary Ward, Louise Creighton and Ethel Harrison, the three chief authors, makes it clear that they were far from being mere pawns in a male political power game."

Generally, scholars have discussed *An Appeal against Female Suffrage* and the Forward Policy as components of an overall survey of prosuffrage texts. Bush notes, "unappealing though anti-suffrage beliefs may nowadays seem, they were as much a part of Victorian and Edwardian women's history as suffragism itself." Despite the Forward Policy's eventual failure as a movement, critics appreciate the appeal for its significance as a social document and as a voice in the late-nineteenth-century conversation about empire and gender politics. Scholars also view the document as pivotal in the development of women's social energies and education. According to Penelope Tuson in *Playing the Game: The Story of Western Women in Arabia* (2003), the exchanges in the *Nineteenth Century* begun by Ward's appeal illustrate the "complexities and contradictions of feminist, or woman's activist, politics at the turn of the century."

BIBLIOGRAPHY

Sources

Bush, Julia. "British Women's Anti-Suffragism and the Forward Policy, 1908-14." *Women's History Review* 11.3 (2002): 431-54. Web. 21 June 2012.

Dilke, Mary Margaret. "The Appeal against Female Suffrage: A Reply. II." *Literature of the Women's Suffrage Campaign in England.* Ed. Carolyn Christensen Nelson. Toronto: Broadview, 2004. 37-43. Web. 5 July 2012.

Fawcett, Millicent Garrett. "From 'The Appeal against Female Suffrage: A Reply. I.'" *Literature of the Women's Suffrage Campaign in England.* Ed. Carolyn Christensen Nelson. Toronto: Broadview, 2004. 30-36. Web. 5 July 2012.

Munhend, Rosemary J., and LuAnn Fletcher. *Victorian Prose: An Anthology.* New York: Columbia UP, 1999. Print.

Tuson, Penelope. *Playing the Game: The Story of Western Women in Arabia.* New York: St. Martin's, 2003. Print.

Further Reading

Argyle, Gisela. "Mrs. Humphry Ward's Fictional Experiments in the Woman Question." *Studies in English Literature, 1500-1900* 43.4 (2003): 939-57. *Literature Resource Center.* Web. 21 June 2012.

Bush, Julia. *Women against the Vote: Female Anti-Suffragism in Britain.* Oxford: Oxford UP, 2007. Print.

Reynolds, K. D. *Aristocratic Women and Political Society in Victorian Britain.* New York: Oxford UP, 1999. Print.

Roberts, Marie. *The Opponents: The Anti-Suffragists.* London: Routledge/Thoemmes, 1995. Print.

Sutherland, John. *Mrs. Humphry Ward: Eminent Victorian, Pre-Eminent Edwardian.* New York: Oxford UP, 1990. Print.

Y., G. "The Work of Mrs. Humphry Ward." *Twentieth-Century Literary Criticism.* Ed. Marie Lazzari. Vol. 55. Detroit: Gale Research, 1995. *Literature Resource Center.* Web. 21 June 2012.

Eleanor Fogolin

DECLARATION OF SENTIMENTS

Elizabeth Cady Stanton

OVERVIEW

Principally authored by Elizabeth Cady Stanton and presented on July 19, 1848, at the first women's rights convention in Seneca Falls, New York, the *Declaration of Sentiments* outlines a series of grievances in response to the marginalization of women and proposes eleven resolutions to help women achieve equality in all aspects of their lives. The declaration details specific injustices: women's lack of voting, property, and divorce rights; their exclusion from public participation in religion and education; and a woman's forced obedience to a husband who can "deprive her of her liberty." Stanton also included an action plan for building a movement, calling on more women to organize similar conventions throughout the country. Modeled after the *Declaration of Independence,* the *Declaration of Sentiments* connects the nascent campaign for women's rights with a well-known American symbol of liberty while underscoring the point that the *Declaration of Independence,* which was ostensibly all inclusive, used language that was ambiguous with respect to women.

Stanton presented the declaration to a crowd of three hundred men and women, and it soon generated widespread ridicule among religious leaders and members of the press. Some members of the growing women's rights movement, including Stanton's sister Harriet, distanced themselves from the document and removed their signatures because of its controversial inclusion of a resolution supporting women's right to vote. The *Declaration of Sentiments* was the first thorough statement in the United States addressing the political, economic, and social repression of women and became a model for subsequent feminist political documents and organizations, including the International Council of Women, which was formed in 1888. The *Declaration* provided a theoretical framework firmly grounded in the highest ideals of the American Revolution for women to act as a separate class in demanding equal rights.

HISTORICAL AND LITERARY CONTEXT

The *Declaration of Sentiments* responds to the social and political injustices experienced by American women in the 1840s as they sought greater control over their lives. By law a woman and her children were considered the property of her husband and had no independent civil existence without him. Married women were largely prohibited from owning or inheriting property and were excluded from publicly participating in elections or education. Their employment prospects were dim: they could obtain few jobs—for example, as domestic workers and teachers—and those positions paid less than half of what a man received doing the same work.

By the time the *Declaration of Sentiments* was read in 1848, some progressive individuals throughout the country had begun working for women's rights, but the cause had not yet gained national attention. Many of the outspoken advocates pushing for change had gained recognition and experience through their involvement with the abolitionist movement, which taught them how to organize, publicize, and articulate a political protest. Starting in 1832, journalist William Lloyd Garrison (1805-79) organized antislavery societies that welcomed the full participation of women, including the well-spoken activist Lucretia Mott (1793-1880) and Stanton (1815-1902). The two women met at an antislavery convention where women were barred from participation by event organizers. From this incident a seed was planted for a convention dedicated to the rights of women, and Stanton took the lead in drafting the document.

The *Declaration of Sentiments* took ideas for its content from the *Declaration of Independence* and borrowed from the structure of past declarations by including a systematized listing of grievances and resolutions. Written in 1776, the *Declaration of Independence* famously justified the independence of the United States by listing colonial grievances against King George III and asserting the colonies' natural and legal rights, including the right to revolution. Stanton saw her declaration as an extension and a revision of the *Declaration of Independence,* composing what she believed was a truer expression of natural rights because of its inclusion of women. The *Declaration of Sentiments* substitutes the injustices imposed on women by men for the eighteen grievances perpetuated by George III against the colonists. Eleven resolutions lay out concrete ideas about how to improve women's lives and strengthen the overall *Declaration* by demanding that women have the same rights as men and be granted civic participation equal to their male counterparts.

Key Facts

Time Period:
Mid-19th Century

Movement/Issue:
Feminism; Women's suffrage

Place of Publication:
United States

Language of Publication:
English

ELIZABETH CADY STANTON: FEMINIST ICON AND SOCIAL REFORMER

A driving force behind the Seneca Falls Convention and the drafting of the *Declaration of Sentiments,* Elizabeth Cady Stanton is remembered for her role in shaping the early women's rights movement. Unlike many of her contemporaries, Stanton reaped the benefits of a formal education at Johnstown Academy, where she excelled in Latin, Greek, and mathematics. The privileged daughter of a judge, she continued her education at Troy Female Seminary. As a young woman she developed a strong relationship with her cousin, Gerrit Smith, who was an active member of the New York abolitionist movement and who helped Stanton foster her own antislavery sentiments.

In 1851 Stanton was introduced to Susan B. Anthony, who would become one of Stanton's primary writing partners. Unable to commit to a rigorous travel schedule until her seven young children were grown, Stanton wrote the speeches that Anthony presented at public appearances at various women's rights conventions. Over the years the two women remained close friends and allies and shared similar political beliefs. Along with Matilda Joslyn Gage, the two founded the National Woman Suffrage Association in 1869 in response to a split in the American Equal Rights Association over whether the group should support the Fifteenth Amendment. Stanton and Anthony believed that the amendment should not be ratified unless it granted women the right to vote. Later in her career Stanton dedicated herself to social reforms related to women's concerns other than suffrage. She collaborated with Gage and Anthony to write the first three volumes of *The History of Woman Suffrage* and wrote her most cherished speech, "The Solitude of Self," in 1892. She continued to write until her death in 1902.

The *Declaration of Sentiments* initiated the first organized women's rights and suffrage movements in the United States. It inspired a multitude of passionate speeches and a body of literature that illuminated the separate treatment of women and fought for their civil rights. Beginning with political essays such as Harriet Taylor Mill's "The Enfranchisement of Women" (1851) and speeches such as Sojourner Truth's "Ain't I a Woman" (1851), feminist writers kept up the momentum created by the *Declaration of Sentiments* as women drove toward social reforms and the right to vote. Literature reflected this struggle and provided a platform for women to voice their opinions and depict their experiences. Authors such as Charlotte Perkins Gilman used their prose to enter into American political discussion by challenging the conventional roles of women. She and other early twentieth-century women writers experienced a resurgence in popularity during the 1960s and 1970s, when the second wave of feminism revisited questions surrounding the experiences of women initially raised by the *Declaration of Sentiments.* The document continues to generate significant scholarly interest because of its pivotal role in the campaign for women's rights.

THEMES AND STYLE

The *Declaration of Sentiments* accuses the U.S. government of failing to live up to its democratic vision by denying women their natural rights. In modeling her manifesto after the *Declaration of Independence,* Stanton borrowed from and revised the Founding Fathers' principle of natural rights, which she used to challenge the social and political order of the new nation. The most famous revision in the *Declaration of Sentiments* comes in the second paragraph, in which Stanton asserts that "all men and women are created equal." Her adaptation of Thomas Jefferson's famous phrase boldly calls out for the equality of the sexes and, by mimicking the logic and phrasing of the *Declaration of Independence,* addresses the ways in which American democracy has not lived up to the ideals of the Revolution. Keeping the revolutionary spirit of the original, Stanton argues, "Whenever any form of government becomes destructive of these ends, it is the right of those who suffer from it to refuse allegiance to it, and to insist upon the institution of a new government." In this way, she rhetorically transformed revolutionary thought into public moral action for the betterment of women's lives.

The *Declaration of Sentiments* cloaks itself in the authority of the *Declaration of Independence.* The document retains the format and much of the same wording as the original in order to set up parallels that establish an ethos for the women's rights movement. By altering the *Declaration of Independence* to reflect the treatment of women, Stanton connects the movement to a larger audience. She strengthens her argument for the natural rights of women by making biblically based appeals. In the third resolution Stanton maintains "that woman is man's equal—was intended to be so by the Creator, and the highest good of the race demands that she be so." Invoking the Christian ethos, she deftly counters arguments against women's rights that were rooted in Christian doctrine.

The *Declaration of Sentiments* adopts a tone of defiance in order to make a rousing emotional appeal that persuades readers and listeners to action. Giving a voice to a large group of society that had previously been discouraged from speaking out, the document erupts in fiery language that spells out the crippling social limitations imposed on women by society. Just as the framers of the *Declaration of Independence* outlined the injustices perpetuated by King George III against the colonies, Stanton also details the ways in which men have sought to "establish … an absolute tyranny" over women. Such bold and passionate language worked to win support from fellow women, while reliance on the ideology of natural rights and the ethos created from referencing the *Declaration of*

Independence helped Stanton secure supporters who might otherwise have been wary of such a forceful presentation.

CRITICAL DISCUSSION

After the *Declaration of Sentiments* was introduced and debated at the Seneca Falls Convention in 1848, it received mixed reactions from within the women's movement. Many women's rights advocates, including Stanton's fellow organizer, Mott, felt that the inclusion of a resolution calling for women's right to vote was too extreme and would hurt the overall reception of the declaration. Nationally, public reaction to the convention tended toward ridicule and sarcasm rather than outrage or positive engagement. Newspapers reporting on the convention responded to the gathering by reiterating the popular beliefs of the time— namely, that a woman's place was in the home. The convention in general and the declaration in particular received respect from prominent activists throughout the country. Frederick Douglass, writing in the *North Star,* commented on the "marked ability and dignity" that characterized the event. Horace Greeley wrote in the *New York Tribune,* "When ... asked to say in sober earnest what adequate reason he can give, for refusing the demand of women to an equal participation with men in political rights, he must answer, None at all .... It is but the assertion of a natural right, and such must be conceded." However, many abolitionists regarded the plight for women's rights as an unnecessary distraction from the more urgent cause of African American male suffrage in the North and ultimately the goal of universal emancipation. Stanton welcomed all responses to the declaration; she felt that any responses, even negative ones, helped generate awareness of the problem and were first steps toward change.

The *Declaration of Sentiments* inspired a host of women to take action and organize similar conventions throughout the country, and it remains one of the most influential documents of the women's rights movement. Christine Bolt succinctly summarizes the declaration's contributions in *The Women's Movement in the United States and Britain from the 1790s to the 1920s,* writing, "It is hard to see how a better beginning could have been made." In her book *An Unfinished Battle: American Women 1848-1865,* Harriet Sigerman posits that the *Declaration of Sentiments* provided "a road map for ... the women's rights movement for decades to come." The women's rights movement of the late nineteenth century went on to address the issues initially raised by the *Declaration of Sentiments.* Eventually, winning the right to vote emerged as the central issue, because the vote was seen as a means by which all other reforms could be attained. In the time since the declaration was first read, it has garnered much feminist scholarly attention for its pivotal role in initiating the women's rights movement in the United States as well as significant

rhetorical analysis for its manipulation of the *Declaration of Independence.*

The majority of scholarship surrounding the *Declaration of Sentiments* has focused on its role in shaping the American women's rights movement, particularly its influence on later forms of feminism. Discussing the declaration's impact on American society, Judith Wellman argues in *The Road to Seneca Falls* that the convention occupies a fulcrum point in history between the American Revolution and the Civil War at which time individuals searched to define the core meaning of citizenship. Other scholars, positioning the "Declaration of Sentiments" as radically different from the *Declaration of Independence,* have taken to analyzing Stanton's manifesto as a document of political theory. In her book *Cannon Fodder: Historical Women Political Thinkers,* Penny A. Weiss takes issue with seeing the *Declaration of Sentiments* as a minor corrective text to the original. Instead Weiss calls for the increased study of the *Declaration of Sentiments* as a unique text as well as one in a line of feminist texts rather than as simply a complement to the *Declaration of Independence.*

Portrait of Elizabeth Cady Stanton, painted by Anna E. Klumpke in 1889. Stanton was the principal author of the "Declaration of Sentiments" and an early proponent of women's rights. NATIONAL PORTRAIT GALLERY, SMITHSONIAN INSTITUTION/ART RESOURCE, NY

BIBLIOGRAPHY

Sources

Bolt, Christine. *The Women's Movement in the United States and Britain from the 1790s to the 1920s.* Amherst: U of Massachusetts P, 1993. Print.

Sigerman, Harriet. *An Unfinished Battle: American Women 1848-1865.* New York: Oxford UP USA, 1998. Print.

Stanton, Elizabeth Cady. "The *Declaration of Sentiments* and Resolutions." CUNY Libraries. Web. 4 June 2012.

Weiss, Penny A. *Cannon Fodder: Historical Women Political Thinkers.* University Park: Pennsylvania State UP, 2009. Print.

Wellman, Judith. "The Seneca Falls Convention: Setting the National Stage for Women's Suffrage." *History Now: American History Online.* Gilder Lehrman Institute of American History, Spring 2006. Web. 4 June 2012.

Further Reading

Davis, Sue. *The Political Thought of Elizabeth Cady Stanton.* New York: New York UP, 2010. Print.

Dubois, Ellen Carol. *Feminism and Suffrage: The Emergence of an Independent Women's Movement in America, 1848-1869.* New York: Cornell UP, 1999. Print.

———. *Woman Suffrage and Women's Rights.* New York: New York UP, 1998. Print.

Hoff, Joan. *Law, Gender and Injustice: A Legal History of U.S. Women.* New York: New York UP, 1994. Print.

McMillen, Sally. *Seneca Falls and the Origins of the Women's Rights Movement.* New York: Oxford UP USA, 2009. Print.

Wellman, Judith. *The Road to Seneca Falls.* Urbana: U of Illinois P, 2004. Print.

Elizabeth Orvis

DECLARATION OF THE RIGHTS OF WOMEN AND OF THE FEMALE CITIZEN

Olympe de Gouges

OVERVIEW

Olympe de Gouges's *Declaration of the Rights of Women and of the Female Citizen,* published in September 1791 amid the tumult of the French Revolution, calls for full citizenship rights for women—the "imprescriptible" rights of liberty, property, security, and freedom from oppression. These are the same rights expressed in the *Declaration of the Rights of Man and Citizen* and adopted by the National Assembly as the foundation for a new French government two years earlier. That declaration, however, failed to consider women as citizens, and the new government framework provided both the source of outrage and the literary template for de Gouges's scorching declaration, which argues that rights derived from natural law extend equally to men and women. Her declaration addresses a wide audience—the men of the revolution generally (in the introduction), the National Assembly (the seventeen articles modeled on the *Declaration of the Rights of Man),* and the women of France (the postscript). A constitutional monarchist, de Gouges dedicated the *Declaration* to Marie-Antoinette.

The National Assembly barely noticed the *Declaration of the Rights of Women,* and the popular Parisian press mocked its author. Nevertheless, de Gouges continued to speak out for universal human rights and also publicly opposed the tactics of Robespierre and the execution of the king and queen of France in 1793. She herself was beheaded that same year, primarily for her outspokenness as a monarchist. Although the *Declaration* had little practical impact— women did not enjoy full citizenship in France until 1944—it is considered significant for, as Susan P. Conner puts it in the *Women's Studies Encyclopedia,* its coherent expression of the "the aims of many French Revolutionary activists."

HISTORICAL AND LITERARY CONTEXT

The *Declaration of the Rights of Women* reflects the disappointment some women felt when the revolution in which they had played such an active role did not recognize them publicly. The October 5, 1789, Women's March on Versailles, which forced Louis XVI and Marie-Antoinette to return to Paris, is the most dramatic example of female participation in the

revolution, though women had been involved in many other ways in the preceding months: writing petitions, hosting salons, and even storming the Bastille along with men. Yet when the new government was formed, women found themselves excluded. After the Women's March, the anonymous "Women's Petition" was submitted to the National Assembly, exposing the hypocrisy of the *Declaration of the Rights of Man* in proclaiming the French a free people while allowing "thirteen million slaves shamefully to wear the shackles of thirteen million despots!"

On September 14, 1791, after an unsuccessful attempt to flee Paris, King Louis XVI reluctantly accepted the Constitution. On the same day the king acquiesced, de Gouges published her pamphlet. She was troubled by the king's flight, but she was even more outraged that women under the new government were not even considered "passive citizens," with active citizenship being reserved for white, independent, tax-paying males. She was also frustrated at being marginalized or ignored in her work as both a playwright and a political writer.

The *Declaration of the Rights of Women* was by far the boldest petition for equal rights for women that a "citoyenne" had ever delivered. The hundreds of other petitions women had offered were so locked in the received culture that they did little more than ask for certain limited rights, especially in regard to inheritance, divorce, and recognition and support of illegitimate children. In July 1790 the *philosophe* Condorcet published a bolder statement on women's rights, "On the Admission of Women to the Rights of Citizenship," asserting that if natural law entitles men to social and political rights, it entitles women to them no less. Some women's clubs and the intellectual *Cercle Social* embraced Condorcet's views, but the argument in favor of female rights remained on the fringes.

Although several other feminist declarations followed the *Declaration of the Rights of Women,* they do not appear to have been influenced by de Gouges's document. The most notable is the British writer Mary Wollstonecraft's *Vindication of the Rights of Women* (1792), which calls for broader education for women but stops short of pronouncing men and

Key Facts

Time Period:
Late 18th Century

Movement/Issue:
Feminism; Women's rights

Place of Publication:
France

Language of Publication:
French

THE BEHEADING OF OLYMPE DE GOUGES: THEATER AT THE GUILLOTINE

Article 10 of the *Declaration of the Rights of Women,* often quoted for its foreshadowing of de Gouges's death, asserts that "woman has the right to mount the scaffold, so she should have the right equally to mount the rostrum." It was not, however, her *Declaration* that led de Gouges to the scaffold. Instead, she was brought to trial for calling for a direct vote by the people of France on whether they wanted monarchy, federalism, or republicanism as their form of government. In so doing, she violated a decree prohibiting any effort to restore the monarchy. She was arrested on July 20, 1793.

She had already imagined a prominent role for herself on the public stage, as she had been working on a play in which her character advises the queen on how to hold on to the throne. Although purely fiction, the play was used against de Gouges to prove her collusion with the queen. In "Performing Justice: The Trials of Olympe de Gouges," Janie Vanpée describes how the melding of theater and reality was obvious even in de Gouges's last words. "From the scaffold, gazing at the spectators with defiance and confidence, she exclaimed, 'Children of the Fatherland, you will avenge my death.' Fusing reality with theatre one last time, she turned the reality of her death into the performance of her life."

women equals. Possibly because of its stronger feminist statement, de Gouges's *Declaration of the Rights of Women* remained little known or acknowledged until feminist researchers brought it to light again in the twentieth century.

THEMES AND STYLE

The unifying themes of the *Declaration of the Rights of Women* are that natural law entitles women to the same rights as men and that the tyranny of men is all that stands in the way of those rights. Article 4 states the position directly: "the only limits on the exercise of the natural rights of women are perpetual male tyranny." The document argues that laws drawn from "nature and reason" must reform these limits, not just for the sake of women's rights but also for the benefit of a healthy public life and government.

The rhetorical strength of the *Declaration* is rooted in its subversion of the *Declaration of the Rights of Man.* At times, de Gouges moves from a specific point in the *Declaration of the Rights of Man* to a universal, overarching concept. For example, whereas article 16 of the *Declaration of the Rights of Man* asserts that there is no constitution if the observance of law is not assured, the same article in the *Declaration of the Rights of Women* crumbles the foundation of any constitution that "the majority of individuals comprising the nation have not cooperated

in drafting." In other places, de Gouges reinterprets more general principles as special concerns of women. The general right of free speech in article 11 in the *Declaration of the Rights of Man* becomes, in Gouges's article 11, the specific right for a woman to "say freely, I am the mother of a child which belongs to you, without being forced by a barbarous prejudice to hide the truth."

The *Declaration of the Rights of Woman* displays great stylistic variety. The introduction combines biting sarcasm ("Man, are you capable of being just? It is a woman who poses the question; you will not deprive her of that right at least.") with a reverence for nature and its ways ("Everywhere you will find [men and women] mingled; everywhere they cooperate in harmonious togetherness in this immortal masterpiece."). The preamble begins in the formal language of public discourse by asserting "the natural, inalienable, and sacred rights of woman" as an equal; yet it concludes by differentiating women, referring to them in flowery prose as "the sex that is as superior in beauty as it is in courage during the sufferings of maternity." The seventeen articles adopt, for the most part, the straightforward style of the *Declaration of the Rights of Man,* but the postscript, addressed to women, is emotionally charged: "Oh, women, women! When will you cease to be blind? What have you received from the Revolution? A more pronounced scorn, a more marked disdain." Contending that "marriage is the tomb of trust and love," de Gouges offers as the final part of her *Declaration* a "form for a social contract between man and woman" that outlines in legalistic language the assurance of communal wealth for a couple.

CRITICAL DISCUSSION

Though destined for nearly two hundred years of obscurity, the *Declaration of the Rights of Women* did make a fleeting impression upon its initial appearance. Some of its specific proposals briefly became law in 1792, when women and illegitimate children were given limited civil rights. Furthermore, de Gouges made a somewhat shocking impression with her willingness to identify herself openly as a *femme de lettres,* defying the "conventions of anonymity, discretion, and modesty by flaunting herself in all her texts," as Janie Vanpée puts it in her 1999 essay in *Theater Journal.* Mainly, however, *Declaration,* like the rest of de Gouges's writing, was ignored, and when the women's clubs were banned in 1793 during the Reign of Terror, the political voices of females were silenced.

In England and the United States, the movement for women's rights slowly gained strength during the nineteenth and twentieth centuries, increasingly echoing de Gouges's sentiments. However, in her piece for *Feminist Issues,* Marie Josephine Diamond writes that histories of the French Revolution during the same period "either completely ignored women or assigned them to marginalia, demonology, or hagiography."

In 1904 the work of de Gouges came briefly out of obscurity when Alfred Guillois published a psychological study of her. Guillois "diagnosed" her with "paranoia reformatoria," a term he coined, reducing her political activity to mental illness. Not until the rise of feminist scholarship in the 1970s—and the subsequent bicentennial of the French Revolution—did de Gouges emerge from the darkness.

Modern scholarship on de Gouges and her writings explores gender, language, identity, and perspectives on natural law. In *Rebel Daughters: Women and the French Revolution,* Joan Wallach Scott argues that de Gouges exposed a paradox in revolutionary political theory: "the relative and highly particularized aspect, the undeniable [male] embodiment, of its claim to universality." Other scholars follow de Gouges as an example of the trend during the French Revolution to blend theater and public discourse, especially since so much of her writing was for the theater. In an essay for *Eighteenth-Century Studies,* Gregory Brown explores the "construction of social identities, especially gender, through language," with de Gouges as a subject of special interest. Religious philosophers argue that without recognizing the wise Creator that de Gouges saw presiding over a divine order, scholars may miss, as Tina Beattie puts it in a 2008 article in *Religion and Human Rights,* "the fleeting historical moment when the scholastic understanding of natural law broke free of its androcentric moorings in order to provide a potent argument for the full and equal rights of the woman citizen of the modern state."

A 1784 portrait of French writer Olympe de Gouges. Arguing for women's rights, de Gouges based her 1791 *Declaration of the Rights of Woman (Les Droits de la Femme)* on the 1789 *Declaration of the Rights of Man and Citizen.* BRIDGEMAN-GIRAUDON/ ART RESOURCE, NY

BIBLIOGRAPHY

Sources

Beattie, Tina. "'Justice Enacted Not These Human Laws' (Antigone): Religion, Natural Law, and Women's Rights." *Religion and Human Rights* 3.3 (2008): 247-49. *Political Science Complete.* Web. 11 July 2012.

Brown, Gregory S. "The Self-Fashionings of Olympe de Gouges, 1784-1789." *Eighteenth-Century Studies* 34.3 (2001): 383-401. ASECS. Web. 6 July 2012.

Conner, Susan P. "Declaration of the Rights of Woman (Les Droits de la Femme)." *Women's Studies Encyclopedia.* Ed. Helen Tierney. Westport: Greenwood, 2002. Web. 7 July 2012.

"Declaration of the Rights of Women and the Female Citizen." *Liberty, Equality, Fraternity: Exploring the French Revolution.* George Mason University. Web. 2 July 2012.

De Gouges, Olympe. "Women's Petition to the National Assembly." *Liberty, Equality, Fraternity: Exploring the French Revolution.* George Mason University. Web. 5 July 2012.

Diamond, Marie Josephine. "The Revolutionary Rhetoric of Olympe De Gouges." *Feminist Issues* 14.1 (1994): 3-23. Religion and Philosophy Collection. Web. 11 July 2012.

Scott, Joan Wallach. "'A Woman Who Has Only Paradoxes to Offer': Olympe de Gouges Claims Rights for Women." *Rebel Daughters: Women and the French Revolution.* Ed. Sara E. Melzer and Leslie W. Rabine. New York: Oxford UP, 1992. Print.

Vanpée, Janie. "Performing Justice: The Trials of Olympe de Gouges." *Theater Journal* 51.1 (1999): 47-65. Web. 8 July 2012.

Further Reading

Godineau, Dominique. *The Women of Paris and Their French Revolution.* Berkeley: U of California P, 1998. Print.

Hesse, Carla. *The Other Enlightenment: How French Women Became Modern.* Princeton: Princeton UP, 2003. Print.

Levy, Darline Gray, Harriet Branson Applewhite, and Mary Durham Johns, eds. *Women in Revolutionary Paris.* Urbana: U of Illinois P, 1979. Print.

Scott, Joan Wallach. "The Uses of Imagination: Olympe de Gouges in the French Revolution." *Only Paradoxes to Offer: French Feminists and the Rights of Man.* Cambridge: Harvard UP, 1996. Print.

Carol Francis

A MOUZELL FOR MELASTOMUS

Rachel Speght

❖ *Key Facts*

Time Period:
Early 17th Century

Movement/Issue:
Early European feminism;
Public debate over the
nature of women

Place of Publication:
England

**Language of
Publication:**
English

OVERVIEW

Written by nineteen-year-old Englishwoman Rachel Speght in 1617, *A Mouzell for Melastomus* (*A Muzzle for Melastomus*) critiques a centuries-old trend of disparaging women in print, arguing instead that good women are valuable people created in God's image. As a direct response to *Arraignment of Lewd, Idle, Froward, and Unconstant Women* (1615) by Joseph Swetnam, the tract uses biblical exegesis to counter Swetnam's insulting language and ideas. By refuting Swetnam's tract, the pamphlet takes part in the larger literary *querelle des femmes,* or the discussion about the nature of women, and it remains the only verifiable example of a female writer engaging in this debate under her own name. Addressed to all participants in the debate, but particularly to women of all classes and ages, *Mouzell* testifies to the rhetorical skill and biblical knowledge of an educated young woman from London. It also contributed to the broader religious political debate that involved a movement to resist the rule of King James I.

After its publication, *Mouzell* was complimented and criticized by subsequent participants in the *querelle des femmes.* Some writers and critics called the volume naive and even prudish, while others praised the courage and intelligence of its author, who presents a logical argument in two parts. Speght opens with a tightly organized polemical statement and then (in a separate but appended pamphlet) counters Swetnam's errors point by point. In the end Speght's work helped to publicize a more female-friendly style of scriptural interpretation, emphasizing that women and men alike could receive divine grace and take part in learned public debates. *Mouzell* also fueled the publication of other pamphlets and tracts that tackle Swetnam's accusations, including the pseudonymous works *Ester Hath Hang'd Haman* (1617) by Ester Sowernam and *The Worming of a Mad Dogge* (1617) by Constantia Munda. In this way *Mouzell* helped to create a profitable niche genre of polemical literature dealing with the "woman question."

HISTORICAL AND LITERARY CONTEXT

A Mouzell for Melastomus responds to the misogynist accusation that women are not only subordinate to men but also inherently flawed. After the rise of vernacular translations of the Bible during the sixteenth century, misogynistic writers could more easily cite passages from such books as Genesis and Ephesians to back up their opinions—claiming, for example, that Eve's original sin indicated universal female waywardness. Apologists for women sought to critique these interpretations of scripture without questioning the veracity of the divine words themselves. They argued that women were being framed as uniformly sensual, self-indulgent, and inferior without good reason. Instead, they pointed out, scripture itself demanded respect for women, who were created by God as helpers and companions for men.

As this debate developed, misogynists also began to cite and lament the immoral behavior of noblewomen at the Jacobean court. In 1613 the Countess of Essex received an annulment, allowing her to marry her lover and in 1615 was convicted of murder. These scandals also coincided with a more general trend of female cross-dressing, lampooned in the contemporary pamphlets *Hic Mulier* and *Haec Vir.* As the goddaughter of a physician who practiced at court, Speght lived in the midst of this atmosphere of gender bending and transgression. She was also the daughter of a Calvinist minister, however, surrounded by middle-class piety. In her work she acknowledges the existence of both "good and bad" women and makes it clear that she defends only the good.

In a broader European context, the argument over the nature of women—or *querelle des femmes*—had become a recurring literary trope by the time of Swetnam and Speght. Beginning in the fifteenth century, partially in response to the work of the French protofeminist writer Christine de Pizan, the *querelle* invited debate about the personhood status of women, asking whether they were trustworthy, rational, bestial, or even capable of learning. In England famous medieval characters, such as Geoffrey Chaucer's Wife of Bath, had weighed in on the debate, but new publications on the subject were relatively rare at the turn of the seventeenth century. One such work, however, was *Salve Deus Rex Judaeorum* (1611) by Aemilia Lanyer. Lanyer's text, written in verse rather than prose, attempts some of the same arguments and uses some of the same rhetorical strategies that Speght employs in *Mouzell.* The publication of Swetnam's vituperative tract reignited the *querelle* in the Jacobean era, providing new fodder for misogynists and their opponents.

As the first substantial counterargument to Swetnam's tract—and the first work to reveal Swetnam's name to the public—*Mouzell* served a vital purpose in moving the debate forward. The title, meaning "a muzzle for the black mouth," implies that Speght is seeking to silence Swetnam, who is behaving like a dog on the loose. This metaphor inspired the later pamphleteer Munda, who calls Speght "the first Champion of our sex that would encounter with the barbarous bloodhound." Speght's tract also provided material for pamphlets that disagreed with hers, including Sowernam's tract. While literary history has tended to overlook Speght's writing, the recent interest in female authors has brought *Mouzell* back into curricula and anthologies.

THEMES AND STYLE

Speght's polemic explicitly sets out to comfort godly women, reassuring them that "if the feare of God reside in their hearts, [in spite of] all adversaries, they are highly esteemed … in the eyes of their gracious Redeemer." Opening with a letter to "all of [Eve's] sex, both rich and poore, learned and unlearned," Speght stakes the claim that no Christian woman deserves to be slandered and that Swetnam's tract must be refuted to reinforce this idea. This bold, universal claim contrasts strikingly with Speght's personal modesty in the letter: she apologizes for her "insufficiency in literature and tendernesse in yeares," even as she calls herself a David willing to fight Goliath, armed with the truth. By stressing both her moral correctness and her lack of qualifications to write, Speght hints that even a comparatively uneducated woman can find errors in Swetnam's text—meaning that the female sex is capable of Christian learning and of discussing that learning in public with modesty.

In *Mouzell* Speght deploys classical quotations within a scholarly, argumentative framework, displaying her learning to persuade her audience and to engage with Swetnam on his terms. Mocking her opponent for his "disordered" logic, his lack of "Grammer sense," and his "mingle mangle invective against Women," Speght produces a treatise that comments clearly on four scriptural moments, as well as their misinterpretation by misogynists. She also explains the "excellency of women" in the Aristotelian scholarly vocabulary of the four causes, and she peppers her text with marginal citations of scripture, illustrating her points in a Protestant style. In her appended reply to Swetnam's errors, Speght goes into more detail about her organizational strategy, explaining that the structure of her pamphlet directly corresponds to the structure of Swetnam's text in order to refute his arguments. With each of these features, Speght displays her classical education, knowledge of proper rhetorical style, and background in scriptural interpretation, making her a worthy opponent not only for Swetnam but for more earnest and scholarly antifeminist writers as well.

PRIMARY SOURCE

A MOUZELL FOR MELASTOMUS

140

Thus having (by God's assistance) removed those stones, whereat some have stumbled, others broken their shins, I will proceed toward the period of my intended task, which is to decipher the excellency of women, of whose creation I will, for order's sake, observe. First, the efficient cause, which was God; secondly, the material cause, or that whereof she was made; thirdly, the formal cause, or fashion, and proportion of her feature; fourthly and lastly, the final cause, the end or purpose for which she was made…

141

[…] The material cause, or matter whereof woman was made, was of a refined mould, if I may so speak. For man was created of the dust of the earth (Gen. 2:7), but woman was made of a part of man, after that he was a living soul. Yet was she not produced from Adams foot, to be his too low inferior, nor from his head to be his superior, but from his side, near his heart, to be his equal, that where he is Lord, she may be Lady. And therefore saith God concerning man and woman jointly, 'Let them rule over fish of the sea, and over the fowls of the Heaven, and over every beast that moveth upon the earth' (Gen. 1:26). By which words, he makes their authority equal, and all creatures to be in subjection unto them both. This being rightly considered doth teach men to make such account of their wives, as Adam did of Eve, 'This is bone of my bone, and flesh of my flesh' (Gen. 2:23), as also, that they neither do or wish any more hurt unto them, than unto their own bodies. For men ought to love their wives as themselves, because he that loves his wife, loves himself (Ephes. 5:28). And ever man hated his own flesh (which the woman is) unless a monster in nature.

Thirdly, the formal cause, fashion, and proportion of woman was excellent, for she was neither like the beasts of the earth, fowls of the air, fishes of the sea, or any other inferior creature, but man was the only object, which she did resemble. For as God gave man a lofty countenance, that he might look up toward Heaven, so did he likewise give unto woman. And as the temperature of man's body is excellent, so is woman's. For whereas other creatures, by reason of their gross humours, have excrements for their habit, as fowls, their feathers, beasts, their hair, fishes, their scales, man and woman only, have their skin clear and smooth (Gen. 1:26). And (that more is) in the image of God were they both created; yea and to be brief, all the parts of their bodies, both external and internal, were correspondent and meet for other.

SOURCE: *Women's Writing of the Early Modern Period, 1588-1688: An Anthology,* edited by Stephanie Hodgson-Wright, Edinburgh University, 2002. Pp. 140, 141.

Stylistically Speght's tract is characterized by a mixture of bold and modest language. As a young, female, nonnoble writer, Speght knows her vulnerability, and she actively seeks the protective patronage of more powerful "Honourable or Worshipfull"

By openly challenging another author's disrespectful attitude toward women during the seventeenth century, Rachel Speght helped set the stage for modern feminism. RYAN MCVAY/ STONE+/GETTY IMAGES

women. At the same time, her religious conviction gives her the boldness to call Swetnam a "monster" and to accuse him of blasphemy against God for willingly misinterpreting scripture. The result is a paradoxical tone that balances humility and daring. While Speght calls Swetnam's work "the excrement of your roving cogitations," and Swetnam himself "a fit scribe for the Divell," she also acknowledges her own lack of perfection, explaining that she is "young in yeares, and more defective in knowledge." Although self-effacement was an expected authorial strategy, particularly for a young woman, Speght's willingness to acknowledge her own deficiencies is also a key component of her argument, implying that even young, incompletely educated women can skillfully defend the female sex.

CRITICAL DISCUSSION

A Mouzell for Melastomus was published to mixed critical reaction. While the pseudonymous Munda rose to defend Speght's work in 1617, the more worldly Sowernam mocked Speght's naïveté. In the tract *Ester Hath Hang'd Haman,* Sowernam points out that Speght had lived a sheltered lifestyle and declares that Speght's writing cannot therefore defend the entire range of female experience. Meanwhile rumors arose that Speght's father had actually written *Mouzell,* publishing it under his daughter's name. Speght acknowledges the "variety of verdicts" about the *Mouzell* in a 1621 publication but reiterates her claim to its authorship, before moving on to publish poetry about education and about the Christian process of preparing for death. While *Mouzell* garnered mixed reviews, it also launched Speght's career as an author and provided subject matter for future participants in the *querelle des femmes.*

The literary responses to Swetnam's tract began to taper off after 1620, and with this trend Speght's tract fell into relative oblivion. Only eight copies of the original publication are known to survive. Nevertheless, her work has enjoyed a recent upswing in popularity because of a renewed focus on historical women's writing. In 1996 *Mouzell* was republished alongside Speght's other work in a volume edited by Barbara K. Lewalski. This critical edition of Speght's work encouraged the development of new scholarship on the author's role in the *querelle des femmes,* as well as her Calvinist outlook and her economic and social position as a writer.

Modern scholars have begun to focus on Speght's political engagements, over and above her gendered status. For example, in a 2010 article in *English Literary Renaissance* Christine Luckyj seeks "to avoid reading Speght as a woman writing chiefly in opposition to men … plac[ing] her within a community of writers, preachers, and publishers defined not by gender but by religious politics." Luckyj argues that Speght and Swetnam share a militant Protestant outlook that underpins their argumentation. Lisa Schnell, in an essay in *Debating Gender in Early Modern England* (2010), wonders if Speght functioned almost as a "sacrificial virgin" in the print marketplace because her publisher could take advantage of her earnest piety to sell more books and prolong the profitable *querelle des femmes.* Whether Speght was a crafty self-fashioner or a naive new author, *Mouzell* effectively refutes Swetnam's tract from a Calvinist, female perspective.

BIBLIOGRAPHY

Sources

Lewalski, Barbara K. "Female Text, Male Reader Response: Contemporary Marginalia in Rachel Speght's *A Mouzell for Melastomus.*" *Representing Women in Renaissance England.* Ed. Claude J. Summers and Ted-Larry Pebworth. Columbia: U of Missouri P, 1997. 136-62. Print.

Luckyj, Christina. "*A Mouzell for Melastomus* in Context: Rereading the Swetnam-Speght Debate." *English Literary Renaissance* 40.1 (2010): 113-31. *Wiley Online Library.* Web. 29 Aug. 2012.

Munda, Constantia. "The Worming of a Mad Dog." *Half Humankind: Contexts and Texts of the Controversy about Women of England.* Ed. Katherine Henderson and Barbara F. McManus. Urbana: U of Illinois P, 1985. 244-62. Print.

Schnell, Lisa J. "Muzzling the Competition: Rachel Speght and the Economics of Print." *Debating Gender in Early Modern England.* Ed. Cristina Malcolmson and Mihoko Suzuki. New York: Palgrave Macmillan, 2002. 57-77. Print.

Speght, Rachel. *The Polemics and Poems of Rachel Speght.* Ed. Barbara Kiefer Lewalski. Oxford: Oxford UP, 1996. Print.

Further Reading

Kelly, Joan. "Early Feminist Theory and the *querelle des femmes,* 1400-1789." *Signs: Journal of Women in Culture and Society* 8.1 (1982): 4-28. *JSTOR.* Web. 29 Aug. 2012.

Lilley, Kate. "'Imaginarie in Manner': Rachel Speght's *Dreame* and the Female Scholar-Poet." *Reading the Early Modern Dream: The Terrors of the Night.* Ed. Katharine Hodgkin, Michelle O'Callaghan, and S. J. Wiseman. New York: Routledge, 2008. 97-108. Print.

Luckyj, Christina. "Rachel Speght and the 'Criticall Reader.'" *English Literary Renaissance* 36.2 (2006): 227-49. *Wiley Online Library.* Web. 29 Aug. 2012.

McManus, Barbara. "Eve's Dowry: Genesis and the Pamphlet Controversy about Women." *Women, Writing, and the Reproduction of Culture in Tudor and Stuart Britain.* Ed. Mary E. Burke, Jane Donawerth, Linda L. Dove, and Karen Nelson. Syracuse: Syracuse UP, 2000. 193-206. Print.

Speight, Helen. "Notes and Documents: Rachel Speght's Polemical Life." *Huntington Library Quarterly* 65.3 (2002): 449-63. *JSTOR.* Web. 29 Aug. 2012.

Nancy Simpson-Younger

Speech at the American Women's Rights Convention at Akron, Ohio

Sojourner Truth

✥ *Key Facts*

Time Period:
Mid-19th Century

Movement/Issue:
Women's rights
movement

Place of Publication:
United States

**Language of
Publication:**
English

OVERVIEW

In a speech delivered on May 28, 1851, in Akron, Ohio, itinerant preacher and former slave Sojourner Truth put her stamp on the nascent American women's rights movement, arguing on the basis of her own experience and her interpretation of the Bible that women should receive equal rights under the law and be allowed to actualize those rights. Held approximately three years after the first American Women's Rights Convention at Seneca Falls, New York, the Akron convention took place at a time when participants in the movement were still in the process of shaping their agenda and defining how their own goals intersected with those of the antislavery movement. In this context, Truth used her personal history both to call attention to the unrecognized capabilities of all women and to emphasize the full humanity of people of African descent.

Because Truth was illiterate, her speech was not written down and is known only through the accounts of others. The most famous of these accounts, written by Frances Dana Gage in 1863, includes some material that differs from more contemporary accounts, especially the "ar'n't I a woman?" refrain (often rendered "ain't I a woman?") now closely associated with the speech and with the claim that Truth rescued a meeting that threatened to devolve into chaos due to heckling by opponents of women's rights. Accounts from 1851 record little external opposition but mention some internal strife over whether or not the movement's aims should be more radical. They suggest that Truth's speech was an appreciated and possibly controversial contribution to the conversation but perhaps not as crucial as Gage later suggested. Nevertheless, with or without Gage's additions, Truth's ideas have played a continuing role in American conversations about rights for women and African Americans, not only in the nineteenth century but also during feminism's "second wave" in the mid- to late twentieth century.

HISTORICAL AND LITERARY CONTEXT

Truth's speech addressed some of the key concerns of the mid-nineteenth-century American women's movement, including debates over women's physical and mental capacities and the role of scripture in justifying their exclusion from active participation in public civic and religious life. While some women's rights activists wished to pursue the vote, the majority were more concerned with changing laws deriving from the concept of *couverture,* the idea that a woman's legal identity was subsumed in her husband's when she married. Often justified as a form of protection for the supposedly weaker sex, couverture made it difficult to impossible for women to control real property, claim wages, or gain custody of their children in the event of separation or divorce. Women's lack of access to education, and of a public voice in influential cultural institutions such as the church, compounded the difficulty of creating change.

By 1851 there were signs of progress, including the passage of Married Women's Property Acts and the founding of high schools and colleges for women. Truth, born into slavery in New York around 1797 and originally named Isabella, was in a unique position to speak to and to symbolize the movement's concerns. Because she had been legal property herself, her experience reflected the limitations that a lack of a legal identity could impose. As a black woman denied the protections women supposedly required, she could also speak to female strengths, both physical and mental. Despite her lack of formal education, her extensive understanding of scripture and theology—gained entirely through listening—allowed her to intervene effectively in religious arguments about women's equality.

Truth's Akron speech drew on oral traditions with which she was familiar, including sermons in the Methodist and African Methodist Episcopal Zion tradition. Her thinking on women's role in the church may have been influenced by her contact with the theology of the Quakers, or Society of Friends, who had female pastors. She also followed the traditions of antislavery polemic in calling attention to the physical hardships of slavery, including grueling labor, harsh punishment, and scant rations. For the most part, however, both her arguments and her method of delivery were strikingly original, especially to the ears of white listeners raised in Calvinist denominations.

Some of the most cited elements of the 1851 speech, including the "ar'n't I a woman?" refrain and Truth's baring of her arm to show its strength, derive from Gage's account. "Ar'n't I a woman?" is probably a reworking of the antislavery slogan "Am I not a Woman and a Sister?" Its rhetorical effectiveness is underlined by its centrality in the numerous sung and spoken performances of Gage's version of the speech that emerged in the late twentieth century. Despite its doubtful authenticity, the refrain has served to carry forward words and images that can be more confidently attributed to Truth, including her recollection of the hard labor she did as a slave and her reinterpretation of biblical texts to emphasize women's agency.

THEMES AND STYLE

Accounts of the speech agree on Truth's central argument: women are more powerful than the men who seek to limit female rights want to admit. According to the most complete contemporary account—written and published soon after the speech by Marius Robinson, editor of the *Anti-Slavery Bugle* and the meeting's recording secretary—Truth, after referring to the physical prowess she displayed in slavery, went on to ask, "As for intellect, all I can say is, if a woman have a pint and a man a quart—why can't she have her little pint full? You need not be afraid to give us our rights for fear we will take too much, for we can[']t take more than our pint'll hold." At the conclusion of the speech, she repeated the idea that men who opposed equal rights for women and African Americans felt beleaguered, caught "between a hawk and a buzzard."

In making her argument, Truth drew not only on personal experience and homely metaphors but also on a text that she and many of her listeners considered to be the ultimate authority: the Bible. Other speakers had already offered interpretations of the Bible that supported women's rights. In Robinson's account, Truth referred to a "Lady" who "has spoken about Jesus, how he never spurned woman from him," and Truth added her own parallel arguments, referring to Jesus's close relationship with Mary and Martha, the sisters of Lazarus. She also reminded listeners through a rhetorical question appearing in both accounts—"[H]ow came Jesus into the world?" in Robinson's transcript and "Whar did your Christ come from?" in Gage's—that, according to Christian theology, "man" played no role in Jesus's incarnation. Finally, in a passage that Gage places at the end of the speech and Robinson in the middle, Truth reinterpreted the biblical passage most often used to underline women's supposed moral weakness—Eve's yielding to temptation in the Garden—and suggested that it instead demonstrated women's strength. In an image she also used in other speeches, Truth, according to Robinson, suggested that "if woman upset the

PRIMARY SOURCE

"AIN'T I A WOMAN?"

Well, children, where there is so much racket there must be something out of kilter. I think that 'twixt the negroes of the South and the women at the North, all talking about rights, the white men will be in a fix pretty soon. But what's all this here talking about?

That man over there says that women need to be helped into carriages, and lifted over ditches, and to have the best place everywhere. Nobody ever helps me into carriages, or over mud-puddles, or gives me any best place! And ain't I a woman? Look at me! Look at my arm! I have ploughed and planted, and gathered into barns, and no man could head me! And ain't I a woman? I could work as much and eat as much as a man—when I could get it—and bear the lash as well! And ain't I a woman? I have borne thirteen children, and seen most all sold off to slavery, and when I cried out with my mother's grief, none but Jesus heard me! And ain't I a woman?

Then they talk about this thing in the head; what's this they call it? [member of audience whispers, "intellect"] That's it, honey. What's that got to do with women's rights or negroes' rights? If my cup won't hold but a pint, and yours holds a quart, wouldn't you be mean not to let me have my little half measure full?

Then that little man in black there, he says women can't have as much rights as men, 'cause Christ wasn't a woman! Where did your Christ come from? Where did your Christ come from? From God and a woman! Man had nothing to do with Him.

If the first woman God ever made was strong enough to turn the world upside down all alone, these women together ought to be able to turn it back, and get it right side up again! And now they is asking to do it, the men better let them.

Obliged to you for hearing me, and now old Sojourner ain't got nothing more to say.

SOURCE: "Ain't I a Woman?," 1851, Internet Modern History Sourcebook, Fordham University.

world," she should be given the "chance to set it right side up again."

Truth adopted a folksy idiom that made a strength of her humble background and lack of formal education. Gage renders the Akron speech in dialect, while Robinson records it in mostly standard English, emphasizing in his introduction its "great simplicity." In both accounts, Truth's confidence in the significance of her experience and the validity of her perspective comes through. Gage portrays Truth as rebuking "a little man in black"—a minister—who opposed women's rights, while Robinson has her prefacing her reinterpretation of the Bible with "I can't read, but I can hear." In keeping with her own remarks about pints and quarts, Truth presented herself as comfortable offering her own thoughts in her own idiom and letting her listeners make of them what they wished.

Sojourner Truth with President Lincoln at the White House in 1861. © World History Archive/ Alamy

CRITICAL DISCUSSION

While it seems unlikely that Truth's speech played the crucial role in the convention recalled by Gage, contemporary records suggest that it was well received. Listeners were intrigued both by Truth's appearance—she was tall, sinewy, and dark-skinned, presenting a marked physical contrast to many of her more privileged colleagues—and by what Robinson refers to as "her strong and truthful tones." Robinson calls her speech "one of the most interesting and unique of the Convention," while the *New York Tribune* reported that "she delighted her audience with some of the shrewdest remarks made during the session."

The speech's greatest period of influence, however, came more than one hundred years later, as participants in the second wave of feminism sought to define women's capabilities and to navigate the oft-fraught relationship between the women's movement and the movement for racial equality. Gage's account offered material both for those who wished to cite a longstanding tradition of the two movements working together and for those who wanted to call attention to white feminists' tendency to see their own and their foremothers' experiences as the norm, discounting or even exploiting the differing nature of black women's experiences. As Nell Painter argues in *Sojourner Truth: A Life, A Symbol* (1996), Truth became a "symbol" for both African American and European American participants in the women's movement, with each group finding different meanings in her example. Much recent scholarship, including Painter's, has focused on examining the varying meanings carried by the stories told about

Truth and on seeking to gain a better understanding of the historical figure behind the legends.

Earlier biographical and theoretical works relied on Gage's account of the Akron speech, which was republished in 1870s and 1880s editions of the dictated autobiography Truth sold to support herself. However, scholars in the 1990s, including Painter, Carleton Mabee, and coauthors Erlene Stetson and Linda David, began unearthing the contemporary accounts of the speech and trying to piece together some idea of its actual content. As Painter writes, these scholars' studies, though different, "have one tactic in common: [they] all treat Frances Dana Gage's version of Truth critically," viewing it as one instance of a "symbolic Sojourner Truth" that is worthy of study as a cultural phenomenon but must be recognized as distinct from the historical. While both Gage's account of the speech and the speech itself are worthy of study, they conclude, the two must be treated as separate though related entities.

BIBLIOGRAPHY

Sources

Gage, Mrs. F.D. "Sojourner Truth." *National Anti-Slavery Standard* 2 May 1863: 4. *Sojourner Truth as Orator: Wit, Story, and Song.* Ed. Suzanne Pullon Fitch and Roseann M. Mandziuk. Westport: Greenwood, 1997. 103-04. Print.

Painter, Nell Irvin. *Sojourner Truth: A Life, A Symbol.* New York: W. W. Norton, 1996. Print.

"Women's Rights Convention, Akron Ohio, May 28, 1851." *Anti-Slavery Bugle* [Salem] 21 June 1851: 4. *Sojourner Truth as Orator: Wit, Story, and Song.* Ed. Suzanne Pullon Fitch and Roseann M. Mandziuk. Westport: Greenwood, 1997. 107-08. Print.

"Woman's Rights Convention, Akron Ohio, May 28, 1851." *New York Tribune* 6 June 1851: 7. *Sojourner Truth as Orator: Wit, Story, and Song.* Ed. Suzanne Pullon Fitch and Roseann M. Mandziuk. Westport: Greenwood, 1997. 141. Print.

Further Reading

Jones, Jacqueline. *Labor of Love, Labor of Sorrow: Black Women, Work, and Family from Slavery to the Present.* 2nd ed. New York: Basic Books, 2009. Print.

Mabee, Carleton, and Susan Mabee Newhouse. *Sojourner Truth: Slave, Prophet, Legend.* New York: New York UP, 1993. Print.

Narrative of Sojourner Truth. Ed Nell Irvin Painter. New York: Penguin, 1998. Print.

Peterson, Carla. *Doers of the Word: African-American Women Speakers and Writers in the North (1830-1880).* New Brunswick: Rutgers UP, 1995. Print.

Stetson, Erlene, and Joan David. *Glorying in Tribulation: The Life Work of Sojourner Truth.* East Lansing: Michigan State UP, 1994. Print.

Washington, Margaret. *Sojourner Truth's America.* Urbana: U of Illinois P, 2009. Print.

Catherine E. Saunders

A VINDICATION OF THE RIGHTS OF WOMAN, WITH STRICTURES ON POLITICAL AND MORAL SUBJECTS

Mary Wollstonecraft

OVERVIEW

Mary Wollstonecraft's *A Vindication of the Rights of Woman, with Strictures on Political and Moral Subjects* (1792) argues for female education on the basis that its denial subjugates women and impedes civilization's advance. Written at a time when women in England could not own property or leave a marriage without losing their children, *A Vindication* demonstrates that the qualities perceived as inferior feminine traits result from women's upbringing and status. Wollstonecraft's thirteen-chapter book begins with a dedication to Charles Maurice de Talleyrand-Périgord, whose report on public education to the French National Assembly recommended that girls should be educated with boys only until the age of eight. Like the French revolutionaries, Wollstonecraft draws on the Enlightenment principles of reason, illustrating why these principles must apply to women if tyranny is to be eradicated. In addition, doctrines of the Protestant Reformation, which sought to remove intermediary authorities between the soul and God, fueled her argument that a woman should develop, by process of reason, her own moral character. Wollstonecraft suggests that this development of virtue will make women better wives and mothers, resulting in the improvement of all.

A Vindication of the Rights of Woman shocked some, but many contemporary readers accepted Wollstonecraft's arguments for female education, if not her more radical belief that, aside from physical strength, there are few essential differences between men and women. A second edition was printed within the first year. However, in the aftermath of the French Revolution, the British became suspicious of radical ideas, and after Wollstonecraft's death the revelation that she had borne a child out of wedlock further discredited her. In the United States, however, the book continued to be reprinted, and it contributed to the women's rights movement led by Susan B. Anthony, Elizabeth Cady Stanton, and others. Today *A Vindication of the Rights of Woman* is recognized as a foundational feminist declaration of equal rights for women.

HISTORICAL AND LITERARY CONTEXT

A Vindication of the Rights of Woman argues that Enlightenment ideals, which had led the American colonies and the French to reject tyranny and create constitutions establishing rights for all citizens—except women—must also apply to women. In Great Britain the vote was restricted to a fraction of the population: men possessing substantial property. When a woman married, her husband assumed ownership of her property as well as her person. Education was denied the lower classes. Middle-class girls in the eighteenth century were educated in the home, learning domestic and ornamental skills (music, dancing, dress, and sewing) and a smattering of other subjects. Slavery was permitted in the colonies, though not in Great Britain itself, and abolition was being debated, with implications for other human rights.

One of Wollstonecraft's earlier works, *A Vindication of the Rights of Men* (1790), responds to Edmund Burke's *Reflections on the Revolution in France,* in which Burke retracts his initial approval of the Revolution and supports aristocratic values. Wollstonecraft asserts that society should be based on reason, not tradition. While some Enlightenment thinkers, such as the utilitarian leader Jeremy Bentham, had argued for women's suffrage and equal participation in government, most believed that women were inferior to men. For example, Jean-Jacques Rousseau's republican political philosophy argued against hierarchy, except regarding gender. Accordingly, the National Assembly of France's *Declaration of the Rights of Men* (1789) excludes women. In 1791 Olympe de Gouges issued the pamphlet *Les droits de la femme: à la reine (The Declaration of the Rights of Woman)*, rewriting the official declaration to include women. Wollstonecraft's *A Vindication of the Rights of Woman* provided a rationale for inclusion.

Significant works arguing for educational reform leading to greater liberty were published by the empiricist philosopher John Locke as well as some Dissenters. These Protestants who broke with the Church of England were prohibited from attending the universities at Cambridge and Oxford and established their

✣ *Key Facts*

Time Period:
Late 18th Century

Movement/Issue:
Feminism; Women's education

Place of Publication:
England

Language of Publication:
English

MARY WOLLSTONECRAFT'S QUEST FOR AUTONOMY

As a child, Mary Wollstonecraft witnessed her father's drunken violence toward her mother and vowed to achieve independence, a nearly unimaginable goal for a middle-class female in eighteenth-century England. First she tried one of the traditional routes and served as a paid companion. Then, more daringly, she opened a school for girls, resulting in her first book, *Thoughts on the Education of Daughters: With Reflections on Female Conduct, in the More Important Duties of Life* (1787). As a governess, Wollstonecraft witnessed upper-class privilege at its worst and returned to London determined to survive by writing.

Wollstonecraft watched history unfold in France, where the Revolution of 1789 ended feudalism, permitted a free press, and enfranchised nearly half of the male population. While the radical thinkers with whom she associated were inspired, not all intellectuals saw these developments as positive. She responded to Edmund Burke's warning of democracy's danger with her own book: *A Vindication of the Rights of Man, in a Letter to the Right Honourable Edmund Burke* (1790). This text established Wollstonecraft as an intellectual force.

Shortly after completing her next book, *A Vindication of the Rights of Woman*, Wollstonecraft traveled to Paris, where she saw the revolution take a darker turn. She also fell in love, bore a child out of wedlock, and attempted suicide when her lover proved unfaithful. Her next relationship, with her colleague William Godwin, was more in accord with her ideals and desire for independence; Wollstonecraft and Godwin married but maintained separate living quarters. Unfortunately, at age thirty-eight Wollstonecraft died of an infection following childbirth, a tragic and common fate for women of that era.

own institutions of higher education. In his "Essay on a Course of Liberal Education for Civil and Active Life" (1765), the Dissenter Joseph Priestley promotes a more practical and experiential course of education than the accepted study of the classics. In her *Letters on Education* (1790), Catherine Macauley argues many of the same points as Wollstonecraft. Like Paine's *The Rights of Man* (1791), these polemical pieces were part of a lively conversation carried on in political pamphlets, the tool by which those denied the vote could influence the powerful.

A Vindication of the Rights of Woman lay dormant for a time. In 1818 Wollstonecraft's daughter, Mary Wollstonecraft Godwin Shelley, authored the Gothic novel *Frankenstein*. Later in the nineteenth century, the Victorian novelist George Eliot wrote an essay on Margaret Fuller and Mary Wollstonecraft. Lucretia Mott, Sarah Grimke, and Margaret Fuller admired *A Vindication* and built on its author's foundation in their writing and speeches advocating for women's rights in the United States in the nineteenth century. Wollstonecraft continued to influence twentieth-century writers, such as the novelist Virginia Woolf, who wrote feelingly of Wollstonecraft's politics and personal tribulations. While equal education for both genders is now standard in developed countries, Wollstonecraft's questions about what is inherent in gender and the pitfalls of objectifying women remain pertinent.

THEMES AND STYLE

The central theme of *A Vindication of the Rights of Woman* is that denying equal education to women is an act of subjugation injurious to humanity. This subjugation causes women to rely on outward appearances and makes them figuratively, and sometimes literally, prostitutes. Education would allow women to be independent human beings, better educators of their children, and virtuous by choice rather than by force. Wollstonecraft's opening dedication to Talleyrand states, "Contending for the rights of woman, my main argument is built on this simple principle, that if she be not prepared by education to become the companion of man, she will stop the progress of knowledge and virtue; for truth must be common to all, or it will be inefficacious with respect to its influence on general practice." The book further asserts that cultivating such traits as weakness and ignorance in one gender means that virtue is relative. Such a view cannot be reconciled with belief in a supreme creator who has endowed humanity with reason.

A Vindication enters into conversation with significant male Enlightenment figures and builds on a shared foundation of faith in a just, rational creator and in human reason to create a better society. Divided into chapters, the book first presents the need for reason to be applied to this topic and then discusses beliefs that keep women subordinate, detailing the errors perpetrated by philosophers, particularly the influential Rousseau. Subsequent chapters explore how women's perceived inferiority distorts ideas about modesty and parent-child relations. Wollstonecraft then arrives at her specific recommendations for education, declaring that free, national day schools for all should be established. Both sexes should be educated together, except individuals destined for the trades, who would spend half the day in separate courses. The final chapter reinforces the point by recounting the errors into which uneducated women fall. Full of examples and digressions, each chapter returns to Wollstonecraft's claim that equal education will correct the problems she outlines.

Wollstonecraft seeks to maintain a reasonable rather than a passionate tone. She does not want her readers to think that she will "violently ... agitate the contested question respecting the equality or inferiority of the sex," but she also avoids "flowery diction." Wollstonecraft only partly achieves these aims: extended analogies become ornate, and sharp turns of phrase reveal her anger at injustice. This contrast between intent and practice demonstrates

Wollstonecraft's ambivalent relationship with the popular discourse of sentiment, which she writes encourages the "exquisite sensibility, and sweet docility of manners, supposed to be the sexual characteristics of the weaker vessel." Nevertheless, in critiquing the discourse that has led so many women astray, the author notes that she "cannot avoid feeling the most lively compassion for those unfortunate females"; she cannot avoid terms popularized by sentimental discourse. Mediating between flowery diction and analogies from the natural world, Wollstonecraft's rhetoric aims to persuade men to consider changing educational policy and to convince women to give up the "regal homage which they receive" by way of courtesies—a practice that deceives them into thinking they have power when they are slaves.

CRITICAL DISCUSSION

Upon publication, *A Vindication of the Rights of Woman* received positive reviews in radical periodicals, while conservative journals ignored or reviled it. Readership was large enough that a second, corrected printing came out that same year. Many readers agreed with Wollstonecraft's ideas about education, paying little attention to the work's larger implications regarding gender equality. Following Wollstonecraft's death after childbirth, her husband, William Godwin, published a memoir of his wife's life. The revelations that her first child was illegitimate and that she cohabited with Godwin prior to their marriage shocked both conservatives and radicals, leading to the neglect of *A Vindication* by nineteenth-century English readers.

Though Americans also disapproved of Wollstonecraft's behavior, *A Vindication* remained in print in the United States and contributed to the developing women's rights movement. The first American book-length consideration of women, written in 1818 by Hannah Mather Crocker (a descendent of the influential Puritan Mather family), states that "Mary Wollstonecraft was a woman of great energy and a very independent mind: her Rights of Woman are replete with fine sentiments, though we do not coincide with her opinion respecting the total independence of the female sex." In their article in *American Journal of Political Science*, Eileen Hunt Botting and Christine Carey point out that in 1866 Mott tried to restore Wollstonecraft's reputation in a speech given to the New York Women's Rights Convention, calling Wollstonecraft a "pioneer of this movement." In 1881 Susan B. Anthony and Elizabeth Cady Stanton published their *History of Women's Suffrage,* dedicating it to Wollstonecraft's memory.

Feminists of the 1970s rediscovered Wollstonecraft and proclaimed her their foremother, with some qualifications. For example, in *Women, Resistance and Revolution* (1974), Sheila Rowbotham observes that Wollstonecraft "cannot conceive of women becoming the agents of their own liberation. She can only hope to convince reasonable men to assist in the

Mary Wollstonecraft, author of *A Vindication of the Rights of Woman.* © LEBRECHT MUSIC AND ARTS PHOTO LIBRARY/ ALAMY

emancipation of their companions." More recently, scholars have critiqued the Orientalism inherent in Wollstonecraft's warning that Christian men should not deny that women have souls, as it was thought that Islam did. Literary critics are now exploring how the text challenges the boundaries between Enlightenment discourse and romanticism. Barbara Taylor has argued that "if the *Rights of Woman* is a work of Enlightenment philosophy … it is one that highlights important tensions in Enlightenment thought, particularly in enlightened thinking on gender issues." Wollstonecraft's work is still making an impact in countries outside the English-speaking world. For example, Tanzanian woman's advocate Salma Maoulidi notes in *Women's Studies Quarterly* that women should indeed be educated but that the struggle must go "beyond moral persuasion and instead call for more stringent institutional measures to check violations against women that occur as a result of their sex—for example, sexual harassment policies."

BIBLIOGRAPHY

Sources

Botting, Eileen Hunt, and Christine Carey. "Wollstonecraft's Philosophical Impact on Nineteenth-Century American Women's Rights Advocates." *American Journal of Political Science* 48.4 (2004): 707-22. *Proquest.* Web. 11 June 2012.

Crocker, Hannah Mather. *Observations on the Real Rights of Women and Other Writings.* Ed. Constance J. Post. Lincoln: U of Nebraska P, 2011. *Google Books.* Web. 11 June 2012.

Janes, R.M. "On the Reception of Mary Wollstonecraft's *A Vindication of the Rights of Woman.*" *Journal of the History of Ideas* 39.2 (1978): 293-302. *JSTOR.* Web. June 2012.

Maoulidi, Salma. "Mary Wollstonecraft: Challenges of Race and Class in Feminist Discourse." *Women's Studies Quarterly* 35.3-4 (2007): 280. *GenderWatch*. Web. 11 June 2012.

Rowbotham, Sheila. *Women, Resistance and Revolution.* Harmondsworth: Penguin, 1974. Print.

Taylor, Barbara. "Feminists versus Gallants: Manners and Morals in Enlightenment Britain." *Representations* 87.1 (2004): 125-48. *JSTOR*. Web. 11 June 2012.

Wollstonecraft, Mary. *A Vindication of the Rights of Woman with Strictures on Political and Moral Subjects.* Ed. Deidre Shauna Lynch. New York: Norton, 2009. Print.

Further Reading

Chernock, Arianne. "Cultivating Woman: Men's Pursuit of Intellectual Equality in the Late British Enlightenment." *Journal of British Studies* 45.3 (2006): 511-31. *JSTOR*. Web. 11 June 2012.

Godwin, William. *Memoirs of Mary Wollstonecraft.* 1798. London: Constable, 1928. Web. 11 June 2012.

Gunther-Canada, Wendy. *Rebel Writer: Mary Wollstonecraft and Enlightenment Politics.* DeKalb: Northern Illinois UP, 2001. Print.

Jones, Louis Worth. "Mary Wollstonecraft." *A Dictionary of Unitarian and Universalist Biography.* Unitarian Universalist History and Heritage Society, 2000. Web. June 2012.

Taylor, Barbara. *Mary Wollstonecraft and the Feminist Imagination.* Cambridge: Cambridge UP, 2003. Print.

Todd, Janet. *Mary Wollstonecraft: A Revolutionary Life.* New York: Columbia UP, 2000. Print.

Wach, Howard M. "A Boston Vindication: Margaret Fuller and Caroline Dall Read Mary Wollstonecraft." *Massachusetts Historical Review* 7 (2005): 3-35. *JSTOR*. Web. 11 June 2012.

"Wollstonecraft, Mary: Introduction." *Antiquity-18th Century, Topics and Authors.* Ed. Jessica Bomarito and Jeffrey W. Hunter. Detroit: Gale, 2005. 523-26. *Gale U.S. History in Context.* Web. 6 June 2012.

Robin Morris

SUBJECT INDEX

Bold *volume and page numbers (e.g.,* **3:269–272***) refer to the main entry on the subject.*
Page numbers in italics refer to photographs and illustrations.

A

N

V

AUTHOR INDEX

The author index includes author names represented in The Manifesto in Literature. *Numbers in* **Bold** *indicate volume, with page numbers following after colons.*

Title Index

The title index includes works that are represented in The Manifesto in Literature. *Numbers in* **Bold** *indicate volume, with page numbers following after colons.*